For Reference

Not to be taken from this room

Novels
for Students

Novels
for Students

**Presenting Analysis, Context and Criticism on
Commonly Studied Novels**

Volume 6

*Marie Rose Napierkowski
and Deborah A. Stanley, Editors*

Carol Jago, Santa Monica High School, Advisor
Kathleen Pasquantonio, Novi High School, Advisor

Foreword by Anne Devereaux Jordan, Teaching and Learning Literature

The Gale Group

DETROIT • SAN FRANCISCO • LONDON • BOSTON • WOODBRIDGE, CT

National Advisory Board

Novels for Students

Staff

Series Editors: Marie Rose Napierkowski and Deborah A. Stanley.

Contributing Editors: Betsy Currier Beacom, Robert Bennett, Karen R. Bloom, Chloe Bolan, Sara L. Constantakis, Sharon Cumberland, Carl Davis, Jane Elizabeth Dougherty, Scott Gillam, Catherine L. Goldstein, Margaret Haerens, Jhan Hochman, Jeremy Hubbell, Motoko Fujishiro Huthwaite, Arlene M. Johnson, David Kelly, Paul Loeber, Nancy C. McClure, Tabitha McIntosh-Byrd, Patrick J. Moser, Wendy Perkins, Diane Telgen, Beverly West, and Donna Woodford.

Editorial Technical Specialist: Karen Uchic.

Managing Editor: Joyce Nakamura.

Research: Victoria B. Cariappa, *Research Team Manager.* Andy Malonis, *Research Specialist.* Julia C. Daniel, Tamara C. Nott, Tracie A. Richardson, and Cheryl L. Warnock, *Research Associates.* Jeffrey Daniels, *Research Assistant.*

Permissions: Susan M. Trosky, *Permissions Manager.* Maria L. Franklin, *Permissions Specialist.* Sarah Chesney, *Permissions Associate.*

Production: Mary Beth Trimper, *Production Director.* Evi Seoud, *Assistant Production Manager.* Cindy Range, *Production Assistant.*

Graphic Services: Randy Bassett, *Image Database Supervisor.* Robert Duncan and Michael Logusz, *Imaging Specialists.* Pamela A. Reed, *Photography Coordinator.* Gary Leach, *Macintosh Artist.*

Product Design: Cynthia Baldwin, *Product Design Manager.* Cover Design: Michelle DiMercurio, *Art Director.* Page Design: Pamela A. E. Galbreath, *Senior Art Director.*

Copyright Notice

ISBN 0-7876-2115-3
ISSN 1094-3552
Printed in the United States of America.

10 9 8 7 6 5 4 3 2 1

Table of Contents

The Informed Dialogue:
Interacting with Literature

When we pick up a book, we usually do so with the anticipation of pleasure. We hope that by entering the time and place of the novel and sharing the thoughts and actions of the characters, we will find enjoyment. Unfortunately, this is often not the case; we are disappointed. But we should ask, has the author failed us, or have we failed the author?

We establish a dialogue with the author, the book, and with ourselves when we read. Consciously and unconsciously, we ask questions: "Why did the author write this book?" "Why did the author choose that time, place, or character?" "How did the author achieve that effect?" "Why did the character act that way?" "Would I act in the same way?" The answers we receive depend upon how much information about literature in general and about that book specifically we ourselves bring to our reading.

Young children have limited life and literary experiences. Being young, children frequently do not know how to go about exploring a book, nor sometimes, even know the questions to ask of a book. The books they read help them answer questions, the author often coming right out and *telling* young readers the things they are learning or are expected to learn. The perennial classic, *The Little Engine That Could, tells* its readers that, among other things, it is good to help others and bring happiness:

> "Hurray, hurray," cried the funny little clown and all the dolls and toys. "The good little boys and girls in

the city will be happy because you helped us, kind, Little Blue Engine."

In picture books, messages are often blatant and simple, the dialogue between the author and reader one-sided. Young children are concerned with the end result of a book—the enjoyment gained, the lesson learned—rather than with how that result was obtained. As we grow older and read further, however, we question more. We come to expect that the world within the book will closely mirror the concerns of our world, and that the author will *show* these through the events, descriptions, and conversations within the story, rather than *telling* of them. We are now expected to do the interpreting, carry on our share of the dialogue with the book and author, and glean not only the author's message, but comprehend how that message and the overall affect of the book were achieved. Sometimes, however, we need help to do these things. *Novels for Students* provides that help.

A novel is made up of many parts interacting to create a coherent whole. In reading a novel, the more obvious features can be easily spotted—theme, characters, plot—but we may overlook the more subtle elements that greatly influence how the novel is perceived by the reader: viewpoint, mood and tone, symbolism, or the use of humor. By focusing on both the obvious and more subtle literary elements within a novel, *Novels for Students* aids readers in both analyzing for message and in determining how and why that message is communicated. In the discussion on Harper Lee's *To*

Kill a Mockingbird (Vol. 2), for example, the mockingbird as a symbol of innocence is dealt with, among other things, as is the importance of Lee's use of humor which "enlivens a serious plot, adds depth to the characterization, and creates a sense of familiarity and universality." The reader comes to understand the internal elements of each novel discussed—as well as the external influences that help shape it.

"The desire to write greatly," Harold Bloom of Yale University says, "is the desire to be elsewhere, in a time and place of one's own, in an originality that must compound with inheritance, with an anxiety of influence." A writer seeks to create a unique world within a story, but although it is unique, it is not disconnected from our own world. It speaks to us *because* of what the writer brings to the writing from our world: how he or she was raised and educated; his or her likes and dislikes; the events occurring in the real world at the time of the writing, and while the author was growing up. When we know what an author has brought to his or her work, we gain a greater insight into both the "originality" (the world of the book), and the things that "compound" it. This insight enables us to question that created world and find answers more readily. By informing ourselves, we are able to establish a more effective dialogue with both book and author.

Novels for Students, in addition to providing a plot summary and descriptive list of characters—to remind readers of what they have read—also explores the external influences that shaped each book. Each entry includes a discussion of the author's background, and the historical context in which the novel was written. It is vital to know, for instance, that when Ray Bradbury was writing *Fahrenheit 451* (Vol. 1), the threat of Nazi domination had recently ended in Europe, and the McCarthy hearings were taking place in Washington, D.C. This information goes far in answering the question, "Why did he write a story of oppressive government control and book burning?" Similarly, it is important to know that Harper Lee, author of *To Kill a Mockingbird,* was born and raised in Mon-

roeville, Alabama, and that her father was a lawyer. Readers can now see why she chose the south as a setting for her novel—it is the place with which she was most familiar—and start to comprehend her characters and their actions.

Novels for Students helps readers find the answers they seek when they establish a dialogue with a particular novel. It also aids in the posing of questions by providing the opinions and interpretations of various critics and reviewers, broadening that dialogue. Some reviewers of *To Kill A Mockingbird,* for example, "faulted the novel's climax as melodramatic." This statement leads readers to ask, "Is it, indeed, melodramatic?" "If not, why did some reviewers see it as such?" "If it is, why did Lee choose to make it melodramatic?" "Is melodrama ever justified?" By being spurred to ask these questions, readers not only learn more about the book and its writer, but about the nature of writing itself.

The literature included for discussion in the *Novels for Students* series has been chosen because it has something vital to say to us. *Of Mice and Men, Catch-22, The Joy Luck Club, My Antonia, A Separate Peace* and the other novels here speak of life and modern sensibility. In addition to their individual, specific messages of prejudice, power, love or hate, living and dying, however, they and all great literature also share a common intent. They force us to *think*—about life, literature, and about others, not just about ourselves. They pry us from the narrow confines of our minds and thrust us outward to confront the world of books and the larger, real world we all share. *Novels for Students* helps us in this confrontation by providing the means of enriching our conversation with literature and the world, by creating an *informed* dialogue, one that brings true pleasure to the personal act of reading.

Sources

Harold Bloom, *The Western Canon, The Books and School of the Ages,* Riverhead Books, 1994.

Watty Piper, *The Little Engine That Could,* Platt & Munk, 1930.

Anne Devereaux Jordan
Senior Editor, *TALL*
(*Teaching and Learning Literature*)

Introduction

Purpose of the Book

The purpose of *Novels for Students* (*NfS*) is to provide readers with a guide to understanding, enjoying, and studying novels by giving them easy access to information about the work. Part of Gale's "For Students" Literature line, *NfS* is specifically designed to meet the curricular needs of high school and undergraduate college students and their teachers, as well as the interests of general readers and researchers considering specific novels. While each volume contains entries on "classic" novels frequently studied in classrooms, there are also entries containing hard-to-find information on contemporary novels, including works by multicultural, international, and women novelists.

The information covered in each entry includes an introduction to the novel and the novel's author; a plot summary, to help readers unravel and understand the events in a novel; descriptions of important characters, including explanation of a given character's role in the novel as well as discussion about that character's relationship to other characters in the novel; analysis of important themes in the novel; and an explanation of important literary techniques and movements as they are demonstrated in the novel.

In addition to this material, which helps the readers analyze the novel itself, students are also provided with important information on the literary and historical background informing each work. This includes a historical context essay, a box comparing the time or place the novel was written to modern Western culture, a critical overview essay, and excerpts from critical essays on the novel. A unique feature of *NfS* is a specially commissioned overview essay on each novel by an academic expert, targeted toward the student reader.

To further aid the student in studying and enjoying each novel, information on media adaptations is provided, as well as reading suggestions for works of fiction and nonfiction on similar themes and topics. Classroom aids include ideas for research papers and lists of critical sources that provide additional material on the novel.

Selection Criteria

The titles for each volume of *NfS* were selected by surveying numerous sources on teaching literature and analyzing course curricula for various school districts. Some of the sources surveyed included: literature anthologies; *Reading Lists for College-Bound Students: The Books Most Recommended by America's Top Colleges;* textbooks on teaching the novel; a College Board survey of novels commonly studied in high schools; a National Council of Teachers of English (NCTE) survey of novels commonly studied in high schools; the NCTE's *Teaching Literature in High School: The Novel;* and the Young Adult Library Services Association (YALSA) list of best books for young adults of the past twenty-five years.

Input was also solicited from our expert advisory board, as well as educators from various areas. From these discussions, it was determined that each volume should have a mix of "classic" novels (those works commonly taught in literature classes) and contemporary novels for which information is often hard to find. Because of the interest in expanding the canon of literature, an emphasis was also placed on including works by international, multicultural, and women authors. Our advisory board members—current high school teachers—helped pare down the list for each volume. If a work was not selected for the present volume, it was often noted as a possibility for a future volume. As always, the editor welcomes suggestions for titles to be included in future volumes.

How Each Entry Is Organized

Each entry, or chapter, in *NfS* focuses on one novel. Each entry heading lists the full name of the novel, the author's name, and the date of the novel's publication. The following elements are contained in each entry:

• Introduction: a brief overview of the novel which provides information about its first appearance, its literary standing, any controversies surrounding the work, and major conflicts or themes within the work.

• Author Biography: this section includes basic facts about the author's life, and focuses on events and times in the author's life that inspired the novel in question.

• Plot Summary: a description of the major events in the novel, with interpretation of how these events help articulate the novel's themes. Lengthy summaries are broken down with subheads.

• Characters: an alphabetical listing of major characters in the novel. Each character name is followed by a brief to an extensive description of the character's role in the novel, as well as discussion of the character's actions, relationships, and possible motivation.

Characters are listed alphabetically by last name. If a character is unnamed—for instance, the narrator in *Invisible Man* the character is listed as "The Narrator" and alphabetized as "Narrator." If a character's first name is the only one given, the name will appear alphabetically by the name. Variant names are also included for each character. Thus, the full name "Jean Louise Finch" would head the listing for the narrator of *To Kill a Mockingbird,* but listed in a separate cross-reference would be the nickname "Scout Finch."

• Themes: a thorough overview of how the major topics, themes, and issues are addressed within the novel. Each theme discussed appears in a separate subhead, and is easily accessed through the boldface entries in the Subject/Theme Index.

• Style: this section addresses important style elements of the novel, such as setting, point of view, and narration; important literary devices used, such as imagery, foreshadowing, symbolism; and, if applicable, genres to which the work might have belonged, such as Gothicism or Romanticism. Literary terms are explained within the entry, but can also be found in the Glossary.

• Historical and Cultural Context: This section outlines the social, political, and cultural climate *in which the author lived and the novel was created.* This section may include descriptions of related historical events, pertinent aspects of daily life in the culture, and the artistic and literary sensibilities of the time in which the work was written. If the novel is a historical work, information regarding the time in which the novel is set is also included. Each section is broken down with helpful subheads.

• Critical Overview: this section provides background on the critical reputation of the novel, including bannings or any other public controversies surrounding the work. For older works, this section includes a history of how novel was first received and how perceptions of it may have changed over the years; for more recent novels, direct quotes from early reviews may also be included.

• Sources: an alphabetical list of critical material quoted in the entry, with full bibliographical information.

• For Further Study: an alphabetical list of other critical sources which may prove useful for the student. Includes full bibliographical information and a brief annotation.

• Criticism: an essay commissioned by *NfS* which specifically deals with the novel and is written specifically for the student audience, as well as excerpts from previously published criticism on the work.

In addition, each entry contains the following highlighted sections, set apart from the main text as sidebars:

• Media Adaptations: a list of important film and television adaptations of the novel, including source information. The list also includes stage adaptations, audio recordings, musical adaptations, etc.

• Compare and Contrast Box: an "at-a-glance" comparison of the cultural and historical differences between the author's time and culture and late twentieth-century Western culture. This box includes pertinent parallels between the major scientific, political, and cultural movements of the time or place the novel was written, the time or place the novel was set (if a historical work), and modern Western culture. Works written after the mid-1970s may not have this box.

• What Do I Read Next?: a list of works that might complement the featured novel or serve as a contrast to it. This includes works by the same author and others, works of fiction and nonfiction, and works from various genres, cultures, and eras.

• Study Questions: a list of potential study questions or research topics dealing with the novel. This section includes questions related to other disciplines the student may be studying, such as American history, world history, science, math, government, business, geography, economics, psychology, etc.

Other Features

NfS includes "The Informed Dialogue: Interacting with Literature," a foreword by Anne Devereaux Jordan, Senior Editor for *Teaching and Learning Literature* (*TALL*), and a founder of the Children's Literature Association. This essay provides an enlightening look at how readers interact with literature and how *Novels for Students* can help teachers show students how to enrich their own reading experiences.

A Cumulative Author/Title Index lists the authors and titles covered in each volume of the *NfS* series.

A Cumulative Nationality/Ethnicity Index breaks down the authors and titles covered in each volume of the *NfS* series by nationality and ethnicity.

A Subject/Theme Index, specific to each volume, provides easy reference for users who may be studying a particular subject or theme rather than a single work. Significant subjects from events to broad themes are included, and the entries pointing to the specific theme discussions in each entry are indicated in **boldface.**

Each entry has several illustrations, including photos of the author, stills from film adaptations (when available), maps, and/or photos of key historical events.

Citing Novels for Students

When writing papers, students who quote directly from any volume of *Novels for Students* may use the following general forms. These examples are based on MLA style; teachers may request that students adhere to a different style, so the following examples may be adapted as needed.

When citing text from *NfS* that is not attributed to a particular author (i.e., the Themes, Style,

Historical Context sections, etc.), the following format should be used in the bibliography section:

"Night." *Novels for Students.* Eds. Sheryl Ciccarelli and Marie Rose Napierkowski. Vol. 5. Detroit: Gale, 1998. 34–5.

When quoting the specially commissioned essay from *NfS* (usually the first piece under the "Criticism" subhead), the following format should be used:

Miller, Tyrus. Essay on "Winesburg, Ohio." *Novels for Students.* Eds. Sheryl Ciccarelli and Marie Rose Napierkowski. Vol. 5. Detroit: Gale, 1997. 218–9.

When quoting a journal or newspaper essay that is reprinted in a volume of *NfS,* the following form may be used:

Malak, Amin. "Margaret Atwood's The Handmaid's Tale' and the Dystopian Tradition," in *Canadian Literature* , No. 112, Spring, 1987, 9–16; excerpted and reprinted in *Novels for Students,* Vol. 5, eds. Sheryl Ciccarelli and Marie Rose Napierkowski (Detroit: Gale, 1998), pp. 61–64.

When quoting material reprinted from a book that appears in a volume of *NfS,* the following form may be used:

Adams, Timothy Dow. "Richard Wright: Wearing the Mask," in *Telling Lies in Modern American Autobiography* (University of North Carolina Press, 1990), 69–83; excerpted and reprinted in *Novels for Students,* Vol. 5, eds. Sheryl Ciccarelli and Marie Napierkowski (Detroit: Gale, 1999), pp. 59–61.

We Welcome Your Suggestions

The editor of *Novels for Students* welcomes your comments and ideas. Readers who wish to suggest novels to appear in future volumes, or who have other suggestions, are cordially invited to contact the editor. You may contact the editor via e-mail at: **CYA@gale.com@galesmtp.** Or write to the editor at:

Editor, *Novels for Students*
The Gale Group
27500 Drake Rd.
Farmington Hills, MI 48331–3535

Literary Chronology

1667: Jonathan Swift was born November 30, 1667, in Dublin, Ireland, to Abigaile and, posthumously, Jonathan Swift.

1688: The Anglican-dominated Parliament secretly planned with William of Orange, the Protestant husband of King James's daughter Mary, to steal the throne from King James II, a Catholic who had come to power in 1685. No one was killed in the coup, hence its name. King William subsequently sided with Spain in a war with France, and Jonathan Swift satirized this war between the English (the Lilliputians) and the French (the Blefuscudians) in *Gulliver's Travels.*

1702: Jonathan Swift's writings and editing of the Tory newspaper the *Examiner* helped end the war between England and France in 1713, but Queen Anne did not reward him and later ruined Swift's chances of a career in the Church of England.

1726: Jonathan Swift satirized George II, the future king of England, and the politics of the Whigs and Tories in Book One of *Gulliver's Travels.*

1745: Jonathan Swift died in a mental institution on October 19, 1745.

1811: Harriet Beecher Stowe was born on June 14, 1811, to Lyman and Roxana Beecher, in Litchfield, Connecticut.

1835: Samuel Langhorne Clemens, better known as Mark Twain, was born in Florida, Missouri in 1835. He grew up in nearby Hannibal, Missouri, and his childhood memories of life along the Mississippi River figured prominently in *The Adventures of Tom Sawyer,* his famous story of a mischievous boy.

1850: The Fugitive Slave Law, which prohibited Northerners from helping escaped slaves to freedom and even required that they help slave catchers to recapture escaped slaves, was passed in 1850. The law was Harriet Beecher Stowe's impetus for writing Uncle Tom's Cabin and also plays a significant role in Toni Morrison's Beloved.

1852: The first installment of Harriet Beecher Stowe's *Uncle Tom's Cabin; or, Life among the Lowly* appeared in *National Era* on June 5, 1851. The publication of the entire book followed in 1852.

1876: *The Adventures of Tom Sawyer,* written by Samuel Langhorne Clemens under the pen name Mark Twain, was published in 1876 and introduced readers to life in the frontier region along the banks of the Mississippi River.

1877: Hermann Hesse was born on July 2, 1877, in Calw, Württemberg, Germany.

1878: Upton Sinclair, author of *The Jungle,* was born in 1878.

1894: Aldous Huxley was born on July 6, 1894, to Leonard and Judith Arnold Huxley, in Laleham near Godalming, Surrey, England.

1896: Harriet Beecher Stowe died on July 1, 1896, in Hartford, Connecticut, and was buried in Andover, Massachusetts.

1899: Ernest Hemingway was born on July 21, 1899, in Oak Park, Illinois.

1906: *The Jungle*, Upton Sinclair's muckraking expose of the meatpacking industry, was published in 1906. Within that same year and as a direct result of *The Jungle*'s impact on public opinion, the Pure Food and Drug Bill was passed.

1910: Samuel Langhorne Clemens, better known as Mark Twain, died in 1910, thirty-four years after the publication of his famous *Adventures of Tom Sawyer*.

1913: Albert Camus was born on November 7, 1913, to Lucien and Catherine Sintès Camus, in a French colony in Mondovi, Algeria.

1914: Henry Ford invents the modern factory assembly line in order to mass-produce his Model T automobile which he designed in 1908. Aldous Huxley was impressed by Ford's production techniques and made Ford a god to his characters in *Brave New World*.

1917: Carson McCullers was born Lulu Carson Smith on February 19, 1917, in Columbus, Georgia.

1922: Hermann Hesse's novel about the founder of Buddhism, *Siddhartha: Eine indische Dichtung (Siddhartha)* was published.

1929: Ursula K. LeGuin was born on October 29, 1929, in Berkeley, California, to anthropologist Alfred Kroeber and author Theodora Kracaw Kroeber Quinn.

1931: Toni Morrison was born Chloe Anthony Wofford on February 18, 1931, in Lorain, Ohio.

1931: Author E. L. Doctorow was born in 1931 in the Bronx, New York.

1932: Aldous Huxley's *Brave New World* was published.

1940: Maxine Hong Kingston was born in 1940 to Chinese immigrant parents, and grew up in Stockton, California.

1940: Carson McCullers's *The Heart Is a Lonely Hunter* was published in 1940.

1942: Isabel Allende was born on August 2, 1942, in Lima, Peru, to Francisca Llona Barros and Tomas Allende, cousin of Salvador Allende, the future president of Chile.

1942: Albert Camus completed *The Stranger* in May, 1941, and the book was published in July, 1942.

1943: Upton Sinclair, author of *The Jungle*, was awarded the Pulitzer Prize in 1943 for *Dragon's Teeth*, a novel about Nazi Germany.

1946: Hermann Hesse received the Nobel Prize for Literature in 1946. This award recognizes an author whose complete work is of the most distinguished idealistic nature in the field of literature.

1952: Ernest Hemingway's *The Old Man and the Sea* was published and received that year's Pulitzer Prize.

1954: Ernest Hemingway received the Nobel Prize for Literature in 1954. This award recognizes an author whose complete work is of the most distinguished idealistic nature in the field of literature.

1957: Albert Camus received the Nobel Prize for Literature in 1957. This award recognizes an author whose complete work is of the most distinguished idealistic nature in the field of literature.

1960: Albert Camus was killed in an automobile accident on January 4, 1960.

1961: Ernest Hemingway committed suicide on July 2, 1961, in Ketchum, Idaho.

1962: A leukemia victim, Hermann Hesse died from a cerebral hemorrhage on August 9, 1962, in Montagnola.

1963: Aldous Huxley died of cancer in Los Angeles, California, on November 22, 1963, the same day that President John F. Kennedy was assassinated.

1964: The Civil Rights Act of 1964 outlawed discrimination based on race, color, national origin, religion, or gender.

1967: Carson McCullers died in 1967, having lived a life filled with health problems including breast cancer and several strokes.

1968: Prizewinning journalist and author Upton Sinclair died in 1968.

1969: Ursula K. LeGuin's *The Left Hand of Darkness* was published in 1969 and received that year's Nebula Award as well as the 1970 Hugo Award, the most prestigious science fiction awards.

1973: On September 13, 1973, a military coup ousted Chilean President Salvador Allende. The events surrounding the coup had a lasting impact on Isabel Allende and became the focus of her novel *The House of the Spirits*.

1975: E. L. Doctorow's *Ragtime* was published in 1975 and received the National Book Critics' Circle Award the following year.

1976: *The Woman Warrior* by Maxine Hong Kingston was published in 1976.

1987: Toni Morrison's *Beloved* was published in 1987 and won the Pulitzer Prize for Fiction the following year.

1993: Toni Morrison became the first African-American and only the eighth woman to win the Nobel Prize for Literature in 1993.

Acknowledgments

The editors wish to thank the copyright holders of the excerpted criticism included in this volume and the permissions managers of many book and magazine publishing companies for assisting us in securing reproduction rights. We are also grateful to the staffs of the Detroit Public Library, the Library of Congress, the University of Detroit Mercy Library, Wayne State University Purdy/Kresge Library Complex, and the University of Michigan Libraries for making their resources available to us. Following is a list of the copyright holders who have granted us permission to reproduce material in this volume of *NfS*. Every effort has been made to trace copyright, but if omissions have been made, please let us know.

COPYRIGHTED EXCERPTS IN *NFS*, VOLUME 6, WERE REPRODUCED FROM THE FOLLOWING PERIODICALS:

American Literature, v. 31, January, 1960; v. 49, May, 1977. Copyright © 1960, 1977 Duke University Press, Durham, NC. Both reproduced by permission.

American Studies, v. 32, Fall, 1991 for "The Problem with Classroom Use of Upton Sinclair's *The Jungle*" by Louise Carroll Wade. Copyright © Mid-American Studies Association, 1991. Reproduced by permission of the publisher and the author.

California Slavic Studies, v. X, 1977 for "A Camp through the Eyes of a Peasant: Solzhenitsyn's *One Day in the Life of Ivan Denisovich*" by David Pike. Reproduced by permission of the publisher.

Contemporary Literature, v. XXVIII, Winter, 1987. ©1987 by the Board of Regents of the University of Wisconsin System. Reproduced by permission of The University of Wisconsin Press.

Criticism, v. XXXI, Fall, 1989 for "Questioning Race and Gender Definitions: Dialogic Subversions in *The Woman Warrior*" by Malini Schueller. Copyright © 1989 Wayne State University Press, Detroit, Michigan. Reproduced by permission of the publisher.

Extrapolation, v. 21, Fall, 1980. Copyright © 1980 by Kent State University Press. Reproduced by permission.

The International Fiction Review, v. 20, 1993. © copyright 1993 International Fiction Association. Reproduced by permission.

Kansas Quarterly, v. 21, Fall, 1989 for "*Ragtime* as Auto-Biography" by Marshall Bruce Gentry. © copyright 1989 by *The Kansas Quarterly*. Reproduced by permission of the publisher and the author.

Literature and Psychology, v. XVII, 1967. Copyright © 1968 by Leonard F. Manheim and Morton Kaplan. Reproduced by permission.

The Massachusetts Review, v. XXI, Winter, 1980. 1980. Reproduced from *The Massachusetts Review*, The Massachusetts Review, Inc., by permission.

The Mississippi Quarterly, v. XLI, Winter, 1987-88. Copyright 1987-88. Mississippi State University. Reproduced by permission.

The New Republic, v. 175, October 30, 1976. © 1976 The New Republic, Inc. Reproduced by permission of *The New Republic.*

The New York Times Book Review, September 13, 1987. Copyright © 1987 by The New York Times Company. Reproduced by permission.

Nineteenth-Century Fiction, v. 39, December, 1984 for "'The Crown without the Conflict': Religious Values and Moral Reasoning in *Uncle Tom's Cabin*" by Thomas P. Joswick. © 1984 by The Regents of the University of California. Reproduced by permission of The Regents and the author.

Revista Hispanica Moderna, v. XLVII, June, 1994. Reproduced by permission.

San Jose Studies, v. IX, Winter, 1983 for "The Importance of Food in *One Day in the Life of Ivan Denisovich*" by Alfred Cismaru. Copyright © 1983 by the San Jose State University Foundation. Reproduced by permission of the publisher and the author.

Studies in American Fiction, v. 18, Spring, 1990. Copyright © 1990 Northeastern University. Reproduced by permission.

Tamkang Review, v. XIV, Autumn, 1983-Summer, 1984. Reproduced by permission.

Texas Studies in Literature and Language, v. XXXIV, Summer, 1992 for "The Hairy Maid at the Harpsichord: Some Speculations on the Meaning of *Gulliver's Travels*" by Dennis Todd. Copyright © 1992 by the University of Texas Press. All rights reserved. Reproduced by permission of the publisher.

COPYRIGHTED EXCERPTS IN *NFS*, VOLUME 6, WERE REPRODUCED FROM THE FOLLOWING BOOKS:

Beckham, Richard H. From "Huxley's *Brave New World* as Social Irritant: Ban It or Buy It?" in *Censored Books: Critical Viewpoints.* Nicholas J. Karolides, Lee Burress, John M. Kean, eds. The Scarecrow Press, Inc., 1993. Copyright © 1993 by Nicholas J. Karolides, Lee Burress, John M. Kean. Reproduced by permission.

Elliott, Robert C. From *The Power of Satire: Magic, Ritual, Art.* Princeton University Press, 1960. Copyright © 1960 by Princeton University Press. Renewed 1988 by Mary C. Elliott. Reproduced by permission of the Literary Estate of Robert C. Elliott.

Firchow, Peter Edgerly. From *The End of Utopia: A Study of Aldous Huxley's* **Brave New World.** Bucknell University Press, 1984. Reproduced by permission.

Rideout, Walter B. From *The Radical Novel in the United States, 1900-1954: Some Interrelations of Literature and Society.* Harvard University Press, 1956. Copyright 1956 President & Fellows of Harvard College. Copyright renewed 1984 by Walter Bates Rideout. All rights reserved. Reproduced by permission of the author.

Tarrow, Susan. From *Exile from the Kingdom: A Political Rereading of Albert Camus.* University of Alabama Press, 1985. Copyright © 1985 by The University of Alabama Press. All rights reserved. Reproduced by permission.

Trilling, Diana. From *Claremont Essays.* Harcourt Brace & World, 1964. Copyright © 1962, renewed 1992 by Diana Trilling. First published as a preface to the 1962 Crowell-Collier edition to *Tom Sawyer.* Reproduced with the permission of The Wylie Agency, Inc.

Ziolkowski, Theodore. From *The Novels of Hermann Hesse: A Study in Theme and Structure.* Princeton University Press, 1965. Copyright © 1965 by Princeton University Press. Reproduced by permission of Princeton University Press.

PHOTOGRAPHS AND ILLUSTRATIONS APPEARING IN *NFS*, *VOLUME 6, WERE RECEIVED FROM THE FOLLOWING SOURCES:*

AP/WIDE WORLD PHOTOS: Allende, Isabel, photograph. AP/Wide World Photos. Reproduced by permission. —Allende, Salvador, 1970, photograph. AP/Wide World Photos. Reproduced by permission. —Camus, Albert, photograph. AP/Wide World Photos. Reproduced by permission. —Ford Motor Company Model T assembly line, photograph. AP/Wide World Photos. Reproduced by permission. —George and Charlie, newborn cows created through cloning and genetic engineering, 1998, photograph. AP/Wide World Photos. Reproduced by permission. —Huxley, Aldous, photograph. AP/Wide World Photos. Reproduced by permission. —McCullers, Carson, photograph. AP/Wide World Photos. Reproduced by permission. —Morrison, Toni, New York City, 1987, photograph by David Bookstaver. AP/Wide World Photos. Reproduced by permission. —National Women's Liberation Party, photograph. AP/Wide

World Photos. Reproduced by permission. —One-room schoolhouse, circa 1886, photograph by Jacob Riis. AP/Wide World Photos. Reproduced by permission. —Shanghai street scene, photograph. AP/Wide World Photos. Reproduced by permission. —Solzhenitsyn, Alexander, photograph. AP/Wide World Photos. Reproduced by permission. —Thomas, Jonathan Taylor, in a scene from *Tom Sawyer*, photograph. AP/Wide World Photos. Reproduced by permission. —Winfrey, Oprah, with Danny Glover in a scene from *Beloved*, photograph. AP/Wide World Photos. Reproduced by permission.

ARCHIVE PHOTOS: Hemingway, Ernest, 1937, Africa, photograph. Archive Photos, Inc. Reproduced by permission. —Rollins, Howard, in the film *Ragtime*, photograph. Archive Photos, Inc. Reproduced by permission.

BETTMAN ARCHIVE/NEWSPHOTOS, INC.: Doctorow, E. L., photograph. The Bettmann Archive/Newsphotos, Inc. Reproduced by permission.

MIRIAM BERKLEY: Kingston, Maxine Hong, photograph by Miriam Berkley. Miriam Berkley. Reproduced by permission.

CORBIS/ADAM WOOLFITT: El Oued Dunes, photograph. Corbis/Adam Woolfitt. Reproduced by permission.

CORBIS/AFP: Demonstrator at Day of Political Protest, photograph. Corbis/AFP. Reproduced by permission.

CORBIS/ARNE HODALIC: Cuban fisherman, photograph. Corbis/Arne Hodalic. Reproduced by permission.

CORBIS-BETTMAN: Armed guard at stadium, photograph. Corbis/Bettmann. Reproduced by permission. —Chinese section of hunger parade, photograph. Corbis/Bettmann. Reproduced by permission. —Ford, Henry I, 1946, Dearborn, Michigan, photograph. Corbis-Bettmann. Reproduced by permission. —Girl dancing at Love-In, photograph. Corbis-Bettmann. Reproduced by permission. —Hesse, Hermann, photograph. Corbis-Bettmann. Reproduced by permission. —St. Patrick's Cathedral, Dublin, Ireland, photograph. Corbis-Bettmann. Reproduced by permission. —Sellers, Catherine, and Marc Cassot with Albert Camus in stage production of *Sensitive Translator*, photograph. Corbis-Bettmann. Reproduced by permission. —Sinclair, Upton, photograph. Corbis-Bettmann. Reproduced by permission. "Southern Industry," c. 1850, engraving. Corbis-Bettmann. Reproduced by permission. Swift, Jonathan, painting. Corbis-Bettmann. Reproduced by permission.

THE KOBAL COLLECTION: Courtenay, Tom, in *One Day in the Life of Ivan Denisovich*, movie still. The Kobal Collection. Reproduced by permission. —Locke, Sondra and Alan Arkin, from the film *The Heart Is a Lonely Hunter*, photograph. The Kobal Collection. Reproduced by permission. —*Siddhartha*, movie still, photograph. The Kobal Collection. Reproduced by permission.

LIBRARY OF CONGRESS/CORBIS: Packing house workers splitting hog backbones, 1906, Chicago, Illinois, photograph. The Library of Congress/Corbis. Reproduced by permission.

NBC/THE KOBAL COLLECTION: Danson, Ted, in the television movie *Gulliver's Travels*, photograph. NBC/The Kobal Collection. Reproduced by permission.

REUTERS/CORBIS-BETTMAN: Worshipers bowing before seated Buddha, 1989, Singapore, photograph. Reuters/Corbis-Bettmann. Reproduced by permission.

UPI/CORBIS-BETTMAN: Engineering camp of Union soldiers, Civil War era, photograph. UPI/Corbis-Bettmann. Reproduced by permission. —Firing squad executing Bolsheviks, January 16, 1920, photograph. UPI/Corbis-Bettmann. Reproduced by permission. —LeGuin, Ursula K, photograph. UPI/Corbis-Bettmann. Reproduced by per-

Contributors

Betsy Currier Beacom: Freelance writer, North Haven, CT. Entry on *The Adventures of Tom Sawyer*.

Robert Bennett: Doctoral student at the University of California, Santa Barbara, and adjunct instructor in English. Original essay on *Siddhartha*.

Karen R. Bloom: Doctoral candidate at Emory University. Original essay on *Gulliver's Travels*.

Chloe Bolan: Original essay on *The Left Hand of Darkness*, and original essay and entry on *One Day in the Life of Ivan Denisovich*.

Sharon Cumberland: Assistant professor at Seattle University. Original essay on *Uncle Tom's Cabin*.

Carl Davis: Associate professor of English at Northeast Louisiana University. Original essay on *The Old Man and the Sea*.

Jane Elizabeth Dougherty: Freelance writer, Medford, MA. Original essay on *The House of the Spirits*.

Scott Gillam: Author and freelance writer; B.A. and M.A. in English. Entry on *The Old Man and the Sea*.

Jhan Hochman: Instructor at Portland Community College. Original essay on *Brave New World*.

Jeremy Hubbell: Freelance writer; M.Litt., University of Aberdeen. Entry on *The Stranger*.

David J. Kelly: Professor of English, College of Lake County (IL). Original essays and entries on *The Heart Is a Lonely Hunter* and *Ragtime*, and entries on *The Jungle* and *The Left Hand of Darkness*.

Nancy C. McClure: Educational consultant and freelance writer, Clarksburg, WV; Ed.D, West Virginia University. Entry on *The Woman Warrior*.

Tabitha McIntosh-Byrd: Freelance writer; M.Litt., University of Aberdeen. Original essay on *The Adventures of Tom Sawyer*.

Patrick J. Moser: Assistant professor at the University of California-Davis. Original essay on *The Stranger*.

Wendy Perkins: Assistant Professor of English, Prince George's Community College, Maryland; Ph.D. in English, University of Delaware. Original essay on *Beloved*.

Diane Telgen: Entries on *Beloved* and *The House of the Spirits*.

Beverly West: Author and freelance writer. Entry on *Brave New World*.

Donna Woodford: Doctoral candidate, Washington University, St. Louis, MO. Original essay on *The Woman Warrior*.

The Adventures of Tom Sawyer

Mark Twain
1876

Mark Twain's publication in 1876 of his popular novel *The Adventures of Tom Sawyer* reversed a brief downturn in his success following the publication of his previous novel, *The Gilded Age.* Twain wrote *The Adventures of Tom Sawyer* while he and his family were living in Hartford, Connecticut, and while Twain was enjoying his fame. The novel, which tells of the escapades of a young boy and his friends in St. Petersburg, Missouri, a village near the Mississippi River, recalls Twain's own childhood in a small Missouri town. The friendship of Tom Sawyer and Huck Finn is one of the most celebrated in American literature, built on imaginative adventures, shared superstitions, and loyalty that rises above social convention. Twain's American reading audience loved this novel and its young hero, and the novel remains one of the most popular and famous works of American literature. The novel and its characters have achieved folk hero status in the American popular imagination. Scenes such as Tom Sawyer tricking his friends into whitewashing Aunt Polly's fence for him, Injun Joe leaping through the window of the courthouse after Tom names him as Dr. Robinson's murderer, and Tom and Becky lost in the cave have become so familiar to American readers that one almost doesn't have to read the book to know about them. But the pleasure of reading *The Adventures of Tom Sawyer* has kept readers coming back to the novel for over a century.

Beyond the fact that *The Adventures of Tom Sawyer* is fun to read, there is another reason for

Mark Twain

the novel's contemporary popularity: It introduces the character of Huckleberry Finn, who, with the publication of Twain's 1884 novel, *The Adventures of Huckleberry Finn,* would become one of the greatest characters in American literature.

Author Biography

Samuel Langhorne Clemens, more commonly known by his pseudonym, Mark Twain, was born in 1835 in what he later called "the almost invisible village" of Florida, Missouri. When he was a young child, Twain moved with his family about twenty miles away to Hannibal, Missouri, which is situated on the Mississippi River. Hannibal, Twain later said, was a town where "everybody was poor but didn't know it, and everybody was comfortable and did know it." Hannibal became Twain's model for the fictional town of St. Petersburg in *The Adventures of Tom Sawyer,* and in Hannibal began Twain's lifelong love for the great Mississippi River. As a boy, Twain played often near the Mississippi, fascinated by the many steamboats traveling up and down the river, and for fun he would build his own small rafts and float upon the river himself. Twain's childhood activities in Hannibal are often compared to those of Tom Sawyer in St. Petersburg, and Twain wrote in his autobiography about how certain characters in the novel had been suggested by persons he had known in Hannibal. In 1847, when Twain was twelve years old, his childhood was cut short when his father died. Young Sam Clemens was forced to leave school and begin working. He became apprenticed to a typesetter for a local newspaper, and began his long association with journalism.

For the next thirty years, Twain worked in the newspaper business, mainly as a writer; traveled extensively, including trips to the West, Europe, and the Middle East; learned how to pilot a riverboat on the Mississippi River and obtained his pilot's license, working for a while as a riverboat captain; served briefly in the Confederate Army during the Civil War; panned for gold; and married Olivia Langdon, the sister of his friend Charles Langdon. Trained as a journalist, Twain wrote about many of his experiences during this period, and his first two books, *Innocents Abroad* and *Roughing It,* are fictionalized accounts of his trips to Europe, the Middle East, and the American West. Twain's success with these two books brought him greater fame and put him in demand as a public speaker. He was known as a great storyteller both on and off the page, and when he published *The Adventures of Tom Sawyer* in 1876, it buoyed and secured his reputation as a teller of rollicking adventure tales.

Plot Summary

The Adventures of Tom Sawyer depicts the life of an imaginative, troublesome boy in the American West of the 1840s. The novel is intensely dramatic in its construction, taking the form of a series of comic vignettes based on Tom's exploits. These vignettes are linked together by a darker story that grows in importance throughout the novel—Tom's life-threatening entanglement with the murderer Injun Joe.

Vignettes

The novel opens with a stern Aunt Polly searching for her nephew Tom in order to punish him. The reader, also looking for Tom, is introduced to the basic elements of his life—exploits and punishments. Aunt Polly finds Tom, and he and his half-brother Sid are presented to readers as contrasting versions of boyhood. Tom is the prototypical appealing bad boy while Sid is the obnoxious goodie-goodie. The reader is on Tom's side from this point onward.

The story moves through a series of chapter-length vignettes featuring Tom and his richly imaginative life. These include the most famous scene in the novel, and arguably the most famous scene in American literature—whitewashing the fence. Sentenced to re-paint Aunt Polly's fence, Tom is desperate to get out of it by any means necessary. He spends the day persuading a series of local boys that whitewashing is fun. This "reverse-psychology" is so convincing that the boys not only beg to take over, they actually bribe him with their most treasured possessions. At the end of the day Tom is loaded with this juvenile largesse, and is rewarded by Aunt Polly for a job well done.

The episodic structure continues with scenes of mock warfare, the appearance of Becky Thatcher—with whom Tom falls instantly in love—and a thematically important episode in which Tom imagines and stages his own death scene. A Sabbath School episode shows Tom using his largesse to barter for the paper equivalent of 2000 successfully memorized verses, and he presents them to the teacher to get his reward. His real ignorance is quickly and embarrassingly exposed.

Next readers are introduced to a boy who will become—in a later novel—one of the most important characters in American fiction: Huckleberry Finn. Huck is a sort of comic figure in his clown's outfit of discarded adult's clothes. After talking to Huck, Tom goes to school, where he "courts" Becky Thatcher. They get engaged, but Tom mentions a prior relationship and Becky is devastated. Hurt, Tom takes out his frustration by playing Robin Hood with a friend. Here readers discover that his inability to learn simple Bible verses is due to lack of interest, since he is capable of memorizing whole pages of his favorite books.

Injun Joe

When Tom and Huck go to the town cemetery, the story that threads the novel together begins. In a scene straight out of the novels Tom loves, Injun Joe and Muff Potter enter the graveyard with young Dr. Robinson in order to "snatch" bodies. While Tom and Huck watch, Injun Joe attacks the doctor, and the men fight. After Muff is knocked unconscious, the scene climaxes with the grisly stabbing of Dr. Robinson. The boys run away, and Joe makes Potter believe that he is the murderer.

From this point, the shadow of Injun Joe hangs over Tom's adventures. The boys decide not to tell anyone for fear of reprisals, and they swear in blood to stay silent. Tom's depression over the murder deepens when Becky refuses to forgive him. The discovery of Dr. Robinson's body "electrifies" the village, and Tom and Huck go to the crime scene. They watch as Muff is arrested and confesses to the murder.

Their consciences troubled, both boys try to appease their guilt over Muff's false arrest by taking the condemned man food and gifts. Convinced that he is unloved, Tom decides to take up a life of crime. Together with Huck and Joe Harper, he decides to live out another of his favorite stories and become a pirate. They raft away and watch as a search is conducted for drowned people. Tom realizes that the "drownded people" are themselves— the town thinks that they are dead. Tom has gotten his earlier wish: he will be able to witness his own funeral. After sneaking home and watching his heartbroken Aunt, Tom makes his plans, and the boys make a dramatic entrance in the middle of their own funerals.

The trial of Muff Potter grows closer, and Tom gets into more scrapes, culminating in a heroic act in which he saves Becky from punishment and she forgives him. The happiness does not last; the trial is now due. In a dramatic turn, Tom is called to the stand by Muff's lawyer. As he exonerates Muff, Injun Joe flees from the building.

Though Tom is terrified at first, time passes and it seems less likely that Joe will come back for revenge. Tom returns to his favorite occupations, and he and Huck go searching for buried treasure in a haunted house. While the boys hide in the loft, two strangers enter the building; one of them is Injun Joe in disguise. The men have stolen money, and while they are burying it they find more—thousands of dollars in gold. They take it and leave, Joe vowing to get his revenge. The boys decide that the target of Joe's revenge must be Tom himself.

The boys decide to track down the "treasure" and go in search of Joe. They find him at a tavern, and Huck begins his surveillance of the men. Tom, however, is distracted by a newly-returned Becky and her plans for a picnic. On the day of the excursion, Becky arranges to stay at a friend's house. After eating, the village children decide to play in the caves. As they play, the story returns to Huck, on watch for Injun Joe. He follows Joe and his partner out of their lair and listens as Joe explains who the real object of his revenge is: the Widow Douglas. The widow's husband had once had Joe horsewhipped, and he has decided to "slit her nostrils."

Panicking, Huck runs for help. Some townsmen scare off the villains, but fail to catch them. Huck tells them that one of the villains is Injun Joe, but keeps quiet about the treasure.

It is not until the next day that the village realizes that Becky and Tom are missing. A desperate search through the caves begins and Tom's wish to stage his funeral seems to have come terrifyingly true this time. In a "flashback" readers find out what has happened. Wandering away from the others, Tom and Becky become lost in the caves. As their supplies run out and they search for an escape route, they narrowly miss bumping into Injun Joe, who is hiding in the caves. Scared, they retreat, and Becky seems near death.

Next, the novel jumps to celebrations in the village—the children have been found. Through the narrative device of Tom telling his story to his family, we learn that the children escaped when Tom found a side route out. Weeks pass and the children begin to recover, while Injun Joe seems to be forgotten. Tom is told that the caves have been sealed up for two weeks, and the horrible truth becomes clear. Joe is still in there. When the doors to the caves are opened, Injun Joe's dead body is found lying at the entrance.

Tom and Huck realize that the treasure is in the caves, and they retrieve it. They return to an excited crowd, and the Widow Douglas announces that she plans to adopt Huck. Tom blurts out that Huck is rich. The story is told, and the money is invested for them, while poor Huck is civilized almost to death. Escaping back to his old life, he can only be enticed back by Tom's promise that they will be "robbers" together, for which they both need to be respectable. With that promise of further adventures, the novel closes.

Characters

Aunt Polly

The sister of Tom and Sid's dead mother, Aunt Polly has taken in both boys to live with her and her daughter Mary. Aunt Polly loves Tom but is both exasperated and amused by him. She is always shaking her head and wringing her hands over his behavior, but her soft heart prevents her from punishing him very strictly.

Widow Douglas

Huck Finn saves the Widow Douglas from Injun Joe when he overhears Injun Joe's plans to mu-

Jonathan Taylor Thomas as the title character in the movie Tom and Huck.

tilate her and enlists the help of the Welshman and his sons to protect her. A pious and good-hearted woman of St. Petersburg, the Widow Douglas later takes Huck Finn into her home with the intention of "civilizing" him.

Huckleberry Finn

Referred to by the narrator as both the "juvenile pariah of the village" and as a "romantic outcast," Huckleberry Finn is "cordially hated and dreaded by all the mothers" of St. Petersburg and secretly admired by their children. The son of the town drunkard, who is usually absent from the village and thus from his parental responsibilities, Huck sleeps in hogshead barrels or on doorsteps, wears castoff men's clothing, swears, smokes, and lives by his own rules. Huck and Tom Sawyer are good friends because, although Tom is "under strict orders not to play with" Huck, he admires Huck so much that he disobeys Aunt Polly's orders and secretly finds ways to play with his outcast friend. Viewed by adults as being "idle and lawless and vulgar and bad," Huck actually possesses a conscience and a heart. When he goes to the Welshman to report Injun Joe's threats against the Widow Douglas, he admits to the older man that he worries about his character and the way he is perceived by others. He confesses that "sometimes [he] can't

sleep much, on account of thinking about [his bad reputation] and sort of trying to strike out a new way of doing." Huck saves the Widow Douglas from Injun's Joe's revenge, and she in turn takes Huck in and attempts to "civilize" him, with clean clothes and church and polite manners. But Huck is miserable under her protective care and runs away, explaining later to Tom, "It's awful to be tied up so."

Joe Harper

Tom Sawyer's "bosom friend," Joe is a member of Tom's pirate gang and as such calls himself "the Terror of the Seas." When the "pirates" run away on a short-lived pirating adventure, Joe is the first to admit to homesickness.

Injun Joe

Known as a "half-breed," meaning he is half white and half Native American, Injun Joe is the villain of the novel and a force of evil in St. Petersburg. He is an angry, vengeful, amoral man who thinks nothing of robbing Hoss Williams's grave, killing Dr. Robinson, stealing gold, or threatening old widows and young boys. Injun Joe's name, which is an abbreviated slang pronunciation of "Indian Joe," shows that his identity is so closely tied to his being a Native American that the townspeo-

Media Adaptations

- In 1930 *The Adventures of Tom Sawyer* was adapted by Paramount as a film entitled *Tom Sawyer*. It was directed by John Cromwell and stars Jackie Coogan and Mitzi Green.

- The novel was also adapted as a film entitled *Tom Sawyer* by Selznick International in 1938. Directed by Norman Taurog and starring Walter Brennan and May Robson, the film is available on video, distributed by Trimark.

- A 1939 film adaptation, *Tom Sawyer, Detective* (Paramount), was directed by Louis King and starred Porter Hall, Donald O'Connor, Elisabeth Risdon, and Janet Waldo.

- In 1973 Clemens's novel was adapted into a musical film version (United Artists) entitled *Tom Sawyer*, directed by Don Taylor and starring Johnnie Whitaker, Jodie Foster, Celeste Holm, and Warren Oates. Available on video (MGM Home Entertainment) and with a musical score composed by Robert and Richard Sherman, this film received three Academy Award nominations.

- In 1995 Disney adapted the novel as a film entitled *Tom and Huck* directed by Peter Hewitt and starring Jonathan Taylor Thomas as Tom Sawyer and Brad Renfro as Huckleberry Finn. This version is also available on video (Walt Disney Home Video).

- Read by Pat Bottino, *The Adventures of Tom Sawyer* is available on cassette from Blackstone Audiobooks.

---

ple—and the narrator—cannot think of him except in terms of his being an Indian. When Injun Joe, Muff Potter, and Dr. Robinson are in the cemetery to rob Hoss Williams's grave, Injun Joe begins to argue with Robinson about money. He points out that years before, Robinson had treated him poorly when he was in need, and he tells Robinson, "I swore I'd get even with you if it took a hundred

years…. Did you think I'd forget? The Injun blood ain't in me for nothing." The inhabitants of St. Petersburg appear to be basically decent, good people; yet Injun Joe represents a dark force among them, embodying the possibilities of human evil.

Mr. Jones
See The Welshman

Amy Lawrence
Tom was in love with Amy before Becky Thatcher arrived in St. Petersburg.

Mary
Tom Sawyer's cousin, Mary is Aunt Polly's daughter and treats Tom sweetly, patiently helping him learn his Scripture verses and get dressed up for church.

The Model Boy
Hated by all the boys in town, the Model Boy is "the pride of all the matrons" because he is so polite and well-behaved.

Willie Mufferson
See The Model Boy

Muff Potter
Set up by Injun Joe to take the blame for Dr. Robinson's murder, Muff Potter is disreputable enough to be a believable murderer. Unable to recall what really happened on the night of the murder because Dr. Robinson had knocked him unconscious in a scuffle, Potter denies killing the doctor. Out of guilt for their secret knowledge of the truth, Tom and Huck are kind to Potter when he is in jail, and in spite of his mortal fear of Injun Joe, Tom finally tells the truth about the murder at Potter's trial, resulting in Potter's freedom.

Dr. Robinson
Dr. Robinson is killed by Injun Joe after they set out together on a midnight grave robbery. Tom and Huck are silent witnesses as Injun Joe takes revenge on the young doctor for having insulted him five years before.

Ben Rogers
Ben is the first boy Tom dupes into whitewashing Aunt Polly's fence for him.

Sid Sawyer
Tom's younger half-brother, Sid is "a quiet boy" with "no adventurous, troublesome ways,"

and so he and Tom do not get along with each other. Sid takes pleasure in tattling on Tom when Tom has gotten into mischief.

Tom Sawyer

Mischievous but lovable, Tom Sawyer is a fictional character so well known that he has become a folkloric figure. Even those who have not read *The Adventures of Tom Sawyer* may be familiar with the episodes in which Tom tricks his friends into whitewashing his aunt's fence for him, spies on his own funeral, acts as the surprise witness against Injun Joe at Muff Potter's murder trial, and gets lost in the cave with his beloved Becky Thatcher. Tom's Aunt Polly takes good care of Tom and his half-brother Sid, although often Tom exasperates her when he gets into trouble. He sneaks out his window at night to go on adventures with his friend Huck Finn, believes in superstitions, and yearns to lead what he sees as the exciting life of a pirate or robber. He can't sit still in church or in school and always finds some diversion, such as watching a bug, to make the time pass more quickly. Tom is happiest when he is off having thrilling adventures with his friends: searching for buried treasure, running away for a few days to a sandbar in the Mississippi River in a game of pirates, or hiding in the cemetery at midnight. He adores Becky Thatcher, the new girl in town, and shows off to get her attention. Tom is a boy of strong emotions and great imagination, and in spite of his mischievous ways he has a good heart: his rescues of Becky when she is heading for trouble with the schoolmaster and of Muff Potter when he is on trial for murder show that Tom knows the right thing to do.

Becky Thatcher

Becky is the new girl in town, daughter of the "august" Judge Thatcher. When Tom sees Becky for the first time, with her blue eyes and "yellow hair plaited into two long tails," he falls in love with her immediately, forsaking his old love, Amy Lawrence. At Becky's picnic, Tom and Becky become lost together in the cave and are missing for five days. During their ordeal inside the cave, Becky fears for her life and depends upon Tom for reassurance and support.

Judge Thatcher

Becky Thatcher's father, Judge Thatcher is a respected county judge, brother to St. Petersburg's lawyer Thatcher.

Rebecca Thatcher

See Becky Thatcher

The Welshman

The Welshman listens carefully to Huck when Huck reports that he has overheard Injun Joe's threats of injuring the Widow Douglas. The Welshman and his grown sons hurry out to investigate the trouble and later welcome Huck back into their house, a rare experience for the outcast Huck.

Themes

Friendship

Children's friendships are at the center of *The Adventures of Tom Sawyer*. Tom's family—Aunt Polly, Mary, and Sid—does not always appreciate him and does not figure into his rich imaginative life. However, Tom's friends—Joe Harper and Huck Finn in particular—look up to him precisely because he is so imaginative and adventurous. The boys see each other as they want to be seen, and together they create an exciting world of intrigue and adventure. The friendship between Tom and Huck especially is highlighted in the novel. Tom admires Huck for his freedom from adults' rules, and he knows that his association with Huck makes him appear daring, an image he relishes. Tom also cares about Huck, concerned that he is alone in the world. When the boys return from their pirating adventure to attend their own funerals, Tom and Joe are smothered with affection by their families while Huck stands awkwardly alone, with no one to welcome him home. Tom points out to Aunt Polly that "it ain't fair. Somebody's got to be glad to see Huck." Tom and Huck share a deep belief in superstitions and a love of adventure, imagining themselves as pirates and robbers in partnership with one another. Tom is so loyal to Huck that he repeatedly disobeys Aunt Polly's orders not to play with Huck, and Tom proudly announces to the schoolmaster that he was late for school because he was playing with the forbidden Huck, even though he knows he will be punished for it. The boys often use dramatic conventions to represent their loyalty to one another. For example, after they secretly observe Injun Joe's murder of Dr. Robinson in the cemetery, Tom writes an oath that "they will keep mum about this and … wish they may drop down dead in their tracks if they ever tell and Rot." Tom and Huck then sign the oath with their own blood.

Topics for Further Study

- Research white Americans' attitudes toward Native Americans in the mid-19th century. Does Injun Joe's status as evil incarnate reflect the popular view of Native Americans in that period?

- Consider the life of Huckleberry Finn in terms of today's standards: How would a homeless child, the son of an alcoholic who has essentially abandoned him, be treated in the United States today? What factors in Huck's world make it possible for him to live as he wishes, sleeping outside in barrels and on doorsteps and wearing rags? How can Twain romanticize a child like Huck, and why would Huck not be considered romantic in today's society?

- The role of women in *The Adventures of Tom Sawyer* seems to be that of a civilizing force: Aunt Polly trying to teach Tom how to behave, the Widow Douglas taking Huck in to "introduce him to society," the young ladies on Examination Evening reading essays with titles such as "Religion in History" and "Filial Love." Research attitudes toward women in 1840s American culture. What kinds of tasks were white women expected to fulfill, and what was their role in helping to shape their world?

- In the 1840s, Missouri represented the American frontier. What did this mean? What form of government existed for Missouri then, and how was it enforced? What attitudes did people "back East" have about those who had moved out West to the frontier, and how did the frontiersmen and women see themselves?

Because Tom is a child of the community, and thus assured of adult protection, he feels safe enough to testify against Injun Joe in Muff Potter's murder trial. But Tom keeps secret Huck's knowledge of the same situation, because Huck fears Injun Joe's retaliation and knows he is without serious protection. Huck and Tom's friendship rises above the social conventions of St. Petersburg. They are friends because each likes the other for who he is, and it matters little to either that their society frowns upon their friendship.

Imagination

Tom Sawyer's imagination rules his life and shapes his world. He takes every opportunity to make a game of life, embarking on such romantic endeavors as digging for buried treasure or organizing his friends into a band of pirates with names like "the Black Avenger of the Spanish Main," "Huck Finn the Red-Handed," and "the Terror of the Seas." Perhaps not always completely original in their imaginings, Tom and his friends play Robin Hood by reciting dialogue that they have memorized from the book. Although he claims to reject many of the rules of the adult world, Tom has his own clear rules about how pirates must behave, what social class robbers must come from, and how certain superstitions work. His imaginings may free him from his rulebound world, but they often place him in another such world. His imaginative world and his "real" world—the mundane life of St. Petersburg—do not often collide. Yet when these two worlds do collide—such as when Tom and Huck witness the murder in the cemetery, and when Tom realizes how badly he hurt Aunt Polly when he ran away to play pirates, and when Tom and Becky's adventure in the cave turns life-threatening—Tom is able to understand the limits of imagination. In each case, Tom's empathy for another person—Muff Potter, Dr. Robinson, Aunt Polly, Becky—causes him to realize that he needs to stop pretending and deal with the situation at hand.

Truth and Falsehood

The first words Tom Sawyer speaks in *The Adventures of Tom Sawyer* are a lie. Aunt Polly is looking for Tom and shouting his name, and when she finds him hiding in the closet and asks him what he is doing, he replies, in an obvious lie, "Nothing." She points to the jam all over his mouth and hands and asks what it is, and he replies, "*I* don't know, aunt," another obvious lie. Tom is thus introduced as a mischievous boy who gets into trouble, although Aunt Polly's laughter upon Tom's escape from her disapproval shows that his lies and disobedience are essentially unimportant to her. Tom lies frequently throughout the novel, mostly about where he's been or what he's been doing, and mostly to avoid getting into trouble. However, when telling the truth really matters, Tom knows he must not lie. When he first returns home after his pirating adventure, he feels bad about having hurt Aunt

Polly by scaring her with his long absence, so he lies to her about having had a dream about her when he was away on his pirating adventure. When she later discovers that the story of the dream had all been a lie, Tom realizes that "what had seemed like a good joke before, and very ingenious … merely looked mean and shabby now." His conscience prods him finally to tell her the truth of what really happened. But this time, Aunt Polly doesn't believe him, and she refuses to until she finds the piece of bark in his jacket pocket with the note to her on it that he had said he had written. Tom's conscience again leads him to tell the truth when he decides he must help Muff Potter. Because he cannot in good conscience let Potter be convicted of Dr. Robinson's murder, Tom decides to be a witness at Potter's murder trial, even though he knows by doing so he places himself in some danger with Injun Joe. In spite of the ease with which lying comes to him, Tom's conscience and his ability to tell the truth when he should place him in stark contrast to Injun Joe. Injun Joe, a man without a conscience and thus capable of evil, lies and misrepresents himself for the purpose of personal gain.

Style

Point of View

The novel's narration is third person, limited omniscient, with Tom Sawyer as the central consciousness. This means that the story is told about Tom's world and is particularly focused on him by a narrator who is able to understand the motivations and feelings of some of the characters. This point of view earns the reader's amused admiration of an unlikely hero. Tom is a mischievous boy, an orphan, who cares nothing for school or church or any other polite social conventions but instead spends most of his time pretending that he is a pirate or a robber, sneaking out his window at midnight to have secret adventures with his friends in places like cemeteries, and entirely likely to have in his possession objects like dead cats. Tom Sawyer's character is a realistic portrayal of a young boy who gets into trouble constantly, trying the patience of the adults around him while making them smile. The novel's point of view makes Tom sympathetic by showing how he often feels guilty or sorry or brave. A more objective narration of Tom's antics—one that does not look into his mind—might make him seem only naughty and tiresome. The glimpses into his often noble inten-

tions as he conjures up his schemes serve to temper his character: he is not a bad boy, just an imaginative one.

Setting

The Adventures of Tom Sawyer is set in the 1840s, mainly in St. Petersburg, Missouri, a small fictional village where everyone knows everyone and the people are unsophisticated. When Judge Thatcher, the county judge, visits the village church during the Sunday service, the children are fascinated, impressed that he has come from "Constantinople, twelve miles away—so he had traveled, and seen the world." Yet in spite of their lack of worldliness, the people of St. Petersburg attempt to keep up "civilized" practices such as having their children memorize Scripture passages and recite poems and other readings at school on Examination Evening. The adults of the village watch out for each other's children: when Tom and Becky are discovered to be lost in the cave, the entire town turns out to help search for them.

St. Petersburg is a true community. Even the threat of evil, embodied by Injun Joe, is squelched by the human desire to help others. For example, Huck swallows his fear of Injun Joe and goes to the Welshman to help save the Widow Douglas, and the Welshman gladly goes to the Widow's aid. In this safe world, Tom Sawyer can feel secure in his human connections but also free to exercise his imagination. St. Petersburg mirrors Twain's childhood home of Hannibal, Missouri. St. Petersburg, like Hannibal, is situated along the Mississippi River, a source of transportation, beauty, and power. The river's presence near St. Petersburg makes the boys' pirate adventure possible and reminds them of the great world beyond their tiny village.

Realism

Realism involves the portrayal of characters and situations that appear to be drawn from real life. In the nineteenth century, realism often involved characters and settings that were ordinary and far from genteel. While *The Adventures of Tom Sawyer* takes a somewhat romantic view of childhood in general—full of freedom and imaginative adventures—most of the children in the novel are themselves not romanticized. Tom and his friends get dirty, spit, sneak around behind their elders' backs, and carry around dead cats. Although he can also be charming and appealing, Tom lies to Aunt Polly, shows off to gain Becky Thatcher's attention, scratches himself when his clothes itch, and tricks his friends into doing his work: in short, he is human, possessing flaws and weaknesses. Twain's illustration of both sides of Tom—the appealing and the exasperating—makes Tom more realistic. Huck Finn's character, too, is shown in some depth, which also makes him more realistic. Huck is romanticized by many of the other children in town, as they envy what appears to be his utter freedom from rules and constraints. However, he has moments when he worries about his status in the world and wishes he weren't such an outcast, and his dark moments make him more real.

Historical Context

The Gilded Age

Mark Twain's 1873 novel, *The Gilded Age,* which he wrote in collaboration with his Hartford neighbor Charles Dudley Warner, gave its name to the mood of materialistic excess and cynical political corruption that started with the Grant administration in 1869 and prevailed in the 1870s and beyond. To be gilded is to be coated in gold, so the phrase "The Gilded Age" refers directly to the opulent tastes and jaded sensibilities of America's wealthy during this period. The appearance of *The Adventures of Tom Sawyer* during the Gilded Age represents a nostalgic look back at a simpler, less expansionist and less industrialized time in American history.

Expansion was a major theme of American society in the post-Civil War period. When the war ended in 1865, the United States was bigger, more powerful and richer than ever before, and it continued to grow. The way post-war Americans behaved and saw themselves was different: as a group they possessed greater energy, greater ambition, and a greater sense of potential. The American economy was becoming increasingly more industrialized. The transcontinental railroad was built, immigrants from Europe were pouring into the cities, westward expansion was occurring, and new farming technologies made it possible for farmers to grow more crops more successfully. The population was growing rapidly, helping to create a large labor pool, and labor unions were on the rise. The growth of industry, supported by the war and the demand it created for supplies, created enormous wealth for many Americans. Powerful businessmen such as Andrew Carnegie, John D. Rockefeller, and J. P. Morgan built their companies—U.S. Steel, Standard Oil, and Morgan Bank, respectively—into

multimillion-dollar enterprises and became known by their detractors as "robber barons." The very wealthy flocked to summer vacation colonies like Newport, Rhode Island, where they built huge summer "cottages" that often were opulent mansions. Money and power were equated with each other during this period, and some of the rich and powerful were not above political corruption. At the time, U.S. senators were elected by the state legislators rather than by the voting public, and it was not uncommon for a legislator to accept bribes for electing a wealthy man's senator of choice.

However, not every American during this period was wealthy or able to vote; many Americans remained disenfranchised and poor. Women did not yet have the right to vote, and the women's suffrage movement had been underway for years. Black Americans also could not vote, and beginning at the end of Reconstruction in the 1870s, the legal apparatus that kept blacks separate from white society came into being, as Jim Crow laws were enacted by Southern states in an effort to suppress blacks. The Ku Klux Klan also began its brutal work in this period, with its goal of frightening and murdering Southern blacks into submission. The U.S. Army's main opponent during this time was Native Americans, who were being suppressed and forced onto reservations. So while the Gilded Age, as it is now called, was about controlling the population and exploiting the land and other resources, all in the service of expanding the power of American culture and society, many Americans remained powerless.

American Literature of the 1870s

American literature following the Civil War began to reflect Americans' new sense of nationalism and diversity. Realism dominated the literary scene, as the arts began to portray ordinary people in their everyday lives. The three major literary figures of the last twenty-five years of the nineteenth century—Twain, Henry James and William Dean Howells—did much to bring realism into the forefront of American letters. In the 1870s alone, Twain published *The Gilded Age* (1873) and *The Adventures of Tom Sawyer* (1876), along with many other shorter works; James published his first two popular and successful works of fiction, *The American* (1877) and *Daisy Miller* (1878); and Howells, while he published several novels during the 1870s, achieved more success as the powerful editor of the *Atlantic Monthly,* the most influential literary magazine of the time. Howells was a friend and editor

Compare & Contrast

- **1840s:** Slavery of Africans was widely practiced throughout the Southern states of the nation. Slaves were considered the property of their owners and possessed no civil rights: they could not vote, legally marry, or own property.

  1876: Following the Civil War and the abolition of slavery in the United States, the radical wing of the Republican party attempted to remake the South without slavery. This period of reformation, called Reconstruction, ended in 1876. The civil rights gains made during Reconstruction were lost following the end of President Ulysses S. Grant's administration.

  Today: African Americans possess full civil rights under the U.S. Constitution and hold positions of power in the U.S. government, including seats on the Supreme Court, in the Senate, and in the President's Cabinet. In spite of these gains, race relations continue to be a divisive issue in American society.

- **1840s:** In 1840, Missouri was the westernmost state in the Union. Presidents Polk and Tyler pursued policies to fulfill America's so-called "manifest destiny" to expand to the shores of the Pacific Ocean. The war with Mexico resulted in the annexation of the Southwest. Texas became a state in 1845; California, virtually unknown in 1840, became a state in 1850.

  1876: Colorado entered the Union. Alaska had been purchased by the United States in 1872. The West was rapidly becoming populated, and in 1890 the U.S. government declared the frontier closed.

  Today: Alaska and Hawaii became the 49th and 50th states in the 1950s, and in the 1990s the physical boundaries of the United States appear fixed, but some wish to make Puerto Rico the 51st state.

- **1840s:** Industrialization was just beginning in the United States. Steam power transformed water transportation from rafts to steamboats. Steam was also beginning to transform travel on land with railroads. Samuel B. Morse's telegraph, a new means of communication, first operated successfully in 1844.

  1876: Industrialization was transforming the country, and the Philadelphia Centennial Exhibition celebrated technology. Alexander Graham Bell's telephone was introduced at the Exhibition. The transcontinental railroad had been finished in 1869, and by 1876 the railroad had become central to the industrial economy.

  Today: The information economy has succeeded the industrial economy. While the railroad was at the center of the industrial economy, the computer is at the center of the information economy. The Internet has produced a global communication network, and travel by automobile and airplane has largely replaced rail travel.

- **1840s:** From 1840 to 1855, about 3.5 million immigrants came into the United States, attracted by the promise of wealth and freedom. Most of the immigrants in this period came from Ireland and Germany.

  1876: Changing the population and the way American cities developed, immigration had become by 1876 a huge influence on American culture. In 1876, the nation was on the verge of its largest-ever influx of immigrants: nine million in the last twenty years of the nineteenth century.

---

to both Twain and James, whose bodies of work could not be more different from each other.

Twain's work from this period brought him wide popularity: it is mostly humorous, focusing on characters who are typically uncultivated and not part of the Eastern establishment. In contrast, James's work, which was never especially popular with the reading audience, subtly probes the social conventions that shape the world of the wealthy, educated, and civilized American. Howells saw the

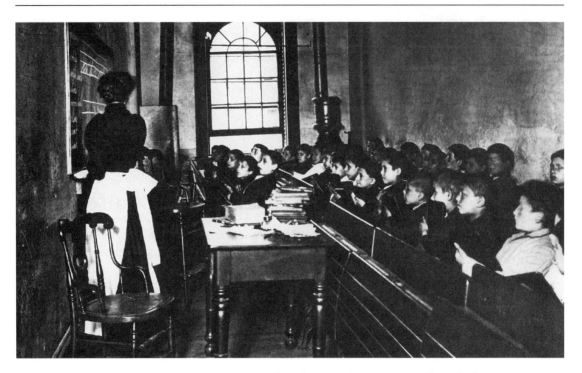

Though taken in the northern city of New York, this photograph gives some idea of what a schoolroom looked like in the late 1800s, when The Adventures of Tom Sawyer *was published.*

genius in both writers and their work and helped to guide them in their careers.

While Twain and James were the best-known and most influential writers of their day, many other writers and styles of writing were also emerging in the 1870s. The nation's expansionist mood was reflected by the proliferation of regional, or "local color," writers, who wrote about their own corners of the rapidly growing nation. Local color writing, another form of realism, generally sought to preserve through fiction the small-town ways that were being threatened by industrialization. By the 1870s, writers such as Bret Harte, Joel Chandler Harris, and Sarah Orne Jewett had begun publishing their work on the West, the South, and New England, respectively. In the next ten to twenty years, Kate Chopin, Mary E. Wilkins Freeman, Charles W. Chesnutt, and Hamlin Garland would add their regional voices—New Orleans, New England, the South, the Midwest—to the mix.

Critical Overview

Often discussed alongside its critically acclaimed and more popular sequel, *The Adventures of Huckleberry Finn, The Adventures of Tom Sawyer* is generally thought by critics to be artistically a lesser work than *Huckleberry Finn.* Yet in spite of its shortcomings as a work of art, *The Adventures of Tom Sawyer* has remained popular around the world throughout the more than 120 years since its publication in 1876. Twain himself called this novel his "hymn to boyhood."

About Twain in general, Henry Nash Smith says that "there can be no doubt that Mark Twain was an artist of the people. His fresh handling of the materials and techniques of backwoods storytellers is the clearest example in our history of the adaptation of a folk art to serious literary uses." Walter Blair discusses in his article "*Tom Sawyer*" the novel's sources, both autobiographical and literary. Twain is widely known to have used people and places from his childhood in the writing of *Tom Sawyer,* and Blair also shows in his article that "Literary influences ... shaped both incidents and the over-all pattern of *Tom Sawyer.*" In his 1960 book *Mark Twain,* Lewis Leary refers to the fact that upon its publication, *The Adventures of Tom Sawyer* "placed Mark Twain once more at the head of best-seller lists." Leary states, "Probably no more continuingly popular book has ever appeared in the United States." Leary discusses the construction of the novel, claiming that although it seems "loose and shambling ... there is artistry in it also ... [and] ... perhaps because [Twain] worked long over it, this first independent novel ... is better constructed than any he was to write again."

Granville Hicks writes in *The Great Tradition* (1935) that *The Adventures of Tom Sawyer* starts out as seeming to be more than just a boys' book. Hicks believes that the novel begins as "a fine and subtle portrayal of the Missouri frontier." However, Hicks goes on to say that Twain's artistic powers were limited and that the book ends "in the tawdry melodrama of conventional juvenile fiction." In short, Hicks feels that Twain's book does not deliver on its promise. In *Mark Twain: An Introduction and Interpretation*, Frank Baldanza claims that Twain's reputation "is based firmly on the unparalleled achievement of his books about boys," namely *The Adventures of Tom Sawyer* and *The Adventures of Huckleberry Finn*. Baldanza calls *Tom Sawyer* "a delightful book," one that "gives a genial and warmhearted backward glance at boyhood in Missouri" yet that also is "a serious and adult book." Baldanza sees the seriousness of the novel in the fact that "in the moral sphere, both Tom and Huck pay plentifully for their natural desires and impulses." John C. Gerber, in his book *Mark Twain*, acknowledges that "*Tom Sawyer* may not have the art or the profundity of *Huckleberry Finn*, but as an idyll of boyhood it has no peer anywhere." Gerber defends *Tom Sawyer* as a portrait of "boys as they are" and as a comic work. Like so many other critics, Gerber highlights the book's broad popularity, pointing out that *Tom Sawyer* "has been translated into over two dozen foreign languages and its sales, domestic and foreign, extend into the millions." According to Gerber, *The Adventures of Tom Sawyer* is second in popularity among Twain's books only to *Huckleberry Finn*.

Contemporary criticism about both *Tom Sawyer* and *Huckleberry Finn* often looks at the treatment of race and racism in these novels and the world they portray. While *Huckleberry Finn* has become controversial in some circles because of its use of language that degrades African Americans, *Tom Sawyer* does not offend in the same way, perhaps because slavery and its implicit racism exist more in the background of this novel than they do in *Huck Finn*. Shelley Fisher Fishkin points out in *Lighting Out for the Territory: Reflections on Mark Twain and American Culture* that "the Hannibal of Twain's youth, like the St. Petersburg of both *Tom Sawyer* and *Huckleberry Finn*, was a slaveholding society; but only in *Huckleberry Finn* would this

fact struggle to the foreground. The world of childhood fantasy, play, and adventure had preoccupied him in *Tom Sawyer*." Fishkin sees none of Twain's growing "moral indignation" in *Tom Sawyer*, and she speculates that "Twain may have suspected that to recreate the boyhood pastoral of *Tom Sawyer* effectively, he had to suppress that troublesome thing called a 'conscience' that had begun to make him ask some difficult questions—such as whether that boyhood world was not so 'innocent' after all."

Criticism

Tabitha McIntosh-Byrd

McIntosh-Byrd is a doctoral candidate at the University of Pennsylvania. In the following essay she explores the ways in which Mark Twain's Adventures of Tom Sawyer *can be read as a powerful critique of American identity.*

The Adventures of Tom Sawyer is an extremely difficult work to approach analytically because it is so embedded in the reader's own childhood. It is read in classrooms throughout the English-speaking world, and has become iconographic of childhood itself—especially American childhood. Indeed, this has been its reception from its initial publication. The first review, written by William Dean Howells in 1876, called it "a wonderful study of the boy-mind" which exists beyond the control or comprehension of adult society. His comments appeared in *Atlantic Monthly* before the book was even published, and thus set the framework for the way in which the novel would be read. Clemens himself did not read his book this way, a fact that is suggested by his initial conviction that the story was written for an adult audience. Though his wife persuaded him to publish it as a children's book, Tom Sawyer's story can still be recovered as a novel for adults—a savage satire on adult hypocrisy and American cultural identity.

Tom Sawyer is generally read as the first truly American novel: a cathartic attempt by Clemens to write his own childhood and the childhood of America into a coherent literary whole. His success is attested to by the timeless status of Tom as a sort of "Every-Boy" for American culture—the literary epitome of the ingenuity, imagination, and pluck which form the basis of America's understanding of its own national character. In this reading, Tom's flouting of authority is a paradigm for American

What Do I Read Next?

- Twain's masterpiece, *The Adventures of Huckleberry Finn* (1884), reintroduces the character of Huck Finn, Tom Sawyer's best friend. While floating down the Mississippi River on a raft, Huck and runaway slave Jim escape the bonds of civilization and gain insight into human nature and conscience. Many critics consider *Huckleberry Finn* to be one of the greatest American novels of all time.

- Twain's *Roughing It* (1871), a book which grew out of his journey to the West with his brother, is a humorous, loosely-constructed travel narrative that relies on the American storytelling tradition.

- Twain's lifelong love affair with the Mississippi River is expressed in his *Life on the Mississippi* (1883), a compilation of travel narrative, anecdotes, history of the river, observations on American society, and stories from Twain's boyhood.

- *The Autobiography of Mark Twain* (1958 edition edited by Charles Neider), which Twain worked on for years before his death, is a book in which Twain says he speaks "freely" because "I shall be dead when the book issues from the press."

---

self-determination in the face of tyranny, his character expressing the intrinsic essence of freedom from tyranny and restraint. If we accept this and then look more closely at the structural motifs and internal parallels of Clemens' novel, a very different picture of the national character begins to emerge. The novel, like the village in which it is set, seems to be bathed in perpetually fair weather and sunshine. There is, however, always a darker side. Just as the sunshine of the village is belied by the dank, labyrinthine caves, so the novel has deeper and more disturbing resonances than are at first apparent.

To find this darker side, we must start by questioning the validity of Howells' distinction between the adult and the child mind in the novel. Are Tom's behavior, responses, needs, and follies *really* any different from those of the adults around him? In two early scenes this distinction would seem to be untenable. The first is the Sabbath School scene where Tom's "wily fraud" wins him a Bible. Several direct parallels are made here between the behavior of the adults and the children. Faced with the unexpected appearance of a guest of honor, adults and children alike respond with the same show of self-importance:

> Mr. Walters fell to "showing off".... The librarian "showed off".... The young lady teachers "showed off".... The little girls "showed off" ... the little boys "showed off" ... and above it all the great man sat and beamed ... for he was "showing off" too.

The only thing that differentiates the individuals in the Sabbath School is the method with which they express the same desire to be noticed. This series of comparisons suggests that public altruism, making spit-wads, enforcing discipline, and fulfilling the duties of public office should all be understood as essentially the same act. More subtly, the language that Clemens uses to describe Tom's actions in this episode is insidiously reflective of the adults that surround him. Tom's successful and hard-nosed bartering for the chits that will win him a Bible is described in the language of the adults' economy. In this way, the chits become "certified checks," which represent "warehoused" knowledge on the "premises" of Tom's brain. Judge Thatcher encourages him to say that he would rather have this "warehoused" knowledge than "any money" he could be offered, which draws the analogy tighter. Tom's gathering of this paper "wealth" is done to elevate himself above his peers and impress the powerful. If this wealth performs the same function in the adults' economy as it does in the children's, then the acquisition of money is being presented as foolish, egotistical, and child-like.

The second incident again takes place in church. Bored during a long service, Tom falls back on teasing a pinch-bug and then watches with smothered amusement as it torments a stray poodle. Despite their public show of faith and piety, the adults of St. Petersburg partake of exactly the same feelings:

> Other people, uninterested in the sermon, found relief in the beetle and they eyed it too ... the whole church was red-faced and suffocating with suppressed laughter.

Just as the Temperance Tavern in the village contains a secret and squalid whisky-drinking den, so the church-going community hides its secret boredom beneath a show of public faith. Just as Tom goes to church because his Aunt compels him, so the villagers go to church because the need to appear acceptable to their peers compels them. In this insistent parallel, the motivations of human beings are presented, again, as identical in essence. The desire to show off and the compulsion to go to church are both shown to be expressions of the same need to be accepted. Further, because it is the adults' own need that compels them, they are shown as more willfully self-deluded. After all, the children have no choice but to be told what to do. The adults give up their own pleasure on purpose.

The fact that both of these scenes take place within the church is indicative of an implicit critique of the role of religion in St. Petersburg culture that threads throughout the text—a critique that finds its main expression through the subtle development of the role of books within the text. Again, this is created through a series of oblique parallels. Tom's relationship to books and the Book (the Bible) is contrasted throughout. While he cannot successfully commit a single verse of the Good Book to memory, he has whole pages of his favorite books memorized. The deliberate juxtaposition of these failures and feats of memory suggests a basic similarity among all of the books in question—a sneaky way, as it were, of suggesting that all of the books in question are nothing more or less than fiction. With this juxtaposition firmly established, Tom's relationship to fiction becomes more understandable as satire. Just as the adults of the church act out their public lives in accordance to the teachings of the Book, so Tom acts out his public life in accordance with books. The charity that the village women want to posthumously extend to Injun Joe is thus performance, in the same way that Tom's posturing and playing is a performance of his favorite stories. The language of the Bible pervades the language of the adults and the language of adventure novels pervades Tom's language. The comparison that this provokes, like the comparisons between adult and child public behavior, devalues and deflates the self-importance of adult life.

There are darker aspects to these parallels. The single most important aspect of Tom's vivid fictions is that they are all actualized during the course of the novel. Tom is saturated in the lore of swashbuckling, Robert Louis Stephenson-style adventures. This is harmless until one by one his obsessions take form in village life. Tom dreams of piracy and buried treasure. Lo and behold, there is an actual theft and real buried treasure hidden by a man who, like Tom's pirates, wears a patch over one eye. Tom fantasizes about a literary-romantic version of his own funeral. By the end of the novel his real funeral has only been averted by luck. Tom stages and provokes mock-battles and wars. Almost immediately he is witness to an actual fight, with real bloodshed, resulting in a horrible murder. If we maintain the implicit conjunction between the Bible and Tom's books, this can be read as a very serious critique of the abuses of religion. Tom's utter belief in fiction shapes the world around him for the worse, and by extension, the adults' utter belief in the Bible is shown to warp the world in which they live. Biblical stories and romantic yarns become one and the same thing—both of them foolish and dangerous when they are acted out.

Ultimately, then, the reader is forced to ask questions that have painful answers. What does it mean if, as so many readers and critics have said, Tom is, in some essential way, America; if his story is America's story, and his character America's own? When we look at the bare bones of Tom's life and the evidence outlined above, it means that Clemens' America is an orphan country of unknown origins that begins—like the novel—in *media res.* It has no history and no future, existing in the framed bookends of the author's comments at the beginning and end of the tale. As he says:

> It being strictly the history of a *boy* it must stop here; the story could not go much further without becoming the history of a man.

If Tom is America, then America too will never have a "man's history." In place of history it has only narrative—fictions and performances through which it lives out a permanent pre-adolescence with no possibility for maturity. The adults of *The Adventures of Tom Sawyer* are as childish as the children are adult—there is no distinction to be made, and hence no maturing wisdom to be counted on. We open where we end—in the middle of a fiction, with the end of an adventure and the start of a new one. In this disturbing world, the danger of these imagined adventures, as Tom's story so vividly illustrates, is that every last one of them comes true. Writing in the 1870s in the aftermath of the Civil War, Clemens has set his novel in the 1840s. Tom's blustering aggression, his acting out of battles, and his fascination with death and heroism become far less amusing when we keep these dates in mind. Seen through this lens, the book becomes a savage indictment of a country that has brought itself to the brink of death because it is infatuated with vainglorious stories of heroism, battle, and divine sanction. What is more, because it has learned nothing from its experiences, it is—like Tom—doomed to repeat them.

Source: Tabitha McIntosh-Byrd, in an essay for *Novels for Students*, Gale, 1999.

Cynthia Griffin Wolff

In the following excerpt, Wolff asserts that Tom Sawyer is a protest against the female-dominated moral code of Twain's day and the lack of suitable masculine role models for boys.

Initially Twain had intended [*The Adventures of Tom Sawyer*] to be a kind of *bildungsroman:* as Justin Kaplan reports, it was to have had four parts—"'1, Boyhood & youth; 2 y[outh] & early manh[ood]; 3 the Battle of Life in many lands; 4 (age 37 to [40?])....'" Yet the finished novel shows no sign of this early intention. In fact, Twain writes his "conclusion" with a kind of defensive bravado: "So endeth this chronicle. It being strictly a history of a *boy,* it must stop here; the story could not go much further without becoming the history of a *man.*" At least one reason for the author's decision may be found in the very nature of the world he was moved to create. There are no available men in it—no men whom Tom can fancy himself imitating—no newspaper office with a garrulous editor, no general store owner to purvey gossip and candy, no lawyer lounging in an office buzzing with flies and heavy with the odor of musty books. Of course there *is* Judge Thatcher, "a fine, portly, middle-aged gentleman with iron-gray hair." But Judge Thatcher presides in the county seat, twelve miles away; he enters the novel only very briefly in chapter IV (to witness Tom's triumph-turned-humiliation in Bible class) and thereafter disappears entirely until chapter XXXII, when he is summoned to rejoice in the safe return of the children from the cave. Many adults who have not read *Tom Sawyer* since the days of their youth are apt to recall Judge Thatcher as a rather more vivid personage than he truly is in the novel. Perhaps we are recollecting cinematic images, or perhaps our own imaginations supply his presence because we feel compelled to remedy the novel's deficiencies and "normalize" the town. But the stubborn fact remains. The town is not normal, certainly not congenial to a boy's coming of age.

It is, of course, a matriarchy (and in this respect, contrasts markedly with the various patriarchal systems that Huck encounters in his journey down the river), a world that holds small boys in bondage. The town that we are shown in this book is saturated with gentility, that is, with women's notions. A man may dispense Bible tickets or conduct the ceremony on Sundays; but the church service, the Sunday School exercises, the daily ritual of family prayers—these are all clearly defined as fundamental components of something that Aunt Polly (and other women like her) have defined as "duty" or "morality." Similarly, the mayor himself may judge the elocution contest; but this masculine salute to "culture" merely reinforces already established female allegiances to the melancholy and banally "eloquent" in literature. The very opening word of the novel establishes the situation. "'Tom!'" The boy's name called by his impatient aunt. "'Tom!'" The demanding tone permeates the novel, no other voice so penetrating or intrusive. What is a male child to do against this diminutive drill master? Surrender is out of the question: the dismal results of capitulation greet him in mournful, not quite masculine figures. Mr. Walters, the superintendent of the Sunday School, "a slim creature of thirty-five, with a sandy goatee and short sandy hair; he wore a stiff standing-collar ... a fence that compelled a straight lookout ahead, and a turning of the whole body when a side view was required." And, more contemptible, "the Model Boy, Willie Mufferson [who took] as heedful care of his mother as if she were cut glass. He always brought his mother to church, and was the pride of all the matrons. The boys all hated him, he was so good."

Rebellion, however, is no easy thing to manage. Tom cannot bring himself to dislike Aunt Polly. Occasionally, he admits to loving her; and when he genuinely saddens her (as during his disappearance to the island), he discovers that "his heart [is] full of pity for her." Pity and its cousin guilt: these are Aunt Polly's most formidable weapons (no less so for being used without guile). "'She never licks anybody,'" Tom complains as he sets about beginning to whitewash the fence. "'She talks awful, but talk don't hurt—anyways it don't if she don't cry.'" Tom might be able to contend with open anger, but he receives only reproaches that insinuate themselves into that budding thing called "conscience." Discovered after a stealthy trip abroad at night, "Tom almost brightened in the hope that he was going to be flogged; but it was not so. His aunt wept over him and asked him how he could go and break her old heart so; and finally told him to go on, and ruin himself and bring her gray hairs with sorrow to the grave, for it was no use for her to try any more. This was worse than a thousand whippings, and Tom's heart was sorer now than his body. He cried, he pleaded for forgiveness, promised to reform over and over again." In Tom's world, female children are no easier to deal with than their adult models. Becky Thatcher rules him by alternating tears with lofty reproaches; and although Tom's angry feelings toward her are a good deal more available to him than any genuinely hostile feelings he might have toward the generation of mothers, he nonetheless continues to wish for a more direct and "manly" emotional code. "He was in a fine rage.... He moped into the schoolyard wishing she were a boy, and imagining how he would trounce her if she were."

With no acceptable model of "free" adult masculinity available, Tom does his best to cope with the prevailing feminine system without being irretrievably contaminated by it. His principal recourse is an entire repertoire of games and pranks and superstitions, the unifying motif of which is a struggle for control. Control over his relationship with Aunt Polly is a major area of warfare. Thus the first scene in the book is but one type of behavior that is repeated in ritual form throughout the book. Tom, caught with his hands in the jam jar—about to be switched.

> "My! Look behind you, aunt!" The old lady whirled round, and snatched her skirts out of danger. The lad fled, on the instant, scrambled up the high board fence, and disappeared over it. His Aunt Polly stood surprised a moment, and then broke into a gentle laugh. "Hang the boy, can't I never learn anything? Ain't he played me tricks enough like that for me to be looking out for him by this time?"

Crawling out his bedroom window at night is another type of such behavior, not important because it permits this or that specific act, but significant as a general assertion of the right to govern his own comings and goings. Bartering is still another type of this behavior. Trading for blue Bible coupons or tricking his playmates into painting the fence—these are superb inventions to win the prizes of a genteel society without ever genuinely submitting to it.

The logical continuation of such stratagems would be actual defiance: the rebellion of authentic adolescence to be followed by a manhood in which Tom and his peers might define the rules by which society is to be governed. But manhood never comes to Tom; anger and defiance remain disguised in the games of childhood.

Twain offers these pranks to us as if they were no more than humorous anecdotes; Aunt Polly is always more disposed to smile at them than to take them seriously. However, an acquiescence to the merely comic in this fiction will blind us to its darker side. A boy who seeks to control himself and his world so thoroughly is a boy deeply and constantly aware of danger—justifiably so, it would seem, for an ominous air of violence hangs over the entire tale. It erupts even into the apparently safe domestic sphere.

When the children depart from their schoolmaster in chapter XXI to begin the lazy summer recess, they leave him disgraced—his gilded, bald pate blazing as the ultimate spectacle in the school's pageant. "The boys were avenged. Vacation had come." Mr. Dobbin (even his name invites laughter) is hilariously humiliated, and he is apt to linger in our memories primarily as the butt of a good joke. Yet for most of the children most of the time, he is a source of genuine terror.

The one "respectable" man whom Tom sees regularly, Mr. Dobbin, is a sadist. Having reached maturity with the unsatisfied ambition to be a doctor, he spends his free time perusing a book of "anatomy" (that is, a book with pictures of naked people in it). His principal active pleasure is lashing the children, and the preparations for the approaching commencement exercises merely provide an excuse to be

> severer and more exacting than ever.... His rod and his ferule were seldom idle now—at least among the smaller pupils.... Mr. Dobbin's lashings were very vigorous ones, too; for although he carried, under his wig, a perfectly bald and shiny head, he had only reached middle age and there was no sign of feebleness in his muscle. As the great day approached, all the tyranny that was in him came to the surface; he seemed to take a vindictive pleasure in punishing the least shortcomings.

If the village itself (with taverns, courthouse, jail, and deserted slaughter-house) is composed of the elements of crime and punishment, then Mr. Dobbin might be construed as one of the executioners—disarmed at only the final moment by the boys' "revenge" and exiting to catcalls and laughter. The joke is a fine exercise in imaginative power, but it does not fully succeed in countering the potency of the masculine "muscle" that is used with such consistent vindictiveness and violence....

Given the precarious balancing of control and violence in Tom's fantasies, we can easily comprehend his terrified fascination with Injun Joe's incursions into the "safety" of St. Petersburg. Accidentally witness to Injun Joe's murderous attack, Tom's first response is characteristic: he writes an oath in blood, pledging secrecy. "Huck Finn and Tom Sawyer swears they will keep mum about this and they wish they may Drop down dead in Their tracks if they ever tell and Rot." It is an essentially "literary" maneuver, and Tom's superstitious faith in its efficacy is of a piece with the "rules" he has conned from books about outlaws. However, Injun Joe cannot easily be relegated to the realm of such villains. It is as if one element in Tom's fantasy world has torn loose and broken away from him, roaming restlessly—a ruthless predator—genuinely and mortally dangerous.

He has murdered a man, but perversely, he does not flee. Instead, he loiters about the town in disguise, waiting for the moment to arrive when he can take "revenge." Humiliated once by the Widow Douglas's husband (no longer available to the Indian's rage), Joe plans to work his will upon the surviving mate. "'Oh, don't kill her! Don't do that!'" his nameless companion implores.

> "Kill? Who said anything about killing? I would kill *him* if he was here; but not her. When you want to get revenge on a woman you don't kill her—bosh! you go for her looks. You slit her nostrils—you notch her ears like a sow! ... I'll tie her to the bed. If she bleeds to death, is that my fault? I'll not cry, if she does."

It is almost a parody of Tom's concocted "rules" for outlaws; even Injun Joe flinches from killing a woman. Sadistic torture (of a clearly sexual nature) is sufficient.

His grievance is twofold: against the absence of the man who would be his natural antagonist; and then against the woman who has inherited the man's property and authority. Seen in this light, his condition is not unlike the hero's. Tom, denied the example of mature men whom he might emulate, left with no model to define an adult nature of his own. Tom, adrift in a matriarchal world—paying the continuous "punishment" of guilt for the "crime" of his resentment at genteel restraints, conceiving carefully measured fantasies within which to voice (and mute) his feelings. Injun Joe is Tom's shadow self, a potential for retrogression and destructiveness that cannot be permitted abroad.

Yet genuine vanquishment is no easy task. No other adult male plays so dominant a role in the novel as Injun Joe. Indeed, no other male's name save Huck's and Tom's is uttered so often. The only contender for adult masculine prominence is that other angry man, Mr. Dobbin. But the schoolmaster's vicious instincts are, in the end, susceptible to control through humor: he can be humiliated and disarmed by means of a practical joke. After all is said and done, he is an "acceptable" male, that is, a domesticated creature. The Indian, an outcast and a savage, is unpredictable; he may turn fury upon the villagers or act as ultimate executioner for Tom. When Tom's tentative literary gestures prove insufficient, desperate remedies are necessary. Twain invokes the ultimate adventure. Death.

Death has several meanings for Tom. On the one hand, it is the final loss of self—a relinquishment of control that is both attractive and frightening. Confronted with reverses, Tom sometimes longs for the blissful passivity of death, deterred primarily by the sneaking fear that "guilt" might be "punishable" even in the unknown land to which he would travel.

> It seemed to him that life was but a trouble, at best, and he more than half envied Jimmy Hodges, so lately released; it must be very peaceful, he thought, to lie and slumber and dream forever and ever, with the wind whispering through the tree and caressing the grass and the flowers over the grave, and nothing to bother and grieve about, ever any more. If he only had a clean Sunday-school record he could be willing to go, and be done with it all.

On the other hand, properly managed, "death" might be the ultimate assertion of control, the means a boy might use in this puzzling female world to win a satisfactory "self" after all. "Ah," Tom's fantasy runs, "if he could only die *temporarily!*"

The triumph of "temporary death" and the fulfillment of that universal fantasy—to attend one's own funeral and hear the tearful eulogies and then to parade boldly down the aisle (patently and impudently alive)—is the central event in the novel. The escapade is not without its trials: a terrible lonesomeness during the self-imposed banishment and a general sense of emptiness whenever Tom falls to "gazing longingly across the wide river to where the village lay drowsing in the sun." Yet the victory is more than worth the pain. Temporarily, at least, Tom's fondest ambitions for himself have come true. "What a hero Tom was become, now! He did not go skipping and prancing, but moved with a dignified swagger as became a pirate who felt that the public eye was on him." He has definitely become "somebody" for a while—and he has achieved the identity entirely upon his own terms.

Yet this central miracle of resurrection is merely a rehearsal. Its results are not permanent, and Tom must once again submit to death and rebirth in order to dispatch the specter of Injun Joe forever.

The escapade begins light-heartedly enough: a party and a picnic up river into the countryside. Yet this moderated excursion into wilderness turns nightmare in the depths of the cave. "It was said that one might wander days and nights together through its intricate tangle of rifts and chasms, and never find the end of the cave.... No man 'knew' the cave. That was an impossible thing." Existing out of time, the cave is a remnant of man's pre-history—a dark and savage place, both fascinating and deadly. Once lost in the cave, Tom and Becky must face their elemental needs—hunger, thirst, and the horror, now quite real, of extinction. For Tom alone, an additional confrontation awaits: he stumbles upon Injun Joe, who has taken refuge in this uttermost region. The temptation to despair is very great; however, "hunger and wretchedness rise superior to fears in the long run.... [Tom] felt willing to risk Injun Joe and all other terrors." Thus he begins his long struggle out. Holding a length of a string lest he be separated from Becky, he tries one dark pathway, then another, then "a third to the fullest stretch of the kite-line, and was about to turn back when he glimpsed a far-off speck that looked like daylight; dropped the line and groped toward it, pushed his head and shoulders through a small hole and saw the broad Mississippi rolling by!" Born again upon his beloved river, Tom has earned his reward.

Afterwards, as Tom recounts his adventures to an admiring audience, he becomes a "hero" once again—now the hero of his own adventure story. Even more, he has become rich from finding buried treasure; Judge Thatcher conceives a great opinion of his future and says that he hopes "to see Tom a great lawyer or a great soldier some day." Endowed with an excess of acceptable identities which have been conferred upon him as the result of his exploits (no clearer, certainly, about the particulars of the adult male roles identified by them, but nonetheless christened, as it were, into the "rightful" inheritance of them), Tom seems to have surmounted the deficiencies of his world.

Yet it is a hollow victory after all. Just as Tom must take on faith the pronouncement of his future as a "great lawyer" or a "great soldier" (having no first-hand information about these occupations), so we must accept the validity of his "triumph." The necessary condition for Tom's final peace of mind (and for his acquisition of the fortune) is the elimination of Injun Joe. And this event occurs quite accidentally. Taking the children's peril as a warning, the villagers have shut the big door to the cave and triple-bolted it, trapping Injun Joe inside. When the full consequences of the act are discovered, it is too late; the outcast has died. "Injun Joe lay stretched upon the ground, dead, with his face close to the crack of the door.... Tom was touched, for he knew by his own experience how this wretch had suffered.... Nevertheless he felt an abounding sense of relief and security, now."

Tom's final identification with the savage, valid as it certainly is, gives the lie to the conclusion of this tale. What do they share? Something irrational and atavistic, something ineradicable in human nature. Anger, perhaps, violence, perhaps. Some unnamed, timeless element.

> The poor unfortunate had starved to death. In one place near at hand, a stalagmite had been slowly growing up from the ground for ages, builded by the water-drip from a stalactite overhead. The captive had broken off the stalagmite, and upon the stump had placed a stone, wherein he had scooped a shallow hollow to catch the precious drop that fell once in every three minutes with the dreary regularity of a clock-tick—a dessert-spoonful once in four-and-twenty hours. That drop was falling when the Pyramids were new; when Troy fell; when the foundations of Rome were laid; when Christ was crucified; when the Conqueror created the British empire; when Columbus sailed; when the massacre at Lexington was "news." It is falling now; it will still be falling when all these things shall have sunk down the afternoon of history and the twilight of tradition and been swallowed up in the thick night of oblivion.... It is many and many a year since the hapless half-breed scooped out the stone to catch the priceless drops, but to this day the tourist stares longest at that pathetic stone and that slow-dropping water when he comes to see the wonders of McDougal's Cave. Injun Joe's cup stands first in the list of the cavern's marvels; even "Aladin's Palace" cannot rival it.

Whatever Injun Joe represents in this fiction—whatever his complex relationship may be to Tom—he cannot be dealt with by summary banishment. Shut up by fiat; locked away. It is an ending with no resolution at all.

Taken seriously as a psychological recommendation, the ultimate disposition of the problem of Injun Joe offers no solution but that of denial. Lock away the small boy's anger; lock away his anti-social impulses; shut up his resentments at this totally feminine world; stifle rebellion; ignore adult male hostility: they are all too dangerous to traffic with.

Thus Tom's final "self" as we see it in this novel is a tragic capitulation: he has accommodated himself to the oddities of his environment and given over resistance. A resolution to the story is established not by changing the bizarre quality of the fictional world (not even by confronting it), but by contorting the small hero into compliance. He becomes that worst of all possible things—a "Model Boy"—the voice of conformity in a genteel society. Huck complains. "'The widder eats by a bell.... Everybody's so awful reg'lar a body can't stand it.'" And Tom responds. "'Well, everybody does that way, Huck.... If you'll try this thing just awhile longer you'll come to like it.... Huck, we can't let you into the gang if you ain't respectable you know.'"

He has even lost his sense of humor.

The fault is Twain's, of course. Tom has earned the right to "be somebody"; but his creator's vision has faltered. Twain averts his attention from the struggle that should be central and shrinks from uncivilized inclinations. In the end, his hero must settle for security in a world that will always be run by its women.

Source: Cynthia Griffin Wolff, "*The Adventures of Tom Sawyer:* A Nightmare Vision of American Boyhood," in *The Massachusetts Review,* Vol. XXI, No. 4, Winter, 1980, pp. 637–625.

Diana Trilling

In the following essay, Trilling analyzes Twain's portrayal of childhood and parental responsibility in Tom Sawyer.

Mark Twain once said of *Tom Sawyer,* "It is *not* a boys' book at all. It will be read only by adults." We can suppose he was speaking defensively, with the extravagance of an irritated author. He had brought to the book his full powers of serious communication and he had no wish for it to be thought of as a mere children's book, what publishers call a "juvenile." Yet ever since its publication in 1876 until quite recently, the audience for *Tom Sawyer* has of course been primarily a youthful one. In fact, the American public has regarded it as one of those books peculiarly apt to induct any sensitive boy, and even any spirited girl, into the wholesome pleasures of reading.

This situation has now significantly altered. In the last few decades there has been a considerable change in American child life, so that *Tom Sawyer* has come closer to fulfilling Mark Twain's prophecy than at any previous time in its history. Much more than it is now thought to be a book *for* children, it is regarded as a classic *of* childhood, especially to be read by adults of college age with an interest in the American past. It would seem that American youngsters can no longer empathize—to borrow the language of current psychology, which

is not without its responsibility for the change—with Mark Twain's little hero. For the big-city child in particular, there is a barrier to be got over before he can find his counterpart in Mark Twain's remembrance of himself as a small boy.

The nature of the difficulty is obvious enough. In today's most advanced view of what constitutes emotional health in the young, Tom is little less than certifiably disturbed. If he is not entirely committed to delinquency, he is manifestly deficient in those restraints upon instinctual conduct which have come to define a young person's potentiality for life in society. From the first chapter of the novel, in which Tom ducks out of the house for a day of truancy from school, a deed in defiance of his good Aunt Polly which he at once embellishes by lying and cheating and then compounds by beating up a boy who happens to walk toward him on the same road, we are in the company of someone whose relation to authority must seem to us to be alarmingly negative, who respects no principle of behavior other than the demand for the quick gratification of desire. In conduct like Tom's, from the very outset of the book, the young reader of our time is bound to recognize a deviation so extreme that he tolerates it only at a certain risk to his own moral well-being. Would Tom Sawyer, as Mark Twain introduces him, be welcome in a contemporary American school, especially an enlightened one? Clearly not. So much at odds with himself and society, Tom Sawyer can be sympathetic only to the view of history.

And as Tom's story progresses, his author can give us but small promise of his rehabilitation. Tom fails dismally at school: unable to concentrate on his age-appropriate job of learning, he squanders his mental powers in infantile sadomasochistic fantasies. For the teachings of religion he substitutes wild primitive superstitions; reality has but the weakest hold on this unhappy victim of magical thinking. Tom has no proper goals of achievement and his exhibitionism is insatiable: he schemes to win a prize he does not deserve. He chooses his friends as we might expect: his great crony is Huckleberry Finn, the outcast ambitionless son of a drunkard, a boy who *likes* to sleep in empty hogsheads and beg for his food and idle away his days on the river. And with such as Huck, Tom indulges in dark rituals of blood-brotherhood, prowling the graveyards and back alleys of St. Petersburg, consorting with the lowest of low village characters. Witness to a murder, he conspires to keep his guilty knowledge a secret. He runs away from home, inflicting cruel suffering on his family. And when remorse strikes him, as occasionally, miraculously, it does, he handles his emotional conflict by still further indulging his antisocial impulses. Yet such is the behavior his poor, deluded author can allude to as Tom's "adventurous, troublesome ways," and in which he would have us see his own beginnings. And not only see them but celebrate them.

It was not until 1884, eight years after *Tom Sawyer,* that Mark Twain published *Huckleberry Finn.* As between the two books it is of course *Huckleberry Finn* that has always been the more admired, rightly so since it is the larger, more complex work. But Mark Twain retained a special affection for his earlier effort to recapture the scene of his childhood in Hannibal, Missouri. In a letter of his later years he wrote of *Tom Sawyer:* "It is simply a hymn, put into prose form to give it a worldly air." When Mark Twain calls *Tom Sawyer* a "hymn" he precisely intends the double connotation of music and sacredness, and certainly the book is nothing if not sung: the human voice is Mark Twain's instrument. And it is also nothing if not a celebration of something sacred, despite its funniness. What is sacred is the condition of grace in which we find Tom in early life. The hymn is a celebration not of God, nor of man as he has attained to what we are pleased to call his civilized maturity, but of boyhood. In every page of Tom's history Mark Twain proclaims his passionate belief that civilization, as it erodes instinct, destroys that which is most valuable in man: affection, honor, loyalty, manly pride, joy, imagination, community with nature. The book is first a hymn; second, with almost religious conviction, it is doctrine.

Mark Twain's position in American letters is so high, and his reputation for humor so prevailing, that we are likely to forget that this most amiable of authors seldom had a good word to say for any man, any full-grown man; women are of course something else again. Throughout his writing, maturity is virtually synonymous with corruption, hypocrisy, meanness, bombast; the men in *Tom Sawyer* are prime examples of Mark Twain's law of deterioration through growth. Alone among the male adults who touch Tom's life, Muff Potter, the town drunkard, boasts even the virtues of generosity and helpfulness; and Muff, like Jim in *Huckleberry Finn,* is still a child in spirit. The schoolmaster in *Tom Sawyer* is an ignorant bully, the Sunday-school superitendent a pious toady, the eminent judge a pompous ass; the owners of temperance taverns traffic in whiskey and harbor the town's most villainous ruffians. Such are the good citizens of St. Petersburg—and always ready for a

good clean hanging even if, like Muff Potter, the victim is guilty only of the crime of never having joined their respectable masquerade.

And yet these people with so little claim to virtue have another aspect to their characters which Mark Twain reveals, as it were, unwittingly. When Tom and his cronies are off being pirates and the whole town thinks they have drowned, the men of St. Petersburg search hard and long for them before they give over to their grief, which is genuine. Or when Becky and Tom are lost in the caves, the men push themselves to extremes of exhaustion trying to rescue them, and with no histrionics of heroism. Selflessness of this kind in people who are otherwise meanly self-engrossed is of course in the American pattern. Today, too, given the proper crisis, and especially if the drama involves a child, we can count on the sudden generous effort of people of ordinarily small spirit. But the difference is notable between the attitude that the townspeople in *Tom Sawyer* bring to their rescue missions and what we might expect today were children to be in difficulties like those of Tom and his friends. There is no word of reproach spoken of Tom for having been on the river when he should have been at home or in school, or for involving Becky in the adventure of the cave. No syllable of criticism is directed at Aunt Polly for having raised a boy so little to be relied upon. Twice Tom disappears, in circumstances where his fault is clear, but there is no hint on the part of neighbors or friends of adverse moral judgment on his character or upbringing. Corrupt and unfeeling as the adult world of St. Petersburg may be, it retains a concept of innocence—innocent childhood and innocent parenthood—which is now gone from American life. For, whatever our present-day concern with children—and it could scarcely be greater—we now bring to any violation of the childhood norm an extraordinary readiness of moral judgment, and on parents no less than on the child. In terms of "advantages," Tom and his friends may be markedly under-privileged compared to children today—to see the difference we have only to catalog the contents of Tom's pockets, the mad odds and ends of string and metal that make up his "worldly wealth." But Tom is accepted in all his quirkiness and error and mess as no boy today can hope to be. Indeed, the more serious the trouble in which Tom lands, the less, not the more, he is blamed.

Understandably, Mark Twain records this side of the life he knew as a child without conscious emphasis. In the 1870s he could have no premonition of a time when the idea that "boys will be boys" would be thought morally dangerous. It is not hard for us to imagine Mark Twain's horror if he had been told, for instance, that a century after Tom's boyhood, properly conscientious parents would signalize Halloween by providing their children with costumes, paper bags and lists of neighbors prepared to give them treats. But particularly in the character of Tom's Aunt Polly, he thoroughly documents the large faith that his society had in children, or at least the fatalism which underlay its refusal to assign ultimate blame when children misbehaved. His guardian's rearing of Tom rests on two beliefs: in God's mysterious ways and in childhood, or perhaps in progress. The strongest motive in Aunt Polly's character is her sense of duty: this together with her affectionateness; and the two are often in strenuous conflict. It is the burden of her duty to her ward to inculcate in him the moral and social law as it has been established in her cultural tradition, which is at the same time her religious tradition: he must not steal or lie, he must obey his elders (at least he must be aware when he does not), he must be polite and he must wash (if only on Sundays), and he must go to church (in decent attire) and learn the Scriptures (at least he must show the signs of effort), and he must go to school; he must also be punished when he does wrong, preferably with a whipping. And it is the burden of her profound love for Tom that she must impose upon him these requirements of proper conduct, to most of which he has, understandably, the greatest natural resistance. It is a particular trial to her spirit that she must punish him. The whippings she administers so regularly truly hurt her more than they do him; and when he escapes her switch, she is relieved.

Thus, the rod which is so ready to hand for Aunt Polly is never the extension of an adverse judgment on Tom for being such a troublesome little boy. It is the instrument of her defined duty to a child, any child in error, and it is an expression of her love—if you love a child, you want to do your best by him. For Aunt Polly, that is, the rules that govern a good woman in the rearing of her young have something of the same magical power that the rituals of superstition have for Tom. Often, as Tom goes through one of his elaborate mumbo-jumbos to fend off evil or to ensure the fulfillment of a wish, he is suddenly assailed by doubt that his method is really the right one, that it will work. But he has nothing with which to replace the tribal lore, and how can a boy risk *not* doing what his tribal lore prescribes? Just so, Aunt Polly questions the tenets of child-rearing in which she has been trained, but she dares not risk violating them.

The impact upon a child of a moral authority as benign and generalized as Aunt Polly's is very different, of course, from an authority rooted in individual judgment, and it is small wonder that Tom not only dearly loves his aunt but suffers no break in his attachment to her because of her frequent whippings. He accepts her punishments in the spirit in which they are administered: they are his aunt's duty to him and evidence of her devotion to his welfare; they convey no possible mitigation of her affection or of her essential and continuing approval of him. And, similarly, the beatings administered by the schoolmaster are part of the traditional, impersonal routine; they, too, leave no emotional scar; at their most severe, they scarcely hurt. While the schoolmaster no doubt brings to the exercise of his duty a certain nasty satisfaction that is wholly absent from Aunt Polly's corporal punishment of Tom, this represents no vital breach in the impersonal system of childrearing that Mark Twain knew as a boy. It merely describes a difference in the characters of the two persons.

The result is that a boy like Tom Sawyer who, in our contemporary view, is grievously at the mercy of impulse, in reality has enough conscience for any civilized man. In our present-day world we have come to think of guilt as a most undesirable state of feeling rather than what it is if it but be kept in sound proportion to instinct: the clue to our humanity. Certainly Tom's well-educated sense of wrong and the remorse he suffers when he seriously misbehaves and gives pain to others is the key to his special lovableness. It is conscience that makes it necessary for Tom to break his vows of secrecy about the murder and, at considerable danger, save Muff Potter from being hanged. It is conscience—the ability to confront his guilt without exaggerating it—that permits the particular tenderness with which Tom treats Becky when the two of them are lost in the caves. And it is guilt at the pain he has given his aunt by disappearing from home that makes him return in the night to leave her a note of reassurance. That Tom decides not to leave the note because he is all at once struck by the beautiful possibility of attending his own funeral makes, finally, the difference between someone able easily to conform to social dictate, a "Model Boy," and the boy who grew up to be Mark Twain. It is the difference, to put it another way, between the ordinary, or ordinarily, decent youngster and a potential hero of the imagination....

And it is not alone for Tom but for Huck, too, that the capacity for guilt and for love, or at least for genuine respect, live in the strongest connection. Unlike Tom Sawyer, Huck has known almost no adult affection in his life—none at all from his vagrant father, certainly, and little enough from the townspeople of St. Petersburg. What, we wonder, has molded his character so close to that of his friend and made him, too, so loving and brave and decent. It is an inquiry to which Mark Twain feels no need to address himself, except, perhaps, by negative implication. Unimpeded by the influences of civilization, Huckleberry Finn has been free to develop nobly; he exists in a state of nature. He is boyhood pure, unindebted even to an Aunt Polly for his decency of feeling. When the Widow Douglas undertakes to adopt Huck and train him, like Tom, in the ways of society, Huck cannot make the compromise that Tom has made. He is full of gratitude and loyalty to this kindly woman, he honors her teachings, but he cannot submit to clothes and a bed and washing and having the Scriptures read to him. Civilization is almost literal death to Huck rather than the mere encumbrance it is for Tom. He chooses life and leaves society, and in making the choice becomes his author's new and greatest hero.

In *Tom Sawyer* the tension between the Model Boy principle and the Huck Finn principle is surely strong enough. But it is not yet fierce, and its product is Tom, a boy whose sweet geniality is unmatched in fiction but who represents compromise and therefore, for all his appeal, a sacrifice of stature. While his story unmistakably has its point of departure in doctrine, doctrine in *Tom Sawyer* is not yet as urgent as it will be when it is Huckleberry Finn's boyhood rather than Tom's that Mark Twain celebrates—in, *Huckleberry Finn* we will have more than a hymn, a choral symphony, with distant but sure echoes of tragedy. The special reverberations of the later book have, however, their chief source in nature. Compared to *Huckleberry Finn, Tom Sawyer* is a town book. Its fields and woods are neighborly, the river lies beyond it. The river is where you go to *from* the main scene of action; it is not itself the main scene of action. It is not yet the great Mississippi.

Some years ago, crossing the country by train, I looked from the window and saw, below me, a narrow muddy river, bordered by a town. Suddenly I realized I was crossing the Mississippi into Missouri, into Mark Twain country. The catch I felt in my throat was for Tom Sawyer's place, not Huck's. This was not the *real* Mississippi I had reached so accidentally and casually. The real Mississippi,

Huck's Mississippi, was yet for me to discover, and it would require a special expedition, for which my encounter with the world of Tom Sawyer was only a preparation.

Source: Diana Trilling, "Tom Sawyer, Delinquent," in her *Claremount Essays,* Harcourt Brace Jovanovich, 1964, pp. 143–225.

Sources

Frank Baldanza, "Boy Literature," in *Mark Twain: An Introduction and Interpretation,* edited by John Mahoney, Holt, Rinehart and Winston, 1961, pp. 103-123.

Walter Blair, *"Tom Sawyer,"* in *Mark Twain: A Collection of Critical Essays,* edited by Henry Nash Smith, Prentice-Hall, 1963, pp. 64-82.

Shelley Fisher Fishkin, "Excavations," in *Lighting Out for the Territory: Reflections on Mark Twain and American Culture,* Oxford University Press, 1997, pp. 92-93.

John C. Gerber, *"The Adventures of Tom Sawyer,"* in *Mark Twain,* edited by David J. Nordloh, Twayne, 1988, pp. 67-77.

Ronald Gottesman and Arnold Krupat, "American Literature 1865-1914," in *The Norton Anthology of American Literature,* Vol. 2, 4th edition, Norton, 1994, pp. 1-8.

Granville Hicks, *The Great Tradition,* Macmillan, 1935, pp. 43-44.

Robert Lacour-Gayet, *Everyday Life in the United States before the Civil War, 1830-1860,* Unger, 1969, p. 8.

Lewis Leary, *Mark Twain,* University of Minnesota Press, 1960, pp. 22-24.

Henry Nash Smith, "Introduction," in *Mark Twain: A Collection of Critical Essays,* edited by Henry Nash Smith, Prentice-Hall, 1963, pp. 1-12.

For Further Study

Bernard DeVoto, *Mark Twain's America,* Chautauqua Institution, 1932.

> DeVoto, who published his book following the publication of Albert Bigelow Paine's biography of Twain, called his own book "an essay in the correction of ideas." The book looks at Twain's works in the context of his American culture.

William Dean Howells, review in *Atlantic Monthly,* Vol. 37, May, 1876.

> In this glowing review written before the novel's American publication, Howells singles out Clemens' depiction of the "boy-mind" as especially wonderful.

William Dean Howells, *My Mark Twain,* Dover, 1997.

> Howells was "the dean of American letters" during Twain's day, and also Twain's close friend and editor. In this book, Howells presents his personal account of his friendship with Twain.

Jim Hunter, "Mark Twain and the Boy-Book in 19th-Century America," *College English,* Vol. 24, 1963.

Hunter provides a valuable survey of contemporary boys' literature, showing the role of the "Bad Boy" that Clemens adapted for Tom Sawyer.

Justin Kaplan, *Mr. Clemens and Mark Twain: A Biography,* Simon and Schuster, 1966.

A groundbreaking biography of Twain when it was first published, Kaplan's book made use of material about Twain's life and work that had been previously unavailable to biographers.

Charles A. Norton, *Writing Tom Sawyer: The Adventures of a Classic,* McFarland and Co., 1983.

Norton traces the creation of the novel, suggesting that Clemens' main motivation in writing it was to present an acceptable version of his childhood to his wife's family.

Dennis Welland, *The Life and Times of Mark Twain,* Crescent Books, 1991.

Lavishly illustrated, this book covers Twain's life and culture, organizing its information through a geographical approach.

Beloved

Toni Morrison

1987

After publishing four novels, Toni Morrison had already established herself as one of the most popular and successful black female writers of her time. With the publication of her fifth novel, *Beloved,* however, critics worldwide recognized that here was an author with a depth and brilliance that made her work universal. In this tale set in Reconstruction Ohio, Morrison paints a dark and powerful portrait of the dehumanizing effects of slavery. Inspired by an actual historical incident, *Beloved* tells the story of a woman haunted by the daughter she murdered rather than have returned to slavery. Part ghost story, part realistic narrative, the novel examines the mental and physical trauma caused by slavery as well as the lingering damage inflicted on its survivors. In prose both stark and lyrical, Morrison addresses several of her enduring themes: the importance of family and community, the quest for individual and cultural identity, and the very nature of humanity.

Although *Beloved* was hailed by many reviewers as a masterpiece when it first appeared in 1987, the novel inspired considerable controversy several months after its publication. After it failed to win either the National Book Award or the National Book Critics Circle Award, accusations of racism were leveled. Demonstrating their support of the author, forty-eight prominent black writers and critics signed a tribute to Morrison's career and published it in the January 24, 1988 edition of the *New York Times Book Review. Beloved* subsequently won the Pulitzer Prize for fiction, and the

secretary of the jury addressed the issue by stating that it "would be unfortunate if anyone diluted the value of Toni Morrison's achievement by suggesting that her prize rested on anything but merit." Despite the controversy, few have contested the excellence of the novel, and *Beloved* remains one of the author's most celebrated and analyzed works. As critic John Leonard concluded in the *Los Angeles Times Book Review,* the novel "belongs on the highest shelf of American literature, even if half a dozen canonized white boys have to be elbowed off…. Without *Beloved* our imagination of the nation's self has a hole in it big enough to die from."

Author Biography

Toni Morrison was born Chloe Anthony Wofford on February 18, 1931, in Lorain, Ohio. Growing up during the Depression, Morrison witnessed the struggle of her parents, George and Ramah Wills Wofford, as they worked multiple jobs to support their four children. In the face of hard and often demeaning work, her parents held on to a sense of pride and self-respect which they passed on to their children. Because of their experiences with racism, they also emphasized the value and strength of African-American individuals, families, and communities. Music and storytelling were also valued in Morrison's home, and dreams and ghostly apparitions were often featured in the stories people told each other. Reading was highly regarded in the family—one grandfather was a figure of respect because he had taught himself to read—and Morrison learned the skill at an early age. As she matured, Morrison became a capable student and read widely, from Russian novels to Jane Austen. While these works did not speak directly to her experience as a young black woman, they taught her about creating setting and atmosphere. As she told Jean Strouse in *Newsweek:* "I wasn't thinking of writing then—I wanted to be a dancer like Maria Tallchief—but when I wrote my first novel years later, I wanted to capture that same specificity about the nature and feeling of the culture I grew up in."

After high school, Morrison attended Howard University, where she studied English and classic literature in preparation for becoming a teacher. She graduated in 1953 and then enrolled in graduate school at Cornell University. After earning her master's degree in 1955, she became an English instructor at Texas Southern and then Howard Uni-

Toni Morrison

versity. During this time the author met and married architect Harold Morrison, with whom she had two sons. After the marriage ended in divorce in 1964, Morrison moved to New York, where she worked as an editor with Random House. Although working in the publishing industry, it took her several tries to find a publisher for her first novel. When *The Bluest Eye* was published in 1969, reviews were generally positive and established the young author as one to watch. Her next works, *Sula* (1973) and *Song of Solomon* (1977), fulfilled the promise of her early works. The former earned a nomination for the National Book Award, while the latter won the National Book Critics Circle Award and became the first work by a black author since Richard Wright's *Native Son* to be a Book-of-the-Month Club selection. Morrison was earning more than just critical acclaim, however. When her fourth novel, *Tar Baby,* was published in 1981, it remained on bestseller lists for four months.

Meanwhile, Morrison was still working at Random House, where she influenced several upcoming African-American writers. In addition to editing their works, she edited several nonfiction collections. While preparing the 1974 anthology *The Black Book,* Morrison came across the shocking but true story of Margaret Garner, a runaway slave who attempted to murder her children rather than allow them to be captured and sent back into slavery. For the author, Garner's story epitomized one of the chief horrors of slavery: the deliberate separation of families and the destruction of the bond between parent and child. Morrison used this story as a springboard for her novel *Beloved,* creating a haunting tale of the challenge of memory and the strength of family.

Morrison left publishing in 1985 for academia, and since 1989 has been the Robert F. Goheen Professor of the Humanities at Princeton University. In 1993 she was awarded the Nobel Prize in Literature, becoming the first African American and only the eighth woman to earn the accolade. The National Book Foundation similarly honored her in 1996 with its Medal for Distinguished Contribution to American Letters. Morrison continues to teach, lecture, and write, attempting to create stories that have meaning for both author and reader. As she stated in *Black Women Writers: A Critical Evaluation,* fiction "should be beautiful, and powerful, but it should also work. It should have something in it that enlightens; something in it that opens the door and points the way. Something in it that suggests what the conflicts are, what the problems are. But it need not solve those problems because it is not a case study, it is not a recipe."

Plot Summary

Part I

In *Beloved,* Morrison chronicles the hardships Sethe and her family endure before, during, and after the American Civil War. The novel opens with a description of the "spiteful" atmosphere of 124 Bluestone Road in rural Ohio in 1873, where Sethe, her daughter Denver, and a troublesome spirit live. They are soon joined by two others: Paul D., who knew Sethe from their years as slaves on a Kentucky plantation, and a strange woman who calls herself Beloved. All quickly become caught up in conflicts that have their roots in the past, which Morrison reveals to the reader in the fragmented flashbacks of Sethe's memory. The novel's complex interweaving of past and present produce a compelling portrait of a black family's struggle with the devastating and inescapable effects of slavery.

Paul D. Garner comes to Ohio looking for Sethe, who, while pregnant, had escaped Sweet Home eighteen years ago after sending her baby girl and two sons ahead to her mother-in-law's

house on Bluestone Road. He meets Denver, a teenaged girl consumed with a loneliness that "wore her out" after her brothers ran off and her grandmother died. As they reminisce about the past, Sethe shows Paul her back, covered with scars that resemble a tree with many branches. After he responds sympathetically, the spirit begins to shake the house. When Paul smashes everything in the house, the spirit flees. Paul decides to stay and share Sethe's bed, which upsets Denver, who wants all of her mother's attention.

On their way home from a carnival, Sethe, Denver, and Paul find a sickly but well-dressed young woman named Beloved sitting near the steps of the house. They take her in and nurse her back to health. Denver feels a special patience with and possessiveness of this young woman whose illness seems to have erased the memory of her past. As she recovers, Beloved hovers around Sethe "like a familiar," her eyes displaying a "bottomless longing." Soon, against his will and in secret, Paul begins to have sex with Beloved after she comes to him one night.

One day Sethe takes Denver and Beloved with her to the Clearing in the woods, where Baby Suggs often preached and offered solace to black men, women, and children. In the Clearing, Sethe senses a strange connection between Beloved and her daughter, also named Beloved, who died soon after Denver's birth. Sethe has told Denver only part of the story of her birth and the surrounding events in order to shield her daughter from the past. She tells Denver that when she ran away from Sweet Home, a white girl named Amy, also on the run, aided her delivery. Then a black man named Stamp Paid helped her get to Baby Suggs' home where she was reunited with her children. When the schoolteacher, Sweet Home's cruel overseer, found her there, she chose jail rather than a return to a life of slavery.

When Denver was seven, she suspected but refused to hear the complete truth about her dead sister and so encased herself in a silence "too solid for penetration" for the next two years. Sethe had left out of the story the details about how Beloved died. Soon after Sethe arrived at Baby Suggs' she saw the schoolteacher arrive on horseback with the sheriff, one of the schoolteacher's nephews (who had been especially cruel to her), and a slave catcher. Inside the shed at the back of the house the men found Sethe and her children, whom she had just tried to kill so they would not have to return to Sweet Home. She succeeded in killing only one of her children, Beloved, before Stamp Paid was able to stop her.

Sethe tells the full story to Paul, including the details of what she suffered under the control of the schoolteacher at Sweet Home, after Stamp Paid shows him a newspaper clipping about the event, which he calls "the Misery." She tries to explain to Paul that her great love for her children prompted her need to kill them so they would not have to suffer the horrors of slavery that she endured. Yet her story shocks Paul, who insists, "your love is too thick…. There could have been a way. Some other way…. You got two feet, Sethe, not four." A distance immediately springs up between them, and Paul moves out.

Part II

Stamp feels "uneasy" ever since he told Paul about "the Misery." Since that time, Sethe and Denver have been ostracized from the black community, due partly to the infanticide, but also to Sethe's proud refusal to ask for help. When Stamp tries to visit Sethe, he hears "loud, urgent [voices], all speaking at once" coming from the house. He determines they are the voices of the suffering ghosts of blacks who have been killed by whites. No one comes to the door when Stamp knocks on it. After Paul left Bluestone Road, certain incidents prompted Sethe to determine that Beloved was the reincarnation of the daughter she lost, which initially fills her with joy and a sense of peace. She decides to cut herself off from the outside world that Paul had introduced her to and then closed off, and focus instead on her daughters and her hopes that her sons will return.

Stamp finds Paul living in the church basement and expresses regret that no one in the community offered him a place to stay. He tries to explain that Sethe's actions resulted from her great love for her children and not from any mental imbalance. Paul admits, though, that he is afraid of her. When, despondent over the situation, he implores, "How much is a nigger supposed to take?" Stamp responds, "All he can." Paul then cries out, "Why?"

Part III

At first Sethe, Denver, and Beloved played together, happily cut off from the rest of the world, but "then the mood changed and the arguments began." Sethe and Beloved close out Denver when both determine that Beloved is Sethe's lost daughter. Their battles revolve around Beloved's recounting of the anguish she has experienced and Sethe's pleas for forgiveness and accounts of what

she has suffered for her children. Denver notes, however, that Sethe's inability to leave the subject alone suggests that she "didn't really want forgiveness given; she wanted it refused, And Beloved helped her out." At this point Denver's concern shifts from Beloved's safety in her mother's presence to Sethe's as she confronts Beloved's anger. She is also anxious about the fact that since Sethe has been fired from her position at a local restaurant, there has been no food for them to eat.

When Denver asks a woman in the neighborhood for help, food starts appearing in the yard. Denver decides she must find a job to help support her family and is hired by Mr. Bodwin, a white abolitionist who had helped get Sethe released from jail. Word of the family's distress reaches the entire black community and, as a result, one morning, thirty women congregate outside their home. There the women begin to pray and sing in an effort to chase the ghosts of the past. In the midst of this congregation, Mr. Bodwin arrives to pick up Denver for work. When Sethe sees a white man arriving at her home, she appears to flash back to the past, confusing him with one of the four white men who came to return her to slavery, and so tries to kill him with an ice pick. As the women, including Denver, wrestle the pick away from her, Beloved, who had been standing on the porch observing the scene, seems to disappear.

Soon after the incident, Paul returns to Bluestone Road. Finding Sethe in a dazed state, he realizes she has given up on life as Baby Suggs had before she died, and tells her, "Me and you, we got more yesterday than anybody. We need some kind of tomorrow." When Sethe cries out that she has lost Beloved, her best thing, Paul tells her, "You your best thing," as he holds her hand. The novel closes with Sethe's questioning, "Me? Me?"

Characters

Beloved

There are several signs that seem to indicate that the mysterious stranger who suddenly turns up at 124 Bluestone is the spirit of Sethe's daughter returned in flesh. She has "new skin, lineless and smooth," is the same age Sethe's baby would have been had she lived, and her name is "Beloved," the same word carved on the baby's gravestone. She has little memory of where she has been or why she is here, but somehow knows to ask Sethe "where your diamonds?" and "your woman she

Scene from the movie Beloved, *starring Oprah Winfrey as Sethe and Danny Glover as Paul D.*

never fix up your hair?" Sethe responds by telling the girl stories that were too painful to recall to anyone else. Beloved devours the stories and cannot take her eyes off of Sethe. She also has an "anger that ruled when Sethe did or thought anything that excluded herself." She drives away the suspicious Paul D by seducing him, and gets Sethe to eliminate Denver from their games. The way that she begins to punish Sethe for leaving her suggests the ghost is finally taking revenge for her murder, while her sudden disappearance from the house seems supernatural.

Is Beloved really a ghost, however, or is her acceptance in the house a case of mistaken identity? There are hints that she is actually an escapee from a slave ship, where she lost her mother. She tells Denver of where she was before: a dark place with "nothing to breathe down there and no room to move in" until she came up to "the bridge." Denver interprets this as a picture of the underworld, but it could easily be the hold of a slave ship as well. Beloved's stream of consciousness chapter— telling of a place with little water or daylight and a "little hill of dead people"—also seems to describe the suffering of a slave hold during the Atlantic passage. Critic Deborah Horvitz offers another interpretation of Beloved's character in *Studies in American Fiction:* "she represents the

spirit of all the women dragged onto slave ships in Africa and also all Black women in America trying to trace their ancestry back to the mother on the ship attached to them." Thus Beloved's descriptions of the ship's passage reflect the experiences of Sethe's own mother; her search for "the woman with my face" mirrors Sethe's loss of her own mother; and Beloved's abandonment by her mother, who "goes into the water," resembles the desertion suffered by Sethe's dead daughter. "As the embodiment of Sethe's memories," the critic concludes, "the ghost Beloved enabled her to remember and tell the story of her past, and in so doing shows that between women words used to make and share a story have the power to heal."

Edward Bodwin

Edward Bodwin is one of the abolitionist siblings who assist Baby Suggs when she first arrives in Cincinnati. "He's somebody never turned us down," Stamp Paid says, and it is primarily Bodwin's efforts that save Sethe from the gallows after she murders her daughter. He also helps Sethe find a job after she is released from prison. Bodwin's most distinguishing features are his snow-white hair and his dark velvety mustache, an interesting combination of black and white that leads his enemies to call him a "bleached nigger." Even

Media Adaptations

- After a decade of working to bring the novel to the screen, producer-star Oprah Winfrey finally brought out a film version of *Beloved* in 1998. Directed and co-produced by Oscar-winner Jonathan Demme, the film starred Winfrey as Sethe, Danny Glover as Paul D, Kimberly Elise as Denver, and Thandie Newton as Beloved.

- An unabridged audio recording of *Beloved* by the author is available from Random House Audio; an abridged version read by actress Lynn Whitfield is also available from Random House Audio.

when Sethe comes at him with an ice pick, Bodwin chooses not to interpret her actions as a personal attack and continues aiding the family by giving Denver a job in his home.

Miss Bodwin

Miss Bodwin is one of the abolitionist siblings who provide Baby Suggs with a house and a job after she is freed from Sweet Home. She is described as "the whitewoman who loved [Baby Suggs]," and her kindness extends to Sethe and her daughter after Baby Suggs's death.

Buglar

Sethe's second son finally leaves home, presumably to fight in the Civil War, after a mirror shatters simply from his looking at it. Denver remembers fondly how he and Howard would make up "die-witch!" stories. One of the few things Sethe tries to remember is the way her son looked—not the fact that he would not let her near him after his sister's death, or how he always slept hand-in-hand with his brother after that day.

Paul D

"For a man with an immobile face," Sethe thinks of Paul D, "it was amazing how ready it was to smile, or blaze or be sorry with you." Perhaps it is this ability to "produce the feeling you were feeling" that makes him "the kind of man who could walk into a house and make the women cry." But the cruelty of slavery has left Paul D with a "tobacco tin buried in his chest where a red heart used to be. Its lid rusted shut." He is the only man left from Sweet Home; his brothers Paul F and Paul A were sold away or hung, while Sixo was burned and Halle was broken. Paul D is sold from Sweet Home and put into a Georgia prison after trying to kill his new master. He is kept in a hole in the ground and put to work on a chain gang. A hard rain that turns their cells to mud also allows the gang to escape. A tribe of sick Cherokee frees him from his chains and points the way north.

Since then Paul D has wandered around, thinking he could not stay in any one place for more than a couple of months. Seeing Sethe, however, "the closed portion of his head opened like a greased lock," and he tells her, "We can make a life, girl." The way he makes people respond to him at the carnival starts to convince even Denver that this might be true. Beloved's arrival changes things, however. The girl seduces Paul, and his inability to resist her leads him to doubt his manhood. When Sethe explains the newspaper clipping to him, Paul D condemns her, moving quickly "from his shame to hers." He leaves the house, but his rusted tin has sprung open, making him wonder for the first time "what-all went wrong." Paul D returns to Sethe after Beloved leaves—but not because of it: "Paul D doesn't care how It went or even why. He cares about how he left and why." Their shared history makes it more bearable, and he realizes that "only this woman Sethe could have left him his manhood like that. He wants to put his story next to hers."

Denver

Isolated in the house with her mother Sethe, lonely Denver's only companions are from the past: memories of her brothers, her imaginings of her father, her mother's stories of Denver's birth, and the baby ghost that haunts the house. The reader is allowed hints of the kind of bright, happy child Denver might have been had Sethe not isolated the family from the community. But Denver "had taught herself pride in the condemnation Negroes heaped upon them," and is also proud of her secret knowledge about the ghost. Another way she deals with her isolation is by creating an emerald play world in a section of boxwood bushes. There her imagination "produced its own hunger and its own food, which she badly needed because loneliness wore her out." The only story Denver wants to hear is the one of her birth; she "hated the stories her mother told that did not concern herself…. The rest was a gleaming, powerful world made more so by Denver's absence from it." Thus she feels threatened by Paul D's arrival, and sobs out her loneliness for the first time in ten years. The idea that he and her mother might form a "twosome" that would make Sethe "look away from her own daughter's body" is too much to bear. The next day, when the three of them see their shadows holding hands, Sethe thinks it means the three of them might form a family. But Paul D recognizes that Denver has "something she's expecting and it ain't me."

When Beloved appears, it seems to Denver as if this is what she has been waiting for: her sister returned to her in the flesh. Although she loves her mother—the only person left who has not abandoned her—she has uneasy memories about "the thing in Sethe" that could make her harm her children. She begins to transfer her affection to Beloved, who she thinks needs her protection. Thus when Sethe nearly chokes in the clearing, "Denver was alarmed by the harm she thought Beloved planned for Sethe, but felt helpless to thwart it, so unrestricted was her need to love another." But it soon becomes evident to Denver that Beloved may be more of a danger than Sethe is. "Frightened as she was by the thing in Sethe that could come out, it shamed her to see her mother serving a girl not much older than herself." She fears losing her mother—being abandoned yet again—and takes steps to support the family that finally result in Sethe's returning to the community. Denver provides another example of how the rupture of families caused by slavery forces people to survive without the family and community support they should have. As Judith Thurman observes in the *New Yorker*, Sethe never truly finished delivering Denver, so the girl "will be forced to complete the labor by herself."

Amy Denver

See Whitegirl

Ella

Ella is a practical woman who had "been beaten every way but down." Ella and her husband John are part of the Underground Railroad, picking up fugitives after Stamp Paid ferries them across the river. She is friendly with Sethe until the attempt on the children, because "she understood Sethe's rages in the shed twenty years ago, but not her reaction to it." Ella's disapproval of Sethe's proud isolation leads her to ignore Paul D's need for shelter, when she would usually offer to help any black man in need. But when news comes that Sethe's dead daughter is beating her, "it was Ella more than anyone who convinced the others that rescue was in order."

Mr. Garner

Mr. Garner allows his slaves more privileges than most owners do: they are encouraged to think for themselves, suggest and implement improvements to the farm, and even handle guns. He claims he has the only "nigger men" in Kentucky and is proud because it shows he is "tough enough and smart enough to make and call his own niggers men." When he delivers Baby Suggs to the Baldwins, having allowed her son Halle to purchase her freedom, he brags that she never went hungry or received a beating under his care. But his kindness cannot cover the inherent evil of slavery. As Baby Suggs thinks, "You got my boy and I'm all broke down. You be renting him out to pay for me way after I'm gone to Glory." Garner dies of a stroke, which Sixo says was caused by a jealous neighbor.

Mrs. Lillian Garner

Although Mrs. Garner and her husband seem fairly benevolent owners, their attitudes betray how slavery dehumanizes its victims, no matter how kindly the slaves are treated. When Sethe asks Mrs. Garner if her marriage to Halle means a wedding, the woman laughs and pats Sethe on the head as if she were a pet. She calls Baby Suggs "Jenny," assuming that the name on the slave papers is what she calls herself. After her husband's death, Mrs. Garner brings in her schoolteacher brother-in-law to run the farm—not because they need the help, but because she does not want to be the only white person there. She becomes ill with a tumor in her throat, and is thus too weak to intervene when the schoolteacher's methods turn severe.

Howard

Sethe's oldest child leaves home, presumably to fight in the Civil War, after two tiny handprints appear in a cake. Denver remembers fondly how he and his brother would make up "die-witch!" stories and let her have the whole top of the bed. Howard "had a head shape nobody could forget," and it is one of the few things Sethe can remember about him: otherwise, she might recall how he never let her touch him after his sister's death, or how he always slept hand-in-hand with his brother after that day.

Lady Jones

Lady Jones is a light-skinned black with "gray eyes and yellow woolly hair" that make her the focus of envy and hatred within the black community. Because of her light skin she has received privileges, including being picked to receive schooling in Pennsylvania, "and she paid it back by teaching the unpicked." Denver is one of the unpicked, and she attends Lady Jones's school until a fellow student reminds her of her family's shame. Thus it is Lady Jones whom Denver turns to for help feeding the family, and it is Lady Jones's kind "Oh, baby" that "inaugurated [Denver's] life in the world as a woman."

Nelson Lord

Nelson Lord is in Denver's class with Lady Jones. He is "a boy as smart as she was," but it is his question about her family history that leads her to leave school and begin a period of silence. When Denver takes steps to save the family, however, it is Nelson's words that open her mind to the idea of having a self to preserve. At the end of the novel, it is implied that he is courting Denver.

Schoolteacher

The schoolteacher is Mr. Garner's sister's husband, and perhaps provides the best example of the dehumanizing effects of slavery. The schoolteacher comes to oversee Sweet Home after Mr. Garner's death. He sees the opportunity as one for studying the slaves, whom he considers no different than animals. Sethe says she thinks it was the schoolteacher's questions "that tore Sixo up ... for all time," and his listing of her "animal characteristics" strengthens her resolve to resist capture: "No one, nobody on this earth, would list her daughter's characteristics on the animal side of the paper," Sethe says in explaining her actions to Beloved. The schoolteacher teaches his nephews that the slaves are like animals, but he fails to prevent them from "mishandling" them and so there is "nothing there to claim" when they discover Sethe and her children in Cincinnati.

Sethe

Sethe has "iron eyes and a backbone to match." Slavery, however, has "punched the glittering iron out of Sethe's eyes, leaving two open wells" that reflect the emptiness in her soul. She has spent all of her efforts "not on avoiding pain but on getting through it as quickly as possible." She avoids planning anything, because "the one set of plans she made—getting away from Sweet Home—went awry so completely she never dared life by making more." So instead of counting on family or community to aid her, Sethe creates a small, insulated world in which her only goals are to escape memories of the past and protect the one child she has left. By herself, she can face anything: she is "the one who never looked away," who can watch a man get stomped to death or repair a pet dog with a dislocated eye and two broken legs.

Paul D's arrival changes things for Sethe, adding "something she wanted to count on but was scared to." His stories also give Sethe "new pictures and old rememories that broke her heart." Even so, she eventually decides she wants him to stay because he makes her story "bearable because it was his as well." When Paul D discovers the truth behind her escape from the schoolteacher, however, he moves out. Sethe "despised herself for having been so trusting," but soon forgets this trouble when she determines that Beloved is really the ghost of her dead baby daughter. She can forget everything, now, Sethe thinks: "I don't have to remember nothing. I don't even have to explain. She understands it all." Sethe devotes herself to Beloved, cutting Denver out of their games, and subjecting herself to the growing girl's whims. When Denver tells Janey Wagon about their problems, Janey thinks that "Sethe had lost her wits, finally, as Janey knew she would—trying to do it all alone with her nose in the air." But is it insanity or fear of yet again losing her "best thing" that causes Sethe to attacks Mr. Bodwin? In the aftermath, with Beloved gone and Denver growing up, Sethe seems to have given up. She retreats to Baby Suggs's bed, just wanting to rest. But Paul D recognizes, even if she doesn't, that "you your best thing, Sethe," and promises her that together they can build "some kind of tomorrow."

Sixo

One of the Sweet Home men, Sixo is "indigo with a flame-red tongue." His dark color, his night-time dancing, his folk knowledge, and his "knowing tales" indicate he is probably a first-generation slave brought over from Africa. He maintains a relationship with Patsy the "Thirty-Mile Woman" despite the distance and difficulties that keep them apart. After the schoolteacher arrives, his questions "[tear] Sixo up" and he stops speaking English because there "was no future in it." Sixo is captured shortly after the group escape attempt, and his wild singing convinces the schoolteacher "this one will never be suitable." They tie him to a tree and light a fire at his feet, but have to shoot him to stop his laughter and singing. Sixo laughs because he has beaten the white men by fathering a child with the Thirty-Mile Woman ("Seven-O!"), while his song is a "hatred so loose it was juba."

Stamp Paid

Stamp Paid was originally named Joshua, but he renamed himself after he "handed over his wife to his master's son" and gave in to his wife's demand that he stay alive and not take revenge. "With that gift, he decided that he didn't owe anybody anything." This "debtlessness" does not satisfy him, however, and so he takes to helping runaways across the Ohio River, "helping them pay out and off whatever they owed in misery." He is witness to the "Misery" that occurs when the schoolteacher comes to take Sethe back to slavery, and prevents her from killing Denver as well. He is concerned about "truth and forewarning," and so he shows Paul D a newspaper clipping about Sethe's arrest. Stamp Paid has second thoughts about his actions after Paul D leaves 124 Bluestone, however, and thinks maybe he does owe the family something. When he returns to the house to try to set things straight with Sethe, he sees Beloved, and it is through Stamp Paid that the community comes to learn of Sethe's trouble.

Baby Suggs

See Jenny Whitlow

Halle Suggs

Halle is the youngest of Baby Suggs's eight children, and the only one she has been able to see grow to adulthood. He rented himself out on Sundays to buy his mother's freedom, and Paul D figures that strong love is why Sethe chose Halle out of all the Sweet Home men. Sethe similarly remembers a tender care that "suggested a family relationship rather than a man's laying claim." Halle does not appear when it is time to escape Sweet Home, however, and Sethe thinks he is dead—better that than believing he abandoned her and their children. Paul D reveals that he saw Halle alive, however, but empty-eyed and with butter smeared on his face. He pieces together that the final straw for Halle must have been witnessing the attack on Sethe that stole her milk. Baby Suggs claims that she felt Halle die—in 1855, on the same day that Denver was born.

Janey Wagon

Janey Wagon has worked at the Bodwins' since she was fourteen, and helps Denver find a job when she comes asking for help. It is interesting to note the change in Janey's attitude over her years with the Bodwins. When Baby Suggs first visits, young Janey tells her to "eat all you want; it's ours," implying that she feels she is part of the household. Her attitude is a little different some twenty years on, however. Although she says of her employers that she "wouldn't trade them for another pair," she is concerned that the Bodwins want "all my days and nights too," not recognizing that she is her own person, with a life apart from their house.

Whitegirl

Amy Denver is the "whitegirl" who helps Sethe through childbirth shortly after her escape from Sweet Home. Although she is white, she is "trash," and her situation is not so different from many slaves. She is escaping beatings and indentured servitude—paying off the debt her mother incurred coming to America—and has a place and a thing that symbolize freedom for her. Amy is on her way to Boston in a single-minded pursuit of "carmine velvet" when she finds Sethe lying on the wrong side of the Ohio River. Her "fugitive eyes and her tenderhearted mouth" lead Sethe to trust her, and with Amy's encouragement she gets up and crosses the river to freedom. Amy's "good hands" help bring Sethe's baby into the world, and Sethe names the girl Denver in her memory.

Jenny Whitlow

Baby Suggs's life serves as an illustration of how slavery separates families: "Anybody Baby Suggs knew, let alone loved, who hadn't run off or been hanged, got rented out, loaned out, bought up, brought back, stored up, mortgaged, won, stolen or seized." Although her bill of sale says her name is "Jenny Whitlow," she claims the name "Baby Suggs," given to her by a "husband" who escaped and left her when he had the chance. Halle is the only one of her eight children she sees grow to adulthood, and this leads her to say: "A man ain't nothing but a man. But a son? Well now, that's *somebody*." After Halle buys her freedom, Baby Suggs turns the house on Bluestone Road into a place where friends and strangers can meet, refresh themselves, and talk. She also preaches in a nearby field, "offering up to [people] her great big heart." When Sethe attempts to murder her grandchildren rather than see them returned to slavery, Baby Suggs "could not approve or condemn Sethe's rough choice. One or the other might have saved her, but beaten up by the claims of both, she went to bed." She remains in bed, contemplating the harmlessness of colors, until she dies, her great heart finally quitting.

Themes

Race and Racism

"You got two feet, not four," Paul D tells Sethe when she reveals her secret to him, and the dehumanizing effect of slavery is a primary theme of *Beloved*. According to the schoolteacher, slaves are just another type of animal: not only does he list their "animal characteristics," he considers them "creatures" to be "handled," similar to dogs or cattle. In some ways, they are not even worth as much as animals: "Unlike a snake or a bear," he thinks while pursuing the runaways, "a dead nigger could not be skinned for profit and was not worth his own dead weight in coin." Because slaves are treated no better—and sometimes worse—than animals, it leads them to question what it is that makes one human. While Mr. Garner was alive, for instance, Paul D truly believed that he was a man. But after the schoolteacher arrives and puts the bit to him, he learns a different lesson: "They were trespassers among the human race." There is another side to the dehumanizing effects of slavery, however: just as it turns slaves into animals, it turns owners into monsters. As Baby Suggs thinks of white people, "they could prowl at will, change from one mind to another, and even when they thought they were behaving, it was a far cry from what real humans did." Stamp Paid understands this effect as well: "The more coloredpeople spent their strength trying to convince [whites] how gentle they were, how clever and loving, how human, ... the deeper and more tangled the jungle grew inside. But it wasn't the jungle blacks brought with them," Stamp Paid thinks, but "the jungle whitefolks planted in them. And it grew. It spread ... until it invaded the whites who had made it. Touched them every one. Changed and altered them. Made them bloody, silly, worse than even they wanted to be, so scared were they of the jungle they had made."

Freedom

For people treated no better than animals, freedom can be a difficult concept to grasp. When Halle buys his mother's freedom, for instance, Baby Suggs thinks that he "gave her freedom when it didn't mean a thing." When she steps across the Ohio River, however, "she could not believe that Halle knew what

she didn't; that Halle, who had never drawn one free breath, knew there was nothing like it in this world." While under the schoolteacher's bit, Paul D sees Mister, the rooster, and thinks, "Mister, he looked so ... free. Better than me." The reason for this, Paul D explains, is that "Mister was allowed to be and stay what he was. But I wasn't allowed to be and stay what I was." Once he has escaped from prison and earned his first money, Paul D decides that "to eat, walk and sleep anywhere was life as good as it got." Freedom is more than this, however, as Sethe has discovered. While waiting for Halle to turn up, Sethe had to learn to become her own woman. "Freeing yourself was one thing," she thinks; "claiming ownership of that freed self was another." This can be a difficult task, especially if one is tormented by painful memories of slavery. In the end, Paul D comes to agree with Sethe about the nature of freedom: "A place where you could love anything you chose—not to need permission for desire—well now, *that* was freedom."

Motherhood

One of the cruelest effects of slavery is how it severs bonds of love, particularly those between mother and child. Sethe still feels the pain of separation from her mother, while Baby Suggs has lost all but one of her eight children. One reaction to this loss of love is to deny it; as Ella says, "If anybody was to ask me I'd say 'Don't love nothing.'" After having her first three children sold away and a fourth fathered by the man who sold them, Baby Suggs "could not love [that child] and the rest she would not." Sethe similarly understands that she couldn't love her children "proper" at Sweet Home "because they wasn't mine to love." Paul D also knows motherlove is risky: "For a used-to-be slave woman to love anything that much was dangerous, especially if it was her children she had settled on to love." When he nevertheless suggests to Sethe that they have a baby together, Sethe thinks, "Lord, deliver me. Unless carefree, motherlove was a killer." This comment is terribly ironic, of course, coming from a woman who murdered her child for such a love.

Despite the pain motherlove can bring to a woman, the maternal impulse is often too powerful to deny. As Baby Suggs says, "A man ain't nothing but a man. But a son? Well now, that's *somebody*." Sethe similarly thinks her children are "her best thing, her beautiful, magical best thing— that part of her that was clean." A mother's love has no time limits, either, as Sethe tells Paul D: "Grown don't mean nothing to a mother.... I'll pro-

Topics For Further Study

- The Fugitive Slave Law of 1850 changed the way free states were required to deal with fugitive slaves, leading to Sethe's terrible response to her capture. Research the history of the legal status of fugitive and freed slaves in America. Create a timeline tracing these legal developments, and include both Supreme Court decisions and state and federal laws.

- In preparing to write *Beloved,* Toni Morrison read several slave narratives—autobiographies by freed slaves. What was missing from these narratives, said the author, was a portrayal of the inner lives of their subjects. Read one or two such slave narratives, such as those by Frederick Douglass or Harriet Jacobs. Does Morrison's point have validity? Argue for or against this opinion in an essay, comparing the narrative with Morrison's novel and using examples from the text to support your arguments.

- In *Beloved,* Amy Denver has also escaped from a situation where she faced beatings and forced labor. Research the history of indentured servi-

tude in America. Who was subject to such contracts? In what ways was it similar to slavery? In what ways was it different? Write a paper describing your findings.

- Read some African-American ghost stories, such as the folktales in Patricia McKissack's *The Dark Thirty* or Virginia Hamilton's *The People Could Fly* and *Her Stories.* What elements do they have in common with the "ghost story" of *Beloved?* Present your conclusions in an essay, and use examples from the texts.

- One of the important themes in *Beloved* is the significance of the bond between mother and child; Sethe, Denver, and Beloved all suffer to some extent because of a rupture in this bond. Do some research into the psychology of the mother-child relationship. What happens when small children are not permitted to bond with a parent? Compare your findings with what happens to the characters in the novel. Remember to cite both research studies and the novel.

---

tect [Denver] while I'm live and I'll protect her when I ain't." It is this need to care for her children that drives Sethe on to Ohio despite her pain. When telling Paul D about the beating she received before escaping, she keeps repeating, "they took my milk!"—emphasizing how important it was to her to save her milk for her baby. Unfortunately, Sethe's experiences with slavery have twisted her maternal protective impulses. "To keep them away from what I know is terrible," Sethe attempts to murder her own children. This love may be "too thick," as Paul D says, but motherless Sethe never had a chance to learn the difference: "Love is or it ain't," she replies. "Thin love ain't love at all."

Memory and Reminiscence

The physical wounds of slavery heal quickly compared to the mental and emotional scars suffered by its victims. Throughout *Beloved,* charac-

ters struggle with their memories, trying to recall the good things without remembering the bad. Paul D has "shut down a generous portion of his head" so that he will not "dwell on Halle's face and Sixo laughing." Of her first seven children, Baby Suggs can only remember that the oldest liked the burned bottom of bread. "That's all you let yourself remember," Sethe says, and for her "the future was a matter of keeping the past at bay." For Sethe, "rememories" are so powerful that they exist for her as physical objects: "if you go there and stand in the place where it was, it will happen again," she tells Denver. In contrast, Ella seems to have a healthy attitude towards the past: "The past [was] something to leave behind. And if it didn't stay behind, well, you might have to stomp it out." But Sethe has a "rebellious brain" which does not allow her to forget: "there is still more that Paul D could tell me and my brain would go right ahead and take it and never say, No thank you. I don't want to know or have to remember that." Beloved seems to have "disremembered" almost all of her past, and when Sethe comes to believe the girl is her lost daughter she "was excited to giddiness by the things she no longer had to remember." Her words seem to imply that Sethe tortures herself with memories as a sort of punishment. Now that her daughter is returned, however, "I don't have to remember nothing. I don't even have to explain. She understands it all." The conclusion of the novel seems to imply that finally putting the past behind her will enable Sethe to survive. "We got more yesterday than anybody," Paul D tells Sethe. "We need some kind of tomorrow." "Remembering seemed unwise," the narrator similarly notes, and so Beloved is "disremembered"—deliberately forgotten: "This is not a story to pass on."

Creativity and Imagination

Despite the statement that "this is not a story to pass on," stories and the imagination play an important role in the novel. Denver's imagination is her only weapon against loneliness and it "produced its own hunger and its own food." Sethe's "deprivation had been not having any dreams of her own at all." Her brain has been "loaded with the past and [is] hungry for more," leaving her "no room to imagine, let alone plan for, the next day." For Beloved, listening to Sethe's stories "became a way to feed her" and the "profound satisfaction Beloved got from storytelling" allows Sethe to share things that had been too painful to speak about before. When the lonely Denver tells stories to Beloved, she gives her subjects "more life than life had." Denver uses these stories to keep Beloved with her, trying to "construct out of the strings she had heard all her life a net to hold Beloved." Stories have the effect of bringing listener and teller together, for in the telling "the monologue became, in fact, a duet." It is this kind of sharing that allows Sethe to begin to heal, and eventually brings her to the brink of a new life with Paul D. Planning on making "some kind of tomorrow" with Sethe, Paul D thinks that "he wants to put his story next to hers."

Style

Narration/Point of View

For the most part, *Beloved* uses a third-person narrator—one who tells the story by describing the action of other people ("he said," "they did"). Because the narration describes what various characters are thinking and doing, it can also be classified as omniscient ("all-knowing") narration. This third-person narration remains fairly constant throughout the novel, but the point of view (or perspective) from which the story is told changes from section to section. In the first chapter alone, for instance, the point of view switches from Baby Suggs ("Baby Suggs didn't even raise her head") to Sethe ("Counting on the stillness of her soul she had forgotten the other one") to Paul D ("He looked at her closely, then") to Denver ("Again she wished for the baby ghost"). The changing point of view is important to the novel for several reasons. First, by including the thoughts and memories of several different characters, the narrator allows the reader to witness the various ways slavery can violate a person's humanity. Second, the changing point of view allows the reader to gain fuller portraits of each of the characters than if the focus was on a single person. These portraits are made even more intense when Morrison changes the narrative style. In the middle of Part Two, the narration switches from the third person to the first ("I") in four consecutive sections that are told directly by the characters. In these sections, Sethe, Denver, and Beloved contemplate how Beloved's arrival has changed their lives. By adding these first-person sections late in the novel, the author enhances her portrait of these characters, deepening the reader's understanding of them even further.

Flashback

A flashback is a literary device used to present action that occurred before the beginning of the story. In *Beloved,* the narrator structures the story in such a way that past events are related as a way of explaining the present. In the first paragraph, for instance, the narrator says that "by 1873, Sethe and her daughter were [the ghost's] only victims." This sets the main action in 1873, but the paragraphs that follow explain how Baby Suggs and the two boys escaped the ghost prior to that date. Flashbacks are also presented as the memories or stories of several of the characters. When Paul D first sees Sethe, for instance, he begins to recall how the men of Sweet Home reacted to her arrival over twenty years ago. As Paul D and Sethe spend time with each other, they remember moments of their previous time together and tell each other stories of what has happened to them since their time at Sweet Home. There are more direct flashbacks in the narrative as well, when past events are related directly, without present-day comment from the person telling or remembering the tale. Examples of this direct style of flashback occur when Beloved first hears the story of Denver's birth and when Paul D recalls how the Plan went wrong. Deborah Horvitz notes in *Studies in American Fiction* that flashbacks play an important role in the novel, for they reflect one of its important themes. The flashbacks, the critic writes, "succeed in bridging the shattered generations by repeating meaningful and multi-layered images. That is, contained in the narrative strategy of the novel itself are both the wrenching, inter-generational separations and the healing process."

Idiom

Idiom refers to a word construction or verbal expression that is closely associated with a given language or dialect. For example, the English expression "a piece of cake" is sometimes used to describe a task that is easily done. In *Beloved,* Morrison makes use of idiom to help re-create the sense of a specific community, that of African Americans in Reconstruction Ohio. When the characters use words like "ain't" and "reckon" and phrases like "sit down a spell," it helps place their characters within that community. One particularly interesting example of this idiom is the way in which it describes people of different races. In compound words such as "whitegirl," "blackman," and "coloredpeople," a person's race is actually part of the word that describes them. This seems to indicate that there is a fundamental difference between blacks and whites, for if the only difference between them were color one would say "black woman" and "white woman." Instead, the compound words seem to indicate that black and whites are entirely different creatures. These words thus reinforce one of the themes of the novel: that one of the foremost evils of slavery is the way in which it dehumanizes people, both black and white.

Motif

A motif (sometimes called a motiv or leitmotiv) is a theme, character type, image, metaphor, or other verbal element that is repeated throughout a piece of work. Throughout *Beloved,* there is one such motif that is repeated with regularity: a description of the characters' eyes and how they see. "The eyes are windows to the soul," goes the common saying, and the eyes of the novel's characters are likewise revealing. Sethe, for instance, has had the "glittering iron" punched out of her eyes, "leaving two open wells that did not reflect firelight."

When schoolteacher catches up to Sethe, her eyes are so black she "looks blind," and after too much conflict with Beloved her eyes turn "bright but dead, alert but vacant." Similarly, the disturbing thing about Beloved's eyes is not that the "whites of them were much too white" but that "deep down in those big black eyes there was no expression at all." When Paul D recalls his time on the chain gang in Georgia, he remembers that "the eyes had to tell what there was to tell" about what the men were feeling. When the schoolteacher comes upon the scene in the shed, he decides to turn back for home without claiming any of the survivors because he has had "enough nigger eyes for now."

The way people use their eyes is also important. Denver thinks of her mother as one "who never looked away," not even from pain or death. Paul D thinks he is safe from Beloved's advances "as long as his eyes were locked on the silver of the lard can." Denver thinks it is "lovely" the way that she is "pulled into view by the interested, uncritical eyes" of Beloved. It is shortly after Beloved asks Sethe, "you finished with your eyes?" that Sethe realizes Beloved is the ghost of her baby daughter. "Now," she thinks, "I can look at things again because she's here to see them too." But as Beloved drains the energy from Sethe, "the brighter Beloved's eyes, the more those eyes that used never to look away became slits of sleeplessness." When Paul D wants to return to Sethe, he considers how he looks through other people's eyes: "When he looks at himself through Garner's eyes, he sees one thing. Through Sixo's, another. One makes him feel righteous. One makes him feel ashamed." Finally, however, he considers how he looks through Sethe's eyes. After he does this, he returns to the only woman who "could have left him his manhood like that."

Imagery

Imagery refers to the use of images in a literary work. Critics frequently describe Morrison's writing as "lyrical" or "poetic" because her use of vivid, powerful imagery. One such image is that of the "chokecherry tree" on Sethe's back. Instead of having the narrator give a simple description of the oozing wounds on Sethe's back, Amy Denver describes it as a chokecherry tree, complete with sap, branches, leaves, and blossoms. The picture this comparison draws in the reader's mind is much more disturbing than a straightforward description would be. This is just one example of how the author sets beautiful natural images in contrast to the horrors of slavery, the better to highlight its evil.

Historical Context

The Fugitive Slave Law of 1850

One of the central events of the novel—Sethe's attack on her children—is described as "her rough response to the Fugitive Bill." Prior to 1850, U.S. law permitted slave owners to attempt to recover escaped slaves, but state authorities were under no obligation to assist them. Many Northerners saw aiding and protecting fugitive slaves as one way to combat the evil of slavery. Escaped slaves who settled in free states were therefore relatively safe from capture, since their abolitionist communities rarely cooperated with slave owners. This sense of safety was jeopardized by the Fugitive Slave Law of 1850.

As America expanded her borders, slavery was a continuing source of controversy. The addition of territory acquired in the Mexican-American War of 1846-48 sparked heated debates over the status of slavery in these new lands. When Pennsylvania Representative David Wilmot proposed that "neither slavery nor involuntary servitude shall ever exist in any part" of the territory acquired from Mexico, Southern states strongly objected. The Wilmot Proviso was defeated, and Kentucky congressman Henry Clay brokered a new deal. The resulting Compromise of 1850 was a series of bills designed to satisfy both North and South. As well as admitting California as a free state and allowing Utah and New Mexico to decide the slavery issue for themselves, the Compromise of 1850 enacted a much stricter fugitive slave law. Under this law, fugitive slaves were denied a jury trial, facing a court-appointed commissioner instead. This commissioner received ten dollars for certifying delivery of an alleged slave, but only five dollars when he refused it. And not only did federal officials take part in the capture and return of fugitives, but they could compel citizens to help enforce the law—and jail or fine them if they refused.

Anti-slavery forces were outraged by this new law, and often took matters into their own hands to combat it. In cities such as Boston, Detroit, Milwaukee, Syracuse, New York, and Christiana, Pennsylvania, mobs rescued alleged fugitives from their captors and in some cases even killed slave owners. Less confrontational forms of protest increased as well, as the new law inspired an increase in organized assistance to slaves such as the Underground Railroad. In 1852, Harriet Beecher Stowe was inspired by the Fugitive Slave Law to write her classic anti-slavery novel *Uncle Tom's Cabin.* Despite these very visible activities protesting the law, most Northerners complied with it. Of an estimated two hundred African Americans arrested during its enforcement, only twenty were released or rescued; the remainder returned to slavery.

The Rise of the Ku Klux Klan

Even after the abolition of slavery ended the threat of being returned to servitude, African Americans still found their rights and even lives in danger. Many white Southerners found Reconstruction Act of 1867—the Republican government's plan for returning the South to the Union—difficult to swallow. This act replaced the mostly all-white state governments created after the war with five military districts. Each district had 20,000 troops, commanded by a Union general. Southern states were forced to grant new rights to African Americans, and more than a dozen black congressmen and two senators were elected. In response to what they perceived as Republican oppression, white Southerners formed a secret society whose aim was to intimidate these unwanted administrators. The Ku Klux Klan (KKK) grew from a social club into a terrorist organization that used arson, beatings, and even murder to achieve their ends.

Klan activity stepped up after the Fifteenth Amendment, which guaranteed all men the right to vote, was passed in 1870. Not only did this amendment ensure the voting rights of Southern blacks, it expanded the right to vote to African Americans in Northern states. Klan activity was similarly expanded, as its violence spread to northern states. In *Beloved,* Paul D considers Cincinnati "infected by the Klan," which he calls "desperately thirsty for black blood." The KKK terrorized African Americans to keep them from voting, often with great success. Many African Americans were murdered, and their killers had little fear of prosecution. To combat this violence, Congress passed the Ku Klux Act in 1871, which strengthened the penalties for interfering with elections. This led to almost three thousand indictments that year, and the 1872 elections were relatively peaceful. Nevertheless, the Klan had demonstrated its strength, and after the last federal troops left the South in 1877, white supremacists were free to establish a deeply segregated society that openly oppressed African Americans until the civil rights movement of the 1960s.

Toni Morrison and the Post-Aesthetic Movement

Mirroring their increased presence in politics, African Americans also became highly visible as

Even after the Civil War, reminders of the previous slave status of African Americans—like the signs in the commercial district pictured here—were everywhere.

writers during the 1960s. Harlem Renaissance writers such as Langston Hughes and Zora Neale Hurston had been prominent in the 1920s, while Richard Wright and Ralph Ellison achieved both literary and popular acclaim in the 1940s and 1950s. Many of these works were popular because of the way they were able to interpret the black experience for a white audience. In the 1960s and 1970s, however, writers within the "Black Aesthetic Movement" attempted to produce works of art that would be meaningful to the black masses. Writers such as Amiri Baraka, Haki R. Madhubuti,

and Sonia Sanchez created works which highlighted the disparity between blacks and whites and affirmed the value of African-American culture, thus creating a sense of pride and identity in the black community.

In the late 1970s and 1980s, however, many African-American writers chose a slightly different approach. Instead of focusing on the differences between blacks and whites in America—and thus placing themselves within or against a white social context—these "Post-Aesthetic" writers used a wholly African-American context for their work.

Instead of looking to the outside world for solutions or validation, the African Americans in these works found answers within their own families or communities. Toni Morrison is considered one of the most prominent writers within this Post-Aesthetic movement, which includes such authors as Alice Walker, Kristin Hunter, and John Edgar Wideman. By emphasizing the importance of family and community in dealing with life's challenges, Morrison's *Beloved* provides a notable example of this literary movement.

Critical Overview

While Morrison had earned a considerable critical reputation with her first four novels, many initial reviews of *Beloved* showed no hesitation in acclaiming it the masterpiece of a supremely gifted writer. Margaret Atwood, for instance, called the work "another triumph" and added in her *New York Times Book Review* article that "Morrison's versatility and technical and emotional range appear to know no bounds. If there were any doubts about her stature as a pre-eminent American novelist, of her own or any other generation, *Beloved* will put them to rest." *New York Times* critic Michiko Kakutani similarly termed the novel "a work of mature imagination—a magisterial and deeply moving meditation not only on the cruelties of a single institution, but on family, history, and love." In the *Chicago Tribune,* Charles Larson acclaimed *Beloved* as the author's "darkest and most probing novel" and concluded that "Toni Morrison has demonstrated once again the stunning powers that place her in the first ranks of our living novelists."

Despite such emphatically positive remarks and the 1988 Pulitzer Prize, not all critics embraced the novel. In *Commentary,* Carole Iannone faulted the work's "oft-repeated miseries" as both numbing and sensationalistic. "Morrison seems simply unsure how much she wants the past, which means both the immediate past and the historical past, to weigh in the lives and behavior of her characters," the critic added. While noting stretches of "first-class writing" in the novel, *New Republic* critic Stanley Crouch called the work melodramatic "protest pulp fiction" that "rarely gives the impression that her people exist for any purpose other than to deliver a message." Martha Bayles similarly offered the "heretical opinion" that *Beloved* "is a dreadful novel, final proof of Morrison's decline from high promise into fashionable medioc-

rity." The critic maintained that in relying increasingly on magical elements, the author has shifted from "bravely probing the consciences of even the most pitiable black characters ... to predictably blaming white racist oppression for every crime committed by the inhabitants of an enchanted village called blackness." Other reviewers, however, observed that the novel was able to overcome its melodramatic tendencies. While noting that the novel has "a slightly uneven, stepping-stone quality," *Nation* contributor Rosellen Brown nevertheless found *Beloved* "an extraordinary novel. It has certain flaws that attach to its design and occasionally to its long reach for eloquence, and an ending that lacks the power of the tragedy it is meant to resolve. But its originality, the pleasure it takes in a language at the same time loose and tight, colloquial and elevated, is stunning." "Morrison is essentially an operatic writer and as a 'production' Beloved has some of the excesses" of opera, Judith Thurman similarly stated in the *New Yorker.* Nevertheless, the critic concluded that "there's something great in [the novel]: a play of human voices, consciously exalted, perversely stressed, yet holding true. It gets you."

Often a reviewer's opinion of the novel was tied to his or her interpretation of Beloved's character. Those who saw her merely as a ghost were more likely to find the novel less compelling. In the *Times Literary Supplement,* for instance, Carol Rumens found Beloved's portions of the novel unsatisfactory, for "the travails of a ghost cannot be made to resonate in quite the same way as those of a living woman or child." For other critics, however, the riddle of Beloved has proven a complex question with many answers. For Susan Bowers, Beloved is a creature returned from the dead—but as living flesh, not a ghost. "Her physical presence," the critic wrote in *Journal of Ethnic Studies,* "has the effect of Judgment Day on all those whom she encounters," leading the residents of 124 to address "her or his most profound individual anguish, whatever lies at the core of each identity." To Elizabeth House, however, "evidence throughout the book suggests that the girl is not a supernatural being of any kind but simply a young woman who has herself suffered the horrors of slavery." House noted in *Studies in American Fiction* that Beloved's entry into the family is due to a double case of mistaken identity, caused by "the destruction of family ties brought by slavery, and Beloved, seen as a human being, emphasizes and illuminates these themes." Other reviewers see Beloved as a figure who represents "the spirit of all the women dragged onto slave ships in Africa and also all Black women in America trying to trace their ancestry back to the mother on the ship attached to them," as Deborah Horvitz notes in *Studies in American Fiction*. According to the critic, Beloved is a stand-in both for Sethe's mother, dragged from her home in Africa, and Sethe's baby girl, emerged from the spirit world. "Beloved's character is both the frame and center of the book, and it is her story—or her desperate struggle to know and experience her own story—that is the pumping heart of the novel," Barbara Schapiro concluded in *Contemporary Literature*. "Beloved's struggle is Sethe's struggle; it is also Denver's, Paul D's, and Baby Suggs's. It is the struggle of all black people in a racist society, Morrison suggests, to claim themselves as subjects in their own narrative."

Another aspect of the novel to come under critical scrutiny has been the circular structure of its narrative. *Beloved* is told through story and flashback, presenting the past in pieces which the reader has to fit together. This structure is important to the theme of the novel, according to several critics. As Susan Bowers remarked, "the characters' rememorying in *Beloved* epitomizes the novel's purpose of conjuring up the spirits and experiences of the past and thus ultimately empowering both characters and readers." "The splintered, piecemeal revelation of the past is one of the technical wonders of Morrison's narrative," Walter Clemons similarly explained in *Newsweek*. "We gradually understand that this isn't tricky storytelling but the intricate exploration of trauma." By moving "the lurid material of melodrama into the minds of her people, where it gets sited and sorted, lived and relived," Morrison endows it with "the enlarging outlines of myth and trauma, dream and obsession," Ann Snitow noted in *Voice Literary Supplement*. Eusebio L. Rodrigues likened the narrative structure of Morrison's novel to an "an extended blues performance." As he explained in the *Journal of Narrative Technique*, "phrases and images will be used over and over again to generate rhythmic meanings; fragments of a story will recur, embedded in other fragments of other stories. A born bard, the narrator, a blueswoman, will cast a spell on her audience so that fragments, phrases, words accelerate and work together to create a mythic tale."

Morrison's work has also been hailed for its ability to re-create the inner lives of people subjected to oppression and brutality, something the author believed was missing from slave narratives of the nineteenth century. Walter Clemons applauded the author's success in achieving this authenticity: "In *Beloved*, this interior life [of slaves] is re-created with a moving intensity no novelist has even approached before." Barbara Schapiro similarly hailed the novel's psychological realism: "*Beloved* penetrates, perhaps more deeply than any historical or psychological study could, the unconscious emotional and psychic consequences of slavery. The novel reveals how the condition of enslavement in the external world, particularly the denial of one's status as a human subject, has deep repercussions in the individual's internal world." In portraying more than just the physical trauma of slavery, the novel has a "great bridging capacity ... in the way it opens up the imaginations of those who haven't lived it to the memory of slavery and the experience of carrying that memory in your past," according to *Washington Post* contributor Amy E. Schwartz. "Written in an anti-minimalist, lyrical style in which biblical myths, folklore, and literary realism overlap, the text is so grounded in historical reality that it could be used to teach American history classes," Horvitz similarly stated. But the true measure of the novel's worth, the critic concluded, is that "as a simultaneously accessible and yet extremely difficult book, *Beloved* operates so complexly that as soon as one layer of understanding is reached, another, equally as richly textured, emerges to be unravelled."

Criticism

Wendy Perkins

Perkins is an Associate Professor of English at Prince George's Community College in Maryland and has published several articles on British and American authors. In the following essay, she examines how the narrative structure of Beloved *reinforces the novel's focus on the problematic search for identity.*

Toni Morrison's Pulitzer Prize-winning novel *Beloved* has achieved considerable recognition for its moving portrait of an African-American family's struggle against the debilitating effects of slavery. Merle Rubin in the *Christian Science Monitor* declares *Beloved* "a stunning book and lasting achievement," while John Leonard in the *Los Angeles Times Book Review* places it "on the highest shelf of American literature, even if half a dozen canonized white boys have to be elbowed off." In the *Times Literary Supplement*, Jennifer Uglow ad-

What Do I Read Next?

- Morrison's first novel, *The Bluest Eye* (1969), is a contemporary portrayal of the self-hatred and destruction that can occur when African Americans look to white society for validation. Pecola Breedlove is a young black girl who has adopted white child star Shirley Temple as her ideal. In comparison, Pecola feels ugly and longs for blue eyes. After her father rapes her, Pecola's obsession turns to insanity. She gives birth prematurely to a baby who later dies, and withdraws into a fantasy world where she has the bluest eyes of all.

- Told from a male perspective, Morrison's award-winning *Song of Solomon* (1979) relates Milkman Dead's search for identity. Milkman wavers between the altruism of his aunt and the materialism of his father and sets out on a journey of discovery. He overcomes his confusion and dissatisfaction to discover the richness of his African-American heritage, the importance of community, and the nature of love and faith.

- The first novel to appear after Morrison's Nobel Prize, *Paradise* (1998) tells the story of the fictional town of Ruby, Oklahoma, founded by African-American freedmen after Reconstruction. Morrison examines the nature of community, responsibility, and history as she relates the events that lead the townsmen to destroy a nearby convent.

- Winner of the National Book Award, Charles Johnson's *Middle Passage* (1990) is a powerful tale of a newly freed slave who stows away on a New Orleans ship in order to avoid marriage. When the ship turns out to be a slave clipper bound for Africa, Rutherford Calhoun faces a journey that is harrowing in both body and spirit.

- Inspired by the furor over the Fugitive Slave Law of 1850, Harriet Beecher Stowe's classic novel *Uncle Tom's Cabin* (1852) was a pioneering portrayal of the evils of slavery and the humanity of slaves. (The stereotype of an "Uncle Tom" comes from poorly adapted play versions of the novel, not Stowe's Christ-like title character.) The novel sold over three hundred thousand copies during its first year of publication and served as a source of inspiration for many anti-slavery activists.

- A highly acclaimed writer for children and young adults, Virginia Hamilton has collected and retold several books of African-American stories and folktales. *Many Thousand Gone: African Americans from Slavery to Freedom* (1992) uses actual narratives to trace the history of African-Americans, while *Her Stories* (1995) collects folktales, fairy tales, and true stories featuring African-American heroines. Both volumes have illustrations by award winners Leo and Diane Dillon.

- Another young-adult writer has created a searing portrayal of the evils of slavery. In *Nightjohn* (1993), Gary Paulsen tells the story of twelve-year-old Sarny, a slave girl who risks serious punishment when she learns to read.

- One critic likened the public impact of Morrison's *Beloved* to that of another novel that tells of a people's fight to combat prejudice and oppression. Leon Uris's popular bestseller *Exodus* (1957) is an epic tale of the Jewish settlement of modern Israel. In preparing to write the novel, the author read 300 books, travelled 12,000 miles inside Israel, and interviewed more than 1,200 people.

- Harriet A. Jacobs's *Incidents in the Life of a Slave Girl Written by Herself* (1862) was one of the first autobiographies written by an African American. In it, Jacobs relates her birth into servitude, her affair with a white neighbor, her escape from a North Carolina plantation, and her struggles to free herself and her children.

dresses one of the novel's prominent themes when she notes that Morrison's works often concentrate on "the developing sense of self." *Beloved*'s unconventional narrative structure, with its disrupted chronology and fragmented glimpses of the main characters, foregrounds this theme as it delineates the support that can enable and the obstacles that can impede this development.

Sethe's struggles to come to terms with her past are complicated by her inability to establish a clear vision of herself. The novel's nonlinear structure in Part I, which affords readers only brief impressions of her, highlights this problem. She has repressed much of the truth about what she experienced as a slave at Sweet Home, the Kentucky plantation where she grew up. There she was not allowed an identity, especially after Mr. Garner died and his brother-in-law, whom she calls the schoolteacher, took over. Schoolteacher considered his black slaves animals, as evidenced by his careful measurements of their physiques and notations of their "human" and "animal" characteristics. Morrison reinforces this attitude when she shifts the narrative point of view to the schoolteacher when he arrives at Bluestone Road to take Sethe back to Sweet Home. When he witnesses Sethe's attempts to kill her children, he thinks of the abuse she suffered from his nephew and determines he "overbeat" her:

> Suppose you beat the hounds past that point that-away. Never again could you trust them in the woods or anywhere else…. the animal would revert—bite your hand clean off…. you just can't mishandle creatures and expect success.

While at Sweet Home, Sethe was forced to deny herself as a wife and a mother. She was not permitted to marry Halle in a legal ceremony and she felt compelled to keep her love for her children in check. She later admits to Paul, "I couldn't love em proper in Kentucky because they wasn't mine to love." Paul understands that Sethe protected herself by loving "small." When chained like an animal and caged in the ground in Georgia, he notes that he "picked the tiniest stars out of the sky to own…. Anything bigger wouldn't do. A woman, a child, a brother—a big love like that would split you wide open." Paul had suffered under similar abuse at Sweet Home and after he was sent to prison in Georgia for the attempted murder of his new owner. He tells Sethe his own repressed memory from his time at Sweet Home. The worst part for Paul after he was chained, waiting to be taken to a new plantation, was "walking past the roosters looking at them look at me." He focuses on one

in particular named Mister, "who was allowed to be and stay what he was." Paul admits,

> I wasn't allowed to be and stay what I was. Even if you cooked him you'd be cooking a rooster named Mister. But wasn't no way I'd ever be Paul D again, living or dead. Schoolteacher changed me. I was something else and that something was less than a chicken sitting in the sun on a tub.

During their conversations, Sethe and Paul allow only fragments of their past to emerge from what Paul calls his locked and rusted shut tobacco tin, buried deep in his chest. They keep these talks short, acknowledging that "saying more might push them both to a place they couldn't get back from" as they struggle to discover a strong sense of themselves. Sethe often turns to cooking after her conversations with Paul, claiming "nothing better than that to start the day's serious work of beating back the past." However, Sethe's attempts to repress her memories ultimately fail when she finds Beloved at Bluestone Road.

Beloved's presence forces Sethe to confront her past and thus to reconcile her vision of herself. Many critics consider Beloved to be the reincarnation of Sethe's daughter, citing her seemingly supernatural gifts and her strong links to Sethe. In this interpretation, Sethe's buried memory emerges in the form of a ghost. Others, however, argue that Beloved had survived a passage on a slave ship, where she watched her mother throw herself overboard. She then transfers to Sethe all the emotions she experienced toward her mother. Morrison's narrative structure, with its brief glimpses of Beloved's dreams and the lack of detail about where she came from, makes it difficult to arrive at a definitive conclusion about Beloved. Yet whether or not she really is the reincarnation of Sethe's murdered daughter has little bearing on the novel's focus: the difficulties Sethe faces as she tries to determine her identity. Morrison's refusal to provide a clear vision of Beloved reinforces her point that discovering one's true self, especially when that self is a black woman, is problematic.

Soon after Beloved's arrival, Paul shows Sethe the newspaper clipping about "the Misery," which compels her to confront the tragedy of her past and her identity as a mother. Sethe pieces together the fragments of her repressed memory and, for the first time, faces the full implications of her actions, taking the first painful step toward recovery of self. When the "four horsemen" approached Bluestone Road, the moment became apocalyptic for Sethe. The hope that she could be a mother to her children, which she had allowed herself during her twenty-eight days at Baby Suggs', was dashed. She tries to explain to Paul that her actions that day stemmed from her great love for her children, but Paul cannot envision her as a responsible mother. At one point, he views her as almost inhuman:

> "I stopped him," she said.... "I took and put my babies where they'd be safe."
>
> "Your love is too thick," he said.... "What you did was wrong, Sethe."
>
> "I should have gone on back there? Taken my babies back there?"
>
> "There could have been a way. Some other way.... You got two feet, Sethe, not four," he said, and right then a forest sprang up between them; trackless and quiet.

The narrative shift to Paul's point of view and his inability to regard Sethe as a responsible mother illustrates how Sethe's loss of self results not only from the horrors of slavery, but also the problems of identity that arise within the black community. After his words create a gulf between them, Paul acknowledges that he has "moved from his shame to hers...." From his cold-house secret straight to her too-thick love. His own shame and lack of a strong sense of self prevents him from understanding Sethe. As a result he leaves Sethe alone, much like the black community had done. Her ostracism, however, results from what the community considers to be her overweening pride as well as her actions. Morrison's presentation of contrasting visions of Sethe highlight the difficulties Sethe faces in her search for herself.

Sethe's efforts to prove herself to be a good mother redouble when she confronts Beloved's anger and resentment toward her. The novel reveals the complicated dynamics of mother-daughter relationships when it shifts back and forth between Sethe's and Beloved's point of view. Beloved's feelings of betrayal and abandonment counter Sethe's pleas for understanding and acknowledgement of her as a protective and long-suffering mother. In an ultimate expression of her love for her children, Sethe attacks Mr. Bodwin, whom she confuses with the men who came to take her back to Sweet Home. Yet when Beloved disappears, Sethe seems to lose all sense of self and gives up on life. Ultimately, though, Morrison suggests that she may be saved when Paul returns to Bluestone Road and presents her with a new vision of herself, telling her, "You your best thing, Sethe. You are."

Through the presentation of the fragmented landscape of Sethe's past, Morrison effectively delineates the psychological effects of racial oppres- sion. *Beloved* presents a powerful account of a black woman's struggle to overcome those devastating effects and discover a complete sense of self.

Source: Wendy Perkins, in an essay for *Novels for Students*, Gale, 1999.

Elizabeth B. House

In this review, House refutes the commonly held assumption among critics that Beloved is the reincarnated ghost of Sethe's murdered daughter. House supports her interpretation of Beloved as human, arguing that this explanation emphasizes the destructive ways in which slavery impacted people's perceptions of themselves and their relationships.

Most reviewers of Toni Morrison's novel *Beloved* have assumed that the mysterious title character is the ghostly reincarnation of Sethe's murdered baby, a flesh and blood version of the spirit Paul D. drives from the house....

Clearly, ... writers evaluate Morrison's novel believing that *Beloved* is unquestionably a ghost. Such uniform acceptance of this notion is surprising, for evidence throughout the book suggests that the girl is not a supernatural being of any kind but simply a young woman who has herself suffered the horrors of slavery.

In large part, Morrison's Pulitzer Prize-winning fifth novel is about the atrocities slavery wrought both upon a mother's need to love and care for her children as well as a child's deep need for a family: Sethe murders her baby girl rather than have her taken back into slavery; Baby Suggs grieves inconsolably when her children are sold; Sethe sees her own mother, a woman who was brought from Africa on a slave ship, only a few times before the woman is killed; Denver loves her mother, Sethe, but also fears the woman because she is a murderer. These and other incidents illustrate the destruction of family ties brought by slavery, and Beloved, seen as a human being, emphasizes and illuminates these themes.

Unraveling the mystery of the young woman's identity depends to a great extent upon first deciphering chapters four and five of Part II, a section that reveals the points of view of individual characters. Both of these chapters begin with the line "I AM BELOVED and she is mine," and in these narratives Morrison enters Beloved's consciousness. From Beloved's disjointed thoughts, her stream-of-conscious rememberings set down in these chapters, a story can be pieced together that describes how white slave traders, "men without skin," captured the girl and her mother as the older woman picked flowers in Africa. In her narrative, Beloved explains that she and her mother, along with many other Africans, were then put aboard an abysmally crowded slave ship, given little food and water, and in these inhuman conditions, many blacks died. To escape this living hell, Beloved's mother leaped into the ocean, and, thus, in the girl's eyes, her mother willingly deserted her.

In order to grasp the details of this story, chapters four and five of Part II must be read as a poem: thus, examining the text line by line is often necessary. As Beloved begins her narrative, she is recalling a time when she was a young girl, for she says "I am not big" and later remarks again "I am small." However, the memory of these experiences is so vivid that, to her, "all of it is now." One of the first traumas Beloved describes is being in the lower hold of a slave ship. The captured Africans have been crouching, crammed in the overcrowded space for so long that the girl thinks "there will never be a time when I am not crouching and watching others who are crouching" and then she notes that "someone is thrashing but there is no room to do it in." At first the men and women on the ship are separated, but then Beloved says that "storms rock us and mix the men into the women and the women into the men [...] that is when I begin to be on the back of the man." This person seems to be her father or at least a father figure, for he carries the young girl on his back. Beloved says "I love him because he has a song" and, until he dies on the ship, this man sings of his African home, of the "place where a woman takes flowers away from their leaves and puts them in a round basket [...] before the clouds."

These lyrics bring to mind the first scene in Part II, chapter four. Beloved's tale begins with the girl watching her mother as the woman takes "flowers away from leaves [...] she put them in a round basket.... She fills the basket [...] she opens the grass." This opening of the grass is probably caused by the mother's falling down, for Beloved next says, "I would help her but the clouds are in the way." In the following chapter, the girl clarifies this thought when she explains, "I wanted to help her when she was picking the flowers, but the clouds of gunsmoke blinded me and I lost her." Thus, what the girl is remembering is the capture of her mother by the men without skin, the armed white slave traders. Later, Beloved sums up her story by explaining that the three crucial points in her life have been times when her mother left her: "Three times

I lost her: once with the flowers because of the noisy clouds of smoke; once when she went into the sea instead of smiling at me; once under the bridge when I went in to join her and she came toward me but did not smile." Thus, the slave traders' capture of her mother is the first of three incidents that frame the rest of Beloved's memories.

Once incarcerated on the ship, Beloved notices changes in her mother. She remembers seeing the diamond earrings, "the shining in her ears," as they were picking flowers. Now on the ship, her mother "has nothing in her ears," but she does have an iron collar around her neck. The child knows that she "does not like the circle around her neck" and says, "if I had the teeth of the man who died on my face I would bite the circle around her neck [...] bite it away [...] I know she does not like it." Sensing her mother's unhappiness, her longing for Africa, Beloved symbolizes the woman's emotions by ascribing to her a wish for physical items: "She wants her earrings [...] she wants her round basket."

As Beloved continues her tale, she explains that in the inhuman conditions of the ship, many blacks die. She says, "those able to die are in a pile," and the "men without skin push them through with poles," evidently "through" the ship's portholes, for the hills of dead people "fall into the sea which is the color of the bread." The man who has carried her on his back is one of those who succumbs, and as he takes his last breath, he turns his head and then Beloved can "see the teeth he sang through." She knows that "his song is gone," so now she loves "his pretty little teeth instead." Only after the man's head drops in death is the girl able to see her mother; Beloved remembers, "when he dies on my face I can see hers [...] she is going to smile at me." However, the girl never receives this gesture of affection, for her mother escapes her own pain by jumping into the ocean, thus committing suicide. The scene is etched in Beloved's memory: "They push my own man through [...] they do not push the woman with my face through [...] she goes in [...] they do not push her [...] she goes in [...] the little hill is gone [...] she was going to smile at me." Beloved is haunted by this second loss of her mother for, unlike the separation caused by the slavetraders' attack, this time the mother chooses to leave her. The girl agonizes as she tries to understand her mother's action and later thinks that "all I want to know is why did she go in the water in the place where we crouched? Why did she do that when she was just about to smile at me? I wanted to join her in the sea but I could not move."

Time passes and Beloved notes that "the others are taken [...] I am not taken." These lines suggest that when the other slaves are removed from the ship, Beloved, whose beauty is noted by several characters, is perhaps kept by one of the ship's officers. At any rate, she is now controlled by a man who uses her sexually, for "he hurts where I sleep," thus in bed, and "he puts his finger there." In this situation, Beloved longs for her mother and explains, "I wait on the bridge because she is under it." Although at this point she may be on an inland bridge, Beloved is most likely waiting for her mother on the ship's bridge; if she is being kept by one of the vessel's officers, the girl would logically be there. But, wherever she is at this time, Beloved last saw her mother as the woman went into the sea; thus, the girl associates water with her parent and believes she can be found in this element.

Beloved's stream-of-consciousness narrative then jumps to the time, apparently several years later, when she arrives at the creek behind Sethe's house. Morrison does not specify exactly how Beloved comes to be there, but various characters give possible explanations. The most plausible theory is that offered by Stamp Paid who says, "Was a girl locked up in the house with a whiteman over by Deer Creek. Found him dead last summer and the girl gone. Maybe that's her. Folks say he had her in there since she was a pup." This possibility would explain Beloved's "new" skin, her unlined feet and hands, for if the girl were constantly kept indoors, her skin would not be weathered or worn. Also, the scar under Beloved's chin could be explained by such an owner's ill-treatment of her. Morrison gives credence to Stamp Paid's guess by having Sethe voice a similar hypothesis and then note that her neighbor, Ella, had suffered the same fate. When Beloved first comes to live with the family, Sethe tells Denver "that she believed Beloved had been locked up by some whiteman for his own purposes, and never let out the door. That she must have escaped to a bridge or someplace and rinsed the rest out of her mind. Something like that had happened to Ella...." In addition, Beloved's own words suggest that she has been confined and used sexually. The girl explains to Denver that she "knew one whiteman," and she tells Sethe that a white man "was in the house I was in. He hurt me." In a statement that reveals the source of her name, Beloved says that men call her "beloved in the dark and bitch in the light," and in response to another question about her name, she says, "in the dark my name is Beloved."

Whatever situation Beloved has come from, when she reaches the creek behind Sethe's house, she is still haunted by her mother's absence. The lonely girl sees the creek, remembers the water under the ship's bridge where she last glimpsed her mother, and concludes that her lost loved ones are beneath the creek's surface. In her soliloquy, Beloved links the scene to her mother and father figure[s] by evoking images of the African mother's diamond earrings and the father's teeth. She says that she knows the man who carried her on his back is not floating on this water, but his "teeth are down there where the blue is ... so is the face I want the face that is going to smile at me." And, in describing the creek she says, "in the day diamonds are in the water where she is and turtles in the night I hear chewing and swallowing and laughter [...] it belongs to me." The diamonds Beloved thinks she sees in the water are most likely reflected bits of sunlight that make the water sparkle. Similarly, the noises the girl interprets as "chewing and swallowing and laughing" are probably made by the turtles. Alone in the world, Beloved's intense need to be with those she loves undoubtedly affects her interpretation of what her senses perceive.

If Stamp Paid is right and the girl has been locked up for years, then she has not had normal experiences with people or places. She lacks both formal learning and the practical education she would have gained from a family life. These deficiencies also undoubtedly affect her perceptions, and, thus, it is not especially surprising that she does not distinguish between the water under the ship's bridge and that in the creek behind Sethe's house. To the untutored girl, all bodies of water are connected as one.

Apparently, Beloved looks into the creek water, sees her own reflection, and concludes that the image is her mother's face. She then dives into the water, believing that in this element her mother will at last give her the smile that was cut short on the slave ship. Beloved says,

> I see her face which is mine [...] it is the face that was going to smile at me in the place where we crouched [...] now she is going to [...] her face comes through the water ... her face is mine [...] she is not smiling.... I have to have my face [...] I go in.... I am in the water and she is coming [...] there is no round basket [...] no iron circle around her neck. In the water, Beloved cannot "join" with the reflection, and thus she thinks her mother leaves her for a third time; distraught, she says, "my own face has left me I see me swim away.... I see the bottoms of my feet [...] I am alone."

Beloved surfaces, sees Sethe's house, and by the next day she has made her way to the structure. Exhausted by her ordeal, the girl is sleeping near the house when Sethe returns from the carnival. Beloved says,

I come out of blue water.... I need to find a place to be.... There is a house.... I sit [...] the sun closes my eyes [...] when I open them I see the face I lost [...] Sethe's is the face that left me.... I see the smile.... It is the face I lost [...] she is my face smiling at me [...] doing it at last."

Thus, when Beloved awakens and sees Sethe smiling at her, the girl mistakenly thinks that the woman is her long lost mother. In the second half of her narrative, Beloved even more clearly states her erroneous conclusions when she asserts, "Sethe is the one that picked flowers ... in the place before the crouching.... She was about to smile at me when the men without skin came and took us up into the sunlight with the dead and shoved them into the sea. Sethe went into the sea.... They did not push her...."

What finally emerges from combining Beloved's thoughts and the rest of the novel is a story of two probable instances of mistaken identity. Beloved is haunted by the loss of her African parents and thus comes to believe that Sethe is her mother. Sethe longs for her dead daughter and is rather easily convinced that Beloved is the child she has lost.

Morrison hints at this interpretation in her preface to the novel, a quotation from [*The New Testament*] Romans 9:25: "I will call them my people, which were not my people; and her beloved, which was not beloved." As Margaret Atwood notes [in an article in *The New York Times Book Review*], the biblical context of these lines emphasizes Paul's message that people once "despised and outcast, have now been redefined as acceptable." However, Morrison's language, especially in the preface, is rich in meaning on many levels. In view of the ambiguity about Beloved's identity found in the rest of the novel, it seems probable that in this initial line Morrison is suggesting an answer to the riddle of who Beloved really is or, to be more exact, who she is not. The words "I will call ... her beloved, which was not beloved" suggest that the mysterious girl is not really Sethe's murdered daughter returned from the grave; she is "called" Beloved, but she is not Sethe's child. Also, the line "I will call them my people, which were not my people" hints that Beloved mistakenly thinks Sethe and her family are her blood kin.

Seen in this light, Beloved's story illuminates several other puzzling parts of the novel. For example, after Sethe goes to the Clearing and feels that her neck is being choked, Denver accuses Beloved of causing the distress. Beloved replies, "'I didn't choke it. The circle of iron choked it.'" Since she believes Sethe and her African mother are the same person, Beloved reasons that the iron collar her African mother was forced to wear is bothering Sethe.

Beloved's questions about Sethe's earrings are one reason the woman comes to believe that the mysterious girl is her murdered child. Before her death, Sethe's baby girl had loved to play with her mother's crystal earrings. Sethe had "jingled the earrings for the pleasure of the crawling-already? girl, who reached for them over and over again." Thus, when Beloved asks "where your diamonds? ... Tell me your earrings," the family wonders, "How did she know?" Of course, Beloved asks this question remembering the "shining" in her African mother's earrings, the diamonds that were probably confiscated by the slave traders. However, Sethe thinks Beloved is remembering the crystal earrings with which the dead baby played.

This instance of misunderstanding is typical, for throughout the novel Sethe, Denver, and Beloved often fail to communicate clearly with each other. In fact, the narrator describes Beloved's and Denver's verbal exchanges as "sweet, crazy conversations full of half sentences, daydreams and misunderstandings more thrilling than understanding could ever be." This evaluation is correct, for as the three women talk to each other, each person's understandings of what she hears is slanted by what she expects to hear. For example, Denver, believing Beloved to be a ghost, asks the girl what the "other world" was like: "'What's it like over there, where you were before? ... Were you cold?'" Beloved, of course, thinks Denver is asking her about Africa and the slave ship, and so she replies, "'Hot. Nothing to breathe down there and no room to move in.'" Denver then inquires whether Beloved saw her dead grandmother, Baby Suggs, or Jesus on the other side: "'You see Jesus? Baby Suggs?'" and Beloved, remembering the death laden ship, replies that there were many people there, some dead, but she did not know their names. Sethe has a similar conversation with Beloved and begins "Tell me the truth. Didn't you come from the other side?" and Beloved replies "Yes. I was on the other side." Of course, like Denver, Sethe is referring to a life after death world, while Beloved again means the other side of the ocean, Africa.

Encased in a deep and destructive need for what each thinks the other to be, Sethe and Beloved seclude themselves in Sethe's house, Number 124, and the home becomes like a prison cell for the two disturbed women. They separate themselves completely from the rest of humanity, even Denver, and they begin to consume each other's lives: Beloved continually berates Sethe for having deserted her. Sethe devotes every breath to justifying her past actions to Beloved. Their home life deteriorates to the point that the narrator says "if the whitepeople … had allowed Negroes into their lunatic asylum they could have found candidates in 124."

Sethe's and Beloved's obsession with the past clearly affects their perception of what happens when the singing women and Edward Bodwin approach Sethe's house. Ella and the other women are there, singing and praying, hoping to rid Sethe of the ghost they think is plaguing her. Edward Bodwin is the white man who helped Sethe when she was jailed for murdering her baby; now he has come to give Denver a ride to her new job. However, when Sethe comes out of her house and views the scene, her mind reverts to the time when another white man, her slave owner, had come into the yard.

On that fateful day Sethe had killed her child, and she had first sensed danger when she glimpsed her slave master's head gear. When she saw the hated "hat, she heard wings. Little hummingbirds stuck their needle beaks right through her headcloth into her hair and beat their wings. And if she thought anything, it was No. No. Nono. Nonono. Simple. She just flew." Years later, as Sethe stands holding Beloved's hand, she sees Bodwin approach, and her unsettled mind replays her thoughts from long ago. She recognizes "his … hat wide-brimmed enough to hide his face but not his purpose.… She hears wings. Little hummingbirds stick needle beaks right through her headcloth into her hair and beat their wings. And if she thinks anything, it is no. No no. Nonono. She flies." Apparently deciding that this time she will attack the white intruder and not her own child, Sethe rushes toward Bodwin with an ice pick. Ella strikes Sethe, and then the other women apparently fall on the distraught mother, pinning her to the ground.

As this commotion occurs, Beloved also has a sense of *déjà vu*. First, the girl stands on the porch holding Sethe's hand. Then Sethe drops the hand, runs toward the white man and group of black women, and Beloved thinks her mother has deserted her again. Remembering that her African mother's suicide came after the hill of dead black people were pushed from the slave ship, Beloved sees the horrible scene being recreated:

> But now her hand is empty.… Now she is running into the faces of the people out there, joining them and leaving Beloved behind. Alone. Again … [she is running away]. Away from her to the pile of people out there. They make a hill. A hill of black people, falling. And above them all, … the man without skin, looking.

Beloved connects this "hill" of falling people with the pile of dead blacks who were pushed from the ship, and, terrified, the girl apparently runs away.

In his introduction to *The House of the Seven Gables,* Nathaniel Hawthorne notes that romances, one of the literary traditions to which *Beloved* is heir, are obliged to reveal the "truth of the human heart." And, in *Beloved,* Morrison does just that. An important facet of this truth is that emotional ghosts of hurt, love, guilt, and remembrance haunt those whose links to family members have been shattered; throughout the novel, Morrison shows that family ties can be severed only at the cost of distorting people's lives. In *Beloved,* Morrison also shows that past griefs, hurts ranging from the atrocities of slavery to less hideous pains, must be remembered, but they should not control life. At the end of the novel, Paul D. tells Sethe "'me and you, we got more yesterday than anybody. We need some kind of tomorrow.'" And, throughout *Beloved,* Morrison's theme is that remembering yesterdays, while not being consumed by them, gives people the tomorrows with which to make real lives.

Source: Elizabeth B. House, "Toni Morrison's Ghost: The Beloved Who Is Not Beloved," in *Studies in American Fiction,* edited by James Nagel, Northeastern University, Vol. 18, No. 1, Spring, 1990, pp. 17–24.

Margaret Atwood

In her glowing review of Morrison's award-winning novel, Atwood lauds the author's use of the supernatural in Beloved.

Beloved is Toni Morrison's fifth novel, and another triumph. Indeed, Ms. Morrison's versatility and technical and emotional range appear to know no bounds. If there were any doubts about her stature as a pre-eminent American novelist, of her own or any other generation, *Beloved* will put them to rest. In three words or less, it's a hair-raiser.

The supernatural element is treated, not in an *Amityville Horror,* watch-me-make-your-flesh-creep mode, but with magnificent practicality, like the ghost of Catherine Earnshaw in *Wuthering Heights.* All the main characters in the book believe in ghosts, so it's merely natural for this one to be there. As Baby Suggs says, "Not a house in the country ain't packed to its rafters with some dead Negro's grief. We lucky this ghost is a baby. My husband's spirit was to come back in here? or yours? Don't talk to me. You lucky." In fact, Sethe would rather have the ghost there than not there. It is, after all, her adored child, and any sign of it is better, for her, than nothing.

Through the different voices and memories of the book, including that of Sethe's mother, a survivor of the infamous slave-ship crossing, we experience American slavery as it was lived by those who were its objects of exchange, both at its best— which wasn't very good—and at its worst, which was as bad as can be imagined. Above all, it is seen as one of the most viciously antifamily institutions human beings have ever devised. The slaves are motherless, fatherless, deprived of their mates, their children, their kin. It is a world in which people suddenly vanish and are never seen again, not through accident or covert operation or terrorism, but as a matter of everyday legal policy.

Slavery is also presented to us as a paradigm of how most people behave when they are given absolute power over other people. The first effect, of course, is that they start believing in their own superiority and justifying their actions by it. The second effect is that they make a cult of the inferiority of those they subjugate. It's no coincidence that the first of the deadly sins, from which all the others were supposed to stem, is Pride, a sin of which Sethe is, incidentally, also accused.

In a novel that abounds in black bodies—headless, hanging from trees, frying to a crisp, locked in woodsheds for purposes of rape, or floating downstream drowned—it isn't surprising that the "whitepeople," especially the men, don't come off too well. Horrified black children see whites as men "without skin." Sethe thinks of them as having "mossy teeth" and is ready, if necessary, to bite off their faces, and worse, to avoid further mossy-toothed outrages. There are a few whites who behave with something approaching decency. There's Amy, the young runaway indentured servant who helps Sethe in childbirth during her flight to freedom, and incidentally reminds the reader that the 19th century, with its child labor, wage slavery and widespread and accepted domestic violence, wasn't tough only for blacks, but for all but the most privileged whites as well. There are also the abolitionists who help Baby Suggs find a house and a job after she is freed. But even the decency of these "good" whitepeople has a grudging side to it, and even they have trouble seeing the people they are helping as full-fledged people, though to show them as totally free of their xenophobia and sense of superiority might well have been anachronistic.

Toni Morrison is careful not to make all the whites awful and all the blacks wonderful. Sethe's black neighbors, for instance, have their own envy and scapegoating tendencies to answer for, and Paul D., though much kinder than, for instance, the woman-bashers of Alice Walker's novel *The Color Purple,* has his own limitations and flaws. But then, considering what he's been through, it's a wonder he isn't a mass murderer. If anything, he's a little too huggable, under the circumstances.

Back in the present tense, in chapter one, Paul D. and Sethe make an attempt to establish a "real" family, whereupon the baby ghost, feeling excluded, goes berserk, but is driven out by Paul D's stronger will. So it appears. But then, along comes a strange, beautiful, real flesh-and-blood young woman, about 20 years old, who can't seem to remember where she comes from, who talks like a young child, who has an odd, raspy voice and no lines on her hands, who takes an intense, devouring interest in Sethe, and who says her name is Beloved.

Students of the supernatural will admire the way this twist is handled. Ms. Morrison blends a knowledge of folklore—for instance, in many traditions, the dead cannot return from the grave unless called, and it's the passions of the living that keep them alive—with a highly original treatment. The reader is kept guessing; there's a lot more to Beloved than any one character can see, and she manages to be many things to several people. She is a catalyst for revelations as well as self-revelations; through her we come to know not only how, but why, the original child Beloved was killed. And through her also Sethe achieves, finally, her own form of self-exorcism, her own self-accepting peace.

Beloved is written in an antiminimalist prose that is by turns rich, graceful, eccentric, rough, lyrical, sinuous, colloquial and very much to the point. Here, for instance, is Sethe remembering Sweet Home:

> ... suddenly there was Sweet Home rolling, rolling, rolling out before her eyes, and although there was not a leaf on that farm that did not want to make her

scream, it rolled itself out before her in shameless beauty. It never looked as terrible as it was and it made her wonder if hell was a pretty place too. Fire and brimstone all right, but hidden in lacy groves. Boys hanging from the most beautiful sycamores in the world. It shamed her—remembering the wonderful soughing trees rather than the boys. Try as she might to make it otherwise, the sycamores beat out the children every time and she could not forgive her memory for that.

In this book, the other world exists and magic works, and the prose is up to it. If you can believe page one—and Ms. Morrison's verbal authority compels belief—you're hooked on the rest of the book.

The epigraph to *Beloved* is from the Bible, Romans 9:25: "I will call them my people, which were not my people; and her beloved, which was not beloved." Taken by itself, this might seem to favor doubt about, for instance, the extent to which Beloved was really loved, or the extent to which Sethe herself was rejected by her own community. But there is more to it than that. The passage is from a chapter in which the Apostle Paul ponders, Job-like, the ways of God toward humanity, in particular the evils and inequities visible everywhere on the earth. Paul goes on to talk about the fact that the Gentiles, hitherto despised and outcast, have now been redefined as acceptable. The passage proclaims, not rejection, but reconciliation and hope. It continues: "And it shall come to pass, that in the place where it was said unto them, Ye are not my people; there shall they be called the children of the living God."

Toni Morrison is too smart, and too much of a writer, not to have intended this context. Here, if anywhere, is her own comment on the goings-on in her novel, her final response to the measuring and dividing and excluding "schoolteachers" of this world. An epigraph to a book is like a key signature in music and *Beloved* is written in major.

Source: Margaret Atwood, "Haunted by Their Nightmares," *New York Times Book Review,* September 13, 1987, pp. 1, 49–50.

Sources

Margaret Atwood, "Haunted by Their Nightmares," in *New York Times Book Review,* September 13, 1987, pp. 1, 49-50.

Martha Bayles, "Special Effects, Special Pleading," in *New Criterion,* Vol. VI, No. 5, January, 1988, pp. 34-40.

Susan Bowers, "*Beloved* and the New Apocalypse," in *Journal of Ethnic Studies,* Vol. 18, No. 1, Spring, 1990, pp. 59-77.

Rosellen Brown, "The Pleasure of Enchantment," in *Nation,* Vol. 245, No. 12, October 17, 1987, pp. 418-21.

Walter Clemons, "A Gravestone of Memories," in *Newsweek,* Vol. CX, No. 13, September 28, 1987, pp. 74-75.

Stanley Crouch, "Aunt Medea," in *New Republic,* Vol. 197, No. 16, October 19, 1987, pp. 38-43.

Mari Evans, editor, *Black Women Writers (1950-1980): A Critical Evaluation,* Doubleday, 1984.

Deborah Horvitz, "Nameless Ghosts: Possession and Dispossession in *Beloved,*" in *Studies in American Fiction,* Vol. 17, No. 2, Autumn, 1989, pp. 157-67.

Elizabeth House, "Toni Morrison's Ghost: The Beloved Who Is Not Beloved," in *Studies in American Fiction,* Vol. 18, No. 1, Spring, 1990, pp. 17-26.

Carol Iannone, "Toni Morrison's Career," in *Commentary,* Vol. 84, No. 6, December, 1987, pp. 59-63.

Michiko Kakutani, "Did 'Paco's Story' Deserve Its Award?," in *New York Times,* November 16, 1987, p. C15.

Charles Larson, review of *Beloved,* in *Chicago Tribune,* August 30, 1987.

John Leonard, review of *Beloved,* in *Los Angeles Times Book Review,* August 30, 1987.

Eusebio L. Rodrigues, "The Telling of *Beloved,*" in *Journal of Narrative Technique,* Vol. 21, No. 2, Spring, 1991, pp. 153-69.

Carol Rumens, "Shades of the Prison-House," in *Times Literary Supplement,* No. 4411, October 16-22, 1987, p. 1135.

Barbara Schapiro, "The Bonds of Love and the Boundaries of Self in Toni Morrison's *Beloved,*" in *Contemporary Literature,* Vol. 32, No. 2, Summer, 1991, pp. 194-210.

Amy E. Schwartz, "*Beloved:* It's Not a Question of Who Suffered More," in *Washington Post,* April 3, 1988, p. B7.

Ann Snitow, "Death Duties: Toni Morrison Looks Back in Sorrow," in *Voice Literary Supplement,* No. 58, September, 1987, pp. 25-6.

Jean Strouse, "Toni Morrison's Black Magic," in *Newsweek,* March 30, 1981, pp. 52-57.

Judith Thurman, "A House Divided," in *New Yorker,* Vol. LXIII, No. 37, November 2, 1987, pp. 175-80.

For Further Study

Marilyn Judith Atlas, "Toni Morrison's *Beloved* and the Reviewers," in *Midwestern Miscellany,* Vol. XVII, 1990, pp. 45-57.

A thorough survey of critical response to the novel prior to its winning the Pulitzer Prize. The critic suggests that the difficulties critics have had in interpreting the novel lie in its sensitive subject matter and complex design.

Bernard W. Bell, "*Beloved:* A Womanist Neo-Slave Narrative; or Multivocal Remembrances of Things Past," in *African American Review,* Vol. 26, No. 1, Spring, 1992, pp. 7-15.

Discusses *Beloved* as an exploration of the "double consciousness" of Black Americans.

Eileen T. Bender, "Repossessing *Uncle Tom's Cabin:* Toni Morrison's *Beloved,*" in *Cultural Power/Cultural Literacy: Selected Papers from the Fourteenth Annual Florida State University Conference on Literature and Film,* edited by Bonnie Braendlin, Florida State University Press, 1991, pp. 129-42.

Argues that *Beloved* is Morrison's meditated reaction against the sentimental stereotypes of Harriet Beecher Stowe's famous novel. According to Bender, Morrison's novel represents a "new act of emancipation for a culture still enslaved by false impressions and factitious accounts."

Patrick Bryce Bjork, "*Beloved:* The Paradox of a Past and Present Self and Place," in his *Novels of Toni Morrison: The Search for Self and Place within the Community,* Peter Lang Publishing, 1992, pp. 141-62.

Examines the contradictions of personal identity and memory in Morrison's novel.

Marilyn R. Chandler, "*Housekeeping* and *Beloved:* When Women Come Home," in her *Dwelling in the Text: Houses in American Fiction,* University of California Press, 1991, pp. 291-318.

Analyzes *Beloved* and Marilynne Robinson's *Housekeeping* "under the rubric of house and home as ideas in relation to which women in every generation and in every situation have had to 'work out their salvation' and define their identities."

Marsha Jean Darling, "Ties That Bind," in *Women's Review of Books,* Vol. V, No. 6, March, 1988, pp. 4-5.

Praises *Beloved* as a masterpiece of historical fiction which "challenges, seduces, cajoles and enjoins us to visualize, contemplate, to know, feel and comprehend the realities of the material world of nineteenth-century Black women and men."

Christina Davis, "*Beloved:* A Question of Identity," in *Présence Africaine,* No. 145, 1988, pp. 151-56.

Extols Morrison's gift for giving expression to the subjective consciousness of Sethe, a slave whose voice "is clear, its pain full of anguish, its beauty unbearable, its truth stunning."

Stephanie A. Demetrakopoulos, "Maternal Bonds as Devourers of Women's Individuation in Toni Morrison's *Beloved,*" in *African American Review,* Vol. 26, No. 1, Spring, 1992, pp. 51-59.

Argues that *Beloved* "develops the idea that maternal bonds can stunt or even obviate a woman's individuation or sense of self," and that "the conclusion of the book effects a resolution of the tension between history and nature which underlies the movement of the work as a whole."

John N. Duvall, "Authentic Ghost Stories: *Uncle Tom's Cabin, Absalom, Absalom!,* and *Beloved,*" in *Faulkner Journal,* Vol. IV, Nos. 1 and 2, Fall, 1988-Spring, 1989, pp. 83-97.

Compares the ghost story elements in novels by Morrison, Harriet Beecher Stowe, and William Faulkner.

Karen E. Fields, "To Embrace Dead Strangers: Toni Morrison's *Beloved,*" in *Mother Puzzles: Daughters and Mothers in Contemporary American Literature,* edited by Mickey Pearlman, Greenwood Press, 1989, pp. 159-69.

Calls the novel a profound "meditation on the nature of love," examining how the characters use relationships to attempt to create order out of chaos.

Anne E. Goldman, "'I Made the Ink': (Literary) Production and Reproduction in *Dessa Rose* and *Beloved,*" in *Feminist Studies,* Vol. 16, No. 2, Summer, 1990, pp. 313-30.

Argues that *Beloved* and Sherley Anne Williams's *Dessa Rose* "comment implicitly on the gap between mainstream critical theories and modern literary practice" by their construction of strong heroines who integrate themselves through writing, in contrast to the narrative fragmentation of postmodern fiction.

Trudier Harris, "Of Mother Love and Demons," in *Callaloo,* Vol. 11, No. 2, Spring, 1988, pp. 387-89.

Analyzes Morrison's treatment of the "mother love" theme in *Beloved.* Harris argues that in "exorcising" Beloved "the women favor the living over the dead, mother love over childish punishment of parents, reality over the legend of which they have become a part."

Karla F. C. Holloway, "*Beloved:* A Spiritual," in *Callaloo,* Vol. 13, No. 3, Summer, 1990, pp. 516-25.

Critiques *Beloved* as a mythic revisioning within an African-American literary tradition.

Carl D. Malmgren, "Mixed Genres and the Logic of Slavery in Toni Morrison's *Beloved,*" in *Critique,* Vol. XXXVI, No. 2, Winter, 1995, pp. 96-106.

Notes *Beloved*'s incorporation of elements from various genres, including the ghost story and historical novel, and argues that "[it] is the institution of slavery that supplies the logic underwriting the novel, the thematic glue that unifies this multifaceted text."

Barbara Hill Rigney, "'A Story to Pass On': Ghosts and the Significance of History in Toni Morrison's *Beloved,*" in *Haunting the House of Fiction: Feminist Perspectives on Ghost Stories by American Women,* edited by Lynette Carpenter and Wendy K. Kolmar, University of Tennessee Press, 1991, pp. 229-35.

Explains the meaning of history in *Beloved* as "the reality of slavery. The 'rememories' are a gross catalogue of atrocities, gross sexual indignities, a denial of human rights on every level."

Mervyn Rothstein, "Toni Morrison, in Her New Novel, Defends Women," in *New York Times,* August 26, 1987, p. C17.

Interview with Morrison about the genesis of *Beloved.*

Danille Taylor-Guthrie, editor, *Conversations with Toni Morrison,* University Press of Mississippi, 1994.

A collection of interviews with the author, including one with Gail Caldwell on the writing of *Beloved.*

Brave New World

Aldous Huxley
1932

Written in 1931 and published the following year, Aldous Huxley's *Brave New World* is a dystopian—or anti-utopian—novel. In it, the author questions the values of 1931 London, using satire and irony to portray a futuristic world in which many of the contemporary trends in British and American society have been taken to extremes. Though he was already a best-selling author, Huxley achieved international acclaim with this now-classic novel. Because *Brave New World* is a novel of ideas, the characters and plot are secondary, even simplistic. The novel is best appreciated as an ironic commentary on contemporary values.

The story is set in a London six hundred years in the future. People all around the world are part of a totalitarian state, free from war, hatred, poverty, disease, and pain. They enjoy leisure time, material wealth, and physical pleasures. However, in order to maintain such a smoothly running society, the ten people in charge of the world, the Controllers, eliminate most forms of freedom and twist around many traditionally held human values. Standardization and progress are valued above all else. These Controllers create human beings in factories, using technology to make ninety-six people from the same fertilized egg and to condition them for their future lives. Children are raised together and subjected to mind control through sleep teaching to further condition them. As adults, people are content to fulfill their destinies as part of five social classes, from the intelligent Alphas, who run the factories, to the mentally challenged Epsilons, who

do the most menial jobs. All spend their free time indulging in harmless and mindless entertainment and sports activities. When the Savage, a man from the uncontrolled area of the world (an Indian reservation in New Mexico) comes to London, he questions the society and ultimately has to choose between conformity and death.

Author Biography

Aldous Huxley was born on July 26, 1894, in Laleham near Godalming, Surrey, England, but he grew up in London. His family was well-known for its scientific and intellectual achievements: Huxley's father, Leonard, was a renowned editor and essayist, and his highly educated mother ran her own boarding school. His grandfather and brother were top biologists, and his half-brother, Andrew Huxley, won the Nobel Prize in 1963 for his work in physiology. When he was sixteen, Aldous Huxley went to England's prestigious Eton school and was trained in medicine, the arts, and science. From 1913 to 1916 he attended Balliol College, Oxford, where he excelled academically and edited literary journals. Huxley was considered a prodigy, being exceptionally intelligent and creative.

There were many tragedies in Huxley's life, however, from the early death of his mother from cancer when he was just fourteen to nearly losing his eyesight because of an illness as a teenager, but Huxley took these troubles in stride. Because of his failing vision, he did not fight in World War I or pursue a scientific career but focused instead on writing. He married Maria Nys in 1919, and they had one son, Matthew. To support his family, Huxley pursued writing, editing, and teaching, traveling throughout Europe, India, and the United States at various points.

Huxley published three books of poetry and a collection of short stories, which received a modest amount of attention from critics, before he turned to novels: *Crome Yellow* (1921), set on an estate and featuring the vain and narcissistic conversations between various artists, scientists, and members of high society; *Antic Hay* (1923) and *Those Barren Leaves* (1925), both satires of the lives of upper-class British people after World War I; and *Point Counter Point* (1928), a best-seller and complex novel of ideas featuring many characters and incorporating Huxley's knowledge of music. As in *Brave New World,* ideas and themes domi-

Aldous Huxley

nate the style, structure, and characterization of these earlier novels.

Huxley's next novel, *Brave New World* (1932), brought him international fame. Written just before the rise of dictators Adolf Hitler and Joseph Stalin, the novel did not incorporate the kind of dark and grim vision of totalitarianism later found in George Orwell's *1984,* which was published in 1948. Huxley later commented on this omission and reconsidered the ideas and themes of *Brave New World* in a collection of essays called *Brave New World Revisited.* (1958). He wrote other novels, short stories, and collections of essays over the years which were, for the most part, popular and critically acclaimed. Despite being nearly blind all his life, he also wrote screenplays for Hollywood, most notably an adaptations of Jane Austen's *Pride and Prejudice* and Charlotte Brontë's *Jane Eyre.*

Always fascinated by the ideas of consciousness and sanity, in the last ten years of his life Huxley experimented with mysticism, parapsychology, and, under the supervision of a physician friend, the hallucinogenic drugs mescaline and LSD. He wrote of his drug experiences in the book *The Doors of Perception* (1954). Huxley's wife died in 1955, and in 1956 he married author and psychotherapist Laura Archera. In 1960, Huxley was diagnosed with cancer, the same disease that killed his mother and his first wife, and for the next three years his health steadily declined. He died in Los Angeles, California, where he had been living for several years, on November 22, 1963, the same day President John F. Kennedy was assassinated. Huxley's ashes were buried in England in his parents' grave.

Plot Summary

Brave New World opens in the year 2495 at the Central London Hatchery and Conditioning Centre, a research facility and factory that mass-produces and then socially-conditions test-tube babies. Such a factory is a fitting place to begin the story of mass-produced characters in a techno-futurist dystopia, a world society gone mad for pleasure, order, and conformity. The date is A.F. 632, A.F.—After Ford—being a notation based on the birth year (1863) of Henry Ford, the famous automobile manufacturer and assembly line innovator who is worshipped as a god in Huxley's fictional society.

Five genetic castes or classes inhabit this futurist dystopia. In descending order they are named for the first five letters of the Greek alphabet: Alphas, Betas, Gammas, Deltas, and Epsilons. While upper castes are bred for intellectual and managerial occupations, the lower castes, bred with less intelligence, perform manual labor. All individuals are conditioned by electric shock and hypnopaedia (sleep conditioning) to reject or desire what the State dictates. For example, infants are taught to hate flowers and books, but encouraged to seek out sex, entertainment, and new products. Most importantly, they are conditioned to be happiest with their own caste and to be glad they are not a member of any other group. For instance, while eighty Beta children sleep on their cots in the Conditioning Centre, the following hypnopaedic message issues from speakers placed beneath the children's pillows:

> "Alpha children wear grey. They work much harder than we do, because they're so frightfully clever. I'm really awfully glad I'm a Beta, because I don't work so hard. And then we are much better than the Gammas and Deltas. Gammas are stupid. They all wear green, and Delta children wear khaki. Oh no, I *don't* want to play with Delta children. And Epsilons are still worse. They're too stupid to be able...."

> The director pushed back the switch. The voice was silent. Only its thin ghost continued to mutter from beneath the eighty pillows.

> "They'll have that repeated forty or fifty times more before they wake; then again on Thursday, and again on Saturday. A hundred and twenty times three times a week for thirty months. After which they go on to a more advanced lesson."

The story begins in the London Hatchery's employee locker room where Lenina Crowne, a Beta worker, discusses men with another female coworker, Fanny Crowne. The subject of their conversation is Bernard Marx, an Alpha-Plus who is considered abnormally short, a defect rumored to be from an excess of alcohol added to the "blood surrogate" surrounding his developing embryo. Generally perceived as antisocial and melancholic, Bernard is unusually withdrawn and gloomy, despite the fact that social coherence and mood enhancement—especially through promiscuity and regular dosages of the drug "soma"—is State-sanctioned and encouraged. Still, despite Bernard's oddness, Lenina finds him "cute" and wants to go out with him. After all, Lenina has been going out with the Centre's research specialist, Henry Foster, for four months—unusually long in that society. In need of a change from the places they always go—the feelies, which are like films with the sense of touch, and dance clubs with music produced from scent and color instruments—Lenina and Bernard go on holiday to the New Mexico Savage Reservation, a "natural" area populated by "sixty thousand Indians and half-breeds" living without television, books, and hot water, still giving birth to their own children, and still worshiping an assortment of Christian and pagan gods. To prevent the "savages" from escaping, the whole reservation is surrounded by an electrified fence.

Wandering around the Reservation, Lenina is horrified by the sight of mothers nursing their own infants, elderly people who actually look their age because they have not been chemically treated, and a ritual of sacrifice in which a boy is whipped, his blood scattered on writhing snakes. After witnessing this ceremony, Lenina and Bernard meet John, who, unlike them and all they know, was not born from a test tube. His mother, Linda, gave birth to him on the Reservation. On a previous visit from civilization to the Reservation years before, Linda, while pregnant with John, was abandoned by John's father, who returned to civilization after Linda disappeared and was thought to have died. Bernard realizes that John's father is none other than Bernard's archenemy, the Director of Hatching and Conditioning, the man who has tried to exile Bernard to Iceland for being a nonconformist. John's mother, Linda, has always resented the

Reservation, and John, though he wants to become a part of "savage" society, is ostracized because he is white, the son of a civilized mother, and because he reads books, especially Shakespeare's works.

John's status as an outcast endears him to Bernard. John, meanwhile, is becoming infatuated with Lenina, and like Linda, he is excited about going to civilization. At Bernard's request, John and Linda go with Bernard and Lenina to, as John puts it (quoting from Shakespeare's *The Tempest*), the "brave new world" of London. Bernard wonders if John might be somewhat hasty calling London a "brave new world."

Back in London, Bernard suddenly finds himself the center of attention: he uses Linda's impregnation and abandonment, and her son, to disgrace the Director. He then introduces the exotic John (now known as "the Savage," or "Mr. Savage") to Alpha society, while Linda begins to slowly die from soma abuse. John comes to hate the drug that destroys his mother, and he becomes increasingly disenchanted with this "brave new world"'s open sexuality, promiscuity, and contempt for marriage. When John finally confesses his love to Lenina, she is overjoyed and makes overt sexual advances. Because he is appalled at the idea of sex before marriage, however, John asks Lenina to marry him. Now it is her turn to be shocked. "What a horrible idea!" she exclaims.

In the aftermath of this aborted romance, John must face another crisis. He rushes to the Park Lane Hospital in time to see his mother die, and he is shocked when a class of children come in for their conditioning in death acceptance. Lenina's rejection and his mother's death finally drive John over the edge. At the hospital, he begins ranting in the hallways, and then he takes the staff's daily soma ration and dumps it out a window. The angry soma-dependent staff of 162 Deltas attack John. Bernard's friend, Helmholtz Watson, rushes to John's defense as Bernard timidly watches. The police arrive in time to quell the disturbance, arrest the three nonconformists, and deliver them to the office of the Controller, Mustapha Mond. The Controller tells John he must remain in civilization as an ongoing experiment. Bernard and Helmholtz, on the other hand, are to be exiled to separate islands because, says Mond, "It would upset the whole social order if men started doing things on their own."

In the last portion of the novel, John, unable to tolerate the Controller's judgment, flees to the countryside to live a life close to nature without incessant and artificial happiness, a life with a bit of truth, beauty, and even pain. But John is seen one day ritually whipping himself and becomes the center of overwhelming media attention. In a final welter of events, John succumbs to the temptation of the crowd's spontaneous orgy of violence, sex, and soma. The next day, unable to live with himself in this brave new world, John hangs himself.

Characters

Controller
See Mustapha Mond

Fanny Crowne
Like her coworker, Lenina Crowne, Fanny is a nineteen-year-old Beta. Though she shares Lenina's last name and is genetically related to her, she is just a friend. Family connections have no meaning in civilization. Her character is never really developed, serving only as a foil to contrast society's values—which she accepts completely—with Lenina's unconventional behavior.

Lenina Crowne
Lenina Crowne is, like Linda, a Beta. Young and beautiful, she has auburn hair and blue eyes; however, she also suffers from the immune system disorder lupus, which causes skin lesions. Employed at the Embryo Room of the Hatchery, Lenina is a shallow person, completely accepting the values of her society without question. However, part of her longs to form a lasting relationship with one man, a desire that is considered ugly and dirty in a society that believes promiscuity is healthy. For this reason, while she is attracted to Henry Foster, she chooses to date Bernard Marx, too. Bernard is a little unusual because he is discontented, and she finds this attractive in spite of herself and in spite of the warnings from her friend Fanny to stay away from him. When she meets John the Savage, she feels tremendous sexual attraction to him, but she has been taught to look down upon love, passion, and commitment. Unable to escape her conditioning, she fears his attraction to her.

Director of Hatcheries and Conditioning
The Director loves to hear himself talk, and, therefore, greatly enjoys giving guided tours of the Hatchery to visiting students, as he does at the beginning of the book. Like many intelligent Alphas, the Director secretly used to wonder about life out-

At eighty-three years old, Henry Ford poses for a photo in his first automobile. Henry Ford popularized the efficient assembly-line method of production when, in 1913, he used it to produce the Model T.

side of the society over which he has so much control. We find that he once took a trip with a young woman named Linda to the New Mexico Indian reservation to see how the "primitive" people lived. Once there, Linda, who was carrying his child, disappeared. He assumed she was dead and returned without her. The Director tells this story to Bernard, but quickly realizes his revelation is unseemly for a man of his great reputation and returns to acting professionally, even gruffly, with Bernard.

When Linda's baby, John the Savage, comes to London as an adult, he faces the Director and

calls him Father. Everyone reacts as if it were an obscene joke. The Director is horrified and humiliated at the public revelation that he fathered a child, just like a primitive person. His reputation is irreparably ruined.

Henry Foster

Henry Foster is a fair-haired, blue-eyed, ruddy-complected scientist in the London Hatchery and a model citizen. He is efficient, pleasant, and cooperative, working hard at his job and spending his leisure time engaging in mindless, if harmless, activities, such as watching feelies (movies), playing new forms of golf, and having casual sex. Lenina Crowne has been dating him exclusively for four months, a practice that raises eyebrows because romantic commitments are frowned upon. Henry does not realize that Lenina has been faithful to him and would be upset if he knew because, as Fanny points out to Lenina, he is "the perfect gentleman." He expects nice girls to sleep around just as he does. Huxley uses the character of Henry Foster to explain how the Hatchery functions and how average citizens are supposed to behave.

Benito Hoover

Huxley took the name Hoover from U.S. President Herbert Hoover, and Benito from the Italian fascist dictator Benito Mussolini. A friend and colleague of Henry Foster, Benito is one of many men who would like to have sex with Lenina Crowne. He is disapproving of Bernard Marx until Bernard introduces the Savage around. Then, like many other people, Benito fawns over Bernard, bringing him gifts.

John the Savage

John the Savage is the central character in *Brave New World* through whom Huxley compares the primitive and civilized societies of the future. He is the son of the Director and Linda, and was born and raised on an Indian reservation in New Mexico after an accident stranded Linda there (the Director had mistakenly assumed she was dead and returned to civilization without her). John, now twenty, tall, and handsome, was raised in the Indian culture. He has a utopian view of civilization that is based on his mother Linda's tales, and he has a vast knowledge of Shakespeare because he learned to read using the only book available to him: *Shakespeare's Complete Works*. Shakespeare greatly influences John the Savage's perception of the world around him and what it means to be human.

Sometimes called just "the Savage," John represents the idea of the Noble Savage: that a person raised in a primitive world, away from western civilization, has a purity of heart that civilized people lack (although Huxley does not portray the primitive world as a paradise). John the Savage cannot understand why civilized people think that having been born to and raised by your parents is an abomination, or why they do not feel sorrow when confronted with death. He very much loves his mother, and cannot understand why his father rejects him. After several discussions with Mustapha Mond, he

Media Adaptations

- *Brave New World* was adapted as a made-for-television movie in 1980, directed by Burt Brinckerhoff, and starring Kristoffer Tabori as John Savage, Bud Cort as Bernard Marx, and Marcia Strassman as Lenina Crowne.

---

quickly realizes that because his values are completely different from other people's, no place exists for him within civilization.

Linda

A Beta-minus, Linda had worked contentedly in the Fertilizing Room until an incident that occurred twenty years earlier while on a date with the Director. They had visited the New Mexico Indian reservation, where she fell, injuring her head. When she regained consciousness the Director was gone. Pregnant with his child, she was taken in by the Indians, but she never really fit into their world because she had been conditioned to live in civilization. For example, Linda continued to be sexually promiscuous, having sex with the other women's mates, because that was the way a proper girl behaved where she came from—the "Other Place," as she called it.

Linda was very embarrassed to give birth to her son, John, and tried to teach him that civilization was superior to life on the reservation. However, she could not explain why it was superior. Because she had not been conditioned to understand the reasons behind the way things worked in the Other Place, she never lost the values she had been conditioned to accept.

When Linda meets Bernard and Lenina she is anxious but thrilled to return to civilization, but she cannot emotionally handle the return. The embarrassment of being a mother, of being old and fat and no longer physically beautiful, is too much for her, so she chooses to drug herself with soma, eventually dying from an overdose. Her inability to handle the contrast between the primitive world and the civilized one foreshadows her son John's final decision to commit suicide.

Bernard Marx

Like other members of civilization, Bernard Marx is named after a person whose ideas greatly influenced the society in *Brave New World:* Karl Marx. Bernard Marx, an Alpha, is a very intelligent man and a specialist in sleep-teaching. However, he is discontented with society and does not completely accept its values—he hates the casual attitude toward sex, dislikes sports, and prefers to be alone. Some people think Bernard was improperly conditioned—that the chemistry of the womb-like bottle he lived in as a fetus was somehow altered. They point to the fact that Bernard is eight centimeters shorter and considerably thinner than the typical Alpha as evidence that a physical reason exists for his emotional differences. This physical inadequacy makes Bernard self-conscious, and he is particularly uncomfortable around lower-class people, since they remind him that he physically resembles his inferiors.

Bernard is a selfish person, trying to bend the rules of society for his own needs and using other people to boost his own fortune. He vacillates between boasting and self-pity, which annoys his friend Helmholtz Watson. When Bernard discovers the Savage, he realizes that by bringing him back to society he will be able to get revenge against the Director, who has been threatening him with exile to Iceland. The Director's reputation will be ruined when it is revealed he is a father. Bernard also realizes that the Savage will be the key to his acceptance into society, a sort of plaything that everyone will want to see.

Indeed, Bernard brings the Savage home, and suddenly everyone wants to meet and spend time with him and the Savage. Bernard tells himself that people like him because of his discovery, unaware that behind their backs they are gossiping about him, saying that anyone so odd and so self-absorbed is bound to come to a bad end. He relishes his new popularity with women and gets angry at John for not cooperating with his attempts to show him off; he believes John is ruining his chances of finally being accepted. Bernard's popularity is predictably short-lived, and in the end he is indeed exiled to Iceland, which makes him very unhappy.

Mitsima

Mitsima is the Indian elder who teaches John the Savage the ways of the Indian people.

Mustapha Mond

Mustapha Mond is the Controller of world society and an intellectual who secretly indulges his own passion for knowledge, literature, and history, all of which are denied to ordinary citizens in order to keep people from questioning the structure and values of the society that has been created for them. Of medium height and with black hair, a hooked nose, large red lips, and piercing dark eyes, Mustapha Mond has a name that is a play on the words "Must staff a mond." ("Mond" is derived from the French word "monde," which means world.) He is a friendly and happy fellow, faithful to his job and his vision of a utopian society. He enjoys discussing Shakespeare with John the Savage, and treats him like a favorite pupil. Formerly a scientist, as a young man he was given the choice of becoming a controller or an exiled dissident, so he chose the former. As the Controller, he has free will, but he denies it to others. Mond understands the frustrations of Bernard Marx and Helmholtz Watson, who have trouble accepting all of the restrictions of their carefully controlled lives. In the end, however, Mustapha Mond's loyalty is to the society rather than to individuals, so he banishes Marx, Watson, and the Savage to isolated areas where they cannot influence others.

Pope

Pope is an Indian man with whom Linda forms a bond, sleeping with him regularly despite her feeling that she ought to be promiscuous. Pope is amused by John's jealousy and hatred toward him. He introduces Linda to *mescal,* an alcoholic drink made by the Indians, which Linda thinks is a sorry substitute for soma because it gives her a hangover.

Thomas

See Director of Hatcheries and Conditioning

Tomakin

See Director of Hatcheries and Conditioning

Helmholtz Watson

Watson (named by Huxley after John B. Watson, the founder of the Behaviorist School of psychology) is an Alpha-plus, a highly intellectual writer and lecturer. He is a powerfully built, broad-shouldered man with dark curly hair. Although he is a typical handsome Alpha male, he is, like his friend Bernard Marx, a little different from his peers. Watson is just a bit smarter than he is supposed to be, a fact he has only recently discovered.

Watson has a distinguished career as an emotional engineer and writer, penning snappy slogans and simplistic rhymes designed to promote the values of society and pacify people. However, he is frustrated by the limitations of his writing and believes that something more meaningful to write must exist. Because of this unconventional desire, he feels a little like an outsider. He befriends Bernard Marx because he sees in him a similar sense of not belonging, of dissatisfaction, but he is disturbed by Bernard's self-pitying and boastful behavior.

Watson is brilliant, but when the Savage introduces him to Shakespeare's works, he can't completely understand the plays because he is so limited by his conditioning. Watson accepts his exile to the isolated Falkland Islands, hoping that being around other outsiders and living in uncomfortable conditions will inspire his writing.

Themes

Brave New World is Huxley's satirical look at a totalitarian society of the future, in which the trends of Huxley's day have been taken to extremes. When an outsider encounters this world, he cannot accept its values and chooses to die rather than try to conform to this "brave new world."

Free Will versus Enslavement

Only the Controllers of society, the ten elite rulers, have freedom of choice. Everyone else has been conditioned from the time they were embryos to accept unquestioningly all the values and beliefs of the carefully ordered society. Upper-class Alphas are allowed a little freedom because their higher intellect makes it harder for them to completely accept the rules of society. For example, they are occasionally allowed to travel to the Indian reservation to see how outsiders live. It is hoped that exposure to an "inferior" and "primitive" society will finally squelch any doubts about their own society's superiority.

Beyond this, however, no room exists in "civilized" society for free will, creativity, imagination, or diversity, all of which can lead to conflict, war, and destruction. Therefore, dissidents who want these freedoms are exiled to remote corners of the earth. Anyone who feels upset for any reason quickly ingests a dose of the tranquilizer "soma."

Topics for Further Study

- Research Henry Ford's development of the modern assembly line for producing Model T automobiles. Compare his ideas about efficient manufacturing and factory management to the Controller's philosophy of creating humans in factories.

- Compare and contrast the values of the Indians on the Zuni reservation with those of the Londoners in Huxley's novel.

- Discuss Huxley's views of class as revealed in *Brave New World,* and compare his fictional class system with those of real-life societies, such as Victorian England and modern India.

- Research the scientific process of cloning plants and animals and compare your findings with Huxley's description of the "Bokanovsky Process"; discuss the social implications of cloning.

John the Savage believes that the price to be paid for harmony in this society is too great. He sees the people as enslaved, addicted to drugs, and weakened and dehumanized by their inability to handle delayed gratification or pain of any sort. He exercises his freedom of choice by killing himself rather than becoming a part of such a world.

Class Conflict

As a result of conditioning, class conflict has been eliminated in Huxley's future world. The Controllers have decided there should be five social classes, from the superior, highly intelligent, and physically attractive Alphas—who have the most desirable and intellectually demanding jobs—to the inferior, mentally deficient, and physically unattractive Epsilons, who do the least desirable, menial jobs. Huxley makes the Alphas tall and fair and the Epsilons dark-skinned, reflecting the common prejudices at the time the novel was written. All people are genetically bred and conditioned from birth to be best adapted to the lives they will lead and to accept the class system wholeheartedly.

Members of different classes not only look physically different but wear distinctive colors to make sure that no one can be mistaken for a member of a different group. Here, Huxley points out the shallowness in our own society: members of different social classes dress differently in order to be associated with their own class. Only John the Savage can see people as they really are because he has not been conditioned to accept unquestioningly the rigid class structure. Thus, when he sees a dark-skinned person of a lower caste, he is reminded of Othello, a Shakespearean character who was both dark-skinned and admirable. John does not think to judge a person by his appearance. Because Huxley was from a distinguished, educated, upper-class British family, he was very aware of the hypocrisies of the privileged classes. The Controller and Director represent the arrogant hypocrisy of the ruling class.

Sex

The inhabitants of Huxley's future world have very unusual attitudes toward sex by the standards of contemporary society. Promiscuity is considered healthy and superior to committed, monogamous relationships. Even small children are encouraged to engage in erotic play. The Controllers realize that strong loyalties created by committed relationships can cause conflicts between people, upsetting productivity and harmony. Since the needs of society are far more important than the needs of the individual, the Controllers strongly believe that sacrificing human attachments—even the attachment between children and their parents—is a small price to pay for social harmony. Women use contraception to avoid pregnancy, and if they do get pregnant accidentally, they hurry to the abortion center, a place Linda recalls with great fondness. She regrets bitterly having had to give birth in what she feels was a "dirty" affair.

People in Huxley's day were becoming more accepting of casual sex than previous generations, and they had much greater access to birth control. However, as Huxley shows, even with the best technology to prevent pregnancy, people can only maintain their loose sexual mores by sacrificing intimacy and commitment.

Science and Technology

Science and technology provide the means for controlling the lives of the citizens in *Brave New World*. First, cloning is used to create many of human beings from the same fertilized egg. The genetically similar eggs are placed in bottles, where the growing embryos and fetuses are exposed to external stimulation and chemical alteration to condition them for their lives after being "decanted" or "hatched."

Babies and children are subject to cruel conditioning. They are exposed to flowers, representing the beauty of nature, and given electric shocks to make them averse to nature. They are brought to the crematorium, where they play and are given treats so that they will associate death with pleasantness and therefore not object when society determines it is time for them to die. Also, hypnopaedia, or sleep teaching, is used to indoctrinate children. All of these extreme methods of conditioning could conceivably work.

Adults use "soma," a tranquilizer, to deaden feelings of pain or passion. Frivolous gadgets and hi-tech entertainment provide distractions, preventing the childlike citizens from engaging in rich emotional and intellectual lives or from experiencing challenges that might lead to emotional and intellectual growth. Indeed, the Controller feels that technology's purpose is to make the distance between the feeling of desire and the gratification of that desire so short that citizens are continually content and not tempted to spend their time thinking and questioning.

Since books are taboo and knowledge restricted only to the powerful elite minority, the citizens are unaware that technology has been used to limit their lives. In fact, in writing this novel of ideas Huxley aims to make contemporary citizens question the ethics of using technology for social purposes and to realize the dangers of misuse of technology by totalitarian governments.

Knowledge and Ignorance

To control the citizens, the Controllers make sure people are taught only what they need to know to function within society and no more. Knowledge is dangerous. Books are strictly forbidden. Art and culture, which stimulate the intellect, emotions, and spirit, are reduced to pale imitations of the real thing. Existing music is synthetic and characterized by absurd popular songs that celebrate the values of society. Movies appeal to the lowest common denominator. Citizens are conditioned to believe that wanting to be alone is strange. They seek shallow relationships with each other, minus intimacy and commitment, rather than spending time alone thinking. If they did spend time in contemplation, they might, like Bernard Marx and Helmholtz Watson, start questioning the meaning of their lives and the function of the society.

Only the Controller has access to the great literature and culture of the past. He enjoys discussing Shakespeare with John the Savage. Huxley, by making his primitive character have only Shakespeare's works on which to base his perceptions, shows the power of such great literature: that it can capture an enormous range of human experience, to which the citizens of the brave new world are completely oblivious. In the end, however, the people who accidentally attain knowledge have only two choices if they are to survive: they can become oppressors or outcasts.

Style

Point of View

Huxley tells the story of *Brave New World* in a third-person, omniscient (all-knowing) voice. The narrative is chronological for the most part, jumping backward in time only to reveal some history, as when the Director explains to Bernard Marx what happened when he visited the Indian reservation, or when John and Linda recall their lives on the reservation before meeting Bernard and Lenina. The first six chapters have very little action and are instead devoted to explaining how this society functions. This is accomplished by having the reader overhear the tour that the Director, and later the Controller, lead through the "hatchery," or human birth factory, lecturing to some students.

Once familiarized with this future world, the reader learns more about the characters through their dialogue and interaction. For example, Bernard and Lenina's conversation on their date shows how deeply conditioned Lenina is to her way of life and how difficult it is for Bernard to meet society's expectations of how he should feel and behave. Throughout the rest of the book, Huxley continues to reveal the way the society functions, but instead of having the reader overhear lectures, he portrays seemingly ordinary events, showing how they unfold in this very different society. When Huxley finally presents the arguments for and against the compromises the society makes in order to achieve harmony, he does this in the form of a dialogue between Mustapha Mond and John the Savage. The book ends with a sober and powerful description of John's vain struggle to carve out a life for himself as a hermit. This is contrasted with the humorous, satirical tone of much of the book, making it especially moving.

Setting

Set in London, England, six hundred years in Huxley's future, *Brave New World* portrays a totalitarian society where freedom, diversity, and conflict have been replaced by efficiency, progress, and harmony. The contrast between our world and that of the inhabitants of Huxley's futuristic society is made especially clear when Huxley introduces us to the Indian reservation in New Mexico, where the "primitive" culture of the natives has been maintained. Huxley chose London as his main setting because it was his home, but he implies, by mentioning the ten world controllers, that the entire world operates the same way that the society in London does.

Irony and Satire

Brave New World is also considered a novel of ideas, otherwise known as an apologue: because the ideas in the book are what is most important, the characterization and plot are secondary to the concepts Huxley presents. In order to portray the absurdity of the future society's values as well as our contemporary society's values, he uses satire (holding up human folly to ridicule), parody (a humorous twist on a recognizable style of an author or work), and irony (words meaning something very different from what they literally mean, or what the characters think they mean). Ordinary scenes the reader can recognize, such as church services and dates, incorporate behavior, internal thoughts, and dialogue that reveal the twisted and absurd values of the citizens of the future. Because the roots of many of the practices seen in this futuristic society can be found in contemporary ideas, the reader is led to question the values of contemporary society. For example, people today are taught to value progress and efficiency. However, when taken to the absurd extreme of babies being hatched in bottles for maximum efficiency, the reader realizes that not all progress and efficiency is good. Huxley even satirizes sentimentality by having the citizens of the future sing sentimental songs about "dear old mom," only they sing a version in which they fondly recall their "dear old bottle," the one in which they grew as fetuses. Being sentimental about one's origin in a test tube will strike many readers as funny, as well as ironic.

Allusion

Throughout the book, evidence of Huxley's vast knowledge of science, technology, literature, and music can be found. He makes frequent allusions to Shakespeare, mostly through the character of John, who quotes the bard whenever he needs to express a strong human emotion. Indeed, the title itself is from Shakespeare's *The Tempest,* in which the sheltered Miranda first encounters some men and declares, "How beauteous mankind is! O brave new world / That has such people in't!" Huxley also makes many allusions to powerful, influential people of his day, naming characters, buildings, and religions after them. For example, Henry Ford (1863–1947) is as a god; his name is used in interjections (Oh my Ford!), in calculating the year (A.F., or After Ford, instead of A.D., which stands for "anno domini"—in the year of our Lord). Even the Christian cross has been altered to resemble the T from the old Model T car built by Ford.

The character of the Savage is reminiscent of the Noble Savage—the concept that primitive people are more innocent and pure of heart than civilized people. However, Huxley is careful not to portray him as heroic or his primitive culture as ideal. The reader sympathizes with him because he is the person who most represents current values.

One of the more subtle influences on the story, however, is Sigmund Freud (1856–1939), the founder of modern psychoanalysis. The Savage is a prime example of someone who suffers from what Freud termed the Oedipus complex, a powerful desire to connect with one's mother. At one point, when he sees his mother with her lover, he identifies with Hamlet, who also had an Oedipal complex, an overattachment to his mother that prevented him from accepting her as sexually independent of him. Freud believed that childhood experiences shape adult perceptions, feelings, and behaviors, and the characters in the novel are all clearly compelled to feel and act according to the lessons they learned as children, even when faced with evidence that their behavior results in personal suffering.

Historical Context

When Huxley wrote *Brave New World* in 1931 it was at the beginning of a worldwide depression. The American stock market crash of 1929 had closed banks, wiped out many people's savings, and caused unemployment rates to soar. To make matters worse, American farmers were suffering from some of the worst droughts in history, leading to widespread poverty and migration out of the farming belt. People longed for the kind of economic security that Huxley gives to the citizens of his fictional world.

The effects of the crash were beginning to be felt worldwide, including in England, where Huxley lived. However much economic issues were on his mind, Huxley was also very much aware of the social and scientific changes that had begun to sweep the world in the beginning of the century, and particularly through the 1920s. Technology was rapidly replacing many workers, but politicians promised that progress would solve the unemployment and economic problems. Instead, workers were forced to take whatever jobs were available. More often than not, unskilled or semi-skilled laborers worked long hours without overtime pay, under unsafe conditions, and without benefits such as health insurance or pensions. Unlike the inhabitants of the brave new world, they had no job guarantees and no security. Furthermore, they often had little time for leisure and little money to spend on entertainment or on material luxuries.

In order to increase consumer demand for the products being produced, manufacturers turned to advertising in order to convince people they ought to spend their money buying products and services. Also, Henry Ford, who invented the modern factory assembly line, was now able to efficiently mass produce cars. For the first time, car parts were interchangeable and easily obtained, and Ford deliberately kept the price of his Model T low enough so that his workers could afford them. In order to pay for the new automobiles, many people who did not have enough cash needed to stretch out payments over time, and thus buying on credit became acceptable. Soon, people were buying other items on credit, fueling the economy by engaging in overspending and taking on debt.

All of these economic upheavals affected Huxley's vision of the future. First, he saw Ford's production and management techniques as revolutionary, and chose to make Ford not just a hero to the characters in his novels but an actual god. Huxley also saw that technology could eventually give workers enormous amounts of leisure time. The result could be more time spent creating art and solving social problems, but Huxley's Controllers, perceiving those activities as threatening to the order they've created, decide to provide foolish distrac-

Compare & Contrast

- **1920s:** Scientist Ivan Pavlov conducts behavioral experiments and shows that one can create a conditioned response in animals. John B. Watson, establishes the Behaviorist School of thought: he believes that human beings can be reduced to a network of stimuli and responses, which can be controlled by the experimenter.

- **1930s:** German Nobel Prize winner Hans Spemann develops the controversial science of experimental embryology, manipulating the experience of a human fetus in the womb in order to influence it.

- **Huxley's London 731 A.D.:** All humans are cloned from a small number of fertilized eggs, incubated in artificial wombs (bottles), and conditioned as embryos and fetuses for their future lives.

- **Today:** In 1978, the first human baby conceived *in vitro* (in a test tube) is born. In 1997, a sheep is cloned for the first time, raising the possibility of cloning humans.

- **1920s:** Totalitarian rulers Joseph Stalin in Russia and Benito Mussolini in Italy come to power.

- **1931:** Totalitarian rulers Francisco Franco (Spain) and Adolf Hitler (Germany) are a few years away from power. In China, communist dictator Mao Tse-tung is fighting for dominance but will not win power until the late 1940s.

- **Huxley's London 731 A.D.:** The world is a totalitarian state ruled by the Controllers, who use technology, brainwashing, and pre-birth conditioning rather than violence and intimidation to control their citizens.

---

tions to preoccupy their workers. These future workers do their duty and buy more and more material goods to keep the economy rolling, even to the point of throwing away clothes rather than mending them.

In Huxley's day, people's values and ideas were changing rapidly. The 1920s generation of youth rejected the more puritanical Victorian values of their parents' generation. Men and women flirted with modern ideas, such as communism, and questioned the rigid attitudes about social class. Some embraced the idea of free love (sex outside of marriage or commitment), as advocated by people like author Gertrude Stein (1874–1946). Others were talking publicly about sex, or using contraceptives, which were being popularized by Margaret Sanger (1883–1966), the American leader of the birth-control movement. Women began to smoke in public, cut their hair into short, boyish bobs, and wear much shorter, looser skirts. These new sexual attitudes are taken to an extreme in *Brave New World*.

Scientists were also beginning to explore the possibilities of human engineering. Russian scien-

tist Ivan Pavlov (1849–1936) showed that one can create a conditioned response in animals. For example, he rang a bell whenever he fed a group of dogs, and over time Pavlov's dogs began to salivate at the sound of a bell, even when no food was presented to them. Pavlov's fellow scientist, John B. Watson (1878–1958), founded the Behaviorist School of psychology: he believed that human beings could be reduced to a network of stimuli and responses, which could then be controlled by whoever experimented on them. In the 1930s, German Nobel Prize winner Hans Spemann (1869–1941) developed the controversial science of experimental embryology, manipulating the experience of a human fetus in the womb in order to influence it. The eugenics movement—which was an attempt to limit the childbearing of lower-class, ethnic citizens—was popular in the 1920s as well.

Meanwhile, the fad of hypnopaedia, or sleep teaching, was popular in the 1920s and 1930s. People hoped to teach themselves passively by listening to instructional tapes while they were sleeping. Although the electroencephalograph, a device invented in 1929 that measures brain waves, would

When Huxley wrote Brave New World, *foreshadowing a future characterized by sterility and an absence of individuality, he could not possibly have known about these newborn transgenic cows, "created" in 1998 through cloning and genetic engineering.*

totalitarian state that would come about would be incorporated into author George Orwell's futuristic anti-utopian novel *1984* (1948) and strongly influenced by Huxley's *Brave New World.*

Critical Overview

When *Brave New World* was published in 1932 it sold well in England and modestly in the United States, but it eventually brought Huxley international fame on both sides of the Atlantic. It was clear to critics that Huxley had written a novel of ideas, in which the characters and plot were not as well-developed as the book's themes, which bring up many important concepts, from freedom to class structure. Huxley used humor and satire to point out the excesses and shallowness of contemporary culture.

Today, *Brave New World* is considered an archetypical dystopian novel portraying a seemingly utopian world that is, upon closer inspection, a horror. Critics generally agree that while Huxley was not a particularly innovative writer, his ideas were provocative and fresh and his writing eloquent. He was appreciated for both his analysis of post-World War I English life and, on a larger scale, his promotion of humanistic values through literature.

prove that people have a limited ability to learn information while asleep, it also proved that hypnopaedia can influence emotions and beliefs. Meanwhile, the ideas of Viennese physician Sigmund Freud (1856–1939), the father of modern psychoanalysis, were also becoming popular. He believed, among other things, that most psychological problems stem from early childhood experiences. Huxley incorporated all of these technological and psychological discoveries into his novel, having the Controllers misuse this information about controlling human behavior to oppress their citizens.

Brave New World was written just before dictators such as Adolf Hitler in Germany, Benito Mussolini in Italy, Joseph Stalin in Russia, and Mao Tse-tung in China created totalitarian states in countries that were troubled by economic and political problems. These leaders often used extreme tactics to control their citizens, from propaganda and censorship to mass murder. Huxley could not have predicted what was on the horizon. The grim

Criticism

Jhan Hochman

Hochman, who teaches at Portland Community College, provides an overview of the unique setting Huxley constructed for his novel and how the work is an argument for individualism.

Aldous Huxley's most enduring and prophetic work, *Brave New World* (1932), describes a future world in the year 2495, a society combining intensified aspects of industrial communism and capitalism into a horrifying new world order. Huxley's title, taken from Shakespeare's play *The Tempest,* is therefore ironic: This fictional dystopia is neither brave nor new. Instead, it is so controlled and safe that there is neither need nor opportunity for bravery. As for being "new," its unrelenting drives toward management and development, and its obsessions with predictable order and consumption, are as old as the Industrial Revolution. Coupling horror with irony, *Brave New World,* a masterpiece of modern fiction, is a stinging critique of twentieth-century industrial society.

Huxley's observations about capitalist and communist societies show that what are usually thought of as vastly different systems also have some similarities. James Sexton calls the common denominator "an uncritical veneration of rationalization." The common denominator might also be characterized as the drive to ensure the industrialization of society by forms of propaganda and force, either frequent and obvious (as with the former Soviet Union) or more infrequent and subtle (such as in the United States and Europe). For proof that Huxley was commenting on modern societies, the reader need look no farther than the names of the characters residing in his futuristic London. There is Bernard Marx (named after Karl Marx, 1818-1883, the philosopher and economist whose theories were adopted by communist societies), Sarojini Engels (named after Friedrich Engels, 1820-1895, Marx's colleague and supporter), Lenina Crowne (named after V. I. Lenin, 1870-1924, the leader of the Russian Revolution in 1917 and Premier from 1918-24), and Polly Trotsky (named after Leon Trotsky, 1879-1940, the Russian revolutionary and writer).

The most damning critique of Western industrialism is indicated by the "God" worshipped in this future world-society: American car manufacturer and assembly line innovator, Henry Ford (1863-1947). In Huxley's dystopia, not only does calendar time begin with Ford's birth (the novel takes place in "A.F. 632"—A.F. stands for "After Ford"), but industry board rooms are sanctuaries for worshipping the Lord, Ford. Even a former religious locale, Stoke Poges (a famous English Christian cemetery), is made over into a golf course, and the Christian-named London square and district, Charing Cross, is renamed "Charing T." The letter "T" (referring to Ford's popular automobile, the "Model T"), is mounted, like a decapitated crucifix, on public buildings and necklaces. Because Ford was a man and the Model T was a car named by a letter in the alphabet (whose small letter resembles a crucifix), one might infer that salvation can only be had in this world, not the next. And the way to this non-eternal salvation is found through the production and consumption of products made in factories not so unlike those once producing Ford's Model T, the first successfully mass-produced car from an assembly line.

One special product that is mass-produced on assembly lines in A.F. 632 is the human being. To insure that there are enough–but not too many— workers and consumers, human life is carefully controlled from conception to death by two methods: outright control of the numbers and types of babies born and subconscious conditioning of people's thoughts. Factories with conveyor belts containing bottled embryos of the five preordained castes are inoculated against all future disease, treated with hormones and proteins, and placed in different environments to influence their growth. In this way, embryos are fashioned to have different levels of intelligence and different physical attributes, depending on the caste for which they have been selected. The factory, The Central London Hatchery and Conditioning Centre, makes viviparous reproduction (live birth from parents) obsolete. Huxley develops here the impersonal generation of children he began in his first novel, *Crome Yellow* (1921). Children are therefore bred to work and associate only with people in their caste; they can never be corrupted by parents who might pass on views that are counter to the ethics of production and consumption.

Once "hatched" or "decanted," infants are conditioned by hypnopaedia (repeated messages played during sleep) and negative stimulus (electric shock) to, for instance, hate nature. The reason for this desirable hatred of nature is simple: an appreciation of nature takes people away from their duties of production and consumption; citizens are therefore made to believe that they can live in a natural environment only if they are wearing special clothing. Continuously conditioned by repeated messages to be happy with their own caste and world, people are distracted from possible thoughts of rebellion by participating in sports, watching entertaining shows that also serve as subtle propaganda, enjoying casual and frequent sex, and by using the drug "soma," a kind of mood-stabilizer regularly handed out free-of-charge in the workplace. Soma is named after a hallucinogenic drink used in Hindu sacrificial ceremonies.

However, there is one last impediment which must be overcome: old age. Because aging would interrupt work (production) and play (consumption) the five castes are kept young through chemical treatments, making them fully capable of producing and consuming until they die. London hospitals in A.F. 632 are only necessary for the dying, and no one grieves for the dying because they are conditioned not to and because lack of familial bonds makes people only friends at best. The maxim "ending is better than mending" applies to

What Do I Read Next?

- *1984* (1948) George Orwell's dystopian novel, was written after *Brave New World* and after the rise and fall of Hitler and Stalin. It paints a far more grim, violent, and oppressive picture of the future. Unlike Huxley, who wrote his novel before television began to appear in American homes, Orwell incorporates into his futuristic vision a role for television, an invention whose influence and possibilities, good and bad, were just beginning to be imagined at the time the book was written.

- *Brave New World Revisited* (1958) is a collection of essays Aldous Huxley published to expand upon the trends explored in *Brave New World.* In it, Huxley talks about the social and scientific developments since writing the book, and he reveals what he would change in the book if he were to rewrite it. Most significantly, he says in retrospective he wishes he would have incorporated some of the grimmer aspects of totalitarianism, which revealed themselves in the 1930s, and would have given the Savage more than just two choices, sanity or insanity. He would have allowed the Savage some sort of compromise, a way to live within a flawed society.

- *Point Counter Point* (1928) is a novel Huxley wrote before *Brave New World,* and it is con-

sidered one of his finest. The complex narrative structure imitates the rhythms, harmonies, and dissonance in music (counterpoint is a musical term referring to a contrasting melody structure). The main character, Philip Quarles, wants to write novels like the one he is in, which incorporate musical ideas. Other characters, his wife and friends, have very different experiences, dreams, and perceptions, and are mouthpieces for Huxley's many ideas.

- *This Perfect Day* (1970) by Ira Levin is another futuristic novel about a totalitarian society with very different values from that of contemporary society. As in *Brave New World,* citizens dull their pain and fears through drugs and are genetically very similar. Those who have some genetic differences have a greater tendency to be dissatisfied with the pacified society, which is controlled by a huge computer that dispenses mood-altering drugs.

- *The Handmaid's Tale* (1985) by Margaret Atwood is the story of a woman named Offred who lives in the Republic of Gilead, an oppressive society of the future in which women's roles are severely limited. Gilead is, in fact, America in the future after right-wing extremists have taken over and virtually enslaved women in service to men.

---

all products, including people, in this disposable society.

The total scientific control of the human organism might lead some readers to think that *Brave New World* is a denouncement of science. This is unlikely, since Huxley came from a family of eminent scientists and, before becoming blind, he wanted to be a doctor. As Keith May commented, "The chief illusion which *Brave New World* shatters has less to do with an unthinking faith in scientific progress than with the assumption that truth, beauty, and happiness are reconcilable goods on the

plane of ordinary, unregenerate human activity." One might also say, however, that truth and beauty have no place in A.F. 632, but must be, as Mustapha Mond says near the end of the book, hidden or eradicated. The trinity of truth, beauty, and happiness has been replaced by the holy pair, stability and happiness, necessary elements of production and consumption.

From birth to death, the life Huxley describes in *Brave New World* is a fully engineered existence in which both people and their environment are remade to society's specifications. George Wood-

---

cock states that "it seemed evident to him [Huxley] that any human attempt to impose an ideal order on Nature or on men would be perverted by man's limitations. So for all his love of order in geometry and architecture and music, he distrusted it in political or social planning." Jerome Meckier characterizes over-engineering and mania for order as an excess of rationality: In *Brave New World* "the rational is raised to an irrational power until, for example, the goal of sanitation reform in the nineteenth century, namely cleanliness, replaces godliness."

In A.F. 632 there are no schools or libraries because it is believed that thinking and learning lead to the instability and unhappiness of individuals and society and interrupt society's greatest goods: consumption and production. Furthermore, there is no mention of money, wealth, or financial institutions. One might cautiously infer from these absences that differences of education and economic class have been replaced by biological castes, a system far more effective at insuring stability, the ideal atmosphere for practices of production and consumption.

For contrasts to *Brave New World*, the reader should consult Huxley's last novel, *Island* (1962). Whereas the earlier novel creates a future dystopia, the latter describes a contemporary utopia. Both worlds have much in common: children are not the property of their parents, sex is open and shameless, peace and order reign, and drugs are accepted. What separates Brave New Dystopia from Island Utopia are the methods by which these ideals are accomplished. In *Island* children freely circulate among a village community of loving adults; sex is neither forced nor encouraged but simply accepted as normal; peace and order are not enforced, but result from the way children are raised; and a particular drug is used occasionally to pry open what artist and poet William Blake (1757-1827) called the "doors of perception" (the sense organs), which also happens to be the name of a nonfiction work by Huxley published in 1954.

In the end, *Brave New World* is an argument for individualism, but not the kind scornfully referred to by Marxists and socialists as "bourgeois individualism" (bourgeois is a French word referring to middle-class property owners, or those who want to be free of government regulations on wealth). Huxley, as is shown more clearly in *Island,* is against any society that encourages the bourgeois individual, a person who accrues wealth at the expense of workers, customers, and the community. Instead, he is interested in an economically free social individual, one who is free to be alone, one who can write, read, think, say, work, play, and otherwise do whatever he or she wants. Such an individual is the polar opposite of the characters in *Brave New World* in which it is said, "When the individual feels, the community reels." For further evidence of Huxleyan individualism, the reader should also consult the nonfiction essays of *Brave New World Revisited* (1958) and the fascinating account of Huxley's experience with the drug peyote in *The Doors of Perception* (1954).

Huxley's lasting contribution to English literature is probably best characterized as the "novel of ideas" as defined by the fictional Philip Quarles in Huxley's fourth novel, *Point Counter Point* (1928): "The character of each personage must be implied, as far as possible, in the ideas of which he is the mouthpiece. In so far as theories are rationalizations of sentiments, instincts, dispositions of the soul, this is feasible." Frederick Hoffman says that while this might seem a monstrous way to construct a novel, "Ideas, as they are used in Huxley, possess ... *dramatic* qualities. Dominating as they very often do the full sweep of his novels, they appropriate the fortunes and careers which ordinarily belong to persons." *Brave New World* is living evidence that the novel of ideas can become a classic, applicable to its own time as well as today.

Source: Jhan Hochman, in an essay for *Novels for Students,* Gale, 1999.

Richard H. Beckham

In the following excerpt, Beckham argues against censoring Brave New World, *claiming that the satire provides an insightful reflection of our human behavior and societal values.*

It is obvious why someone who believes in censorship might choose to object to *Brave New World.* This world is a world of sexual promiscuity, a world with a drug culture in the most literal sense of that expression, a world in which the traditional family—in fact, any family at all—has been vilified and rendered taboo, a world in which religion has been reduced to orgiastic rituals of physical expression. It is a world in which art panders to the sensations of mass communications and a world in which the positive values of Western democracy have been ossified into a rigid caste system, in which the members of each caste are mass produced to the specifications of assembly line uniformity.

Readers who have strict standards of sexual behavior, who believe in chaste courtships and monogamous, lifetime marriages confront in this novel a society in which sexual promiscuity is a virtue and in which the sole function of sexuality is pleasure, not reproduction. Since reproduction is achieved by an elaborate biogenetic mass production assembly line, the citizens of *Brave New World* do not need normal human sexual activity to propagate the species. In fact, such activity is discouraged by the state so that the carefully monitored population controls are not disrupted. Women are required to wear "Malthusian Belts"—convenient caches of birth control devices—in order to forego pregnancies. The sole function of sex in this society is pleasure, and the sole function of pleasure is to guarantee the happiness of *Brave New World* and thus assure a stable, controllable population. State encouraged promiscuity assures that loyalty to one's lover or family will not undermine one's loyalty to the state. Thus, "Everyone belongs to everyone else," and the highest compliment a man can offer a woman is that she is "very pneumatic"—a euphemism suggesting that her movements during sexual intercourse are especially pleasurable. Unlike Orwell, who in the novel *1984* placed severe taboos on sexual activity, since as private and personal act it might permit or encourage rebellion against the state, Huxley prophesizes that in the future the state will use sex as a means of population control on the basis of the psychological truism that men and women condition themselves to avoid pain and to seek pleasure.

Lest the pleasure of frequent and promiscuous sexual activity not be sufficient to distract the population and dissuade them from rebellion, Huxley foresees a culture in which widespread and addictive use of drugs offers a second means of assuring a frictionless society. "A Soma in time saves nine,"—a hypnopaedic slogan drilled into the heads of Brave New Worldians from nursery days on—conveys the message that individuals are to protect themselves from normal pain by frequent doses of this widely available and socially acceptable narcotic.

One of the most important uses for Soma is to insulate people from the effects of rapid aging which afflict *Brave New World* inhabitants after an artificially induced period of extended youth. In this "perfect" society—the future as heaven—most of the human qualities of life have been altered and adapted so that they are devoid of crisis and pain. Just as the inhabitants of this world age only during a brief period shortly before death and just as

the drug which eases them through this period has no unpleasant side effects, so they are insulated against the normal stresses and tensions of family life. They have no parents to contend with since in Huxley's inspired anticipation of the consequences of biogenetic engineering, they are conceived through artificial insemination, carried in assembly line placentas made of sow's peritoneum, and decanted rather than born. *Brave New World* inhabitants spend their nursery years in state-run institutions where they are conditioned for future life. Those normal mortals who recall the pain of adolescence would be spared such in *Brave New World;* there is no adolescence. As adults, the inhabitants enjoy youth and vitality until near the time of their deaths. People never have to contend with the stress of accommodating themselves to the authority of parents, nor do they know the stress, pain, heartache—nor the joy—of nurturing and raising children.

The birth and childhood of *Brave New World* inhabitants is greatly reduced from the human world in which we daily live. After perusing the early chapters of this novel, the sensitive reader becomes aware that reduction is one of its recurrent themes, and that this reduction usually involves those attributes of life which make us most human. The purpose behind these reductions is to make all existence subservient to the state. Such subservience requires that even such basic institutions of human civilization as religion and art be sapped of their vital force.

With lives so devoid of pain and so concentrated in the physical and the immediate present, the Worldians have little need for the comfort or solace of religion. If religion is that aspect of man's culture which speaks to the spirit, then Worldians have an absence of spirit of which they are unaware. The reduction of religion is symbolized in the icon which replaces the cross as the dominant religious image—a T. The worship of a supernatural savior has been supplanted by worship of a lord of the assembly line, Henry Ford, and the sign of Our Ford is taken from the model name of one of his early cars. The four arms of the cross have been reduced to the three arms of the T.

Religion lends continuity to civilization, and so does art. Each is an important constituent of the emotional component of human life. But, like religion, art in *Brave New World* has been reduced to trafficking in sensation—slight, transitory, physical responses as opposed to the profound, sustained, psychological responses of emotion. The

"Feelies"— *Brave New World's* multi-sensory version of the movies—well illustrates this pandering to sensation; rather than celebrating the ideas and emotions of human life, the "Feelies" are designed to give its participants a sensory overload of neural stimulation—the sight and feel of bare flesh on a bearskin rug, for example.

Thus art and religion are controlled by the state and subordinated to the support of the state, but the nature of that state is quite different from what a contemporary reader might expect. In the 1990s, citizens of Western Democracies see their form of government as the best form yet developed by man. As Huxley projects this important facet of human life into the future, he foresees neither Western Democracy nor its historical competitor, Eastern Communism, as the most likely political system. Instead of either he sees a five-tiered caste system occasioned through the perfection of biogenetic engineering and other modern devices of social control. Every man is created biologically equal to all others in his caste. The leisured classes are conditioned to consume, and the working classes are conditioned to manufacture what those other classes consume. Society functions almost as simply as the physical law of equal and opposite reactions.

If Huxley had perversely set out to oversimplify and reduce the most important philosophical and scientific ideas of modern times to a facile society representing a serious projection of what the world will surely become, then one might at least understand the objections of those who seek to censor the book. Neither Marx nor the founders of Western Democracy prevail. The Worldians seem to extrapolate from some of the world's great religions—Islam, Christianity, Judaism—such belief as is useful for their purpose. Freud's insights into family relationships are read only in their negative connotations, and these connotations then become the basis for social organization. Darwin's discoveries about adaptation and heredity are seen not as patterns for understanding how nature works but rather as patterns for manipulating nature to nefarious ends. The history of modern technology culminates in a culture where man eases his way through life on drugs, is free of painful involvement with other human beings, and is sustained by the state's manipulation of mass consumption and mass communication.

But Huxley does not offer *Brave New World* as an ideal. Neither does he render it as an idle fantasy portraying what life might be like in the future. *Brave New World* is a satire, and the pleasur-

able perfection of society in A.F. 689 is measured against the norm of Twentieth Century society in general and against the norm of a particular primitive society still currently extant. Brave New World has its critics both from within and without. The critic from within is Bernard Marx. Because of some abnormality in his birthing process, he is not a perfect Alpha specimen, which suggests that human imperfection and mechanical malfunction have not been completely eliminated in this brave new world. The critic from without is John Savage. As the child of Linda from the dominant culture and the adopted son of a Native American on a reservation in the American Southwest, he is a half-breed belonging to neither the progressive nor the traditional societies in the book.

Marx introduces some of the universal human norms in the book. He is in the society, but not of it. He is physically smaller than other members of his caste—the dominant Alphas—and this physical distinction seems to generate in him envy and alienation, which are uncommon in the society. He rebels against his superior, and when he finds Linda and her son on the reservation and discovers her past association with his superior, he brings them back to the "World" in order to humiliate his boss. Though he has a professional, psychological interest in the two, he is so flattered by the attention he receives because of his connection with the famous pair that he begins to pander to the society of which he has previously been so harshly critical. Marx is important in a technical sense because it is from his point of view that we see the activities of the society—activities which he both participates in and criticizes.

John, or the savage, articulates the values of both a minority culture, the Native Americans and of the culture of the past. To the degree to which he has assimilated the culture of the Native Americans, he is a child of nature communicant with the earth, sky, wind and water. He is free of the artificial and urban environment in which Bernard spends his life. Though his mother is from the dominant society, John is born outside that society and thus escapes its state-supported brainwashing nurture and its prescriptions against artifacts of earlier times. His education he obtains from the *Bible* and Shakespeare—two of the most important cultural forces in modern Western civilization. It is by the norms of this literature that he executes his criticism of this "Brave New World."

Bernard and John convey to the reader the dilemma of modern life which Huxley expresses in the novel. Through their knowledge humans gain greater and greater control over their environment. As they gain control and are better able to manage their own destiny, they also greatly increase the danger of losing their humanity—the sum total of those facets of life by which people define and know themselves. This point is literally and symbolically illustrated through the tragic conclusion of the novel. John falls victim to that most human of human emotions—love. Yet he cannot reconcile his love for Lenina Crown in a satisfactory way. John cannot accept her as "pneumatic," as "belonging to everybody else," after the fashion of his mother's culture. Nor can he remold her into the image of the beloved he holds from the Biblical and Shakespearean cultural guides he learned in his childhood. John is caught out of time. He cannot go back to his old culture, nor can he assimilate the new. His only option in a world where he has become a freak to be gawked at is suicide. As his body swings from the rope gyrating toward all points of the compass, Huxley suggests that we too may be creating a world in which ironically there is no place for human life and for human emotion.

One of the objectors to this novel comments on its pessimism and tragedy as reasons why it should not be taught. Such an objection overlooks the tone of the book. As satire, the book's purpose is to examine the failings of human behavior in order to encourage reform. Such examinations are painful when we recognize our faults through them. But pain and growth and regeneration are part of the human condition and prove that Huxley's prophesy has not yet come true. And certainly if we try to prevent people—especially young people—from being exposed to the tragic, we would have to eliminate much world literature which has been universally proclaimed great.

Source: Richard H. Beckham, "Huxley's Brave New World as Social Irritant: Ban It or Buy It?" in *Censored Books: Critical Viewpoints,* edited by Nicholas J. Karolides, Lee Burress, and John M. Kean, Scarecrow, 1993, pp. 136–41.

Peter Edgerly Firchow

In the following excerpt, Firchow discusses how Huxley faced a distinct challenge in developing unique and interesting characters in a world where uniformity is strictly enforced.

One of the chief problems Huxley had with *Brave New World,* according to Donald Watt [in *Journal English and Germanic Philology,* July, 1978], was with the characters. On the evidence of the revisions, Watt concludes that Huxley seems first to have thought of making Bernard Marx the rebellious hero of the novel but then changed his mind and deliberately played him down into a kind of anti-hero. After rejecting the possibility of a heroic Bernard, Huxley next seems to have turned to the Savage as an alternative. According to Watt, there are in the typescript several indications, later revised or omitted, of the Savage's putting up or at least planning to put up violent resistance to the new world state, perhaps even of leading a kind of revolution against it. But in the process of rewriting the novel, Huxley also abandoned this idea in favor of having no hero at all, or of having only the vague adumbration of a hero in Helmholtz Watson.

Watt's analysis of the revisions in *Brave New World* is very helpful and interesting; he shows convincingly, I think, that Huxley was unable to make up his mind until very late in the composition of the novel just what direction he wanted the story and the leading male characters to take. From this uncertainty, however, I do not think it necessary to leap to the further conclusion that Huxley had difficulty in creating these characters themselves. Huxley's supposedly inadequate ability to create living characters, the result of his not being a "congenital novelist," is a question that often arises in discussions of his fiction, and in connection with longer and more traditionally novelistic novels like *Point Counter Point* or *Eyeless in Gaza* (1936) appropriately so. But *Brave New World* is anything but a traditional novel in this sense. It is not a novel of character but a relatively short satirical tale, a "fable," much like Voltaire's *Candide.* One hardly demands fully developed and "round" characters of *Candide,* nor should one of *Brave New World.*

This is all the more the case because the very nature of the new world state precludes the existence of fully developed characters. Juliets and Anna Kareninas, or Hamlets and Prince Vronskys, are by definition impossibilities in the new world state. To ask for them is to ask for a different world, the very world whose absence Huxley's novel so savagely laments. Character, after all, is shaped by suffering, and the new world state has abolished suffering in favor of a continuous, soma-stupefied, infantile "happiness." In such an environment it is difficult to have characters who grow and develop and are "alive."

Despite all this, it is surprising and noteworthy how vivid and even varied Huxley's characters are. With all their uniformly standardized conditioning, Alphas and Betas turn out to be by no means alike: the ambitious "go-getter" Henry Foster is different from his easy-going friend Benito Hoover; the unconventional and more "pneumatic" Lenina Crowne from the moralistic and rather less pneumatic Fanny Crowne; the resentful and ugly Bernard Marx from the handsome and intelligent Helmholtz Watson. Huxley, in fact, seems to work consistently and consciously in terms of contrastive/complementary pairs to suggest various possibilities of response to similar situations. So, too, Helmholtz and the Savage are another pair, as are the Savage and Mond, Mond and the DHC, Bernard and Henry Foster. The most fully developed instance of this pairing or doubling technique is the trip that Bernard and Lenina make to the Indian reservation, a trip that duplicates the one made some years earlier by the DHC and a "particularly pneumatic" Beta-Minus named Linda. Like the DHC, Bernard also leaves Lenina, another pneumatic Beta, (briefly) behind while returning to civilization, and during this interval she, too, is lusted after by a savage, much as Pope and the other Indians lust after Linda. Even the novel as a whole reveals a similar sort of doubling structure, with the new world state on the one hand and the Indian reservation on the other.

Within limits, the characters, even some of the minor and superficial characters like Henry Foster, are capable of revealing other and deeper facets of their personality. Returning with Lenina from the Stoke Poges Obstacle Golf Course, Henry Foster's helicopter suddenly shoots upward on a column of hot air rising from the Slough Crematorium. Lenina is delighted at this brief switchback, but "Henry's tone was almost, for a moment, melancholy. 'Do you know what that switchback was?' he said. 'It was some human being finally and definitely disappearing. Going up in a squirt of hot gas. It would be curious to know who it was—a man or a woman, an Alpha or an Epsilon....'" Henry quickly jolts himself out of this atypical mood and reverts to his normally obnoxious cheerfulness, but for an instant at least there was a glimpse of a real human being.

Much more than Henry, Bernard Marx and Helmholtz Watson are capable of complexity of response. The latter especially and partly through his contact with the Savage grows increasingly aware of himself as a separate human entity and of his dissatisfaction with the kind of life he had led hitherto. As an Emotional Engineer and contriver of slogans, Helmholtz has been very successful, as he also has been in the capacities of lover and sportsman; but he despises this success and seeks for a satisfaction for which he has no name and which he can only dimly conceive. He comes closest to expressing it in the poem that eventually leads to his exile, the poem in which an ideal and absent woman becomes more real to him—in the manner of Mallarmé's flower that is absent from all bouquets—than any woman he has ever actually met.

In the end Helmholtz agrees to being sent into frigid exile in the Falkland Islands. The reason he chooses such a place rather than possible alternatives like Samoa or the Marquesas is because there he will not only have solitude but also a harsh climate in which to suffer and to gain new and very different experiences. His aim, however, is not, as some critics have suggested, to seek mystic experience; he simply wants to learn how to write better poetry. "I should like a thoroughly bad climate," he tells Mustapha Mond. "I believe one would write better if the climate were bad. If there were a lot of wind and storms for example...." This hardly represents a search for mysticism and God; in this novel only the Savage, and he in only a very qualified way, can be described as seeking after such ends. Helmholtz merely wants more and better words....

The same is true of Bernard Marx. Despite the apparent fact that Huxley once had more exalted intentions for him, Bernard belongs very much to the familiar Huxleyan category of the anti-hero, best exemplified perhaps by Theodore Gumbril, Jr., the so-called Complete Man of *Antic Hay* (1923). Like Gumbril, Bernard is able to envision and even seek after a love that is not merely sexual, but, like Gumbril again, his search is half-hearted. He is willing to settle for less because it is so much easier than trying to strive for more. Bernard is weak and cowardly and vain, much more so than Gumbril, and this makes him an unsympathetic character in a way that Gumbril is not. Nevertheless Bernard is undoubtedly capable of seeing the better, even if in the end he follows the worse.

Bernard is certainly a more fully developed character than Helmholtz; he is, in fact, with the exception of the Savage, the character about whom we know most in the entire novel. Just why this should be so is a question worth asking, just as it is worth asking why Bernard is the first of the novel's three malcontents to be brought to our attention.

Bernard's importance resides, I think, in his incapacity. The stability of the new world state can be threatened, it is clear, from above and from below. In the case of Helmholtz the threat is from above, from a surfeit of capacity; in Bernard's case it is from below, from a lack of sufficient capacity. This is not simply to say that Bernard is more stupid than Helmholtz, which he probably is, but rather that because of his physical inferiority he has developed a compulsive need to assert his superiority. It is this incapacity which, paradoxically, seems to make Bernard the more dangerous threat, for it compels him to rise to a position of power in his society; he wants to be accepted by his society, but only on his own terms, terms that are not acceptable in the long run if stability is to be maintained. Helmholtz, on the other hand, is a loner who really wants to have nothing to do with the society at all, and in this sense he represents much less of a threat. The Savage, on the other hand, though most violent and uncompromising in his hatred of and desire to destroy the new world state, is really no threat at all, for he originates from outside the society and is a kind of *lusus naturae*. There is never likely to be another Savage, but it is very probable that there will be or that there are more Bernards and Helmholtzes.

Both Bernard and Helmholtz are fairly complex characters. What is surprising, however, is that the same is true of Lenina Crowne. She seems at first to be nothing more than a pretty and addle-brained young woman without any emotional depth whatever. And at first it is true that this is all she is; but she changes in the course of the novel into something quite different. She changes because she falls in love.

The great irony of Lenina's falling in love is that she does not realize what it is that has happened to her; like Helmholtz she has no name for the new feeling and hence no way of conceiving or understanding what it is. She can only think of love in the physiological ways in which she has been conditioned to think of it; but her feeling is different.

So subtle is Huxley's portrayal of the change in Lenina that, as far as I know, no critic has ever commented on it. Yet Lenina is clearly predisposed from the very beginning to a love relationship that is not sanctioned by her society. As we learn from her conversation with Fanny, Lenina has been going with Henry Foster for four months without having had another man, and this in defiance of what she knows to be the properly promiscuous code of sexual behavior. When Fanny takes her up on this point of unconventionality, Lenina reacts almost truculently and replies that she "jolly well [does not] see why there should have been" anyone other than Henry. Her inability to see this error in her

sexual ways is what predisposes her for the much greater and more intense feeling that she develops for the Savage.

The stages of her growing love for the Savage and her increasing mystification at what is happening within herself are handled with a brilliantly comic touch. There is the scene following Lenina's and the Savage's return from the feelies when the Savage sends her off in the taxicopter just as she is getting ready to seduce him. There is the touching moment when Lenina, who had once been terrified of pausing with Bernard to look at the sea and the moon over the Channel, now lingers "for a moment to look at the moon," before being summoned by an irritated and uncomprehending Arch-Songster. There is Lenina's increasing impatience with the obtuseness of Henry Foster and his blundering solicitousness. There are the fond murmurings to herself of the Savage's name. There is the conference with Fanny as to what she should do about the Savage's strange coldness toward her. There is her blunt rejection of Fanny's advice to seek consolation with one of the millions of other men. There is the wonderful scene in which she seeks out the Savage alone in his apartment, discovers to her amazement that he loves her, sheds her clothing, and receives, to her even greater amazement, insults, blows, and a threat to kill. There is the final terrible scene at the lighthouse when Lenina steps out of the helicopter, looks at the Savage with "an uncertain, imploring, almost abject smile," and then "pressed both hands to her left side [i.e., to her heart], and on that peach-bright, doll-beautiful face of hers appeared a strangely incongruous expression of yearning distress. Her blue eyes seemed to grow larger, brighter; and suddenly two tears rolled down her cheeks." Again the Savage attacks her, this time with his whip, maddened by desire, by remorse, and by the horde of obscenely curious sightseers. In the end, however, desire triumphs and the Savage and Lenina consummate their love in an orgy-porgian climax. When the Savage awakens to the memory of what has happened, he knows he cannot live with such defilement. For him the end is swift and tragic. For Lenina, however, there is no end; her tragedy—and for all the comedy and irony in which her love for the Savage is immersed, the word *tragedy* is not entirely inappropriate—her tragedy is that she has felt an emotion that she can never express or communicate or realize again.

The characters of *Brave New World*, it is safe to conclude, are not merely made of cardboard and *papier-mâché*. That they are nonetheless not full and complete human beings is quite true; but for all the technology and conditioning and impulses toward uniformity, there is still something profoundly human about them. As Lenina's development in the novel indicates, it is possible, as it were, to scratch the plasticized "doll-like" surface of a citizen—at least of an Alpha or Beta citizen—of the new world state and draw actual blood. In this sense and to this degree, Huxley's vision of the perfectly planned future is not without hope; for all the genetic engineering and conditioning, basic humanity remains much the same as it always was. Its imperfections and its needs, even under such greatly altered conditions, inevitably reappear. And it is for this reason, I think, that Huxley's vision is so extraordinarily powerful and compelling; because in the people he portrays we can still somehow recognize ourselves.

Source: Peter Edgerly Firchow, in his *End of Utopia: A Study of Aldous Huxley's Brave New World,* Bucknell University Press, 1984, 154 p.

Sources

Frederick J. Hoffman, "Aldous Huxley and the Novel of Ideas," in *Aldous Huxley: A Collection of Critical Essays,* edited by Robert E. Kuehn, Prentice Hall, 1974, pp. 8-17.

M. May Keith, *Aldous Huxley,* Harper & Row, 1972.

Jerome Meckier, *Aldous Huxley: Satire and Structure,* Chatto & Windus, 1969.

Guinevera A. Nance, *Aldous Huxley,* Continuum, 1988.

James Sexton, "*Brave New World* and the Rationalization of Industry," in *Critical Essays on Aldous Huxley,* edited by Jerome Meckier, G.K. Hall, 1996, pp. 88-102.

Grover Smith, editor, *Letters of Aldous Huxley,* Chatto & Windus, 1969.

Philip Thody, *Huxley: A Biographical Introduction,* Scribner's, 1973.

George Woodcock, *Dawn and the Darkest Hour: A Study of Aldous Huxley,* Faber & Faber, 1972.

For Further Study

Robert S. Baker, *The Dark Historic Page: Social Satire and Historicism in the Novels of Aldous Huxley, 1921-1939,* University of Wisconsin Press, 1974.
> Baker discusses Huxley's aversion to "historical thought."

Sybille Bedford, *Aldous Huxley: A Biography,* Knopf, 1974.
> Bedford's biography is based on published works, documentaries, and personal accounts.

Milton Birnbaum, *Aldous Huxley's Quest for Values,* University of Tennessee Press, 1971.
> This is an exploration of Huxley's ability to articulate the pulse of twentieth century thought.

Peter Bowering, *Aldous Huxley: A Study of the Major Novels,* Oxford University Press, 1969.
> Bowering examines nine of Huxley's eleven novels.

Lawrence Brander, *Aldous Huxley: A Critical Study,* Bucknell University Press, 1970.
> Brander's study is of Huxley's novels, essays, short stories, and travelogues.

Thomas D. Clareson, "The Classic: Aldous Huxley's 'Brave New World'," in *Extrapolation,* Vol. 3, no. 1, December, 1961, pp. 33-40.
> An analysis of *Brave New World,* praising the universalism of Huxley's vision and ideas, by an American educator and critic. Clareson is also considered an authority on the genre of science fiction.

Peter Firchow, *Aldous Huxley: Satirist and Novelist,* University of Minnesota Press, 1972.
> Firchow's focus is satire in Huxley's essays and novels.

Sisirkamar Ghose, *Aldous Huxley: A Cynical Salvationist,* Asia Publishing, 1962.
> Ghose studies Huxley's times, religious world-view, and his novels.

Alexander Henderson, *Aldous Huxley,* Russell and Russell, 1964.
> This is a study of Huxley's life, four novels, criticism, poetry, and travel books.

Julian Huxley, editor, *Aldous Huxley: 1894-1963,* Harper & Row, 1965.
> This is a book of tributes to Huxley made by friends, family, and admirers after his death.

Gulliver's Travels

Jonathan Swift

1726

Although in its abridged form *Gulliver's Travels* (1726) is known as a classic children's adventure story, it is actually a biting work of political and social satire by an Anglican priest, historian, and political commentator. Anglo-Irish author Jonathan Swift parodied popular travelogues of his day in creating this story of a sea-loving physician's travels to imaginary foreign lands. Structurally, the book is divided into four separate adventures, or travels, which Dr. Lemuel Gulliver undertakes by accident when his vessel is shipwrecked or taken over by pirates. In these fantastic tales, Swift satirizes the political events in England and Ireland in his day, as well as English values and institutions. He ridicules academics, scientists, and Enlightenment thinkers who value rationalism above all else, and finally, he targets the human condition itself.

Like all of Swift's works, *Gulliver's Travels* was originally published without Swift's name on it because he feared government persecution. His criticisms of people and institutions are often scathing, and some observers believe he was a misanthrope (one who hates mankind). Other critics have suggested that while Swift criticized humans and their vanity and folly, he believed that people are capable of behaving better than they do and hoped his works would convince people to reconsider their behavior. Swift himself claimed he wrote *Gulliver's Travels* "to vex the world rather than divert it." He succeeded in that aim, as the book is considered one of the best examples of satire ever written. Swift's sharp observations about the cor-

ruption of people and their institutions still ring true today, almost three hundred years after the book was first published.

Author Biography

Swift was born in 1667 in Ireland of English parents. Swift's father died shortly before he was born, leaving Jonathan, his sister, and their mother dependent on his father's family. Their mother moved to England and left him with a nurse for his first three years. He attended Ireland's best schools, including Trinity College in Dublin, which is where he was in 1689, when civil unrest forced him and other Protestants to flee Ireland for England. In England, Swift began to work as secretary to scholar and former Parliament member Sir William Temple and lived at his home until Temple's death in 1699. Swift was exposed to many new books, ideas, and important and influential people during this time. Ordained as an Anglican (Episcopalian) priest in 1695, Swift wanted a career in the church. Unfortunately, his satirical writings, such as *A Tale of a Tub* and *Battle of the Books* (both 1704) offended Queen Anne, who made sure he could not get a decent position. Swift found a job as an Anglican clergyman in Ireland instead.

During this period, Swift met a woman he called Stella, whose real name was Esther Johnson, and wrote his *Journal to Stella* (1710–1713). No one really knows if the two were just friends or were romantically involved, although rumors persisted that the two had secretly married. At this time Swift also changed his political allegiance from the Whigs, who were more religiously tolerant, to the Tories, whom he felt were more supportive of the Anglican Church. Still, Swift felt that each man should worship God according to his own conscience. His attitude toward the bickering over small religious differences is symbolized in *Gulliver's Travels* (1726) by the silly dispute in Lilliput over which end of an egg one should crack.

Swift became involved with another woman, Esther Vanhomrigh (called Vanessa), in 1713, but resisted her attempts to make the relationship serious. He continued to write important works, including *A Modest Proposal* (1729) in which he suggested that the wealthy eat the babies of the Irish poor. He was, of course, using satire to point out the callousness of the wealthy toward the poor.

Jonathan Swift

Swift's pseudonymously written *The Drapier's Letters,* published in 1724, denounced England's plan to force the Irish to use a new currency that would prevent the Irish from trading with other countries. Swift hated how England took advantage of the Irish. This popular and controversial essay actually forced the English to discard their currency plan, making Swift an Irish hero to this day (the Irish carefully guarded his anonymity to protect him). He spent several years writing *Gulliver's Travels,* inspired by an assignment to parody travelogues given him by his group of writing friends, the Scriblerus Club.

Although Swift had hoped for a better position in the church after Queen Anne's death in 1714, the Tories' loss of power meant he could not hope to improve his status. He remained dean of St. Patrick's Cathedral until 1742, when Swift was declared of unsound mind. Although some early biographers attributed his mental weakness to senility caused by syphilis (some say this disease had prevented him from marrying), modern biographers now suggest he was the victim of an inner ear disease which was compounded by memory loss and speech difficulty caused by a stroke. Regardless, he was sent to a mental institution, where he died in 1745. He was buried next to Esther Johnson in St. Patrick's Cathedral.

Plot Summary

At its simplest level, *Gulliver's Travels* is the story of Lemuel Gulliver and his voyages around the world. Prefaced by two letters attesting to the truth of the tales, the adventures are told by Gulliver after his return home from his final journey. *Gulliver's Travels* is divided into four Parts or Books, each about a different place. Because of this structure, the book as a whole has a very sketchy plot; it feels more like weekly episodes than one long narrative. The individual books also feel very choppy, since Gulliver has a habit of stumbling from one adventure or crisis to the next. The book seems more cohesive if readers recognize that each part reflects Gulliver's character and is related to all the other parts. For example, Part I discusses things being disproportionately small, and Part II discusses things being disproportionately large.

Part I: A Voyage to Lilliput

Part I, entitled "A Voyage to Lilliput," is the most famous section of *Gulliver's Travels.* Lured by the prospect of adventure and easy money, Lemuel Gulliver signs up as a "surgeon," or ship's doctor, for a voyage through the East Indies in Asia. Unfortunately for Gulliver, he is shipwrecked. He swims to an unfamiliar shore and, exhausted by his efforts, goes to sleep. When he awakes, he finds himself tied up by a crowd of extremely tiny and well-armed people. Gulliver is taken prisoner, shipped to the capital, and presented to the Emperor. A cross between court pet and circus attraction, Gulliver makes friends with many of the courtiers and learns about the history, society, politics, and economy of Lilliput. For many years, Lilliput has been at war with its sister island Blefuscu over whether to break soft-boiled eggs at the big or little end. This clash parodies the French-English and Catholic-Protestant conflicts of Swift's time, and many of the characters in this section correspond to actual political figures of the day.

Although he aids Lilliput by stealing the Blefuscudian navy, Gulliver is resented by many of the Emperor's courtiers. He eventually hears of a plot to accuse him of treason and sentence him to be blinded and starved to death. Frightened by this prospect, he swims over to Blefuscu and presents himself as a visitor from the Lilliputian emperor. The Blefuscudian emperor treats him well, even after a message from Lilliput demands his return. An Englishman-sized rowboat washes up on shore, however, and, taking advantage of the opportunity, Gulliver departs Blefuscu and Lilliput. He is even-

tually rescued by a passing English ship and returns home to England and his family.

Part II: A Voyage to Brobdingnag

Gulliver is only home two months when he sets out on Part II, "A Voyage to Brobdingnag." After encountering a terrible storm, Gulliver's ship puts in to another unfamiliar shore for much-needed food and water. He goes ashore with the landing party but is abandoned by the crew when they discover there are giants living there. Gulliver is captured by a farmer, who displays him as a circus wonder at local fairs. The farmer's daughter, Glumdalclitch, teaches Gulliver to speak the language and the two become good friends. Eventually, the farmer sells Gulliver to the Queen of Brobdingnag, who allows Glumdalclitch to join the court as Gulliver's keeper.

Once at court, Gulliver has a series of violent, physical misadventures because of his size. Once, he is taken into the country and allowed to walk around a meadow on his own. Poor Gulliver has not yet learned the limits of his size in Brobdingnag, however. As he reports, "There was a Cowdung in the Path, and I must needs try my Activity by attempting to leap over it. I took a Run, but unfortunately jumped short, and found my self just in the Middle up to my Knees." Gulliver spends most of his time discussing history, politics, philosophy, and economics with the King. The King frequently dismays Gulliver by displaying his "ignorance," that is, finding certain aspects of Gulliver's England repulsive. When Gulliver offers to teach him about gunpowder so he can rule over his subjects with force, for example, the King rejects him in horror. In the end, Gulliver is carried off by a giant bird and dropped into the sea, where he is rescued again by an English ship. Disoriented by the size of things on shipboard and then in England, Gulliver takes some time to adjust to people of his own size. Eventually he gets used to other English people again and resolves to stay at home for the rest of his life.

Part III: A Voyage to Laputa, Balnibarbi, Glubbdubdrib, Luggnagg, and Japan

As usual, however, Gulliver is unable to keep his resolution. He is tempted by the prospect of easy money yet again and embarks on Part III, "A Voyage to Laputa, Balnibarbi, Luggnagg, Glubbdubdrib, and Japan." Gulliver's misfortunes begin when he and his crew are seized by pirates, who abandon him alone on a deserted island. In despair,

Gulliver begins to make the best of his bad lot when he is astonished to see a giant floating island appear in the sky. The inhabitants carry him up to them and make him welcome on the island, which they call Laputa. The Laputans control a non-floating island named Balnibarbi and live entirely by the rules of science and mathematics: even their bread and meat are carved into geometric shapes. The men are so consumed in thought that they have servants, called flappers, to bring them out of a trance into conversation. Women, who are excluded from these activities and entirely ignored by the men, frequently try to escape to Balnibarbi. After some persuasion, Gulliver is allowed to descend to Balnibarbi, where he witnesses the destructive effects of not enough practical thinking on agriculture, economics, education, and architecture.

In the most famous section of Part III, Gulliver visits the Grand Academy, Swift's parody of London's Royal Society. There he meets men devoting their lives to absurd experiments such as extracting sunlight from cucumbers and turning human waste into its original components. Gulliver proceeds from Balnibarbi to Luggnagg via the island of Glubbdubdrib, which is run by magic. There the governor raises several historical leaders and philosophers from the dead, giving Gulliver a chance to wonder at the corruption and brutishness of these supposedly great men. In Luggnagg, Gulliver hears of a race of people called Struldbruggs, who live forever. Gulliver imagines what he would do if he were a Struldbrugg, but when he meets them he realizes that eternal life does not necessarily mean eternal youth. The Struldbruggs actually have both infinite age and infinite infirmity, and they are miserable, senile people. Disgusted with all he has learned about himself and different ways of thinking, Gulliver sets sail for Japan, where he catches a ship for Amsterdam and returns home.

Part IV: A Voyage to the Country of the Houyhnhnms

Gulliver's last voyage, Part IV, is called "A Voyage to the Country of the Houyhnhnms" (pronounced whin-hims). Part IV examines less what humanity creates, such as science or gunpowder or government, and more what humanity is. Appropriately, Gulliver is left on an alien shore by a mutiny, a betrayal and abandonment that sets in motion the wheels of Gulliver's detachment from his own people. He encounters two types of inhabitants: the rational Houyhnhnms and the vicious, crude Yahoos. The Houyhnhnms are talking horses who have established a society based on rea-

son rather than emotion, while the Yahoos are hairy humanoids who are used by the Houyhnhnms as slaves. As usual, Gulliver learns the language and converses with the inhabitants about society, government, history, and philosophy. The Houyhnhnms do not know deceit, lying, or other vices, and are governed by reason. Neither, however, do they know fairness or love: certain color Houyhnhnms are restricted to a servant class and the race as a whole has no great attachment for spouses or children. Gulliver comes to admire the Houyhnhnms and loathe the Yahoos, who really are quite disgusting and violent.

Soon Gulliver is unable to appreciate the difference between humans and Yahoos:

> When I thought of my Family, my Friends, my Countrymen, or human Race in general, I considered them as they really were, Yahoos in shape and Disposition, perhaps a little bit more civilized, and qualified with the Gift of Speech; but making no other Use of Reason, than to improve and multiply those Vices, whereof their Brethren in this Country had only the Share that Nature allotted them. When I happened to behold the Reflection of my own Form in a Lake or Fountain, I turned away my Face in Horror and detestation of my self; and could better endure the Sight of a common Yahoo, than of my own Person. By conversing with the Houyhnhnms, and looking upon them with Delight, I fell to imitate their Gait and Gesture, which is now grown into a Habit; and my Friends often tell me in a blunt Way, that I "trot like a Horse"; which, however, I take for a great Compliment: Neither shall I disown, that in speaking I am apt to fall into the Voice and manner of the Houyhnhnms, and hear my self ridiculed on that account without the least Mortification.

The Houyhnhnms also have difficulty distinguishing Gulliver from the Yahoos, however. In spite of his best efforts to learn to be like the Houyhnhnms, they eventually find Gulliver too much like a Yahoo and sentence him to exile. Devastated, Gulliver builds a boat and sets sail. Long after his rescue by a Portuguese ship and return home, Gulliver consistently expresses his deep hatred for humanity, whom he calls Yahoos. Part IV concludes with Gulliver very slowly learning to accept his wife, his family, and other humans again, but still full of self-hatred and misanthropy.

Characters

Blefuscudians

Big-Enders and inhabitants of the island across the water from Lilliput, the Blefuscudians are supportive of the rebel Big-Ender refugees. They rep-

Ted Danson in the title role of the television movie Gulliver's Travels.

resent both Catholic France—with whom England went to war several times—and Ireland—a mostly Catholic country to which English Catholics fled for political asylum.

Skyresh Bolgolam

High Admiral of Lilliput and counselor to the Emperor, Skyresh Bolgolam is the enemy of Gulliver from the start. He brings Gulliver a list of demands or conditions for Gulliver to stay in Lilliput and also teams up with Flimnap to draw up articles of impeachment, which are leaked to Gulliver by an unnamed member of the court.

Brobdingnagians

The Brobdingnagians are a race of giants who live on Brobdingnag, a country in the Arctic Sea that Gulliver visits in Part II. Gulliver is repulsed by the flaws in their skin, which appear monstrous to him. He soon realizes their form of government is superior to those of Europe. Swift implies they are moral giants as well as physical giants in comparison to the Englishman Gulliver.

Emperor of Lilliput

A fingernail taller than his subjects, the Lilliputian Emperor is a handsome man with strong features, an olive complexion, and a regal bearing.

He wears Low Heels as an expression of his political beliefs. (Swift intends him to represent King George I, who was sympathetic to the Whig political party, represented by the Low Heels.) He is corrupt, petty, arrogant, obsessed with foolish ceremonies and political shenanigans—in short, a symbol of bad politicians everywhere.

The emperor is not quite twenty-nine years old but has ruled successfully for seven years. One controversy the emperor has faced is a religious conflict caused by a debate over which end of an egg to open—the big end or the little end. After his grandfather was injured by a Big End, the government outlawed their usage. Rebel Big Enders (representing Catholics) have been persecuted by Little Enders (representing Protestants) and many have fled to Lilliput's enemy, Bledfuscu (representing France).

The emperor wants to punish the Big-Ender Blefuscudians, just as the Whig party wanted to be harsher toward the Catholic French and Spanish than the Tories wanted to be when England was settling the War of the Spanish Succession. Gulliver helps repel an attack by the Bledfuscudian navy but refuses to conquer and enslave the attackers. As a result, while the emperor is respectful toward Gulliver, he is easily persuaded by his counselors to turn against him.

Media Adaptations

- A live-action miniseries *Gulliver's Travels* was made for television in 1996 by Charles Sturridge from a screenplay by Simon Moore. The film starred Ted Danson as Gulliver, as well as Mary Steenburgen, Peter O'Toole, Ned Beatty, Alfre Woodard, Geraldine Chaplin, Ned Beatty, John Gielgud, Kristin Scott Thomas, and Omar Sharif. Longer and containing more of the book's plot than other film versions of *Gulliver's Travels,* this version nevertheless takes some big liberties, adding a secondary plot featuring Gulliver's wife (Steenburgen) and son. However, much of Swift's satire is maintained and the special effects are far superior to those in earlier versions (much of the work was done by Jim Henson Productions). Available on two videos from Hallmark Home Entertainment.

- The 1939 animated film *Gulliver's Travels,* directed by Dave Fleischer with screenplay by Dan Gordon, Ted Pierce, Isidore Sparber, and Edmond Seward, featured the voices of Lanny Ross and Jessica Dragonette. Nominated for two Academy Awards, for Best Score and Best Song (for the song "Faithful Forever"). The film cuts several episodes from the plot and eliminates most of Swift's satire, but the animation is of exceptionally high quality for the era. Available from Congress Entertainment, Moore Video, and Nostalgia Family Video.

- The partially animated *Gulliver's Travels* (1977), directed by Peter Hunt from a screenplay by Don Black, starred Richard Harris (as Gulliver), Catherine Schell, Norman Shelley, and Meredith Edwards, and the voices of Michael Bates and Denis Bryer. The film cuts much from the plot and eliminates most of Swift's satire, making the movie cloying and childish at times. Available from Video Treasures, Hollywood Home Entertainment, and Reader's Digest Home Video.

- Containing animation effects from Ray Harryhausen, *The Three Worlds of Gulliver* (1960; also known as *The Worlds of Gulliver*), was directed by Jack Sher from a screenplay by Arthur Ross and Jack Sher, and starred Kerwin Mathews (as Gulliver), Jo Morrow, and June Thorburn. The film cuts much from the plot, focusing on Gulliver's adventures in Lilliput and Brobdingnag, and adding a character as a love interest for Gulliver. Much of Swift's satire is maintained, however. Available from Columbia Tristar Home Video.

- Two animated versions of *Gulliver's Travels* from 1979 include a short version aimed at children and narrated by Vincent Price, available from AIMS Multimedia on video, and a slightly longer version from Hanna Barbera Productions featuring the voices of Ross Martin and Janet Waldo, available on video from Worldvision Home Video, Inc. and Goodtimes Entertainment.

- An unabridged audio reading of *Gulliver's Travels,* narrated by Norman Dietz, is available on eight cassettes (10 hours, 45 minutes) from Recorded Books, Inc., 1989. Abridged versions include an audio dramatization originally presented on NBC Theater (a radio program), narrated by Henry Hull, available on one cassette from Metacom audio library classics, 1991; and a dramatization read by Ted Danson, available on two cassettes from Simon & Schuster Audioworks, 1996.

Empress of Lilliput

The empress likes Gulliver at first; he charms her by kissing her hand. However, when he extinguishes the fire in her quarters of the palace by urinating on the building, she is repulsed and turns against him. She represents Queen Anne, who denied Swift a position in the Church of England because she thought his satirical writings were vulgar, even though one of those writings, *A Tale of a Tub,* defended the Church of England against the

Puritans and Roman Catholics. Queen Anne also ungratefully exiled Swift's friend, Bolingbroke, after he'd gone through the trouble of negotiating a peace with France, thereby ending the War of Spanish Succession.

Quinbus Flestrin
See Dr. Lemuel Gulliver

Flimnap

Flimnap is Lord High Treasurer of Lilliput and the best rope dancer in the emperor's cabinet. Swift meant him to represent politician Robert Walpole, leader of the Whigs (represented by the fictional Low Heels). Walpole is recognized as England's first prime minister, and Swift considered him a corrupt symbol of an oppressive party. Political office in Lilliput is gained through rope-dancing competition, and Flimnap, the ultimate politician, can turn somersaults in the air. He would have hurt himself in his acrobatics had he not been caught by a cushion, which is Swift's allusion to how George I's mistress, the Duchess of Kendall, helped save Walpole's political career in 1721.

Flimnap is an archconservative who gets upset when he realizes how much it will cost the kingdom to continue to support Gulliver, and thus turns against him. He is suspicious of Gulliver as well, thinking that his wife is somehow having an affair with him. He urges the emperor to get rid of Gulliver by any means necessary and helps draw up charges of treason against Gulliver. Unlike Skyresh Bolgolam, Flimnap is two-faced—pleasant to Gulliver's face but secretly his enemy.

Glumdalclitch

Glumdalclitch is the nine-year-old daughter of the Brobdingnagian farmer who discovers Gulliver in his field. Gulliver names her Glumdalclitch, meaning "little nurse." She is kind to Gulliver, whom she treats like a precious doll, and is allowed to continue being his nursemaid when he becomes the possession of the king and queen.

Governor of Glubbdubdrib

The governor of Glubbdubdrib, whom Gulliver meets on his third voyage, is the most powerful sorcerer on an island of magicians. He is able to summon spirits of the dead and calls up famous politicians and philosophers of old for Gulliver's entertainment. Swift included this section mostly to show how modern historians gloss over the corruption of conquerors and kings and "how degenerate the human race was in the past."

Grildrig
See Emperor of Lilliput

Golbasto Momaren Evlame Gurdilo Shefin Mully Ully Gue
See Emperor of Lilliput

Dr. Lemuel Gulliver

Dr. Lemuel Gulliver is a medical doctor with an itch to sail the seas rather than make money by cheating his patients—a practice of many of his fellow doctors. He is honest, hardworking, and curious, good with languages (which helps in his travels), and has a well-rounded education. Swift portrays Gulliver as a typical middle-class Englishman of the time, complete with wife and children. In his fictional letters at the front of the book, we see a cranky, eccentric (perhaps crazy?), and misanthropic Gulliver, but the letter from his editor suggests to us that Gulliver is an honest person, well-liked by his neighbors, and hints that we will learn much more about him in the pages that follow.

As a character, Gulliver is quite inconsistent. At times he seems to be the mouthpiece for Swift himself, voicing the author's opinions. At other times, he is quite proud and arrogant, even unlikable. Often, he is naive and easily influenced by others. Even his name, "Gulliver," suggests he is gullible. (As for his first name, "Lemuel" is a character in the Bible who is urged by his mother to judge rightly and plead the cause of the poor and needy; morality figures greatly in Gulliver's adventures.) Swift intends for readers to be skeptical about Gulliver's perceptions and morality. Gulliver is a detailed person and seems honest, so we should not doubt his facts. How he interprets those facts, however, is something we should question. In doing so, readers will begin to question their own prejudices and human failings, their own opinions and beliefs, and their own institutions.

Gulliver is at first called Quinbus Flestrin (which he translates as Man Mountain) by the Lilliputians, and then is given the honorable title of Nardac by the emperor after he captures the enemy's fleet. The Brobdingnagian girl who takes care of him renames him Grildrig, meaning "little dwarf." The Brobdingnagians also refer to him as a *splacknuck* after an animal of the region that is about his size. By the end of the book, Gulliver is unmistakably a misanthrope (hater of humankind), preferring the company of horses to humans, even his own family. This "madness" is the result of his fourth and final voyage, in which he was confronted with the imperfections of humanity.

Mary Burton Gulliver

Dr. Gulliver's wife, daughter of Edmond Burton, figures little into the story. After the second voyage, Gulliver criticizes her for being too thrifty, since he left her with plenty of money. She is not happy about Gulliver's choice to keep going to sea, although she agrees to allow the third voyage because it will help the family.

Houyhnhnm

Pronounced "Whin-ems," like a horse's whinny, the Houyhnhnm are a race of intelligent horses Gulliver encounters in Book IV. They are different from horses in eighteenth-century England because they are the masters over the human-like Yahoos who toil for them. The Houyhnhnm have an nearly utopian or ideal society and are unfamiliar with the concepts of lying, deceit, jealousy, or hatred. They love all Houyhnhnm equally, enabling them to choose their partners not according to love or passion but according to genetics—that is, which pairings would produce the healthiest offspring. They school their children communally and govern themselves democratically.

Critics have long argued whether Swift presents the Houyhnhnm as an ideal society or whether they, too, are set up for satire. Those who argue the latter view point out how casually the Houyhnhnm treat the death of a spouse or loss of a child. Gulliver admires the Houyhnhnm greatly, but he can never be one of them any more than he can digest their horse's diet. He is a human, and hates this reality, but Swift implies that Gulliver ought to accept his human nature. After all, for all their positive attributes, the Houyhnhnm can't feel passionate love as humans can.

Laputans

Inhabitants of the flying island encountered in Part III, the Laputans have one eye perpetually inward (symbolizing introspection) and one eye perpetually skyward (symbolizing lofty ideals). They are brilliant, completely impractical, and so caught up in their intellectual pursuits that their servants have to slap them around to get their attention so that they can have conversations. They wear ill-fitting garments with celestial symbols on them, worship science and music, and oppress other lands, demanding taxes. Those who don't pay up are pelted with rocks. Although the Laputans threaten to smash those below with their island, they never

do so because it might hurt the island. The Laputans represent Enlightenment thinkers who worship ideas at the expense of practicality. Note that "Laputa" is a play on "La puta," which is Spanish for "prostitute": the Laputans have prostituted science by fixing on knowledge for knowledge's sake, instead of putting intellectual theory to practical use.

Lilliputians

The Lilliputians are six-inch-tall people Gulliver encounters on his first travel in Book I. They live near Van Diemen's Land (Australia). Swift implies that with their petty politics, they are moral midgets as well as physical midgets in comparison to the Englishman Gulliver.

Pedro de Mendez

The captain of the Portuguese ship that rescues Gulliver on his fourth and final travel, he is extremely kind and sympathetic to Gulliver, helping him to return to England. Gulliver has been traumatized by his most recent travel and the realization that mankind in general is more Yahoo than Houyhnhnm. Thus, while Mendez is a contrast to the Yahoos, Gulliver has trouble appreciating the goodness of Mendez. Swift likely created this character to remind the reader that even if mankind is corrupt and selfish, individuals exist who are kind and good.

Lord Munodi

Lord Munodi is the former governor of the rebellious city Lagado on Balnibari, the island oppressed by the Laputans in the third voyage. Unlike his neighbors' fields and homes, Munodi's house and land are intact and prosperous because he ignored the newfangled advice of the Projectors, scientists who insisted that farmers try new "improvements" that in the end were disastrous. Munodi represents the sensible man who does not toss away tradition and insist that newer is always better.

Reldresal

Lilliput's Principal Secretary of Private Affairs, Reldresal is second only to Flimnap at rope dancing. He explains to Gulliver many of the Lilliputians' customs and the origin of the war against the Blefuscudians, asking him to help in the war effort. When Gulliver falls out of favor with the court, Reldresal proposes "mercy" in the form of putting out his eyes instead of taking his life. Reldresal represents one of George I's counselors.

Slamecksans

Lilliputians who belong to the Low Heels political party, representing the real-life Whigs of England.

Struldbruggs

In Book III, Gulliver encounters the Struldbruggs in the kingdom of Luggnagg. The Struldbruggs have immortal life but not immortal youth, so they become senile and frail. Swift uses the Struldbruggs to examine society's fear of death.

Richard Sympson

Richard Sympson is Gulliver's fictional cousin, who gets the book of *Gulliver's Travels* published. In a letter to the reader, he defends his editorial work on the book, setting up the idea that Gulliver is focused on details at the expense of a larger vision, which guides the reader into being skeptical about Gulliver's perceptions of events but not his facts. Sympson also defends Gulliver himself, who seems like a cranky character, suggesting that once the reader has read of these adventures he will have more sympathy for Gulliver. Thus, Sympson is less a character than a device.

Tramecksans

The Tramecksans are Lilliputians who belong to the High Heels political party, representing the real-life Tories of England.

Yahoos

The Yahoos are a barbaric race of filthy, repulsive humanoids who live in the country of the Houyhnhnm. They resemble human beings so much that the Houyhnhnm have trouble believing that Gulliver is not one of them. They represent mankind at its very worst. Gulliver begins to use the term "Yahoo" to refer to any human who is barbaric, cruel, and immoral, and later calls all humans "Yahoos."

Themes

Human Condition

Gulliver's Travels is political satire in the form of an adventure novel. Swift creates several fantasy worlds to which his character, Lemuel Gulliver, travels, and where he learns that English institutions, such as the government and social structure, are not necessarily ideal.

Swift subscribed to the pre-Enlightenment, Protestant idea that man is by nature sinful, having fallen from perfection in the Garden of Eden. While man is a rational animal, his rationality is not always used for good. Therefore, one should not hold up rationality as the greatest human quality, as many Enlightenment thinkers did. It is the human condition, Swift felt, to sin: to be deceitful, cruel, selfish, materialistic, vain, foolish, and otherwise flawed. Rationality and institutions such as governments, churches, and social structures (schools, for example) exist to rein in man's tendency to sin, to keep him in line.

These beliefs of Swift's are evident throughout *Gulliver's Travels*. Naive Gulliver encounters his physical and moral inferiors, the Lilliputians, and sees that they have well-thought-out but illogical and even unethical ideas about justice, schooling children, and choosing political leaders. On the contrary, Gulliver's physical and moral superiors, the Brobdingnagians, do not suffer war or strife because their political and social structures are far superior to England's. Part III is a scathing indictment of how Enlightenment thinkers value rationality, science, discoveries, and new ideas over traditional, practical ways of doing things. Note, for example, that only Count Munodi's arm thrives because he does not embrace the Projectors' newfangled ways. Practicality and tradition, Swift believed, have great value. Finally, in Part IV, Swift contrasts the best that man was (in the Garden of Eden before the Fall), represented by the Houyhnhnm, with the debased state to which he can fall, represented by the Yahoo. While Swift suggests that we can never return to that state of perfection, because it is the human condition to sin, we can at least rise above our Yahoo-ness.

Politics

Swift was not only a clergyman but a political writer and activist, writing for the Tory paper at one point in his career and writing political pamphlets. He was deeply involved in the battles between the Whigs and Tories and active in trying to help England's oppression of Ireland. He and some of his friends were also the victims of petty politics. No wonder Swift chose to ridicule the worst aspects of politics in *Gulliver's Travels*.

Most of Swift's scathing political satire can be found in Part I, which mirrors the events in England in Swift's day. The petty Lilliputian emperor represents the worst kind of governor, pompous and too easily influenced by his counselors' selfish ambitions. He is also a stand-in for King George I, from his identification with the Whig party (the fictional Low Heels) to his betrayal of his friend and helper, Gulliver (who represents Swift and his Tory friends Oxford and Bolingbroke), to his ridiculous means of choosing his advisors and rewarding them with meaningless ribbons (which represent titles and other useless favors bestowed by George I on his cronies). The king and his cabinet demand a cruel and, Gulliver thinks, unjust punishment of the rebel Blefuscudians, just as George I and the Whigs wanted to punish France more severely than the Tories did when negotiating the Treaty of Utrecht that ended England's war against France and Spain.

Then, too, Swift explores the duties and purpose of government in Parts I, II, and IV. By having Gulliver discuss his system of government and compare it to the ones he discovers, Swift raises questions about government's role in public education, provisions for the poor, and distribution of wealth. Part of what makes *Gulliver's Travels* so provocative and timely even today is that Swift doesn't provide simplistic answers to these questions. His observations about partisan politics, unchecked corruption, and dubious qualifications of political leaders unfortunately ring true even in contemporary America.

Culture Clash

When people of two different cultures come in contact with each other, they often experience "culture clash": they are surprised and a unsettled when they are confronted with the other's customs. Gulliver is the odd man out whenever he travels to other countries, and is curious about the customs of the people he meets. He is quite surprised at times by the differences between his way of life and theirs. He discusses English institutions and customs at length with both the Brobdingnagians and the Houyhnhnm. He is confident, even arrogant, in his belief that once these foreigners hear of British ways they will be impressed by his people. To his surprise, disappointment, and frustration, they ask obvious questions about flaws and shortcomings of British institutions and customs. The Brobdingnagian king is horrified at the concept of gunpowder, and he tells Gulliver that his race must be "the most pernicious race of little odious vermin that nature ever suffered to crawl upon the surface of the earth." The Houyhnhnm simply can't understand the concept of lying, and are amazed and horrified to hear that in England, horses are enslaved by men, because in their country the humanoid Yahoos are their slaves. The more Gulliver tries to explain England's ways, the more

Topics for Further Study

- Discuss how Gulliver's travels change him and the way he perceives his fellow man.

- Research actual historical explorers of the 1600s and early 1700s. Compare and contrast their voyages with Gulliver's journeys, and quote from actual historical accounts if you can find them.

- Based on having read *Gulliver's Travels,* would you say Jonathan Swift was a misanthrope (a person who hated mankind)? Support your argument with quotes and examples from the text.

- Investigate philosophical thought of the 1600s and early 1700s regarding the nature of man. Compare the analyses of philosophers such as René Descartes, Thomas Hobbes, Gottfried Leibniz, and John Locke with Gulliver's opinions as expressed in the novel.

- Explain why Swift gave Gulliver the habit of describing people, places, items, and events in specific, sometimes almost scientific, detail.

shocked and repulsed the Houyhnhnm and Brobdingnagians are, and the more the reader sees how blind Gulliver is to the shortcomings of his own kind. The contrast between Gulliver's way of life and the foreigners', even that of the Lilliputians and Laputans, is intended to nudge readers into asking hard questions of their own culture.

Custom and Tradition

Swift is one of the most acclaimed satirists of the English language because of his clever use of language and symbolism to make his points in a humorous way. Satire, or holding up to ridicule human vices and folly, often involves irony, or words that mean more than the characters realize, or something entirely different altogether. The gullible Gulliver's straightforward reporting of absurdities creates this irony. For example, he tells us matter-of-factly that the Lilliputians bury their dead head first because they believe that when the end of the world comes the flat earth will flip upside down, leaving them right side up for the afterlife. He also notes that many Lilliputians no longer actually believe this is necessary, but follow tradition anyway. This passage is satirical as well, because it is representative of all sorts of traditions, religious and otherwise, that human beings create and cling to long after they've stopped believing in them.

Science and Technology

Swift also parodies the scientists of his day in order to make his point that science for its own sake is not a lofty ideal. Science, and the ability to reason, ought to be used for practical ends, he felt, to address and solve the many real-life problems. He drew upon actual scientific experiments in Part III, when the scientists of Balnibarbi defy the law of nature with such ludicrous experiments as extracting sunshine from cucumbers. The absurdity of their impracticality—for example, they can't even sew clothes for themselves that fit because their way of measuring is so screwball—makes them objects of ridicule.

Style

Point of View

Lemuel Gulliver himself narrates the story of *Gulliver's Travels,* but this first-person narrator is not completely reliable. Though Gulliver is very exact with the details of his travels, and we know him to be honest, sometimes he doesn't see the forest for the trees. Swift deliberately makes Gulliver naive and sometimes even arrogant for two reasons. First, it makes the reader more skeptical about the ideas presented in the book. Second, it allows the reader to have a good laugh at Gulliver's expense when he doesn't realize the absurdity of his limited viewpoint. He certainly sounds foolish when extolling the qualities of gunpowder to the peaceful Brobdingnagians, for example. Also, at the end of the novel, the reader can see that Gulliver has turned into a misanthrope (hater of humanity), but can hear in his voice both here and in the introductory letter to his publisher that he is proud and arrogant in his belief that humans are Yahoos. Because by the end of the book readers are accustomed to being skeptical of Gulliver's perceptions, one can guess that his misanthropy has something to do with his arrogance. Humans simply can't be

perfect and if we hold ourselves to that ideal we will hate humanity, but Gulliver can't see this truth. Swift claimed that it was not he that was misanthropic, but Gulliver, the narrator he created.

Setting

Although the fantastic lands that provide the setting for *Gulliver's Travels* seem unreal today, modern readers should keep in mind that the settings would not have seemed so farfetched to Swift's contemporaries. The novel was written in the 1720s, and Gulliver travels to areas that were still unknown or little explored during this time. The book was written before the discovery of the Bering Strait between Alaska and Russia, for example, where Brobdingnag is supposedly located. It was also before the discovery of an effective means of measuring latitude, which meant it was very difficult for sailors to navigate and explore new territory accurately. Travelogues, or accounts of journeys to foreign lands, were very popular at this time, so the reading public was accustomed to hearing of new geographical discoveries. Thus Gulliver's explorations to new lands, while unusual, would have seemed little different than the strange tales of "exotic" lands in America, Asia, and Africa. Like the travelogues it parodies, *Gulliver's Travels* even provides maps of Gulliver's journeys in the book to lend more truthfulness to the story.

Structure

Structurally, *Gulliver's Travels* is divided into four parts with two introductory letters at the beginning of the book. These letters, from Gulliver and his editor Sympson, let us know that Gulliver is basically a good person who has been very much changed by the amazing journeys to follow. Part I follows Gulliver's journey to Lilliput and its tiny people; Part II to Brobdingnag and its giants; Part III to several islands and countries near Japan; Part IV follows Gulliver to the country of the Houyhnhnm. The first and second parts set up contrasts that allow Swift to satirize European politics and society. The third part satirizes human institutions and thinking and is subdivided into four sections that are set in Laputa, Balnibarbi, Glubbdubdrib, and Luggnagg. The first two sections are seen as a critique of sciences and scholars; the Glubbdubdrib section looks at history; and the Luggnagg section at Swift's fears about getting old. The final section moves from criticizing humanity's works to examining the flawed nature of humanity itself.

Utopia

The idea of a perfect society, with institutions such as government, school, and churches that are flawless in design, began with the ancient Greeks and was explored by Thomas More's *Utopia* (1516). Many writers before and since Jonathan Swift have toyed with the idea of utopia, and some contemporary writers have even written novels about anti-utopias (properly known as dystopias), in which utopian visions have gone terribly wrong—for example, George Orwell's *1984* and Aldous Huxley's *Brave New World.* Both of these authors were fans of *Gulliver's Travels.*

Gulliver finds a near-utopia in the land of Brobdingnag, where war and oppression are unheard of. In this section, Swift incorporated many of the ideas of the social engineers of his day. Swift's impatience with utopian theories is also evident, however. Because the Brobdingnagians are humanlike, their utopia is not completely perfect. They can be insensitive, treating Gulliver as some sort of pet or toy, and their society includes poor beggars. In Luggnagg, Gulliver is told of a race of men who are immortal, and he imagines that their wisdom must be great, making their society well-ordered and their people happy and content. Unfortunately, everlasting life does not combat the effects of old age, and the immortals are objects of pity and disgust. Swift comes close to creating a perfect utopia with the Houyhnhnm, but suggests that man can never really fit in a perfect society, because he is by his nature flawed. Therefore, he can only strive for the ideal, and never reach it.

But would we want to? The Brobdingnagian society is imperfect, but the people are wise and humane. While the Houyhnhnm society does not have grief, lying or deceit, greed or lust, ambition or opinion, it also doesn't have love as we know it. All the Houyhnhnm love each other equally. They chose their mates according to genetics rather than love or passion, and they raise their children communally, because they love all the children equally. Gulliver wants to rise above the human condition and be a Houyhnhnm, but Swift implies that this is neither possible nor necessarily desirable.

Allegory

An allegory is when characters or events in a work of fiction represent something from reality, such as actual people, places, events, or even ideas. In *Gulliver's Travels,* and especially in Part I, many of the things Gulliver experiences can be linked to actual historical events of Swift's time. For instance, the religious/political controversy between the Big Enders and Little Enders corresponds to actual conflicts between Protestants and Catholics that led to several wars. Lilliput stands for England, while Blefuscu stands for England's longtime enemy, France. The two-faced Treasurer Flimnap corresponds to the Whig leader Sir Robert Walpole, while the Empress's outrage at Gulliver's extinguishing a palace fire with his urine mirrors the complaints Queen Anne had about Swift's "vulgar" writings. The numerous allegories to be found in the novel added to satire Swift's readers would have enjoyed. They have also provided critics throughout the years with valuable material for analysis.

Historical Context

England in the 1720s

While Swift was writing *Gulliver's Travels* in the 1720s, England was undergoing a lot of political shuffling. George I, a Hanoverian prince of Germany, had ascended the British throne in 1714 after the death of Queen Anne ended the Stuart line. Although he was not a bad or repressive king, he was unpopular. King George had gained his throne with the assistance of the Whig party, and his Whig ministers subsequently used their considerable gains in power to oppress members of the opposition Tory party. Swift had been a Tory since 1710, and bitterly resented the Whig actions against his friends, who often faced exile or worse. Understanding how events in Europe and England led to this political rivalry can help the reader of Swift's novel better understand his satire.

The Restoration

The Restoration era began in 1660, a few years before Swift was born. At this time Charles Stuart (King Charles II) became king of England, restoring the Protestant Stuart family to the throne. Charles II supported a strong Church of England, also known as the Anglican Church. He was supported by the Tories, a political party made up mostly of church officials and landowning noblemen. Protestants who did not support the Anglican church teamed with Roman Catholics to form the opposing Whig party. The main source of contention between the parties was the Test Act of 1673, which forced all government employees to receive communion according to the Anglican church's customs. In effect, this prevented non-An-

Compare & Contrast

- **1720s:** Robert Walpole is England's first prime minister, and German-born King George I gives him a great deal of authority to run the country.

  Today: Britain's ruler is only a figurehead and the prime minister is the leader who wields real power. The House of Lords and House of Commons still make up the Parliament.

- **1720s:** The Great Awakening begins to sweep the American colonies, as people are converted to Protestantism by charismatic evangelists. In England, John Wesley, an Anglican priest, begins to form the Evangelical Methodist movement in 1729.

  Today: Worldwide, of 1.9 billion Christians, almost half (968 million) are Roman Catholic, 70 million are Anglican (Episcopalian), 218 million are Eastern Orthodox, 395 million are Protestant, and 275 million belong to other denominations.

---

glicans from holding government jobs. Swift himself supported the act, and even switched from Whig to Tory in 1710 because he believed a strong Church of England was necessary to keep the balance of power in the government. Throughout his life, he felt that institutions such as the church and government had to be strong in order to rein in people's tendency toward chaos and sin; he explored this idea in *Gulliver's Travels.* Over the years, however, Swift came to believe the Tories were as much to blame as the Whigs for engaging in partisan politics, locking horns over minor issues and bringing the government to a stalemate. Whenever one party was in favor with the reigning king and in power in the Parliament, it attacked the other party, exiling and imprisoning the opposition's members. Swift satirized their selfish and petty politics in Part I of *Gulliver's Travels,* where the Lilliputian heir (who represented George II, the future king of England) has to hobble about with one short heel and one high as a compromise between the two parties that wear different heights of heels.

The Glorious Revolution and War of Spanish Succession

Charles II's brother King James II, a Catholic, came to the British throne in 1685. He immediately repealed the Test Act and began to hire Whigs for his government. The Anglican-dominated Parliament secretly negotiated with William of Orange, the Protestant Dutch husband of James's Protestant daughter Mary, to take over the throne. In December 1688, William did so, and James II fled to France without a fight. This was called the Glorious Revolution because no one was killed in the coup.

Soon after King William III and Queen Mary II came to power, the Catholic Louis XIV of France declared war on Spain over trade and religious issues. William entered the war on the side of Spain, a war the English called William's War. This conflict was satirized by Swift in the war between the Lilliputians (England) and Blefuscudians (England with the Spanish, Dutch, and Germans as allies) was fighting France, it was also warring with Ireland. Irish Catholics wanted freedom from British rule, and England feared that France could invade their country through a sympathetic Ireland. Peace came about in 1697, but England got almost none of the spoils of war—land in Spain. In order to appear strong, William declared war again, this time on the Spanish and the French. This began the War of Spanish Succession.

In 1702 William died and his daughter Queen Anne ascended the throne. The war waged on while at home the Whigs and Tories fought amongst themselves. Many of the Whigs were merchants who were profiting from the war, and they wanted the fighting to continue. The landowning Tories wanted the war to cease, because it devalued their property. Swift helped the Tories in their efforts to stop the war by becoming editor of their newspa-

Author Jonathan Swift served as dean of St. Patrick's Cathedral (pictured here) in Dublin, Ireland.

per, the *Examiner*. His influential writings, along with his friend Bolingbroke's secret negotiations with France, helped end the war in 1713 with the Treaty of Utrecht. Queen Anne seemed ungrateful for these efforts, as she later exiled Bolingbroke and destroyed Swift's chances of a career in the Church of England. Swift was forced to return to Ireland to find a job as an Anglican priest.

Ireland

Catholic Ireland had been dominated by the British since the fifteenth century, because England had always been paranoid about a French or Spanish invasion coming through Catholic Ireland. Eng-

land's restrictive policies had driven Ireland and its people into poverty, which angered Swift. He was incensed when the scientist Sir Isaac Newton, given the task of overseeing the economics of Ireland, supported a currency law that would further destroy the economy of the Irish. His anonymously written *The Drapier's Letters,* inspired the Irish people to unite against England and force the law to be repealed. The Irish protected Swift's anonymity, and for his role, Swift is a hero in Ireland to this day.

The Enlightenment

In the midst of all this political back and forth, the optimistic Age of Enlightenment was flourishing. Intellectuals, philosophers, and scientists such as John Locke, Francis Bacon, and Isaac Newton were opening the doors to exploration in many fields, asking new questions, and experimenting. They discarded the old idea that man is by nature sinful because of Adam and Eve's fall from grace in the Garden of Eden. Man's ability to reason, they claimed, could save him from his tendency to sin. Man could create a utopia, or perfect society, that solved the problems of humankind. Swift vehemently disagreed. He felt that reason could just as easily be misused for foolish or selfish purposes as good ones, and man could never rise above the tendency toward sin to be able to create utopia on earth. His satire of the folly of Enlightenment scientific and theological musings and experiments in Part III of *Gulliver's Travels* is followed by his portrayal of a utopian society, the Houyhnhnm's, into which man can never fit.

Critical Overview

Gulliver's Travels was quite a success in its time. The first printing sold out immediately and the book was translated into French, Dutch, and German. It appealed to people from all social classes and ages, and readers thought the book was a humorous adventure tale, suitable even for children to read (the separate category of books especially for children did not come about until a generation after Swift's death). Gulliver was perceived as a "happy fellow." (Note, however, that the original editor of the work had toned down some of the satire, which was not restored to the text until 1735.) By the end of the 1700s, however, people were beginning to see past the fun adventure plot and become aware of Swift's hidden messages. Many were shocked by the negativity of the book and condemned it. Writer William Makepeace Thackeray said the message of the book was "horrible, shameful, blasphemous … filthy in word, filthy in thought" and "obscene," and certainly proof that Jonathan Swift was "about the most wretched being in God's world."

Sir Walter Scott obviously thought *Gulliver's Travels* had some merit or he wouldn't have published a collection of Swift's works in 1814. He noted that the work was "unequalled for the skill with which [the narrative] is sustained, and the genuine spirit of satire of which it is made the vehicle." He also declared, however, that the book was "severe, unjust and degrading" and dismissed early

fans as people who, like Swift, had obviously been in a "state of gloomy misanthropy." Swift was accused again and again of being a bitter misanthrope who hated mankind, a pessimist who wouldn't acknowledge the good qualities of human beings. For a time only Part III was considered acceptable reading, and Part IV was considered exceptionally offensive right up through the 1800s. In 1889, Edmund Gosse urged "decent" people to avoid reading Part IV because of the "horrible foulness of this satire." And in 1882 Leslie Stephen speculated that the "oppressive" tone of "misanthropy" in Parts III and IV must have been the result of Swift's bitterness over ill health and dashed ambitions and suggested that readers skip them altogether. His contemporary, Churton Collins, said the book had "no moral, no social, no philosophical purpose." The novel's controversial messages about politics and the nature of man even led to censorship. In later editions, right up until 1899, the Lindalinian revolt at the end of Part III was excised because it was (probably correctly) interpreted as a symbol of the righteousness of a potential Irish revolt.

However, despite the early controversies, critics over the years have come to hail *Gulliver's Travels* as the greatest satire by the greatest prose satirist in the English language. An early fan, William Hazlitt, said in 1818 that Swift's object had not been to spew venom but to "strip empty pride and grandeur" and "to show men what they are, and to teach them what they ought to be." Novelist Aldous Huxley (author of the antiutopian novel *Brave New World*) said in the early twentieth century that Swift was an incurable sentimentalist and romantic who resented reality. Indeed, most critics today think that Swift has been misunderstood, probably since many readers have mistakenly assumed that Gulliver, who certainly is a misanthrope at the end, is a mouthpiece for Swift.

Swift's bitterness, contemporary critics argue, is not the product of insanity or illness but the inevitable result of a caring, compassionate, religious man who had seen the worst side of human nature. As a young man, Swift had tried to serve his country through work with political parties, and wanted to serve in the Church of England, but petty politics destroyed his and his friends' plans and drove them into exile. In Ireland, Swift saw the greed of the British drive a country of people to poverty and desperation. He tried, in *Gulliver's Travels,* to alert people to the ugliness of human behavior. Yet at the same time, he hoped that the novel, and his other works, would rouse them to strive to do better. Swift denied that he hated people. He wrote, "I have ever hated all Nations, professions, and Communityes and all my love is toward individuals." His inclusion of the kindly, charitable Captain Pedro de Mendez in the end of the book supports Swift's claim that he believed there are good, admirable individuals in the world.

As for novel itself, critics have generally agreed that Part III is the weakest and least unified of the four sections, possibly because it was the last written. Some have claimed the fourth section of Part III is an unnecessary departure from the major themes of the book, focusing as it does on Swift's fears of growing old and senile (which, in fact, he did). Also, in Part III, Gulliver is merely an observer, which makes the voyage less engaging than the others.

Critics have agreed about what Swift was satirizing in each of the first three voyages. They have disagreed, however, on how to interpret the fourth voyage. Do the Houyhnhnm and Yahoos represent the dual nature of humanity, good and evil? Or do the Houyhnhnm represent Swift's view that utopian thinkers are foolish in their attempts to imagine a perfect human society? Critics since 1950 have generally agreed that the Houyhnhnm are symbols of unattainable human perfection which can be the ideal we strive for, even if we fall short, and the Yahoos represent how far into ugliness we can fall if we lose sight of our ideals.

Critics have suggested that Swift intended the novel to be both an attack on mankind and its follies and a honest assessment of mankind's positive and negative qualities. It is also considered a critique of the greatest moral, philosophical, scientific, and political ideas of Swift's time. The greatest and most lasting accomplishment of *Gulliver's Travels* may be its ability to encourage readers of any society at any time to raise important questions about mankind's limitations, how we can structure our institutions to bring out the best in people, and what it means to be human.

Criticism

Dennis Todd

*In the following essay, Bloom, a doctoral candidate at Emory University, explores the historical and cultural background of Swift's satire and ex-*plains the differing interpretations of the ending of Gulliver's Travels.

Jonathan Swift's *Gulliver's Travels,* first published in 1726, was an instant hit, one of the top three sellers of the eighteenth century. It was only one of Swift's many significant works, however. Of his prose writings, the most famous include his attack on modern literature, *The Battle of the Books;* a critique of English oppression of the Irish, *A Modest Proposal;* and *A Tale of a Tub,* his defense of Protestantism and the Church of England. He is also well-known as a poet, particularly for his poems criticizing romance, such as *Cassinus and Peter* and *A Beautiful Young Nymph Going to Bed. Gulliver's Travels* addresses almost all of Swift's primary concerns and involves some of the most important questions in literature and the development of the novel.

Gulliver's Travels remains Swift's most famous and popular work. Ricardo Quintana calls it a "satire taking the form of four imaginary voyages," a formulation which explains why the story does not have the traditional plot structure of rising action-climax-denouement. Because Swift depicts the ills and sins of his society, *Gulliver's Travels* can feel like a string of episodes tied together. The book gets its unity from Gulliver himself, since his perceptions drive the story and the satire. Swift uses Gulliver and his voyages primarily to examine problems with contemporary society, such as the evils of politics, humanity's frequent foolishness, and the importance of a thoughtful, self-aware, balanced perspective. In this sense, *Gulliver's Travels* addresses issues that still worry people today. A recent television version also testifies to the book's continued appeal. Although this version is generally faithful in many places, however, it is no substitute for the book.

Swift's story takes place simultaneously at two points in time and at two levels of meaning. First, it is a recollection: Lemuel Gulliver tells the story of his adventures after they are finished. The story of Gulliver sitting at home writing about his voyages is the "frame narrative," the story of the telling of the story. Like a frame around a painting, it gives shape to Gulliver's character and to the events that he recounts. As Richard Rodino writes, "Swift the author writes the story of Gulliver the author writing the story of Gulliver the character." Second, all the events except the frame narrative take place in the past. These two levels of time enable Swift to create a work that also has two levels of meaning: the straightforward story of Gulliver's adventures,

What Do I Read Next?

- Many have said that *A Modest Proposal* by Jonathan Swift (1729) is the best satirical essay ever written. In it, he suggests that the problem of poverty among the Irish (which Swift, incidentally, blamed on British policies) would be solved if Irish babies were treated as food and fed to the wealthy. Many of Swift's contemporaries who read the essay were horrified, missing the irony. Swift's real message was that the upper classes ought to change their deplorable callousness toward the poor.

- Swift's *A Tale of a Tub* (1704) is a religious allegory featuring three brothers who represent the Anglican, Roman Catholic, and dissenting Christians (who believe in a personal, non-institutional form of Christianity). Swift uses his satire and fiction writing abilities to make his point that Anglicism is the happy medium between the egotistic individualism of other Protestants and the rigid institutionalism of the Catholic church.

- Swift's *The Battle of the Books* (1704), published along with *A Tale of a Tub,* is a satire about the purpose of history, which Swift believed was not to pile up facts and events but to develop a moral philosophy. Swift pits ancient books against modern ones in a war that takes place in a library.

- *Utopia* by Thomas More (1516) is a classic work of western philosophy. Saint Thomas More wrote this blueprint for an ideal human society in the form of a dialogue between More and a fictional traveler, Raphael Hythlodaeus, who describes a foreign country where the inhabitants's customs bring out the best in their people.

- *Alice's Adventures in Wonderland* and *Through the Looking Glass* by Lewis Carroll (1865 and 1872 respectively) are, like *Gulliver's Travels,* works of satire disguised as children's adventure stories. Both books are fantastical stories about a little girl named Alice who travels through absurd worlds, having fallen down a rabbit hole or stepped into a mirror.

- *Candide* by Francois Voltaire (1759) is a funny, satirical novel about a simple fellow named Candide who learns from his travels and his teacher, Pangloss, to be less idealistic and more pragmatic. He learns that work is rewarding and decides that everything is not for the best after all.

- *A Connecticut Yankee in King Arthur's Court* by Mark Twain (1889) is a satirical story about a young man, Hank Morgan, who wakes up in England during King Arthur's reign after suffering a blow to the head. He tries to bring democracy to feudal England with less-than-desirable results.

---

and the satire of Swift's world. By making Gulliver look back on his life and explain it, Swift allows readers to see Gulliver as unreliable, a man whose opinions must be questioned.

The two levels of meaning, the adventure and the satire, come from Swift's use of a popular kind of literature, the travel narrative. It is important to remember while reading *Gulliver's Travels* that Swift's world was very different from ours. Captain Cook had not yet sailed around the world; he would not be born until 1728. Lewis and Clark would not head west across North America for an-

other seventy years, and much of the continent was still inhabited only by Native American tribes. It was not unusual to be the first westerners to discover new islands (the Dutch found Easter Island in 1722), to make the first maps of a coast, or to find strange and exotic people, plants, and animals. The eighteenth-century public was as excited to read about travels to strange lands such as Africa, India, and the Middle East, as well as North and South America, as the twentieth-century public is to hear about celebrities. They were also used to a wider diversity of reading material, and, because it was so hard to prove things were true, were more comfortable with not knowing whether a story was fiction or not.

The travel narrative did more than allow Swift to create an exciting "true" story, however. It also gave him a way to criticize the familiar world of eighteenth-century England. Swift "defamiliarized" aspects of English life such as political or social practices by having Gulliver describe them to people who had never encountered them before, or as if they were things he had never seen before. In some cases, this defamiliarization is amusing. When the Lilliputians search Gulliver's pockets, for example, they find a "Globe, half Silver, and half some transparent Metal: For on the transparent Side we saw certain strange Figures circularly drawn, and thought we could touch them, until we found our Fingers stopped with that lucid Substance. He put this Engine to our Ears, which made an incessant Noise like that of a Water-Mill." What is this unusual object? A pocket watch. By making aspects of England such as fashions or the government seem strange to Gulliver or the people he meets, Swift could make those aspects seem strange to his readers, which in turn could make readers see how silly or bad these aspects of their lives really were.

But with his unreliable narrator, Gulliver, Swift could also extend his satire from the foolish things people do to the way they judge and think. When Swift wishes to criticize violence and wars, he has Gulliver describe something very comfortable and familiar to English readers—gunpowder—to someone who knows nothing about it. The response forces readers to question what they otherwise accept as part of life. Gulliver describes how the English put "Powder into large hollow Balls of Iron, and discharged them by an Engine into some City we were besieging; which would rip up the Pavement, tear the Houses to Pieces, burst and throw Splinters on every Side, dashing out the Brains of all who came near." The King of Brobdingnag does not react as Gulliver or the reader expects: "The King was struck with horror at the Description I had given of those terrible Engines, and the Proposal I had made. He was amazed how so impotent and groveling an Insect as I (these were his Expressions) could entertain such inhuman ideas, and in so familiar a Manner as to appear wholly unmoved at the Scenes of Blood and Desolation, which I had painted...." Confronted with the King's reaction, the reader can recognize that blowing people up really is appalling.

Swift uses perspective as his main theme. In the first two books, Gulliver himself is the wrong

size, and Swift exploits the possibilities of Gulliver's inevitable difficulty in perceiving. In Lilliput, where Gulliver is so much bigger than everyone else, he has an exaggerated sense of his own importance and in the correctness of his understanding. In Brobdingnag, where he is so much smaller, Gulliver struggles to make everyone take him seriously. In the second two books, Gulliver thinks differently from the people he meets. The Laputans, for example, prize reason and the scientific method above even common sense, and even Gulliver understands the foolishness of his hosts. In Book IV, however, Gulliver is sucked in by the Houyhnhnms' (whin-hims) philosophy. Seduced into accepting a false either-or (he must be either a Yahoo or a Houyhnhnm, according to the Houyhnhnms, but in fact he is a third creature, a human), Gulliver becomes as extreme as the Laputans, learning to hate humanity, especially himself. Throughout *Gulliver's Travels,* Swift challenges his readers' acceptance of social, political, military, economic, and philosophical practices, and he concludes by reminding his readers of the frailty and foolishness involved in simply being human.

Book IV, the Voyage to Houyhnhnm-land, is considered the darkest and most controversial part of *Gulliver's Travels.* Critics disagree about how much of Lemuel Gulliver's hatred for humanity is really Jonathan Swift's hatred for humanity. This disagreement involves two issues: 1) how much of Gulliver can we equate with Swift, and 2) how should we read the end of *Gulliver's Travels*? Critics sometimes call Gulliver a "persona" for Swift, meaning that Gulliver is a mask which Swift can put on and from behind which he can make certain critical statements. Most scholars, however, agree that Gulliver is not a persona but a character who occasionally gets to say things Swift really means, but more often says things that are the opposite of what Swift means.

The question, how we are to understand the last book, has caused much disagreement among readers since it first appeared in print. There are two ways of reading the message at the end of Book IV, the end of *Gulliver's Travels:* the "hard" and the "soft" readings. The hard reading says that Swift and Gulliver agree about how horrible humanity is and that our last view of Gulliver, stopping his nose with tobacco to avoid smelling other people and afraid to socialize with other "yahoos," is Swift's pronouncement on humanity. Gulliver's description of his happiness living with the Houyhnhnms is an indictment of human society: with the Houyhnhnms, he says, "I did not feel the Treachery or Inconstancy of a Friend, nor the injuries of a secret or open Enemy. I had no occasion for bribing, flattering or pimping, to procure the favour of any great Man, or of his Minion. I wanted no Fence against fraud or Oppression: here was neither Physician to destroy my Body, nor Lawyer to ruin my Fortune … " and so on.

The soft reading takes a very different stand. In this view, Gulliver is the butt of the joke just as other characters and even Gulliver have been elsewhere (think about his offer of gunpowder to the King of Brobdingnag, for example). His refusal to participate in human society is the result of his own unbalanced thinking, a cardinal sin in Swift's book. Instead of accurately depicting his fellow creatures as neither angels nor brutes and beasts, this reading says that Gulliver paints them with the unsubtle and unreliable brush of a fanatic. His daily conversations with his horses back in England are not the inevitable retreat forced on the sensitive man by the world, but a ridiculous affectation of a silly man.

The hard and soft readings are both functions of an anxiety that saturates and motivates *Gulliver's Travels.* After all, satire is the result of someone believing something is wrong with the world. While critics may disagree whether satire is positive—in other words, that it provokes improvement—or negative—in other words, that all it does is complain—they do agree that satire is the result of concern and dissatisfaction. Swift takes on issues that range all over the map of life, from politics and science to women's education and the production of literature. And although he was thinking of the problems facing the English at the beginning of the eighteenth century, Swift's combination of urgent social concern, creative imagination, and the possibilities of literary form appeals to readers of all ages and outlooks. It reminds us that great literature tells us as much about those who create it as it does about ourselves.

Dennis Todd

In the following excerpt, Todd draws parallels between the strange and alien sights Gulliver experiences during his travels and the popular entertainments of Bartholomew Fair, an area of early eighteenth-century London which put dwarfs, giants, and other "monsters" on display. The critic shows how Gulliver is similarly treated as a monster during his journey, and argues that Gulliver accepts and even encourages this role in order to distinguish himself as an individual.

When Gulliver first appears on the shores of the several remote nations he visits, the inhabitants respond to his monstrosity much as Londoners responded to monsters at Bartholomew Fair. The Lilliputians show "a thousand Marks of Wonder and Astonishment" when they first see him, and when he rises to his feet, "the Noise and Astonishment of the People … [were] not to be expressed." In Brobdingnag, Gulliver "was shewn ten Times a Day to the Wonder and Satisfaction of all People." The Laputans "beheld [him] with all the Marks and Circumstances of Wonder." Not even the rational Houyhnhnms are immune to astonishment: "The Horse started a little when he came near me, but soon recovering himself, looked full in my Face with manifest Tokens of Wonder."

These first reactions give way to another, equally mindless response. Astonishment and wonder are succeeded by a desire to be diverted—most obviously in Brobdingnag, where Gulliver is trundled around the country like dwarfs were in England, but also in Lilliput, where the king uses Gulliver like the kings of Europe used giants, as a way of "diverting himself" and of "entertaining the Court." And the Houyhnhnm master, Gulliver reports "brought me into all Company, and made them treat me with Civility, because, as he told them privately, this would put me in good Humour, and make me more diverting."

Turning Gulliver into a diversion is a way of neutralizing the threat of his monstrous difference, a way of managing the radically alien so that it does not disrupt the comforting assurances of the usual. Tied down in Lilliput, Gulliver is addressed by one of the officials:

> … I saw a Stage erected about a Foot and a half from the Ground, capable of holding four of the Inhabitants, with two or three Ladders to mount it: From whence one of them, who seemed to be a Person of Quality, made me a long Speech, whereof I understood not one syllable. This is a deliciously ludicrous moment, for to give a "long Speech" to a monster who obviously does not understand a word of it is to insist on the unexpungeable truth of the normal with a tenacity that verges on the solipsistic. But this is the strategy of the inhabitants in all the lands he visits. He is effortlessly assimilated into each society, leaving their quotidian realities unperturbed.

To be sure, very occasionally some of the creatures are willing to see Gulliver as a monstrous Other whom they allow, if not radically to critique or disrupt their own familiar reality, at least to comment on it. Like the Brobdingnagian king before him, the Houyhnhnm master is willing to listen to Gulliver because he thought "that it was no Shame to Learn Wisdom from Brutes, as Industry is taught by the Ant, and Building by the Swallow." But even the Houyhnhnms have their limits. They do learn from Gulliver the technique of castration that they can apply to their own local problem of pest control, but they appear to learn nothing at all about the confines of their own structures of thought and value that are exposed by the fact that the mere existence of Gulliver causes unprecedented puzzlement and disagreement. And so, in the end, all the creatures turn from his monstrosity and ignore what he might have to tell them about themselves.

In *his* encounter with monsters, Gulliver reacts much more complexly and in a greater variety of ways. Further, he tends (though this is not invariable) to react to the monstrous inhabitants he visits just oppositely from the way the inhabitants react to him, their monstrous visitor. If they assimilate him, thus leaving intact and unquestioned their own sense of the normal, he tends to take the monsters as normative and to assimilate into himself their realities. And yet, for all of this apparent openness to their difference, he gains no more self-knowledge from his dealings with monsters than they do from their dealings with him.

Gulliver achieves no awareness because in his dealings with monsters he is always anxious about his own identity, always caught up (like the gawkers at Bartholomew Fair) in the various strategies of defense against humiliating self-knowledge. Something of a paradigm of his psychology is revealed when he first sees the Brobdingnagians in the beginning of Book II:

> I bemoaned my desolate Widow, and Fatherless Children: I lamented my own Folly and Wilfulness in attempting a second Voyage against the Advice of all my Friends and Relations. In this terrible Agitation of Mind I could not forbear thinking of *Lilliput,* whose Inhabitants looked upon me as the greatest Prodigy that ever appeared in the World; where I was able to draw an Imperial Fleet in my Hand, and perform those other Actions which will be recorded for ever in the Chronicles of that Empire, while Posterity shall hardly believe them, although attested by Millions. I reflected what a Mortification it must prove to me to appear as inconsiderable in this Nation, as one single *Lilliputian* would be among us. But, this I conceived was to be the least of my Misfortunes; For, as human Creatures are observed to be more Savage and cruel in Proportion to their Bulk, what could I expect but to be a Morsel in the Mouth of the first among these enormous Barbarians who should happen to seize me. There are several peculiar features in this passage, not the least of which, given the context, is Gulliver's use of the word "mortification." For at this moment, he is on the brink of a literal death, fearful that he is about to be made "a

Morsel in the Mouth" of the Brobdingnagians, who, like Grim Reapers, are advancing on him "with Reaping-Hooks in their Hands, each Hook about the largeness of six Scythes." But in the face of this death, Gulliver dwells on another kind of "mortification," and the fact that the two are linked by association in his mind (and by etymology in Swift's) is suggestive. For Gulliver's encounter with monsters at this moment precipitates anxieties about his personal identity. The sight of the Brobdingnagians causes him to swing hysterically from fears of the loss of his identity, "mortification," the "death" of the self, to hypertrophied fantasies of immortality (he thinks his actions "will be recorded for ever in the Chronicles of that Empire"). And he swings so violently because he has delivered his sense of his own identity over to others. He is as he is perceived. To be "mortified" is to be seen as "inconsiderable"; to be "the greatest Prodigy" is to be so "attested by Millions." And the double meaning of "prodigy" reveals both the direction Gulliver takes to achieve a comfortable identity and the cost he is willing to pay to achieve it: in order to be distinguished, he is willing to play the monster.

For these reasons, it seems to me that throughout the book most of Gulliver's misperceptions of the significance of the creatures and events he witnesses in these remote nations, his inability to see any important relation between them and himself, his skewed and partial judgments, and his loopy misinterpretations seldom arise from naiveté or stupidity. For if his encounters with monsters provoke a blurring of his identity, these varieties of mis-seeings become ways, often unconscious, by which he reconstructs a sense of himself that he finds pleasing.

This strategy is most obvious in Book I. Gulliver quickly loses sense of the Lilliputians' monstrosity, accepting their perceptions and finally their values as normal, for to see the world as the Lilliputians see it is to see himself to considerable advantage. He can think of himself as having "performed … Wonders" simply by eating and drinking, and he can take pride in urinating, watching with awe that "Torrent which fell with such Noise and Violence from me." And so he willingly plays the monster. He begins "entertaining the Court with … Feats." He is pleased that he can find a way to "divert" the emperor and nobility "after a very extraordinary Manner" by turning his handkerchief into an exercise field. He willingly yields to the king's "fancy of diverting himself" by acting the colossus. The longer he stays in Lilliput, the more he can entertain fantasies of what "so prodigious a Creature … I must appear to them." And the more deeply he implicates himself in the Lilliputian point of view, the more he can see himself as superior not only physically but socially as well. He fails to see the patent physical absurdity in the charge that he has had an affair with a Lilliputian lady not because he is stupid but because it is more flattering to mis-see it in this way; he can revel in visions of himself at the center of court society ("I have often had four Coaches and Horses at once on my table full of Company," he says, proving that the visits by the lady were by no means unique) and as an important player in Lilliputian social and court politics ("I had the Honour to be a *Nardac,* which the Treasurer himself is not; for all the World knows he is only a *Clum-glum"*).

One can see Gulliver's strategy in little in the scene in which the Blefuscudian ministers ask him "to shew them some Proofs of [his] prodigious Strength, of which they had heard so many Wonders." Gulliver readily complies:

> When I had for some time entertained their Excellencies to their infinite Satisfaction and Surprize, I desired they would do me the Honour to present my most humble Respects to the Emperor their Master, the Renown of whose Virtues had so justly filled the whole World with Admiration, and whose Royal Person I resolved to attend before I returned to my own Country. Accordingly, the next time I had the Honour to see our Emperor, I desired his general licence to wait on the *Blefuscudian* Monarch. First, Gulliver has normalized the monsters, fully assimilating himself into their point of view ("our Emperor"). He then attributes to them an inflated stature that is in no ways theirs ("whose Virtues had so justly filled the whole World with Admiration"). He then performs before them, seeing himself as he fancies they see him ("I entertained their Excellencies to their Infinite Satisfaction and Surprize"). From this he reaps "Honour" and "Admiration"—indeed, the honor and admiration mean something only because he has previously attributed to the monsters a worthiness that makes their honor and admiration worth receiving....

To be distinguished, Gulliver has made a spectacle of himself. He has not engaged in the dialectic of monstrosity at all. Refusing to see in the Lilliputians their monstrosity, their sheer difference, he cannot see their monstrous sameness to humans. And not recognizing in their pettiness, vainglory, and power hunger this monstrous identity, Gulliver allows himself to be governed by precisely these same passions and hence becomes a monster—literally, by "entertaining the Court with ... Feats" and allowing the king to use him as a way of "diverting himself" and morally by allowing his vanity to seduce him into the inanities of the Lilliputian social hierarchy and, even worse, into becoming an engine of war.

Gulliver's encounters with monsters are never this simple again. In Brobdingnag, he is so obviously treated as a monster that he himself complains of "being exposed for Money as a publick Spectacle" and of "the Ignominy of being carried about for a Monster." After Lilliput, Gulliver is increasingly mortified. His sense of his identity is continually under attack: he is "mortified" that the "smaller Birds" were not afraid of him, acting as if he were "no Creature at all"; he feels his "most Uneasiness" among the Maids of Honor, who treated him "like a Creature who had no Sort of Consequence." The Struldbruggs are "the most mortifying Sight" he had ever beheld. And among the Houyhnhnms, he is always haunted by his sense of identity with that "ugly Monster," the Yahoo. He is made so conscious of monstrosity both without and within that he can no longer deal in the easy self-deceptions by which he had fashioned his identity in Lilliput.

Still, he does manage his mortifying encounters with monsters by drawing from a repertoire of defenses. At times, he uses simple denial. It is not until he leaves Brobdingnag that he calls his traveling box what it really is, a "Dungeon," instead of what he usually calls it while he is in Brobdingnag, a "convenient Closet," and he never does allow himself to become aware that Glumdalclitch has treated him like a doll. At other times, he simply converts his mortification into anger against others. "Mortified" by the dwarf, Gulliver attacks him for his small stature. Classed among the "little odious Vermin" by the king of Brobdingnag, Gulliver condemns the king's "*Short Views*" for refusing the secret of gunpowder.

Gulliver even continues to try to play the monster, which worked so well in Lilliput. He voluntarily performs for his royal patrons, pleased that the Brobdingnagian queen was "agreeably entertained with my Skill and agility" when he performed his "Diversion" of rowing a boat, pleased that it was her "Diversion ... to see me eat in Miniature." His stunts, particularly his flourishing his sword ("wherein my Dexterity was much admired,"), jumping over cow dung, playing the piano, and even dressing himself, recall the compensatory feats deformed dwarfs performed at Bartholomew Fair.... Such diverting tricks have their rewards. Gulliver thinks that he has "become a Favourite" and fancies that he is "esteemed among the greatest Officers." He even entertains the extraordinary notion that he "might live to do his Majesty some signal Service."

And yet such defenses become more and more insufficient. "I was the Favourite of a great King and Queen, and the Delight of the whole Court," he says of his tenure in Brobdingnag; "but it was on such a Foot as ill became the Dignity of human Kind." Increasingly, Gulliver seems incapable of silencing the voices of the monsters, and he begins to entertain "Mortifying Reflections." He realizes that the Brobdingnagians are a reproach to the petty pride of Europeans, including himself. By the end of his stay in Brobdingnag, having been surrounded by "such prodigious Objects," Gulliver "could never endure to look in a Glass ... because the Comparison gave me so dispicable a Conceit of my self."

Gulliver's self-loathing and misanthropy culminate in Book IV, of course, and to all appearances he seems to enter into the full dialectic of monsters, recognizing in the Yahoos their secret alliance with himself. Initially, he sees the Yahoo as a complete Other: "singular" and "deformed," an "ugly Monster," it appears to be a species other than man. Even after Gulliver recognizes in the Yahoo the "perfect human Figure," he resists identifying it with himself, insisting on distinguishing it from "my own Species." But Gulliver's certitude about what constitutes "my own Species" begins to erode. The more he observes the Yahoos, the more the two species begin to merge in his mind, and in spite of his attempt to keep them separate, he quietly elides them, so that he unselfconsciously begins to call humans Yahoos, and before too long, when he refers to "my own Species," he means "European Yahoos." By the end of his stay with the Houyhnhnms, Gulliver believes that humans *are* Yahoos, and it is within the Yahoo species that he finally classifies himself ("I [am] a poor *Yahoo,*" he tells the Portuguese crew when they find him on the island). His final assessment of man is that he is a "Lump of Deformity," exactly like the "deformed" and "ugly Monster," the Yahoo. His identification of the two species is complete, and he appears to be consumed by self-disgust: "When I happened to behold the Reflection of my own Form in a Lake or Fountain, I turned away my Face in Horror and detestation of my self; and could better endure the Sight of a common Yahoo, than of my own Person."

And yet, for all of his mortification, Gulliver never once truly entertains those "Mortifying Reflections" that Congreve did. Gulliver's apparent acknowledgment of the identity between the Yahoos and himself, it turns out, is his most elaborate defense. Indeed, Gulliver's willingness to see an identity between the two species is suspicious, if for no other reason than that, after his first gestures of resistance, he begins to pursue it with so much relish. Initially, of course, he is appalled. He hears the Houyhnhnms call him Yahoo "to my everlasting mortification." In Brobdingnag, when Gulliver was "mortified," his first impulse (in fantasy, at any rate) was to make himself singular in order to distinguish himself. And this is his initial reaction among the Houyhnhnms. Mortified to learn that the master Houyhnhnm identifies him with that species of monsters, Gulliver conceals the secret of this clothing "in order to distinguish myself as much as possible, from that cursed Race of *Yahoos.*"

But soon, Gulliver no longer tries to distinguish himself. In fact, he presses for the identity. When he is assaulted by the female Yahoo, the incident becomes "Matter of Diversion to my Master and his Family, as well as of Mortification to my self"—but this is a "Mortification" that Gulliver has sought out (and one, significantly, that has led to someone else's "Diversion"). He has purposefully titillated himself by toying with the identification, much as the monster-mongers in London titillated their viewers with the promise of a hidden identity between them and the monsters: "And I have Reason to believe, [the Yahoos] had some Imagination that I was one of their own Species, which I often assisted myself, by stripping up my Sleeves, and shewing my naked Arms and Breast in their Sight." It is an identity he seeks with enthusiasm.

> As I ought to have understood human Nature much better than I supposed it possible for my Master to do, so it was easy to apply the Character he gave of the *Yahoos* to myself and to my Countrymen; and I believe I could yet make farther Discoveries from my own Observation. I therefore often begged his Honour to let me go among the Herds of *Yahoos* in the Neighbourhood.

Armed with his observations, Gulliver returns to teach his master Houyhnhnm the truth that man is a Yahoo. Now, why Gulliver would "give so free a Representation of my own Species, among a Race of Mortals who were already too apt to conceive the vilest Opinion of Human Kind, from that entire Congruity betwixt me and their *Yahoos*" becomes clearer and clearer as Book IV draws to a close:

> At first, I did not feel that natural Awe which the *Yahoos* and all other Animals bear toward [the Houyhnhnms]; but it grew upon me by Degrees, much sooner than I imagined, and was mingled with a respectful Love and Gratitude, that they would condescend to distinguish me from the rest of my Species.

"To distinguish me from the rest of my Species": here is the motive for Gulliver's misanthropy and self-loathing. In order to be distinguished, Gulliver must first identify himself and humankind with the Yahoos; once having done that, he can then distinguish himself from the identity he himself has created by conspicuously doing those things Yahoos cannot do: be self-critical, judge himself, loath his own nature. By identifying himself with the Yahoos, and then by attacking both them and himself, Gulliver distinguishes himself not only from the Yahoos but from the "self" he claims to be, for he makes himself superior to that "self" by condemning it.

In Book IV, Swift reveals that self-loathing can become a mechanism of self-love, that self-love can turn the dialectic of monster-viewing into a parody where the identification of the self with monsters becomes a way to deny any truly "Mortifying Reflections." But for all of its knotted intricacy, Gulliver's final construction of his identity is merely a variation on all his earlier constructions. When he takes leave of the master Houyhnhnm, Gulliver "was going to prostrate myself to kiss his Hoof, but he did me the Honour to raise it gently to my Mouth," and Gulliver is besmitten "that so illustrious a Person should descend to give so great a Mark of Distinction to a Creature so inferior as I." From the beginning, Gulliver has been driven by this desire for "Distinction," and throughout he has been willing to play the monster in order to be distinguished. In so doing, he really does become a monster, for Gulliver is proud that he "passed for a Prodigy" among the Houyhnhnms, proud that they "looked upon it as a Prodigy, that a brute Animal should discover such Marks of a rational Creature." And he makes sure that he continues to pass for a prodigy by identifying himself with the monstrous Yahoos in order to distinguish himself from them. In the end, he becomes to the Houyhnhnm, as well as to himself, the "wonderful Yahoo," the epithet recalling all those wonderful monsters that were on show at Bartholomew Fair.

Back in England, when he is laughed at for imitating the Houyhnhnms' gait and whinny, he can "hear [himself] ridiculed … without the least Mortification" because he has perfected an identity that has put him beyond mortification. Of course, in doing so, he has had to define himself out of the human species (as he reveals with the slip of his pen in the very last sentence he writes when he tells Sympson that he fears he shall be corrupted by continuing to associate with "your Species"). Gulliver, therefore, becomes, like a Yahoo, a true monster, utterly "singular," outside all species. And so it is appropriate that when he returns to England he, like

all monsters, is plagued by "the Concourse of curious People coming to him at his House in *Redriff.*"

Source: Dennis Todd, "The Hairy Maid at the Harpsichord: Some Speculations on the Meaning of *Gulliver's Travels,*" in *Texas Studies in Literature and Language,* Vol. 34, No. 2, Summer, 1992, pp. 239-283.

Robert C. Elliott

In the following excerpt, Elliott argues that Gulliver, an unreliable narrator who attacks others for his own faults, and who fails to make any distinctions between man in the particular and man in the abstract, is as great an object of satire as the beings he observes on his journeys.

If we ask who is the satirist of *Gulliver's Travels,* the answer obviously is Swift—or, if he is not "of" *Gulliver's Travels,* he is the satirist who creates the satire of *Gulliver's Travels.* But in the extended sense of the term we are familiar with Gulliver is also a satirist.…

This of course is the Gulliver of the Fourth Voyage, worlds removed from the ship's surgeon who was charmed with the Lilliputians and quick with praise of "my own dear native Country." That Gulliver, he of the early voyages, is so far from being a satirist that he is often the butt *par excellence* of satire: Swift's satire, of course, and, within the work, the King of Brobdingnag's; but also, in a sense, of his own—his, that is, when he is an old man, sitting down to unaccustomed literary labors to compose his memoirs.…

The Gulliver who writes, then, is Gulliver the misanthrope who stuffs his nose with tobacco leaves and keeps a long table between himself and his wife. It is he who "creates" the ship's surgeon—a man capable of longing for the tongue of Demosthenes so that he may celebrate his country in a style equal to its unparalleled merits. Given the emotional and intellectual imbalance of the old seaman, he is remarkably successful in producing an objective portrait of himself as he was in time long past.

The actual, as opposed to the fictive, situation, of course, is that Swift has created two dominant points of view to control the materials of the *Travels:* that of his favorite *ingénu* (the younger Gulliver) and that of the misanthrope. The technique has obvious advantages. An *ingénu* is a superb agent of indirect satire as he roams the world uncritically recording or even embracing the folly which it is the satirist's business to undermine.… On the other hand, a misanthrope can develop all the great power of direct, hyperbolic criticism. By allowing Gulliver, an uncritical lover of man, to become an uncritical hater of man, Swift has it both ways.

The technique is not that of the novelist, however. Swift pays little regard to psychological consistency; Gulliver's character can hardly be said to develop; it simply changes. If one takes seriously the premise that Gulliver writes his memoirs after his rebirth, then many passages in the early voyages turn out to be inconsistent and out of character. "There are," says Gulliver of Lilliput, "some Laws and Customs in this Empire very peculiar; and if they were not so directly contrary to those of my own dear Country, I should be tempted to say a little in their Justification." ... (The laws from Swift's point of view, from the point of view of reason, are excellent.) Here Gulliver is trapped in a conflict between his patriotism and his reason; as he is an *ingénu* his patriotism wins. But note the tense: "I should be tempted"; that is, now—at the time of writing. Given this tense, and given the logic of the controlling situation, it must follow that this is the utterance of Gulliver as he composes the work. At the time he writes, however, Gulliver is committed so irrevocably to the claims of reason that the appeal of patriotism could not possibly have meaning for him—could not, that is, if we assume general consistency in Gulliver's character....

To define one's life, one enumerates the solid, unproblematic facts that have gone to make it, and one uses solid, unproblematic sentences—simple and straightforward as one's own character....

The lack of modulation is striking. The predominantly declarative sentences set out the things that happen in their concrete particularity, piling them up but making no differentiation among them. There is something monstrous in the way that Gulliver can describe the taking of a geographical fix, the deaths of twelve seamen, the wreck of the ship, the loss of his companions, his inability to sit up after his sleep ashore—all in sentences similar in structure and identical in tone. Ordinarily, by his style a writer judges his material, places it for his reader in the context of moral experience. Here, the lack of modulation in the style is a moral commentary on the writer—on Gulliver....

But while we may equate the impassivity of tone with an impassivity of sensibility, we are overwhelmed by the impression of Gulliver's commitment to hard, undeniable fact. Dr. Johnson speaks finely of Swift's "vigilance of minute attention"; we see it most impressively as Gulliver records his reaction to the Lilliputians. The pages are peppered with citations of numbers, figures, dimensions: I count over thirty such citations in the last three paragraphs of Chapter One, each figure increasing our sense of the reality of the scene; for nothing, we tend to think, is so real as number.... Swift (not Gulliver, now) is parodying the life-style that finds its only meaning in things, that lives entirely in the particularity of externals, without being able to discriminate among them. This explains in part the function of the scatological passages of Parts I and II which have been found so offensive. The style also helps prepare for the satire on language theory in Part III. But, parody or no, Gulliver's style is a marvellous instrument for narration, building easily and with increasing fluidity the substantiality of his world.

Gulliver, then, succeeds in the novelist's great task of creating the illusion of reality. But again we must recall that he is not a novelist. The reality he creates is one of externals only. He does not create a sense of reality about himself—or rather, to step now outside the framework of the *Travels,* Swift does not create a sense of reality about Gulliver. Gulliver is not a character in the sense that Tom Jones, say, is a character. He has the most minimal subjective life; even his passion at the end is hardly rooted in personality. He is, in fact, an abstraction, manipulated in the service of satire....

The paucity of Gulliver's inner life needs little documentation. To be sure, he is shown as decent and kindly and honorable, at the beginning: we are delighted with his stalwart vindication of the honor of the Treasurer's wife, whom malicious gossip accused of having an affair with him. But his life is primarily of the senses. He sees—how superbly he sees!—he hears, smells, feels. Poke him and he twitches; but there is little evidence of rational activity. The *leaping* and *creeping* contest at the Lilliputian court is a diversion for him, nothing more; he sees no resemblance between it and practices in any other court in the world. Except for an occasional (dramatically inconsistent) episode where he is startled into an expression of bitterness, Gulliver's is a life without nuance. The nuances are there, of course, everywhere, but must be supplied by the reader....

[The] over-riding function [of the climactic two chapters of the fourth voyage] is to develop with cold implacability the horror of English civilization as Gulliver sees it....

Against the destructiveness of Gulliver's onslaught, we look for the kind of positives that are evident in the episode of the Brobdingnagian King. We naturally turn to the Houyhnhnms who represent to Gulliver (and surely in some sense to Swift) one pole of an antinomy: "The Perfection of Nature" over against the repulsiveness of Yahoo-man. Both Gulliver and the Houyhnhnms are at pains to point out wherein Houyhnhnm perfection lies. It is first physical: Gulliver is lost in awe of the "Strength, Comeliness and Speed" of the horses, whereas he can view his own person only with detestation.... Houyhnhnm perfection is next mental: the horses' lives are "wholly governed" by reason, an infallible faculty, at least to the degree that there is nothing "problematical" about it; reason strikes them with immediate conviction, so that opinion and controversy are unknown. Their perfection is finally moral. They lead austere lives devoted to temperance, industry, and cleanliness; they have no idea of what is evil in a rational creature, have no vice, no lusts, and their passions are firmly controlled by the rational faculty. Their principal virtues are friendship and benevolence, which extend to the whole race; and love as we understand it is unknown. For Gulliver the Houyhnhnms are the repository of all that is good.

Here are positives in abundance, the only question being whether they are unqualifiedly Swift's positives. Most critics have felt that they are and that *Gulliver's Travels* (to say nothing of Swift's character) suffers thereby....

It seems likely that a close reading of Gulliver's fourth voyage is such a shocking experience as to anesthetize the feeling for the ludicrous of even the most sensitive readers (perhaps *particularly* the most sensitive readers). I do not mean to deny the horror of the work, which is radical; but the horror is ringed, as it were, by Swift's mocking laughter. For example, Coleridge is outraged at the way "the horse discourses on the human frame with the grossest prejudices that could possibly be inspired by vanity and self-opinion." Human limbs, Coleridge stoutly insists, are much better suited for climbing and for managing tools than are fetlocks. Swift lacks "reverence for the original frame of man." True, Swift did lack reverence for human clay; but he also wrote the scene of the Houyhnhnm's denigration of the human body as comedy. It is very funny. It is a kind of parody of the eighteenth century's concern over man's coveting various attributes of the animals, "the strength of bulls, the fur of bears." It is even connected, as we shall see, with the theme of man's coveting suprahuman reason.... The equine chauvinism of the Houyhnhnms, amusing as it is, undercuts their au-

thority; it must raise doubts in our minds about their adequacy as guides to *human* excellence, to say nothing of the adequacy of Gulliver, who wants to become a horse and whose capacities in matters requiring moral and intellectual discrimination have not been such as to inspire confidence.

Our dubieties are likely to be strengthened by a careful reading of the last part of the voyage. Although Gulliver presumes to doubt the reasonableness of the Houyhnhnm decision to banish him, he builds his canoe of Yahoo skins and prepares, brokenhearted, to sail into exile.... He reaches an island, where he is the victim of an unprovoked attack by savages who wound him with an arrow, and is then picked up, against his will, by Portuguese sailors. An odd situation arises here if we remember that it is the misanthropic Gulliver who is writing his memoirs. It is he who in describing the Portuguese insists on their admirable qualities.... Captain Pedro de Mendez "was a very courteous and generous Person"; in his dealings with Gulliver he is shown consistently to be a wise and compassionate man. Yet Gulliver is unable to distinguish morally between the savages who had wounded him and this human being whose benevolence is worthy Houyhnhnm-land. Because the Captain is a man (a Yahoo in Gulliver's terms), Gulliver is perpetually on the verge of fainting at his mere presence.... But the Gulliver who is writing (five years, he says, after his return to England) is of precisely the same mind. He shows not the slightest compunction at his earlier fierce denial of spiritual kinship with the Portuguese; he still stuffs his nose against the hated smell of humanity, keeps a long table between his wife and himself, and talks willingly only to horses.

The violence of Gulliver's alienation, his demand ... for the absolute, incapacitate him for what Lionel Trilling calls the "common routine" of life—that feeling for the ordinary, the elemental, the enduring which validates all tragic art. Each of Gulliver's voyages begins with a departure from the common routine, each ends with a return to it.... This commonplace family represents a fixed point of stability and calm in Gulliver's life, a kind of norm of humble though enduring human values. Gulliver comes from this life, his early literary style is an emblem of it; and it is against the background given by the common routine that his wild rejection shows so startlingly....

In short, Gulliver's *idée fixe* is tested in the world of human experience. The notion that all men are Yahoos cannot accommodate a Don Pedro de Mendez any more than it can accommodate the long-suffering family at Redriff. But this is our own ironic insight, unavailable to Gulliver, who has never been capable of evaluating the significance of his own experience. Gulliver persistently moulds the world according to his idea of it, instead of moulding his idea according to the reality of things—which must include the Portuguese. Such behavior defines comic absurdity as Bergson expounds it. In other contexts this kind of "inversion of common sense" is characteristic of insanity....

The last words of Gulliver's memoir are part of the complex process of discrediting his vision of the world. He ends with a virulent diatribe against pride, a sin of which he himself is conspicuously guilty. [He] whips his own faults in other men....

Gulliver's great function is to lay bare the rottenness at the core of human institutions and to show man what, in Gulliver's view, he is: an animal cursed with enough reason to make him more repulsive and more dangerous than the Yahoos. Satirists have always used the transforming power of language to reduce man to the level of the beast, but few have debased man as systematically and as ruthlessly as does Gulliver. To find parallels one must go to the theologians.... It would be possible in that case to think of Gulliver as a satirist of man within the Christian tradition. But *Swift,* as this essay has tried to show, writes as a humanist, not as a theologian. *His* satire undercuts Gulliver's vision of man, which is shown dramatically, concretely, to be incommensurate with man's total experience. The vision, to be sure, has a certain abstract cogency, and in Houyhnhnm-land it carries conviction; but Gulliver ... fails to assume the human burden of discriminating morally between man in the abstract and John, Peter, Thomas, and Don Pedro de Mendez. Swift, in life and in this work, insists upon that responsibility.

This reading of *Gulliver's Travels* dissolves a logical paradox. Insofar as Gulliver's vision of man obtains, Swift is implicated: if all men are Yahoos, the creator of Gulliver is a Yahoo among the rest, and *Gulliver's Travels* (and all literary works whatsoever) are no more than the noisome braying of an odious beast. As a clergyman, there is a sense in which Swift might have accepted those implications; but as a humanist and an author he could not. He could accept his own involvement in the great range of human folly which Gulliver avidly depicts, but he could not accept the total Yahoodom of man.

Source: Robert C. Elliott, "The Satirist Satirized: Studies of the Great Misanthropes," in his *Power of Satire: Magic, Ritual, Art,* Princeton University Press, 1960, pp. 130-222.

Sources

Michael Foote, Introduction to *Gulliver's Travels* (includes quotes from early reviews), Penguin Books, 1985.

William Hazlitt, "On Swift, Young, Gray, Collins, Etc.," in his *Lectures on the English Poets,* 1818, reprinted by Oxford University Press, 1924, pp. 160–89.

Samuel Holt Monk, "The Pride of Lemuel Gulliver," in *Gulliver's Travels: A Norton Critical Edition, 2nd Edition,* edited by Robert A. Greenberg, 1961 and 1970, pp. 312-330.

Sir Walter Scott, extract from *The Works of Jonathan Swift, D.D., Dean of St. Patrick's Dublin: Life of Swift, Vol. 1,* 2nd edition, A. Constable & Co., reprinted in *Swift: The Critical Heritage,* edited by Kathleen Williams, Barnes & Noble, 1970.

William Makepeace Thackeray, in his *English Humourists of the Eighteenth Century,* Smith, Elder & Co., 1853, reprinted in his *The English Humourists of the Eighteenth Century: The Four Georges, Etc,* Macmillan, 1904, pp. 1–32.

For Further Study

Frank Brady, "Vexations and Diversion: Three Problems in 'Gulliver's Travels,'" in *Modern Philology: A Journal Devoted to Research in Medieval and Modern Literature,* Vol. 75, 1978, pp. 346-367.
    A good overview of approaches to *Gulliver's Travels* and an analysis of the humor, the sense of historical degeneration, and Swift's true intentions. A "soft" school interpretation.

Arthur E. Case, "The Significance of 'Gulliver's Travels,'" in *Four Essays on "Gulliver's Travels"* Princeton University Press, 1945, pp. 97-126.
    A critical assessment of the book *Gulliver's Travels.*

J. A. Downie, "Political Characterization in 'Gulliver's Travels,'" in *Yearbook of English Studies,* Vol. 7, 1977, pp. 108-120.
    Downie argues against the usual reading of *Gulliver's Travels* as a political allegory by demonstrating how such a reading fails in all four books.

Jenny Mezciems, "Swift's Praise of Gulliver: Some Renaissance Background to the Travels," in *The Character of Swift's Satire: A Revised Focus,* edited by Claude Rawson, University of Delaware Press, 1983, pp. 245-281.
    A discussion of how Swift used Renaissance genres to write his book.

Frank Palmeri, *Critical Essays on Jonathan Swift,* G. K. Hall, 1993, pp. 1-10.
    A useful collection of essays about Swift, his historical context, and major themes and techniques in his

work, including *Gulliver's Travels.* Palmeri's introduction offers a very fine historical overview of criticism about Swift.

Ricardo Quintana, "'Gulliver's Travels': Sine Structural Properties and Certain Questions of Critical Approach and Interpretation," in *The Character of Swift's Satire: A Revised Focus,* edited by Claude Rawson, University of Delaware Press, 1983, pp. 282-304.

An excellent summary of formal and interpretive issues and a discussion of the main interpretations to date.

Edward J. Rielly, editor, *Approaches to Teaching Swift's 'Gulliver's Travels',* The Modern Language Association of America, 1988.

An extremely useful guide, containing descriptions of materials for teaching the text, discussions of different methods for introducing students to the issues in the work, examinations of several themes and issues, and a survey of assignments and syllabi to be used in conjunction with the book.

Richard H. Rodino, "'Splendide Mendax': Authors, Characters, and Readers in 'Gulliver's Travels,'" in *PMLA: Publication of the Modern Language Association of America,* Vol. 106, No. 5, 1991, pp. 1054-1070.

A study of Gulliver and his relationship with language, writing, and readers to explain how the book can support both the hard and the soft interpretations.

Pat Rogers, "Introduction," *Gulliver's Travels* (includes quotes from early reviews), Everyman's Library Edition, Alfred A. Knopf, Inc., 1991.

An overview of the history of *Gulliver's Travels,* its writing, influences on it, and critical responses to it.

Peter J. Schakel, editor, *Critical Approaches to Teaching Swift,* AMS Press, 1992.

A collection of essays that model different critical approaches to reader Jonathan Swift's work. There are several essays on *Gulliver's Travels* and a bibliography for teachers.

Frederik N. Smith, "Vexing Voices: The Telling of Gulliver's Story," in *Papers on Language and Literature: A Journal for Scholars and Critics of Language and Literature,* Vol. 21, No. 4, 1985, pp. 383-398.

Smith examines the relationship between Jonathan Swift and Lemuel Gulliver, questioning whether we should read Gulliver as a spokesman for Swift.

Frederik N. Smith, editor, *The Genres of 'Gulliver's Travels',* University of Delaware Press, 1990.

A collection of essays discussing the influence of different eighteenth-century genres, such as travel narratives and the novel, on the work.

Paul Turner, Introduction to *Gulliver's Travels* (includes quotes from early reviews), Oxford University Press, 1986.

A helpful overview of the work.

J. K. Welcher, "Gulliver in the Market Place," in *Studies on Voltaire and the Eighteenth Century,* Vol. 217, 1983, pp. 125-139.

Welcher describes the book's best-seller status in the eighteenth century, and examines the way capitalism appears in the story.

The Heart Is a Lonely Hunter

The Heart Is a Lonely Hunter was Carson McCullers' first novel, published in 1940, when the author was just twenty-three years old. It started out as a short story in a creative writing class, and an early, working draft of the novel, then called *The Mute,* was submitted for a Houghton Mifflin Fiction Fellowship, for which McCullers won a cash prize and a publishing contract. Her editors at Houghton Mifflin convinced her to change the title. Upon its publication, the book was received positively by reviewers, who were all the more enthusiastic about it because of the author's young age. The book introduced themes that stayed with McCullers throughout her lifetime and appeared in all of her works, such as "spiritual isolation" and her notion of "the grotesque," which she used to define characters who found themselves excluded from society because of one outstanding feature, physical or mental. The story takes place in a small town in the South in the late 1930s. The five central characters cross paths continually throughout the course of about a year, but due to the imbalances in their personalities they are not able to connect with one another, and are doomed to carry on the loneliness indicated in the title. An indication of their lack of coping mechanisms is that the one character that the other four confide their hopes and aspirations and theories to is a deaf mute, who cannot fully understand them nor communicate back to them anything more than his nodding acceptance of what they tell him. Throughout her short career, McCullers' novels continued to present characters

Carson McCullers

1940

who were cut off from mankind, although, many critics believe, never as successfully as in this first, brilliant stroke.

Author Biography

McCullers was born Lulu Carson Smith on February 19, 1917, in Columbus, Georgia. Her family had deep roots in the South: her great-grandfather, Major John Carson, owned a two-thousand acre plantation with seventy-five slaves before the Northern army burned the plantation and freed the slaves during the Civil War. Her father, Lamar Smith, was a watchmaker, like Mick Kelly's father, and owned a jewelry shop like the one John Singer works in. From early childhood, Lulu Carson was expected to achieve great fame, and while she was growing up her parents did what they could to encourage her interest in music. She started formal piano lessons at age ten, and progressed swiftly through her studies in music, which were intense and consuming. After a bout with pneumonia at age fifteen, she started to question whether she had the stamina to be a concert pianist, and turned her attention to writing. She kept her parents believing that she was interested in music, and so when she was seventeen she was sent to New York to study at the Juilliard School, but when she arrived, she enrolled at Columbia University, which had better creative writing teachers, including Sylvia Chatfield Bates, who was a major influence. While home for the summer in 1936 she met Jim McCullers, an army corporal who was also interested in writing, and the following summer they were married. Living in North Carolina with him, McCullers was able to devote all of her time to writing: in a few months, she developed an outline and the first chapters of a novel she called *The Mute,* which Bates suggested she submit to a writing competition. It won a $1500 Houghton Mifflin fellowship and a publishing contract, and was published as *The Heart Is a Lonely Hunter* the following year, when the author was twenty-three years old.

Soon after the novel's publication, McCullers and her husband separated. She and *Harper's Bazaar* editor George Davis moved into a house in Brooklyn Heights, where an eccentric cast of famous boarders came and went, among them Christopher Isherwood, Richard Wright, Paul Bowles, Oliver Smith, Benjamin Britten, Gypsy Rose Lee, and W. H. Auden, who oversaw the housekeeping. Visitors included Anais Nin,

Carson McCullers

Leonard Bernstein, Salvador and Gala Dali, Aaron Copeland, Muriel Rukeyser, Granville Hicks, and Truman Capote. McCullers became attached to Swiss novelist Annemarie Larac-Schwarzenbach, and her husband fell in love with the couple's best friend, David Diamond. The couple divorced in 1940, but they stayed in contact, remarrying in 1945. When they were considering divorcing again in 1953, he committed suicide in Paris. During the early 1940s McCullers published a succession of books that made their mark on American literature: *Reflections in a Golden Eye* in 1941; *The Ballad of the Sad Cafe,* a novella, in 1943; and *The Member of the Wedding* in 1946. Tennessee Williams liked *The Member of the Wedding* so much that he helped McCullers develop a script for it, and it opened with great success on Broadway in 1950. As her career accelerated, though, her health deteriorated rapidly. In 1940 she suffered a minor stroke that left her vision temporarily impaired, and strokes in August and November of 1947 left her blind, unable to speak, and permanently paralyzed on her left side at the age of thirty. McCullers had operations for numerous problems: the muscles of her left hand atrophied, her hip was fractured and had to be set twice, and she had a mastectomy after being diagnosed with breast cancer. For the rest of her life she continued writing; creating stage and film adaptations of works already done and producing just one major new work, a play, *Clock without Hands,* in 1961. McCullers died in 1967.

Plot Summary

Part One

The first section of this novel has six chapters—one chapter focused on each of the five main characters, and then the sixth concerning their continuing relationship to one another. The first two chapters take place much earlier than the continuing action of the rest of the novel. The first chapter introduces John Singer, the deaf mute, and it is written in the vague, fable-like tone that all of the parts concerning Singer are told in. His relationship with another mute, Antonapoulos, is explained: they live together and spend their free time together, but after ten years Antonapoulos starts showing erratic behavior—stealing from the cousin he works for, exposing himself in public, etc. Singer spends all of his money trying to make restitution for his friend's crimes, but the cousin has Antonapoulos committed to the state insane asylum two hundred miles away. Singer moves into the boarding house owned by the Kelly family and begins eating his meals at the New York Cafe. The second chapter takes place one night at the cafe: all of the five main characters pass through this chapter, but it is primarily about the cafe owner, Biff Brannon. When he is coming off of his shift and going to bed, his wife is rising to go to work. Brannon admits to his wife that he has a fondness for what he calls "freaks." Their conversation is about how to handle a third main character, Jake Blount, who has spent every night at the cafe since arriving in town twelve days earlier: he gets drunk, doesn't pay his bills, and terrorizes the customers. Mick Kelly, a twelve-year-old girl from town, comes in to buy a pack of cigarettes. Blount leaves briefly and returns with Dr. Benedict Mady Copeland, a black physician, insisting that he will buy him a drink in defiance of segregation laws, until Dr. Copeland shakes his grip and leaves. Singer, the deaf mute, takes Blount home to sleep off his drunkenness.

Throughout the rest of this section the backgrounds of the characters are revealed. Mick Kelly watches after her younger brothers throughout the summer, and she is obsessed with music. She recalls a Mozart melody she heard and she tries to make a violin out of an old ukulele. She is also

brash, offensive, and vulgar to the other members of her family. Jake Blount takes a job with the carnival that moves around town, and he dreams of leading a revolution against social injustice. He strongly opposes racism and holds Marxist views about economic inequality, but he distances himself from everybody except Singer because of his tendency to get drunk and argue. Dr. Copeland does not get along with his children—as an educated black man in the South, he feels that blacks have to rise above their station, and he is disappointed that his children are average. When Singer goes away for a week to visit his friend at the end of this section, all of these characters are worried, because they each feel that he is the one person who understands them.

Part Two

Most of the action in the book takes place in the long middle section, which spans fifteen chapters. Mick enters Vocational High School, and, in order to get to know her new classmates, she throws a party, dressing in girl clothes for the first time; she is disappointed when the rowdy neighborhood children crash the party, although her new classmates do not seem to mind. Biff's wife dies, and he becomes more withdrawn, more self-involved, and he takes on effeminate traits such as wearing perfume. Doctor Copeland's son William is arrested and sent to prison, and, at the request of his daughter, Portia, the doctor attends a family function, at which his father-in-law, a farmer, angers him by talking about God: he lets his anger show, alienating his family further. Mick's younger brother, playing with a rifle, shoots Baby, who is Biff Brannon's niece: her mother agrees to not press charges if the Kelly family will pay for Baby's first-class hospital treatment, but the bills destroy the Kellys financially. In the middle of this section is a chapter about Singer visiting his friend at the asylum, and then writing him a letter. It is through this letter that readers find out what Singer thinks of all of the people who confide in him: he does not generally understand what they are talking about, and thinks they are foolish and crazy. Mick takes piano lessons from a girl at school, practicing in the gymnasium while the boys play basketball.

After weeks of being out of contact, William comes home: due to torture and abuse at the prison farm, he has lost his feet to gangrene. Dr. Copeland, going to see a judge he knows about the matter, is mocked and beaten by a deputy sheriff and thrown in jail for the night, crushing his dignity. Jake, who has seen racial tensions flaring at the carnival, goes to see the doctor upon hearing about these mistreatments: the two of them cordially agree to form an alliance to demand social justice, but they disagree about how to reach their goal, and the argument flares until racial insults are thrown. At the end of this section Singer goes to see Antonapoulos again, only to be told that his friend is dead. He goes home and kills himself.

Part Three

The last section is about what happens after Singer's death and how it affects the surviving characters, who counted on him to be their moral compass whether he understood them or not. This section is divided into four chapters labeled *Morning, Afternoon, Evening,* and *Night,* respectively, of August 21, 1939. Doctor Copeland, the proud, educated man who could not tolerate his father-in-law's simplistic religious groveling, is too ill to care for himself, and so he is taken away to the country, lying in the back of the farmer's old mule-wagon. Jake Blount, who meant to be the man who could bring the races and classes together, takes part in a race riot at the carnival: after holding back at first, he finds himself joining in and swinging his fists ferociously. He leaves town with a sense of having accomplished nothing, but with hope for the next town he will end up in. Mick takes a job at Woolworth's in order to help with the family's mounting bills. It means giving up her dream of studying music. In the end she stops at the New York Cafe to have a beer and a sundae, indicating the mixture of child and adult at which she is frozen. Biff Brannon spends his time in the basement among the newspapers he has collected over the past twenty years, isolated from his customers and employees, living in his own world.

Characters

Spiros Antonapoulos

Antonapoulos is the person that John Singer cares most about in the world, even though there is little evidence that he returned Singer's affection. The book's first chapter concentrates on their ten years of life together and how Antonapoulos behaved more and more badly as years passed—stealing from the restaurant, urinating in public, pushing people around—until his only relative, Charles Parker, has him committed to an insane asylum. Throughout the rest of the book Singer

pines for his friend's companionship, even though most of his memories of him seem to involve Antonapoulos drinking or stealing money or in some other way taking advantage of his friendship.

Jake Blount

People in the town fear and mock Jake Blount because his behavior is wildly uneven, symbolized by the two sets of clothes that he owns: the white linen suit that he arrived in town wearing, and the filthy overalls that he wore for the twelve days following, during which he remained drunk. Blount is an educated and compassionate man, concerned about social equality and willing to fight for the rights of anybody, but his enthusiasm is tainted by the fact that he is so drunk most of the time that his anger and symbolic gestures appear to be just foolishness. The first time he meets Dr. Copeland, for instance, he is drunk and drags the doctor into the cafe, in defiance of the segregationist rules that forbade a black man from drinking in a white establishment: from the doctor's perspective, though, he had come expecting a medical emergency and the drunk who had him by the arm instead tried to buy him a drink. Before he left Biff saw him turn on Blount with "a look of quivering hatred." After sobering up, Blount takes a job as a mechanic at a carnival, working on the carousel, or "flying-jinny." He is well-educated in the literature of social revolution and Marxism, and when he visits Singer's room he brings liquor and talks most of the night about the things he would like to do to liberate the working class. Given the choice of living during any time in history, he tells Biff, he would live in 1775, presumably so that he could participate in the American Revolution. When he hears about Willie Copeland's mutilation in prison, Blount insists that Singer take him to see Willie, saying that he can help. While there he tells a long, complex story about the labor struggle and the ownership of factories, but it ends with him fighting with the doctor until they end up slinging racial slurs at each other. He writes out theories and treatises and manifestos, with titles like "The Affinity Between Our Democracy and Fascism," and distributes them around town. After Singer commits suicide, Blount feels empty and betrayed, and then a calamity happens: after all of his work toward racial understanding, he takes place in a riot between blacks and whites at the carnival. He decides to leave town, and is last seen walking through the cramped, rotting tenements on the outskirts of town: "There was one thing clear. There was hope in him, and soon perhaps the outline of his journey would take form."

Sondra Locke and Alan Arkin in the 1968 movie The Heart Is a Lonely Hunter.

Bartholomew Brannon

See Biff Brannon

Biff Brannon

Brannon is the calmest and most content character in the novel, although not in the beginning. At the start of the novel, Brannon works hard to run the New York Cafe and keep it open day and night. He does not appear to have a very good relationship with his wife of twenty-one years, Alice. They are seldom together because she sleeps while he works and he sleeps while she works, and when they are together they argue about how he treats the customers; she feels that he gives too much food and liquor away to strange people like Blount. "I like freaks," he explains. "I just reckon you certainly ought to, Mister Brannon," she replies, "being as you're one yourself." Later, thinking about that conversation, Biff thinks about his "special friendly feeling for sick people and cripples," and accepts it with neither pride nor disdain. As the novel develops, it becomes evident that Biff himself is androgynous, that he feels that he is part male and part female, which explains his disinterest in sleeping with Alice. He is a big, brutish man who wears his mother's wedding ring on his smallest finger, wears perfume, and arranges decorative baskets "with an eye for color and design." When his sister comes by with her daughter, she tells Biff, "Bartholomew, you'd make a mighty good mother," and he thanks her for the compliment. Locked in his cellar, Biff thinks about how nice it would be to adopt two children, a boy and a girl, but he does not dream of raising them with anyone else. Elsewhere in the book Biff reflects on "the part of him that sometimes wished he was a mother and that Mick and Baby were his kids." Writing to his friend, Singer expresses the opinion that Biff "is not like the others…. He watches. The others all have something they hate. And they all have something they love more than eating or sleeping or friendly company." Critics have suggested that it is Brannon, not Singer, who is the religious center of this novel because he lives by principles of love and acceptance. Like the rest, he is upset by Singer's death, and the novel ends with him sitting in the New York Cafe, keeping his mind occupied with crossword puzzles and flower arrangements, waiting for customers.

Doctor Benedict Copeland

Doctor Copeland is a black man raised in the South but educated in the North, so he sees the disgrace of the racism in the town better than anyone. He is respected by his patients, many of whom have named their children after him, but he has little re-

Media Adaptations

- The 1968 film adaptation of *The Heart Is a Lonely Hunter,* with a screenplay by Thomas C. Ryan and directed by Robert Ellis Miller, was released on video by Warner Brothers in 1985.

- A recording entitled *Carson McCullers Reads from The Member of the Wedding and Other of Her Works* was released on audio LP disc by MGM Records in 1952.

spect for them. He feels that most of the people in town, his own children included, are allowing themselves to be taken advantage of, and he frowns upon gestures, even those made in friendship, that make his race look lazy or weak. The doctor has trouble relating with people. When his daughter tells him that the way he talks to people hurts their feelings, he says, "I am not interested in subterfuges. I am only interested in the truth." At a family reunion he sits by himself, sulking and grumbling and embarrassed that his father-in-law describes God's face as "a large white man's face with a white beard and blue eyes." Doctor Copeland feels more involved with books than with people. He reads Spinoza and Thorstein Veblen and Karl Marx, whom he named one of his sons after (the son goes by the name "Buddy," just as the son he calls William goes by "Willie"). When Willie is tortured in jail and his feet have to be amputated, Dr. Copeland goes to see a judge he knows, but he is stopped in the hall of the courthouse by a deputy sheriff who insults him, accuses him of being drunk, beats him and arrests him, throwing him in a cell with the very lower-class blacks that he has spent his lifetime avoiding. Upon his release and after a long night of drinking and talking with Jake Blount, Dr. Copeland and Jake start planning ways to make people aware of society's injustices. Dr. Copeland is impatient with Jake's plan, which would take a long time, and demands that violent meetings in the street are in order. The two argue, and their discussion about promoting racial har-

mony dissolves into racial insults. In the end, Dr. Copeland, too sick with tuberculosis to care for himself, is taken off to his father-in-law's farm, riding in a wagon piled high with his possessions (his other option was to ride on his son's lap), feeling that his mission is uncompleted and still hungry for justice.

Willie Copeland

Willie is the cook at the New York Cafe, and as such is familiar with all of the main characters. His father is Dr. Benedict Copeland and his sister is Portia. One night, when Willie and his brother-in-law Highboy are drinking at a place called Madame Reba's Palace of Sweet Pleasure, he dances with a girl whose boyfriend starts a fight with him. Defending himself with a razor, he cuts the other man badly and is sent to prison for nine months. In prison, Willie is locked in a freezing shed and hung by his feet from a rope, and after three days he contracts gangrene and must have his feet amputated.

Portia Jones

Portia is the daughter of Dr. Copeland, the only one of his four children who visits with him—the other three, all boys, are constantly reminded of his disappointment with them because he wanted them to be a scientist, a teacher, and a lawyer, to help their race. Portia's husband is Highboy, and the two of them live with and spend their time with her brother, Willie: as Portia explains it to her father, "You see—us have our own way of living and our own plan. Highboy—he pay the rent. I buys all the food out of my money. And Willie—he tends to all of our church dues, insurance, lodge dues and Saturday Night. Us three haves our own plan and each one of us does our parts." Portia is also the housekeeper at the Kelly boarding house, and Mick sometimes explains her troubles to her. When Willie is sent away to prison, Portia writes to him dutifully, and when he comes back crippled she is distraught, but unlike her father she does not believe that there is a way to demand justice.

Bubber Kelly

Early in the novel Bubber is the little brother who tags around after Mick all day long throughout the summer. One day, when another boy from the neighborhood brings over a rifle that his recently deceased father left him, Bubber takes the rifle and points it at a neighbor girl and, after mentioning several times how cute and pretty she looks, fires the gun. The major separation between Bubber and Mick comes when she goes to his hiding place and, to teach him a lesson, tells him that the police will arrest him: "They got electric chairs there—just your size. And when they turn on the juice you fry up just like a piece of burnt bacon. Then you go to Hell." This frightens Bubber more than expected, and his feelings change, so that he is aloof to her. After the shooting incident, he is not known as Bubber anymore, but goes by his given name, George.

George Kelly

See Bubber Kelly

Mick Kelly

Mick is the character who is most like the author, growing up in a Southern town during the course of the novel. When she is first introduced, in the long chapter that brings all of the characters into the cafe, she is a "gangling, towheaded youngster, a girl of about twelve ... dressed in khaki shorts and, a blue shirt, and tennis shoes—so that at first glance she was like a very young boy." "I'd rather be a boy any day," she tells her older sister who criticizes her clothes. In contrast to this childish image is the fact that Mick has come to the cafe to purchase cigarettes. During the summer days, Mick is responsible for her younger brothers, Bubber and Ralph, and is constantly with them. Ralph is so young that he should be wheeled through town in a carriage or a stroller, but since the Kelly family is poor, they can afford neither, so Mick ties him down in an old wagon so that he won't fall out. Mick is fascinated with music, stopping when she hears a radio playing in a room in the boarding house or while passing someone's home, so interested that she knows exactly which yard to go to to hear music in a time of emotional distress. Early in the novel, Mick is trying to make her own violin with a broken, plastered ukulele body, a violin bridge, and strings from a violin, a guitar and a banjo; when her older brother Bill, whom she looks up to, tells her that it will not work she gives up in frustration. Although Mick does not have a wide circle of friends, due largely to her family responsibilities, she is also not a social outcast: when she throws a party for her new classmates at the technical school, wearing a dress and makeup for the first time to assert her sophistication, it is a reasonable success. She ends up disappointed, because the dirty, scruffy neighborhood kids whom she is trying to leave in her past come to the party and mingle with her new friends. Like the other major characters in the book, Mick goes to Singer's room to talk out her problems—he has a radio in his room, although he cannot hear it, and she listens to it when she visits. At the end, she has to give up her dream of studying for a career in music to take a job at Woolworth's. After Singer's death, she realizes that this job is not temporary, that it marks a change in her personality: "But now no music was in her mind. It was like she was shut out from the inside room.... It was like she was too tense. Or maybe because it was like the store took all her energy and time." She tries to convince herself that she will return to music, but ends up repeating it and repeating it unconvincingly.

Harry Minowitz

Harry grew up next door to the Kelly boarding house, and while he is in vocational school he takes a job at the cafe. One summer afternoon, he and Mick go swimming, and the event progresses into a sexual encounter. Afterward, rather than going home, he tells Mick that he is leaving town because "If I stayed home mother could read this in my eyes." Mick discovers that he actually did leave later in the evening, when Mrs. Minowitz phones and asks where he is.

Simms

A sidewalk preacher who captures Jake Blount's attention and acts as his conscience, Simms offers to help Jake find religion, but he backs away when he sees the scar that Jake has given himself by driving a nail through his hand. As Jake leaves, Simms shouts at him that he is a blasphemer, and that God will get him. Later, when Jake is distraught about Singer's death, he goes to Simms and offers to bring interested people into Simms' religious meeting by drawing pictures of "some good-looking naked floozies" on the sidewalk, leading them to him. Simms is outraged and shouts curses at Jake, not forgetting to tell him to come back at "seven-fifteen sharp" to hear God's message.

John Singer

Singer is not the central character in the novel, although he is the central figure in the lives of the other characters. Being deaf and mute, he is forced to watch people carefully when they talk, and that concentration, combined with the fact that they can talk freely with him without fear of being interrupted, gives them the impression that he really understands them and cares about them. In fact, the only person Singer really cares about is the Greek

Topics for Further Study

- World War II had started in Europe when this novel took place, although America did not enter it until a year and a half later. Examine the effect that the war had on race relations in the South: did things get better or worse? Did the war affect the situation at all?

- What kind of music would have been on the jukebox at the New York Cafe? Find out what songs were popular in 1938-40 and make up a soundtrack for this novel.

- Using the details given from the novel, draw a diagram of the Kelly house, showing where each character's room would be.

- Research the laws that are in place today that are meant to prevent the abuses that cost Willy his feet. What legal recourse would he have today? Who would he take his case to? What authorities would be responsible for punishing the offenders?

Antonapoulos, another deaf mute who lived with Singer for ten years and never showed any sign of understanding him any more that Singer understands Mick, Dr. Copeland, Blount, or Brannon when they talk about their lives. Singer spends his life's savings to cover up for the petty thievery and destruction that Antonapoulos causes, and when his friend is sent away to a mental institution he is so lonely that he moves into the Kelly boarding house, because "he could no longer stand the rooms where Antonapoulos had lived." None of his friends in town know about Antonapoulos, and when Singer takes his vacation time to visit him at the asylum, the others are anxious for his return. Singer's reaction to this attention is conveyed in a letter that he sends to the Greek in which he discusses them all. "They are all very busy people," he explains. "I do not mean that they work at their jobs all day and night but that they have much business in their minds that does not let them rest." The letter goes on to explain that he does not enjoy their company, as each of them thinks, but that he has feelings rang-

ing from slight approval of Mick ("She likes music. I wish I knew what it is she hears.") to disgust with Blount ("The one with the moustache I think is crazy.") At the end of the letter about their obsessions he, without irony, goes into his own obsession, stating exactly how many days it has been since he and Antonapoulos were together: "All of that time I have been alone without you. The only thing I can imagine is when I will be with you again." When Singer goes to visit his friend and finds out that he has died, he wanders around in a stupor for half a day, then takes a pistol from the jewelry shop he works at and commits suicide.

Themes

Strength and Weakness

Very early in the book Biff Brannon announces to his wife, "I like freaks." Her response is "I reckon you ought to, Mister Brannon—being as you're one yourself." What Biff has in mind is the affinity he has for the struggling underdog, or, as the book puts it later, "a special feeling for sick people and cripples." Although Brannon himself is physically healthy, his connection to the physically deformed is an indication of the weakness that he sees within himself, a weakness that shows itself in his inability to connect to his wife when she is alive and is even more pronounced in his withdrawal from society after her death. The other main characters display signs of social weakness that range from the obvious to the sublime. Mick Kelly, the only female in the group, is a young girl, wielding no real authority but burdened with responsibility for her younger brothers. She tries to enhance her stature by acting tough, using a boy's name and dressing boyishly and smoking, but her false strength is revealed by the fear she has of being found out after her first sexual encounter. In the end, it is her family's financial vulnerability that dashes her dreams of pursuing a career in music. Jake Blount's weakness is alcoholism, which keeps him from following through with any plans he makes, confusing his thinking and driving him to rage when he has a point to make. Beside the social disadvantage of being black in the South in the 1930s, Dr. Copeland has to deal with the tuberculosis that is eating away his body. John Singer, though stable and respected about town, is shut off from humanity, both by his handicap and by his obsession with Antonapoulos. The novel uses these weaknesses to bring the characters together, both for practical reasons (Blount drinks at Brannon's cafe, Singer boards at the Kelly house) and for commiseration with one another. The other four are drawn to Singer because his weakness is openly displayed, and they feel that he can understand them.

Search for Self

To varying degrees, all of the main characters feel that they understand where they fit into society, but they all are actually missing something that would help them function in their world. This is a part of McCullers' concept of the grotesque: each character has an outstanding aspect that makes them different from the norm, and yet they keep looking for acceptance. The most obvious case of this is Dr. Copeland, who is so isolated by his concept of his intellectualism that he cannot even fit in with his own family, although he cannot give up his intellectualism, either, because it is what makes his illness and society's racism bearable. Similarly, Jake Blount is driven by intellect, except that his thoughts are often interrupted by flashes of anger. In anger, he once quit an organization that he himself had founded, unable to accept the behavior of the other members: "They had stole the fifty-seven dollars and thirty cents from the treasury to buy uniform caps and free Sunday suppers," he tells Singer indignantly. Biff Brannon has an identity problem while his wife Alice is around, because she is a constant reminder of his impotence, but when she dies he is able to incorporate female personality traits in with his own, and he finds peace in that way. The most obvious case of one of the main characters searching for their identity is Mick, who, as an adolescent, has not yet found out who she really is: she throws a party for her new classmates in order to find her place, and explores sexuality with Harry Minowitz, and she gives in to what a career in music can tell her about herself, but ironically, after she has found a self that she is comfortable with, she is denied following the music career because of financial difficulty. Each of these characters goes to Singer because they think that he is like them: ironically, Singer does not identify with any of them, but with the Greek, Antonapoulos, but even though he is deaf Antonapoulos does not see much of himself in Singer. Some of the minor characters, too, bring out the theme of Search for Self, although they do not belong within the circle formed by the main characters. Mick's Dad, for instance, shows this theme by trying to acclimate to a new job after being injured as a roofer, while Portia and Willie and Highboy create an unusual composite identity by spending most of their free time as a threesome.

Race and Racism

This novel was praised by critics, both black and white, for the clear and honest way it dealt with the problems blacks were subjected to. The issue of race is approached slowly and carefully at first. The first black characters, Willie and Portia, are introduced in their menial positions as, respectively, fry cook and maid. To modern readers, their patterns of speech, their dialect, may seem offensive or comical. When Dr. Copeland is introduced, he seems to fit another stock type: that of the black intellectual who resents the social rewards that have not been available to blacks and resents his own people for accepting their second-class citizenship. It soon becomes apparent, however, that McCullers has created characters who are more rounded than stereotypes. Dr. Copeland's high-minded nobility is impressive, but Portia's capacity for love for her brother and for her grandfather when he comes to visit makes the doctor's studies of Marx and Spinoza seem small and unimpressive. The tragedy of what happens to Willie, losing both of his feet while jailed for defending himself in a fight, shocks his family, but it is not presented as being anything so unusual that the authorities would take action about it. When Dr. Copeland goes to speak with a judge of the Superior Court that he knows, he is stalled by a deputy sheriff, then verbally abused, then assaulted and arrested. When he resists arrest he is beaten merciless and tossed in jail. Upon his release he is admonished by his daughter, who explains to him, impatiently, "Father, don't you know that ain't no way to help our Willie? Messing around at the white folks' courthouse? Best thing we can do is keep our mouths shut and wait." On a personal level, there is mixing of races in this novel—Portia is treated like a wise older sister in the Kelly household, and Singer is waiting with Copeland's family when he is released from jail. On a larger level, though, relations between the races break down, as shown by the riot at the carnival or in the way that Dr. Copeland and Jake Blount, trying to form an organization to fight oppression, can only hold their alliance for a few minutes before they start arguing, and as soon as they start arguing racial insults are spoken.

Style

Grotesque

The idea of the grotesque has run throughout American literature, through the works of Melville,

Hawthorne and Poe, and may in fact have to do with the democratic political system, which emphasizes the individual over the collective. In twentieth-century literature, it is usually associated with Southern writers such as William Faulkner and Flannery O'Connor. Put simply, "grotesque" refers to work that portrays characters who each have an exaggerated trait or characteristic, which is used to symbolize their entire personality. McCullers once explained that "Love, and especially love of a person who is incapable of returning or receiving it, is at the heart of my selection of grotesque figures to write about—people whose physical incapacity is a symbol of their spiritual incapacity to love or receive love—their spiritual isolation." Clearly, this applies to John Singer in the novel, a character who is loved by all of the other main characters but who is only perplexed by their attentions. The first chapter establishes the world that Singer lives in—a world where he and his friend Antonapoulos live together, walk to and from work together, and spend their evenings quietly playing chess. Because of his "physical incapacity," his deafness, that world does not change much for Singer, even when his friend moves away and new characters come around. With Singer setting the tone as the most obvious example of the story's use of the grotesque, the other characters are given conditions that are less physically noticeable but hinder their emotional capacity just as badly: Dr. Copeland's tuberculosis makes him anxious that the work he finds important will be completed; Jake Blount's alcoholism causes every nearly-meaningful conversation to deteriorate into ranting; Biff Brannon's androgyny, which some critics have suggested is caused by impotence, makes him self-fulfilled, with no need to connect with anyone else; and Mick's budding adolescence suspends her in a void between childhood and womanhood, distracting her from her love of music until economic circumstances take away that choice, possibly forever.

Structure

This book is not structured like a traditional novel, which would use a more systematic method to follow the ways in which the events in the main characters' lives affect each others', and so by traditional standards it appears to be chaotic, even uncontrolled. The story lines of the five main characters are developed side-by-side with each other, so that readers would have difficulty picking one that is more important than the others. The shape of the novel is in fact based in musical theory, with the three parts organized as a fugue would be. The first section opens with Singer's story alone, like a musical solo, and then weaves in the other voices in balanced increments, playing off of each other and creating distinct harmonies, ending with Singer again—since words are not exchanged in Singer's sections, the story is told completely in narrative, giving these outside chapters a hushed, thoughtful feeling. The second section, fifteen chapters in total, is much busier, still concentrating on one character per chapter but complicating their lives with struggles and misery, giving the full rich tone of an entire orchestra, still following various individual strands but doing so with greater fury. This section ends with the climactic event of the novel, John Singer's suicide. The third section is a coda that does not develop any new ideas but returns to each of the four remaining characters to confirm that they did in fact end up living the destinies that they seemed to be headed for earlier. This section is divided into quarters in a new way, dividing one day, August 21, 1939, into morning, afternoon, evening, and night, echoing Singer's isolation at the end as Biff Brannon shouts to his assistant and receives no response. Basing the design on a musical form reflects both the musical training that Carson McCullers had (and that Mick in the novel would like to have) and the irony that runs throughout of the music that plays on the radio in the room of the deaf man.

Historical Context

Fascism

The character of Mick is so politically naive early in the novel that when she is defacing the wall of a house under construction she includes the name Mussolini along with the comic-strip crime fighter Dick Tracy and the inventor of light bulbs, phonographs and moving pictures, Thomas Edison. At that time in world history, Fascism had reached its height as a political power. The word itself was coined by Benito Mussolini during his rise to power in Italy after World War I ended in 1818—he defined fascism as "organized concentrated authoritarian democracy on a national basis," although most other sources would not forget to include the words "totalitarianism" and "authoritarianism" in their definition. Fascism is unlike Democracy because it gives the government control over all aspects of its citizens' lives; it is unlike Communism because it emphasizes the nation, and not the worker, as being the most essential element in life.

Compare & Contrast

- **1940:** England and France were at war with Germany, Italy and Japan: later that year France, Belgium, the Netherlands, Luxembourg, Denmark, Norway, and Romania fell to the Germans, but the United States did not join World War II until Pearl Harbor was bombed in December of 1941.

  Today: Having been elevated to the status of world power as an outcome of World War II, the United States is almost certain to be involved in any major worldwide conflict.

- **1940:** The first Social Security checks were mailed out to Americans. The first payout to American pensioners totaled $75,844.

  Today: After decades of workers paying into the system, the amount paid out annually by the Social Security Administration is nearly $400 billion.

- **1940:** Plutonium, the radioactive element that fueled the nuclear bombs used in 1945 to end World War II, was first discovered.

  Today: Now that the Soviet Union has disbanded, there are fears that the nuclear bombs they stockpiled between the 1940s and 1990s might fall into the hands of terrorists.

- **1940:** In the South, blacks and whites were not allowed to eat or drink at the same establishments, stay at the same hotels, or ride on public transportation together. At the same time, the persecution of European Jews by the Nazis made government support of racial hatred conspicuous.

  Today: Because of progress made toward civil rights in the 1950s and 1960s, some groups argue that minorities are over-privileged.

- **1940:** Most Americans had radio receivers that provided them with news and entertainment; television broadcasting had been introduced during the 1939 Wold's Fair in New York, but there were only about 100 to 200 sets to receive it. During World War II little was done to expand on the television experiment. Ten years later, just nine percent of U.S. households had television sets, but twenty years later, that number had jumped to 85 percent.

  Today: Television's immense popularity has created a market for literally hundreds of networks, catering to diversified tastes.

---

whites, drinking at fountains whites drank at, attending the same schools, etc., as long as there were equal facilities for them to use. In the South, states took advantage of this ruling to pass laws, called "Jim Crow laws," to ensure racial separation. The problem for blacks was that the "equal" part of the "separate but equal" doctrine was seldom enforced. Black schools received less funding, as did black medical facilities; theaters that allowed whites main-floor seats only allowed blacks to sit in the balcony, far from the stage; and the better restaurants and hotels excluded blacks. Famous and wealthy blacks were sent to ramshackle accommodations while watching any white who cared to walk in enter places that they were kept out of. Early in this novel, for instance, the drunken, dis-

orderly Jake Blount believes that he is doing a big favor for Dr. Copeland, bringing him into the cafe and offering to buy him a drink even though, as one of the patrons tells him, "Don't you know you can't bring no nigger in a place where white men drink?" Dr. Copeland, for his part, is embarrassed to have a low-class wreck like Blount condescend to him. Enforcement of the laws that segregated the races was brutal. Blacks, with almost no political power in the South, had to suffer legal abuse by any whites, even those of the lowest level, as shown in this novel when Dr. Copeland, a respected man in his community, is beaten by a deputy sheriff who does not like his attitude. The legal system seldom sided with blacks, for fear that recognizing some civil rights would encourage them to want more.

Child labor, now recognized as a form of exploitation, was the norm during the Industrial Revolution. Instead of a school picture, these boys posed for a photo that documented their roles as laborers.

In 1848, when the Capitalist economic system had established roots all over the world and the Industrial Revolution had made it strong, Karl Marx and Friedrich Engels published *The Communist Manifesto.* Their fear was that the way the free-market economy divided the world between two groups—the rich, who owned the means of production, and the workers who provided the labor—made slaves out of the laborers. They encouraged workers to unite. In the early twentieth century, Socialism was popular in many countries around the world, and in 1917 Russia was taken over by the Communist Revolution (in general, the distinction between the two is that Socialism advocates changing the government from within the system, while Communism supports revolutionary overthrow). In Italy, as elsewhere, Communism appealed to the poor, and many of the people were suffering in poverty after a post-war economic collapse that made their money practically worthless. Property owners, however, feared that Communism would take away what they had, and many middle-class people equated a Communist take-over with anarchy and chaos. Mussolini, a former Socialist, gained the support of people who had been made to feel powerless because of the economy's collapse and who liked the Fascist party's strong pro-Italy rhetoric.

His rise to power was driven by a combination of the promise to restore order and the violence of Fascist thugs in black shirts who committed murder and arson against socialists. In 1922, violence against Socialists was so bad that they called a national strike against the transportation sector: Mussolini used this politically to take control of the government, gaining citizen support because he got the trains to run on time. Between 1925 and 1930 he turned his control of the government into a dictatorship, with absolute control over all media and all aspects of the people's lives. At the same time, the same elements that brought the Fascist party to government control were at work in Germany, where Hitler was using the promise of order, the threat of Communism and a hatred of people considered "outsiders" (in this case, Jews, blacks, Catholics and Gypsies) to build the Nazi empire.

Segregation

In 1896, the U.S. Supreme Court, in a landmark case called *Plessy v. Ferguson,* ruled that it was legal for states and municipalities to keep blacks and whites apart from each other in public by offering "separate but equal" accommodations. The idea was that laws could be passed forbidding blacks from eating at restaurants frequented by

Outside of the legal system was the Ku Klux Klan, an organization of native-born white Protestant men who hid their identities in robes and hoods while they perpetrated heinous crimes against non-whites, non-Protestants and foreigners. The organization was started in Georgia in 1915, based on a similar organization that had existed after the Civil War. The tactics that they used to intimidate the people they considered undesirable were window-breaking, public cross-burnings, and kidnapping and hanging people, known as "lynching." Legal authorities claimed to be unable to stop the Klan, although in many cases they used their hidden identities as an excuse to let them run rampant. During World War II, from 1941 to 1945, Southern blacks received a taste of equality: they visited European countries where segregation laws did not exist, and the United States Armed Forces, though not completely equal, did have blacks and whites working alongside one another. By the 1950s, public sentiment against racism grew to an extent that the laws had to be changed: the 1954 Supreme Court ruling in *Brown v. the Board of Education of Topeka, Kansas* found that separate schools could not be equal, and so all-white schools had to admit blacks. Integration was extended to other institutions, reversing the Plessy decision.

Critical Overview

The Heart Is a Lonely Hunter was met with almost universal critical acclaim when it was published. Many reviewers found it to be an incredibly polished work, and they were flabbergasted that such a book could be written by an author who was only twenty-three. When Richard Wright, one of America's greatest novelists and the author of the classic *Native Son,* reviewed the book in the *New Republic,* he put its young author in the company of Gertrude Stein, Sherwood Anderson, Ernest Hemingway, and William Faulkner. "Her quality of despair is unique and individual: it seems to me more natural and authentic than Faulkner," he told readers, adding that "she recounts incidents of death and attitudes of stoicism in sentences whose neutrality make Hemingway's terse prose seem warm and partisan by comparison." Wright, who was black, was especially impressed with McCullers' ability to handle black characters without being insulting or condescending. The thing that was most impressive to him was "the astonishing humanity that enables a white writer, for the first

time in Southern fiction, to handle Negro characters with as much ease and justice as those of her own race." Novelist May Sarton reviewed the book in the *Boston Evening Telegraph* and found it to be such an incredible work of literature that minor flaws that would have been acceptable in other novels stood out here as being unnecessary. She found the inclusion of tragedies caused by accident and not by the lives of the main characters, such as Bubber shooting Baby and Mick's sexual encounter with Harry, to weaken the story. "Neither is false," Sarton quickly explains. "Both are believable but neither is necessary. The beauty of the book is that except for these, every action seems inevitable." Rose Feld praised the novel in *The New York Times Book Review,* finding that McCullers possessed a "rich and fearless" imagination and "an astonishing perception of humanity."

After the publication of *The Heart Is a Lonely Hunter,* McCullers' reputation grew, as she continued to produce powerful works of literature that commanded serious consideration. Her next publication, the novel *Reflections in a Golden Eye,* was published in 1941: it was well-received, but it suffered by comparison to the surprise and delight critics had gotten from the first book. "[I]t was then regarded as somewhat disappointing in the way that second novels usually are," Tennessee Williams wrote in the introduction to the 1950 edition. "When the book preceding a second novel has been very highly acclaimed, as was *The Heart Is a Lonely Hunter,* there is an inclination on the part of critics to retrench their favor, so nearly automatic and invariable a tendency that it can almost be set down as a physical law." His essay goes on to look at aspects that could be seen as weak, and to explain how they had been misunderstood. Her third novel, *The Member of the Wedding,* was published in 1946, and it clearly established McCullers not only as a writer with control and skill, but as one with her own vision, as readers became accustomed to the solidity of her style. Now assured that her initial success was not just a fluke, her works received widespread analysis from literary critics. Marguerite Young's review in *The Kenyon Review* looks at the book as an intellectual piece, like a chess game or a modern poem. She explained that "Mrs. McCullers, sometimes depicted as a sensationalist reveling in the grotesque, is more than that because she is first of all a poetic symbolist ... " Her only other major publication was the 1951 collection *The Ballad of the Sad Cafe and Other Works.* The novella in the title is considered one of her best works, but reviewers were divided about McCullers' short fiction. In a review of a book published after her death that collected poems, essays, and short stories, David Madden noted that comparing a timeless book like *The Heart Is a Lonely Hunter* to her short fiction shows readers "how poorly a first-rate talent can sometimes function."

Criticism

David J. Kelly

David J. Kelly is a literature and creative writing instructor at several colleges in Illinois. In this essay he sets the scene in which Baby is shot, and explains why it was necessary to add the scene to the novel's final draft even though it does not immediately involve any of the central characters.

One of the great things about a meticulously-crafted novel like *The Heart Is a Lonely Hunter* is that readers get to watch it unravel slowly, feeling secure with its sense of order, knowing, even during those passages where they cannot see the grand scheme, that the author is in control and most likely is not wasting her readers' time. Another great thing about reading the work of a structure fanatic is that they often plan early what the novel is going to do, where it is going to go, what the characters are going to be like and what their significance will be. Writers usually have *some* idea of what is going to happen, and sometimes they write their ideas down, although they often, when asked, just tap their foreheads, nod, and say, "I've got the whole thing worked out up here...." I do not believe I have ever seen a set of notes as complete as Carson McCullers' "Author's Outline of *The Mute*." I do not know the circumstances under which she would have written such a thorough treatment of the uncompleted book; she might have been just that conscientious, although I suspect that it was written to apply for the grant that eventually won her a publishing contract. I do know that the book that turned out to be *The Heart Is a Lonely Hunter* was very close to *The Mute* in symbolism, themes, and backgrounds of the main characters, but that there are enough differences to see that it was indeed a work in progress. In other words, this is not a summary of a work that is already completed, where the author just describes the actual and symbolic importance of what happened. This is a working plan for things that McCullers intended to happen in the book.

Most of the changes were incidental: Harry Minowitz was originally the non-Jewish Harry West, which would have left out the opportunity to bring up the war in Europe and the rampant anti-Semitism that defines it in this book; Willie Copeland was arrested as a white boy's dupe during a robbery in this version, rather than in a knife fight; Mr. Simms was originally a key player in Biff Brannon's life, not Jake Blount's. Any one of these changes is worth speculating about, because speculating offers readers some insight into the decision-making process, which itself opens the window to the author's intent just a little bit wider. The one that interests me most, though, is the absence of the shooting of Baby in the original plan. It clearly was not in the work at this stage—there is no mention of Baby or anyone like her with another name in the "Outline," and Bubber had no specific shining moment planned for him at that time. In fact, in the section named "Subordinate Characters," under "The Kelly Children," McCullers states directly, "No great interest is focussed on any of these children individually."

I would not presume to second-guess whether adding the "Bubber shooting Baby" episode was a good idea or not. Reviewers have pointed to this as one of the novel's (just slightly) weak points, and critics in general, when they single it out, mention this episode as something that does not fit cleanly into the grand scheme. But the book as a whole works, and it works to an astounding degree, so I think it would just be rude without being productive to question the author's instincts. If I can't ask whether it works, I think my curiosity would be just as well served if I can ask *how* it works: what about the shooting of Baby adds just the right spice to this tale, and helps the novel define itself?

My first assumption is that Bubber's role would have been beefed up anyway, even without the shooting of Baby. In the "Outline," McCullers alludes to him while describing Mick: "Her family does not own a radio and in the summer she roams around the streets of the town pulling her two baby brothers in a wagon and listening to any music she can hear from other people's houses." There's nowhere but up for Bubber to go from this slight, vague inclusion as one of the baby brothers. Later in the "Outline," a distinction is made when talking about Mick's responsibility to watch over "Bubber and the baby," at least elevating him to individuality. That same section goes on to include a paragraph that actually made it into the finished book, about how hard it is for younger siblings, including the phrase, "Bubber—he looks sick but

What Do I Read Next?

- Many of McCullers' other significant works are collected in one volume, called *The Collected Stories of Carson McCullers, Including The Member of the Wedding and The Ballad of the Sad Cafe.* The latest reissue is from Mariner Books in 1998.

- Truman Capote was a friend of McCullers', and many of the characters in his works seem as though they would fit perfectly into her books. One collection that particularly resembles hers is *The Grass Harp,,* reissued in 1993 by Vintage Books. Included in this volume is his acclaimed novella *A Tree of Night.*

- Flannery O'Connor once said, "I have found that anything that comes out of the South is going to be called grotesque by the Northern reader, unless it is grotesque, in which case it is going to be called realistic." O'Connor was a Southern woman writer in the 1950s and 1960s, like Carson McCullers, and like McCullers she was ill most of her life and died young. Her novels are interesting, but O'Connor's most polished work is in her short stories, compiled in *The Collected Stories of Flannery O'Connor.*

- The town described in this book resembles the southern towns in the work of William Faulkner, a Mississippi writer of the generation before McCullers'. Its fragmented style, looking from one character to the next, resembles one of Faulkner's most successful works, *The Sound and the Fury,* published in 1939.

- The name that Sherwood Anderson originally gave to his 1919 book *Winesburg Ohio* was *The Book of Grotesques:* like McCullers' book, it is about different characters in a town who sometimes interact and sometimes do not, but all have distinguishing exaggerated characteristics that affect the ways they exist in their world.

---

he's got guts underneath that." My assumption is that she was using her words loosely when she referred to seven-year-old Bubber as one of two baby brothers. Then, too, is the possibility that Bubber already started to develop a personality during the course of writing this outline. One can see how Mc-Cullers could write a paragraph that comes out so clean and solid that it deserves being kept, and how, from that paragraph, the seeds of identity can grow. A sickly-looking kid with guts can prove a useful tool in drawing out aspects of Mick's personality, given how much she puts into covering her artistic sensibilities up with toughness.

If Bubber, then, was to be a mirror for Mick, a good function—the function that he takes on in the finished work—would be to show how excessive swaggering can get him into trouble. In Mick's case, tough posturing only serves to make her obnoxious, alienating her further: real trouble would prevent the tragedy of her life, in the end, becoming mundane. In a secondary character, though, trouble could be made to stick, frightening her and softening her up. These facts, of course don't even take into consideration the fact that the author needed something to ruin the Kelly family financially.

Enter Baby. Four years old, Baby presents the unlikely hope of her mother, Lucile, for a better life: she plans to give Baby a permanent, gives her dancing and expression and piano lessons, and tells Biff, the child's uncle, "I feel like I got to push Baby all I can. Because the sooner she gets started on her career the better it'll be for both of us." At this point, Baby is a part of Biff's life, functioning to show us the kind of idealistic dreamer he would attach himself to—his fondness for Baby helps redefine just what kind of "freaks" he is attracted to. Baby is such a strange character in her physical beauty that it is plain to see this early that she will either succeed spectacularly, in a triumph of vacuous prettiness over the strong defeated characters with way more substance, or she will fail, flattening her mother's dreams in a town where dreams just get flattened. The potential for tragedy is

---

heightened by the fact that Biff delights in her so much, which bodes poorly for Baby because this book is an exercise in the ways that its main characters, unable to express themselves, suffer. The tragedy that Baby Wilson seems headed for is one of her mother's doing, and it looks like one that we would look back on at the end and feel that Biff should have put a stop to things before they went so far.

The reason some critics disagree with the shooting is that it seems unprepared by the story. The point is well taken, considering that everything else is so carefully prepared and metered. A certain segment of the population would also say that the randomness of the act is good, that it mirrors the unpredictability of life, that it breathes some fresh air into a book too tightly woven. "Life-like" is not the virtue in a stylized piece like this that it would be in another piece of fiction, but the capacity to surprise readers should always be considered a good thing.

The surprising thing about the shooting is that it comes from a secondary character and draws more attention to Bubber than anyone but the five main characters generally earn in the novel. As I have mentioned, it is better for the book that a character near Mick plunge into trouble without the trouble actually threatening Mick's future bland career at Woolworth's. Bubber certainly jumps, with that one shot, from a tiny, nearly anonymous role, past Willie and even past Portia, to a status almost as vivid as the foggiest of the main characters, Biff. He introduces a scary element of violence in the book, and not even intentional violence, but a destructiveness that can well up in a child at the same time that he is admiring something's beauty. The same mixed emotions are alluded to earlier in the book, when Mick writes on a wall the names of the artist, Mozart, and the dictator Mussolini, and then "a very bad word—PUSSY, and beneath that she put her initials, too." Oddly, not much is made of the psychological aspect of Bubber raising a gun against another child, just of the social aspect, with the "end of childhood" that he undergoes by changing from his nickname to "George" foreshadowing the end, where Mick the tomboy worries over a run in her stockings. Some critics have referred to the shooting as "an accident," although it seems he had a good long time to put the gun down and it's clear that his finger went to the trigger deliberately. The book's about alienation, and the whole mood might be spoiled if anyone cared to find out what was running through someone else's mind, so Bubber's destructive impulse is written off as just one of those childhood things.

The last we see of Baby, we have come to understand what this incident means to her: she could not participate in the soiree, so she "began to yell and cut up during one of the dances" until she is taken outside and spanked. Finally, she seems to be finding her place in this miserable town, with Jake and Mick and Dr. Copeland, who all raise their voices in disappointment. There is no place in this town for the fortunate, the blessed, or the beautiful. Under other circumstances, she might have been a good character to have lurking around in the corners, just for contrast, to show that there are people who don't end up shouting to vent their souls, but this is the human condition that McCullers is examining here, and no one, especially not a little talent-show princess, is going to escape it.

Source: David J. Kelly, in an essay for *Novels for Students,* Gale, 1999.

Janice Fuller

In the following excerpt, Fuller explains how McCullers used the structures and patterns found in the musical conventions of counterpoint and fugue as the framework for her novel to successfully deliver and explicate the novel's theme—the "insurmountable isolation of human beings."

The influence of music manifests itself in a number of ways in Carson McCullers' fiction. While critics in general note the frequent direct references to music in her works, most of them focus on the way music functions as a "minor symbol" and as an "extended correlative" or mirror of theme and character. Few critics, however, have examined music's role as "architectural framework," as Barbara Nauer Folk [in "The Sad Sweet Music of Carson McCullers," *Georgia Review,* 16, 1962.] calls it. This omission is surprising since, as Virginia Spencer Carr [in her book *The Lonely Hunter: A Biography of Carson McCullers,* 1975] points out, McCullers herself in later life came to acknowledge her musical studies as the source of the excellent "sense of form and structure" admired by students of her fiction....

The work by McCullers in which the sense of musical form seems strongest is *The Heart Is a Lonely Hunter,* a novel in which direct references to music abound Willie's harmonica tunes, the music from Biff's mandolin, the mechanical music of the flying-jinny, and the "singing moan" of Doctor Copeland's voice accompany the classical music Mick enjoys in the dark and composes in her "inner room." To speak of the novel's structure using the analogy of music does not seem unreasonable since in her outline for "The Mute" (later published as *The Heart Is a Lonely Hunter*) McCullers herself [as recorded in her book *The Mortgaged Heart,* 1971] employs musical terminology in discussing her plans for the novel's form:

> This book is planned according to a definite and balanced design. The form is contrapuntal throughout. Like a voice in a fugue each one of the main characters is an entirety in himself—but his personality takes on a new richness when contrasted and woven in with the other characters in the book.

In using technical language to refer to counterpoint in general and the fugue as a more specific pattern or style of counterpoint, McCullers sets up certain expectations. Counterpoint, based upon a Latin phrase meaning "note against note" or "melody against melody," consists of two or more melodic lines that are played at the same time. Fugue, a more specific term, refers to the "mature form of imitative counterpoint" perfected by J. S. Bach [Willi Apel, *The Harvard Dictionary of Music,* 1972]. Counterpoint and the fugue, in particular, are associated with a number of conventions. When the completed novel *The Heart Is a Lonely Hunter* is considered in light of these conventions, it is clear that McCullers, for the most part, faithfully followed the original plan of her outline. In fact, the novel's conformity to many of the conventions provides a key to the structure and meaning of the novel....

Perhaps the most obvious convention of counterpoint followed in *The Heart Is a Lonely Hunter* is the independence of musical voices. Counterpoint, including the fugue, consists of a number of separate voices or melodic lines. Each of these lines must be musically sound, interesting and, most importantly, independent in terms of rhythm and movement. In *The Heart Is a Lonely Hunter,* each of the five main characters or "voices"—John Singer, Biff Brannon, Jake Blount, Dr. Benedict Mady Copeland, and Mick Kelly—is interesting enough and his story complete enough to have been developed into its own novella. For example, the story of Dr. Copeland's struggle to lead his people out of oppression and face the reality of his own children's fates does not depend upon the other characters' stories for its development. Instead, it stands as an intriguing tale in its own right. Furthermore, McCullers gives each of the five individuals a unique character that goes beyond the obvious differences of race, age, profession, sex, and physical ability. Such distinctness of characteriza-

tion is evident in idiosyncrasies such as Dr. Copeland's studying the philosopher Spinoza and Biff's wearing his deceased wife's perfume. The uniqueness of the five characters is underscored by the distinct narrative styles McCullers develops to suggest the "inner psychic rhythms of the character" [as recorded in her book *The Mortgaged Heart,* 1971]. Biff's "voice," for instance, can be heard in the section in which McCullers introduces him:

> The place was still not crowded—it was the hour when men who have been up all night meet those who are freshly wakened and ready to start a new day.... The mutual distrust betwen the men who were just awakened and those who were ending a long night gave everyone a feeling of estrangement.

The style of this passage could hardly be mistaken for that used by McCullers to focus on Mick:

> When Mick had finished half of the cigarette she smashed it dead and flipped the butt down the slant of the roof. Then she leaned forward so that her head rested on her arms and began to hum to herself.

The distinctness and independence of each character are also ensured by McCullers' introducing each character individually in the novel's first part. Like the staggered entrances of voices typically used in counterpoint, each character, beginning with John Singer, is introduced in a separate chapter, which, as McCullers' outline suggests, presents the "salient points of each person." McCullers conforms to this contrapuntal convention of independence of voices in order to emphasize and even enact her theme of the insurmountable isolation of human beings. Thus, from the outset of the novel through its concluding treatment of the surviving four characters in isolated chapters in part three, McCullers, as Richard Cook [in his book *Carson McCullers,* 1975] suggests, "preserves the separateness of each person even as she holds them together in a lonely community of suspicion and misunderstanding."

Conventional counterpoint is also characterized by imitation among voices. In the fugue, this imitation involves recurrent motifs as well as the imitation of the subject or theme—that is, a short melody introduced by "one voice alone, being taken up ('imitated') by the other voices in close succession and reappearing throughout the entire piece in all voices at different places" [Willi Apel, *The Harvard Dictionary of Music,* 1972]. Such an imitative technique occurs in *The Heart Is a Lonely Hunter,* in which, as Dayton Kohler suggests, "themes and character motifs appear early in the novel, only to be dropped and later resume." In the first chapter of the novel, McCullers uses John

Singer's relationship with Antonapoulous to introduce the novel's central theme—the persistent attempt by the individual, in the face of the one-sided nature of love, to overcome the isolation of the self. In the next four chapters of Part One, McCullers "imitates" this theme by presenting the reader's first glimpses of Biff, Mick, Jake and Dr. Copeland in the context of their failed relationships and their resulting states of isolation. The theme reappears in all the "voices" throughout the rest of the novel as the various characters unsuccessfully attempt to communicate with other human beings. Of course, the most exact imitation in the novel results from the way in which each of the four characters' one-sided relationship with John Singer mirrors Singer's relationship with Antonapoulous. As McCullers herself suggests in her outline for the novel, the way each of the four characters creates an understanding of Singer "from his own desires" and makes Singer "the repository of his most personal feelings and ideas" has an "exact parallel" in Singer's imputing great dignity and wisdom to Antonapoulous.

McCullers also uses imitation in *The Heart Is a Lonely Hunter* by associating distinctive motifs with certain characters and causing those motifs to reappear in other "voices." For example, Dr. Copeland's blindness to the potential for human communion in the form of Portia as he attempts to reach all of the black community is echoed in Mick's desire to bring her brother Bill and John Singer into her "inner room" while letting her potential relationship with "Bubber" be destroyed. This motif reappears in Singer's failure to take advantage of the accessible and potentially gratifying relationships with his four "disciples" because of his obsession with Antonapoulos. McCullers introduces another motif through Mick's figurative movement back and forth between her "inner room" of the self and the outer world of human interaction. This motif is repeated and objectified in Biff's movement between the upper room where he reads and plays his mandolin and the public café as well as in Singer's wanderings from his boarding-house room through the streets of the town. These motifs and the imitation of the central subject or theme unify the novel and give universality to the independent characters of the novel by suggesting that the continued struggle to break out of the isolation of the self is part of the human condition....

Despite the existence of both social and individual considerations in the novel, *The Heart Is a Lonely Hunter* is also analogous to counterpoint in its emphasis on the horizontal rather than the vertical elements of structure. While homophonic or harmonic music focuses primarily on the simultaneous occurrence of sounds in pleasing and harmonious combinations, counterpoint is more concerned with the melodic line of each voice. Thus, vertical relationships among notes are incidental. Dissonance or clashing of notes occurs as often as consonance and harmony. In the same way, McCullers focuses on the actions and perceptions of individual characters rather than their collective attempts at interaction or communion. Except for those occasions when other characters seek out Singer for "conversation," the encounters between the central characters are random, as when Jake and Dr. Copeland collide and exchange angry glances on the stairs. The encounters that do occur—Biff's attempts to talk to Mick in the café, the bedroom confrontation between Jake and Dr. Copeland—are generally discordant. In fact, the two occasions in which all five of the "voices" are brought together—their first meeting in Biff's café in Part One and their later accidental meeting in Singer's room—are among the most tense and dissonant scenes in the novel. Even the interaction between Singer and the other four characters, whether in Singer's room, in the café, or at Dr. Copeland's party, is markedly one-sided, more like unison music than harmony among separate voices. This linear focus, in which each "voice" remains a "stranger in a strange land," underscores a pervasive loneliness in the novel....

Perhaps because of this linear structure, *The Heart Is a Lonely Hunter* has a texture that resembles the typical texture of four-and five-voice counterpoint. Because the listener is unable to follow four or five lines of equal importance for any length of time, the composer of counterpoint uses a variety of strategies to vary the texture of the music: temporarily eliminating or subordinating one or more voices and shifting the focus of attention from one voice to another. In a similar way, each chapter of *The Heart Is a Lonely Hunter* centers on one of the five central characters, the focal character being indicated not only by the character's name being mentioned normally within the first sentence or paragraph and the action's centering around him but also by a shift to the narrative style associated with that character. But, like most contrapuntal music, McCullers' novel does not (except possibly in Singer's chapters) allow the texture to be reduced to a single "voice." Even when the action centers on a single character, the reader gets enough glimpses of other central characters—through

Harry Minowitz's mentioning Jake Blount to Mick or Singer's appearing at Dr. Copeland's party or Mick's stopping by Biff's café for a sundae—to remind him that their lives or "melodies" are continuing, though temporarily subordinated, in the background....

In describing the form of McCullers' novels in general, Marvin Felheim [in "Eudora Welty and Carson McCullers," *Contemporary American Novelists,* 1964] speaks of a typical movement from order—through an opening that is an "exact, economical" statement of "what is going on"—to disorder. This disorder, which occurs in Part Two of *The Heart Is a Lonely Hunter,* corresponds in musical terms to the development section of the fugue—generally a freer, longer section in which episodes alternate with complete or partial restatements of the theme and, thus, heighten the listener's interest. In Part Two, which is nearly three times longer than Part One, the length of the chapters and the appearance of the five central "voices" follow no regular pattern. Furthermore, the actions of outside forces—Harry Minowitz, Baby Wilson, the prison officials guarding Willie—intrude upon the lives of the central characters and often increase their sense of alienation. In the face of this greater loneliness, the central characters continue vainly to reach out to other people, most often John Singer.

Part Three of *The Heart Is a Lonely Hunter,* while not a full recapitulation of Part One, creates a return through a sense of balance and completion. True to the plan of McCullers' outline for the novel, the "technical treatment" of the final section is quite similar to that of the first part. Each of the four surviving characters is allowed a chapter to restate his or her variation of the subject or theme, and, as Edgar MacDonald [in "The Symbolic Unity of *The Heart Is A Lonely Hunter,*" in *A Festschrift for Professor Marguerite Roberts on the Occasion of Her Retirement from Weshampton College University of Richmond, Virginia,* 1976] points out, these final chapters precisely reverse the Part I order of appearance of the four mourners." Smith [in "A Voice in a Fugue," *Modern Fiction Studies,* 1979] goes even further to suggest that the brevity of each chapter and, thus, the "rapid succession" of "voices" as they repeat the theme are analogous to *stretto,* a technique often successfully used in the concluding sections of fugues....

The particular ways in which McCullers deals with the demands and conventions of counterpoint and the fugue make *The Heart Is a Lonely Hunter* a less than pessimistic treatment of man's struggle as a "lonely hunter" to come to terms with his inevitable isolation and disillusionment. Through the use of the contrapuntal fugue with its linear but imitative treatment of individual voices and its varied texture, McCullers is able to represent five distinct characters struggling in touchingly similar ways to break out of the lonely inner room of the self.

Source: Janice Fuller, "The Conventions of Counterpoint and Fugue in *The Heart Is a Lonely Hunter,*" in *The Mississippi Quarterly: The Journal of Southern Culture,* edited by Robert L. Phillips Jr., Mississippi State University, 1987–88, pp. 55–67.

David Madden

In this excerpt, Madden examines the parallel positions of Mick Kelly and Doctor Copeland. He describes how each character finds relief in solitude yet desires connection with others. However, the others are also beset by the same personal dilemma of opposing needs, thus everyone remains solitary and misunderstood.

The theme of *The Heart Is a Lonely Hunter* could hardly be more vital and universal: the immemorial, individual dilemma of loneliness, the spiritual isolation of human beings. It is not a realistic novel about the modern South, nor is it, despite certain critics or whatever McCullers' original intention may have been, a political polemic against capitalism and racism. The memorable characters are all excruciatingly real, but they retain a poetic simplicity which raises them to the level of universal significance. I do not mean "spiritual" in either the religious or even the mystical sense. I, and I think McCullers, mean that inexplicable force in each man which makes him ask why, which compels him to go deeply beneath the surface complex of himself into a more intensive, extensive reality. The validity of McCullers' vision of the psychic realm of her characters, or of man, depends a great deal upon the accuracy and consistency with which she achieves a very acute psychological understanding of her characters and of nature of loneliness which moves them so grotesquely....

McCullers was only 21 when she wrote this book, but she was too mature to condemn abstractions either, although it is a rather abstract, paradoxical conflict that she is primarily concerned with: everyone hungers for human understanding while simultaneously desiring an inviolable privacy.

The need for privacy is no less crucial than the need for understanding, but in the context of society both needs are frustrated, or, in the desperate attempt to satiate one, the other is neglected or deprived....

Mick [Kelly] is a unique, individual adolescent and will be a neurotic, bitter woman; Biff is already neurotic. Copeland, obsessed with the one true purpose, and Blount, obsessed with the gospel of social reform, are both subject to monomania, and it is in this light that we see them.

The portrait of Mick is complete. We see her in various situations, reacting variously, exhibiting in her own eccentric way all the characteristics of an adolescent girl trying to achieve womanhood, but fearing to succeed. Unable to identify with her unsympathetic, older sisters, who ignore her, Mick used to follow, take her cues from her older brother Bill. But when the novel opens, she realizes, "Sometimes she hated Bill more than anyone else in the world. He was different entirely from what he used to be." In growing up, he has failed her. The mother is too busy to answer questions, and one assumes that Portia, the Negro cook, is the only adult female from whom Mick can learn what a girl must do....

But Mick knows "that always there had been one person after another... But she had always kept it to herself and no person had ever known." There had been male and female schoolmates and female teachers whom she had secretly loved. Now all she has is Bubber, her little brother, Mr. Singer, and her father. There is a fine scene between Mick and her father in which their mutual longing for familial love and sympathy very nearly achieves satisfaction. "Yet for some reason she couldn't tell him about the things in her mind — about the hot, dark nights."

More than any of the other characters, Mick needs solitude, privacy. "Some things you just naturally want to keep private. Not because they are bad, but because you just want them secret." But when they are about to "poison" her, she "throws" them at her "idea" of Singer; she responds to his impersonal air as she could not respond to her father's intense personal need. Having no physical room of her own, she imagines one as existing in her own mind. The only person allowed in that room is Mister Singer. It is filled with dreams of the future, with music she has heard or imagined herself.

Mick not only writes music and spends her lunch money for private piano lessons, but she also paints very imaginatively. She is trying to make a violin, which, along with other fragments of things, she keeps in a special box. (When she is famous, she will print M. K. on all her possessions.) She takes long walks at night, where ordinary girls would be afraid to go, and one time she sits under a window, thrills to a Beethoven symphony, coming over the radio. "Wonderful music like this was the worst hurt there could be." To divert herself from it, she subjects herself to physical pain by scraping rocks against her thigh until her hand is bloody.

Always now she is aware of a feeling of change. "All the time she was excited. In the morning, she couldn't wait to get out of bed and start going for the day. And at night she hated like hell to have to sleep again." She daydreams of herself as a heroine, saving Mr. Singer from disaster, conducting an orchestra with all her heroes and friends in the audience. Refusing to wear her sister's cast-off clothes, she also refuses to take the same courses in school; she takes mechanical shop. She has in her mind plans (as strong as those for music) for belonging to one of the "bunches" of kids in school. She decides that a party will help. She is surprised when the seemingly grown-up kids respond gaily to the party-crashing antics of the younger kids in the neighborhood, but relieved, too. "And about the bunch she wanted to be with everyday. She would feel different in the halls now, knowing that they were not something special but like any other kids. It was O.K. about the ruined party. But it was all over. It was the end." Realizing this night that she has changed, she dismisses the party and dresses for the last time in her tomboy clothes.

"Mick, I come to believe we all gonna drown," says Bubber, watching the relentless rain. What he says is very true, certainly; this is what is happening to all Mick's plans. First, she loses Bubber's companionship when, with childlike cruelty but more out of her extravagant imagination, she frightens him with the prospect of the electric chair in Sing Sing for having shot Baby Wilson. That night, Mick, sorry, kisses his little body desperately. But "After he shot Baby the kid was not ever like little Bubber again." Everyone began to call him by his right name, George. McCullers' insight into George's behavior, his change suddenly from a quiet, sweet child to an introverted, solitary premature adolescent, is frighteningly real. "But he was a different kid—George—going around by himself always like a person much older and with nobody, not even her, knowing what was really in his mind." She retreats further into the "inside room."

Mick's self-respect becomes insidiously impaired as the family grows poorer. "They were nearly as poor as factory workers. Only nobody could look down on them." She follows Mr. Singer, talks to him. "For some reason it was like they had a secret together. Or like they waited to tell each other things that had never been said before", except that he tells her nothing. She imitates his habits. Ironically, she believes that Brannon hates her because she and Bubber once stole some candy from the café. Actually, he is one of the few people with whom she might have freely, naturally talked. Harry, her Jewish neighbor, is her friend; they talk, play together and plot to kill Hitler. Harry has a crush on Jake Blount, whose raging against society gives Harry, who is hypersensitive about his Jewishness, new ideas.

McCullers subtly builds up the process of sexual awakening. Sitting on the steps talking to Harry, Mick notices that "There was a warm boy smell about him." Confused, she reverts to their early childhood horse-play, but in the midst of it they become aware of each other's bodies....

When they go swimming in the country, Mick suggests that they swim naked. Facing each other's nudity, they are suddenly very bashful. But lying on the grass, they naturally succumb to the urges within them. Afterwards, Harry thinks they have sinned, so he runs away to work in Birmingham. "She felt very old, and it was like something was heavy inside her. She was a grown person now, whether she wanted to be or not."

Later, although her family kindly forbids it, she is obliged to work in the ten-cent store. Once, in need of Mr. Singer, she goes to look for him but is frightened by the darkness that as a child she had loved. After Singer's suicide, she feels trapped into womanhood and servitude....

Educated in the North, Doctor Copeland returned to the South to lead his people out of sickness and servitude. He has read the great writers on spiritual and economic freedom and named his children after them. To them, "He would talk and talk, but none of them wanted to understand." He was almost Calvinistic in the way of life he wanted to prescribe for his family: "He knew how the house should be. There could be no fanciness—no gaudy calendars or lace pillows or knick-knacks—but everything in the house must be plain and dark and indicative of work and the real true purpose." But his wife, Daisy, taught them meekness, submission, superstition. Years later, Portia says,

"Us talk like our own Mama and her peoples and their peoples before them. You think out everything in your brain. While us rather talk from something in our hearts that has been there for a long time. That's one of them [our] differences."

"You all the time using that word—Negro," said Portia. "And that word haves a way of hurting peoples' feelings ..."

When *her* talk hurts *his* feelings, he refuses her gentleness: "No. It is foolish and primitive to keep repeating this about hurt feelings." His stern dedication to his "true purpose" has alienated all his children but Portia; yet between them no understanding and mutual sympathy is possible.

Meeting his son for the first time in a long time, he can not submit to his desire for common emotional expression, can only reproach him for not becoming the ideal leader of his people Copeland had tried to teach him to be. All his life Copeland has carried within him the hurt and humiliation of the white man's domination. To protect himself from the excessive emotional responses he naturally feels compelled to make, he has adopted a stoic attitude. The fervor of his dedication to ideas, "to the one strong true purpose," his obsession with his mission, his really valiant devotion to his duty as a doctor, divert his thoughts and energies and become media for sublimation of violence and forces of repression upon the real violence, the genuine Negro feelings smouldering inside him, that cause him such frustration and anxiety. Dying of TB, he realizes that he has failed, but actually he has probably saved himself from the gallows. When he was young,

> The feeling that would come on him was a black, terrible, Negro feeling. He would try to sit in his office and read and meditate until he could be calm and start again.... But sometimes this calmness would not come. He was young and the terrible feeling would not go away with study.

When he is old, the Negro blues of his people, that wonderful emotional cathartic, tries to come out of him: "it happened that he began swaying slowly from side to side and from his throat there came a sound like a kind of singing moan." But even the singing he suppresses, does not surrender to. One time, years ago, he struck down his wife with a poker. Then "He wrestled in his spirit and fought down the evil blackness" with very hard work and a lofty, impossible ideal. When, with the dignity of a white man, he goes to the court house to object to the atrocity perpetrated upon his son, Willie, in prison, he is beaten as though he were a lowly "nigger."

He waited for the terrible anger and felt it arise in him ... he broke loose suddenly from their grasp. In a corner he was surrounded. They struck him on the head and shoulders with their clubs. A glorious strength was in him and he heard himself laughing aloud as he fought.... He kicked wildly with his feet ... even struck at them with his head ... Someone behind kicked him in the groin and he fell to his knees on the floor.

The old, suppressed violence finally came out and was suppressed again by other forces.

Copeland and Blount are afflicted with the same problem. They try to sublimate their personal frustrations into public causes and their manner of fighting for these causes further intensifies their neuroses by alienating the very people they wish to convince; this increases their own loneliness, and the poison of narcissism festers in their spirits. Copeland is happiest when he is being listened to even though he knows it will do no good; his joy comes from the feeling of being respected, of being unlike other Negroes, of having a part of himself become absorbed into the minds of his listeners. "In the room there was a murmur. Hysteria mounted. Doctor Copeland choked and clinched his fists. He felt as though he had swelled up to the size of a giant. The love in him made his chest a dynamo, and he wanted to shout so that his voice could be heard throughout the town."

That he might have found a friend in Blount is indicated in the scene in which they talk all night, but finally end in disagreement. Although the torment in their souls is similar, their ideas and their race ultimately conflict. More than the success of their reform programs, they need friendship, an end to loneliness. "Yet now he [Copeland] could not clearly recall those issues which were the cause of their dispute." Copeland was more at peace when he could talk to the uncomprehending deaf-mute, Singer. Even when men have the opportunity to admit into their solitude a kindred spirit, the habit and nature of introversion prevent it. Copeland goes, a sick, broken failure, to his wife's father's farm where he will die alone in a house full of his own people. Hope, a feeble hope that the future will be better is all any of them have. "I will return soon," Doctor Copeland says. The reader is less optimistic....

Source: David Madden, "The Paradox of the Need for Privacy and the Need for Understanding in Carson McCullers' *The Heart Is a Lonely Hunter*," in *Literature and Psychology*, edited by Leonard F. Manheim and Morton Kaplan, University of Hartford, Connecticut, 1967, pp. 128–140.

Sources

Virginia Spencer Carr, *Understanding Carson McCullers*, Columbia: University of South Carolina Press, 1990.

Rose Feld, "A Remarkable First Novel of Lonely Lives," *New York Times Book Review*, June 16, 1940, p. 6.

David Madden, "Transfixed among the Self-Inflicted Ruins: Carson McCullers' *The Mortgaged Heart*," *Southern Literary Journal*, Vol. 5, Fall, 1972, pp. 137-162.

May Sarton, "Pitiful Hunt for Security: Tragedy of Unfulfillment Theme of Story That Will Rank High in American Letters," *Boston Evening Telegraph*, June 8, 1940, pp. IV-1.

Tennessee Williams, "This Book," *Reflections in a Golden Eye*, by Carson McCullers, New York: New Directions, 1950.

Richard Wright, "Inner Landscape," *The New Republic*, Vol. 103, August 5, 1940, p. 195.

Marguerite Young, "Metaphysical Fiction," *Kenyon Review*, Vol. IX, No. 1, Winter, 1947.

For Further Study

Richard M. Cook, *Carson McCullers*, Ungar, 1975.
　　The twenty-five pages that Cook devotes to the novel cover all of the major themes and characters.

Oliver Evans, *The Ballad of Carson McCullers: A Biography*, Coward McCann, 1966.
　　Published during McCullers' lifetime, this book contains the early synopsis of the novel, "Author's Outline of *The Mute*" (which was the original title of *The Heart Is a Lonely Hunter*). Invaluable to students of this book.

Lawrence Graver, "Penumbral Insistence: McCullers's Early Novels," in *Carson McCullers*, edited and with an introduction by Harold Bloom, Chelsea House Publishers, 1986, pp. 53-67.
　　In a few pages, Graver gives a concrete understanding of the characters in this novel and of the characters in *Reflections in a Golden Eye* and *The Ballad of the Sad Cafe*.

Margaret McDowell, *Carson McCullers*, Twayne, 1980.
　　McDowell's analysis of this novel is divided into themes: "Isolation as Man's Fate," "The Quartet—the "Spokes of the Wheel,'" "The Use of Black Characters," "A 'Contrapuntal' Novel," and "The Sense of Violence Held Tenuously in Check."

Louise Westling, *Sacred Groves and Ravaged Gardens: The Fiction of Eudora Welty, Carson McCullers, and Flannery O'Connor*, University of Georgia Press, 1985.
　　This book explores the influence of Southern culture on the writings of women, an aspect that is often ignored in male-oriented literary criticism.

The House of the Spirits

Isabel Allende
1982

Until the publication of Isabel Allende's *House of the Spirits,* few female writers had emerged from the "Boom" of Latin American literature that began in the 1960s. When the translation of *La casa de los espíritus* appeared in 1985, however, Allende received the kind of international attention that had previously been reserved for writers such as Colombian Nobel Prize-winner Gabriel García Márquez. In fact, *The House of the Spirits* has frequently been compared with García Márquez's masterpiece *One Hundred Years of Solitude* because of Allende's mixture of magical and realistic elements and her multi-generational plot. While there are some similarities between the two works, *The House of the Spirits* is distinguished by its author's unique perspective as a woman and a Chilean.

The novel follows three generations of Trueba women—Clara, Blanca, and Alba—as they struggle to establish their independence from Esteban Trueba, the domineering family patriarch. The political backdrop to this family story is the growing conflict between forces of Left and Right, culminating in a military coup that leads to a stifling dictatorship. While the country is never specifically named as Chile, its political history reflects that of the author's homeland. In 1973, military forces deposed the legally elected administration of President Salvador Allende, Isabel's uncle. "I think I have divided my life [into] before that day and after that day," Allende told *Publishers Weekly* interviewer Amanda Smith. "In that moment, I realized that everything was possible—that violence

was a dimension that was always around you." Because of this realization, *The House of the Spirits* has a political element that is more explicit than many other works of magic realism. This makes it "one of the best novels of the postwar period, and a major contribution to our understanding of societies riddled by ceaseless conflict and violent change," Bruce Allen observed in the *Chicago Tribune Book World.* "It is a great achievement, and it cries out to be read."

Author Biography

Allende (pronounced "Ah-*yen*-day") was born August 2, 1942, in Lima, Peru, the daughter of Chilean diplomat Tomás Allende and his wife, Francisca Llona Barros. Her father was a first cousin of Salvador Allende, her godfather, who later became president of Chile. Allende's parents divorced when she was just two years old, and her mother took her to live with her grandparents. Allende's grandparents had a profound influence on her, and she has said they served as the models for the characters of Esteban and Clara Trueba in *The House of the Spirits.* Allende's mother later remarried, and her new husband was also a diplomat whose assignments took the family abroad. By the time she was fifteen, the author had lived in Bolivia, Europe, and the Middle East.

Allende became a noted journalist in Chile, authoring regular magazine columns, editing a children's magazine, and even hosting a weekly television program. At the same time, she tried her hand at producing plays and writing short stories for children. Allende married engineer Miguel Frías in 1962, and the couple had two children, Paula and Nicolás. In the meantime, her uncle Salvador Allende was elected President of Chile on his fourth attempt at the office. When his government fell to a military coup on September 13, 1973, the author's life took a dramatic change. Like her character Alba, Allende joined the efforts of church-sponsored groups in providing food and aid to the needy and families of the victims of the regime. For fifteen months, the author helped many people escape the military's persecution at the risk of her own life, witnessing events that she would later incorporate into her first novel. "Because of my work as a journalist I knew exactly what was happening in my country, I lived through it, and the dead, the tortured, the widows and orphans, left an unforgettable impression on my memory," the author wrote in *Discurso Literario.* "The last chap-

Isabel Allende

ters of *La casa de los espíritus* narrate those events. They are based on what I saw and on the direct testimonies of those who lived through the brutal experience of the repression."

Because of her family connections, Allende lost her job, and fear for their safety led her family to flee Chile for Caracas, Venezuela in 1975. Despite her considerable experience as a journalist, she found it difficult to find work as a writer. Instead she worked as a teacher and administrator for several years before taking a position with one of the leading newspapers in the country. The exiled author felt isolated, however, and was concerned about the ailing grandfather she had left behind. Wanting him to know she had not forgotten him, she began writing a letter recounting all the family stories she had learned. This letter turned into the manuscript for her first novel, *La casa de los espíritus,* and after finding a Spanish agent, the work was published in 1982. Despite being banned in Chile, copies found their way to Chilean readers, and the novel earned worldwide popularity upon translation.

Allende's subsequent works have gained similar success with critics and readers. *De amor y sombra* (1984; translated as *Of Love and Shadows*), *Eva Luna* (1987), and *Cuentos de Eva Luna* (1990; translated as *Stories of Eva Luna*) all take place in

Latin America or the Caribbean and deal with similar themes of love, literature, and survival. Her 1991 work *El plan infinito* (translated as *The Infinite Plan*) takes place in America. The author herself relocated to the United States in 1988, having married American lawyer William Gordon that year. Allende also used her own experiences as inspiration for writing the 1995 autobiography *Paula,* which recounts the author's thoughts as she sat by her dying daughter's bedside. Despite her continuing success, she remains best known for her first work, *The House of the Spirits.*

Plot Summary

Clara

The House of the Spirits begins by introducing readers to Severo and Nívea del Valle and two of their daughters: Rosa, the oldest, and Clara, the youngest. Clara, who has been denounced by the local priest as possessed by the devil, predicts a death in the del Valle family, which is tragically fulfilled when Rosa accidentally drinks poison meant for Severo. As a result of Rosa's death, her fiancé Esteban Trueba, who has been working at the mines hoping to make his fortune, tells his sister Férula that he will instead restore their family's estate, Tres Marías. During his tenure there, Esteban rapes one of the tenants on his estate, Pancha García, and impregnates her, a pattern he will continue with other women on the estate. After he has had relations with all the young women on the estate, Esteban begins going to the local brothel, where he meets Tránsito Soto and assists her by giving her fifty pesos to leave town.

After nine years in the countryside, Esteban returns to the city to see his dying mother and is betrothed to Clara, who has recently broken a nine-year silence by announcing that she will marry Rosa's fiancé. Clara gives birth to a daughter, Blanca, and twin boys whom she names Jaime and Nicolás against Esteban's wishes. Esteban meets Tránsito Soto again and she tells him she wants to start a whores' cooperative. After finding his sister Férula in bed with Clara, Esteban banishes her from the house, and Clara's clairvoyant powers fail in locating her. When the family is at Tres Marías, Férula appears as a ghost and Clara insists on returning to the city, knowing that Férula is dead.

Blanca

When next the Truebas return to Tres Marís, Blanca and her childhood playmate Pedro Tercero García begin a love affair. Clara divines that Blanca is having an affair after a massive earthquake which breaks all of Esteban's bones. Following the earthquake, Pedro García sets Esteban's bones, his son Pedro Segundo becomes foreman of the estate, and his grandson Pedro Tercero begins preaching socialist ideas to the tenants. Clara takes on the domestic duties of the estate, working closely with Pedro Segundo and shutting the city house. Esteban fires Pedro Tercero for insubordination, but he and Blanca continue their affair. When Count Jean de Satigny, a guest at the estate, asks for Blanca's hand, she refuses him. Soon after the death of Pedro García, Jean tells Esteban that Pedro Tercero and Blanca are lovers. After Clara points out that though they are like Esteban in taking lovers from other social classes, Blanca and Pedro Tercero have done so out of love, an enraged Esteban hits her. Pedro Segundo leaves Esteban's employ and Esteban swears revenge on Pedro Tercero, finding him with the help of Esteban García, his own illegitimate grandson. After he chops off three of Pedro Tercero's fingers, Esteban refuses Esteban García the reward he has promised him.

Esteban orders Jean de Satigny to marry the pregnant Blanca. Clara assures Blanca that Pedro Tercero still lives, and also predicts that Esteban Trueba will win his election by a small margin. Meanwhile, Blanca's brother Jaime, a doctor who helps the poor and disagrees with his father's conservative politics, performs an abortion on Nicolás' girlfriend Amanda, whom he secretly loves. By the time she gives birth to her daughter Alba, Blanca has discovered her husband's erotic photographs of the servants and has left him. Alba grows up thinking that her father has died, but Blanca continues her affair with her true father, Pedro Tercero. As a child, Alba has her first encounter with Esteban García, who nearly molests her.

Alba

Clara dies on Alba's seventh birthday and her grieving husband begins to shrink. After his son Nicolás' naked protest gives Esteban a heart attack, he gives Nicolás money to leave the country. Esteban constructs a mausoleum for Clara and Rosa and when he kisses Rosa's corpse, it disintegrates in his hands. Esteban becomes obsessed with the "Marxist cancer," but Blanca continues to see Pedro Tercero, now a popular singer of socialist songs, though she will not marry him because she is afraid of losing her class status. Esteban meets Tránsito Soto again and murmurs Clara's name while he has sex with her.

At the university, Alba joins Miguel's political cause out of love for him, and when she is unmasked as Esteban Trueba's granddaughter by Esteban García, Miguel's love for her overcomes his sense of betrayal. Jaime leaves his father's house because he supports the Candidate and agrees to help Miguel's drug-addicted sister, his lost love Amanda. The Candidate becomes the President, and Pedro Tercero joins the government, after which Blanca rejects his final marriage proposal. Esteban Trueba is helping to sabotage the economy, but the younger Truebas work for the survival of the new government. After the peasants of Tres Marías take Esteban prisoner, Blanca and Alba ask Pedro Tercero to rescue him and he agrees. During this visit, Pedro Tercero's love for Blanca is rekindled, while Alba learns that Pedro Tercero is her father. After Pedro Tercero rescues Esteban, they discover their personal hatred is extinguished, but hatred in the rest of the country is on the rise. Jaime is shot and killed during a coup which Esteban celebrates; when Esteban offers his services to the new regime he learns of his son's death and the destruction of the democratic system. Esteban is disgusted with himself after he orders the peasant village at Tres Marías destroyed. After the funeral of the Poet, which becomes the symbolic burial of freedom, Esteban admits that he has made a mistake, enabling Blanca and Pedro Tercero to flee the country and asking her forgiveness, which she grants by telling him she loves him.

Alba's terrible nightmare comes true when she is arrested and tortured by Esteban García, but she refuses to give up Miguel. When Alba is at her lowest point, in solitary confinement, Clara appears to her and tells her to write in order to survive. Meanwhile, on the outside, Esteban gets Transíto Soto to help him secure Alba's release. After the two restore the house and write their story, Esteban dies in Alba's arms. Alba is pregnant, possibly as a result of having been raped, and she realizes that her grandfather's evil created the evil of Esteban García and vows to break that terrible chain. Alba is left, at the end of the novel, waiting for Miguel's return and her daughter's birth.

Characters

Amanda

With her "exotic appearance"—long black hair, heavily made-up eyes, and beaded necklaces—Amanda is passionately loved by both Trueba brothers. Amanda has a "free, affectionate, adventurous" personality, yet is practical enough to realize the immature and selfish Nicolás is not a good match for her. She has a "very old soul," aged prematurely by her extreme poverty and her responsibility for her young brother Miguel. While it is Jaime who would be able to take care of her, it is twenty years before the two begin a relationship. By this time, unfortunately, Jaime no longer feels capable of any deep emotion but compassion. Amanda joins him at the clinic, and works there even after his death. During the terror she is detained by the police and questioned about her brother's revolutionary activities. Weakened by her grief and her years of drug use, she dies in custody without betraying her brother, just as she had promised him years before.

Barrabás

Barrabás arrives at the del Valle household with the rest of Uncle Marcos's effects, barely recognizable as a puppy. Clara recognizes him at once for what he is, adopts him, and nurses him back to health. The huge dog seems to be the living embodiment of the mythical beasts Rosa embroiders on her tablecloth. He is devoted to Clara, even accompanying her on sleepwalks, and dies on her engagement day, stabbed in the back with a butcher's knife.

Countess

See Alba Trueba

Nívea del Valle

Clara's mother, Nívea, is a good example of the first stage of feminism in Chile. She demonstrates for women's rights while still being a dutiful mother of fifteen. While she jokes with her friends that women will not have the strength to take advantage of their rights as long as they wear corsets and long skirts, "she herself was not brave enough to be among the first to give up the fashion." She treats her favorite daughter, Clara, "as if she were an only child, creating a tie so strong that it continued into succeeding generations as a family tradition." Nívea dies in a car accident with her husband, Severo, in which she is decapitated. Clara locates the head after others are unable to find it, and after spending years in the Trueba basement it is eventually buried with Clara in the mausoleum.

Rosa del Valle

The oldest of the del Valle daughters, Rosa is "the most beautiful creature to be born on earth since the days of original sin." She has yellow eyes and green hair, and has a "maritime grace" that makes her resemble a mermaid. She becomes Esteban Trueba's fiancée because he is the only man brave enough to approach her. Nevertheless, while he is away making his fortune, Rosa scarcely thinks of him as she dreamily embroiders strange creatures on an endless tablecloth. Her mother senses that Rosa "was not destined to last very long in the vulgar traffic of this world" and so she learns nothing about managing a household. Nívea's premonition is accurate, for Rosa is killed with a flask of poisoned brandy meant for her father. She is even more beautiful in death, and decades later is completely unchanged when Esteban Trueba steals her body to place it in the family mausoleum.

Severo del Valle

Clara's father, Severo, is "an atheist and a Mason," but since he has political ambitions he attends church faithfully. He joins the Liberal party despite being a member of the upper class, and is invited to run as a Congressional representative for a southern district "that he had never set foot in and had difficulty finding on a map." He gives up his life-long political ambitions, however, after his daughter Rosa is poisoned. He ironically wishes that "none of his descendants would ever get mixed up in politics," although that is exactly what happens. Severo dies in a car accident, a victim of his "weakness for modern inventions."

Alba de Satigny

See Alba Trueba

Count Jean de Satigny

The Count de Satigny is a frequent visitor to Esteban Trueba's home at Tres Marías. While some people mock his concern with appearance and etiquette, he still becomes a figure of high social standing. After Blanca refuses his marriage proposal, he is considerate enough to win her friendship. When he discovers the true nature of Blanca's relationship with Pedro Tercero, however, he betrays them to Esteban, leading to a terrible family fight. A few months later, when Esteban learns Blanca is pregnant, he forces the Count to marry her and legitimize the child. "He did not know whether to feel sorry for himself for having fallen victim to these savage aborigines, or to rejoice at being on the verge of fulfilling his dream of marrying a rich, young, beautiful South American heiress." Satigny settles for the second interpretation, but the marriage does not last long. When

Isabel's uncle, Salvadore Allende, served as president of Chile from his election in 1970 until his assassination during a military coup in 1973.

Blanca discovers the Count's collection of pornographic photographs, she leaves without looking back. The family never hears from him again until called to identify his body, felled by a stroke during old age.

Ana Díaz

Ana is one of Alba's fellow students at the university, and is somewhat disdainful when she learns that Alba is the granddaughter of Esteban Trueba. She is more understanding when they meet again as captives of the police. She is "indomitable," and helps Alba survive her captivity. It is Ana who gives Alba a notebook and suggests she write everything down to "get out whatever's worrying you inside, so you'll get better once and for all."

Esteban García

Because of his grandmother Pancha's reminders, Esteban García grows up keenly aware that he is the grandson of Esteban Trueba, even if his grandfather scarcely notices his existence. He first comes to Trueba's notice when he offers to reveal the hiding place of Pedro Tercero. Trueba gives him a slap instead of a reward, however, leaving the boy weeping with rage. When young Este-

Media Adaptations

- Danish director Bille August made a film version of *The House of the Spirits* starring Jeremy Irons as Esteban, Meryl Streep as Clara, Glenn Close as Férula, Antonio Banderas as Pedro Tercero, and Winona Ryder as Blanca. The film was not particularly successful, with many critics claiming the Anglo actors were hopelessly miscast. One critic even suggested that the only worth of the adaptation was as a "potential camp cult film."

ban comes to ask his grandfather for help in entering the police force, he molests Alba, recognizing "she embodied everything he would never have, never be." On her fourteenth birthday he gives Alba her first "kiss," giving her nightmares of a green beast trying to suffocate her. His hatred is cemented when she orders him to take her home after leaving the university strike. After the coup he becomes a colonel and Alba becomes his private prisoner, there for him to "avenge himself for injuries that had been inflicted on him from birth."

Pancha García

The daughter of Pedro García, Pancha is just fifteen when Esteban first spots her working on the plantation. A peasant of Indian extraction, she "had the beauty of early youth," although Esteban could see "that it would quickly fade, as it does with women who are born to have many children, work without rest, and bury their dead." Esteban uses and then discards Pancha, even as she bears him a child. Her son Esteban is the only bastard he admits is his, even though he sires many more with the women of Tres Marías. Pancha later dies of chicken fever, beyond the help of her father Pedro's remedies.

Pedro García

Pedro is an elderly man when Esteban Trueba takes over the operation of Tres Marías. He claims his grandfather had fought for independence against the Spaniards and tells marvelous stories. He knows almost as much about herbs and healing as the *curandera,* and it is Pedro García and not the gringo technician who finds the cure for the ant plague. It is also old blind Pedro who sets Esteban's bones "so perfectly that the doctors who examined Trueba afterward could not believe such a thing was possible." He dies an old man, of sound mind and clear memory although blind and deaf.

Pedro Segundo García

The son of Pedro García, Pedro Segundo ("the Second") becomes the foreman on the Tres Marías plantation, a position which "brought him no more privileges, but only more work." Although he is most likely the same age as Esteban Trueba, he "looked older." Pedro Segundo is more intelligent than the other peasants, but Trueba never treats him as a friend and Pedro Segundo looks on his *patrón* with a "mixture of fear and resentful admiration." He is loyal and dependable, however, and never speaks against Trueba or his policies. Clara learns to treat him as a friend and partner when she takes charge of the plantation after the earthquake, and Pedro Segundo "valued her as much as he detested Esteban Trueba." He comforts her after Trueba knocks her teeth out over her defense of Blanca's relationship with Pedro Tercero. Pedro Segundo never sees any of the family after that point, for he leaves the plantation rather than witness what might happen when Trueba takes his revenge on his son.

Pedro Tercero García

Although he physically resembles his father, Pedro Segundo, Pedro Tercero ("the Third") is willing to defy Esteban Trueba and fight against the injustice of the social order. Despite his father's beatings and Trueba's warnings, Pedro Tercero continues to discuss "revolutionary" ideas of justice he learns from Leftist leaning teachers, priests, and union members. But while he believes he must struggle against injustice, he also "knew his place in the world"—one that will never allow him to have a legitimate relationship with the daughter of Esteban Trueba. When Trueba discovers his secret affair with Blanca, Pedro is forced to hide from the *patrón*'s anger. A confrontation leads to Pedro Tercero losing three fingers to Trueba's ax. He recovers and learns to play the guitar again and soon is recording songs of revolution that make him famous. Although his fame brings him many women, none of them is Blanca's equal. He begins to secretly meet with her once again, but she refuses to allow him to recognize Alba as his daughter and turns down his proposals. Even though he is "disillusioned with political organizations" and "had no ambition for either money or power," after the Candidate's election he is drawn into an administrative post in the government. The pressures of the job lead him to give Blanca a final ultimatum: marry him or never see him again. When she refuses again they remain apart for two years, until she asks his help in rescuing her father from the revolutionary tenants who have taken him hostage. Esteban Trueba returns the favor after the coup makes Pedro Tercero a fugitive, arranging for him to escape the country with Blanca. The two live in exile in Canada, where finally "they both felt completely fulfilled in the peace of satisfied love."

Sebastián Gómez

Sebastián Gómez is a professor at the university which Alba attends. He assists the students with their occupation of a university building during the strike, and is naively hopeful that students and workers all over the country will join their cause. He never complains during the occupation, although he wears braces on his crippled legs. Although he is an "ideologue" against injustice, he still believes that women should not be involved in "men's affairs" such as the strike. His naive idealism also leads him to declare that the government is "not a dictatorship and it never will be." Ironically, he is betrayed by his students and is killed by the political police during the first raid on the university after the coup.

Uncle Marcos

Nívea del Valle's brother, Uncle Marcos is a "weather-beaten and thin" world traveller with a pirate's mustache and the manners "of a cannibal," according to Severo del Valle. His first funeral occurs after he disappears while trying to fly a mechanical bird to the mountains. He returns unharmed, however, and after yet another journey sets up a fortune-telling shop with Clara. Clara is closest to her uncle, not only because of her clairvoyance but because she loves his stories of exotic lands. Uncle Marcos has written accounts of his travels and stores these journals and his books of fairy tales in the family junk room. Although Uncle Marcos dies while Clara is still a child, his stories live on as they entertain and instruct Blanca, Pedro Tercero, and Alba.

Father José Dulce María

Father José Dulce María is a Spanish priest with revolutionary ideas that have led to his being sent to San Lucas, "that hidden corner of the world." He turns Biblical stories into Socialist parables, and is an important influence on Pedro Tercero. He not only teaches the boy philosophy, but also instructs him in "how to cultivate his natural poetic gifts and to translate his ideas into songs." Father José also takes Pedro Tercero in after his encounter with Esteban Trueba and heals him "in both body and soul."

Miguel

Amanda's younger brother Miguel is around five when he first encounters the big Trueba house on the corner. He calls Clara "Mama" and Jaime "Papa" and is inseparable from his sister until Clara convinces her to allow him to attend school. As an adult, he is a revolutionary who believes violence is the only way to effect radical change. He is a natural leader, and during the building occupation "seemed to be the only one who knew what to do." He loves Alba even after he discovers she is the "bourgeois" granddaughter of Esteban Trueba, and they create a love nest in the basement of the big house. Nevertheless, Miguel realizes that Alba's commitment to the cause is for love, not political conviction, and insists that she remain uninvolved in any of his guerilla activities. Jaime believes that Miguel is one of those with a "dangerous idealism and an intransigent purity that color everything they touch with disaster," but he is fond of the young man because of his "natural gaiety" and "capacity for tenderness." After the coup, Miguel goes into hiding and manages to evade capture. He is also the one who comes up with the idea to use Tránsito Soto to arrange Alba's release. It is implied in the Epilogue that Miguel will remain in Chile as long as he has to in order to bring about the political change he so passionately wants.

Mora Sisters

The three Mora sisters "were the only people who possessed irrefutable proof that souls can take on physical form." They learn of Clara's existence through "telepathic contact" with her, and are soon frequent visitors at the big house. Nicolás spends quite a bit of time with them during his unsuccessful attempts to develop his own powers of perception, and it is through them that he meets Amanda. The sisters are associated with the scent of wild violets, which is how their presence is announced at several points in the novel. It is the last surviving sister, Luisa Mora, who prophetically warns Alba of the danger that waits for her if she remains in the country after the coup.

Nana

Nana is the Indian caretaker of all the children in first the del Valle and later the Trueba family. After Rosa's death, it is Nana who is able to comfort the guilty Severo del Valle, who believes the poison was intended for him: "He felt that this woman, as warm and generous as the earth itself, would be able to console him." She is an important member of the del Valle and Trueba households, and yet apart, born to "live on borrowed happiness and grief" without ever truly having her own life. She dies of fright during the earthquake, and the chaos caused by the disaster ensures that "none of the many children she had raised with so much love attended her funeral."

Tránsito Soto

Esteban Trueba first meets Tránsito when she is a "skinny adolescent" working at the Red Lantern brothel in the countryside. She has the voice of a "hoarse bird" and a tattoo of a snake around her navel. Esteban likes her because of her practical nature and her "amusing" claim that she will go far in life. When he lends her fifty pesos, he does not know that her repayment of the debt will come to be an important one. She uses the money to move to the city, lead a successful prostitutes' cooperative, and obtain wealth and power. It is ironic that Trueba admires her so, for her success comes from feminine empowerment and Socialist practices.

Alba Trueba

Alba is the product of Blanca's illicit affair with Pedro Tercero García, although she does not learn her true parentage until she is an adult. Her name, which can be translated as "dawn," forms the "last in a chain of luminous words" that serve as names for the women in the novel. She has greenish hair, like her great-aunt Rosa, but otherwise she looks like no other member of the family. Like her predecessors, Alba is also a solitary child, preferring to play imaginary games in the basement of the big house or with her uncle Jaime. Like her grandmother, she has a "wild imagination" and enjoys Uncle Marcos's tales, told as variations by her mother Blanca. She becomes the only focus for Esteban's love and tenderness, since he has already destroyed his relationships with the rest of the family. He agrees that she should have a decent education, since she is "too plain to attract a well-to-do husband."

Alba attends university and despite her grandfather's warnings to avoid love, falls instantly for Miguel, a brash young law school student. She follows him to student protests but manages to keep her activities—including a love nest in the basement—secret from her grandfather. Alba has the same generous spirit as her grandmother, for she smuggles Blanca's hoarded food supplies out to the poor and also gives many of the weapons hidden by her grandfather to Miguel's guerilla movement. After the coup, she helps victims of political persecution find asylum and works with local priests to help feed the poor. "She realized that they had returned to the old days when her Grandmother Clara went to the Misericordia District to replace justice with charity." Her efforts convince Esteban that something has gone wrong in the country, especially after the secret police seize her in the middle of the night. She is tortured, but a vision of Clara convinces her that survival should be her goal. With the aid of Ana Díaz and other women in the prison, Alba recovers and begins to write. Upon her return home, she recreates the family story at her grandfather's urging, so "you'll be able to take your roots with you if you ever have to leave." The act of writing, she discovers, will help her "reclaim the past and overcome terrors of my own," and so she begins with the first lines of her grandmother's diary: *Barrabás came to us by sea ...*

Blanca Trueba

The oldest child and only daughter of Esteban and Clara, Blanca looks like an armadillo when she is born. She soon flourishes under Clara's care, and is very close to her mother, as the similarity of her name (which translates as "white") suggests. Her mother treats her as an adult, and as a result, as a very young child "Blanca looked like an intelligent midget" because of her ability to speak and take care of herself. She is still a child when she first meets Pedro Tercero at Tres Marías, and she runs naked to play with the boy and falls asleep on his stomach. This incident foreshadows their future relationship, when they become lovers and are discovered in the same position by Esteban. As a child, Blanca is romantic and sentimental and considered "timid and morose" by her teachers. Only in the country, when she is with Pedro Tercero, does she bloom and become happy. She exchanges secret messages with him and sneaks out of her room to meet him by the river. The commotion when her father discovers their relationship causes the family to split apart.

Blanca is pregnant, however, and when her father discovers this he tells her he has killed Pedro Tercero and forces her to marry Count Jean de

Satigny. She is "a practical, worldly, diffident woman" with a "modern, pragmatic character," so she tries to make the most of her marriage and lead the "idle life that was her true vocation" until discovering the Count's unpleasant hobby. She only loves Pedro Tercero, but refuses to run away with him, not wishing to give up her social position or face the ridicule of his working-class friends. For romantic Blanca, her "poetic fantasies" are better than discovering that "the grandiose love that had withstood so many tests would not be able to withstand the most dreadful test of all: living together." Her refusals separate them for a time, but they reunite over the crisis of her father's kidnapping. The repression after the coup finally forces Blanca to make a decision: she hides Pedro Tercero from the police and then enlists her father's help in escaping the country. Only then can the two men overcome the hatred that had poisoned their lives until then, and Blanca ends up a successful artist in Canada, living "completely fulfilled in the peace of satisfied love."

Clara del Valle Trueba

The youngest of the del Valle children, Clara has an unusual ability to see things, just as her name (which translates as "white" or "clear") suggests. As a child she is "extremely precocious and had inherited the runaway imagination of all the women in her family," and enjoys the stories and books of her Uncle Marcos. Her family accepts her ability to move saltcellars and predict earthquakes, only becoming concerned when the local priest claims she is possessed by the devil. When she witnesses the autopsy of her sister Rosa, it fills her with "the silence of the entire world" and she stubbornly remains mute for the next nine years. Instead she reads voraciously and writes in her notebooks, diaries which prove to be invaluable to her granddaughter Alba in the future. To the dismay of her politically ambitious father, Clara's psychic abilities increase as she grows older, but her mother realizes that the only way to deal with her unusual daughter is to "love her unconditionally and accept her as she was." She is allowed to keep to herself and "in later years would recall her childhood as a luminous part of her existence."

At age nineteen, however, Clara sees her future is with Esteban Trueba and decides she will "marry without love." Esteban, in contrast, falls deeply in love with the woman who has the advantage of charm, if not beauty, over her late sister Rosa. Clara is not a very good manager, being too distracted by the "world of apparitions," and

leaves the running of the household to her sister-in-law Férula. After Blanca's birth and the family's move to Tres Marías, however, "she seemed to have been cured of her habit of speaking with invisible spirits and moving the furniture by supernatural means." She works to educate the people on the plantation, trying to teach the women about equality. After Férula's departure and the earthquake, she becomes a more practical person, as the death and destruction she witnesses "put her in touch with the basic needs to which she had been oblivious." She often invokes Esteban's anger and frustration, but is able to defuse his temper with either a few short words or her own inattentiveness. When she supports Blanca's relationship with Pedro Tercero, however, Esteban loses control and strikes her, knocking out several teeth. She refuses to speak to her husband ever again, and moves back to the big house in the city. She resumes her psychic experiments, but is sadder than before. She dies on Alba's seventh birthday, having made up her mind to die. She believes that "dying is like being born: just a change," and Esteban believes that she walks the halls of the big house after her death. This may just be a manifestation of his guilt and desire, however, for it is only after Clara's death that he allows himself to tell her "everything I couldn't say before."

Esteban Trueba

The patriarch of the Trueba family, Esteban is a passionate, hard-working man who is determined to succeed. He is also quick to anger, frequently cruel, and intolerant of those less fortunate than himself. He allows no contradiction of his strict conservative beliefs, and thinks he is justified in ruling his plantation with an iron hand because he has improved the peasants' standard of living. "It would be lovely if we were all created equal, but the fact is we're not," he says, arguing that his workers would be lost without him. He takes the same attitude toward women, wanting to possess Clara "absolutely, down to her last thought," taking advantage of plantation women, and declaring that a woman's duty is "motherhood and the home." His greatest failing is his inability to control his temper, which leads him to hurt those he loves the most. To his regret he always "gets carried away with his punishment," as when he whips Blanca after discovering her with Pedro Tercero or when he beats Clara when she defends her daughter. When Tres Marías is returned to him after the coup, he dismisses all the tenants and burns down the buildings he once worked so hard to build. Afterwards, "despite the pleasure of his revenge, he was unable to sleep. He felt like a father who has punished his children too severely."

Having come from a noted but impoverished household, Esteban is ambitious for both power and money. He is successful in achieving both, becoming a wealthy *patrón* and senator. He is less successful in his personal life, however. His relationships with his children "only worsened with time," and after Clara's death, he notes that he had "only two friends" to try to cheer him up. Férula's curse seems to come true and he shrinks with time. It would be hard to feel sympathy for Esteban, except for two things: the first-person narration that shows how deeply he both loves and suffers; and the tolerance and understanding he finds in his old age. The consequences of the coup have taught him that his judgment is not perfect, and he is not so adamant in having his way. His granddaughter Alba has also mellowed his demeanor, for he has "transferred all his finest sentiments to Alba" and treats her with tolerance and indulgence. He makes no protests over her relationship with Miguel, an orphaned revolutionary, and also mends his differences with Pedro Tercero and Blanca. Thus a man who lived with so much passion and violence dies a peaceful death, "without pain or anguish, more lucid than ever and happy, conscious, and serene."

Ester Trueba

Esteban and Férula's mother has been so afflicted with arthritis that she is "like a living corpse." She came from a rich family, but fell in love with and married a "good-for-nothing" immigrant instead of a man of her own class. Her family's money squandered, Ester Trueba is left to the care of her son Esteban and daughter Férula. She dies bedridden and suffering from gruesome wounds, leaving her son guilty and angry "at not having loved her and cared for her enough."

Férula Trueba

Esteban's sister Férula has spent her life taking care of her mother, and it has left her bitter and resentful. Esteban observes that she was a "beautiful woman," but "already the ugliness of resignation could be glimpsed through her pale, peach-toned skin." While she "took pleasure in humiliation" and performs her duties without complaint, she knows just how to make the recipients of her service feel guilty. She is prepared to hate her new sister-in-law, but Clara's openness disarms her and Férula becomes her most devoted friend.

As passionate as her brother, Férula "was one of those people who are born for the greatness of a single love," and it is only with Clara that she permits herself "the luxury of giving in to her overwhelming desire to serve and be loved." Her passion leads her to be jealous of her brother, and the conflict between them causes Esteban to send her away. Six years later her ghost leads the family to her impoverished apartment, where she has obviously refused to use any of the funds sent by her brother. Even in death, she fills Esteban with anger over "her spirit of sacrifice, her severity, her vocation for poverty, and her unshakable chastity, which he felt as a reproach."

Jaime Trueba

One of the twin sons of Esteban and Clara, Jaime has the same desire to help the unfortunate as his mother had. He displays an early interest in the writings of Karl Marx, and as an adult is "tall, robust, timid, and studious." Although he is "peevish" and dislikes dealing with people, he is "generous and candid and had a tremendous capacity for kindness." He creates a tunnel of books in his room in the big house, and studies medicine so that he may help the poor. He ignores his father's disapproval and attends Socialist meetings and, unknown to his father, is the best friend of Pedro Tercero. His one passion is for his brother's lover Amanda, whose "vulnerability was more seductive than anything that had attracted him before." His love for Nicolás is greater than that for Amanda, however, and by the time they begin a relationship, twenty years after first meeting, he is no longer capable of feeling anything but compassion for her. His work with the poor brings him into contact with the President, and so he is with the leader on the day of the coup. He refuses to lie about the President's death, and so the military tortures and executes him. Jaime, who was "preoccupied and more or less continued to be until the day they killed him," provides another example of a person who believes "it can never happen here."

Nicolás Trueba

One of the twin sons of Esteban and Clara, Nicolás "inherited the adventurous spirit of his great-uncle Marcos and his mother's propensity for making up astrological charts and reading the future." He is "as pretty as a girl" and is much smarter than his brother, but Jaime frequently serves as his protector. As a young man Nicolás is interested in girls and the supernatural, trying to develop his powers by studying with the Mora sisters despite his father's insistence that such matters are for women. He has no talent, however, and turns to business ventures such as a dancing school, selling advertising on a zeppelin, and selling chicken sandwiches. He is an innocent, however, as Amanda tells him when he offers to marry her and legitimize their child: "Can't you see my soul is very old and you're still a child?" He searches for spiritual fulfillment in yoga, drugs, travel, and vegetarianism, and in writing a book on the names of God and the attainment of nirvana. He teaches Alba to conquer fear through visualizing it, and sets up an academy called the "Institute for Union with Nothingness." The embarrassment he causes his father leads Esteban to banish him from the country with enough money to settle down. Nicolás founds another institute in North America, and there finds success in combining his quest for God with his skill in business.

Themes

Love and Passion

While most of the characters of *The House of the Spirits* experience passionate love, they often discover that passion is not enough to sustain a relationship. Esteban has a deep passion for his wife Clara, but his love is possessive: "he wanted far more than her body; he wanted control over that undefined and luminous material that lay within her." His desire to control what he loves fuels his anger, leading him to punish those he loves when they do not comply with his expectations. Férula's love for Clara similarly becomes a "jealous passion that resembled that of a demanding husband more than it did that of a sister-in-law," and leads to her banishment from the house. But unpossessive love is not complete, either, unless it is tempered with common sense. Amanda, for instance, knows that Nicolás is too immature to make a good husband and refuses to turn their "free love" relationship into a marriage. Blanca is unable to run away with Pedro Tercero because she fears her "grandiose love" will not survive the commonplace nature of everyday life together. Instead, she "fed [her love] with fantasies, idealized it, savagely defended it, stripped it of prosaic truth, and turned it into the kind of love one found in novels." The most successful loves portrayed in the novel are unconditional, involving both giving and receiving. Alba and Miguel love each other without restrictions or conditions, which allows their love to survive his

periods of concealment as well as her torture and imprisonment. This healthy attitude toward love is also expressed in parent-child relationships. Nívea del Valle, for instance, understands that the best way to deal with Clara's unusual abilities is to "love her unconditionally and accept her as she was." Blanca and Alba learn that the impaired children to whom they teach ceramics "worked much better when they felt loved, and that the only way to communicate with them was through affection." This is a lesson that Esteban finally learns, when at last he manages to love his granddaughter Alba without the anger that has crippled the rest of his relationships.

Sex Roles

The struggle of women to achieve equality and self-determination forms an important part of the novel, and is reflected in the clashes of the various female characters against Esteban Trueba. Although Esteban believes that a woman's duty is "motherhood and the home," he recognizes that this role is a difficult one: "I would not have liked to be a woman," he says to Férula when she expresses her bitterness at having to stay with their infirm mother. Interestingly enough, Esteban has nothing but respect for the most unconventional woman he knows, Tránsito Soto, whose ambition has made her into a successful businesswoman. Nevertheless, he treats women like property, raping peasant women without guilt, paying female workers less than men, and expecting his female relatives to obey his orders without question. He frowns on Nívea del Valle, who fights for the right to vote, and forbids Clara to teach the hacienda's workers about women's rights. Clara continually defies her husband's expectations, however, and essentially lives her life as she wants to, using his house to hold spiritualist sessions and minister to the poor. Blanca similarly defies her father by taking Pedro Tercero for her lover, even though she gives in to Esteban by marrying Jean de Satigny. By the time his granddaughter grows up, Esteban "had finally come to accept ... that not all women were complete idiots," and agrees that Alba "could enter one of the professions and make her living like a man." The struggle for equality has made women strong, however, as Alba discovers after she is rescued from the empty lot where the political police have dumped her. The woman who takes her in is "one of the stoical, practical women of our country," and the risks she takes to help a stranger make Alba realize that "the days of Colonel García and all those

Topics For Further Study

- Read Gabriel García Márquez's novel *One Hundred Years of Solitude,* to which *The House of the Spirits* has often been compared, if not accused of imitating. Make a note of the comparisons and the differences between the two works. In an essay, argue whether or not Allende's work is more than just an imitation of García Márquez's novel. Support your argument with examples.

- Research the history of Chile during the administration of Salvador Allende. Create a month-by-month timeline that illustrates the major developments—such as strikes or congressional actions—that led to the fall of his government. In a different color, add events from the novel that correspond to these developments.

- Do some research on the Internet and find a sampling of domestic violence statistics from various countries and cultures around the world. For those countries you select, also find out what kinds of laws protect the legal rights of women. Draw up a chart with your findings. Is there a correlation between women's legal status and domestic violence? Report your conclusion in a short essay.

- Author Gabriel García Márquez has said the key to writing in the magic realist style is to report on fantastic events with a perfectly "straight face." Start with an everyday subject, like a day at school or a meeting with friends, and try writing your own short story in the style of "magical realism."

- In *The House of the Spirits,* the character Clara demonstrates mental powers such as the ability to predict the future (clairvoyance), move objects (telekinesis), and communicate without words (telepathy). Investigate the history of such extrasensory perception (ESP). In an essay, compare previous scientific inquiries into ESP with what researchers believe today.

---

like him are numbered, because they have not been able to destroy the spirit of these women."

Justice and Injustice

Just as Esteban believes that women have their place in life, he also feels strongly about the role of the "lower classes." He believes his tenants "are like children, they can't handle responsibility," and is leery of letting them learn more than basic reading and math skills "for fear they would fill their minds with ideas unsuited to their station and condition." He does not recognize the injustice that his *patrón* system perpetuates and is unable to see in the intelligent Pedro Segundo "any virtues beyond those that marked him as a good peon." The clear-seeing Clara, however, recognizes the injustices created by class differences. As a young girl she sees the "absurdity" in her upper-class mother preaching about oppression and inequality to "hard-working women in denim aprons, their hands red

with chilblains." When she takes Blanca with her to visit the poor, she explains that "this is to assuage our conscience…. But it doesn't help the poor. They don't need charity; they need justice." The election of the Socialist Candidate does little to ease class inequities, however, as the upper-class Conservatives conspire to undermine the government by arranging food shortages. After the coup, food returns to stores but the poor cannot afford it, and Alba sees a return to "the old days when her Grandmother Clara went to the Misericordia District to replace justice with charity." But, as the upper class discovers, the coup does not mean a return to the old class order; instead, the military forms a new class: they were "a breed apart, brothers who spoke a different dialect from civilians." Esteban García is a member of this new ruling class, and it is his perverted desire for "justice"— fed by his grandmother Pancha's tales of his parentage—that leads him to torture Alba. She comes to understand that the Colonel's purpose was not to gain information about Miguel, "but to avenge himself for injuries that had been inflicted on him from birth."

Science and Technology

The twentieth century is one of "light, science, and technology," as Severo del Valle believes. Esteban Trueba is similarly enchanted with scientific developments, and attempts to improve life at Tres Marías through technology. Science is not perfect, however, as it can do nothing to cure Clara's silence or discover why Esteban is shrinking. Similarly, many scientific improvements to the hacienda end up useless, such as the kerosene stove that becomes a henhouse because no one can learn how to use it. Old Pedro García often demonstrates the limits of science, as he dispels the hacienda's ant plague just by talking to the insects and sets Esteban's broken bones by touch so well that "the doctors who examined Trueba afterward could not believe such a thing was possible." Science and magic are not so different from each other, however. If sufficiently advanced, science becomes a kind of magic, as one cannot understand how it works and must take it on faith. Thus Father Restrepo calls the del Valle car "satanic," while the peasants of Tres Marías believe the news reports on the radio are "fairy tales, which did nothing to alter the narrowness of their existence." Clara recognizes this connection between science and magic: "If you can't understand how the telephone works," she tells Nicolás during his fruitless attempts to develop psychic powers, "how do you expect to understand miracles?"

Language and Meaning

Words and stories have a special significance in *The House of the Spirits*. Old Pedro García is respected and loved for his storytelling ability, and Nívea tells young Clara wild stories about their family in the hope that she will ask questions and thus regain her speech. Férula is such a gifted storyteller that "her listener felt as if he were there," and Pedro Tercero's story-songs create more converts than all the pamphlets he distributes. Language has power, and Clara believes that "by giving problems a name they tended to manifest themselves ... ; whereas if they remained in the limbo of unspoken words, they could disappear by themselves." Names have importance as well, as the names of Clara, Blanca, and Alba form "a chain of luminous words" which connect them to each other. Clara is convinced that Spanish and Es-

peranto are the only languages of interest to beings from other dimensions, while Esteban believes that English is superior to Spanish in describing the world of science and technology.

It is the written word, however, that has the most significance in the novel—after all, the family's story could not have been retold without Clara's notebooks, which "bore witness to life." Uncle Marcos's books of travel and fairy tales "inhabit the dreams of his descendants," giving Clara, Blanca, and Alba a shared mythology. The writing in Clara's notebooks reflects her state of mind, and her correspondence with Blanca "salvaged events from the mist of improbable facts." Jaime constructs a room with books, and Nicolás fills fifteen hundred pages with a treatise on spirituality. Even the government recognizes the might of the written word: "With the stroke of a pen the military changed world history, erasing every incident, ideology, and historical figure of which they disapproved." When the political police come for Alba, the culmination of their destruction comes when they set "an infamous pyre" that was fed with Jaime's collection, Uncle Marcos's books, Nicolás's treatise, and "even Trueba's opera scores." Thus, it is fitting that Alba battles this violence through writing, as both Clara's ghost and Ana Díaz suggest to her. Using Clara's notebooks, Blanca's letters, and other family documents, Alba can come to understand and survive through writing: "I write, she wrote, that memory is fragile and the space of a single life is brief, passing so quickly that we never get a chance to see the relationship between events.... I want to think that my task is life and that my mission is not to prolong hatred but simply to fill these pages."

Style

Narration/Point of View

While much of *The House of the Spirits* seems to have very straightforward third-person ("he/she") narration, in fact there are three distinct narrative voices in the novel. The first voice is that of an unnamed first person ("I") narrator whom the reader does not discover is Alba until the epilogue. From this narrator's opening paragraph, the reader is made aware that this account has been reconstructed from Clara's notebooks. After this disclosure, however, the majority of reconstruction is told in the third person, with all characters referred to as "he" or "she." This second narrative voice is omniscient, or "all-knowing," able to relate what the various characters are thinking or feeling. This method of telling a story as a re-creation is not so unusual, except that it is interrupted at times by yet another narrative voice. This third voice belongs to Esteban Trueba, whose first person ("I") accounts serve to express either his intense passion or his acute suffering. (It is also interesting that all but the first of Esteban's encounters with Tránsito Soto are told in his voice.) Esteban's first-person accounts serve two purposes: first, they reinforce the idea that the novel has been reconstructed from the family histories, both written and oral. More important, however, is the way in which Esteban's words reveal the emotions he does not express in front of others. Without Esteban's narration, it would be easy to dismiss him as a cruel, heartless tyrant; including his heartfelt declarations, however, shows him to be a complex character struggling to battle his inner demons of passion and anger.

Setting

Although the setting of the novel is never explicitly named as Chile, the history of that country forms an important part of the plot. The political turmoil that engulfed Chile in the 1970s after the election of "the Candidate" Salvador Allende is reflected in the increasing impact that political events have in the lives of the characters. The more specific settings of the novel, however, have their own significance as well. The Tres Marías hacienda provides a good setting for illustrating the class conflict that is an important theme in the novel. Pedro Tercero's ability to come and go as he pleases from the hacienda reflects his more direct challenges to Esteban Trueba's authority. Similarly, "the battle of the sexes is cleverly manifested in the continuous struggle for space in the house," as Ronie-Richelle García-Johnson notes in *Revista Hispanica Moderna*. Esteban has designed the "big house on the corner" to demonstrate his own wealth and power, but it more accurately reflects the personality of his wife, Clara. Even when he is turning the salon of the house into a political meeting place, Clara manages to continue her spiritualist meetings and charity work by adding rooms and staircases to the back of the house. The split between the couple caused by Esteban's violence also becomes evident in the house, as "an invisible border arose between the parts of the house occupied by Esteban Trueba and those occupied by his wife." Little Alba recognizes that "her grandmother was the soul of the big house on the corner," and the

loss Esteban feels after her death is mirrored in a similar decline of the house.

Foreshadowing

Foreshadowing is the technique of hinting at future events or setting up an explanation of later developments. Allende frequently uses foreshadowing in *The House of the Spirits* to hint at the fate facing her characters. The foreshadowing occurs not only in Clara's prophecies, but also in direct comments by the narrator. As early as Chapter 1, the narrator remarks that Rosa's poisoning is just "the first of many acts of violence that marked the fate of the del Valle family." A more specific remark comes in Chapter 7, when after reuniting with her brother Miguel after his first day of school, Amanda impulsively tells him that she would sacrifice herself for him. When the narrator adds that "she did not know then that one day she would have to," this anticipates Amanda's end, when she dies in police custody during questioning about her brother. Another instance of foreshadowing occurs at the end of Chapter 12, when the last surviving Mora sister comes to warn Alba that she is in danger. Esteban dismisses her words as crazy, but, the narrator notes, "later he would recall Luisa Mora's prophetic words, when they took Alba away in the middle of the night, while the curfew was in force." The frequent use of foreshadowing throughout the novel helps create a sense of fate at work and reinforces the violence of the political system, as the reader is constantly reminded that despite magical or pleasant interludes, dire events are yet to come.

Magical Realism

Because of its mixture of realistic everyday events with supernatural occurrences, *The House of the Spirits* fits within the literary genre known as magic realism or magical realism. A term first coined by Cuban writer Alejo Carpentier, magical realism is a style of writing which treats myth and magic with the same acceptance and objectivity as "truth." The abilities that allow Clara to play the piano with the cover closed and predict the future are just a few of the magical elements that appear in the novel. The Mora sisters possess a photograph containing "irrefutable proof that souls can take on physical form," and Férula's ghost appears to the entire family to announce her death. Every time Esteban comes to the big house, Blanca's rubber plant "lowered its leaves and began to exude a whitish fluid, like tears of milk, from its stem." *The House of the Spirits,* however, is much more frankly realistic in its portrayal of political turmoil than many other works of magical realism. There are almost no magical incidents in the later portions of the novel, particularly after the coup that leads to political repression. While this wide difference in tone may seem out of place, it actually serves to heighten the horror of the military's regime. Which is really more unbelievable, the author seems to be asking, a woman with psychic abilities or a government that tortures and murders thousands of its citizens?

Historical Context

Chile and the Turmoil of the 1970s

Although the setting of *The House of the Spirits* is never explicitly named, there are several historical events—from the 1933 earthquake to the election and overthrow of Salvador Allende—that clearly place the action in Chile. Occupying most of the southeastern coast of South America, Chile was part of the territory conquered by the Spanish in the 1500s. The country formally declared independence in 1818, but the nineteenth century was marked by both internal and external conflicts. By the 1910s, when the novel opens, Chile had enjoyed several years of relative peace and prosperity. The country's deposits of nitrate—an essential component of gunpowder—proved profitable during World War I. The wealth did not spread to workers such as miners, farm laborers, and factory workers, and so in the 1920s the country entered a period of strikes and political conflict which saw an increase in the kinds of radical political movements which so disturb Esteban Trueba throughout the novel. Salvador Allende was the cofounder of one of these parties, the Socialist Party, and was elected to the Chilean national congress in 1937 and to the senate in 1945. It was as a Socialist that he ran for president in four consecutive elections: 1952, 1958, 1964, and 1970. At the front of a Leftist coalition, Allende came in a close second in the 1958 election, but it was the 1970 election that finally brought him to power.

In a three-way race, Allende's Unidad Popular alliance won 36.3% of the popular vote—more than any other candidate, but not the majority required for election. Congress awarded him the presidency, but only after Allende signed a series of constitutional amendments that promised to protect the basic freedoms of political parties, labor unions, the media, and civic organizations. Allende's attempts to effect a peaceful transition to socialism—including the redistribution of land to peasants and

the nationalization of businesses—were undercut by a broad array of forces, however. Radicals in his party led thousands of illegal land seizures and openly thwarted the president's efforts to compromise with the opposition in Congress. Wealthy Conservatives undermined the government by decreasing food production and encouraging trucking strikes that created food shortages. Several American business interests, worried about losing holdings to nationalization, encouraged the delay or cancellation of loans to Chile and even actively tried to subvert the government. The American Central Intelligence Agency, concerned about the spread of Communism, tried to bribe Chilean Congress members to prevent Allende from becoming president and unsuccessfully encouraged the Chilean military to overthrow the regime. By 1973, Allende's support had eroded: strikes were widespread, terrorism was waged by both right and left, and in June a tank regiment attacked the presidential palace. Hoping to restore order, Allende named the commanders of the armed forces to his cabinet that August. After congressional opposition called on the military to restore civil order, Allende's military ministers resigned and conservative forces in the military gave the president an ultimatum to resign. When Allende refused, the military took control of the government on September 11. Allende died during an attack on the presidential palace, the victim of either a self-inflicted gunshot wound (as the military claimed) or a military execution (as his allies and family alleged).

The military established a new government, led by General Augusto Pinochet, and moved quickly to stifle dissent. An estimated five to fifteen thousand Chileans were killed or tortured, or "disappeared," during and immediately after the coup; thousands of others fled into exile. Political parties, the Congress, trade unions, and any other organizations that opposed Pinochet were soon outlawed, and as many as forty thousand Chileans were arrested. Under the military government, torture became an accepted practice during the interrogation of political prisoners. In 1980, Pinochet imposed a new constitution that included a weak Congress with many members chosen undemocratically by the regime. The constitution also allowed military vetoes of most congressional decisions and allowed the government to suspend civil rights to deal with threats to "national security." While the regime's strict control initially led to improvements in Chile's economy, the upturn only benefited a small portion of the population. By 1982, the year *The House of the Spirits* was pub-

Compare & Contrast

- **Chile:** The country of Chile occupies 748,800 square kilometers of land—roughly twice the size of Montana—and in the late 1990s had an estimated population of just over 14.5 million people.

  United States: The United States covers 9,158,960 square kilometers of land, and in the late 1990s had an estimated population of over 270 million people.

- **Chile:** With a long history of political activism, modern-day Chile has over half a dozen different political parties; in order to form majority governments, however, these parties come together in two coalitions: the Coalition of Parties for Democracy (CPD) and the Union for the Progress of Chile (UPP).

  United States: Politics in the United States are controlled by two political groups: the Republican Party and the Democratic Party. While there have been several third-party movements throughout the twentieth century, none has seriously influenced the outcome of national elections since Theodore Roosevelt's Bull Moose Party during the presidential election of 1912.

- **Chile:** While the Chilean economy has opened up more to world trade since President Augusto Pinochet left office, the country's economy is

still strongly dependent on natural resources—particularly copper mining, fishing, and forestry. In 1996, the estimated gross domestic product per person was $8,400.

  United States: America enjoys one of the most powerful, diverse, and technologically advanced economies in the world. In 1997, the estimated gross domestic product per person was $30,200.

- **Chile:** At the end of 1998, the most controversial issue facing Chile was the proposed extradition of former President Augusto Pinochet from England to face charges of human rights abuses. Supporters of the General considered the action a blow to Chile's sovereignty, while his opponents argued that dictators should be held legally responsible for atrocities committed during their regimes.

  United States: At the end of 1998, the most controversial issue facing the American government was the impeachment of President Bill Clinton over his attempts to conceal an inappropriate relationship with a White House intern. Supporters of the president said the charges were trumped up by political opponents, while his opponents maintained that Clinton had obstructed justice and abused his power in trying to keep his actions secret.

---

lished, an international recession made it clear that the economic benefits of Pinochet's dictatorship were paltry, especially when compared to the loss of freedoms suffered by Chileans. Massive protests occurred, and in 1983 the military cracked down once again. Pinochet's 1980 constitution had allowed for a plebiscite in 1988, however, when the public would say "yes" or "no" to another term in office for the general. Pinochet was firmly convinced he would win, and allowed the vote to take place. A majority voted "no," and Pinochet agreed to step down. In presidential elections the following year, Pinochet's candidate lost to Patricio Ayl-

win. The return to democracy was peaceful, although Pinochet retained his position as leader of the military and opposed efforts to prosecute it for human rights abuses. World attention was focused on the brutality of Pinochet's regime in 1998, however, when he faced extradition from England to Spain to answer charges of assassination and torture.

"The Poet" and the Latin American "Boom"

Throughout *The House of the Spirits,* Allende frequently makes reference to "the Poet," a man revered and respected for his work. Even the Count de Satigny, a European, says the Poet's work "was the best poetry ever written, and that even in French, the language of the arts, there was nothing to compare it to." By the time Jaime and Nicolás are adults, the Poet is "a world-renowned figure, as Clara had predicted the first time she heard him recite in his telluric voice at one of her literary soirées." While the Poet is never named in the novel, it is clear that Allende is referring to Pablo Neruda, a Chilean poet who won the Nobel Prize for Literature in 1971. Neruda was not Chile's first Nobel laureate—poet Gabriela Mistral won the accolade in 1945—but he is considered one of the most important Latin American poets of the twentieth century. His works included such classics as *Residencia en la tierra* ("Residence on Earth," 1933), *Alturas de Macchu-Picchu* ("The Heights of Macchu Picchu," 1948), and his epic *Canto general de Chile* ("General Song of Chile," 1943, revised 1950). Through these works and many others, Neruda became noted worldwide for his innovative techniques and explorations of love, death, and the human condition. Neruda was a dedicated Communist who was nominated for president in 1970, but ended his candidacy and threw his support to the eventual winner, Salvador Allende. Neruda died less than two weeks after the military overthrow of Allende's government, and in the novel his funeral becomes "the symbolic burial of freedom."

Neruda was not the only Latin American writer to receive international recognition, however. The 1960s saw the beginning of the "Boom" in Latin American literature that brought numerous translations of Spanish-language works to English-speaking readers and critics. Writers such as Argentinean Jorge Luis Borges, Guatemalan Miguel Angel Asturias (Nobel, 1967), Colombian Gabriel García Márquez (Nobel, 1982), Peruvian Mario Vargas Llosa, and Mexicans Octavio Paz (Nobel, 1990) and Carlos Fuentes became familiar names to readers and academics. By the 1980s, most of the works by these well-known writers were appearing in translation and some were even adapted as English-language films. Few women writers emerged from the Boom, however, and so when the translation of Allende's *House of the Spirits* was published 1985, it was justly hailed for bringing a fresh, feminine perspective to the portrayal of Latin American life.

A Chilean Army soldier guards prisoners in Santiago's National Stadium, used as a detention center following the coup d'etat that overthrew Marxist president Salvador Allende.

Critical Overview

Because of the author's family background and the political subject matter of *The House of the Spirits,* Allende's best-selling first novel was bound to cause a stir in literary circles. Most initial reviews of the work made it clear, however, that it was the author's talent, not her political credentials, that made *The House of the Spirits* well worth the wide readership it attained. *Washington Post Book World* critic Jonathan Yardley explained that "*The House of the Spirits* does contain a certain amount of rather predictable politics, but the only cause it wholly embraces is that of humanity, and it does so with such passion, humor and wisdom that in the end it transcends politics; it is also a genuine rarity, a work of fiction that is both an impressive literary accomplishment and a mesmerizing story fully accessible to a general readership." While observing that some of the minor characters are one-dimensional, *New York Times* reviewer Christopher Lehmann-Haupt added that "Clara, Blanca, and Alba Trueba … are complex and vivid women. And the story's dominant character, the tragically ill-tempered Senator Esteban Trueba, is so appalling and appealing that he easily transcends ideology." "Slowly, this fine, stirring, generous novel casts its powerful spell," Hermione Lee stated in the *Observer*. While the critic expressed some reservations about Esteban's narration and the sentimental treatment of love, she noted that the novel "is a much more redoubtable and complex narrative, and much more grimly truthful, than at first appears."

Not all early reviews were positive, however. Paul West attributed the "runaway vogue" of *The House of the Spirits* to the popularity of the family chronicle genre and found that the magical elements detracted from the focus on the characters. "As *The House of the Spirits* advances," the critic wrote in the *Nation,* "it calms down into the book Allende probably wanted to write, and would have had she not felt obliged to toe the line of magical realism." D. A. N. Jones similarly objected to the magical elements, writing in the *London Review of Books* that "bizarre little fantasies come sputtering out with an inconsequential brevity, like ideas thrown up at a script conference for a Latin American soap opera or horror film." But other critics praised what *Chicago Tribune Book World* contributor Bruce Allen called "Allende's gift for dramatic detail": "The most remarkable feature of this remarkable book," the critic explained, "is the way in which its strong political sentiments are made to coexist with its extravagant and fascinating narrative." Suzanne Ruta similarly observed that Allende's "fidelity to the magic realist formula … worked because history provided ample ballast and counterweight to her flights of fancy." While there is "something a bit precious about the story of grandmother Clara, mother Blanca, and daughter Alba," the critic concluded in the *Women's Review of Books* that "it took courage to turn the ugly reality of 1973 and after into a kind of fairy tale. I read it and wept."

Because of its style and plot, it was inevitable that many reviewers would make comparisons between Allende's novel and Colombian author Gabriel García Márquez's masterpiece *One Hundred Years of Solitude. Village Voice* contributor Enrique Fernández, for instance, stated that "only the dullest reader can fail to be distracted by the shameless cloning from *One Hundred Years of Solitude.*" While faulting the ending of the novel for using one of García Márquez's "hoariest clichés"—the discovery of a manuscript—*Time* critic Patricia Blake noted that "Allende is not just an epigone [poor imitator] of García Márquez.

Writing in the tradition of Latin America's magic realists, she has a singular talent for producing full-scale representational portraits with comic surreal touches." Many other critics agreed that while Allende may have used *One Hundred Years* as a model, *The House of the Spirits* is her own unique achievement. A *Publishers Weekly* reviewer made the comparison with García Márquez and declared that "Allende has her own distinctive voice, however; while her prose lacks the incandescent brilliance of the master's, it has a whimsical charm, besides being clearer, more accessible, and more explicit about the contemporary situation in South America." *New York Times Book Review* contributor Alexander Coleman likewise remarked that Allende's work differs from the fatalism of García Márquez's work in that it is "a novel of peace and reconciliation, in spite of the fact that it tells of bloody, tragic events. The author has accomplished this not only by plumbing her memory for the familial and political textures of the continent, but also by turning practically every major Latin American novel on its head." The critic added: "Rarely has a new novel from Latin America consciously or unconsciously owed more to its predecessors; equally rare is the original utterance coming out of what is now a collective literary inheritance." In a *Latin American Literary Review* article devoted to comparing the two works, Robert Antoni determined that there are significant differences, including the feminine, first-person voice; the presentation of Clara's manuscript as history, not prediction; and the interesting dialogue created by including Esteban Trueba's voice in the narrative. In Allende's work "historical writing replaces magical writing, tragic sentiments replace comic sentiments," the critic concluded. "All this amounts to a novel which—more consciously than unconsciously—may begin as an attempt to rewrite *One Hundred Years of Solitude,* but which discovers itself as a unique statement."

Further assessments of the novel have examined it from a feminist perspective, analyzing the author's depiction of the patriarchal society of Latin America. Critics have also paid attention to the role that writing and storytelling play in the novel, thus presenting an examination of the nature and uses of art. Reviewers have generally come to value *The House of the Spirits* not only as a commentary on turbulent political times in Chile but also as a powerful piece of humanistic fiction. Sara Maitland noted in the *New Statesman* that *The House of the Spirits* "seemed to me to take South American 'magic realism' a step further in the direction I have always felt it could go—to a fictional technique which can carry universal meaning within its own specific location of character and place." Coleman suggested that *The House of the Spirits* is well worth comparison with the best works of the Latin American "Boom." As he concluded in the *New York Times Book Review,* Allende is "the first woman to approach on the same scale as the others the tormented patriarchal world of traditional Hispanic society and to argue that the enraged class violence in Latin America is a debate among men who are not only deaf but who have fixed and unalterable ideas on all subjects. And she has done all this in an absorbing and distinguished work that matches her predecessors' in quality as well as scope."

Criticism

Jane Elizabeth Dougherty

Dougherty is a Ph.D. candidate at Tufts University. In the following essay, she explores themes of connection and interconnection in The House of the Spirits.

Isabel Allende, the author of *The House of the Spirits,* wrote the novel after fleeing her own country, Chile, after a military coup much like the one she describes, and much of the action in the book is connected to her personal experiences and the larger history of Chile. The novel is a narrative of connection, both structurally and thematically: the primary narrator, Alba, continually connects the events in the story to their causes and effects, and presents her own family, the Truebas, as a microcosm of the society as a whole. The actions of the Trueba family have consequences not only in the personal realm, but in the political and cosmic realms as well, showing the ways in which these realms are interconnected, in the past, present, and future, among the dead, the living, and the yet-to-be-born.

Allende uses the technique of "magic realism" to show her themes of interconnectedness. P. Gabrielle Foreman writes that "magic realism, unlike the fantastic or the surreal, presumes that the individual requires a bond with the traditions and the faith of the community, that s/he is historically constructed and connected." Magic realism, then, implies that the magical and the real are implicated in and reflected in each other. A massive earthquake hits the country just as Clara discovers her daughter Blanca's illicit affair with Pedro Tercero,

and all of Esteban's bones are broken as a result, suggesting that the earthquake is a cosmic reflection of the cataclysmic nature of the love between Blanca and Pedro Tercero. But magic, Allende implies, has its limits: when Férula is banished from the Trueba house, Clara tries to locate her with her magic powers but concludes that "you can't find someone who doesn't want to be found." Though Allende is often compared to the Colombian writer Gabriel García Marquez, as Foreman writes, "Allende inverts his technique—the stronger the historical moments, the more distant the magical—as if to counter the threat of history becoming 'merely' enchanted and so subsumed." Instead, Allende, through her narrator Alba, shows that the relationships among the characters determine both the private and public events of the story.

The relationships in and among the Trueba family are a microcosm of the larger society: Esteban Trueba's rape of Pancha García is a reflection of the exploitation of the peasant classes by the upper classes, and their grandson Esteban García's rape of Alba reflects the rage of the poor towards the privileged. Alba recognizes that the two rapes are interconnected and vows at the end of the story to break the chain of evil which has afflicted her family and her country. She also offers other, more hopeful examples of relations between the exploited and the privileged when she writes of her parents' long and loving affair and her own relationship with Miguel, suggesting, as Norma Helsper writes, "the superior resilience of love in comparison to hate." Helsper notes that while Allende portrays the traditional family as a "respectable facade that hides the truth of rape, adultery, battering and domination," by the end of the novel "Alba has begun to forge a new model family which will include Chileans of all social classes and political tendencies." Alba is able to forge her new, interconnected family after a visit from her grandmother, Clara, who magically appears to her when she has begun to await her own death:

> She stayed like this for a long time. When she had nearly achieved her goal, her Grandmother Clara, whom she had invoked so many times to help her die, appeared with the novel idea that the point was not to die, since death came anyway, but to survive, which would be a miracle. With her white linen dress, her winter gloves, her sweet toothless smile, and the mischievous gleam in her hazel eyes, she looked exactly as she had when Alba was a child. Clara also brought the saving idea of writing in her mind, without paper or pencil, to keep her thoughts occupied and to escape the doghouse and live. She suggested that she write a testimony that might one day call at-

What Do I Read Next?

- Allende's second novel, *Of Love and Shadows* (1984), is an even more overtly political work than her first. Journalist Irene Beltrán and photographer Francisco Leal are assigned to do a story about a fifteen-year-old peasant girl alleged to possess miraculous powers. The couple falls in love, but their future is jeopardized by their discovery of evidence of atrocities committed by the military personnel.

- In her 1987 work, *Eva Luna,* Allende tells the story of another storyteller, a woman who tells tales to survive in a politically unstable Latin-American society. Set in a country similar to Venezuela, it tells the story of the orphan Eva Luna and how she survives to find success and fulfillment in a career as a scriptwriter for television. Several of the main character's stories are separately recounted in another collection, *The Stories of Eva Luna* (1990).

- Allende's novel *The House of the Spirits* has often been compared to the work of Colombian Nobel-winner Gabriel García Márquez. His most famous book is the 1968 masterpiece *One Hundred Years of Solitude,* which follows several generations of the Buendía family as they influence the small town of Macondo.

- García Márquez is also a noted journalist. In 1986 he published *Clandestine in Chile,* a non-fiction account of an exile's return to the Chile during the rule of General Pinochet.

- Another magical tale of thwarted love is Mexican novelist Laura Esquivel's acclaimed work *Like Water for Chocolate* (1989), about a woman whose true love marries her sister in order to stay close to her. Both the novel and the film based upon it were extremely successful throughout the world.

- American author Alice Hoffman also tells tales that combine the magical with the everyday. Her 1995 novel *Practical Magic,* made into a 1998 film starring Nicole Kidman and Sandra Bullock, tells the tale of two sisters whose mystical abilities often cause more problems than they solve.

- Edward Boorstein's 1977 work *Allende's Chile: An Inside View* is a nonfictional if partisan account of the government of Salvador Allende. Boorstein worked for the Allende government and lived in Santiago during many of the demonstrations that took place both for and against the government. His account is written from a Leftist perspective and examines the role of corporate and U.S. interests in the fall of Allende and his party.

---

tention to the terrible secret she was living through, so that the world would know about this horror that was taking place parallel to the peaceful existence of those who did not want to know, who could afford the illusion of a normal life, and of those who could deny that they were on a raft adrift in a sea of sorrow, ignoring, despite all evidence, that only blocks away from their happy world there were others, these others who live or die on the dark side.

Here, Allende connects magic with creativity. Rather than having the capacity to alter historical and personal events, magic instead is the means through which we can survive them. Even at her most alone, in solitary confinement and close to death, Alba is connected with the spirits, who in turn connect her with her own spirit, the magical

creativity within her. In this scene, the dead care for the living, so that the living may in turn care for the yet-to-be-born. Moreover, Clara suggests that Alba write her story to connect with others who do not realize their connection to the suffering of those "on the dark side," and in spite of being able to live in denial about these connections, because of the suffering of others are themselves "adrift on a sea of sorrow" without knowing it. As Z. Nelly Martinez notes, "Allende suggests that it is only by aligning themselves with 'spirit,' 'magic,' or 'Eros,' that human beings may recover their wholeness and thereby recover the wholeness which is, in fact, the world—an interrelatedness that celebrates cooperation rather than competition, and deliverance rather than repression." Allende stresses that aligning oneself with magic is a choice; because of their interconnectedness, the female characters enable one another in making this choice. As Nora Glickman writes, "Nívea's stories are imprinted in Clara's journals. Blanca's letters mold Alba's character, the latter's life testimony reaches the reader in episodic segments that Alba announces, elaborates, orders and revises to offer that reader the most sensible way to rescue the past." The sharing of writing and stories among the various generations of females symbolizes their shared spirit, which enables them, as Clara enables her granddaughter, to endure.

By contrast, throughout the story, Esteban Trueba has disavowed or destroyed his connections with others. His need to possess Clara only further distances her and his refusal to acknowledge his illegitimate offspring leads to the rage of Esteban García, which nearly destroys the person he loves most. Esteban fails to see the consequences of his support for the destruction of the popularly-elected regime, his destruction of the tenant village at Tres Marías, and his unwillingness to accept Pedro Tercero. As Richard McCallister writes, "His rape of Pancha García is revenged by Esteban García's rape of Alba, his early support for the overthrow of democracy is revisited in his political impotence under the military regime. Indeed, his acts of usurpation in the name of establishing a patriarchal lineage work precisely to prevent it from happening," which is shown most clearly in Esteban's initial support for the coup which leads to the death of his son Jaime. It is only when Esteban sees the impact his actions have had on others that he can find an inner peace which has always eluded him, and as Martinez writes, "to symbolize [Esteban's] redemptive awareness, Allende makes him assist in the telling of the story, done by the narrator, Alba, who most adequately fulfills the role of artist in the novel." Thus, the interconnected narratives of Alba and Esteban are interspersed throughout the novel such that the structure reflects the overlapping themes of interconnectedness. Moreover, Esteban's redemption is symbolized by his use of his own magical creativity, which occurs not only through his recognition of the harm he has done to others but by his alignment with Clara's gentle spirit, an alignment which is symbolized by his gradual shrinking to Clara's height.

As Martinez writes, Allende's novel ends with Alba's recognition that "the past, existing only as memory and hence open to transformation, loses its grip over the present as well as its power to ef-

fectively predetermine the future." In vowing to love her unborn daughter as she has been loved, even though that daughter may be the result of a rape, Alba vows to transform the future. As Helsper notes, Allende "proposes the family as a model for her divided country: members of this family have oppressed, wounded, and tortured each other, but they are the same ones who must now heal one another. The family she posits is all of Chile." In connecting the political, personal, and cosmic realms of her narrative, Allende offers Alba's spirit as a reflection of the spirit of all her fellow citizens and as a witness to us as readers of our own interconnectedness.

Source: Jane Elizabeth Dougherty, in an essay for *Novels for Students* Gale, 1999.

Ronie-Richele Garcia-Johnson

In the following excerpt, Garcia-Johnson presents a "spatial examination of the treatment of women" in Allende's House of the Spirits.

The temporal setting of the action in *The House of the Spirits* spans fifty years—from the early twenties to about 1974. Historically, and fictionally, within the novel, these were the years in which the women's movement began to gather strength, and then gain progress. While it is apparent that Allende has traced the development of women's struggle for freedom in her novel, some critics have suggested that Nivea, Clara, Blanca, and Alba are allegorical characters which epitomize women at various phases of Chilean social and political history....

A thorough and complex understanding of *The House of the Spirits* demands spatial interpretation, and thus a spatial examination of the treatment of women in the novel is imperative as well. There are treasures hidden in the spaces and rooms of Allende's novel, where the idea that bodies and structures are both houses, and that they are inseparable and essential, is fundamental. Careful examination reveals that, besides the bloody political battle between the military and the liberals, there is another war in the work. The battle of the sexes is cleverly manifested in the continuous struggle for space in the house; the main house in *The House of Spirits* is a divided one. Allende's magnificent representation of the fight for dominance between men and women, the discordant coexistence of the male and female, is a prime example of the author's perception and presentation of a universal theme.

Allende utilized spatial symbolism to emphasize and parallel the actions of female characters as they sought to overcome the tyranny of patriarchy. In her novel, structures, and the spaces they contain, serve as metaphors for or symbols of social and political barriers. Rather than allowing these metaphorical or symbolic obstacles to determine their lives, the women of the Trueba family overcame them. Clara, Blanca, and Alba managed to defeat Esteban Trueba, who, with traditional notions of honor, of a woman's "place," and of sexuality, attempted to possess and confine these women. The Trueba women confronted Esteban in his own space, usurped his control of that area, expanded their lives into alternative spaces, or left Trueba's property altogether. Trueba and "his" women were contenders struggling to dominate the space they should have shared; by the end of the novel, Trueba found that he had lost the battle and the war.

Trueba's attitude towards women, "possessing" them, and keeping them within his own structures became apparent spatially in the beginning of the novel. After he learned of Rosa the Beautiful's death, he regretted not having married her sooner and he thought that, if he had known that she was to die, he would have "built her a palace studded with treasures from the ocean floor," "kidnapped her and locked her up," and only he "would have had the key." According to Trueba, his betrothed would have never been "stolen" from him by "death" if he had kept her to himself. Like many traditional fathers and husbands, Trueba regarded his women jealously and attempted to confine them as treasure in a chest to maintain their loyalty. So intense was Trueba's determination to keep his women with him that he prepared a tomb with a place for not only himself, but for his wife and his long-dead Rosa. No one, or thing, was going to "steal" his women from him again.

No structure, however, could keep Clara isolated and protected from the outside world. Clara had inherited her mother Nivea's determination to have her own way; she was a strong, willful woman. While Nivea enthusiastically promoted feminist causes, Clara quietly continued her own fight for freedom within her own home, the home that Trueba had built for her. Clara did not have to physically and permanently leave the structure of the house to escape the domination of her husband. She found freedom and battled Trueba with various spatial manuevers. She existed, spiritually, in another space or dimension, and brought the outside world inside the space of the house to her. She

manipulated the space within the house as she pleased and, when all other techniques failed, she locked herself up, in her own secluded space, out of Trueba's reach....

Clara had developed the habit of seeking alternative mental spaces in which to dwell as a child in her father's home. She would escape her immediate reality as she read a book, or imagined herself in far-away places. Her "magic" and her attempts to move articles about with the power of her mind distanced her from the "real" world. Once she was married, Clara maintained her secret, interior universe. As she prepared to give birth to her first child, she announced: "I think I'm going to levitate." Clara "meant that she wanted to rise to a level that would allow her to leave behind the discomfort and heaviness of pregnancy and the deep fatigue that had begun to seep into her bones. She entered one of her long periods of silence..." ... Clara was pregnant with more than a physical child, she was pregnant with love, creativity, and what would later be born as a text.... Whether Clara's silence is interpreted as a retreat, a refuge ... or as a clever victory over the mundane, it is clear that she entered an alternative space ... as she "levitated" in silence.

Although, at the moment when Clara was preparing to give birth Trueba understood that this silence was a "last refuge," he later became distressed. He "wanted control over that undefined and luminous material that lay within her and that escaped him even in those moments when she appeared to be dying of pleasure." The patriarch "realized that Clara did not belong to him and that if she continued living in a world of apparitions ... she probably never would." Trueba could build a house to contain wife, and he could enter the space within her body, but he would never be allowed to enter the home she had built for herself inside her own head. Clara had defeated male domination.

Clara's magic and the happiness she found as she practiced it was attractive to artists, poets, and spiritualists. The "big house on the corner" became a gathering place for these marginal people as Clara invited them into the space of her home. Clara also opened her home to the unfortunates who needed food and shelter. By encouraging these people to enter the exterior world that represented her interior self, Clara let them into the space that was forbidden to Trueba. Not surprisingly, Trueba objected to the carnivalization of his home and the daily parade that marched through it. He insisted that the "big house on the corner" was not a thoroughfare and coldly ordered that the celebration of the everyday be stopped. Clara and her children, especially Nicolás, continued to live as they pleased, and to fill the space as they desired, while Trueba was out of town. Upon his return, the atmosphere of the house changed, and the party was over—temporarily. Trueba continually struggled to dominate the space of the house in the city and his family fought back with determined consistency.

As she found herself trapped in a particular space and time, and could not divorce Trueba, Clara had to manipulate her immediate area. She attempted to move objects with the power of her mind, and she redefined the limits of the structure Trueba had built for her in the "big house on the corner."

> In response to Clara's imagination and the requirements of the moment, the noble, seignorial architecture began sprouting all sorts of extra little rooms, staircases, turrets, and terraces. Each time a new guest arrived, the bricklayers would arrive and build another addition to the house. The big house on the corner soon came to resemble a labyrinth.

The use of the word labyrinth is telling, for it suggests a space that, rather than possessing a masculine, linear order, is as complex as the intuition of a woman. Trueba's perfect, logical space was transformed by a woman. Instead of allowing his space to enclose her, she opened it and recreated it to suit her.

The struggle for space came to a climax while Clara was still alive and surrounded by her eccentric friends and Trueba campaigned for the office of Senator of the Republic. Clara needed space for her continuous spiritual celebrations, and Trueba needed space for the operations of his political party.

> The house filled with political propaganda and with the members of his party, who practically took it by storm, blending in with the hallway ghosts, the Rosicrucians, and the three Mora sisters. Clara's retinue was gradually pushed into the back rooms of the house...

The house became a house divided as "an invisible border arose between the parts of the house occupied by Esteban Trueba and those occupied by his wife." As the house has traditionally represented the unification of its occupants, the "invisible" spatial division within the house is a symbol, not only of the Trueba's spliced relationship, but of the separation of the sexes.

Trueba believed that the spirituality that captivated his wife and her friends was for women only. Before Nicolás departed to India, he told him "I hope you return a man, because I'm fed up with all your eccentricities." He considered his other son, Jaime, to be eccentric as well, because he cared for the underprivileged and didn't want to join his father in business. Jaime, therefore, was not a "well-adjusted man." Other readers have noticed that with some special exceptions, such as Jaime, Pedro Tercero García, and the prostitute Tránsito Soto, the men in the novel operate with logical thinking while the women depend on their spiritual and emotional strength to survive. This presentation of men and women is based on beliefs which are prevalent in Latin America. The author of *The House of the Spirits* herself has stated that "at times science is efficient than magic." As the "big house on the corner" in Allende's novel is a symbol for the family, the house naturally reflects the fact that the family, and the world, exists only because of the differences between two groups: women and men. It is not surprising that Allende chose to represent the schism spatially; as she spoke of her childhood, she noted that men and women were "segregated," and this implies a spatial understanding of the problem.

In the arena of the house in the city, Clara was victorious as she defended her independence. While the "façade of the house underwent no alterations" the most intimate interior of the house belonged to, was dominated by, and represented Clara. Even "the rear garden," once a perfect, strict emulation of "a French garden" became hers, "a tangled jungle in which every type of plant and flower had proliferated and where Clara's birds kept up a steady din, along with many generations of cats and dogs." The house belonged to Clara....

By manipulating the space of the house, it began to represent Clara, instead of Trueba. Gone was the house that Trueba had desired, planned, and built. His house was not a reflection of himself, as he had wanted, but of Clara, the family, and his relationship to them. One might venture as far to say that the house was female. With spatial symbols, Allende communicates the message that, although the patriarchy may seem to be in control, women and traditionally feminine spirits prevail behind the façade.

After Trueba slapped her and knocked her teeth out as she tried to defend her daughter, Clara's response to his physical violence was twofold. First, she refused to speak him and then, she locked herself in her room. Clara's denial of access to the space of her room, of her body—the spaces which Trueba had violated—was a powerful weapon. Even more potent was her refusal to allow Trueba to enter her mental space; she would never verbally communicate with him again. Clara had once again defeated Trueba with his own space; he was the one who had built and decorated her room. While some have mistaken both of these manuevers for passivity, spatial analysis demonstrates that Clara's actions were far from passive, and thus provides evidence to support Agosín's assertions regarding feminine silence in the novel. Clara had refused the masculine body access to her feminine world, and she swore not to enter masculine verbal space. Trueba was, more than frustrated, defeated; he could not touch Clara's soul, let alone control it.

Blanca, Trueba's only daughter, continued the tradition of independence begun by her grandmother. Although she did not rally for women's suffrage, or practice magic like her mother to assert her freedom, Blanca defied her father. Trueba would have never sanctioned the love that Blanca had for the peasant leader Pedro Tercero García. The house that divided Blanca and Pedro Tercero García was the elaborate symbol of elite wealth and social grace; her home at The Three Marias sharply contrasted with the little hut in which her peasant lover lived. It would have been absurd for Pedro to cross into Trueba's space, to visit the big house, and it would have been scandalous for Blanca to debase herself by setting foot in the peasant's quarters. Nevertheless, Blanca asserted her freedom with her actions and by symbolically passing through space.

Instead of opening her window and waiting for her lover to climb over a wall and into her father's space, Blanca crossed the barriers of her father's home herself. She waited until her father was asleep, until the landscape was hidden in the darkness, to lock her bedroom door and leave her father's house and domination. She would slip out the window, climb down a trellis covered with flowers, and run in the darkness. She did not go to the peasant quarters to meet her lover—that space, technically, belonged to her father. Instead, she and Pedro Tercero García met far from the structures, the houses and the huts, which symbolized the tyranny imposed over both of them and found each other by the banks of the stream, which for them, represented the flow of life, freedom, and passion.

Trueba's characteristic reaction to Blanca's defiance was to violently regain his powerful authority over her. He beat her and forced her to marry the Count. When Blanca arrived at the big house the morning after her wedding to visit her mother, Trueba ordered her to return quickly to her husband. By leaving the hotel to go to her mother's house

and space, Blanca was symbolically negating her marriage. Trueba sent Blanca away, out of his space. He could not tolerate the fact that his daughter had willfully negated his position by leaving his house in order to meet Pedro Tercero García. Trueba knew that, by leaving the protective space of his house, Blanca had escaped his masculine domination, and that she aspired to sexual freedom by inviting a man of her own choice to penetrate her physical space. While Blanca did obey her father and marry the Count, she did manage to keep a sacred space within her womb for the product of her union with Pedro: Alba. Later in the novel, Blanca subverted her father's dominion with the brazenly defiant act of bringing Pedro into Trueba's home.

While Clara didn't care to concern herself with the daily up-keep of the house, Blanca, and later, Alba, became devoted to its maintenance. They would feed the members of the household, keep the birds singing, the plants green, and do the gardening. During Trueba's absence, these women effectively ran the household. Bachelard discussed the idea that, while men build the external house, its is the women who, immersed in the day-to-day project of maintenance, make the house livable, or better—make it a home. "In the intimate harmony of walls and furniture, it may be said that we become conscious of a house that is built by women, since men only know how to build a house from the outside." In fact, as time passed, the women of the "big house on the corner" were responsible for the renovation and rebirth of the house.... At the end of the novel it is Alba who convinces her father to renew the house and resurrect the garden, the symbol of freedom. Allende's message seems to be that with love and patience, women maintain their nations as well as their homes.

Alba's youth coincided with the late sixties and the early seventies, a time of sexual revolution. Despite the ideas of the youths, those of the older, empowered generations did not look favorably upon these developments. Trueba would never have consented to Alba having a pre-marital sexual relationship with anyone. He wouldn't have tolerated mere courtship if her suitor were someone like Miguel, a radical leftist. Like her mother, however, Alba did not let her grandfather's attitude stop her from loving the man of her choice....

Alba did not run away from her home to live as she desired. Although at first she and Miguel would meet in his apartment, she found that the most comfortable solution was to bring Miguel into Trueba's home, where "in the labyrinth of the rear rooms, where no one ever went, they could make love undisturbed." The use of the word "labyrinth" reminds the reader that the house was still Clara's house, even though, after her death, it deteriorated for lack of her laughter. "One by one the lovers tried out all the abandoned rooms, and finally chose an improvised nest in the depths of the basement." Alba would lead Miguel in through the garden (the symbol of freedom) into the basement. It is spatially significant that the lovers went to the basement because their love, like the basement was "underground"—a secret.

The basement is, as the reader will remember, also a metaphor for the womb [Campos, Rene. "*La casa de los espíritus* : mirada, espacio, discurso de la otra historia." *Los libros tienen sus propios espíritus*, 1986.] Alba was leading Miguel to the most intimate of spaces, the space where life, (and text, in the cases of Clara and Alba,) is created. Their entrance into the basement was symbolic of sexual intercourse as well as of a more profound act of love. Alba and Miguel rearranged the space Trueba had created, as had her grandmother Clara, although they transformed the basement into a love nest. Alba and Miguel utilized the long-forgotten artifacts they found to turn their underground "nest" into an "nuptial chamber." Although they occupied the same space that Alba's grandparents had, Alba and Miguel shared a more fruitful love, and they did so by transforming the vestiges of an old world into a new "home."

Of all the actions of the women who had gone before her, Alba's spatial statement was by far the most assertive. Instead of preserving her intimate space with silence and magic, as Clara had, or leaving her "father's" home as Blanca had, Alba lived as she pleased in the space where she had grown up. This spatial relationship represents a confrontation with the patriarchy. Alba and Miguel's complicity as they recreated the basement, the history of the Truebas, to suit themselves, suggests that a new generation, women and men alike, would overcome that patriarchy....

The patriarchy, however, manipulated more than the freedom of the Trueba women. Just as Trueba attempted to control "his" women within the structures he had built for them, those with power in the country of which Allende wrote dominated the lives of workers, farmers, and every underprivileged citizen within the political structure. As Alba, and all the women of *The House of the Spirits* battled for their freedom as women, they struggled for political justice. The struggle for in-

dependence was not just a feminine one; it was a fight for the rights of all classes, creeds, and sexes. Clara had always been interested in the welfare of the poor. Blanca not only loved a leftist peasant, she hid this wanted man in her father's home after the Coup. Alba hid weapons for the resistance forces and her radical, guerrilla lover in her grandfather's home. She took food from the cupboards and sold furniture, including the portrait of her grandmother Clara, to feed the poor who were starving as a result of the Military's policies. Alba directly defied the government, and her grandfather, the symbol of conservatism, as she utilized Trueba's space and that which it contained. In *The House of the Spirits,* feminism and leftist liberalism were united in the struggle to preserve the Chilean home; feminine auras and the forces of freedom alike dwelt in the "house of the spirits."

Source: Ronie-Richele Garcia-Johnson, "The Struggle for Space: Feminism and Freedom in *The House of the Spirits,*" in *Revista Hispanica Moderna,* Vol. XLVII, No. 1, June, 1994, pp. 184–193.

Peter G. Earle

In the following article, Earle discusses the tradition of Latin American literature as demonstrated in Allende's House of the Spirits.

The story began urgently, if unpretentiously, after a long-distance telephone call from Santiago de Chile to Caracas. Isabel Allende's grandfather, in his ninety-ninth year, was about to die. More precisely, he'd decided his time had come. Despite opposing ideologies, their family relationship had been close; and now, although from the remote region he was about to enter she couldn't expect a reply, she sat down to write him a long letter. Her purpose was to keep him living, in conformity with his own idea of immortality. "My grandfather theorized that death didn't really exist. Oblivion is what exists, and if one can remember those who die—remember them well—they'll always be with him and in some way will live on, at least in spirit." ["Entrevista con Isabel Allende," with Michael Moody, *Hispania* 69, March, 1986.]

"Living on" was a persistent tradition in Isabel Allende's family on her mother's side, and her late grandmother—the main model for Clara del Valle, "Clara la clarividente," in *The House of the Spirits*—had been practicing since premature death what Grandfather had always preached in life, with her periodic messages and visitations. The letter to Grandfather got longer, and longer. A year later (1982) it had grown to five-hundred pages. It was a diary in retrospect, a family chronicle, an autobiography, a political testimony, a group portrait and contemporary history, a series of experiments with magic. In other words, a novel. Allende was a journalist in search of a complementary medium. Aesthetically, she would now participate in the basic ritual of Latin American literature: a celebration of reality. Ethically, she wanted to bear witness to social injustice, political violence, and repression—having been motivated by the betrayal and murder by right-wing conspirators of an uncle on her father's side, President Salvador Allende....

In what circumstances was the novel under consideration written? ... Allende stressed the importance of the "moment of history the writer is born into," especially in Latin America, a world of great "struggles and defeats, brutality and magic." Increasingly aware of the New World's five-hundred-year tradition of violence, she matured intellectually with her uncle's socialist movement and became a novelist at her reactionary grandfather's death. Thus, her book is the celebration of a momentous social struggle in which those two figures were principals. Only fictitious names are used in the story, for places as well as for people, but the implications are obvious: this was to be a composite testimony of many voices (like *One Hundred Years of Solitude,* with which superficial comparisons have often been made), written with a recent exile's sense of urgency, and a family member's intimacy. The political dispersion of the family she tells about is microcosmic, for contemporary Chilean history is also one of dispersion, beginning the day after Salvador Allende's election in 1970 with a complex opposition program that included technical and financial assistance from our Central Intelligence Agency and State Department and accelerating after September 11, 1973, when military forces led by General Pinochet carried out their *coup d'état.*

Soon after Allende's election, Secretary of State Henry Kissinger declared at a National Security Council meeting, "I don't see why we have to stand by and watch a country go communist due to the irresponsibility of its own people." In *The House of the Spirits* President Allende's niece has her principal male character say of the impoverished tenant farmers at Tres Marías, his country estate, "They're like children, they can't handle responsibility." A closer and more impetuous father-figure than the always distant Kissinger, Esteban Trueba was also unwilling to stand by and watch. In his paternalized utopia no one would go hungry, everyone would do his assigned work, and all would learn reading and writing and simple arithmetic—that is, enough to follow simple instructions and read signs, to write brief messages, and to count, *y nada más,* "for fear they would fill their minds with ideas unsuited to their station and condition." When, near the beginning of the century, Esteban took over the administration of Tres Marías—it had been in the family for generations—it was "a lawless heap of rocks, a no-man's-land." He quickly put things in order and regimented his tenant farmers; within a year the "heap of rocks" was a lucrative agricultural enterprise.

But behind this organizational rigor was an unbridled temperament, and deep sentimental frustrations. His fiancée, Rosa del Valle of memorable beauty, dies in the first chapter, which is narrated—like several other sections of the story—in first person singular by Esteban Trueba himself. Rosa's death is caused by brandy laced with rat poison from a decanter sent as an anonymous "gift" to her father, a prominent member of the Liberal Party. The extraordinary Rosa had bright green hair and the aura of "a distracted angel." Ensconced in the white satin of her coffin, she impressed her grieving fiancé as having been "subtly transformed into the mermaid she had always been in secret." Her autopsy and preparation for viewing are secretly witnessed by her little sister Clara in a semitraumatic state, immediately after which Clara enters a nine-year period of unbroken silence. Her first words will be to announce, in one of the many psychic predictions over her lifetime, that she'll soon be married.

In chapter 2 we are told that not only did Clara, *la clarividente,* foresee her marriage but also the identity of her husband-to-be: Rosa's fiancé, whom she hadn't seen since her sister's funeral and who was fifteen years her senior. Two months later, to be sure, Esteban visits the del Valle residence and immediately formalizes their engagement.

The family was to grow in its strange diversity through three generations, but Clara and Esteban would always constitute its vital, antithetical nucleus. The latter embodies privileged power; the former, humanitarian resistance. History, for Trueba, was paternity and—whenever the situation called for it—aggression. One of his first rituals in organizing Tres Marías as a community was to start populating it, ranging through the wheatfields on horseback in pursuit of the peasant girls, raping and impregnating more than a few.... History was procreation, and the father's subsequent attempts to deal with the results of procreation. The most troublesome outcome of his sexual escapades in the environs of Tres Marías was Esteban García, his natural grandson born of an offspring of Pancha García, his first wheatfield victim. After a childhood of deprivation and growing resentment, the grandson has nothing but the grandfather's first name for an inheritance. Since childhood he had wanted to become a policeman. And he became one.

During the ugly reprisals taken by the military government in the aftermath of the President's death (in a series of obvious allusions to the Pinochet regime's repressions starting in September, 1973), García reappears, having risen to the rank of lieutenant colonel in the political police. It is he who presides over the interrogation, confinement, and prolonged torture of his privileged cousin Alba, a university student who has been active in the socialist underground and Esteban Trueba's only recognized grandchild. Alba undergoes her torture partly in trauma, partly in an unconscious state. In the process she's raped an undisclosed number of times, and in the Epilogue we're told that one of the culprits is Colonel García. Third in a lineage of strong-willed women, Alba is the human instrument through which Esteban Trueba is made to pay psychologically for a lifetime of large- and small-scale transgressions. That is, instead of retaliating in a direct, physical way against the aged patriarch, Trueba's bastard grandson chooses to punish him through his "legitimate" counterpart: revenge against the privileged by the underprivileged, against the upper-class child of affluence by the peasant-child of want.

The principal antecedent to this reprisal comes in chapter 6. Trueba is then informed by Jean de Satigny, his daughter Blanca's effete and dandified suitor, that Blanca is having nighttime trysts. The secret lover, it turns out, is her childhood playmate at Tres Marías, Pedro Tercero García, who has grown up with revolutionary ideas and composes revolutionary songs for the guitar (including one based on a fable told to him years before by the first Pedro García: once there was a chicken coop invaded nightly by a fox who stole eggs and ate baby chicks; eventually the hens organized, and one night they surrounded the fox and pecked him half to death). About three weeks later Esteban García—then a boy of twelve—presents himself and offers to lead his grandfather to Pedro Tercero's hiding place in the woods. Agreeing to pay a reward, Trueba sets out with a pistol. Surprised in bed, the intended victim is still able to leap out, to dodge the only shot Trueba gets to fire and, a second later, to disarm his assailant by hurling a piece of firewood at him. Whereupon Trueba seizes an ax and swings—and Pedro Tercero, in a reflex-at-

tempt at self-defense, loses three fingers from his right hand. Shock and loss of blood notwithstanding, he rushes from the cabin and escapes in the dark. Adding literal insult to literal injury, Trueba then refuses to pay the boy his promised reward, slaps him, and snarls, "There's no reward for [double-crossers]!"

No reward *then*. But ultimately Esteban García was to obtain one of sorts. Years later, at the very moment Senator Trueba of the Conservative Party was celebrating with champagne the Socialist president's overthrow, "his son Jaime's testicles were being burned with an imported cigarette." After refusing to accept his captors' offer of freedom in return for saying on television that the late president in a drunken state had committed suicide, Jaime is beaten a second time, left with hands and feed bound with barbed wire for two days and nights, then shot together with several other prisoners in a vacant lot. In the interests of good government and domestic tranquillity, the lot and the cadavers are dynamited immediately after the execution. Two weeks later the Senator is told the circumstances of his son's death, but he refuses to believe the eyewitness account. Only when Jaime appears months later as a ghost, "covered with dried blood and rags, dragging streamers of barbed wire across the waxed parquet floors," does he realize that he had heard the truth. It is in this penultimate chapter (13, "The Terror") that he concludes he had been wrong and that, after all, "the best way to overthrow Marxism" had not been found.

Systematic oblivion (it never happened; there's no proof), censorship, … disinformation (the President, it has been reported, committed suicide in a drunken state), and the infinite ways of "disappearing" people (such as dynamiting political prisoners' corpses) are some of the methods by which authoritarian regimes maintain themselves in power. The Brazilian critic Antonio Callado remarked in 1974 that contemporary Latin America was "full of new ruins" (e.g., democracy in Uruguay and Chile, the Revolution in Mexico), that Latin Americans have displayed a peculiar resistance to "becoming historical," because they're "always trying to start again" amidst a detritus of infringed constitutions and derelict or disabled governments. ["Censorship and Other Problems of Latin American Writers," *Working Paper* No. 14, Center of Latin American Studies, University of Cambridge, 1974, 18–19.] The attempted starting-again, we could add, is more often ultraconservative or reactionary than revolutionary, and more motivated by frustration than by hope.

But against this antihistorical resistance, of which the cantankerous Esteban Trueba is a representative figure, another, more imaginative, more perceptive resistance arrays itself. In *The House of the Spirits* Clara, Blanca, and Alba are its persistent mainstays over three generations. Light is freedom and hope, and the luminous names of the three women are clearly symbolic. The dramatic nucleus of the book is the struggle between Trueba and the forces he generates, on the one hand, and the female members of his family, on the other. He is the blind force of history, its collective unconscious, its somatotonic (i.e., aggressive, vigorous, physical) manifestation. They embody historical awareness and intuitive understanding. Trueba is a semicomic version of the "world historical personalities" conceived of by Hegel; never happy, "they attained no calm enjoyment; their whole life was labor and trouble; their whole nature was nothing but their master passion." [Hegel, *The Philosophy of Hegel,* 1956.] But unlike the three illustrious examples offered by Hegel—Alexander the Great died young, Julius Caesar was murdered, Napoleon Bonaparte ended up in humbling exile—Esteban Trueba lives through the problems and outrages he helps create. Possessed by a terrible temperament, violent and arbitrary in his treatment of peasant girls, his sharecropping tenants, his wife and daughter, and his political enemies, and subject to furniture-smashing tantrums, he is not permitted to recognize—or forced to acknowledge—the consequences of his acts until he's close to death. His author, it seems, decided to put off his death until he could be made to witness the full historical effect of his own retrogressive ideas and actions, and of his collaboration and conspiracy with like-minded people. Until that time of punitive recognition he is subjected ... to recurrent experiences of loneliness and frustration. His estrangement from his family (although he ends his isolation at Tres Marías and joins them in "the big house on the corner") leads him, halfway through the novel, to venture into politics as a Conservative Party candidate for the Senate, "since no one better personified the honest, uncontaminated politician, as he himself declared."

Symbolically in that same chapter (7), having won election as Senator, he becomes convinced that his body and brain are shrinking and travels to the United States for diagnosis. Symbolically in that chapter ("The Brothers") his two sons manifest themselves as ideologically incompatible with him and with each other: Jaime is socially and socialistically committed; Nicolás, the childlike seducer, equates the highest good with pleasure and later

will found an Institute for Union with Nothingness and be arrested for singing Asiatic psalms naked before the gates of Congress. And, symbolically, in that chapter Alba is born (feet first, we're later told), harbinger of a new era.

Clara "la clarividente" died when Esteban was seventy, with twenty-nine years still to go, and when Alba was seven. Did the seven and its multiple of ten portend survival and good fortune for the old man and his granddaughter? Clara, Blanca, and Alba, I've already observed, embody historical awareness and intuitive understanding. Their role throughout the novel is the preservation of moral and social conscience and civic responsibility. Clara departs this life at a relatively young age, but she'll often return as a spirit to the halls and bedrooms of "the big house on the corner," and in chapter 14 ("The Hour of Truth"), to Alba's tomb-like prison cell. The latter apparition occurs at the crucial moment when Alba, having undergone the worst of the tortures directed by Esteban García, has decided to stop eating, drinking, and even breathing, in hopes of a quicker death. Clara succeeds in convincing her granddaughter that "the point was not to die, ... but to survive." Further, she strengthens Alba's will to live by urging her to write—"in her mind, without paper or pencil"—not only to forestall madness by keeping her mind occupied, but to preserve a testimony that sooner or later and one way or another must be revealed to the outside world. Her reason is that, given the ways in which the *inside* world works (through torture, deceit, abuse, betrayal, and cowardly concealment), no one has a right to ignorance or forgetfulness, and the true heart of literature is neither pleasure nor knowledge, but survival. The paragraph in which Allende describes how Alba tries to reconstruct what has happened to her could easily be adapted to an essay or textbook on the function of memory within the creative process:

> Alba tried to obey her grandmother, but as soon as she began to take notes with her mind, the doghouse [i.e., her undersized, dark prison cell] filled with all the characters of her story, who rushed in, shoved each other out of the way to wrap her in their anecdotes, their vices, and their virtues, trampled on her intention to compose a documentary, and threw her testimony to the floor, pressing, insisting, and egging her on. She took down their words at breakneck pace, despairing because while she was filling a page, the one before it was erased. This activity kept her fully occupied. At first, she constantly lost her train of thought and forgot new facts as fast as she remembered them. The slightest distraction or additional fear or pain caused her story to snarl like a ball of yarn. But she invented a code for recalling things in

order, and then she was able to bury herself so deeply in her story that she stopped eating, scratching herself, smelling herself, and complaining, and overcame all her varied agonies.

Of course, after Alba is set free—and it is through the intervention of Tránsito Soto, a prostitute friend of Esteban Trueba's from many years back who owes him a favor, that her release is made possible—she tells us in the first-person singular Epilogue that her grandfather was the one "who had the idea that we should write this story." He also helped write it, with a memory that was intact "down to the last second of his ninety years." More basic still is the contribution of Grandmother Clara, who had superior psychic powers but a poor memory; but even before becoming deliberately mute at the age of ten she had begun to write copiously in her notebooks about everything that happened in her eccentric family. It is only after finishing the book and then returning to the first page that we can identify with certainty the "I" in the phrase, "never suspecting that fifty years later I would use her notebooks to reclaim the past and overcome terrors of my own." Clara's notebooks—arranged not chronologically but according to the importance of events—are mentioned on the last page in the same context as they were on the first....

Clara the Clairvoyant was, then, the creative spirit who at the same time that she bore witness to history was able on occasion to alter it and even to perceive its predetermined elements (for the same reason she frequently foresaw what was going to happen). If observation of what occurs, changing the course of what occurs, and understanding what must occur are the three most important attributes of the narrative writer, then Clara fully and dynamically symbolizes the narrative writer. Although she kept forgetting things—menial everyday details—she forced her memory to work through writing (the Notebooks). Although Esteban Trueba pampered her and regaled her with luxuries including a canopy bed with gauze curtains "that looked like a sailboat on a sea of silken blue water," she had a keen social conscience and on her first stay at Tres Marías immediately sensed the workers' "resentment, fear and distrust" upon which Colonel García as a boy was nurtured. Although with distracted sweetness she "lived in a universe of her own invention," she simultaneously endured the abuses of society and her husband—who knocked out four of her front teeth when he discovered that their daughter Blanca was Pedro Tercero García's secret lover.

Clara became immune to surprise (her nursemaid tried for several years to frighten her into speaking during the nine-year silence).

Clara interpreted dreams.

Clara predicted with demonstrated accuracy deaths, earthquakes, and evil actions.

Clara was able to move objects without touching them.

Clara could invoke ghosts.

Clara played Chopin on the piano without raising the lid over the keyboard. And so forth.

Only a writer endowed with a comparably wide range of secret powers is likely to exercise effectively the art of survival in the twentieth century. By the art or literature of survival I mean the ultimate power of testimony through the creative use of memory. That is, creative memory enables testimony to transcend obstacles, ignorance, and repression....

In *The House of the Spirits* magic and the flights of fancy are the instrumental privilege of a select few: the "extraordinary women" to whom Isabel Allende dedicates her novel. Amidst the abuse and the madness that surround them, orientation is not lost. When Alba is finally released one night on a garbage-strewn vacant lot, she is granted provisional freedom, a possibility of putting things together again if only in writing. She doesn't know whether the child in her womb was engendered by a rapist or by Miguel, for whom she'll wait. She considers what has happened to her as "another link to the chain of events that had to complete itself." Yet she is determined "to break that terrible chain" that hatred has so relentlessly fashioned. She finds her basic hope in Grandmother Clara's insightful Notebooks, and in the pages she herself is engaged in writing.

Source: Peter G. Earle, "Literature as Survival: Allende's *The House of the Spirits,*" in *Contemporary Literature,* Vol. 28, No. 4, Winter, 1987, pp. 543–554.

Sources

Bruce Allen, "A Magical Vision of Society in Revolt," *Chicago Tribune Book World,* May 19, 1985, pp. 37-38.

Isabel Allende, "Sobre *La casa de los espíritus*" (Spanish language), *Discurso Literario,* Vol. 2, Autumn, 1984, pp. 67-73.

Robert Antoni, "Parody or Piracy: The Relationship of *The House of the Spirits* to *One Hundred Years of Solitude,*" *Latin American Literary Review,* Vol. XVI, No. 32, July-December, 1988, pp. 16-28.

Patricia Blake, "From Chile with Magic," *Time,* Vol. 125, No. 20, May 20, 1985, p. 79.

Alexander Coleman, "Reconciliation among the Ruins," *New York Times Book Review,* May 12, 1985, pp. 1, 22-23.

Enrique Fernández, "Send in the Clone," *Village Voice,* Vol. XXX, No. 23, June 4, 1985, p. 51.

Ronie-Richelle García-Johnson, "The Struggle for Space: Feminism and Freedom," *Revista Hispanica Moderna,* Columbia University Hispanic Studies, Vol. XLVII, No. 1, June, 1994, pp. 184-93.

Review of *The House of the Spirits, Publishers Weekly,* Vol. 227, No. 9, March 1, 1985, p. 70.

D. A. N. Jones, "Magical Realism," *London Review of Books,* August 1, 1985, pp. 26-7.

Hermione Lee, "Chile Con Carnage," *Observer,* June 7, 1985, p. 21.

Christopher Lehmann-Haupt, Review of *The House of the Spirits, New York Times,* May 9, 1985, p. 23.

Sara Maitland, "Courage and Convictions," *New Statesman,* Vol. 114, No. 2937, July 10, 1987, p. 27.

Suzanne Ruta, "Lovers and Storytellers," *Women's Review of Books,* Vol. VIII, No. 9, June, 1991, p. 10.

Amanda Smith, "PW Interviews: Isabel Allende," *Publishers Weekly,* May 7, 1985.

Paul West, "Narrative Overdrive," *Nation,* Vol. 241, No. 2, July 20 & 27, 1985, pp. 52-4.

Jonathan Yardley, "Desire and Destiny in Latin America," *Washington Post Book World,* May 12, 1985, pp. 3-4.

For Further Study

Robert M. Adams, "The Story Isn't Over," in *New York Review of Books,* Vol. XXXII, No. 12, July 18, 1985, pp. 20-23.

Mixed review of the novel that praises Allende's use of magical elements and mood of reconciliation. The critic does fault the author for failing to take proper advantage of her eccentric but "entertaining" female characters.

Lori M. Carlson, review of *The House of the Spirits,* in *Review,* No. 34, January-June, 1985, pp. 77-78.

Praises Allende's "precise structuring of character development" and notes that the novel remains compelling even if very reminiscent of García Márquez's *One Hundred Years of Solitude.*

Susan de Carvalho, "Escrituras y Escritoras: The Artist-Protagonist of Isabel Allende," in *Discurso Literario,* Vol. 10, No. 1, 1992, pp. 59-67.

Examines the self-exploration of the narrators in Allende's *Eva Luna* and *The House of the Spirits.*

P. Gabrielle Foreman, "Past-On Stories: History and the Magically Real, Morrison and Allende on Call," in *Feminist Studies,* Vol. 18, No. 2, Summer, 1992, pp. 369-88.

Comparative study in which Foreman examines the "interrelation of history, ontology, and the magically

real" in Allende's *The House of the Spirits* and Toni Morrison's *Beloved.*

Ambrose Gordon, "Isabel Allende on Love and Shadow," in *Contemporary Literature,* Vol. 28, No. 4, Winter, 1987, pp. 530-42.

A review of Allende's second novel, *Of Love and Shadows,* that includes a generally positive assessment of *The House of the Spirits.* Gordon notes that the novel's "bizarre detail" and "jumbled history" do not necessarily mean the work is not valuable. Concludes that the novel works as a skillful "weapon" of protest against the Pinochet government.

Patricia Hart, *Narrative Magic in the Fiction of Isabel Allende,* Fairleigh Dickinson University Press, 1989.

A book-length study of the magic realist elements of Allende's work.

Ruth Y. Jenkins, "Authorizing Female Voice and Experience: Ghosts and Spirits in Kingston's *The Woman Warrior* and Allende's *The House of the Spirits,*" in *Melus,* Vol. 19, No. 3, Fall, 1994, pp. 61-73.

Examines the "connections between the supernatural and female voice" in Allende's *The House of the Spirits* and Maxine Hong Kingston's *The Woman Warrior,* stating that "both authors narrate and preserve authentic female experience."

Claudia Marie Kovach, "Mask and Mirror: Isabel Allende's Mechanism for Justice in *The House of the Spirits,*" in *Postcolonial Literature and the Biblical Call for Justice,* University Press of Mississippi, 1994, pp. 74-90.

Examines the ways in which Allende propagates a "prophetic vision of female integrity and justice" in *The House of the Spirits,* focusing on the role of memories in the book and Allende's narrative strategies.

Marilyn Berlin Snell, "The Shaman and the Infidel," in *New Perspectives Quarterly,* Vol. 8, No. 1, Winter, 1991, pp. 54-58.

Interview in which Allende discusses Latin American literature, magic realism, and the major themes of her work.

Gail Tayko, "Teaching Isabel Allende's *La casa de los espíritus,*" in *College Literature,* Vols. 19-20, Nos. 3-1, October, 1992-February, 1993, pp. 228-32.

Discusses how *The House of the Spirits* could be utilized in the classroom, concluding that the work "interweaves sexual, political, and economic oppression and affirms the national identity of Chile through its focus on the familial sphere. In doing so the novel powerfully raises the issues that are so important for students to confront."

Michael Toms, interview with Isabel Allende in *Common Boundary,* May/June, 1994, pp. 16-23.

An interview in which Allende discusses her writing technique, how personal experience has affected her works, her literary influences, and her career as a journalist

Robert Wilson, "A Latin Epic of Marxism and Magic," in *USA Today,* June 7, 1985, p. 4D.

Mostly positive review of the novel that nevertheless faults the author's treatment of President Allende's rise and fall for leaving her characters behind.

The Jungle

Upton Sinclair
1906

Since its first publication in 1906, Upton Sinclair's *The Jungle* has stirred generations of readers to outrage. It is the story of an economic system that destroys Jurgis Rudkus and his family, treating them no better than the cattle that are slaughtered and vivisected in the book's most horrific and memorable scenes. The novel is not only taught in English classes, as a powerful example of early-twentieth century naturalism, but it is also a perennial favorite of sociology teachers, who use it to convey just how terrible conditions for workers were a hundred years ago and how dangerous the threat of food contamination really was before corporate greed was put in check by government regulation. *The Jungle* is a rare example of a work of fiction that is so true to its source and so powerfully written that it changed the course of government regulation: it is generally credited with getting the 1906 Pure Food and Drug Act passed. The story starts with a family of Lithuanian immigrants moving into the Packingtown district of Chicago, hoping to find a decent place to live and to find jobs to support themselves. They are foiled at these basic requirements: everything costs more than it should, especially since real estate agents and merchants take advantage of their ignorance, and work, when it is available, is brutal and degrading. The book's first half is packed with the gruesome descriptions that have become its legacy, with details of diseased meat shoveled off dirty floors into sausage grinders and sick or injured people preparing meat. In the second half, Jurgis Rudkus, hav-

ing lost his house and family, strikes out on his own, nearly starving on the streets, unable to find work. Stepping into a meeting-hall to get warm, he is enlightened to the Socialist Party's philosophy, and he goes on to read more and attend more meetings, confident that socialism is the solution to society's problems. By the end, the character of Jurgis is just barely significant, as his function is limited to just occasional agreement with the speeches that the author presents for the readers.

Author Biography

Upton Sinclair is best known today as the author of *The Jungle,* which is probably a legacy he would accept, since it is true that this novel did indeed affect society in the way he wanted all of his books to do. He was a prolific writer throughout his long life, and everything he wrote was written with the intent of changing society. Sinclair was born in 1878 with a volatile social background: his mother came from a wealthy and respected Baltimore family, and his father, a salesman, struggled without much success to give her the lifestyle she had been accustomed to. One of the reasons his father was unsuccessful at business was that he was an alcoholic, which is why Sinclair, when he grew up, supported laws that prohibited the sale and use of alcohol (this cause was popular enough to be passed into federal law from 1920 to 1933, a period referred to as "Prohibition"). The first stories and books Sinclair published were not political in nature. When he was eighteen, he started selling stories to Street and Smith, a well-known publisher that printed popular fiction which was inspirational and usually poorly written. His first novels, published when he was in his early twenties, were romances, with titles like *Springtime Harvest* and *Prince Hagen.* Sinclair's writing took a sharp turn toward social realism in 1904, with the publication of *Manassas:* in researching the history of slavery for this novel about a plantation owner's son, he grew more and more outraged with the unfairness of American social structure, and his anger showed in his work.

After reading *Manassas,* Fred Warren, the publisher of the radical newspaper *Appeal to Reason,* issued a challenge to Sinclair to write a novel about current social problems: as a result, Sinclair went to Chicago in the autumn of 1904 to research the meat packing industry, and his research produced *The Jungle.* The book became a best-seller,

Upton Sinclair

and its graphic descriptions of the horrible sanitary conditions in the industry led to calls for government action. The huge companies that were obviously the models for the book, such as Swift, Armour, and Nelson Morris, claimed that Sinclair made up the horrors he described, but independent investigations confirmed conditions to be just as bad as he said, if not worse. In the end, government standards for the handling of all food products became tougher because of *The Jungle.*

Sinclair went on to support changes in all aspects of American life. He arranged a communal living experiment in New Jersey, which lasted from 1906 until it burned down in 1914. In 1914 he used the same method that had worked for *The Jungle* when he went to Colorado to investigate a violent coal miners' strike and the oppressive conditions that caused it, resulting in the novel *King Cole.* Also written in this same way was his most successful novel, *Oil!,* published in 1927 and credited with weakening John D. Rockefeller's monopoly in the petroleum industry. In the 1920s Sinclair was one of the founders of the American Civil Liberties Union, which to this day provides support to people whose Constitutional rights are violated. In 1934 he was the candidate for Governor of California on the Democratic ticket: although he did not win, his strong showing brought national attention to his Socialist views. He continued writing throughout all of his social activity, winning a Pulitzer Prize in 1943 for *Dragon's Teeth,* a novel about Germany under the Nazis' control that was part of his eleven-book series about wealthy secret agent Lanny Budd. He died in 1968, having written ninety books of fiction, political history, social criticism and autobiography throughout his ninety-year life.

Plot Summary

Life in Packingtown

The novel's first seventeen chapters, roughly half of its length, examine the struggles and compromises faced by one extended family from the eastern European country of Lithuania. They attempt to settle into a comfortable life in America, only to find themselves destroyed by the economic system. The book starts with hope, with the marriage of Jurgis Rudkus to Ona Lukoszaite. At the wedding, the key people in their lives are introduced—his father, her cousin, her stepmother who has six children, and so on. The wedding scene also introduces a sense of how strict their budget is and how greatly they fear unemployment. The narrative then slips backward by a year to explain their situation by presenting their courtship in the Imperial Forest in Lithuania, the financial disaster that occurred when her father died, and the decision to move to America. It soon becomes clear that this is Jurgis Rudkus' story, since most of the details related are about him. On first immigrating, Jurgis is ecstatic and confident, and by the time of his marriage he still feels able to fend for his family, although responsibilities make his life difficult. A major financial burden is the house that the family buys: although they take much caution before signing for it, the real estate agent takes advantage of their poor grasp of English and the monthly payments turn out to be considerably more than the sum that they had to struggle to meet. To meet expenses, Ona goes to work sewing casings on hams, Jurgis' father Antanas takes a lowly job sweeping floors, Cousin Maria paints cans, and Ona's stepmother has to leave her children unsupervised to work in a sausage factory. With all of them working at different jobs in the meatpacking industry, the book is able to present the horrible details that are the book's main claim to fame: the methods of disguising tainted meat with brine, or putting it in sausage; the rats and vermin that crawl across the meat and are packaged with it; the bribes to inspectors. The family's financial situation continues to worsen, and their fear of losing their home increases. Jurgis twists his ankle and has to be bedridden, forcing him to later take a job in the toxic fertilizer plant. Cousin Marija loses her position for complaining that she has been cheated on her pay, and takes a job trimming rancid meat. Ona develops "womb trouble" from going back to work too soon after their son's birth. When Ona is pregnant with a second child, she fails to come home one snowy night, and Jurgis finds out that the foreman where she works has forced her to work in a house of prostitution downtown, threatening the jobs of all of her family if she refused. Jurgis rushes to the plant, finds the man, and beats him bloody, for which Jurgis is sent away to jail for a month.

Travelling Alone

Jurgis has trouble finding his family upon his release from jail, because they have been evicted and the house has been sold to new owners. After asking around, he finds them living in an unheated attic, where, the very night he arrives, Ona is giving birth. Without money they cannot get adequate medical help, and Ona and the baby die. Because the man he assaulted was influential, Jurgis' name is blacklisted by meatpackers throughout the country. With considerable trouble he finds a job at a harvester plant, but it shuts down nine days after his hiring. A social worker gets him a job at a steel mill near the Indiana border. When he finds out that his young son has drowned while playing in a flooded street, Jurgis feels no more bond to city life, and he leaves town on a freight train, travelling the countryside in the fresh air and sleeping in fields and barns. This life reminds him of his home country, and he is happy with it, but when winter comes he returns to Chicago. Working briefly at digging tunnels under the city for the subway system, his arm is broken in an accident, leaving him in danger of freezing in the streets. He runs into a rich drunk man who takes him home to supper: this man gives Jurgis a hundred-dollar bill to pay the cab driver and then, forgetting, has his butler pay the cab. After dinner, when the rich man falls asleep at the table, the butler throws Jurgis out, and when he tries to cash the hundred-dollar bill at a saloon, the bartender will only give him change for a dollar, denying that he brought in anything more. Jurgis assaults the man and ends up in jail again.

Life of Crime

In jail Jurgis renews his acquaintance with Jack Duane, whom he met during his last jail term; this time, however, he agrees to become Duane's partner in crime. When they are released they perform a simple, vicious street mugging, cracking a man's skull and taking his wallet and leaving him to freeze. Jurgis' life of crime progresses quickly, from street crimes to gambling to political graft. The political boss of the Packingtown district enlists Jurgis to assure that a weak politician of the opposing political party will defeat the Socialist candidate that their own party has nominated, and so he arranges a job for Jurgis at the same packinghouse that he used to work at, because party regulars cannot campaign for the opposition. With the election won, Jurgis stays on, and when the workers go out on strike the political bosses offer him the chance to become a foreman by staying and working with the scab laborers that they bring in. Jurgis is richer than ever, thanks to his life of crime. It all falls apart when he runs into the man who raped his wife and forced her into prostitution: he assaults the man again, losing his job and political connections, and it costs him the three hundred dollars he has saved to stay out of jail.

Socialism

Alone and on the street again, Jurgis runs into an old friend who tells him where to find Cousin Marija, giving him an address that turns out to be a house of prostitution. Marija explains that she is taking care of what is left of the family with her wages as a prostitute, and that she would not quit her job, even if Jurgis could support them all financially, because she is addicted to opium. One day, Jurgis goes into a meeting hall to warm up, not caring about the meeting being held, but a beautiful woman behind him notices him dozing and suggests that he might be interested if he paid attention. He listens, and he becomes enthralled with socialist philosophy. After the speech he goes to talk with the meeting chairman and is assigned to a party member who tutors him, giving him readings and explaining them to him. When he finally lands a job as a porter at a hotel, his surprised mentor explains that the hotel owner is one of the state's leading socialists. Jurgis is then able to sit in on conversations when famous socialists pass through town. The book ends with Jurgis and his socialist friends gathering in a hall on election night, exuberant about the huge increase in votes that Socialist candidates are gathering all across America in the 1904 elections.

Characters

Marija Berczynskas

Ona's cousin, an orphan, Marija decided to join the family in coming to America just before they left on their journey. She is a big, strong, loud woman who just starts to find happiness in her courtship with Tamoszius Kuszkeika when the canning factory that she works in shuts down after the holidays, when the demand is slow. When she attends a union meeting, Marija is not too shy to stand up and complain about the way she has been treated, even though the meeting is conducted in English and she only speaks Lithuanian. When the cannery starts up again, Marija is fired almost immediately: she says that it is for belonging to the union, although others know that she has also been arguing with her boss. The only place she can find work is in trimming the meat of diseased cattle, at half the pay she was making before. While Jurgis is in jail, it is reported to him that Marija has gangrene from a cut she received at work, and that the company doctor says she might have to lose her hand. She survives that injury, though. Near the end of the novel, Jurgis runs into a friend who tells him where to find Marija, whom he has not seen in over a year. She is living and working in a house of prostitution and supporting Teta Elzbieta with the money that she makes. Jurgis offers to make enough money to allow her to move out, but Marija explains that she really does not mind the life of a prostitute and that she is bitter about the way that people are taken advantage of in legal jobs. The main reason that she wants to stay at the house is that she is hooked on morphine, which she started taking when she came to the house, and she would not make enough money to support her habit anywhere else.

Phil Connor

Connor is the boss of the ham packaging department that Ona works in. When Ona is pregnant with her second child, Connor tries seducing her, and then rapes her one night when everyone else is gone. Then, with a combination of threats and promises, he convinces her to work as a prostitute at the house run by her forelady, Miss Henderson. When Jurgis finds out, he goes to the plant, beats Connor, and is sent to jail. Later, after finding success in politics, Jurgis runs into Connor again and again attacks him, only to find that his political connections cannot help him out of trouble because Connor's political connections are stronger.

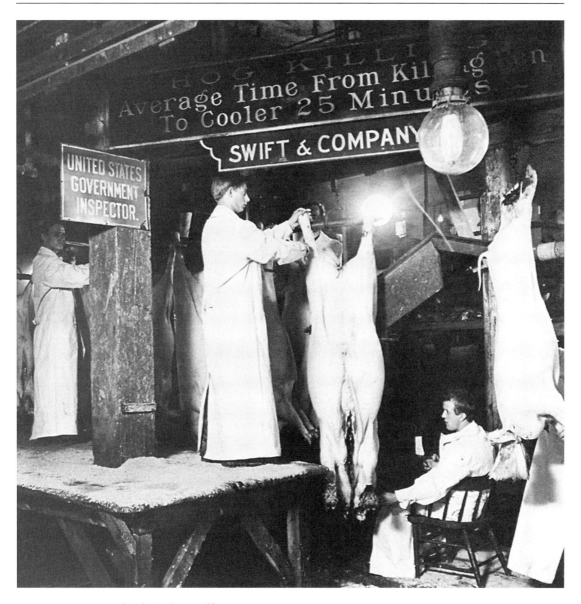

Meat inspectors at Swift & Co. in Chicago.

Dede Antanas

See Antanas Rudkus

Jack Duane

Jurgis meets Duane when he is in jail for beating Connor up. Duane takes a liking to Jurgis, and offers to help him make money, but Jurgis is not interested in illegal activity. Later, after Jurgis runs into Duane the second time he is in jail, he is eager to earn money, no matter what it takes. He finds Duane when he is released, and together they mug a man and leave him with a concussion, freezing on the street. He introduces Jurgis to a high-moneyed life of crime, and to other criminal connections.

Tommy Hinds

Tommy Hinds is a hotel owner, and, although Jurgis does not know it when he applies for a job as the hotel's porter, he is also one of the state's most prominent Socialists. He hires Jurgis to replace the old porter, who was a Socialist but drank too much, and is delighted to find that Jurgis is studying Socialism: "'By Jove!' he cried, 'that lets me out. I didn't sleep at all last night because I had discharged a good Socialist!'" Hinds' hotel is staffed by other Socialists, and he takes Jurgis

Media Adaptations

- An audio recording of *The Jungle* was made by Blackstone Audio Books in 1994, read by Robert Morris.

- An unabridged recording of *The Jungle,* narrated by George Guidall, was released by Recorded Books, Inc. in 1998.

- Audio Book Contractors released an audio version entitled *Upton Sinclair's The Jungle* in 1998.

around to party meetings and teaches him about the Socialist philosophy.

Alena Jasaityte

During the wedding scene at the beginning of the novel, Alena is young and good-looking, but pompous: "she would really be beautiful if she were not so proud," the narrator says. She is engaged to a well-paid delivery-truck driver and spends a half-week salary on her dress. Much later, Jurgis runs into her on the street when he is desperate for food and shelter. Alena is well-dressed, but cannot give him anything because, she says, she left her purse at home. She is the one who tells him to find Marija at the house of prostitution.

Freddie Jones

One of the most colorful characters in the novel, Freddie's dialogue is written in drunken half-words and incoherent statements. He is a son of a wealthy family who meets Jurgis begging on the street one night and takes a liking to him. Because he is drunk, Freddie is full of self-pity, and when Jurgis explains that he has no money, Freddie says that he does not have much either, because his parents have sailed to Europe and he has almost spent what they left him and they have not responded to his telegram asking for more. He gives Jurgis a hundred-dollar bill to pay a cab to take them to his house, but he forgets it and has the but-ler pay the cab when they arrive. When Freddie falls asleep at the dinner table, the butler throws Jurgis out.

Tamoszius Kuszleika

The fiddler at Jurgis and Ona's wedding, he is a popular figure in Packingtown, invited to parties by people too poor to hire a musician because they know that he will not be able to resist playing for free while he is celebrating. After a while, a courtship develops between Tamoszius and Marija, but the economic troubles of the family continually distract them: first, when Marija loses her job, and then when Jurgis goes to jail and the house is lost. When Jurgis runs into Marija near the end of the novel, she says that Tamoszius had contracted blood poisoning and lost a finger, so he could not play his violin any more. He "went away," and she had not seen him in over a year.

Elzbieta Lukoszaite

Ona's step-mother, who brought her six young children to America with her. At first, she stays home to keep house while the other adults work. Soon financial troubles become so bad that the family relies on the money that her boys make by selling newspapers on street corners. They are spending time with rough characters and prostitutes, and the only way they can quit working and go back to school is if Elzbieta goes to work, so she obtains a job in the sausage plant.

Jonas Lukoszaite

Jonas is the brother of Ona's step-mother Elzbieta, the one who has the idea to come to America in the first place because he knows of a man who moved to Chicago and became rich. After living with the family for a few years and contributing to the household expenses, Jonas disappears one spring day—there is speculation that, since he was single and unattached, he might have gone to find a better life. It is also suggested that if he had died in the meat-processing plant the company might just have disposed of his body, rather than paying death benefits: "When, for instance, a man had fallen into one of the rendering tanks and had been made into pure leaf lard and peerless fertilizer, there was no use letting the fact out and making his family unhappy."

Stanislovas Lukoszaite

The oldest of Teta Elzbieta's six children, Stanislovas goes to work at age fourteen in the lard-canning department at Durham's, where he puts cans on the conveyor belt for ten hours a day. In the winter, he becomes lost in a snowstorm on his way home from work, and his fingers freeze at the first joint. After that, he is terrified of going out in the snow, and has to be threatened and beaten to go to work on snowy days. Jurgis finds out near the end of the book how Stanislovas died: fetching beer for workers in an oil factory, he drank some and fell asleep, and when he was locked inside of the factory overnight, rats killed him and ate his flesh.

Antanas Rudkus

Jurgis' old father ("Dede" means "Grandfather" in Lithuanian) had one other son in Lithuania, but he went into the army ten years before the novel began and was never heard from again. After they move to America, Jurgis does not want his father to work, but Antanas is still in the habit of working hard for many years, and he would not feel good about being idle while the rest of the family is struggling so hard to pay the bills. He has trouble finding a job because no one wants to hire an old man who is incapable of much physical labor, but, by agreeing to pay one-third of his salary to a man with business connections, he is hired as a "squeedgie man" at the Durham factory. There it is his job to push around brine on the floor of the room where beef is pickled. The pickling solution leaks through his boots and infects a sore on his foot, but Antanas stays at his work until one day he collapses on the floor, and two fellow workers have to carry him home. As he lies in bed, sick, Jurgis hires a worker to come to the house and tell him that Durham's is holding his job until he is well enough to return, although it is not true. Antanas dies a few days later.

Jurgis Rudkus

Jurgis is the protagonist, or main character, of this story: after the extended wedding scene which introduces all of the characters, the narrative stops on Jurgis and stays with his experiences throughout the book. In the beginning, he is a tall, strong young man, although by the novel's end a few years later his health is ruined by his experiences. Jurgis comes from *Brelovicz*, "The Imperial Forest," in Lithuania, which is where he met Ona and fell in love with her. In America, he initially feels that his salary, along with the rent paid by relatives in his house, should cover the family's expenses, so that his elderly father and petite bride will not have to go to work. When expenses mount, Jurgis' first reaction is, "I shall have to work harder." He soon

finds that circumstances will always rise to keep him from addressing problems with hard work alone. When the demand for beef slackens, Jurgis' hours are cut, and when he injures his leg at work, he has to stay home and let it heal, or he will be crippled forever. When his leg heals, the only job Jurgis can find is in the fertilizer plant, where the smell of chemicals and animal remains permeates his skin so badly that the stench is on him for months after he leaves. After assaulting the man who raped Ona and forced her into prostitution, Jurgis goes to jail: while he is there, the bank forecloses on his house, and the day he is released Ona dies during childbirth. With the help of a social worker, Jurgis lands a clean, well-paying job at a steel mill in South Chicago, but he breaks his shoulder at work and is left unemployed. When his little son dies, drowned in a flooded street, Jurgis leaves Chicago and takes off on the road, stopping to work on farms only when he really needs money and sleeping out under the open sky. This is the only section of the novel that shows Jurgis as content, even happy. When winter comes, he returns to the city, but still cannot find a job. A rich person gives him a hundred-dollar bill, but when he tries to change it a bartender cheats him: the commotion Jurgis raises lands him in jail again. This time he is disillusioned with the world, and cultivates his connections with criminals. Upon his release he makes a good wage in crime, rising from mugging to politics. In order to move from political work to steady work he becomes a strike breaker in a meat plant, doing the jobs of his former coworkers, who are out on strike, but he loses his job and his political connections when he once again assaults the man who raped his wife. In the last section of the book, Jurgis stumbles across Socialism and realizes that it is the one true way, the answer to all of the questions he ever had. He attends lectures and reads Socialist literature at every opportunity. He lands a job at a hotel that is, coincidentally, owned by one of the state organizers of the party. This man takes Jurgis to meetings with other socialists from all walks of life, so that they can learn what the working life is like from someone who has suffered economic oppression.

Ona Rudkus

Ona is very small and young when she comes to America. Although the book opens with her wedding to Jurgis, the next chapter tells the reader what happened before the wedding: they were actually not married until more than a year after arriving. Jurgis waits before marrying her because he wants to own the house Ona will live in and have a job so he can provide for her. She does not have a very striking role in the story, but Ona's function in the novel is important: she is an emblem of decency, and she provides Jurgis with a reason to struggle against the corruptive elements of poverty while she is alive (a function that is carried over after her death by little Antanas, their child). His love for her is so strong and pure, and she is so small and frail, that when the snow is high he carries her to work at the factory in his arms. After the birth of little Antanas, Ona develops "womb-trouble," and she is ill all of the time, although she is unwilling to admit this to Jurgis. Ona works in the cellar at Brown's, sewing casings on hams. When she is carrying their second child, Ona begins having fits of hysteria, coming home at night crying and shuddering. One snowy night she does not come home at all, explaining that she stayed with a friend, and when it happens again Jurgis confronts her and finds out the truth. The boss of her department, Connor, forced her to have sex with him, she explains, and then he forced her to work downtown as a prostitute by threatening not just her job, but Jurgis' and Marija's too. Jurgis goes to jail for assaulting Connor, and he returns to the family to find Ona in labor in an unheated attic. She dies during childbirth.

Mike Scully

Scully is the legendary political boss who runs the Packingtown district on behalf of the owners of the big packing houses. Scully has the power to give out political favors to the rich and jobs to the poor through an organization he started called the "War-Whoop League." At the end of his spree as a criminal, Jurgis works for Scully to elect a weak member of the opposing party, but when he is sent to jail Scully refuses to help him.

Teta Elzbieta

See Elzbieta Lukoszaite

Themes

American Dream

The novel explains that after the death of Ona's father in Lithuania his farm was sold, and the family paid two-thirds of their inheritance to a local magistrate in order to avoid losing all of it. That was when Ona's brother Jonas suggested that they all move to America. He had heard about a friend

who went to America and became rich (the friend later turns out to actually be making just a modest living with his delicatessen in Chicago). In calculating the money he could earn in America, Jurgis Rudkus does not account for the fact that, while the pay rate is higher, the cost of living is greater too. But the promise of wealth is not even as important in their decision-making as the promise of social equality. The book explains their thinking: "In (America), rich or poor, a man was free, it was said; he did not have to go into the army, he did not have to pay out his money to public officials,—he might do as he pleased, and count himself as good as any other men. So America was a place of which lovers and young people dreamed." The central theme of this book focuses on this particular group finding the American Dream of wealth and freedom to be an illusion. They are not free to do as they wish, but instead spend all of their time and energy trying to meet their financial needs, destroying themselves physically and morally in the process. The clearest example of this is the fact that Ona has to work as a prostitute in order to assure that her family members can keep their dangerous, mind-numbing jobs at the packing house. One of the greatest lures of the American Dream has always been the promise of land ownership, which is related to freedom, but that is denied the Rudkus family too, when they lose their house and all they have put into it after missing a few payments. In the end, Jurgis finds that socialism offers him more prosperity and freedom than the competitive American system, because it focuses its attention on the good of all, rather than making the rich and poor opponents.

Class Conflict

Most of the problems faced by Jurgis' family are caused by the fact that they have nothing, and that those who do have things actively strive to keep them from benefiting from their own hard work. Not only do the packinghouse owners benefit from the workers' labor, but they also benefit from promoting hostility among the workers, because resentment toward each other keeps them from organizing into unions. The plant managers are forced by the people above them to eke more and more work out of the low-level employees. European laborers look down on black workers from the south, whom they see as lazy and wild. After the deaths of his wife and child, and after he has been out from the bottom of the social ladder and experienced the freedom of the countryside, Jurgis becomes determined to be a winner in his struggle in society, even if it means taking advantage of his fellow men. The mugging that starts his life of crime bothers his conscience, but his partner helps him rationalize it as fair because the victim probably deserved it: Jurgis points out that the man had never done them any harm and his friend explains, "He was doing it to someone as hard as he could, you can be sure of that." His subsequent descent into the criminal world leads him to gambling and crooked politics, crimes that are more and more abstract, taking advantage of those at the bottom of society (where Jurgis so recently was) while keeping him blind to the cost they are paying for his luxury. The final irony is when he becomes a strike breaker, creating the same near-impossible conditions that destroyed his family when he was in the lower class. Abuse of the social order is captured most keenly when Jurgis and two policemen, trying to suppress striking workers, go into a tavern, and the policemen empty the cash register, with no moral justification, simply because they have the power to do it. After that, the book turns its attention to socialism's philosophy of classlessness, espousing a system where merit is given to people for working hard and helping society, not for taking advantage or for holding tight to the privileges of their social class.

Individualism

From the start, Jurgis' response to financial difficulty is, "Leave it to me; leave it to me. I will earn more money—I will work harder." He is young and strong, and, as the novel explains, "he could not even imagine what it would feel like to be beaten." This attitude also shows in his old, ailing father, Dede Antanis, who is so determined to fend for himself that he pays a substantial part of his salary back to the man who arranges his brutal job, which eventually sends him to his grave. The novel shows all of these immigrants to be mistaken in their belief that they are in control of their fates, but it is just as harsh toward those who refuse to take individual responsibility. There are numerous examples of characters who feel that living within a corrupt system permits an individual to loosen his or her morals, and their individual corruption serves to make society harsher, which leads to even more corruption, and so forth. Even when someone in the novel tries to help another person for selfless reasons, such as the social worker in Chapter 21 who arranges for her fiancé at the steel works to hire Jurgis, the gesture is never powerful enough to overcome the heartless competitiveness of society at large. The only time Jurgis is able to celebrate his

Topics for Further Study

- Many of the incidents included in *The Jungle* are based on actual events. Research the 1904 beef strike in Chicago and other cities, the International Harvester Trust created in 1902, the settlement house movement, or the Socialist movement in the early years of the twentieth century, and report on the background of Sinclair's fictionalized events.

- What steps are taken by the government to assure that meat sold today is sanitary and safe to eat? Examine the inspection process and explain it visually with a chart that shows the steps of the process.

- Music often helps people to understand the mood of a different time or culture. Find some songs that would have been popular in Chicago in 1905, and explain how their lyrics and melodies reflect the way of life described in *The Jungle*.

own individuality is when he is roaming through the countryside, but that is not necessarily a good thing, since his freedom is due to the fact that those closest to him are dead. The message conveyed by the book's socialist ending is that individualism does not have to mean isolation, as it does in a competitive capitalist system: it can mean individual progress put to use for the common good. Unlike other collectivist philosophies which have sought to ignore or even crush individual thought, the type of socialism advocated in *The Jungle* supports a combination of individualism with voluntary cooperation.

Style

Narration

Most of this book is told from Jurgis Rudkus' point of view, giving readers information that Jurgis would have experienced or heard about and providing access to his feelings and opinions. The book's first chapter provides the most obvious exception to its overall narrative structure. Chapter 1 has an omniscient narrator who is not identified with any particular character, shifting attention from one wedding participant to the next, like a movie camera panning a crowd scene. A reader who was only familiar with the first chapter would not be able to tell that this is a book about Jurgis: the characters who receive the most attention in that part of the book are Ona's cousin Marija Berczynskas and the fiddler Tamoszius Kuszleika, who in fact only receives passing mention throughout the rest of the tale. Once the narration settles on Jurgis, from Chapter 2 on, its hold is loose, slipping every so often into the point of view of another character. For example, in the course of describing the work situations of other characters, such as Ona or Elzbieta, the narration will say what these characters thought, which is actually a violation of the pattern established in the rest of the book, which only gives access to Jurgis' mind.

Plot

The Jungle was written the way that was most common in the nineteenth century, the way that Charles Dickens and Mark Twain produced novels: as a continuing serial for a newspaper, with new installments in each edition. As a result, the plot of the book is choppy and uneven, with less care taken in connecting one chapter to the next than is taken to ensure that each individual chapter is solid within itself. The impression that readers retain about Jurgis' life is not necessarily about his growth from bright-eyed innocent to dedicated socialist, but of the individual situations that he passes through in moving from the beginning to the end. While it is true that the turmoil of each step, such as going to jail, being injured, or becoming a political operative, might be important in molding Jurgis into the man he eventually becomes, each episode is important because it is an interesting story in itself, apart from the rest of the work. The individual pieces work well separately, each with a structure that makes it satisfying. The connection between the book's parts is so weak that, as Sinclair himself explained, the preachy, long-winded speeches in the final chapters are not the fulfillment of some overall design: they were written hastily simply to finish the book by his publisher's deadline.

Setting

The Jungle is most often examined as a book about the Chicago stockyards, in spite of the fact that the main character quits being a part of stockyard life before the book is half over. The vivid details of the packinghouse scenes had much to do with the book's overall social significance. In 1906, when it was published, this book delivered the news of just what conditions were like, performing a function that is now expected from the news media. The packinghouse scenes are still powerful today, even though the conditions described in the book no longer exist in the United States. Modern readers can relate to the dehumanizing effects of boring, repetitive assembly-line labor and of employers who put profits before the health of their workers. Even though these packinghouses and their particular methods are gone, the drive to get employees to do more work for less money still exists, as does the practice of handling merchandise, whether it is meat or information, as expediently as the law allows. By symbolically linking the fates of the immigrants with the treatment of the butchered food products, the book establishes a nearly perfect link between setting and theme, which, even more than the sheer mass of gruesome details, accounts for the impact of the stockyard setting upon the minds of readers throughout the decades.

Naturalism

This book is a classic example of the Naturalist movement in literature, which developed in the nineteenth century with the writings of French novelist Emile Zola. Naturalist theories do not separate man from nature, as many ways of thought do, but they explain man's behavior as being a result of environment, and thus they explore the social environment for the weaknesses that cause bad behavior. Because it looks at the world in terms of external causes and effects and does not account for the effect that free will can have on a person's situation, Naturalist literature is often considered depressing and hopeless. Writers like Upton Sinclair, who intend their works to produce social change, have traditionally used Naturalist techniques to shock their readers about what is happening in the world. The problem with combining social dedication with impartial description is that, with the number of incidents required to make a novel, writers tend to strain credibility in their attempt to make the world look as harsh as possible. Independently, the brutal and oppressing events that happen to Jurgis Rudkus in this book might serve to stir readers to outrage, but collectively they raise the question of whether the "nature" presented in the story is not manipulated to give Jurgis more bad luck than any one person would normally have.

Historical Context

Immigration

The Jungle was written specifically to draw attention to the working conditions faced by laborers in America, specifically the immigrants who came, mostly from Europe, and had no choice but to work long hours for whatever meager pay they could get. Throughout the end of the nineteenth century and into the twentieth, their situation became increasingly difficult. One reason was that a great number of unskilled laborers came to America at the time, so that employers could offer low wages for miserable jobs and always find someone willing to do the work. The United States population more than doubled, for instance, between 1850 and 1880, growing from 23 million to 50 million people; twenty years later, it was up by fifty percent more, to 76 million. Some of this was due to the country's expansion and acquisition of new western territories, but much of it was due to the fact that Europeans left hard conditions at home for the abundance of the new land. For example, the Irish potato famine of 1845-1847 caused millions of Irish people to leave their land in search of a new life. Th first wave of immigrants came from western Europe. As word about America's strong economy spread deeper into the continent and travel became easier (by locomotives across land and steamships across oceans), people came from more distant countries, including Lithuania, where the Rudkus family of the novel came from. As the number of unskilled workers grew, urban areas bulged with their increased populations, and industries developed machines that simplified and standardized tasks so that workers could handle them without much skill or training or grasp of the language. In the early part of the twentieth century, the United States government passed new laws that severely limited immigration, which had been growing every year, reaching a high in 1910, when fifteen percent of the population was foreign-born.

Organization of Labor

It was in the early part of the twentieth century that unions began their rise to power, eventually reaching a level of influence in national politics that many people in the second half of the century took for granted. Because of the violent up-hill struggles faced by unionization, such as the one described in *The Jungle,* it sometimes seems as if unions are a twentieth-century development. Actually, the impulse for workers to band together in fighting for rights, and for employers to try to isolate and manipulate the workers, is as old as the country itself, practically required by the American system of capitalism. The concept extends back to the twelfth century in Europe, where workers in specific trades banded together with one another to form guilds: these organizations kept wages secure by limiting the number of people who could work at the trade, and they assured the quality of goods by assuring that the guild members were properly trained. Through the centuries the formal organization of the guild declined, although the concept of people in one profession banding together for the common good has lived on. In the early 1800s, there were unions among shoemakers, printers, and other crafts persons. In 1827, a collection of these smaller unions banded together in Philadelphia to form the Mechanics Union of Trade Associations; though it was only in existence for a few years, it provided a basic design for unions of the future, enabling its members to use the power of several professions in one location, rather than calling out a strike of one profession spread out across the country. At the same time, workers in the country's coal mines found their conditions so perilous and their chances of surviving without the mines so hopeless that they brought unionization to rural settings. Early union activity almost always led to violence if it was not called off quickly: the government generally sided with employers, denied the unions' right to exist, and provided police or armed militia squads to break up demonstrations. Notable events in the struggle for unionization are the Haymarket Massacre in Chicago in 1886, during which police fired into a crowd of striking workers, setting off a chain reaction of violence, and the Homestead strike of 1892 that resulted when a Pittsburgh steel works cut wages and fired workers and sent 300 armed thugs to prevent a strike. The brutality of the company owners and the cooperation of the government against its citizens in cases like these swayed public opinion toward unionization.

Socialism

With its emphasis on the rights of the workers and on the sins of the property owners, it is only natural that many activists in the labor movement, like Upton Sinclair, would be supporters of socialist philosophies. Early on, the goals of socialism and communism were closely linked, because both

Compare
&
Contrast

- **1906:** The Pure Food and Drug bill introduced, in part, as a result of revelations made in *The Jungle,* was opposed by conservative politicians. Republican Senator Nelson W. Aldrich, 64, asked, "Is there anything in the existing condition that makes it the duty of Congress to put the liberty of the United States in jeopardy? … Are we going to take up the question as to what a man shall eat and what a man shall drink, and put him under severe penalties if he is eating or drinking something different from what the chemists of the Agricultural Department think desirable?"

  Today: The debate still continues about whether government safety standards are an infringement of manufacturers' freedom.

- **1906:** The worst earthquake to hit an American city shook San Francisco, registering 8.3 on the Richter scale. The resulting fire lasted three days. In the end, 2,500 died, 250,000 were left homeless, and damages were estimated at over $400 million.

  1989: An earthquake crippled San Francisco, measuring 7.1 on the Richter scale (which means that its impact was one-tenth of the 1906 quake). The quake killed 90 people and caused $6 billion in property damage, mostly due to the collapse of the double-deck Nimitz Highway and the buckling of the Bay Bridge.

  Today: A growing number of scientists are convinced that a major tremor, greater than any on record, is due to shake California's San Andreas Fault within the next fifty years.

- **1906:** Investigation of an outbreak of typhoid fever in a private kitchen lead researchers to the discovery that similar outbreaks occurred in places where Mary Mallon had previously worked. "Typhoid Mary," as she came to be called, was put into virtual solitary confinement from 1906-1910 because of her ability to infect others.

  1981: Scientists started noticing symptoms of abnormalities in the immune systems of gay American men, mirroring the symptoms of Kaposi's sarcoma, a form of cancer found often in Africa but rare in the rest of the world. Their findings eventually came to be known as Acquired Immune Deficiency Syndrome, or AIDS.

  1985: The first blood test for the HIV virus, which causes AIDS, was approved for use in the United States. Unsafe sharing of needles among intravenous drug users is recognized as a significant cause in spreading the virus.

  Today: The spread of AIDS has been so prevalent that it is no longer dismissed as the problem of just a few social groups. Inhibitors have been developed that can prolong the lives of AIDS victims, but it is still considered a terminal disease.

- **1906:** On Christmas Eve, radio operators on ships off of the Atlantic seaboard heard the first broadcast of a human voice. Inventor Reginald Fessenden read the Christmas story from the gospel of St. Luke over the airwaves that had only been used up to that time to broadcast Morse code. Previous radio transmissions had been to specific receivers.

  1920: The world's first radio station, KDKA in East Pittsburgh, began transmission. Only about 5000 Americans had radio receivers. The following year 75,000 sets were sold.

  1948: The technology boom that followed the end of World War II led to the growth of television: in 1945 there were only 5000 television sets in America, but by 1948 there were over a million.

  Today: Information media are increasingly carried over wires, as in the cases of the Internet and cable television, while personal communication devices like telephones and pagers send signals through the air.

Workers at a Swift & Co. packing house splitting hog backbones, Chicago, Illinois, 1906.

supported the equal distribution of wealth and the breaking down of the social class system. Since the United States' chief rival throughout much of the twentieth century was the communist Soviet Union, many Americans have tended to block out the ideas of socialism as a threat. When Sinclair was writing, however, the Russian Revolution was still ten years in the future, and the cause of socialism was supported by Americans of all backgrounds, although its support was chiefly within the labor movement. In 1877 the Socialist Labor Party was formed in the United States, and in 1901 the Socialist Party was formed by one of the key histor-

ical figures of the century, Eugene V. Debs, who ran for president five times, once while in prison on a charge of "pacifism." In 1904, while Sinclair was in Chicago researching *The Jungle,* labor leader "Big Bill" Haywood called workers and socialists from around the world to Chicago for what he called a "Continental Congress of the working class." Out of that convention came an Industrial Workers Manifesto and the seeds of a new socialist labor union, the Industrial Workers of the World. The I.W.W. was more driven by political beliefs than other unions, and it reached a peak membership of 100,000 before America joined World War

I in 1917. Its membership shrank considerably when the government arrested socialists during the war, on charges of treason. Though the I.W.W. never regained the height of its political power, it still exists today.

Critical Overview

Critics have never shown much agreement about the depth of Upton Sinclair's talent as a writer. Some feel that he was, at best, a weak storyteller, who hid his inability to create believable characters behind his sincere effort for political reform, while others have suggested that it was his political agenda that made it hard to see just how talented he really was. Most critics admit that he was fairly talented, though not exceptionally so, and almost all grant that he was scrupulously faithful to the details he wrote about. Sinclair's friend George Bernard Shaw, the Nobel Prize-winning playwright, suggested to people who asked what had happened in his lifetime that they should not look to newspapers but rather should read Upton Sinclair's novels. Bernard Dekle, who repeated the Shaw story in a 1969 article called "Upton Sinclair: The Power of a Courageous Pen," considered the author a "superb journalist": though that opinion says nothing of his ability as a novelist, Dekle goes on to quote Sir Arthur Conan Doyle (creator of Sherlock Holmes), calling Sinclair, "one of the greatest novelists in the world." Important literary critic Walter B. Rideout described the books of Upton Sinclair as comprising "one of the great information centers in American literature." Another much-admired critic, Granville Hicks, centered in on the quality that gave Sinclair the ability to be such a detailed and credible recorder of the world around him: "Sinclair," Hicks wrote, "has always had the ability to withdraw himself from the struggle and to write with an astonishing degree of objectivity."

But even those critics who praised his ability to capture events in words still acknowledge what Rideout referred to as his "artistic limitations." Rideout pointed out a discrepancy between Sinclair's fictional structure and his social message, explaining that they were separated from one another, instead of complimenting each other the way they should in a good work of art. Hicks, after marveling at his objectivity, recognized that Sinclair's writing, "if seldom downright bad ... is not very distinguished." Even though he wrote his review

during Sinclair's lifetime, he considered the author's works to be "historical fiction" because of the way they were meant to leave a record of the times. That, in Hicks' view, was the source of the problem: as he explained, "flatness of character is, I think, an inherent defect in the genre in which Sinclair is writing." In other words, even a really great writer would have trouble creating well-rounded characters if limited by the facts of history, and Sinclair was even more limited by his undistinguished talent.

One last area of contention comes from those who have disagreed about the level of objectivity in Sinclair's writing, and about how well it served the causes he supported. Few writers have openly criticized Sinclair for his support of the workers against people of privilege, and many have been willing to overlook the problems with his writing because they have considered him to be an overall positive influence. One critic who refused to give him any consideration for good intentions, however, was Van Wyck Brooks. Brooks rejected the claim that Sinclair's books recorded objective reality, pointing out that complete objectivity is impossible: "Mr. Sinclair, like the rest of us, has seen what he wanted to see and studied what he wanted to study." Since the world Sinclair presented to his reader could not be exactly the same as the real world, Brooks tried to describe what Sinclair's world was really like, characterizing it as one where "all the workers wear halos of pure golden sunlight and all the capitalists have horns and tails." Sinclair's supporters might still claim that it was his right to present reality as he saw it, but Brooks went even further, explaining that Sinclair's greatest failure was in not doing what he himself had set out to do: instead of showing workers to be proud and independent, Brooks claimed, Sinclair's over-simplifications made them look helpless and naive, like infants. The implication of Brooks' critique is that he personally supported the working class as much as Sinclair did, but that he did not think it did any good to overstate their problems or to understate their abilities to cope.

Criticism

James Woodress

In the following essay, Woodress explores Sinclair's motivation and methods in writing The Jungle, *and notes of this novel, which provoked action*

What Do I Read Next?

- In 1962, a few years before his death, Sinclair published his view of his long life and many accomplishments in *The Autobiography of Upton Sinclair* (Harcourt, Brace). While *The Jungle* and the social changes that resulted from it are clearly the most notable accomplishments in his life, his life was filled with other publications and deeds that make it notable, including the founding of the American Civil Liberties Union and breaking the Rockefeller oil trust with his novel *Oil!*.

- Leon Harris' biography *Upton Sinclair: American Rebel*, published in 1975 by Thomas Y. Crowell Company, is a thorough picture of the author's life. It paints a generally positive picture of the author's life, a picture that his critics might find a little too rosy.

- Theodore Dreiser's book *Sister Carrie* was published a few years earlier than *The Jungle*, in 1900. It shocked readers of the day with its grim realism and frank sexuality, presenting what might be the best example of the realistic style that Sinclair used to make his social message powerful. Dreiser's later and more famous book, *An American Tragedy* (1925), about a famous murder in Chicago, also reflects Sinclair's style and social concerns.

- James R. Barrett's book *Work and Community in the Jungle: Chicago's Packinghouse Workers, 1894-1922* is an explanation of the social situation that Sinclair wrote about. Published in 1987, this book makes an excellent companion piece to *The Jungle,* and was published along with the authoritative 1988 version of the novel (for which Barrett wrote the notes) by the University of Illinois Press.

- Emile Zola is considered the father of the Realist movement, and was certainly one of the most dedicated social critics to ever write novels. Much of Sinclair's style can be seen in the work of Zola. Almost all of his books are considered classics and are read today, but in particular *The Dram Shop* from 1877, concerning alcoholism, might interest Sinclair readers, since it is a theme that is visited frequently in *The Jungle.*

- Another follower in the Realistic vein was James T. Farrell, who wrote a trilogy of books about an Irish-Catholic boy growing up in Chicago. The books were published throughout the 1930s, and then collected together in 1938, in a volume called *Studs Lonigan,* with a new introduction by the author.

---

from a figure no less influential than President Theodore Roosevelt, "No book ever published in the United States produced such an immediate response."

The Jungle, Upton Sinclair's one claim to a place in literary history, was not so much a novel as it was a tract for the times. Sinclair intended it not as a work of art but as an instrument for changing people's minds. He thought of it as an expendable round of ammunition in the battle for social justice. The novel is better judged as propaganda than as literature, but it has compelling power and interests readers today long after the circumstances under which it was written passed into

history. Sinclair's considerable ability as a storyteller, coupled with the fierce indignation of a born reformer, made *The Jungle* perhaps the most memorable document of the muckraking movement. He was incensed by the appalling conditions he observed among the workers in the Chicago stockyards and was determined to do something to improve them.

Sinclair recalled the novel's provenance in 1946 when he wrote an introduction for a new edition. He remembered being sent in 1904 by the *Appeal to Reason,* a socialist magazine, to investigate conditions in the meat-packing industry. This was at a time when American business answered to no one for safety, sanitary conditions, product reliability, or working conditions. Unions were weak or non-existent, and business squeezed as much profit as it could from low wages. A good many magazines, chief of which was *McClure's,* were then busily publishing exposes of corruption and malpractice in both industry and government. After the scandal of lethal "embalmed beef" sold to the army during the Spanish-American War, the meatpacking industry seemed a prime subject for investigative reporting.

Sinclair spent seven weeks in Chicago living among and interviewing the stockyard workers and studying conditions in the packing plants. He found that he could go anywhere in the stockyards provided he wore old clothes and carried a lunch pail. One day outside the slaughter-houses he chanced upon a Lithuanian wedding supper and dance, spent the afternoon and evening watching and talking to the newly married couple and their relations, and realized that this immigrant group could provide his point of view for his propaganda novel. He invented Jurgis Rudkus and his family and depicted their lives in and about the stockyards. The story, which begins with the happy wedding scene, moves from joy to ever-increasing misery, as the Lithuanians are exploited inside the packing plant and cheated outside of it. The novel is never dull, at least the early chapters that involve the slaughterhouse and life behind the stockyards are not. Here the novel has all the melodrama of a soap opera, and Jurgis suffers more disasters than the early Christian martyrs. Later Sinclair couldn't resist writing a polemic for the Socialist Party, and the novel even ends with a speech that Sinclair had delivered himself at a mass meeting in Chicago on behalf of Eugene V. Debs, the perennial socialist candidate for President in that era.

The Jungle was written in a one-room cabin outside Princeton, New Jersey. He offered the book to Macmillan, publisher of the romances he had written earlier, but that firm would not publish it unless some of the more lurid details about the packing industry were deleted. Meantime, it had been appearing in the *Appeal to Reason* where it was creating a sensation. Sinclair published the book himself with aid from Jack London and others, following which Doubleday Page took it over. Sinclair's purpose in writing the book was to improve the lot of the packinghouse workers, but his account of the lack of proper sanitation, the processing of spoiled and diseased meat, particularly the report of men who fell into the lard vats and were rendered into lard, shocked the public. Sin-

clair said of his book: "I aimed at the public's heart and by accident hit it in the stomach."

No book ever published in the United States produced such an immediate response. Sinclair remembered being summoned to the White House by Theodore Roosevelt to tell his story, after which the President ordered an investigation of the Chicago slaughterhouses. Consumers shuddering over what they might be eating bombarded their senators and representatives with demands for action. Before the year was out Congress passed its first law to regulate the meat, food, and drug industries. No politician could ignore the outcry for reform produced by *The Jungle.*

The contemporary reader finds the socialist propaganda ladled generously into the novel hard to get through, and even the most dramatic chapters are written in a pedestrian style. The organization of the story, moreover, is loose and rambling. But despite its faults the novel has the air of truth and conveys a sense of terrible urgency. This, of course, is the result of its being true. Sinclair was writing a kind of work that might be called the reportorial novel or the novel of social protest, of which there have been many more recent examples. There is relatively little work of the creative imagination in *The Jungle,* for the bulk of it consists of closely observed detail and innumerable facts. Today the same material probably would be cast in the form of non-fiction, the sort of multi-part documentary that often appears in the *New Yorker.* Any student of American history and cultures owes it to himself to read *The Jungle* in order to understand more clearly the impulse behind the labor movement, the drive for regulatory agencies, and the need for social conscience on the part of all citizens.

Source: James Woodress, *The Jungle,* in *Reference Guide to American Literature,* third edition, St. James Press, 1994, pp. 995-96.

Lewis Carroll Wade

In the following excerpt, Wade examines the fallacies upon which Sinclair based his disturbing novel The Jungle.

There is no doubt that *The Jungle* helped shape American political history. Sinclair wrote it to call attention to the plight of Chicago packinghouse workers who had just lost a strike against the Beef Trust. The novel appeared in February 1906, was shrewdly promoted by both author and publisher, and quickly became a best seller. Its socialist message, however, was lost in the uproar over the relatively brief but nauseatingly graphic descriptions of packinghouse "crimes" and "swindles." The public's visceral reaction led Senator Albert Beveridge of Indiana to call for more extensive federal regulation of meat packing and forced Congress to pay attention to pending legislation that would set government standards for food and beverages. President Theodore Roosevelt sent two sets of investigators to Chicago and played a major role in securing congressional approval of Beveridge's measure. When the President signed this Meat Inspection Act and also the Food and Drugs Act in June, he graciously acknowledged Beveridge's help but said nothing about the famous novel or its author.

Teachers of American history and American studies have been much kinder to Sinclair. Most consider him a muckraker because the public responded so decisively to his accounts of rats scurrying over the meat and going into the hoppers or workers falling into vats and becoming part of Durham's lard. Many embrace *The Jungle* as a reasonably trustworthy source of information on urban immigrant industrial life at the turn of the century. Few raise questions about Sinclair's credentials as either a journalist or historical novelist. If doubts arise, they are quickly dismissed....

Drawing on old records and new scholarship, this article looks first at Sinclair's motives for writing the novel, then compares what he says about packers, packinghouse products, immigrant workers and their community with the historical evidence. In concludes that contrary to the author's 1906 claim that it was "so true that students may go to it, as they would a work of reference," *The Jungle* often strays quite far from the truth. As a result, the book misinforms readers about life in what Sinclair called "Packingtown" but which residents and reporters knew as "Back of the Yards." ...

Capitalist packers were the most fearsome monsters in Sinclair's jungle. They were "the incarnation of blind and insensate Greed.... devouring with a thousand mouths, trampling with a thousand hoofs." They could live in the lap of luxury because they cheated cattle raisers, set high market prices on their meat products, bribed federal inspectors to pass diseased animals, and chiseled on workers' wages. To them [as Sinclair records in his *Autobiography*] "a hundred human lives did not balance a penny of profit." Their plants were "honeycombed with rottenness": "bosses grafted off the men" who in turn were "pitted against each other." As a result, Packingtown "was simply a seething

cauldron of jealousies and hatreds; there was no loyalty or decency anywhere." Female employees, "mostly foreign, hanging always on the verge of starvation," were at the mercy of foremen "every bit at brutal and unscrupulous as the old-time slave drivers." Things "quite unspeakable" went on in the packinghouses and "were taken for granted by everybody; only they did not show ... because there was no difference in color between master and slave." ...

Those in the path of the Chicago packers fought a noisy rear guard action. Dairy farmers called margarine a "cheap, nasty grease" capable of transmitting tuberculosis and trichinosis. Congress placed a modest tax on it in 1886, but the Department of Agriculture's Division of Chemistry pronounced it safe and nutritious. As Chicago chilled beef invaded eastern markets, local slaughterers and butchers dubbed it "stale" or "dead" meat, implying that it absorbed ammonia from cooling machinery or was chemically "embalmed" to prolong its life. Customers liked its superior taste and lower price and thus ignored the warnings. Opponents then accused Chicago packers of using diseased animals and said only local inspection in their own states at the time of slaughter could safeguard consumers. Several states banned Chicago beef, but the Supreme Court overturned these laws in 1890. Meantime, European countries banned American pork products until the federal government certified that they were free of trichinae. Congress in 1890–91 authorized the Department of Agriculture's Bureau of Animal Industry to inspect livestock before and after slaughter and, at the request of packers or foreign governments, conduct microscopic examinations of pork before certifying it. The large packers quickly availed themselves of this service, and by 1900 federal meat inspectors, graduates of veterinary colleges and protected by civil service, were working in 149 packinghouses in 46 cities.

Criticism of Chicago meat products surfaced again during the Spanish-American War. General Nelson A. Miles, still smarting from the packinghouse workers' insolence to his soldiers during the Pullman strike, blamed the sickness of American troops in Cuba and Puerto Rico on the canned meat and chilled beef prepared in Chicago. He told [as noted by Louise Carroll Wade in "Hell Hath No Fury Like a General Scorned," in The *Illinois Historical Journal,* Autumn, 1986] the War Investigating Commission that the former was defective, the latter what "you might call embalmed beef." Major General Leonard Wood, trained at Harvard

Medical School, testified that the chilled beef was nutritious and wholesome, while academic and government chemists (including Dr. Harvey W. Wiley, chief of the Division [later Bureau] of Chemistry from 1883 to 1912) gave clean bills of health to samples of the canned beef. After visits to the packinghouses and voluminous testimony, the Commission declared that the canned beef was "generally of good quality" and that "no refrigerated beef ... was subjected to or treated with any chemicals." Undaunted, General Miles asked for a military court of inquiry into his beef charges. It ruled that Miles had no justification for "alleging" that the beef was "embalmed" or "unfit for issue." These two investigations revealed that careless handling of the refrigerated beef and the practice of eating canned meat opened days before contributed to intestinal illnesses, but drinking contaminated water was the major factor. Medical doctors and researchers soon tracked typhoid to poor sanitation and pinned malaria and yellow fever on mosquitos. Despite exoneration of Chicago meat and scientific explanations for the illnesses, historian Graham A. Cosmas [in his book *An Army for Empire,* 1971] concedes that the "sensational charges, not the sober refutations, stuck in the minds of thousands of ordinary citizens."

Foes of the packers kept the rotten beef charges alive, and, as Floyd Dell noted, this "more or less prepared" the public for *The Jungle.* Simons rejoiced that "the world knows now the story of the infamous part played ... by the packers of Chicago." Charles Edward Russell asked "How did they manage to emerge unharmed from the terrible 'embalmed-beef' revelations of the Spanish War? How did they escape prosecution when more American soldiers fell before their deadly beef than were hit by all the Spanish guns?" *The Jungle* claimed "the 'embalmed beef' ... killed several times as many United States soldiers as all the bullets of the Spaniards." And in May 1906 Sinclair issued a press release stating that Philip Armour's 1901 death was due—not to pneumonia—but to "worry incidental" to hushing up the company's responsibility for those deaths....

Another aspect of food safety was the question of whether meat and milk from tubercular cattle could infect people. When Dr. Robert Koch discovered the bacillus in 1882, he thought it caused the same disease in man and beast. No one knew how tuberculosis was transmitted, but veterinarians advocated stringent livestock inspection as a public health measure. While doctors did not rule out infection through meat or milk, they thought cook-

ing meat and boiling milk could eliminate the risk. Since they suspected the White Plague spread through lung discharges of sick individuals, they emphasized disinfection of premises and careful disposal of sputum so it could not dry out, pulverize and travel through the air. Disagreement sharpened after Koch declared in 1901 that bovine and human tuberculosis were caused by different bacilli and conjectured that people seldom if ever contracted tuberculosis from cattle. American doctors generally supported Koch, and some even suggested that money spent on livestock inspection be used to identify and treat patients. Most veterinarians and many British doctors disputed Koch, and insisted, as did Dr. Daniel E. Salmon, head of the Bureau of Animal Industry from 1884 until 1905, that "No slaughter-houses should be allowed to operate without inspection." Ironically, there was widespread agreement that thorough cooking rendered all meat safe, even pork, and the Bureau of Animal Industry began phasing out microscopic examination for trichinae in 1902, abandoning it completely by 1907.

Meantime, those seeking environmental factors in the transmission of tuberculosis decided that it was endemic in dark, crowded slums and workplaces and spread from there. Explained Robert Hunter, the germs "live for months in darkness or in places artificially lighted" and eventually become "pulverized dust which is blown about through tenements, theatres, street cars, railway trains, offices, and factories." Dr. Alice Hamilton of Hull House also fingered "germ-laden dust ... whirled in the air by gusts of wind." Back of the Yards physician Dr. Caroline Hedger insisted that in the interior packinghouse rooms with electric lights "germs could live almost indefinitely unless removed." She found it "revolting to think of the chances for infection of food in a situation like this." Adolphe Smith believed that the "sharp angles, nooks, and corners" of the packinghouses harbored "sputum of tuberculous workers ... for weeks, months, and years" and that the disease was "especially prevalent" among packinghouse workers. There was a distinct possibility, therefore, that the packers were exporting "the bacilli in the provisions ... sent from Chicago all over the world."

The Jungle effectively heightened fears about contamination and adulteration of packinghouse products. In the novel men and women labor in "dark holes, by electric light." Many cough incessantly, spit at random, and stack meat in sputum on the floor. The packers are said to prefer tubercular cattle because they "fatten more quickly." They hire "regular alchemists" to concoct meat products out of knuckle joints, gullets, skins, moldy scrap ends and those poisoned rats, appropriately spiced, colored and preserved. Other illustrations were excised by Doubleday. One involved an unmarried worker who gave birth in a "dark passage" and dropped the baby "into one of the carts full of beef, that was all ready for the cooking-vats." Black strike-breakers (with "woolly heads" and "savages" for ancestors) spread "diseases of vice" in the canned meat, "loathsome" afflictions which caused fingers and parts of the faces "to rot away and drop off." In *The Brass Check,* Sinclair professed "bitterness" when he finally realized that he "had been made into a 'celebrity' … simply because the public did not want to eat tubercular beef." But in September 1905, when he was trying to persuade Macmillan to publish the manuscript, he assured them that "with the spoiled meat sensations that are in it … you can count upon making the book a success."

President Roosevelt, supplied with advance copies of *The Jungle* by Marcosson and Sinclair, was concerned about the accusations against federal inspectors and the implications for public health. He asked the Department of Agriculture to investigate, and early in March a committee visited eighteen Chicago plants that used federal inspection and three that did not. Its report provided detailed information about the inspection service and the physical conditions within the plants. The investigators found good, fair and bad conditions, often within the same plant and sometimes in the same room. In one establishment, for example, there were dirty windows and unpainted walls in the hog-killing area but clean workbenches and a clean vitrified brick floor. The cattle-killing area had "good light and ventilation," tiled side walls, but dirty overhead beams. The beef-canning section was "well whitewashed, lighted, and ventilated, and was clean," although the cooking room had dirty meat receptacles and no fans to carry off the steam. There were dressing rooms, lockers and wash basins for some but not all employees. Some toilets were "clean, well flushed, painted, and whitewashed," others "dark and insanitary." The plants not using federal inspection were generally unsanitary throughout [as recorded in "Report of the Department Committee on the Federal Meat-Inspection Service at Chicago," by the Bureau of Animal Industry, in *Annual Report,* 1906].

Annoyed by the report's detail and refusal to generalize about sanitary conditions, the President felt that it did not give him "clear, definite an-

swers." So he asked the same men to address specific criticisms in Smith's *Lancet* articles, Sinclair's novel and Hedger's forthcoming article. The committee tried again to explain to Roosevelt that sanitary conditions were uneven. Hedger's charge of excessive dirt fit "certain rooms of certain establishments, but it is absolutely unfair as a generalization." Sinclair "selected the worst possible condition which could be found in any establishment" and "willfully closed his eyes to establishments where excellent conditions prevail." The novelist's assertion that poisoned rats went into the meat hoppers was a "deliberate misrepresentation of fact [according to the "Supplemental Report on Certain Publications Reflecting on the Meat Inspection," Bureau of Animal Industry, Annual Report, 1906]." They also took this opportunity to call attention to Adolphe Smith's statement: "When a carcass, or a portion of a carcass, is condemned, in spite of stockyard gossip and scandal, I believe that it is conscientiously destroyed." Smith also had "some difficulty in believing" stories about the use of bruised hams and defective meat.

The President sequestered both of these April reports, for he had dispatched Commissioner of Labor Charles P. Neill and James B. Reynolds to make yet another investigation. Interestingly, both men had toured the stockyard and packinghouses on previous occasions without registering any complaints about procedure. Neill and Reynolds spent several weeks in Packingtown but delayed writing their report until commanded to do so the first weekend in June. In [the U.S. Congress, House Documents, No. 873 "Conditions in the Chicago Stock Yards"] the authors say they verified everything by "personal examination." They did find dirty windows, floors, workbenches and meat receptacles, some toilets improperly located and unsanitary, and many rooms that were poorly ventilated. They were critical of the use of electric lights: "Most of the rooms are so dark as to make artificial light necessary at all times." They did not mention rats. But they departed from their own guidelines to hypothesize that aged meat "might be treated with chemicals" and to say that unidentified physicians thought tuberculosis "disproportionately prevalent" among packinghouse workers.

Briefly and grudgingly they acknowledged seeing clean brick and cement floors, model cooling and meat storage facilities, and eating rooms for the women in the packinghouses. Federal agents conducted the post-mortem inspections "carefully and conscientiously" and examined hog flesh under microscopes with "great care." In a section of the report headed "Uncleanliness in handling products" they buried their approval of the entire chilled-meat operation:

> After killing, carcasses are well washed, and up to the time they reach the cooling room are handled in a fairly sanitary and cleanly manner. The parts that leave the cooling room for treatment in bulk are also handled with regard to cleanliness.

When called before the House Agriculture Committee, both Neill and Reynolds said their criticisms applied only to the canning and preservation of meat. Packinghouse workers were "a strong, sturdy class of foreigners," not tubercular wrecks, and they saw clean rooms and sanitary metal carts, tubs and cutting tables "in quite a number of places." Asked about their relationship to Sinclair, Reynolds replied, "We had letters from Mr. Sinclair, and he sent parties to us to give evidence." We "made an attempt to verify certain statements, but found it impossible to do so."

During the last week of May, Sinclair fed his scary version of what would be in the Neill-Reynolds [May 26, 27, and 28, 1906] report to the *New York Times*—plants "overrun with rats," lard made from hogs that had died of cholera, food prepared by "ignorant foreigners or negroes" who had "no knowledge" of sanitation. Roosevelt's June 4 letter accompanying the actual report stressed the negative and ignored the positive observations because "legislation is needed ... to prevent the possibility of all abuses in the future." The House Agriculture Committee finally forced the President to release the two Department of Agriculture reports, but the newspapers gave them short shrift. Nor did anyone ask why Dr. Wiley had found "so little to criticize and so much to commend" in Packingtown, or why so many visitors and journalists trooped through the plants without mentioning unsanitary conditions, or how millions could consume Chicago meat without ill effects. Said the *Outlook* [on June 9, 1906], "the suspicion that poisoned, diseased, and putrid meat is packed and distributed for the use of the American people has ... spread widely—not to say wildly. Even if this suspicion is unfounded, nothing but Federal legislation can allay it." And so Congress bowed to public opinion and the President's wishes and endorsed the essence of the Beveridge bill extending federal inspection to all parts of the packinghouses.

If *The Jungle* misrepresents packers and packinghouse products, it is even more misleading about the workers and their community. In order to prove that they exist in an "inferno of exploitation," Sin-clair lets bosses, realtors, merchants, politicians, priests, saloon keepers and the midwife cheat the Rudkus clan. Jurgis is "helpless as a wounded animal, the target of unseen enemies," his wife too child-like to cope, and stolid Elzbieta, the linchpin of the group, reminds him of "the angleworm, which goes on living though cut in half ... she asked no questions about the justice of it, nor the worthwhileness of life in which destruction and death ran riot." Little wonder the journal published by the packinghouse workers' union called the novel "greatly overdrawn" and objected to a plot in which the immigrants experience "only slavery, injustice and death" [as reported in "Amalgated Meat Cutters and Butcher Workmen, *Official Journal,* May, 1906].

Sinclair wanted readers to believe that packinghouse workers were "rats in a trap," that prostitutes fared better than "decent" girls, and that "if you met a man who was rising ... you met a knave." John R. Commons of the University of Wisconsin studied the Chicago packinghouse workers in 1904 and described the great variety of jobs commanding wages from 15 cents an hour for new unskilled hands to 50 cents an hour for the highly skilled "butcher aristocracy." He found [as noted in his article "Labor Conditions in Meat Packing and the Recent Strike," *Quarterly Journal of Economics,* November, 1904] that Irish and German newcomers in the 1880s had moved up, "accumulated money," and were fanning out into other jobs. Bohemians dominated the skilled ranks, while newly-arrived Slovaks and Lithuanians filled the lower positions. He did meet one Slovak who had been in Packingtown for ten years and "worked himself up to a 50-cent job." Another academic investigator, Carl William Thompson, studied the district in 1906 and came to similar conclusions. Even laborers were able to save part of their earnings, and "Slovak and Lithuanian girls working ... at the low wage of five dollars a week also save a considerable fraction of their income." A recent study of Chicago's low-wage women workers who chose to live apart from family and relatives found that most managed to do so. Ernest Poole's protagonist [in Antanas Kaztauskis's autobiography dictated to Ernest Poole from "Lithuania to the Chicago Stockyards," advanced from five dollars per week in his first job to eleven dollars per week and said that was "very common. There are thousands of immigrants like me." ...

The novel's impact upon readers in 1906 assures its place in American history. As John Braeman so aptly said, "During the excitement aroused by Upton Sinclair's *The Jungle,* the federal government stepped forward as the defender of the public well-being." But is the book "journalistic novel writing," as Sinclair claimed? Mark Sullivan rejected it as muckracking journalism and referred to the author as a "propagandist." Stockyards area resident Ralph Chaplin considered it "very inaccurate." And Mary McDowell, more familiar with the packinghouses and neighborhood than either Sullivan or Chaplin, said the novel "was filled with half-truths." In a review [published in the *New Republic* on September 28, 1932] of Sinclair's first autobiography, Edmund Wilson ventured the opinion that he chose sides "before he knew what it was all about" and the resulting "vision of good and evil at grips in all the affairs of the world ... would always have prevented Sinclair from being a first-rate newspaper man."

Does *The Jungle* have value as historical fiction? While novelists have the right to give free rein to their imaginations, the historical novelist needs what Cushing Strout calls a "veracious imagination." Sinclair does not meet Stout's criteria[as found in his book *The Veracious Imagination,* 1981]—respect for "both the documentable and the imaginative without sacrificing either to the other." Turn of the century evidence buttressed by recent scholarship exposes the many ways in which Sinclair loaded the dice to convince readers that packinghouse workers led heart-breaking lives in a capitalist jungle. In the process he distorted the truth about the packers and their product and about immigrant workers and their community....

Source: Lewis Carroll Wade, "The Problem with Classroom Use of Upton Sinclair's *The Jungle,*" in *American Studies,* Vol. 32, No. 2, Fall, 1991, pp. 79–101.

Walter B. Rideout

In his essay, Rideout explains how Jurgis's conversion to Socialism by the end of The Jungle *is believable, despite scholarly discussion of the system being out of place in the gritty novel.*

Lincoln Steffens tells in his *Autobiography* of receiving a call during the early years of muckraking from an earnest and as yet little-known young writer.

> One day Upton Sinclair called on me at the office of *McClure's* and remonstrated.
>
> "What you report," he said, "is enough to make a complete picture of the system, but you seem not to see it. Don't you see it? Don't you see what you are showing?"

Having just been converted to Socialism, Sinclair was sure he "saw it," and in the late autumn of 1905 his friend Jack London was writing to the Socialist weekly *The Appeal to Reason* in praise of a new book which it was serializing.

> Here it is at last! The book we have been waiting for these many years! The *Uncle Tom's Cabin* of wage slavery! Comrade Sinclair's book, *The Jungle!* and what *Uncle Tom's Cabin* did for black slaves, *The Jungle* has a large chance to do for the wage-slaves of today....

The Jungle is dedicated "To the Workingmen of America." Into it had gone Sinclair's heartsick discovery of the filth, disease, degradation, and helplessness of the packing workers' lives. But any muckraker could have put this much into a book; the fire of the novel came from Sinclair's whole passionate, rebellious past, from the insight into the pattern of capitalist oppression shown him by Socialist theory, and from the immediate extension into the characters' lives of his own and his wife's struggle against hunger, illness, and fear. It was the summation of his life and experience into a manifesto. The title of the book itself represented a feat of imaginative compression, for the world in which the Lithuanian immigrant Jurgis and his family find themselves is an Africa of unintelligibility, of suffering and terror, where the strong beasts devour the weak, who are dignified, if at all, only by their agony.

After their pathetically happy marriage, the descent of Jurgis and Ona into the social pit is steady. They are spiritually and, in the case of Ona, physically slaughtered, more slowly but quite as surely as the cattle in the packing plant. Disease spread by filthy working and living conditions attacks them, they endure cold in winter and clouds of flies in summer, bad food weakens their bodies, and seasonal layoffs leave them always facing starvation. When illness destroys Jurgis's great strength, he realizes that he has become a physical cast-off, one of the waste products of the plant, and must take the vilest job of all in the packing company's fertilizer plant. The forced seduction of his wife by her boss leads him to an assault on the man and thirty days in jail. Released without money, he returns to his family evicted from their home and Ona dying in childbirth. After being laid off from a dangerous job in a steel plant, Jurgis becomes successively a tramp, the henchman of a crooked politician, a strikebreaker in the packing plant strike of 1904, and finally a bum. Having reached the bottom of the social pit, he wanders into a political meeting to keep warm and hears for the first time,

though at first unaware that he is listening to a Socialist, an explanation of the capitalist jungle in
which he has been hunted. The sudden realization
of truth is as overwhelming to Jurgis as it had been
to Jurgis's creator. He at once undertakes to learn
more about Socialism, is given a job in a hotel
owned by a Socialist, and is eventually taken to a
meeting of radical intellectuals where he hears all
the arguments for the Industrial Republic which
Sinclair wants his readers to know. Jurgis throws
himself into the political campaign of 1904, the one
in which the Party actually made such astonishing
gains, and the book concludes exultantly with a
speech first given by Sinclair himself, proclaiming
the coming victory of the Socialists, at which time
Chicago will belong to the people.

The "conversion" pattern of *The Jungle* has
been attacked as permitting too easy a dramatic solution; however, aside from the recognized fact that
many conversions have occurred before and since
Paul saw the light on the road to Damascus, it
should be noted that in *The Jungle* Sinclair carefully prepares such an outcome by conducting Jurgis through all the circles of the workers' inferno
and by attempting to show that no other savior except Socialism exists. Perhaps a more valid objection to the book is Sinclair's failure to realize his
characters as "living" persons, a charge which, incidentally, may be brought against many noncon-
version novels. Jurgis is admittedly a composite
figure who was given a heaping share of the troubles of some twenty or thirty packing workers with
whom Sinclair had talked, and the author's psychology of character is indeed a simple one. Although in the introductory wedding scene Jurgis
and the other major characters are sharply sketched
as they had appeared to the writer at an actual wedding feast in Packingtown, during the remainder of
the book they gradually lose their individuality, becoming instead any group of immigrants destroyed
by the Beef Trust. Yet paradoxically, the force and
passion of the book are such that this group of lay
figures with Jurgis at their head, these mere capacities for infinite suffering, finally do come to
stand for the masses themselves, for all the faceless ones to whom things are done. Hardly individuals, they nevertheless collectively achieve
symbolic status.

Sinclair's success in creating this jungle world
emphasizes by contrast what is actually the book's
key defect. Jurgis's conversion is probable enough,
the Socialist explanation might well flash upon him
with the blinding illumination of a religious experience; but practically from that point onward to the

conclusion of his novel Sinclair turns from fiction
to another kind of statement. Where the capitalist
damnation, the destruction of the immigrants, has
been proved almost upon the reader's pulses, the
Socialist salvation, after its initial impact, is intel-
lectualized. The reader cannot exist imaginatively
in Jurgis's converted state even if willing, for Jurgis hardly exists himself. What it means to be a Socialist is given, not through the rich disorder of felt
experience, but in such arbitrarily codified forms
as political speeches, an essay on Party personalities, or the long conversation in monologues about
the Cooperative Commonwealth which comprises
most of the book's final chapter. *The Jungle* begins
and lives as fiction; it ends as a political miscellany.

The fact that Jurgis's militant acceptance of
Socialism is far less creatively realized than his previous victimization is indicative of how Sinclair's
outraged moral idealism is attracted more to the
pathos than the power of the poor, and suggests his
real affinity for the mid-Victorian English reform
novelists. More specifically, *The Jungle* is reminiscent of the work of the humanitarian Dickens,
whose social protest had "thrilled" the young rebel.
There are frequent resemblances between the two
writers in narrative method, in presentation of character, in the tendency of both to intrude themselves
with bubbling delight or horrified indignation into
the scene described. Whole paragraphs on the wedding feast of Jurgis Rudkus and Ona recall, except
for the Lithuanian, the manner of Dickens with the
Cratchits' Christmas dinner, and Madame Haupt,
fat, drunken, and filthy, might have been a midwife
in Oliver Twist's London. Finally, the temper of
Sinclair's protest is curiously like that of Dickens.
Where the latter urges only the literal practice of
Christianity as a remedy for the cruelties he describes, Sinclair, to be sure, demands the complete
transformation of the existing order of things by the
Socialist revolution; yet the revolution that the or-
ator so apocalyptically envisages at the conclusion
to *The Jungle* is to be accomplished by the ballot
and not by the bullet. Sinclair's spirit is not one of
blood and barricades, but of humanitarianism and
brotherly love.

Source: Walter B. Rideout, "Realism and Revolution," in
his *The Radical Novel in the United States, 1900–1954:
Some Interrelations of Literature and Society,* Harvard University Press, 1956 pp. 19–46.

Sources

Van Wyck Brooks, "Upton Sinclair and His Novels," *Sketches in Criticism,* Dutton, 1932, pp. 291-98.

Bernard Dekle, "Upton Sinclair: The Power of a Courageous Pen," *Profiles of American Authors,* Tuttle, 1969, pp. 70-74.

Melvyn Dubofsky, *'Big Bill' Haywood,* St. Martin's Press, 1987.

James R. Green, *The World of the Worker: Labor in Twentieth-Century America,* Hill and Wang, 1980.

Granville Hicks, "The Survival of Upton Sinclair," *College English,* Vol. 4, no. 4, January, 1943, pp. 213-220.

Daniel Nelson, *Shifting Fortunes: The Rise and Decline of American Labor, from 1920 to the Present,* Ivan R. Dee, Inc., 1997.

Walter B. Rideout, *The Radical Novel in the United States, 1900-1954: Some Interrelations of Literature and Society,* Harvard University Press, 1956.

Upton Sinclair, *The Autobiography of Upton Sinclair,* Harcourt Brace World, 1962.

Jon A. Yoder, *Upton Sinclair,* Frederick Ungar, 1975.

For Further Study

William A. Bloodworth Jr., *Upton Sinclair,* Twayne, 1977.
A brief, comprehensive, scholarly look at the author's career and how his political activities intertwined with his social goals.

Floyd Dell, *Upton Sinclair: A Study in Social Protest,* Doran, 1927.
Dell was a prominent writer and social activist in Sinclair's time, and his critical study tends to view Sinclair and his achievements favorably.

Melvyn Dubofsky, *We Shall Be All: A History of the Industrial Workers of the World,* Quadrangle Books, 1969.
Over five hundred pages is given to examination of the politicized union that few readers know about today, but that influenced labor relations throughout the twentieth century.

Thomas J. Jablonsky, *Pride in the Jungle: Community and Everyday Life in Back of the Yards Chicago,* Johns Hopkins University Press, 1993.
A full-spectrum look at the area, keeping readers current with the changes that have taken place in the stockyard neighborhood since Sinclair's book was published, and as a result of it.

Harvey Swados, "The World of Upton Sinclair," in *The Atlantic Monthly,* December, 1961, pp. 96-102.
A look at Sinclair as a social force, apart from his literary worth, from a poet and short story writer who, though not a household name, was himself important in the literature of his day.

Louise Carroll Wade, *Chicago's Pride: the Stockyards, Packingtown, and the Environs of the Nineteenth Century,* University of Illinois Press. 1987.
Wade offers a heavily-annotated, scientific look at the neighborhood described in *The Jungle* during its formative years, before the events in the novel take place.

The Left Hand of Darkness

Ursula K. Le Guin

1969

The basic principle of *The Left Hand of Darkness* is one that started in Ursula K. Le Guin's first novel in 1966 and runs through several of her early works: that of the interplanetary expansion started by the first race of humanity on the planet Hain and expanded across the universe, forming the League of All Worlds, eventually expanding to the eighty-three-world collective called the Ekumen. This novel takes place in the year 4870 and concerns an envoy, Genly Ai, who is on a planet called Winter ("Gethen" in the language of its own people) to convince the citizens to join the Ekumen. Winter is, as its name indicates, a planet that is always cold, and its citizens are neither female nor male: they only have gender identities or sexual urges once a month. These conditions have affected the ways that civilizations on Winter have developed, with the most obvious effect being that there has never been a war on the planet. There are, however, arcane rules of politics and diplomacy that the envoy must learn in order to survive. His fortune changes quickly, according to what political faction is in power at the time in the country he is residing in: in one country, for instance, the Prime Minister arranges an audience with the king for him, but the next day the Prime Minister is exiled for treason; in another he has trouble determining which factions among the thirty-three Heads of Districts support him and which want to use him to gain political power. The struggle of Genly Ai as he tries to understand the ways of these people and survive on this hostile planet gives Le Guin the chance to

explore what life would be like without the dualities, such as summer and winter or male and female, that form our way of thinking: the book's title comes from a Gethen poem, which begins, "Light is the left hand of darkness ... " This book received the most prestigious awards given to science fiction writing: a Hugo Award in 1969 and a Nebula Award in 1970.

Ursula K. LeGuin

Author Biography

Ursula K. Le Guin was born on October 29, 1929, in Berkeley, California, where she grew up. Her father was Alfred Kroeber, an internationally-known anthropologist whose influence may have nurtured her understanding of cultural artifacts and traditional myths and legends. Her mother, Theodora Kracaw Kroeber Quinn, was a writer of several biographies and children's books. Le Guin attended Radcliffe College, where she received her B.A., and Columbia University, where she received a master's degree in romance literatures of the Middle Ages and Renaissance. She married Charles A. Le Guin, a French historian, in 1953. Her first short stories appeared in science fiction magazines as early as 1962, and she published three novels, including the first one in her acclaimed *Earthsea* trilogy, in the three years between 1966 and 1968. It was *The Left Hand of Darkness,* though, that made her famous, winning the major science fiction awards: in 1969 the book won the Nebula Award, and in 1970 it earned her a Hugo Award. She has defined herself as a feminist, but not a radical feminist: she has spoken out for women's rights in life and, as in *The Left Hand of Darkness,* she has studied the roles of the genders in her science fiction, but most of her protagonists have been males, especially in her early books. One of the earliest lessons she learned in regard to self-identity and gender came in the same year that this book was published, when *Playboy* magazine published her story "Nine Lives." They asked her to publish it under the name "U. K. Le Guin": she did it, but she went on to resent having had to hide who she was. In her career Le Guin has published over eighty short stories, two collections of essays, ten books for children, seven volumes of poetry, and sixteen novels. She has written a screenplay for *The Left Hand of Darkness* that has not yet been produced.

Plot Summary

In Karhide: Chapters 1-5

Genly Ai, a somewhat naive young black man from Terra, or Earth, is an envoy from the Ekumen, an organization of more than eighty worlds, representing 3,000 countries, spanning one hundred light years from border to border, whose purpose is to develop commerce, communications and, possibly, mystical unity. Ai's mission is to convince the country of Karhide on the distant planet called Gethen to join the Ekumen. His story of that mission consists mainly of his own observations with interpolated chapters of Karhide tales and myths, Ekumen data, sayings from Orgoreyn (Karhide's neighbor), and excerpts from the diary of Therem Harth rem ir Estraven, prime minister of Karhide to mad King Argaven XV.

The planet Gethen is called Winter by the Ekumen because it is in the grip of an Ice Age. Ai is constantly challenged by the unrelenting cold, by the Karhide custom of *shifgrethor,* and by the androgynous nature of all the people who populate Winter. In Ai's dealings with Estraven, he fails to understand *shifgrethor,* a method of saving face by avoiding confrontation. When Estraven is exiled, thanks to his rival Tibe who convinces the King that Estraven is a traitor, Ai fails to understand the reason. He has an interview with the King and discovers that Estraven had been in favor of the Ekumen, although Ai thought he'd been against it. Through future miscommunications and clarifying explanations concerning Estraven, Ai eventually understands *shifgrethor.*

Estraven's androgynous nature further obscures him to Ai. Although all of Winter's androgynes are referred to as "he," the fact is they are neither "he" nor "she" until they enter *kemmer,* a state of estrus lasting a few days a month, analogous to a woman's cycle. Then, depending on the chemistry between partners, one will develop as a male, the other as a female. The same person can be a child-bearing mother to some children and a father to others. No wonder Ai is confused. However, the people of Winter are confused by Ai and can't believe everyone in the Ekumen is either a male, like Ai, or a female. Ai is considered a pervert, a creature always in *kemmer.* The androgynous biology, which eliminates sexual issues of male dominance and female dependency due to child bearing and rearing, is the underpinning for the culture and politics on Winter, a planet that has no word for war and no experience of it. Yet, despite this, the two countries of Karhide and Orgoreyn seem to be on the brink of war over disputed territory. This gives Ai's peaceful purpose and patient approach elements of tension and timeliness.

In Orgoreyn: Chapters 6-14

Estraven is exiled as a traitor for putting the planet's good over the country's good by wanting to give the disputed territory to neighboring Orgoreyn. He has only a limited time to leave Karhide under pain of death. He must race to the Orgoreyn border where he ends up losing his identification and being exploited as a factory worker. Finally he is discovered by some Commensals, politicians of high status somewhat like senators, and introduced into the socialist politics of Orgoreyn. Ai also travels to Orgoreyn. Since the King has rejected his proposal to join the Ekumen, he thinks perhaps the neighboring country will be interested. Orgoreyn is considerably different from Karhide, a bureaucracy compared to a monarchy; Orgoreyn's Yomesh religion denies the dark yet is an offspring of Karhide's Handdara which espouses both light and dark for "[l]ight is the left hand of darkness"; Orgoreyn's people are supposedly more progressive and yet they live under a corrupt political system

with the darkness of secret police and concentration camp prisons and, on the whole, have less humane values than the people of Karhide. Although Estraven tries to warn Ai of the shifting politics here, again Ai doesn't understand. He ends up being betrayed by a politician with ties to the secret police and is taken away in a truck with other unfortunates to Kundershaden Prison. All are naked, freezing, and hungry. To make matters worse, the technology here isn't even up to present-day standards in the United States, although the point of this is that Winter's people have respected the ecology with each advance. Still, the truck moves slowly, lengthening the torture. Once imprisoned, Ai has little to look forward to until he is rescued through the daring of Estraven. Unfortunately, the road back to Karhide is over the Gobrin Ice.

The Gobrin Ice and Back to Karhide: Chapters 15-20

Ai and Estraven battle the snow and ice, glacier and crevasse, wind and night. Through cooperation, for Ai is physically superior to Estraven while Estraven has superior survival skills, the two become closer. Ai realizes that while Estraven is a forced exile, he himself has chosen to exile himself from his family, friends, and, in fact, several generations by being a space traveler. Ai is 127 earth years old, but because of timejumping is not quite 30.

Ai teaches Estraven telepathy, or mindspeak. Estraven hears Ai's voice as that of his dead brother Arek to whom he swore *kemmering.* Although incest between siblings in not taboo, they are forbidden to swear allegiance for life. Ai begins to understand Estraven better. When Estraven goes into *kemmer,* although both avoid a sexual relationship, Ai sees the full womanly side of Estraven and finally understands his friend as a complete person, and, by extension, understands the androgynous people of Gethen.

When the two return to Karhide, the exiled Estraven is discovered, and as he skis to the Orgoreyn border, he skis straight into the guards who shoot him, a seeming suicide. This too is a Karhide taboo. Estraven dies in Ai's arms asking Ai to clear his name. Ai is successful in convincing the King to join the Ekumen, but when the crew from the spaceship alight, Ai is repulsed by their overt sexuality. In the final chapter he visits Estraven's family who are distraught because Estraven is still considered a traitor. Ai had not cleared his name as he promised, because he didn't want to jeopardize his mission, Gethen's entry into the Ekumen, a mission for which Estraven gave his life. However, Estraven's son Sorve by his dead brother shows the same kind of curiosity as his father, the kind which characterizes human progress: he asks Ai to tell him about other worlds and other lives he has seen.

Characters

Genly Ai

Ai is the main character of the story, often called "Genry" by the Gethenians, who have trouble pronouncing the letter "l" in their language. At the start of the book, he has been on Gethen for two years, trying to become accustomed to the ways of the planet's inhabitants and to get them accustomed to the idea of him. He arrived with basic information about the language and culture because a team of investigators from the Ekumen had come before him and lived among the Gethenians without revealing their identities or their mission. Still, Ai's obstacles are many. For one thing, he knows that it will not be easy to explain to people who have never even thought of air flight that men can arrive from space. In Karhide, the king is reluctant to acknowledge him or discuss his diplomatic mission because admitting the existence of beings who have mastered travel and communications would diminish the king's importance. The new Prime Minister is bound to oppose Ai because the old Prime Minister, who is being forced out of power, supported him. Moving to another country, Orgoreyn, Ai is accepted more easily by the political leaders and believes that they will help him to accomplish his mission; it turns out, though, that their political system is more complex and subtle than Karhide's, and, while he is trying to sort out which factions are sincere about offering help and which have a hidden agenda, Ai is arrested, stripped of his clothes, drugged and sent to a work camp to die of exhaustion. He is rescued by Estraven, the deposed Prime Minister of Karhide, and he realizes that cultural differences had kept him from understanding their relationship previously: he had not understood advice when it was given because Estraven had not stated it directly, thinking that doing so would offend him. During their eighty-one day journey across the frozen land to return to Karhide, where people would cooperate with him now (if only to embarrass Orgoreyn), Ai gets to know and love Estraven and he sees how he has looked to the people of this planet. One day while Estraven is in his sexual cycle, and is being distant

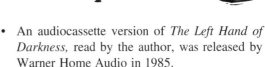

Media Adaptations

- An audiocassette version of *The Left Hand of Darkness,* read by the author, was released by Warner Home Audio in 1985.

so that they will not become involved, Ai realizes how he had misread the situation. "And I saw then, and for good, what I had always been afraid to see, and had pretended not to see in him: that he was a woman as well as a man." He realizes that this fact has made him unable to give his trust and friendship to Estraven because of this dual personality, and that this has been his fatal flaw.

Argavan XV

In the first chapter, Estraven, trying to imply that Orgoreyn might be a better place for Ai to look for acceptance, tells him, "the Commensals of Orgoreyn are mostly sane men, if unintelligent, while the king of Karhide is not only insane but rather stupid." Chapter 3, in which Ai finally is granted an audience with Argavan after half a year's wait, is titled "The Mad King." The book is never clear, however, whether the king is mad or stupid, or if he is just working from a different set of assumptions than everyone else. In being protective of his people, he appears to Ai to be small-minded and frightened: while Ai can see no reason for him to turn down an alliance with the Ekumen, the king sees great reason to be suspicious of the strange alien who makes promises, especially with hostilities against the neighboring country of Orgoreyn increasing and the great chance that Ai's story is just a trick to humiliate him. Added to his natural suspicions is the advice of his Prime Minister, Tibe, who recently ascended to his position precisely because he encouraged the king's fears. At the end of the story, when Argavan agrees to host a landing party of Ai's comrades, he is disappointed that Ai called them before asking permission, but other than that he seems to believe that all that has happened was according to his plan: "You've served

LeGuin wrote The Left Hand of Darkness *during the Sixties, a time when gender-bending, free-love scenes—like this one at a love-in in Los Angeles, California—were common.*

me well," he tells Ai. Again, it is not clear whether he is delusional or cunning.

Ashe

Estraven's *Kemmering,* or spiritual partner, for seven years, Ashe bore two sons with him. Ashe left three years earlier to join a Fastness at Orgny and became celibate. Before Ai goes to Orgoreyn, Ashe gives him money to take to Estraven.

Estraven

See Therem Harth rem ir Estraven

Faxe

Faxe is the leader of the Handdarata, a religious sect living in the area known as Ariskostor Fastness. A Fastness is a religious place like a monastery, where people can retreat from the world, spending "the night or a lifetime." Faxe is the Weaver of the Foretellers of the Handdarata, which means that he is at the center of the spiritual ceremony they use to foretell what will happen in the future. He is the one to weave the power of the other participants—the Zanies, the Pervert, the Celibates, etc.—into an answer for the question asked. He is also the one to explain, later, that knowing the future is generally useless: the reason

the Handdarata developed Foretelling, he says, was "to exhibit the perfect uselessness of knowing the answer to the wrong question." In the end, when Ai has called his ship to come to Gethen, Faxe shows up as a council member from the Indwellers of Handdarata Fastness, a sign that he was worried about what Tibe had been doing to the government.

Obsle

One of the thirty-three Commensals in Orgoreyn, he is cheerful, amused at seeing Estraven in his exile. He recalls the old times that they had together when Estraven was Prime Minister, but the pattern to his seemingly innocent questions implies that he is most interested in finding out information about the situation in Karhide.

Therem Harth rem ir Estraven

In the beginning of the book, Genly Ai is indebted to Estraven for having arranged an audience with the king, but he is also frustrated because he sees Estraven as being cold and aloof, and he is angry because he feels that, as Prime Minister, he should have done more to make the audience go more smoothly. What Ai does not realize at the time is that Estraven is out of favor with the government, and in fact will be sent into exile the next morning. Several of the book's chapters are written as excerpts from Estraven's diaries, so readers are able to develop a sense of what he is trying to accomplish and what he feels his limitations are, which is an understanding that Ai is incapable of. Estraven accepts his exile almost passively: he takes a menial job in Orgoreyn, and when the Commensal rescues him and he is taken to be a dependent of Commensal Yegey, he does not use the opportunity to sell out the government that banished him. Throughout the story, Estraven works diplomatically to help Ai achieve his goal, but his maneuvering is so diplomatic that Ai does not recognize its implications, and counts him as untrustworthy, if not actually a foe. When he risks his life to save Ai from the prison farm in Pulefen, there can be no doubt that his loyalty is to Ai's cause. On the trip across the ice to safety, Ai learns that Estraven, far from being a self-serving politician, is actually a spiritual man whose actions were hard to understand, in part, because he was not acting for the good of his country (as a politician should) but for the good of the whole world. It is Estraven's planning that makes it possible for them to cross back into Karhide, and even though Ai promises to have his exile called off when the treaty between planets is put into place, he still charges into armed guards, knowing that they would have orders from Tibe to kill him, after an old friend has betrayed his trust.

Thessicher

At the very end of their journey back into Karhide, when they are out of supplies, Ai and Estraven run into Thessicher. When he was Prime Minister, Estraven helped Thessicher buy his farm, so Thessicher repays him by allowing them to stay the night, even though he could be in serious trouble for harboring an exile. His kindness turns out to be treachery, though, when Estraven overhears him on the radio alerting Tibe's troops that Estraven is there.

Tibe

The cousin of King Argavan, who is made Prime Minister by having Estraven exiled. Although there has never been a war on the planet Winter, it seems that one could erupt at any moment: Tibe works to incite hostilities and border disputes between his country and Orgoreyn. At one point, Estraven points out that Tibe's political style is like that of the Orgota in its "new-style" deception and efficiency. In the end, when the king wants to take credit for the aliens landing and bringing new wonders to the world, Tibe is exiled for having opposed the idea.

Pemmer Harge Tibe

See Tibe

Themes

Growth and Development

In establishing the basic facts of life on Gethen, this novel raises the fundamental question of "nature" versus "nurture": which cultural traits are learned and passed on from generations, and which are direct results of one's immediate surroundings? Since the people on this planet have no gender distinctions, their society is less restrictive about where citizens can go and what jobs they can take; the phrase "The king is pregnant" may sound strange to Earth ears because the associations that go with the word "king" are not the same as those that go with "pregnancy," but nobody on Gethen is fazed by the announcement. What does startle them is that humans are capable of sexuality every day, instead of being on monthly cycles. The effects of having sexuality kept aside for certain occasions are, first, that when they *are* in their "kemmer" or their sexual cycle, they are overpowered by it, and that without its distraction throughout most days they are able to concentrate on wholeness and not differences. The spiritually enlightened Gethenians have developed the ability to band together and tell the future, although they see no real benefit in it; the advanced members of the Ekumen know how to reach out to the minds of others, a skill developed from the basic concept of differences. The other main factor influencing development on Winter is the fact that it is in an Ice Age. There are no birds, and so they have no model for air flight, and therefore no basis for space flight; much of their body energy goes toward producing heat, leaving them with somewhat underdeveloped muscles; and, as indicated by the Creation Myth in Chapter 17, in which a house made of the corpses of Edondurth's brothers provides warmth, they have learned all their lives to be more careful with resources than cultures are when waste is not a matter of life and death.

Sex Roles

When asked by his Gethenian friend how women on Earth are different from men, Genly Ai

Topics for Further Study

- In the novel, Genly Ai draws the "yin and yang" symbol for Estraven. Study the ancient Chinese Naturalist movement that developed the philosophy of yin and yang, and explain it in a way that would help readers understand this book better.

- Research the problems of extreme cold faced by Arctic expeditions, such as Admiral Robert Peary's expedition to the North Pole in 1909. Write your findings in the form of a guide for travelers.

- Many people feel that an envoy from another world may have already visited Earth. Search the Internet or supermarket tabloids for stories from people who claim to know things about alien visitors. Devise a scale that will help observers test how true these stories are.

- Several science fiction books have used a device like the ansible communicator that would be able to transmit messages instantly across space. Is such a thing possible? Why or why not? Discuss the scientific principles involved.

---

responds, "It's extremely hard to separate the innate differences from the learned ones. Even where women participate equally with men in the society, they still do all of the childbearing, and so most of the child-rearing...." After mulling over how little the differences are between men and women, yet how different their roles in society, he concludes, "In a sense, women are more alien to me than you are. With you I share one sex, anyhow...." One of the most discussed ideas in this novel is that it creates a race of people on Gethen who are not encumbered with having to live up to the expectations of gender identity, and so their characteristics develop in response to environment and situation. This makes it difficult for Genly Ai, raised on Earth, to be an effective envoy, because he has trouble determining what they are thinking. He is used

to thinking of human identity as divided into two separate groups, to seeing people as either like him or unlike him, and this leads him to some bizarre and unfounded conclusions about his hosts. For example, he finds the lack of war in their history to be more of a fault than an achievement: "They lacked, it seemed, the capacity to *mobilize*. They behaved like animals, in that respect; or like women. They did not behave like men, or ants." His inability to see them for who they really are makes him disappointed early in the book, when Estraven is not as aggressive with the king on his behalf as he thinks he could be. Because they do develop sexual identities every twenty-six days, and pregnancy can fix a Gethenian into the maternal role during the time of carrying and nursing the child, it is not accurate to say that they are asexual: they are ambisexual. Rather than having no sexes, they have experience with both roles. Because of the limitations of the English language, it is difficult for readers to get a true sense of this sexlessness, because the narrative continually describes characters as "he."

Politics

Because Genly Ai is a stranger, he does not know the cultural expectations in Karhide or Orgoreyn, but as a diplomat he is required to live among the highest levels of government and therefore experiences concentrated forms of each culture's thought patterns. In Karhide, where the government is a monarchy, people are more direct about what they think. It is the Karhide government that allows Ai to live openly as an alien from another planet, that broadcasts news about his arrival on the radio. While Ai feels that Estraven, as the Karhidian Prime Minister, was not entirely open with him, it is later learned that Estraven behaved that way out of politeness, not for personal gain: in a country so dominated by one man's will, there is not much to be gained by tricky political maneuvering. Similarly, in Orgoreyn there is much to be gained by deception: with thirty-three Commensals, the balance of power is subject to change quickly. The Orgota are friendlier with Ai, but that is because friendliness is necessary when one is surrounded by enemies, and the Commensals are in a constant state of siege from each other. When the faction that opposes Ai comes to power, he is not publicly exiled, as Estraven is from Karhide; he is dragged away naked in the night and the world is told that he has died.

Survival in Nature

Most of the last half of the book is a detailed account of the trip that Ai and Estraven make across the ice in order to reach relative safety in the country that they both left under threat. It is only in fighting the elements together that they are able to learn about each other, observing strengths and weaknesses that lead them to conclusions about the other's culture. Isolated in their tent at night, they tell stories and give opinions that they never had the chance to share when they were in society, to such an extent that the mind-speaking technique that Ai teaches has strange results: to Estraven, Ai's voice sounds just like Estraven's brother's, and when Ai hears Estraven he thinks that the voice he is hearing is his own. Relying on each other for survival, they form a bond unlike any that they could have formed when they were both playing social roles and at the same time trying to guess what social role the other was playing.

Style

Structure

The structure of this novel is a cluster of information from various sources. The main one, in terms of quantity and prominence, is the report of Genly Ai to the Stabile on Ollul, which, as he explains as the first chapter starts, is presented in the form of a first-person narrative, "because I was taught as a child on my homeworld that Truth is a matter of the imagination." Alternating with these chapters are chapters taken from the journals kept by Estraven. The journals are also written in the first person, but since they were not created for public consumption they offer a more candid impression of Estraven than Ai gives from his observations. Juxtaposing the two against each other gives a rounded view of the self/other conflict that is at the heart of the story. Also interwoven between the chapters dominated by these two characters are fragments of civilization on Gethen/Winter: ethnological reports, accounts of native myths and legends, and descriptions of religious ceremonies. These fragments allow the culture that Genly Ai encounters to speak for itself, so that readers are not forced to know it only from his limited experiences and biased perspective. The relevance of these fragments to the overall story is sometimes easy to guess—for instance, the chapter titled, "Estraven the Traitor," an ancient East Karhidish tale, clearly reflects the support that Estraven in the

novel gives Ai. Others, such as the story of Meshe in Chapter 11, are less directly related to the action, and are therefore more open to the interpretation of the reader, just like ancient myths and legends in our own world are.

Point of View

The central consciousness of this novel is Genly Ai: he is the one who is strange to the ways of the people of Winter, and readers experience the planet through his eyes. Since he is from Earth, he can report his experiences in relation to how they affect a body that his reader can understand. A temperature of negative ten degrees, for instance, might be uncomfortable to a Karhidian or to the Hainish, but to Earthlings it is dangerous. This Earthly perspective makes it difficult, at first, for readers to tell the truth of the situation that is being presented. "If this is the Royal Music," he says in Chapter 1, "no wonder the kings of Karhide are all mad," little expecting that the last half of the book will be a desperate three-month race through sub-Arctic conditions to the safety of the "mad" king. In the same chapter he notes, "I don't trust Estraven, whose motives are forever obscure; I don't like him; yet I feel and respond to his authority as surely as I do the warmth of the sun." The people that he does like and trust, such as Commensals Obsle and Yegey in Orgoreyn, arrange for him to disappear from society and be sentenced to death. If this book had been written in a more objective point of view, the turns in the plot would not come as surprises to readers, and the point of how difficult it is for a person to enter into another world would be lost.

Setting

During the chapters that take place in urban settings, the extreme cold that prevails over this planet is not very relevant. Housing accommodations in Erhenrang, the capital of Karhide, and in the Orgoreyn capital of Mishnory are slightly different than Earth's, more collective in order to conserve heat, but in general social life is not much different than it would be in a cold city like Minneapolis or Buffalo. The coldness of Winter may have affected the way that civilizations on the planet developed, but it is not an important consideration until Ai is taken away to the Pulefen Commensality Third Voluntary Farm and Resettlement Community. Patterned on Siberia, the frozen province of northeast Russia where political dissidents were sent, Pulefen has an isolation that would never be possible in an area that was habitable; also, an escaped prisoner in a more reasonable climate would be hunted down and caught, rather than being left to die. It is the struggle against the brutal elements that brings Ai and Estraven to finally form a bond of trust, as they have to depend on each other's strengths and defer to each other's weaknesses. The physical details of their trek across the ice evokes a solid sense of reality that is different from that felt in the earlier chapters, which is appropriate, for the physical world is more real to the characters, too, in these chapters.

Historical Context

The Space Race

The year that *The Left Hand of Darkness* was published, 1969, was the year that the first human, Neil Armstrong, set foot on the moon. The idea had, of course, been present in science fiction for hundreds of years, in books by authors ranging from Daniel Defoe to Edgar Allan Poe. One of the most realistic early works about space travel was Jules Verne's 1865 novel *From Earth to the Moon*, which was the basis for one of the earliest silent movies made at the beginning of the twentieth century; another was H. G. Wells' *The First Men on the Moon*, published in 1901. The first real progress in space exploration came in 1957, when Americans found out with a shock that the Soviet Union, the world's other super power, had put the first artificial satellite, Sputnik I, into orbit. Later in 1957, when the Russians put a living being, a dog, into space in Sputnik 2, the race to put a man on the moon immediately became a priority with the U.S. government, which poured millions of dollars into the space program. The National Aeronautics and Space Agency, NASA, was established in 1958, and in 1959 it had started work on Project Mercury, with the goal of sending animals into space, then robot-operated flights, and finally manned flights. The first human to go into space was the Russian Yuri Gagarin, in April of 1961; the first American was Alan Shepard, the following month. In an address to Congress in May of that year, President Kennedy made a historic declaration that determined the course of the space program: "I believe that this Nation should commit itself to achieving the goal, before the decade is out, of landing a man on the moon and returning him safely to Earth," he said. At the same time that the Mercury project was being carried out, NASA began a separate project, code-named Apollo, with the intent of putting a man on the moon before the end of the 1960s. The one-man rockets of Mercury were replaced with two-man Gemini craft in 1964, but at the same time the Soviets announced that the three-man Voslhod I had been in space. In the middle 1960s the Soviets fell behind, pushing their old technology while the Americans made new advances and gained new ground.

The Feminist Movement

One of the reasons that critics took the androgyny in this novel to be such a strong feminist statement was that the Feminist Movement had not yet made much progress at the time it was published, in 1969. During the 1950s and 1960s, the American public's attention was drawn to racial inequality by the Civil Rights Movement, which was led by such dynamic leaders as Medgar Evers, Ralph Abernathy, Malcolm X, and Martin Luther King Jr. During those years, hundreds of thousands of white Americans were made aware of the unequal treatment of blacks. One of the greatest achievements of the Civil Rights Movement was the passage of the Civil Rights Act of 1964, which changed the face of American society. The bill received strong unexpected supported from President Lyndon Johnson, although, as a rich Texas politician, he had never seemed to be particularly zealous about the rights of minorities before. The Civil Rights Act did not put an end to discrimination, but it made it illegal. While most people focused on the act's provisions regarding racial minorities, it also included language that prohibited discrimination in employment on the basis of sex. As the 1960s progressed, many who had been made politically aware by the struggle for racial equality shifted to other concerns. Some organized the young people on college campuses in the struggle against the Vietnam War; some went from the non-violent tactics of Dr. King's Southern Christian Leadership Conference to militant racial groups such as the Black Panthers; some focused their attention on the unequal treatment of women. In 1966, feminist leader Betty Friedan and others formed the National Organization for Women as a result of their frustration over the fact that, three years later, the sex-discrimination provisions of the Civil Rights Act were not being enforced. There were companies that would only advertise for men to fill open positions, professional organizations that would not admit women members, and open verbal and sexual harassment of females in the workplace. One of NOW's primary missions was to pass an amendment to the Constitution, the Equal Rights Amendment, that would assure fair treatment for women all across the United

Compare & Contrast

- **1969:** The Woodstock Music festival took place on a farm outside of Bethel, New York, drawing between 300,000 and 500,000 young people from across the country to hear three days of music from acts including Jimi Hendrix, the Who, the Grateful Dead, Janis Joplin, and the Jefferson Airplane. The event was surprisingly peaceful, given that many more people showed up than anticipated.

  Today: Modern marketing techniques have tried to reproduce such a massive event, with no luck.

- **1969:** The largest anti-war demonstration in the history of Washington, D.C., occurred on November 15th, when 250,000 people marched on the capitol. Another 200,000 protesters gathered at the same time in San Francisco.

  Today: Lacking outrage at government policies, citizens tend not to band together in such large groups to protest; instead, large demonstrations are often intended to draw attention to areas in which ordinary people can make a difference in their communities. The Million Man March of 1995 is estimated to have brought between 600,000 and 850,000 black men to Washington to demonstrate a commitment to family and personal responsible behavior.

- **1969:** Finding the Students for a Democratic Society to be too complacent, a group calling itself the Weather Underground split off to protest the war by violent means, such as bombing army recruitment offices.

  Today: Anti-government terrorism is more likely to come from right-wing separatists, as shown by the bombing that killed 169 people in Oklahoma City in 1995.

- **1969:** The gay rights movement began when police raided the Stonewall Inn, a bar in Greenwich Village, New York. The gay patrons resisted arrest, leading to a three-day riot in the street.

  Today: Gay activists have made strides in securing the right of gays to gather in public, but they still struggle for rights such as employment security and the benefits enjoyed by legally married couples, such as family medical insurance and the right to adopt children.

- **1969:** The University of California at Los Angeles, in response to a Defense Department order, developed a computer network "node" in order to decentralize information, so that it would not be vulnerable to computer attack. By 1975, over 100 universities and government research facilities had research nodes that shared computer information, and in 1985, the National Science Foundation created a network to link regional networks of academic and research sites in a new Internet.

  Today: Over 180 million Americans have access to the Internet at home, at school, or on the job.

States—Congress approved the ERA in 1972, but it was not ratified by enough states after ten years and it expired in 1982.

Critical Overview

Since the 1960s, Ursula K. Le Guin has been respected by critics both inside and outside of the science fiction genre and by the general reading audience. She was the first female writer to build her reputation within the science fiction world, although other women, notably Doris Lessing, had crossed over into the genre before her. Philippa Maddern credited Le Guin as "the one writer who did the most" to take science fiction "away from adventure stories and the cerebral solutions of physical problems and toward the contemplation of anthropological, ethnological and psychological truths." *The Left Hand of Darkness* is the book

Gender roles were being redefined in 1969, when Left Hand of Darkness *was published. At a 1968 protest against the Miss America Pageant, these women voiced their opposition to what they saw as a practice of objectifying women.*

that caught critics' attention. As thought-provoking as most reviewers found it to be, many still confined the book and its author in the narrow category of her gender even as they admitted that the importance of her work went beyond the narrow category of science fiction. Perhaps because of her pioneer status, coupled with the ambisexuality of the Gethenians in her book, critics have tended to categorize Le Guin as a feminist. As Barbara J. Bucknall pointed out in her 1981 book, however, the feminism in Le Guin's works is not the driving force: it is always secondary to her examination of politics. Keith N. Hull, writing in *Modern Fiction Studies* in 1986, made the point that *The Left Hand of Darkness* is simply too well-written to focus on one aspect and act as if it has no more purpose or significance than that: his long examination asserts that the book "integrates its lesson so thoroughly with Gethenian culture, biology and geography that … the main theme is too rich to be sentimental, no matter how uplifting it may sound when abstracted." Le Guin herself does not categorize herself as a feminist, but as a theorist. In the famous Introduction to *The Left Hand of Darkness* she describes the androg-

yny of the characters as a "thought-experiment," not as a policy or a statement about what the world will eventually come to. "Science fiction is not predictive," she explains, "it is descriptive." It is this kind of dedication to human matters over matters of the physical world that has made her work speak to a far broader audience than her predecessors were able to capture.

Aside from disagreements about her political or social views, criticisms of the quality of Le Guin's works are very rare. When they do come up, they seem to be slightly condescending, praising her on the one hand for being a good science fiction writer while faulting her for not being a better writer in general. Weak plotting and excessive wordiness seem to be the most frequently mentioned problems. Noel Perrin, in a review of a 1982 book of Le Guin's short fiction, offered an explanation for her weaknesses that had to do with her literary rise: she appeared to still, even with the mainstream praise she had received, write like a science fiction writer of the old days. To him, this meant that she overwrote and underrevised, a practice dating back to when science fiction writers had to work hard and publish constantly just to make a

living; given the economic comfort her fame produced, Perrin suggested that she could afford to be
more considered and careful.

Criticism

Chloe Bolan

*Bolan is an English instructor, playwright, es-
sayist and fiction writer, who has published science
fiction. In the following essay, she explores the
problems of androgyny as it relates to the plot, pronoun usage, and the missing scene in* The Left
Hand of Darkness.

An Androgyne is a person possessing the traits
of both sexes, a hermaphrodite—strictly speaking,
a sexual aberrant. But on the planet Winter in Ursula Le Guin's *The Left Hand of Darkness*, everyone is an androgyne, fully functioning as a male at
certain times, a female at others, and favoring neither sex. This intriguing notion, so brilliantly conceived by the author, has elevated the Hugo-and
Nebula-winning novel to classic status. Yet, androgyny is the element most often criticized in this
landmark work, androgyny as it relates to plot and
the choice of pronoun. The plot might have been
made whole, although the pronoun problem remains, had Le Guin fleshed out a missing scene.

World-famous science fiction writer and critic
Stanislaw Lem, of Poland, and critic David Ketterer have both questioned whether androgyny in
The Left Hand of Darkness is integral to the plot.
Ketterer gives a plot summary without mentioning
androgyny as a way to demonstrate this. Even Le
Guin, in her earlier defense of the issue in the essay "Is Gender Necessary? Redux," claimed the
most fundamental theme of the novel was betrayal
and fidelity. Her whole purpose in using androgyny was to eradicate sexual tensions of male dominance and female compliance and describe how a
world would evolve without them. On Winter (or
Gethen), the country of Karhide contrasts with that
of Orgoreyn religiously, politically, and culturally,
despite their androgyny, but neither has experienced war, nor is there a word for it in their separate tongues. However, Le Guin, ever the dualist,
undercuts this argument by suggesting war is coming and the only hope of stopping it is to join the
Ekumen. Seemingly, not even androgyny can forestall the inevitable eruption of combat among supposedly intelligent beings. This would make androgyny a side issue and not integral to the plot.

The main issue of this novel is survival—political, cultural, physical, and psychological. Ai and
Estraven have a plan to ensure Winter's peaceful
survival which will favorably impact the cultures
of Karhide and Orgoreyn instead of turning them
against each other; Ai and Estraven have physically
conquered the Gobrin Ice and resolved the psychological impediment to their friendship when Estraven dies. What remains is hope for the planet
through the Ekumen, the memory of the deep
friendship between a human and an androgyne, and
a bright future in the person of Estraven's son who
asks Ai to tell him stories of other worlds. So, Estraven could have been a man whom Ai was struggling to understand, and the ending would have
been the same.

But Estraven isn't a man and yet his manliness
lingers—which leads to the question of the pronoun. Why did Le Guin refer to the androgynes as
"he"? Until the women's liberation movement in
the 1960s, in a general statement where sex was
not imperative, "he" represented "he" and "she."
With consciousness raising, "he/she" and sometimes "she" began to replace the all-purpose "he."
Although this came into vogue after Le Guin had
written her novel in 1969, she missed an opportunity to impact English at its root. Despite her genius for inventing words, she chose not to "man-
gle" the language, as she says in her original
version of "Is Gender Necessary? Redux." She later
regretted this choice and experimented with "she"
and even invented pronouns for a screenplay of *The
Left Hand of Darkness,* but the novel remains unchanged.

Feminists have long criticized Le Guin for using "he" and exacerbating this issue by her focus
on the stereotypical male roles of Estraven. As
prime minister of Karhide exiled under pain of
death, as an exploited factory worker in Orgoreyn,
as a daring rescuer of Genly Ai from prison, and
as an adventurer crossing the Gobrin Ice in a death-
defying journey, Estraven evokes the masculine
ideal. He's a modern-day action figure, a latter-day
James Bond, an early-twentieth-century Hemingway code hero. He's never seen with a child or tidy-
ing up a hearth. And if this isn't enough, the protagonist, Genly Ai, is another "he."

Although it seems "she" would be as ineffec-
tive as "he," in fact, "she" would better describe
the creature that appears to have sprung whole from
Le Guin's fertile imagination. According to Le
Guin, the androgyne of Gethen has a 26-to 28-day
cycle, paralleling a woman's cycle. *Kemmer,* or estrus, begins on the twenty-first day, and the sexual

What Do I Read Next?

- Three of Le Guin's novels that follow the same cycle as this one—*Rocannon's World, Planet of Exile,* and *City of Illusions*—have been collected into one volume by Nelson Doubleday Inc., called *Three Hainish Novels.*

- Besides this novel, the book by Le Guin that is most often examined in literature and political science classes is *The Dispossessed: An Ambiguous Utopia,* published in 1974.

- Orson Scott Card's classic 1985 science fiction novel *Ender's Game* also uses the ansible as a tool for interplanetary communication, but it examines the effects of travel and communication on war, not diplomacy.

- One of the greatest science fiction novels is Frank Herbert's *Dune* (1965), which has led to a series of interrelated novels about a richly-imagined world.

- Doris Lessing is generally linked to Le Guin because they were among the first women to gain popular attention for their science fiction writing. Not all of Lessing's work is sci-fi: some is fantasy, and some is straight literary fiction. A sampling of Lessing's work can be gained from *The Doris Lessing Reader,* published in 1988.

- Most of Le Guin's introductions to her novels are as thought-provoking as the introduction to *The Left Hand of Darkness.* Many of them, along with some original essays on the craft of science fiction, are collected in *The Language of the Night: Essays on Fantasy and Science Fiction,* published in 1989 by HarperCollins.

---

role of male or female is determined by hormonal dominance in one partner, which determines the opposite role in the other partner. Still, an androgyne has an equal chance of becoming a mother or a father. Nevertheless, when the androgyne becomes a mother, that role is extended by pregnancy and lactation; therefore, an androgyne spends more time

as a female than a male. Also, the mother's line of descent prevails. Finally, Estraven sounds close enough to the female hormone estrogen to subliminally suggest his feminine side. But even if "she" presents a better case than "he," neither pronoun describes the androgyne.

The pronoun "it" is used for inanimate objects or animate ones whose sex is not known or apparent. "It" would certainly be appropriate for an androgyne, especially the ones in *The Left Hand of Darkness* where sex is an issue for only one-fifth of their lives. Considering that sleep takes up one third of a human life, one fifth seems a short time. Yet the implication of "it" denotes a lack of personhood and suggests the androgynes are relegated to the position of beasts. "They," on the other hand, a non-specific sex pronoun, could well describe this group, but not in the singular. Le Guin explains in her essay, "Is Gender Necessary? Redux," that until the sixteenth century "they" *was* the singular and is still used that way colloquially. However, this choice would have been more confusing than illuminating.

Nevertheless, Estraven's uniqueness should be able to shine through. His personality and character do, but any references to sexual characteristics are supplied by Ai, whose "eye" is clouded by bias. This leads to another pronoun, the point of view pronoun in this novel, "I." Aside from the chapters supplying cultural information, most of the novel is narrated in the first person and most of the time that first person is Ai. He approaches Estraven as a man approaches a man, and whenever Estraven acts in what Ai considers a stereotypically feminine way, Ai criticizes him. This perspective characterizes Ai quite well: a man defensive of his knowledge based on human sexuality; prejudiced against the unknown but, nevertheless, knowable androgyne; and unperceptive in general, partially due to the Karhide custom of *shifgrethor* or face saving. Possibly, too, since an androgyne also means an effeminate man, Ai's perspective is justified, although this doesn't speak well for Terra (Earth). Estraven doesn't clarify matters when he becomes narrator, but then he has no need to explain himself.

Perhaps the most disappointing section of the novel occurs when Estraven enters *kemmer* (as a female naturally). Both Ai and Estraven in their separate accounts merely mention they chose not to have a sexual relationship. Their use of the past tense means *kemmer* is over and the chance has passed. Ai further says he had a revelation of Estraven as a complete person after seeing "him" as a female. But this doesn't explain Estraven. Somehow, the core issue of single versus dual sexuality is missing. If *kemmer* is as intense as it's been described, and these two beings love each other as friends and respect each other for their similar goals, and trust each other with their lives, wouldn't the temptation to consummate their feelings be seen as the most passionate struggle of their lives? Or has Estraven's brother Arek intervened as he had in mindspeak? But then, if Estraven so closely identifies the voice of Ai with Arek, wouldn't his passion be doubled? On the other hand, maybe Ai has an extremely low sex drive. Never does he long for a woman nor explain his own sexual needs. The first woman he sees walking off the spaceship seems strange to him. But speculation aside, the real reason a more explicit scene seems necessary is that Ai tells the reader he understands Estraven *through* his androgyny, but that is all the reader is told. The reader is shown nothing. Despite the clever argument that this scene is left to the reader's imagination, so that the complaining reader risks being called unimaginative, wouldn't it be better if the author presented it? The author—who's made up the alien elements and who's drawn such an important conclusion from them? If this scene had been fleshed out, Ai would never again use "he" for Estraven. On the other hand, Estraven's femininity, felt by a man who's never known anything but his own masculinity, might have been so unforgettably intense that "she" would have been the perfect description of Ai's evolving understanding of androgyny. Another possibility is Ai inventing a pronoun because of his experience. "He" remains an impediment and any new ideas Le Guin might have found by facing the scene are lost forever. The scene is left out, and the reader is left on the right hand of light.

Still, many a great novel has minor flaws. The weak integration of androgyny to the plot doesn't weaken Le Guin's creative concept of androgyny; the pronoun choice doesn't take away from Le Guin's great courage in writing a feminist-rooted novel for her overwhelmingly male audience; Mary Shelley's *Frankenstein* has one line devoted to the famous professor bringing his creature to life—a scene that dominates every movie on the subject—and her book has been in publication for more than one hundred years. Besides, Ursula Le Guin's masterpiece has lifted the standard in the world of science fiction and left all of literature the chill of a wintry planet, the warmth of a beautifully evolved but tragic friendship, and the taunt of an androgyne's tantalizing sex life.

Source: Chloe Bolan, in an essay for *Novels for Students,* Gale, 1999.

Barbara Brown

In this excerpt, Brown maintains that The Left Hand of Darkness *explores the past, present, and future aspects of androgyny, recognizing that individuals can only become fully human when sexual differences are transcended.*

Much of the impact of Ursula K. Le Guin's *The Left Hand of Darkness* (1969) results from the fact that the novel is an exploration of the concept of the dichotomous/androgynous one on three time levels: future, present, and past. First and most obviously, it is future directed, presenting a possible androgynous world on the planet Winter. Second, it is rooted in the present. As Le Guin affirms in her introduction to the Ace edition, the purpose of her science fiction is descriptive, not predictive: "I'm merely observing, in the peculiar, devious, and thought-experimental manner proper to science fiction, that if you look at us at certain odd times of the day … we already are [androgynous]." Third, *The Left Hand of Darkness* is directed to the past. In her exploration of androgyny, Le Guin examines a subject whose origins are buried deep in our mythic past.…

The very origins of the word, lying in our past, in ancient Greece suggest a beginning definition. Androgyny is a combination of *andro* meaning male and *gyn* meaning female. It suggests by its form a blending in which human characteristics of males and females are not rigidly assigned. One might simply assert then that the androgyne is the dichotomous one, incorporating male and female psychological duality in one physical entity. There are, though, more complex ideas currently associated with the word. Androgyny is an affirmation that humanity should reject all forms of sexual polarization, emerge from the prison of gender into a world in which individual behavior can and is freely chosen.…

In practical terms, then, the theory of androgyny affirms that we should develop a mature sexuality in which an open system of all possible behavior is accepted, the temperament of the individual and the surrounding circumstances being the determining factors, rather than gender.…

The preceding interpretation of androgyny in the present is certainly part of what concerns Le Guin. However, her presentation of the androgynous beings in *The Left Hand of Darkness* also encompasses the original archetypes. These archetypes express the underlying human conviction that man had once experienced a unity that is now denied by the basic division into male and female. Any review of the creation myths reveals an astounding number of androgynous situations.... Some of the more obvious examples are briefly referred to here. Consider that the Bible includes two versions of creation. In Genesis I, it is an androgynous God who creates both man and woman in his image. In the second version in Genesis, it is the hermaphroditic Adam who produces Eve from his side....

Similarly, this concept of the paradoxical, split yet unified, male and female principle is found in Chinese mythology. This traditional belief is embodied in the *I Ching* or *Book of Changes* dated sometime between 2000 to 1300 B.C. Here the supreme ultimate generates the primary forms, the Yin and the Yang. All nature then consists of a perpetual interplay between this primordial pair. They are Yang and Yin, heat and cold, fire and water, active and passive, masculine and feminine....

According to the perceptions of many writers, we are, indeed, male and female. This recognition of androgyny as our ideal is buried in our mythology, in our literature, in our subconscious, and in our cells. Ursula Le Guin draws upon this past tradition of the mythic and literary androgyne and her recognition of the androgynous behavior in our present society when she writes her future-based novel, *The Left Hand of Darkness*.

Le Guin is aware how difficult her readers will find acceptance of the androgynous principle. To make explicit the need for such a non-Western interpretation of experience, she first establishes the movement from duality to unity on all levels of Genly Ai's experience, then depicts his increasing sensitivity to the peripheral ambiguities of truth that contradict the central facts.

We begin with duality into unity in terms of imagery, setting, characters, action, and philosophy. Traditionally, the right side has been associated with light representing knowledge, rationality, and the male principle; the left with darkness, ignorance, and the female principle. In *The Left Hand of Darkness* the initial description of the setting immediately establishes this light/dark, left/right polarity. The novel opens with "Rain clouds over dark towers ... a dark storm-beaten city." Yet there is one vein of slowly winding gold. This is the parade. Genly, the protagonist, sees these as contrasts, separate facets of the scene. They are, though, part of one unified vision of the world of Winter.

The wider universe is depicted in terms of light and dark. The mad Argaven, King of Karhide, mentions that the stars are bright and blinding, providing a traditional account of the universe. Continuing the description, he expands it, insisting on the surrounding void, the terror and the darkness that counterpoint the rational light of the interplanetary alliance of the Ekumen that Genly symbolizes. The glacier, the heart of Winter, is so bright on the Gobrin Ice it almost blinds Genly and his travelling companion, Estraven, the proscribed first minister of Karhide. Yet it is dark and terrible when they are caught between Drumner and Dremegale, the volcanos, spewing out black smoke and ash.

The action in the novel is often described in terms of dualities. At Arikostor Fastness, Genly specifically mentions the thin strips of light that creep across the circle. They are the counterpoints of the slats of dimness. The weaver, Faxe, a man, is seen as a woman dressed in light in the center of darkness. The foretellers are a part of a bright spider web, light against dark.

Toward the conclusion of his journey, both Genly and the reader perceive the merging pattern of dualities on these levels of setting and action. Light and dark, left and right, and, by implication, male and female become whole. Estraven quotes Tormer's Lay to Genly:

> Light is the left hand of darkness
> and darkness the right hand of light.
> Two are one, life and death, lying
> together like lovers in kemmer,
> like hands joined together,
> like the end and the way.

Genly and Estraven yearn for the dark of the shadow when they are in the antarctic void of the white darkness. Without shadow, without dark, there is a surfeit of light. They cannot see ahead to avoid the threatening changes in the terrain. In total understanding, Genly draws for Estraven the Yang and the Yin, the light and the dark. "Both and one," he says; "A shadow on snow." Both are necessary. Ultimately, Genly recognizes their crossing of the ice is both success and failure: union with the Ekumen, death for Estraven. Both are necessary.

But light and dark, left and right are not the only polarities that are unified as preparatory patterns for the central sexual unification. There is political duality in the opposed states of Orgoreyn and Karhide. Karhide has a slow steady pace of change. In many ways it is disunited. While it speaks to the people's sense of humanity, fostering a sense of strong individualism and family loyalty based on the conception of the hearths, like many democracies it harbors within it the possibility of the rise of fascism and a susceptibility to demagogues.

Orgoreyn is more socialist. Burdened down by the rivalries of its Commensalities, the extensiveness of its bureaucracies, the pettiness of its inspectors, it nonetheless is ordered and unified. It conveys a sense of progress. Still, it terrifies Genly with its failure to respect the rights of the individual. These political polarities exist not only between the two states but also within each, since the individual systems are at the same time both rational and irrational.

Genly, disgusted with this ambiguity, embraces Karhide, then rejects it; accepts Orgota, then flees from it. He seeks a consistent rational pattern. There is none. This is precisely Le Guin's thesis. Ambiguous duality must exist if unification is to occur.

This state of political polarity is unified by the agency of the Ekumen. Not a kingdom but a co-ordinator, it serves as a clearinghouse for trade and knowledge for the eighty-three nations within its scope. Mystical in nature, the Ekumen works slowly, seeking consensus. Estraven immediately recognizes that the Ekumen is a greater weaver than the Handdara. It has woven all aliens into one fabric that reflects both the unity and diversity of the civilized world.

This pattern of unifying dualities is clearly related to the central concern of androgyny. Without an awareness of the possibility of unifying opposites on the imaginative, physical, and political levels, we would not be as willing to alter the present sexual dichotomy we experience. According to Ursula Le Guin, at times we already perceive the androgynous possibilities within us. She suggests we are, nonetheless, unable to explore fully this unified duality. One reason for this limitation is the restrictive way the western mind interprets human experience. (A similar view is promulgated by Taoism and Zen.) This linear approach, characterizing western thought, focuses on scientifically provable facts. As a result it is narrow and exclusive. It fails to incorporate our peripheral senses which, through intuition and mystical awareness, also contribute to knowledge [according to Alan W. Watts in his *The Way of Zen*]. Through the action in *The Left Hand of Darkness,* Le Guin suggests that by utilizing this peripheral vision we, like Genly, can learn to accept life with all its ambiguities, its paradoxes, its flow, its unknowable qualities, with all its androgyny.

At the beginning of *The Left Hand of Darkness,* Genly is limited by the western mode of thought. As a scientist observing a subject, there is a tacit assumption of superiority on his part. He admits early in the first chapter that he judges the Gethenians as aliens. His detached manner leads him mistakenly to assert that the rivalry between Tibe, the traitorous cousin of the King, and Estraven is irrelevant to his cause. He dislikes Estraven because he is obscure, not an easy subject for scientific research. Notably, Genly's poor judgment of Winter's cultures results from his desire to gather the facts and proceed to logical conclusions. He is skeptical of anything that cannot be labeled and categorized.

Only by abandoning his divisive scientific approach can Genly achieve the unification of the warring philosophical and sexual elements within him. First, however, there are many ambiguities he must accept. One of these is Shifgrethor, an ambiguous conveying of information and intent. Not lying, it is a viable mode of behavior, conveying one aspect of truth. The wheel of experience, as Estraven insists, is not factually knowable. It turns independent of human control. On the Gobrin Ice, Genly must accept this ambiguity. No one can predict his success or failure on the glacier. As well, Genly eventually perceives that opposites are not exclusive, not contradictory. Estraven is both patriot and traitor. Genly is both patriot and traitor. Loyal to his mission, he brings Winter into the Ekumen; yet he betrays Estraven by permitting the landing of the starship before forcing Argaven to recall Therem's condemnation. Life is not linear as Genly first believes. Since it is process, the Gethenian system of measuring time is not alien but rather a logical emphasis of the individual's perception as the center of meaningful experience.

Finally, Genly accepts the ambiguous flow of events that makes it an impossibility to contain truth in language. In discussing Therem's behavior with Argaven, he says, "As I spoke I did not know if what I said was true. True in part; an aspect of truth." Often it is the west that affirms that there is one truth that can be logically explicated. It is the east that perceives that truth is flowing and ebbing, inexplicably diffuse, androgynous.

Ironically, this recognition of the many facets of truth is revealed in the beginning of *The Left Hand of Darkness.* Here the enlightened Genly, now looking back with wisdom on his experiences on Winter, declares that truth is a matter of the imagination (eastern) but one can write a report on events (western) containing facts (western). However, those facts, since they are neither solid nor coherent, will glow or dull according to the speaker (eastern).

The unification of all these dualities, the acceptance of these ambiguities, prepares both Genly and the reader to accept the central thematic unity of the sexual hermaphroditism of the Gethenians. In his response to the aliens, Genly reveals what Le Guin assumes the reader's feelings might be to these dichotomous characters. Estraven is first described as "the person on my left." Appropriately he is involved in feminine intrigue; however, he is wearing green, gold, and silver. These are colors not usually associated with both the right (the masculine) and with the left (the feminine). By page 122 Estraven is on Genly's right, all male now, but defying the traditional symbolism of right and left, he is a dark, shadowy figure. Associated with both light and dark, with left and right in a deliberately reversed symbolic order, Estraven is also an ambiguous figure. Neither Genly Ai nor the reader can interpret such a character according to traditional concepts. This world of Winter denies the established polarities of the light and dark, left and right, male and female.

Initially, the mobile responds to this confusion on the basis of his cultural conditioning. While he is repelled by the sexual duality of the Karhiders, he can neither overtly reveal his feelings to his hosts nor covertly admit his distaste to himself. His language, his responses, though, record his uneasiness. Genly first describes Estraven in these revealing terms declaring he was "Annoyed by [his] sense of effeminate intrigue." Later he calls Estraven a strange alien. He is oblivious to the fact that Estraven is the Karhider who has most attempted to befriend him. In a patronizing manner, Genly mentions that his landlady seems male on first meeting but also has "fat buttocks that wagged as he walked and a soft fat face, and a prying, spying ignoble, kindly nature.... He was so feminine." In commenting on the lack of war on Gethen, Genly observes, "They lacked, it seemed, the capacity to mobilize. They behaved like animals, in that respect; or like women. They did not behave like men or ants." Finally, in describing Therem in their later relationship, he affirms, "There was in his attitude something feminine, a refusal of the abstract, the ideal, a submissiveness to the given which displeased me."

At the beginning of *The Left Hand of Darkness,* Genly divides these unified creatures into polarities. He perceives the Gethenians in single bodies responding as both male and female. This merging of the stereotyped roles and responses first shocks and then revolts him.

The completion of his mission, however, brings him to full understanding of the nature of all dualities. They are extremes on a continuum, separated but nonetheless joined, unified. Duality can be unity. Genly must accept this fact and find ease in it. For him the crossing on the ice is a journey to self and universal knowledge. Genly begins by sharing supplies with Estraven; moves to encompassing him with mindspeak; concludes by totally accepting Estraven's nature and, by extension, the androgyny of his own. Toward the conclusion of their journey, Genly admits,

> What I was left with was, at last, acceptance of him as he was. Until then I had rejected him, refused him his own reality. He had been quite right to say that he, the only person on Gethen who trusted me, was the only Gethenian I distrusted. For he was the only one who had entirely accepted me as a human being; who had liked me personally and given me entire personal loyalty, and who therefore had demanded of me an equal degree of recognition, of acceptance. I had not been willing to give it. I had been afraid to give it. I had not wanted to give my trust, my friendship to a man who was a woman, a woman who was a man.

By later drawing the symbol of the Yang and the Yin, light and dark, masculine and feminine, Genly makes visible his emotional and intellectual acceptance of Estraven: the two in the one.

Le Guin, however, does not conclude with Genly's recognition of the androgynous possibility. Her ending suggests that this state of unified duality is a preferable, superior state of existence. In the final chapter, Genly no longer relates to his own species nor they to him. He is alien to the Terran arrivals. Uneasy in his new perceptions, Genly calls the representatives of the Ekumen "a troupe of great, strange animals of two different species, great apes with intelligent eyes, all of them in rut, in kemmer...." He is happy to return to the company of the young Gethenian physician who is described in these terms: "... and his face, a young serious face, not a man's face and not a woman's, a human face, these were a relief to me, familiar, right."

In *The Left Hand of Darkness* Ursula Le Guin suggests we too should accept as right, as familiar, the archetypal androgyny within us. Transcending male, transcending female, we can become fully human.

Source: Barbara Brown, "*The Left Hand of Darkness:* Androgyny, Future, Present, Past," in *Extrapolation,* Vol. 31, No. 3, Fall, 1980, pp. 227–235.

Robert Scholes

Scholes, author of Structural Fabulation, *holds the premise that Le Guin forces readers to examine how sexual stereotyping affects all personal relationships and individual personalities.*

Ursula K. Le Guin works in a very different manner from John Brunner. Her fiction is closer to fantasy than naturalism, but it is just as grounded in ethical concerns as Brunner's work, despite its apparent distance from present actualities. Though some would argue that her political novel, *The Dispossessed* (1974), is her best work, and others might favor her ecological romance, *The Word for World is Forest* (1972, 1976), or her young people's fantasy, *A Wizard of Earthsea* (1968), today's critical consensus is still that her best single work is *The Left Hand of Darkness* (1969).

In *The Left Hand of Darkness* Le Guin moves far from our world in time and space, to give us a planet where life has evolved on different lines from our own. This world, which happens to be in a period of high glaciation, has evolved political institutions in two adjoining countries that resemble feudalism on the one hand, and bureaucracy on the other. But the most important difference between this world and our own is that its human inhabitants are different from us in their physical sexuality. All beings on the planet Gethen have both male and female sexual organs. In a periodic cycle like estrus in animals, Gethenians become sexually aroused—but only one set of sexual organs is activated at this time. These people are potentially hermaphroditic. Most of the time they are neuter, but then they may briefly become a man or a woman, and in that time beget a child or conceive one. Thus the same person may experience both fatherhood and motherhood at different times. There is no privileged sex, exempt from child-bearing and child-rearing. This difference has many ramifications in political and social structure, and in personal behavior—far too many to attempt a discussion of them here. But the major effect of Le Guin's imagining such a fictional world is to force us to examine how sexual stereotyping dominates actual human concepts of personality and influences all human relationships. "What," one of her characters from a "normal" planet asks, "is the first question

we ask about a new-born baby?" What indeed? We all know the answer. The real question of course, is "Why?" Why must we know of any new person what their sex is before we can begin to relate to them? The answer to this involves our realization of how deeply our culture is coded along sexual lines, how much must be undone if a person is to be judged as a person—even in the eyes of the law, which has never kept its blindfold tight enough to ignore the sex of those who appear before it.

Ursula Le Guin has been attacked by radical feminists for not going far enough, for using male protagonists, as she does even in *The Left Hand of Darkness,* and for putting other issues, both political and environmental, ahead of feminism. In fact, it is probably wrong to think of her as a feminist. But I know of no single book likely to raise consciences about sexism more thoroughly and convincingly than this one. And that this is done gently, in a book which manages also to be a fine tale of adventure and a tender story of love and friendship, makes the achievement all the more remarkable. There are few writers in the United States who offer fiction as pleasurable and thoughtful as Ursula Le Guin's. It is time for her to be recognized beyond the special provinces of fantasy and science fiction or feminism as simply one of our best writers.

Source: Robert Scholes, "Science Fiction as Conscience: John Brunner and Ursula K. Le Guin, in *The New Republic,* Vol. 175, No.17, October 30, 1976, pp. 38–40.

Sources

James W. Bittner, "A Survey of Le Guin Criticism," in *Ursula K. Le Guin: Voyager to Inner Lands and to Outer Space,* Kennikat Press, 1979, pp. 31-49.

Barbara J. Bucknall, *Ursula K. Le Guin,* Ungar, 1981.

Keith N. Hull, "What Is Human? Ursula Le Guin and Science Fiction's Great Themes," *Modern Fiction Studies,* Vol. 32, no. 1, Spring, 1986, pp. 65-74.

David Ketterer, "Ursula K. Le Guin's Archetypal 'Winter-Journey,'" in *Modern Critical Views: Ursula K. Le Guin,* Chelsea House, 1986, pp. 11-21.

Ursula Le Guin, "Is Gender Necessary? Redux," in her *Dancing at the Edge of the World,* Harper & Row, 1989, pp. 7-16.

Philippa Maddern, "True Stories: Women's Writing in Science Fiction," *Meanjin,* Vol. 44, no. 1, March, 1985, pp. 110-23.

Noel Perrin, "Ursula Le Guin: Striking Out in a New Direction," *Washington Post Book World,* September 5, 1982, p. 5.

For Further Study

Thomas M. Disch, *The Dreams Our Stuff Is Made Of: How Science Fiction Conquered the World,* Free Press, 1998.
> The author, who has published in almost all genres and is a cult figure in science fiction, has produced an insightful, well-researched, and entertaining history.

John Griffiths, *Three Tomorrows: American, British and Soviet Science Fiction,* Barnes and Noble Books, 1980.
> This exercise in comparative sociology gives readers a good sense of where notions of the unreal come from in the imaginations of authors, including Le Guin's.

N. B. Hayles, "Androgyny, Ambivalence, and Assimilation in *The Left Hand of Darkness,*" in *Ursula K. Le Guin,* edited by Joseph D. Olander and Martin Harry Greenberg, Taplinger, 1979, pp. 97-115.

> This essay looks in depth at the issues in its title, offering an advanced, scholarly study.

Suzanne Elizabeth Reid, *Presenting Ursula Le Guin,* Twayne, 1997.
> Reid gives a clear overview of the author's career and insightful interpretations of her works.

Karen Sinclair, "Solitary Being: The Hero as Anthropologist," in *Ursula K. Le Guin: Voyager to Inner Lands and to Outer Space,* edited by Joe DeBolt, Kennikat Press, 1979, pp. 50-65.
> This early exploration of Le Guin's characters draws upon parallels and themes that are not evident to the reader of just one novel.

George Edgar Slusser, *The Farthest Shores of Ursula Le Guin,* Borgo Press, 1976.
> This early study of Le Guin's career, published when she had been publishing for just thirteen years, offers a good overview of the ideas addressed in the Hainish novels.

The Old Man and the Sea

When *The Old Man and the Sea* was published in 1952 to wide critical acclaim, it had been twelve years since Ernest Hemingway's previous critical success, *For Whom the Bell Tolls.* His major writing effort during the intervening period, *Across the River and Into the Trees,* published in 1950, had been widely dismissed as a near-parody of the author's usual style and themes. *The Old Man and the Sea,* however, was a popular success, selling 5.3 million copies within two days of its publication in a special edition of *Life* magazine. A few complaints about the stilted language of some of the Spanish transliterations came from critics. Some also found Santiago's philosophizing unrealistic. Nevertheless, the story won the Pulitzer Prize for fiction in 1953. A year later, Hemingway was awarded the Nobel Prize for Literature. The Nobel committee singled out the story's "natural admiration for every individual who fights the good fight in a world of reality overshadowed by violence and death," (noted Susan F. Beegel in "Conclusion: The Critical Reputation of Ernest Hemingway"). Although Hemingway's writing continued to be published, much of it posthumously after the author's suicide in 1961, *The Old Man and the Sea* is generally considered by many to be his crowning achievement. The work was especially praised for its depiction of a new dimension to the typical Hemingway hero, less macho and more respectful of life. In Santiago, Hemingway had finally achieved a character who could face the human condition and survive without cynically

Ernest Hemingway

1952

Ernest Hemingway

dismissing it or dying while attempting to better it. In Santiago's relationship with the world and those around him, Hemingway had discovered a way to proclaim the power of love in a wider and deeper way than in his previous works.

Author Biography

Ernest Hemingway was born in Oak Park, Illinois, in 1899. He was the second son of Clarence Hemingway, a doctor, and Grace Hall Hemingway, who had been an aspiring opera singer. While his father encouraged his son's athletic and outdoor skills, his mother fostered her son's artistic talents. In school, Hemingway was an active, if not outstanding, athlete. He wrote poems and articles for the school newspaper, and he also tried his hand at stories. After graduation Hemingway became a reporter on the *Kansas City Star,* where he learned the newspaper's preferred style of simple declarative sentences that was to permanently influence his own style of writing.

In May of 1918, Hemingway volunteered for duty in World War I, serving as an ambulance driver on the Italian front. This experience later served as the source material for *A Farewell to Arms.* He,

like the novel's protagonist, was wounded in the legs. However, instead of being returned to the front he was sent home, where he was greeted as a celebrity. He spent months convalescing at the family cabin in Michigan. Having recovered, in 1920, Hemingway moved to Toronto where he functioned as companion to a disabled youth. There, he again entered the world of writing by working for the *Toronto Star.* After marrying, he became a correspondent with the paper. His position enabled him to begin pursuing a career as a novelist. He and his wife, Hadley Richardson, left for Paris, where Hemingway associated with a group of other authors known collectively as the "Lost Generation." The group included James Joyce, Ezra Pound, Gertrude Stein, and Ford Madox Ford.

Awaiting the birth of their child, the Hemingways returned to Toronto in 1923. Following the birth of their son John, the family went back to Paris. There Hemingway spent a year and a half editing a literary magazine. 1925 to 1929 proved to be a prolific period for Hemingway, who wrote and published the short story collection *In Our Time* and the novels *The Sun Also Rises* and *A Farewell to Arms,* as well as others. The end of the 1920s was marred, however, by his divorce from Hadley in 1927 and by the suicide of his father in

1928. In the same period, Pauline Pfeiffer, whom Hemingway married the same year as his divorce, nearly died while she was giving birth to their child. This experience later found its way into the death of the character Catherine Barkley in *A Farewell to Arms*.

The 1930s, on the other hand, were filled with writing and adventure, as Hemingway hunted in Africa, fished in the Gulf Stream near Cuba, and reported on the Spanish Civil War for the *North American Newspaper Alliance*. During the mid-1930s Hemingway began gathering material for *The Sea*, one part of which eventually became *The Old Man and the Sea*. The other parts, as edited by Charles Scribner, were later published posthumously in 1970 as *Islands in the Stream*.

In 1940 Hemingway left Pfeiffer for Martha Gellhorn. The same year he published *For Whom the Bell Tolls*. Hemingway and Gellhorn then went to China. Next, he became a war correspondent with the U.S. Fourth Infantry Division where he met Mary Welsh. In 1946, one year after divorcing Gellhorn, he married Welsh.

The Old Man and the Sea won the Pulitzer Prize in 1952. Two years later, Hemingway was awarded the Nobel Prize for Literature. But as he approached his sixties, Hemingway's health began deteriorating. The once robust adventurer now suffered from hypertension, mild diabetes, depression, and paranoia. Despite treatment for mental health issues, Hemingway committed suicide on July 2, 1961. He is remembered as one of the great stylistic innovators of modern American literature.

Plot Summary

An Unlucky Boat

The Old Man and the Sea tells the story of Santiago, an aging Cuban fisherman, who alone in his small boat faces the most difficult fight of his life against an enormous marlin. At the beginning of the short novel, Santiago has lost his fisherman's luck; he has gone eighty-four days without catching a marketable fish. Even his closest friend, a village boy he taught to fish, has left him to work on another boat. The local fishermen make fun of Santiago or feel sorry for him, but he himself remains hopeful and undefeated. Every day he rises early, prepares his skiff, and rows far out into the Gulf Stream in search of marlin.

Though ordered by his parents to work on a luckier boat, the boy still loves Santiago, and he visits the old man's simple shack when he can. Once married, Santiago now lives alone in increasing poverty. He has little to eat, and frequently must rely on the boy or others in the village to bring him food and clothing. As they share their meals, Santiago and the boy discuss baseball and the important players of the period, especially "the great DiMaggio." The old man tells of his early life working on ships that sailed to Africa. When he sleeps, Santiago dreams of being young again and seeing "lions on the beaches in the evening."

The Truly Big Fish

Early one morning the old man rises, shares coffee with the boy, and sets out for the far reaches of the fishing grounds. He passes all the other fishermen, who stop to work "the great well," the point where the ocean drops off suddenly to seven hundred fathoms. He watches for flying fish or other signs of bait that might signal the presence of larger fish. Soon he catches a small albacore and, using it for bait, quickly hooks something very large. Though he pulls as hard as he can on the line, Santiago cannot move the great weight on the other end. The big fish refuses to surface and begins to swim out to sea, towing the skiff behind it.

> Eat it so that the point of the hook goes into your heart and kills you, he thought. Come up easy and let me put the harpoon into you. All right. Are you ready? Have you been long enough at table?
>
> "Now!" he said aloud and struck hard with both hands, gained a yard of line and then struck again and again, swinging with each arm alternately on the cord with all the strength of his arms and the pivoted weight of his body.
>
> Nothing happened. The fish just moved away slowly and the old man could not raise him an inch. His line was strong and made for heavy fish and he held it against his back until it was so taut that beads of water were jumping from it. Then it began to make a slow hissing sound in the water and he still held it, bracing himself against the thwart and leaning back against the pull. The boat began to move slowly off toward the north-west.

Alone and unable to release the tightening line, Santiago struggles to hold onto the fish. Without the boy to help him, he knows that either he or the fish will die from this. His body is old but still strong, and he maintains his grip on the line despite his age and increasing discomfort. After several hours, night falls, but he never considers giving up. He realizes that he will need to eat to keep up his strength, and as the sun begins to rise the next day he consumes one of the small tuna he caught the day before.

During the second day, the great fish surfaces just long enough for Santiago to see him. The sight of the great marlin, "two feet longer than the skiff," inspires the old man. He remembers a time in his younger days when he arm wrestled a man in a Casablanca tavern. The match began on a Sunday morning and lasted the entire night, ending the following morning when Santiago forced his opponent's hand to the wood. Night comes again and the old man realizes that he needs to sleep. He wraps the line around his shoulders and cramps his body against it. Then he sleeps and dreams of the lions.

When Santiago wakes it is still dark, though the moon has come out. While he was sleeping, the great fish has risen to the surface, and now Santiago can hear the marlin thrashing and jumping in the distance. As the old man gathers all his strength to hold onto the line, the marlin begins to circle the boat, and Santiago knows he has won. After several turns, the fish pulls closer, brushing the sides of the boat, and the old man, seeing his chance, drives his harpoon into its side. With a final struggle that sends spray over the entire skiff, the fish dies, its dark blood staining the blue water.

Destroyed But Not Defeated

Now many miles out to sea, the old man lashes the great fish to the side of his skiff and sets his small sail for home. After about an hour of smooth sailing, however, his luck runs out. A shark, following the trail of blood left by the huge fish, bites into the body, taking a large piece of flesh. Santiago manages to kill the "dentuso" with his harpoon, but he realizes that more sharks will follow. He begins to wonder whether he committed a sin in killing the great marlin, but before he has time to decide, the sharks close in. Fighting a hopeless battle, the old man kills several of the large "galanos" before he loses first his harpoon and then his knife. By the time the skiff reaches the village, little remains of the great fish but the head and skeleton.

Convinced that he "went out too far" and bears responsibility for the loss of the fish, the exhausted Santiago returns to his shack and falls asleep. The fishermen in the village marvel at the mutilated fish; at eighteen feet, it is the largest marlin they have ever seen. The boy brings the old man food and fresh clothes and watches over him as he sleeps.

Characters

Bodega Proprietor

Although he is unnamed in the story, the bodega proprietor serves the important function of representing those in the village who show their respect and admiration of Santiago by supporting him—in this case, by giving Santiago free coffee and newspapers.

Female Tourist

Although she has only one line in the story, the unnamed female tourist is important since in her mistaking the carcass of the marlin as that of a shark, she acts as a foil for Santiago's extraordinary knowledge of the sea.

Manolin

Manolin is a young man, based on someone Hemingway knew in Cuba who was then in his twenties. In the story, however, Manolin is referred to as "the boy." Like Santiago, Manolin comes from a family of fishermen and has long admired Santiago as a masterful practitioner of his trade. Although Manolin's father has forbidden him to go fishing with Santiago because of the old man's bad luck, Manolin nevertheless continues to visit Santiago and to help him in whatever ways he can. Manolin shows great concern for Santiago's health, especially after he sees how Santiago has suffered in catching the big marlin. As a mark of his friendship and respect for Manolin, Santiago has given him certain responsibilities from an early age, such as fetching bait and carrying the lines. By contrast, Manolin's own father only belittles his son's relationship with Santiago.

Even though Manolin appears only at the beginning and the end of the story, he is an important character. Manolin's conversations with Santiago, and Santiago's longing for the boy's company when he is alone, reveal the character of both men. Santiago is seen as a loving, patient, and brave man, both proud and humble, who accepts and appreciates life, despite all its hardships. Manolin is shown to be someone who loves and respects Santiago, and who realizes that he can learn things from the old man that he cannot learn at home.

Manolin undergoes an important change between the beginning and end of the story. At the beginning he still defers to the wishes of his parents that he not accompany Santiago fishing since the old man's luck has turned bad. By the end of the story, however, Manolin has resolved to go with the old man, lucky or not, in spite of his parents' wishes.

Manolin's Father

Manolin's father forbids Manolin from going out with Santiago after the old man's fortieth day without a fish. By the end of the story Manolin decides to disobey his father out of his love for Santiago.

Old Man

See Santiago

Pedrico

As a friend of Santiago, Pedrico helps the old man by giving him newspapers. After the old man's return from the sea, despite his wounds and exhaustion, Santiago remembers to carry out his promise to give Pedrico the head of the fish carcass.

Santiago

Santiago is an old fisherman of undetermined age. As a young man he traveled widely by ship and fondly remembers seeing lions on the beaches of East Africa. His wife died, and he has taken her picture down because it makes him sad to see it. Now he lives alone in a shack on the beach. Every day he sets forth alone in his boat to make a living.

When the story opens, Santiago has gone eighty-four days without catching a single fish. As a result, he is pitied and regarded by the other fishermen as unlucky. Santiago is still respected by some, however, because of his age and his perseverance. He is a very experienced fisherman who knows well the tricks of his trade, including which fish to use as bait.

Santiago also loves baseball and occasionally gambles. He identifies with Joe DiMaggio, the great center fielder for the Yankees in the 1940s and 1950s. Santiago admires how DiMaggio, whose father was a fisherman, plays in spite of bone spurs in his feet that cause him pain whenever he runs. As an old man, Santiago must also cope with the physical demands of his job in the face of the infirmities of his aging body. Yet he suffers without complaining, and it is this stoic attitude that has won him much respect in the community.

Santiago is not a religious person, but he does think about the meaning of life, and his religious references show that he is very familiar with Roman Catholic saints and prayers. Through the author's revelation of Santiago's own thoughts, and the conversations between Santiago and his relatively young companion, Manolin, readers come to sense that despite his setbacks and shortcomings, Santiago remains proud of himself, and this makes his humility both touching and real. Though he strives to attain the most he can for himself, Santiago also accepts what life has given him without complaint.

Spencer Tracy starring in the title role of the 1956 film The Old Man and the Sea.

This largeness of vision also allows Santiago to appreciate and respect nature and all living creatures, even though he must kill some of these creatures in order to live. For example, the old man recalls how he once hooked, brought in, and finally clubbed to death a female marlin, while her faithful mate never left her side once during the ordeal. "That was the saddest thing I ever saw," the old man comments. "The boy was sad too and we begged her pardon and butchered her promptly."

Hemingway first wrote about the true incident upon which his story is based in an article entitled "On the Blue Water: A Gulf Stream Letter" for the April 1936 issue of *Esquire* magazine. The actual incident took only two days; the fisherman, "half crazy" and crying, was picked up by others after

Media Adaptations

- *The Old Man and the Sea* was adapted as a feature film starring Spencer Tracy as Santiago and Felipe Pazos as The Boy, Warner Brothers, 1958. This film has been praised for some of its visual effects, and the score won an Academy Award.

- It was also the source of a made-for-TV production in 1990 starring Anthony Quinn, Gary Cole, Alexis Cruz, Patricia Clarkson, and Francesco Quinn.

- The novel is also available on a two-cassette sound recording narrated by Charlton Heston.

fighting the sharks; and half the carcass was still left at the end. Hemingway's intentions in creating the character of Santiago may perhaps best be seen in examining how the author altered the true events to shape his telling of *The Old Man and the Sea.*

In Hemingway's later version, Santiago's hooking the fish, hauling it to the boat, fighting the sharks, and then bringing it home takes three days and is completed in heroic fashion with no outside help. Nothing remains of the fish at the end except its skeleton. No mention is made of the fisherman's state of mind other than that he wants to fish again as soon as he can.

Hemingway's changes clearly make Santiago more of a single heroic and tragic figure who fights alone, loses almost everything, and yet still is ready to meet life again. Thus, after a night's sleep and a promise from Manolin that from now on they will fish together, Santiago is making plans not just to resume his life but to strive even harder next time. Similarly, Hemingway turned an anecdote about a piteous, helpless fisherman into a parable of man's tragic but heroic struggle not merely to survive but, as fellow Nobelist William Faulkner expressed it, to endure.

Themes

The Human Condition

In his novella about a fisherman who struggles to catch a large marlin only to lose it, Hemingway has stripped down the basic story of human life to its basic elements. A single human being, represented by the fisherman Santiago, is blessed with the intelligence to do big things and to dream of even grander things. Santiago shows great skill in devising ways to tire out the huge fish he has hooked and ways to conserve his strength in order to land it. Yet in the struggle to survive, this human must often suffer and even destroy the very thing he dreams of. Thus Santiago cuts his hands badly and loses the fish to sharks in the process of trying to get his catch back to shore. Yet the struggle to achieve one's dreams is still worthwhile, for without dreams, a human remains a mere physical presence in the universe, with no creative or spiritual dimension. And so at the end of the story, Santiago, in spite of his great loss, physical pain, and exhaustion, is still "dreaming about the lions"—the same ones he saw in Africa when he was younger and would like to see again.

Love

Against the seeming indifference of the universe, love is often the only force that endures. This force is best seen in the relationship of Santiago and Manolin, which has endured since Manolin's early childhood. Over the years, Santiago has taught Manolin to fish and given him companionship and a sense of self-worth that Manolin failed to get from his own father. Manolin in return shows his love for Santiago by bringing him food and by weeping for him when he sees how much he suffered in fighting the marlin. Manolin also plans to take care of Santiago during the coming winter by bringing him clothing and water for washing.

Santiago's love, of course, extends to other people as well. He loved his wife when they were married, though when she died he had to take down her portrait because it made him feel lonely. Similarly, even in his suffering he thinks of others, remembering his promise to send the fish head to his friend Pederico to use as bait. Santiago's love also extends to include nature itself, even though he has often suffered at its hands. His love for all living creatures, whether fish, birds, or turtles, is often described, as is his love for the sea, which he sees as a woman who gives or withholds favors. Some of the younger fishermen, in contrast, often spoke of the sea as a "contestant" or even an "enemy."

Youth and Old Age

The comparison and contrast of these two stages of human life runs throughout the story. Although Santiago is obviously an old man, in many ways he retains a youthful perspective on life. For example, he is a keen follower of baseball, and admires players like Joe DiMaggio and Dick Sisler for their youthful skills and abilities. His friendship with Manolin is also based partly on Santiago's fond recollections of his own youth. For example, he recalls the time he saw the lions on the beach in Africa or when he beat a well-known player in a hand-wrestling match that lasted all day. His repeated wish that the boy were in the boat is not made just because that would make it easier to fight the fish. He also misses the boy as a companion with his own youthful perspective. Yet Santiago does not admire all youth indiscriminately. For example, he contrasts his own attitude toward the sea as a woman with that of "some of the younger fishermen, those who used buoys as floats and had motorboats," who think of the sea as a male enemy who must be defeated. By the same token, Santiago is aware that not everything about old age is attractive to youth. For example, he keeps from Manolin the knowledge that he doesn't care very much about washing or eating on a regular basis. Santiago is also very aware of the disadvantages of old age. Although he retains much of his youthful strength, for example, he knows that at his age he is no longer able to fight off the sharks that attack his fish. Yet in the end, despite his defeat, Santiago is still able to plan his next fishing expedition and to dream again of the lions who perhaps represent to him the strength and the freedom of youth.

Luck vs. Skill

Many people believe in the concept of destiny, a concept in which spiritual forces and luck are combined. When one is lucky, it is considered a sign that one has the spiritual qualities to succeed. By the same token, when one has been unlucky, as Santiago is considered after eighty-four days of not catching any fish, he is dismissed by Manolin's parents as *salao,* "which is the worst form of unlucky," and therefore someone to avoid. Santiago himself believes to some extent in the concept of luck. He senses that his eighty-fifth day of fishing will be a good one and wants to buy that number in the lottery. Later in the story, when his big fish has already been half-eaten by sharks, he says he would pay "what they asked" for some luck "in any form."

Earlier in the story, however, before he has caught the big fish, Santiago reflects that "It is bet-

Topics for Further Study

- Throughout *The Old Man and the Sea,* Santiago expresses his feelings about nature. Today, the protection of our natural environment is often in the news. Do some research on environmental issues and write an essay comparing Santiago's attitude about nature to modern theories of environmentalism. Would Santiago be considered an environmentalist today?

- Manolin undergoes a change between the beginning and the end of the novel. What do you think causes this change? Find specific examples from the story to support your opinion. Then write an essay comparing the "old" Manolin from the beginning of the story to the "new" Manolin who has emerged by the end.

- Most of Ernest Hemingway's heroes are young men, but Santiago, as the title reveals, is an old man. Why do you think the author chose to tell this story from an older person's perspective? How might the story have been different if the hero had been a young man? Present your ideas in an essay and use examples from the text to support your conclusions.

ter to be lucky [than unlucky]. But I would rather be exact. Then when luck comes you are ready." In this reformulation of the luck-vs.-skill question, Santiago is clearly favoring skill. This preference is shown by his actions throughout the novel, from the way he gauges the strength of the fish by the pull on the line to the manner in which he calculates and conserves his own strength for the battle he knows lies ahead. After his defeat he says the boy should not fish with him because "I am not lucky anymore." Yet Santiago quickly changes his mind about going out with Manolin when the boy says that "we will fish together now, for I still have much to learn." Toward the end, Santiago asks himself "[W]hat beat you" and answers "Nothing. I went out too far." So in the end, Santiago finds that it is matters of judgment and skill that determine success, not luck.

Style

Point of View

All novels use at least one point of view, or angle of vision, from which to tell the story. The point of view may be that of a single character, or of several characters in turn. *The Old Man and the Sea* uses the omniscient, or "all-knowing," point of view of the author, who acts as a hidden narrator. The omniscient point of view enables the author to stand outside and above the story itself, and thus to provide a wider perspective from which to present the thoughts of the old man and the other characters. Thus at the beginning of the tale, the omniscient narrator tells us not only what Santiago and the boy said to each other, but what the other fishermen thought of the old man. "The older fishermen … looked at him and were sad. But they did not show it…."

Setting

The Old Man and the Sea takes place entirely in a small fishing village near Havana, Cuba, and in the waters of the Gulf Stream, a current of warm water that runs north, then east of Cuba in the Caribbean Sea. Hemingway visited Cuba as early as 1928, and later lived on the coast near Havana for nineteen years, beginning in 1940, so he knew the area very well. The references to Joe Dimaggio and a series of games between the Yankees and the Detroit Tigers in which Dimaggio came back from a slump have enabled scholars to pinpoint the time during which the novel takes place as mid-September 1950. As Manolin also reminds readers, September is the peak of the blue marlin season. The story takes three days, the length of the battle against the fish, but as Manolin reminds the old man, winter is coming on and he will need a warm coat.

Structure

Like the three-day epic struggle itself of Santiago against the fish, Hemingway's story falls into three main parts. The first section entails getting ready for the fishing trip; then the trip out, including catching the fish and being towed by it, which encompasses all of the first two days and part of the third; and finally the trip back. Another way of dividing and analyzing the story is by using a dramatic structure devised by Aristotle. In the opening part of the story, or rising action, the readers are presented with various complications of the conflict between the other fishermen's belief that Santiago is permanently unlucky and Santiago and

the boy's belief that the old man will still catch a fish. For example, readers learn that some of the other villagers, like the restaurant owner Pedrico, help Santiago, while others avoid him. The climax of the story, when Santiago kills the fish, marks the point at which the hero's fortunes begin to take a turn for the worse. This turning point becomes evident when sharks start to attack the fish and leads inevitably to the resolution (or denouement) of the drama, in which Santiago, having no effective weapons left to fight the sharks, must watch helplessly as they strip the carcass of all its remaining meat. Perhaps showing the influence of modern short story writers, however, Hemingway has added to the ending what James Joyce called an epiphany, or revelation of Santiago's true character. This moment comes when the author implicitly contrasts the tourist's ignorance of the true identity of the marlin's skeleton to Santiago's quiet knowledge of his skill and his hope, reflected in his repeated dreams of the lions on the beach, that he will fish successfully again.

Symbolism

A symbol can be defined as a person, place, or thing that represents something more than its literal meaning. Santiago, for example, has often been compared to Christ in the way he suffers. His bleeding hands, the way he carries the boat mast like a cross, and the way he lies on his bed with his arms outstretched, all have clear parallels in the story of Christ's crucifixion. In this interpretation of the story, Manolin is seen as a disciple who respects and loves Santiago as his teacher. In this context, the sea could be said to represent earthly existence. Humans, as stated in Genesis, have been created by God to have dominion over all other living creatures, including the fish in the sea. Yet humans like Santiago still suffer because of Adam and Eve's original sin of eating the apple from the tree of knowledge. Santiago, however, says he does not understand the concept of sin. Santiago can also be seen more broadly as a representative of all human beings who must struggle to survive, yet hope and dream of better things to come. Hemingway himself does not seem to mind if his characters, setting, and plot have different meanings to different readers. He once said that he "tried to make a real old man, a real boy, a real sea and a real fish and real sharks. But if I made them good and true enough they would mean many things."

Gregorio Fuentes, a Cuban fisherman, was Hemingway's inspiration for the title character of The Old Man and the Sea. *With a portrait of Hemingway and Fuentes hanging in the background, this photograph was taken in 1994.*

Historical Context

Cuba and the United States in the Early 1950s

Relations between Cuba and the United States were generally friendly during most of the 1950s, as they had been since 1934. That year marked the end of the Platt Amendment, which had given the United States the right to intervene in Cuba's affairs. United States' ownership of many Cuban sugar mills, however, was a continuing source of dispute. In 1952, President Prio Socarras was overthrown in a military coup by General Fulgencio Batista y Zalvidar. Batista had previously ruled as dictator from 1933 to 1940, and would rule again until 1959, when he was overthrown by Fidel Castro. Despite Hemingway's move to Ketchum, Idaho, soon after Castro and his supporters overthrew the Batista regime, Hemingway had supported both the overthrow and what he called the "historical necessity" of the Castro revolution.

Cuban Culture

Cuban culture during the first half of the twentieth century was marked perhaps foremost by an ambivalent view toward the Catholic Church. Unlike other Latin American countries, church and state in Cuba were constitutionally separate during this period. Because of its long Spanish heritage, however, Cuba was still dominated by Catholic cultural influences. The result was a contradictory situation in which 85 percent of the population called itself Catholic, but only 10 percent actually practiced the faith. The effect of these circumstances are seen many times in *The Old Man and the Sea.* For example, when Santiago battles the marlin, he says, "I am not religious, but I will say ten Our Fathers and ten Hail Marys that I should catch this fish, and I promise to make a pilgrimage to the Virgin of Cobre if I catch him." Later after he has killed the fish, Santiago wonders if it is a sin to hope that he will make it back to shore with the fish's meat intact, but he quickly dismisses the thought. "Do not think about sin," he thought. "There are enough problems now without sin. Also I have no understanding of it."

Cubans, like other Latin Americans, place a high value on the innate worth of the individual. Success in life is defined under the code of *personalismo* as the achievement of one's spiritual potential or personal destiny rather than one's financial or career status. Thus Santiago is respected as a skilled and unique individual even though he has not caught a fish in three months. As seen through the eyes of Manolin and the omniscient narrator, Santiago is a heroic and majestic figure who, like Odysseus or Christ, has undergone a great ordeal and provides a model to emulate.

Machismo, or maleness, is an important male goal in traditional Latin American society. *Machismo* is ideally developed in several ways, including military, athletic, and intellectual exercises, and sexual prowess. Most men are not expected to live up to the *machismo* ideal in practice. Yet by cultivating these powers, one can approach being the ideal man. Santiago, for example, is admired because of his physical power of endurance. He takes great pride in having in his youth defeated a powerful Negro in an all-day hand-wrestling contest in Casablanca. Santiago also places a high value on mental qualities like his self-confidence and his vast knowledge of the "tricks" of fishing. Santiago is so confident of these qualities that he can bet "everything [the fish] has against only my will and my intelligence." It has often been noted that in his own

life, Hemingway also strove to challenge himself intellectually through his friendships and writing, as well as physically, through boxing, war service, hunting, fishing, and bullfighting. Although Hemingway is sometimes criticized for what is interpreted as an attraction to violence for its own sake, it is not hard to understand why the Latin American belief in *machismo* appealed to the author.

Critical Overview

The early critical reception of *The Old Man and the Sea* upon its publication in 1952 was very favorable, and its reputation has been generally high ever since, notwithstanding negative reactions in the 1960s by critics like Kenneth Lynn and Philip Young. Yet what the critics have seen worthy of special note in the story has changed noticeably over the years.

The early reviews of Hemingway's first novel since the disastrous reception two years earlier of *Across the River and into the Trees* especially praised the central character, Santiago. In his original 1954 evaluation of the book which Gerry Brenner included in *The Old Man and the Sea: The Story of a Common Man,* Philip Young wrote, "It is the knowledge that a simple man is capable of such decency, dignity and even heroism, and that his struggle can be seen in heroic terms, that largely distinguishes this book." In his book *Ernest Hemingway: Critiques of Four Major Novels,* Carlos Baker noted that critic Clinton S. Burhans saw in Santiago "a noble and tragic individualism revealing what a man can do in an indifferent universe which defeats him, and the love he can feel for such a universe and his humility before it." *The Old Man and the Sea* won the Pulitzer Prize for fiction in 1953 and played a large role in Hemingway's being honored with the Nobel Prize for Literature in 1954.

Though several posthumous volumes of his fiction would follow in the 1970s, Hemingway's suicide in 1961 was the occasion for a major, and perhaps less inhibited, reevaluation of his work. Philip Young's *Ernest Hemingway: A Reconsideration* was one of the most influential of these. According to Young's "wound theory," Hemingway's entire life and art was an attempt to master the traumatic event of his wounding in World War I. To do this, said Young, Hemingway evolved a "code" by which his heroes sought to live. As Young described this hero code, it was a " 'grace under pressure' ... made of the controls of honor and courage which in a life of tension and pain make a man a man and distinguish him from the people who follow random impulses, let down their hair, and are generally messy, perhaps cowardly, and without inviolable rules for how to live holding tight."

In his life and his heroic struggle against the fish, Santiago fits Young's definition. His pride in his physical strength, still noteworthy in his old age, is shown in his fond recollection of the time he beat a "giant" in an all-day hand-wrestling match in Casablanca. In his mental suppression of physical pain, Santiago also reminds the reader of Jake Barnes in *The Sun Also Rises* and Frederic Henry in *A Farewell to Arms*.

Young's "wound theory" and "code hero" concepts continued to influence much of Hemingway criticism in the 1960s and 1970s, despite the posthumous publication during this period of nine new volumes of Hemingway's fiction and nonfiction, including his Toronto newspaper dispatches, his high school literary efforts, his poetry, *A Moveable Feast* (a nonfiction collection of acid-witted accounts of Hemingway's days in Paris as a young writer in the 1920s), and *Islands in the Stream*. In fact, as Susan F. Beegel has pointed out, "the idea of the code hero would smother the originality of lesser critics and stifle alternative views for a long time." The best source of basic facts about Hemingway's life, however, remains Baker's 1969 biography, *Ernest Hemingway*.

Though the Hemingway "industry" of posthumous publications, memoirs of old friends, and newsletters and annuals of Hemingway critics continued to mount, it was not until after 1986, with the publication of *The Garden of Eden,* that Young's theory began to be replaced in most critical readers' minds by Kenneth Lynn's "theory of androgyny," or the state of having both male and female characteristics, as described in Lynn's influential psychoanalytic biography, *Hemingway*. According to Lynn, Hemingway's androgyny was partly the result of his mother's having dressed Ernest as a toddler in girl's clothes that were identical to his older sister's. In *Hemingway's Quarrel with Androgyny*, Mark Spilka sees Santiago's androgyny as a typical example in Hemingway's late fiction of the "return of the repressed" female side of the author's personality.

The androgyny theory allows readers to view Santiago, and indeed Manolin, from a wider perspective. Many people see, for example, that while women themselves play only a small role in the novel, nevertheless, the sea itself is regarded as feminine in Santiago's eyes, unlike some of the other younger fishermen in the story, who regard the sea as a male enemy to be conquered. Santiago describes the sea (*la mar*), like a woman, as "something that gave or withheld great favours." Hemingway also describes how Manolin cries not once, but twice, after seeing the old man's condition soon after he returns to shore. This is perhaps more significant than it may appear, because Manolin, although called "the boy," is actually at least twenty-two years old as noted by Bickford Sylvester in "The Cuban Contest of *The Old Man and the Sea*." A critic laboring under the more rigid notion of the code hero would probably expect Manolin, as a full-grown man, to keep his emotions held in check.

No matter through which prism the reader analyzes Hemingway's great sea story, it seems there will always be new revelations to find. Beegel notes that new areas for study may be found in Hemingway's ecological consciousness or the multicultural background of several of his novels. And with the increased use of the computer to analyze prose text and style, who knows what other discoveries await the Hemingway scholars of the future.

Criticism

Carl Davis

In the following essay, Davis, an associate professor of English at Northeast Louisiana University, describes The Old Man and the Sea *as a brilliant, deceptively simple work that expresses the author's most fundamental beliefs about what it means to be a person. The work might also be seen as an expression of the author's personal struggle with thoughts of suicide.*

From its publication in 1952, *The Old Man and the Sea* has played an important role in defining and confirming Ernest Hemingway's position as a major voice in twentieth-century fiction. Long famous for his short stories and the early novels *The Sun Also Rises* in 1926 and *A Farewell to Arms* in 1929, Hemingway built his public image upon that of his wounded, isolated heroes. His passion for bull fighting, fishing, and big game hunting inevitably led him to dangerous places and activities. He covered the Spanish Civil War as a reporter and later served as a war correspondent during World War II. By the 1950s, he was at the height of his fame, living on a small estate or *finca* in Cuba and

What Do I Read Next?

- *Youth* (1903) and *Typhoon* (1902), both by Joseph Conrad, are sea stories with intriguing parallels to Hemingway's work. It is believed that Hemingway, who read all of Conrad in Paris and Toronto during the twenties, may have consciously or unconsciously used the "central strategy" of *Youth* when writing *The Old Man and the Sea.*

- *For Whom the Bell Tolls* (1940) was Hemingway's last successfully received novel before *The Old Man and the Sea,* and the only previous Hemingway novel in which a Hispanic background plays a major part. It depicts the struggle of Robert Jordan, an American fighting against the Fascists in the Spanish Civil War, to live up to his political and personal ideals without becoming narrowly partisan.

- *Islands in the Stream,* published posthumously in 1970, is the book, as edited, of which *The Old Man and the Sea* was originally envisaged by Hemingway as the fourth part. The first three sections were originally called "The Sea When Young," "The Sea When Absent," and "The Sea in Being."

- *The Nick Adams Stories* (1972) are all Hemingway's short stories, plus a few story fragments, about this recurring fictional character, from the time he first appeared in the early 1920s as a young boy, to his last appearance as an adult and father in 1933. Although written and published at different times in Hemingway's life, they are arranged here by Hemingway scholar Philip Young to illustrate Nick's unfolding life.

---

playing out his role as "Papa" Hemingway, the white-haired, white-bearded symbol of virility and intellectual heroism. With the publication of *The Old Man and the Sea,* a taut, technically brilliant short novel, his reputation as a master craftsman of prose narrative was reaffirmed. More importantly, however, the story of Santiago, the isolated old man who fights a great fish for three days, seemed to bring together all the major elements of Hemingway's life and work. Indeed, it remains a concise expression of what it means for Hemingway to live and act as an individual in the modern world.

On first glance the most striking aspect of *The Old Man and the Sea* is its combination of compression and depth. Like many of Hemingway's early stories, the novel takes full advantage of the author's widely imitated prose style—a mixture of simple sentence structures, limited adjectives, and spare but suggestive description. As he himself explained in his examination of bullfighting in *Death in the Afternoon,* good writing should move like an iceberg, only one-eighth of which appears above the water. The writer who truly knows a subject should be able to leave much of the content unstated, and the reader will "have a feeling of those things as strongly as though the writer had stated them." Accordingly, *The Old Man and the Sea* offers a deceptively simple surface story of an aging fisherman who catches a great fish only to lose him to marauding sharks. The fable-like simplicity of the plot, however, suggests that the story may yield broader symbolic meanings.

One such symbolic interpretation of the novel focuses upon the ancient and often repeated pattern of a hero confronting a natural force. In this reading, Santiago the fisherman is more than just a poor Cuban hoping to break his streak of eighty-four days without a fish. He represents the skillful, courageous individual who willingly undergoes a test of character against an equally worthy opponent. The sea, the feminine and possibly maternal "la mar," becomes the site of his encounter with nature itself. Far away from the other fishermen and even further from any sort of civilized society, Santiago must test his own strengths alone and without help. Not even the boy he has taught to fish can be present at such a moment. Like the bullfighter or the soldier in battle, the old man struggles as though against his own death. However, to catch his "brother," as he calls him, is not to prove himself better than the fish, only its equal. Indeed, Santiago's failure to save the dead marlin from the sharks serves to reaffirm his limits as an individual and remind him of the need for humility in the face of nature's power.

Santiago's actions suggest that he is more than just a courageous individual, however. He also shows great concern for the quality of his work and the precision of his actions. As tutor to the boy, he fills the archetypal or mythic role of the master craftsman who not only represents the height of artistic skill but also upholds the ethical standards of heroic action. He stands above the other fishermen both in terms of experience and skill, but he is also marked, set apart as the one for whom fishing has become more than just a livelihood:

> "Who is the greatest manager, really, Luque or Mike Gonzalez?"
>
> "I think they are equal."
>
> "And the best fisherman is you."
>
> "No. I know others better."
>
> "*Que va,*" the boy said. "There are many good fishermen and some great ones. But there is only you."

Like the "great DiMaggio" whose father was also a fisherman, Santiago stands alone in the level of his commitment to his craft and in his role as the hero who must test himself against his own frailty. His defense against the randomness of experience is precision. Unlike the other fishermen who let their lines drift with the current, Santiago keeps his "with precision.... It is better to be lucky. But I would rather be exact. Then when luck comes you are ready." The value of such a method is confirmed by the presence of the great fish. Just as Santiago goes "far out" beyond the lesser ambitions of the other fishermen, he finds the great fish not simply because he is a better fisherman but because, in a symbolic sense, he deserves it. His "religious" devotion to the precision of his craft has made it difficult for him to catch ordinary fish, reserving him instead for the extraordinary, mythic creature whose quality equals Santiago's "purity."

Such a deep concern with the quality of Santiago's actions reflects Hemingway's own concern with style, both in writing and in behavior. In much of his work, heroic characters face dangerous and even impossible situations as a test of their devotion to an unwritten code or method of behavior. The more courageous the act, the greater its beauty, clarity, and ethical purity. The same can be said of Hemingway's own prose style, which aims to reproduce the uncluttered grace and control of the bullfighter or the boxer. In fact, Santiago's struggle with the great fish may also reflect Hemingway's own difficulties in writing the story itself. The act of catching the great fish only to lose it in the end may suggest the combination of triumph and failure that comes with attempts at artistic perfection.

This fundamentally religious dimension to Hemingway's thinking appears even more forcefully in the novel's many allusions to Christianity and Christ in particular. The name, Santiago, for instance, is Spanish for Saint James, himself a fisherman, like Christ, the symbolic "fisherman" for souls. Also like Christ, Santiago undergoes a test and a type of "crucifixion" when the sharks attack the marlin: "'*Ay,*' he said aloud. There is no translation for this word and perhaps it is just a noise such as a man might make, involuntarily, feeling the nail go through his hands into the wood." Yet Santiago's suffering does not appear to lead to any sort of traditionally Christian resurrection. At the novel's end he is not reborn, literally or spiritually. Though he admits his fault in going too far out, he is simply tired and empty. He acknowledges his weaknesses but upholds the quality of his actions and his "brotherhood" with the fish: "'Half fish,' he said. 'Fish that you were. I am sorry that I went out too far. I ruined us both. But we have killed many sharks, you and I, and ruined many others. How many did you ever kill, old fish? You do not have that spear on your head for nothing.'"

The combination of triumph, endurance, and loss that *The Old Man and the Sea* offers says a great deal about the Hemingway of 1950s. Shortly after the novel's publication Hemingway was awarded the Pulitzer Prize for fiction in 1953. The following year, he received the Nobel Prize for literature for his life's work, though many acknowledge that the success of *The Old Man and the Sea* played a crucial role in the decision. About this same time, however, Hemingway suffered serious injuries in two separate plane crashes in Africa and was even reported dead by many newspapers. For the next seven years he lived in deteriorating health on his ranch in Ketchum, Idaho. In 1961, his ability as a writer severely compromised by his physical problems, Hemingway killed himself. Whether viewed as an act of courage or surrender, such a choice by the author of *The Old Man and the Sea* was no surprise. As the critic Earl Rovit speculates, "Having chosen to do battle with nothing less than eternity on a day-to-day basis, it may have been his way of complying with the rules insofar as the rules required the unconditional surrender of one of the combatants."

Viewed in light of Hemingway's long-held interest in suicide, *The Old Man and the Sea* might also be the author's way of thinking through the ethical and philosophical problems of taking his own life. In this respect, the fish, already a symbol of death in general, becomes the representation of the writer's self, his identity as a living thing. To wrestle with and conquer this "other" identity suggests a measure of self-control, a way of reaffirming your strength as an individual. To lose such a conquest to the attacks of voracious sharks undermines any certainty the individual might have gained from such a victory. Thus suicide, as a method, suggests the ultimate sort of self-control, a removal to safety beyond the mouths of the sharks, an ironic self-taking that precludes the attacks of others.

It is in the context of such crucial issues that *The Old Man and the Sea* continues to evoke comments and questions from its readers. It presents a fundamentally human problem in graceful form and language, proposing not an answer to the limits of individual existence but a way of facing those limits with dignity and grace.

Source: Carl Davis, in an essay for *Novels for Students*, Gale, 1999.

William J. Handy

In this excerpt the critic examines the novel's characters, particularly Santiago, noting that these portraits are the most powerful elements of the novel.

[In] the portrayal of Santiago in *The Old Man and the Sea* there is no uncertainty of being, no confusion of self and values. The old man is presented from beginning to end as one who has achieved true existence. His response to every situation is the response of a spiritually fulfilled man. The story, then, is not concerned with the familiar Hemingway search for values; rather it is concerned with the depiction of conflicting values.

Throughout five carefully delineated sections of the novel, the center of focus is always on the image of the old man. The first section concerns the old man and the boy; the second, the old man and the sea; the third, the old man and the marlin; the fourth, the old man and the sharks; the fifth section returns to the old man and the boy.

In the opening section Santiago is shown to be something of a pathetic figure. He is old, alone, except for the friendship of a young boy, and now even dependent to a degree upon the charity of others for his subsistence. His situation is symbolized by the condition of his sail which was "patched with flour sacks and, furled, it looked like the flag of permanent defeat." For eighty-four days he had fished without success and had lost his apprentice because the boy's parents had considered him "salao," "the worst form of unlucky."

But almost at once the tone of the writing changes. Only in external appearances is the old man pathetic. Hemingway reverses the attitude toward the old man in a single stroke:

Everything about him was old except his eyes and they were the same color as the sea and were cheerful and undefeated.

The contrast in meaning is evident: To be defeated in the business of fishing is not to be a defeated man. The theme begins and ends the novel; never, after the opening lines, does the reader regard Santiago as defeated. The point is made emphatic in the final conversation between the old man and the boy:

"They beat me, Manolin," he said. "They truly beat me."

"He didn't beat you. Not the fish."

And the old man, whose thoughts have been on a much more profound level of contesting, replies,

"No. Truly. It was afterwards."

The novel's concern, then, is with success and failure, more precisely, with kinds of success and kinds of failure. The central contrast is between the two fundamental levels of achievement: practical success and success in the achievement of one's own being. Similarly the novel posits two kinds of defeat: Failure to compete successfully in a materialistic, opportunistic world where this only is the measure of a man and failure to maintain one's being regardless of external defeat. Thus the real story concerns the meaning, in terms of fundamental human values, of human existence.

Almost at once we become aware that the misleading initial depiction of the old man as a somewhat pathetic figure is the direct result of viewing him only from the standpoint of his recent prolonged ill luck. Had Hemingway continued to present Santiago through the eyes that measure a man's worth merely in terms of his practical success or failure, the novel would necessarily have been a naturalistic one. Santiago's skill, determination, and nobility of spirit would simply have contributed to the greater irony of his finally catching a prize fish only to worsen his lot by losing it.

But the key to all of Hemingway's major characters is never to be found … in merely what happens to them. Rather it is to be found in what they essentially are. This is not to discount the importance in Hemingway of environmental forces, both man-made and cosmic, acting to condition and even to determine human destiny. In fact, those whose values do not follow from the shaping forces of environment are few in number, rarely to be encountered. Santiago is one not determined by environment. And in his age and wisdom and simplicity he constantly reminds himself and the boy, who is learning from him, of the distinction. It is a subtle but vital distinction, one which Santiago never loses sight of. When the boy complains to Santiago about the attitude of his new master, Santiago's response is central to the underlying theme of the novel. The boy points out:

> "He brings our gear himself. He never wants anyone to carry anything."
>
> "We're different," the old man said.

The real story of *The Old Man and the Sea* begins with this distinction. In the first section two indistinct characters are introduced who embody the values of the practical world, the boy's father and the successful fisherman to whom the boy is assigned. In the old man and the boy's discussion of their enforced separation, we see the old man's simple recognition of the problem.

> "Santiago," the boy said to him as they climbed the bank from where the skiff was hauled up. "I could go with you again. We've made some money."
>
> The old man had taught the boy to fish and the boy loved him.
>
> "No," the old man said. "You're with a lucky boat. Stay with them."
>
> "But remember how you went eighty-seven days without fish and then we caught big ones every day for three weeks."
>
> "I remember," the old man said. "I know you did not leave me because you doubted."
>
> "It was papa made me leave. I am a boy and I must obey him."
>
> "I know," the old man said. "It is quite normal."

But the old man's response means something more than that it is quite normal for a boy to obey his parents; it means the acknowledgment that materialism is the central criterion for action and values in the practical world. And the passage also suggests that the boy has been taught something more than how to fish; he has been taught love and respect, values which he now finds conflicting with the practical demands of his parents.

The successful fisherman, the unnamed "he" who is the boy's new master, is, in spite of his success at catching fish, totally without respect in the boy's eyes. When Santiago promises to awaken the boy in time for his day's work with his new master, the boy declares,

> "I do not like for him to waken me. It is as though I were inferior."

The missing quality in the boy's new relationship is evident: The old man wakens the boy in order to share living with him; the impersonal 'him' wakes the boy in order to use him.

Both the old man and the boy are keenly aware of their loss of each other, and both plan ways to regain their former partnership....

The novel's second section presents the full significance of what it means to possess the sense of true existence. Just as the "he" who wakes the boy to use him is blocked by his practical ends from the experience of love so also the "younger fishermen" whose intention is to exploit are prevented from regarding the sea as anything more than "a contestant or a place or even an enemy." Again the distinction is one of individual values:

> He always thought of the sea as *la mar* which is what people call her in Spanish when they love her. Sometimes those who love her say bad things of her but they are always said as though she were a woman. Some of the younger fishermen, those who used buoys as floats for their lines and had motorboats, bought when the shark livers had brought much money, spoke of her as *el mar* which is masculine. They spoke of her as a contestant or a place or even an enemy. But the old man always thought of her as feminine and as something that gave or withheld great favours, and if she did wild or wicked things it was because she could not help them.
>
> The moon affects her as it does a woman, he thought.

The passage is an important one in the development of the novel. Hemingway's theme is clear: Success in the achievement of being carries with it the most valued of man's possessions, the capacity for love. And Santiago's capacity is everywhere evident. Once far out in the Gulf the old man takes his place as a true inhabitant of his true environment. He responds to the sea and the sky and the birds and the fish with the pure response of his achieved being:

> He loved green turtles and hawkbills with their elegance and speed and their great value and he had a friendly contempt for the huge, stupid loggerheads, yellow in their armour-plating, strange in their love-making, and happily eating the Portuguese men-of-war with their eyes shut.

One is reminded of the philosopher's statement, "Being consents to Santiago's being responds to the creatures about him."

> During the night two porpoises came around the boat and he could hear them rolling and blowing. He could tell the difference between the blowing noise the male made and the sighing blow of the female.
>
> "They are good," he said. "They play and make jokes and love one another. They are our brothers like the flying fish."

Nowhere in all of Hemingway's works can be found such a direct treatment of genuine sentiment. One is reminded of Pound's statement that the writer in our time must necessarily be ironic and indirect to be effective. But in the simple image of the old man's identification with the creatures of the sea we have a rare instance of positive values being directly and effectively presented. Yet perhaps it is because there is everywhere present the lurking dangers of the dark water and the old man's realistic awareness of those malevolent forces that his love emerges fully as realistic as the ever-present threats which surround him.

Santiago's struggle with the marlin is the principal subject of the long third section. From the moment he feels the fish touch the bait, his feeling is one of joy for the anticipated contest:

> Then he felt the gentle touch on the line and he was happy.
>
> "It was only his turn," he said. "He'll take it."
>
> He was happy feeling the gentle pulling and then he felt something hard and unbelievably heavy.

Throughout the long contest his attitude toward the fish remains constant:

> "Fish," he said. "I love you and respect you very much. But I will kill you dead before this day ends."
>
> Let us hope so, he thought.

The events of the struggle are dramatic: From the time the fish is hooked, about noon of the first day, until the fish is killed, about noon of the third day, the old man is forced to place his own body between the fish and boat. Fastening the line to the boat would result in the breaking of the line by any sudden lurch or swift motion by the fish. Thus the contest means for Santiago the summoning of his greatest efforts in skill and endurance. He carefully plans his strategy: Constant maximum pressure on the line must be maintained in order to wear down the resistance of the fish and to encourage him to surface in an attempt to dislodge the hook. Santiago knew that once having surfaced, the fish would be unable to dive deep again. Nourishment and rest must be systematically apportioned to his body so that he would not lose the battle prematurely through physical exhaustion. All effort must point to the final struggle which would involve not merely skill and physical endurance but will, his own will in mortal contest with the will of the marlin.

But the real power of the novel's impact does not lie merely in the events of the old man's dramatic struggle. It lies, I believe, in Hemingway's successful creation of a new dimension in dramatic portraiture. In each of the five carefully delineated sections of the novel, the reader's attention is always on Santiago. But in each, Hemingway alters with subtle but masterful strokes his changing image of the old man. In each he modifies the dramatic focus to isolate, intensify, and thereby magnify the novel's central and controlling image, the portrait of Santiago.

In the setting of the simple fishing village we are presented with the aged fisherman, initially pathetic in his meager existence, but admirable in his determination to break his run of bad luck, at once lovable in his touching relationship with a young boy and quaint in his concern for American baseball. But as a solitary figure on the sea, against a backdrop of cosmic nature, the image of the old man takes on new and greater proportions. He becomes a being among the beings of the sea, a human force among the forces of the natural world. But it is at the point at which the old man engages the great marlin that a more profound level of meaning is reached. Hemingway marks the shift with characteristic restraint. The change is simple but unmistakable:

> The boat began to move slowly off toward the North West.

It is here, I think, that the reader becomes aware that he is experiencing the achievement in prose which Hemingway had tried vaguely to explain in *Green Hills of Africa.* He had referred there to "a fourth and fifth dimension that can be gotten." And in speaking of the complexity of such writing, he had declared, "Too many factors must combine to make it possible." He had called such prose "much more difficult than poetry," but "one that can be written, without tricks and without cheating. With nothing that will go bad afterwards." In the amazing combination of simple realism of narrative and complex symbolism of image at once contained in *The Old Man and the Sea,* Hemingway has, I believe, constructed his closest approximation to his goal.

Source: William J. Handy, "A New Dimension for a Hero: Santiago of *The Old Man and the Sea,*" in *Contemporary Novels,* The University of Texas, 1962, pp. 62-69.

Clinton S. Burhans Jr.

In this excerpt the critic explores the various levels of the novel, focusing on individualism and interdependence.

In *Death in the Afternoon,* Hemingway uses an effective metaphor to describe the kind of prose he is trying to write: he explains that "if a writer of prose knows enough about what he is writing about he may omit things that he knows and the reader, if the writer is writing truly enough, will have a feeling of those things as strongly as though the writer had stated them. The dignity of movement of an iceberg is due to only one-eighth of it being above water."

Among all the works of Hemingway which illustrate this metaphor, none, I think, does so more consistently or more thoroughly than the saga of Santiago. Indeed, the critical reception of the novel has emphasized this aspect of it: in particular, Philip Young, Leo Gurko, and Carlos Baker have stressed the qualities of *The Old Man and the Sea* as allegory and parable. Each of these critics is especially concerned with two qualities in Santiago—his epic individualism and the love he feels for the creatures who share with him a world of inescapable violence—though in the main each views these qualities from a different point of the literary compass. Young [in *Hemingway*] regards the novel as essentially classical in nature; Gurko [in *College English*] sees it as reflecting Hemingway's romanticism; and to Baker, [in *Hemingway*] the novel is Christian in context, and the old fisherman is suggestive of Christ.

Such interpretations of *The Old Man and the Sea* are not, of course, contradictory; in fact, they are parallel at many points. All are true, and together they point to both the breadth and depth of the novel's enduring significance and also to its central greatness: like all great works of art it is a mirror wherein every man perceives a personal likeness. Such viewpoints, then, differ only in emphasis and reflect generally similar conclusions—that Santiago represents a noble and tragic individualism revealing what man can do in an indifferent universe which defeats him, and the love he can feel for such a universe and his humility before it.

True as this is, there yet remains, I think, a deeper level of significance, a deeper level upon which the ultimate beauty and the dignity of movement of this brilliant structure fundamentally rest. On this level of significance, Santiago is Harry Morgan alive again and grown old; for what comes to Morgan in a sudden and unexpected revelation as he lies dying is the matrix of the old fisherman's climactic experience. Since 1937, Hemingway has been increasingly concerned with the relationship between individualism and interdependence; and *The Old Man and the Sea* is the culminating expression of this concern in its reflection of Hemingway's mature view of the tragic irony of man's fate: that no abstraction can bring man an awareness and understanding of the solidarity and interdependence without which life is impossible; he must learn it, as it has always been truly learned, through the agony of active and isolated individualism in a universe which dooms such individualism.

Throughout *The Old Man and the Sea,* Santiago is given heroic proportions. He is "a strange old man," still powerful and still wise in all the ways of his trade. After he hooks the great marlin, he fights him with epic skill and endurance, showing "what a man can do and what a man endures." And when the sharks come, he is determined " 'to fight them until I die,' " because he knows that " 'a man is not made for defeat.... A man can be destroyed but not defeated.' "

In searching for and in catching his big fish, Santiago gains a deepened insight into himself and into his relationship to the rest of created life—an insight as pervasive and implicit in the old fisherman's experience as it is sudden and explicit in Harry Morgan's. As he sails far out on the sea, Santiago thinks of it "as feminine and as something that gave or withheld great favours, and if she did wild or wicked things it was because she could not help them." For the bird who rests on his line and for other creatures who share with him such a capricious and violent life, the old man feels friendship and love. And when he sees a flight of wild ducks go over, the old man knows "no man was ever alone on the sea."

Santiago comes to feel his deepest love for the creature that he himself hunts and kills, the great fish which he must catch not alone for physical need but even more for his pride and his profession. The great marlin is unlike the other fish which the old man catches; he is a spiritual more than a physical necessity. He is unlike the other fish, too, in that he is a worthy antagonist for the old man, and during his long ordeal, Santiago comes to pity the marlin and then to respect and to love him. In the end he senses that there can be no victory for either in the equal struggle between them, that the conditions which have brought them together have made them one. And so, though he kills the great fish, the old man has come to love him as his equal and his brother; sharing a life which is a capricious mixture of incredible beauty and deadly violence and in which all creatures are both hunter and hunted, they are bound together in its most primal relationship.

Beyond the heroic individualism of Santiago's struggle with the great fish and his fight against the sharks, however, and beyond the love and the brotherhood which he comes to feel for the noble creature he must kill, there is a further dimension in the old man's experience which gives to these their ultimate significance. For in killing the great marlin and in losing him to the sharks, the old man learns the sin into which men inevitably fall by going far out beyond their depth, beyond their true place in life. In the first night of his struggle with the great fish, the old man begins to feel a loneliness and a sense almost of guilt for the way in which he has caught him; and after he has killed the marlin, he feels no pride of accomplishment, no sense of victory. Rather, he seems to feel almost as though he has betrayed the great fish; "I am only better than him through trickery," he thinks, "and he meant me no harm."

Thus, when the sharks come, it is almost as a thing expected, almost as a punishment which the old man brings upon himself in going far out "beyond all people. Beyond all people in the world" and there hooking and killing the great fish. For the coming of the sharks is not a matter of chance nor a stroke of bad luck; "the shark was not an accident." They are the direct result of the old man's action in killing the fish. He has driven his harpoon deep into the marlin's heart, and the blood of the great fish, welling from his heart, leaves a trail of scent which the first shark follows. He tears huge pieces from the marlin's body, causing more blood to seep into the sea and thus attract other sharks; and in killing the first shark, the old man loses his principal weapon, his harpoon. Thus, in winning his struggle with the marlin and in killing him, the old man sets in motion the sequence of events which take from him the great fish whom he has come to love and with whom he identifies himself completely. And the old man senses an inevitability in the coming of the sharks, a feeling of guilt which deepens into remorse and regret. "I am sorry that I killed the fish," he thinks, and he tells himself that "You did not kill the fish only to keep alive and to sell for food. You killed him for pride and because you are a fisherman."

Earlier, before he had killed the marlin, Santiago had been " 'glad we do not have to try to kill the stars.' " It is enough, he had felt, to have to kill our fellow creatures. Now, with the inevitable sharks attacking, the old man senses that in going far out he has in effect tried "to kill the sun or the moon or the stars." For him it has not been "enough to live on the sea and kill our true brothers"; in his

individualism and his need and his pride, he has gone far out "beyond all people," beyond his true place in a capricious and indifferent world, and has thereby brought not only on himself but also on the great fish the forces of violence and destruction. " 'I shouldn't have gone out so far, fish…,' " he declares. " 'Neither for you nor for me. I'm sorry, fish.' " And when the sharks have torn away half of the great marlin, Santiago speaks again to his brother in the sea: " 'Half-fish,' he said. 'Fish that you were. I am sorry that I went too far out. I ruined us both.' "

The old man's realization of what he has done is reflected in his apologies to the fish, and this realization and its implications are emphasized symbolically throughout the novel. From beginning to end, the theme of solidarity and interdependence pervades the action and provides the structural framework within which the old man's heroic individualism and his love for his fellow creatures appear and function and which gives them their ultimate significance. Having gone eighty-four days without a catch, Santiago has become dependent upon the young boy, Manolin, and upon his other friends in his village. The boy keeps up his confidence and hope, brings him clothes and such necessities as water and soap, and sees that he has fresh bait for his fishing. Martin, the restaurant owner, sends the old man food, and Perico, the wineshop owner, gives him newspapers so that he can read about baseball. All of this the old man accepts gratefully and without shame, knowing that such help is not demeaning. "He was too simple to wonder when he had attained humility. But he knew he had attained it and he knew it was not disgraceful and it carried no loss of true pride."

Santiago refuses the young boy's offer to leave the boat his parents have made him go in and return to his, but soon after he hooks the great marlin he wishes increasingly and often that the boy were with him. And after the sharks come and he wonders if it had been a sin to kill the great fish, the old man thinks that, after all, "everything kills everything else in some way. Fishing kills me exactly as it keeps me alive." But then he remembers that it is not fishing but the love and care of another human being that keeps him alive now; "the boy keeps me alive, he thought. I must not deceive myself too much."

As the sharks tear from him more and more of the great fish and as the boat gets closer to his home, the old man's sense of his relationship to his friends and to the boy deepens: "I cannot be too far out now, he thought. I hope no one has been too worried. There is only the boy to worry, of course. But I am sure he would have confidence. Many of the older fishermen will worry. Many others too, he thought. I live in a good town." In the end, when he awakens in his shack and talks with the boy, he notices "how pleasant it was to have someone to talk to instead of speaking only to himself and to the sea." This time he accepts without any real opposition the boy's insistence on returning to his boat, and he says no more about going far out alone.

This theme of human solidarity and interdependence is reinforced by several symbols. Baseball, which the old man knows well and loves and which he thinks and talks about constantly, is, of course, a highly developed team sport and one that contrasts importantly in this respect with the relatively far more individualistic bullfighting, hunting, and fishing usually found in Hemingway's stories. Although he tells himself that "now is no time to think of baseball," the game is in Santiago's thoughts throughout his ordeal, and he wonders about each day's results in the *Gran Ligas.*

Even more significant is the old man's hero-worship of Joe DiMaggio, the great Yankee outfielder. DiMaggio, like Santiago, was a champion, a master of his craft, and in baseball terms an old one, playing out the last years of his glorious career severely handicapped by the pain of a bone spur in his heel. The image of DiMaggio is a constant source of inspiration to Santiago; in his strained back and his cut and cramped left hand he, too, is an old champion who must endure the handicap of pain; and he tells himself that he "must have confidence and be worthy of the great DiMaggio who does all things perfectly even with the pain of the bone spur in his heel."

But DiMaggio had qualities at least as vital to the Yankees as his courage and individual brilliance. Even during his own time and since then, many men with expert knowledge of baseball have considered other contemporary outfielders—especially Ted Williams of the Boston Red Sox—to be DiMaggio's equal or superior in terms of individual ability and achievement. But few men have ever earned the affection and the renown which DiMaggio received as a "team player"—one who always displayed his individual greatness as part of his team, one to whom the team was always more important than himself. It used to be said of DiMaggio's value as a "team player" that with him in the line-up, even when he was handicapped by the pain

in his heel, the Yankees were two runs ahead when they came out on the field. From Santiago's love of baseball and his evident knowledge of it, it is clear that he would be aware of these qualities in DiMaggio. And when Manolin remarks that there are other men on the New York team, the old man replies: "'Naturally. But he makes the difference.'"

The lions which Santiago dreams about and his description in terms of Christ symbols further suggest solidarity and love and humility as opposed to isolated individualism and pride. So evocative and lovely a symbol is the dream of the lions that it would be foolish if not impossible to attempt its literal definition. Yet it seems significant that the old man dreams not of a single lion, a "king of the beasts," a lion proud and powerful and alone, like the one from which Francis Macomber runs in terror, but of several young lions who come down to a beach in the evening to play together. "He only dreamed of places now and of the lions on the beach. They played like young cats in the dusk and he loved them as he loved the boy." It seems also significant that the old man "no longer dreamed of storms, nor of women, nor of great occurrences, nor of great fish, nor fights, nor contests of strength, nor of his wife"—that is that he no longer dreams of great individualistic deeds like the one which brings violence and destruction on him and on the marlin. Instead, the lions are "the main thing that is left" and they evoke the solidarity and love and peace to which the old man returns after hunting and killing and losing his great fish.

These qualities are further emphasized by the symbolic value of the old fisherman as he carries the mast crosslike up the hill to his shack and as he lies exhausted on his bed. His hands have been terribly wounded in catching the great marlin and in fighting the sharks, and as he lies sleeping "face down on the newspapers with his arms out straight and the palms up" his figure is Christlike and suggests that if the old man has been crucified by the forces of a capricious and violent universe, the meaning of his experience is the humility and love of Christ and the interdependence which they imply.

Such, then, are the qualities which define man's true place in a world of violence and death indifferent to him, and they are the context which gives the experience of the old fisherman its ultimate significance as the reflection of Hemingway's culminating concept of the human condition—his tragic vision of man. For in his understanding that "it is enough to live on the sea and kill our true brothers," the fellow creatures who share life with us and whom he loves, the old man is expressing Hemingway's conviction that despite the tragic necessity of such a condition, man has a place in the world. And in his realization that in going alone and too far out, "beyond all people in the world," he has ruined both himself and also the great fish, the old man reflects Hemingway's feeling that in his individualism and his pride and his need, man inevitably goes beyond his true place in the world and thereby brings violence and destruction on himself and on others. Yet in going out too far and alone, Santiago has found his greatest strength and courage and dignity and nobility and love, and in this he expresses Hemingway's view of the ultimate tragic irony of man's fate: that only through the isolated individualism and the pride which drive him beyond his true place in life does man develop the qualities and the wisdom which teach him the sin of such individualism and pride and which bring him the deepest understanding of himself and of his place in the world. Thus, in accepting his world for what it is and in learning to live in it, Hemingway has achieved a tragic but ennobling vision of man which is in the tradition of Sophocles, Christ, Melville, and Conrad.

It is not enough, then, to point out, as Robert P. Weeks does [in the *University of Kansas Review*], that "from the first eight words of *The Old Man and the Sea* ... we are squarely confronted with a world in which man's isolation is the most insistent truth." True as this is, it is truth which is at the same time paradox, for Santiago is profoundly aware that "no man was ever alone on the sea." Nor is the novel solely what Leo Gurko feels it is—"the culmination of Hemingway's long search for disengagement from the social world and total entry into the natural." If the old man leaves society to go "far out" and "beyond all people in the world," the consciousness of society and of his relationship to it are never for long out of his thoughts; and in the end, of course, he returns to his "good town," where he finds it pleasant "to have someone to talk to instead of speaking only to himself and to the sea." To go no further than Santiago's isolation, therefore, or to treat it, as Weeks does, as a theme in opposition to Hemingway's concern with society is to miss the deepest level of significance both in this novel and in Hemingway's writing generally.

For, surely, as Edgar Johnson has shown, the true direction of Hemingway's thought and art from the beginning and especially since 1937 has been a return to society—not in terms of any particular social or political doctrine, but in the broad sense of human solidarity and interdependence. If he began by making "a separate peace" and by going, like Santiago, "far out" beyond society, like the old man, too, he has come back, through Harry Morgan's "'no man alone,'" Philip Rawlings's and Robert Jordan's "no man is an island," and Santiago's "no man is ever alone on the sea," with a deepened insight into its nature and values and a profound awareness of his relationship to it as an individual [a development found in Hemingway's *"Nobody Ever Dies!"*].

In the process, strangely enough—or perhaps it is not strange at all—he has come back from Frederic Henry's rejection of all abstract values to a reiteration for our time of mankind's oldest and noblest moral principles. As James B. Colvert points out [in *American Literature*], Hemingway is a moralist: heir, like his world, to the destruction by science and empiricism of nineteenth-century value assumptions, he rejects equally these assumptions and the principle underlying them—that intellectual moral abstractions possess independent supersensual existence. Turning from the resulting nihilism, he goes to experience in the actual world of hostility, violence, and destruction to find in the world which destroyed the old values a basis for new ones—and it is precisely here, Colvert suggests, in reflecting the central moral problem of his world, that Hemingway is a significant moralist.

But out of this concern with action and conduct in a naturalistic universe, Hemingway has not evolved new moral values; rather, he has reaffirmed man's oldest ones—courage, love, humility, solidarity, and interdependence. It is their basis which is new—a basis not in supernaturalism or abstraction but hard-won through actual experience in a naturalistic universe which is at best indifferent to man and his values. Hemingway tells us, as E. M. Halliday observes, that "we are part of a universe offering no assurance beyond the grave, and we are to make what we can of life by a pragmatic ethic spun bravely out of man himself in full and steady cognizance that the end is darkness [in *American Literature*]."

Through perfectly realized symbolism and irony, then, Hemingway has beautifully and movingly spun out of an old fisherman's great trial just such a pragmatic ethic and its basis in an essentially tragic vision of man; and in this reaffirmation of man's most cherished values and their reaffirmation in the terms of our time rests the deepest and the enduring significance of *The Old Man and the Sea*.

Source: Clinton S. Burhans Jr. "*The Old Man and the Sea:* Hemingway's Tragic Vision of Man," in *American Literature*, March 1959-January 1960, pp. 446-55.

Sources

Carlos Baker, ed., *Ernest Hemingway: Critiques of Four Major Novels*, Scribner's, 1962, pp. 132-72.

Susan F. Beegel, "Conclusion: The Critical Reputation of Ernest Hemingway," from Scott Donaldson, ed., *The Cambridge Companion to Ernest Hemingway*, Cambridge University Press, 1996, p. 276.

Gerry Brenner and Earl Rovit, "The Structure of the Fiction," in *Ernest Hemingway*, Revised Edition, Twayne, 1986, pp. 62-89.

Gerry Brenner, ed., *The Old Man and the Sea: The Story of a Common Man*, Twayne, 1991.

Kenneth Lynn, *Hemingway*, Simon and Schuster, 1987.

Philip Young, *Ernest Hemingway: A Reconsideration*, Pennsylvania State University Press, 1966, p. 274.

For Further Study

Clifford Burhans, "*The Old Man and the Sea:* Hemingway's Tragic Vision of Man," in *American Literature*, January, 1960, p. 447.

Burhans relates *The Old Man and the Sea* to Hemingway's earlier work and finds it a mature statement of the author's philosophy.

Clinton S. Burhans Jr., "*The Old Man and the Sea:* Hemingway's Tragic Vision of Man," in *Hemingway and His Critics: An International Anthology*, edited by Carlos Baker, Hill and Wang, 1961, pp. 259-68.

The critic describes the novel as Hemingway's "mature view of the tragic irony of man's fate."

Rose Marie Burwell, *Hemingway: The Postwar Years and the Posthumous Novels*, Cambridge University Press, 1996.

Burwell's work has gathered considerable acclaim for its supplanting of the wound theory and notions of code heroes with new readings of the late works.

John Griffith, "Rectitude in Hemingway's Fiction: How Rite Makes Right," in *Hemingway in Our Time*, edited by Richard Astro and Jackson T. Benson, Oregon State University Press, 1974, pp. 159-73.

Griffith discusses the author's expressions of "ritual correctness and moral right."

Kenneth Kinnamon, "Hemingway and Politics," from Scott Donaldson, ed., *The Cambridge Companion to Ernest Hemingway*, Cambridge University Press, 1996, pp. 149-69.

Despite the author's noted individualism and scorn for politicians, Kinnamon makes a strong case for a consistent leftism in Hemingway's basic political philosophy.

Harry Levin, "Observations on the Style of Ernest Hemingway," in *Hemingway: A Collection of Critical Essays*, edited by Robert P. Weeks, Prentice-Hall, 1962, pp. 72-85.

Levin discusses Hemingway's "power of connotation" and "oblique suggestion."

Glen Love, "Revaluing Nature: Towards an Ecological Criticism," in *Old West—New West: Centennial Essays*, ed. Barbara H. Meldrum, University of Idaho Press, 1993.

Love chastises critics for failing to respond to environmental issues and suggests that works like Hemingway's "engage such issues profoundly."

Kathleen Morgan and Luis Losada, "Santiago and *The Old Man and the Sea:* A Homeric Hero," in *The Hemingway Review*, Vol. 12, No. 1, Fall, 1992, pp. 35-51.

The critics discuss Homeric influences in the novel.

Toni Morrison, "Disturbing Nurses and the Kindness of Sharks," in *Playing in the Dark: Whiteness and the Literary Imagination*, Harvard University Press, 1992, pp. 63ff.

The author's multicultural interpretations of Hemingway (though Morrison does not refer specifically to *The Old Man and the Sea*) suggests that multiculturalism may be a source of new insights into Hemingway's work.

George Plimpton, "An Interview with Ernest Hemingway," in *Hemingway and His Critics: An International Anthology*, edited by Carlos Baker, Hill and Wang, 1961, pp. 19-37.

The author discusses his working methods and techniques employed in the novel.

Mark Spilka, *Hemingway's Quarrel with Androgyny*, University of Nebraska Press, 1990, p. 189.

Spilka notes that throughout his life, and contrary to his public persona, Hemingway was very dependent on women, and secretly identified with them.

Bickford Sylvester, "The Cuban Context of *The Old Man and the Sea*," from Scott Donaldson, ed., *The Cambridge Companion to Ernest Hemingway*, Cambridge University Press, 1996, pp. 243-68.

A fascinating essay on how Hemingway's wide knowledge of local customs, history, religion, and baseball informs the substance of his novel.

Joseph Waldmeir, "Confiteor Hominem: Ernest Hemingway's Religion of Man," in *Ernest Hemingway: Five Decades of Criticism*, edited by Linda Welshimer Wagner, Michigan State University Press, 1974, pp. 144-52.

The critic explicates Christian symbolism in the novel.

Wirt Williams, "*The Old Man and the Sea:* The Culmination," in *The Tragic Art of Ernest Hemingway*, Louisiana State University Press, 1981, pp. 172-97.

Williams focuses on the "tragic action" of the novel as a struggle of will.

One Day in the Life of Ivan Denisovich

Aleksandr Solzhenitsyn

1963

Aleksandr Solzhenitsyn secretly wrote *One Day in the Life of Ivan Denisovich* during the Cold War, an era during which the Union of Soviet Socialist Republics (USSR) and the United States, the world's superpowers, fought each other psychologically by stockpiling more and more destructive weapons in preparation for a real and possibly world-ending war. One of the few confidants Solzhenitsyn allowed to read his novel said, "There are now three atomic bombs in the world. The White House has one, the Kremlin the second—and you the third" (quoted in David Burg and George Feifer's *Solzhenitsyn*).

When the Twenty-second Congress met in 1961, Nikita Khrushchev defamed Stalin's tyrannical excesses, explaining that they were due to "the cult of personality," and promised they would never again be allowed. Afterwards Stalin's body was removed from Red Square and cremated. The political fire needed to detonate Solzhenitsyn's bomb had been set.

Solzhenitsyn brought his work to the liberal magazine *Novy Mir*. Its famous editor, Aleksandr Tvardovsky, showed it to Khrushchev, who approved its publication. Every copy of the magazine was sold, and each buyer had a long list of friends anxious to read it as well. A second and last printing followed and was immediately sold out. Western publishers acquired the manuscript, and, since the Soviets did not observe international copyright laws, were free to publish translations without the author's approval. The quality of these translations

varied from good to mediocre. Still, the literary merits of the novel with its unities of time and place—one day in a forced-labor camp—and its common-man protagonist accepting his situation without self-pity were clear. However, because of its content, any literary evaluation would be eclipsed by its political importance in disclosing the dark past of Stalinism. Solzhenitsyn's subsequent works continued this exposure.

Author Biography

Aleksandr Solzhenitsyn was born on December 11, 1918, in Kislovodsk, Russia. His father, an artillery officer in World War I, died in an accident before he was born, and his mother raised him on a secretary's salary. He studied mathematics at the University of Rostov and graduated in 1941, after having married fellow student Natalya Reshetovskaya in 1940. He became an artillery officer in the Soviet Army during World War II and was decorated twice for valor. However, in letters to a friend he criticized the dictator Josef Stalin, referring to him indirectly as "the whiskered one" or "the boss" in Yiddish. This led to his being stripped of his rank and medals and sentenced to a Moscow prison. He spent the last four years of his eight-year sentence at a forced-labor camp in Kazakhstan, where he conceived *One Day in the Life of Ivan Denisovich.* During this period he also underwent a cancer operation and his wife was forced to divorce him. When he was finally freed, he was not allowed to return home, but instead was required to stay in Kazakhstan. He taught mathematics and wrote "underground," meaning he kept his writing a secret and hid the papers he wrote for fear of discovery by the KGB, the secret police.

Solzhenitsyn didn't expect his work to be published; he wrote because he had to tell the truth about life in the Soviet Union. However, in 1962, the political climate changed briefly. Premiere Nikita Khrushchev wanted to denounce his predecessor, Josef Stalin, so Solzhenitsyn exposed his underground book to the editors of *Novy Mir,* a liberal magazine. His novella was published, but it soon led to trouble for Solzhenitsyn. Khrushchev fell and the "Iron Curtain" of Soviet secrets shut tightly again. Solzhenitsyn then had to battle the Soviet Writers Union, an organization whose purpose was to publish only those writers who adhered to Socialist Realism, a style that supports and even glorifies the Communist party line. But the world

Aleksandr Solzhenitsyn

had its glimpse of the real Soviet Union, thanks to Solzhenitsyn, and that vision would not fade; in fact, it would intensify. Although Solzhenitsyn's future writings weren't printed in Russia, they were published in the West. *One Day,* along with *The First Circle* and *Cancer Ward,* earned Solzhenitsyn the Nobel Prize in 1970.

In 1974, the KGB struck and Solzhenitsyn was exiled from Russia while in the process of publishing *The Gulag Archipelago.* He moved to Vermont in the United States with his second wife and children, where he stayed until the political climate changed again. The Soviet Union collapsed, and in 1994 Solzhenitsyn, who some consider to be the conscience of Russia, returned to his homeland.

Plot Summary

"Reveille was sounded, as always, at 5 A.M.... "

So begins another day for Ivan Denisovich in a forced labor camp in Siberia, in a pitch-dark room filled with two hundred men, stacked four bunks high. Usually he gets up and finds one of the numerous ways to earn more food, but this morning he's sick. Not sick enough to know he can't work, but sick enough to wonder if he can. He plans on going to the infirmary, but a mean guard, the thin

Tartar, catches him in his bunk and sentences him to solitary confinement for three days. Fortunately for Ivan, he only has him mop the floor of the warders' office. Inside the warders check the thermometer. If it is lower than forty below zero, the men won't have to work outside. It registers sixteen degrees below, but the men know it isn't accurate and there's no talk of fixing it. Ivan does a poor job of mopping: "If you're working for human beings, then do a real job of it, but if you work for dopes, then you just go through the motions."

The beginning segment of the novel firmly establishes the prison setting, its unspoken laws, and the goal of the prisoners: to survive. Ivan recalls his former gang boss from another camp who told the men that even though jungle law reigns, certain behavior signals a non-survivor: "the guy who licks out bowls, puts his faith in the infirmary, or squeals to the screws." Another firmly established theme is Ivan's health. Because he starts the day not feeling well, he tracks his health for the rest of the day. His psychological health is closely tied to his physical health. For example, today is the day his gang finds out whether they are to be reassigned to build on an unsheltered area. Since fuel is such a valuable commodity, they won't be able to make a fire. This could spell death for many of the men who already live on the edge of life. Their gang boss is bribing the prison bosses to keep them off this assignment. Another undermining element is the bread ration. Ivan overhears that it's been cut today. Survival becomes a little more challenging.

After a breakfast of gruel and boiled fish bones, Ivan goes to the infirmary where Nikolay Semyonovich Vdovushkin, the supposed medic, is writing poetry. Vdovushkin takes Ivan's temperature. It's ninety-nine degrees, not high enough to be admitted, so Ivan is sent off to work. Besides, Vdovushkin's patron, the new doctor, Stepan Grigoryevich, believes work is the best cure. But Ivan knows even a horse can die from overwork.

Ivan returns to the barracks and receives his bread ration, which is short. He eats half, then hides the rest in his mattress, sewing it in, in case the guards check for hidden items. As Ivan's gang stands outside waiting to be searched, Caesar Markovich, the rich intellectual who receives two packages a month, is smoking. Both Ivan and the scrounger Fetyukov watch him, hoping he'll pass the butt their way. Ivan waits with a semblance of self-control while Fetyukov hovers around like a dog. Caesar gives the butt to Ivan. This is another rule of prison survival: don't lose your dignity. Ivan

goes to get his identification tag, S-984, repainted on his cap, chest, knee, and back, and the importance of dignity becomes clearer. The men's identities have been reduced to a letter and some numbers.

The feared Lieutenant Volkovoy supervises the frisk—despite the freezing cold—for nonregulation clothing or food, which might indicate an escape attempt. Captain Buynovsky, a newcomer, is caught with a jersey. He protests that this procedure violates Soviet law and is given ten days in solitary confinement. This means a hot meal only once every three days and a cut in bread rations and could easily mean death.

> "The big, red sun,... was slanting through the wires of the gate ... "

As the gang heads to their old work place, thanks to the gang boss bribing their way out of the new and dreaded site, Ivan thinks of his wife and the *kolkhoz* or collective farm they lived on. She wants him to come back and paint carpets since most of the farmers are finding better incomes outside the farm. But, of course, he can't go home. He has been exiled from home.

When the gang arrives at the site to wait for their assignment, Ivan has a chance to think and observe his fellow gang members. He wonders how Aloysha the Baptist can survive on only the prison rations: religious faith is barely tolerated in the atheist Soviet Union. He likes the minorities and the cultural qualities they bring. He likes the deaf prisoner, Senka Klevshin, who has already survived Buchenwald as a prisoner of World War II. Because of Article 58 of the penal code, Klevshin was given a ten-year sentence for "allowing" himself to become a prisoner of war and, therefore, spying for the enemy. Finally the men's assignments come and the work begins.

Ivan is to work with another Ivan, the Latvian. Since the quantity of work they do is tied to their food rations, there is sufficient motivation. For most of the men, losing themselves in work is their best escape. Still, the mind can wander. Ivan recalls how he came to the camps. Like Senka Klevshin, he too was captured by the Germans, but he escaped to rejoin his regiment, violating Article 58. Only those who consistently won battles or who died evaded Article 58.

The men are so busy working that they are late for their lunch of groats. Their portions are always reduced by other prisoners, especially those in the kitchen. However, the gang boss and his assistant always get double portions. The clever Ivan shows

Pavlo, the assistant boss, two extra portions he's managed to steal. Pavlo lets Ivan have one and shows his humanity by giving the Captain the other.

Ivan overhears a debate about art between Caesar and prisoner K-123. Caesar praises the Eisenstein film *Ivan the Terrible* for its artistic merits while K-123 criticizes any artist who bends himself to the political regime, in this case, Stalin's. All art is a sore point in the Soviet Union, where freedom is not a value. The prime value is following the Communist party line.

Before the men return to work, they listen to Tyurin tell his story of imprisonment. His father was a *kulak* who resisted the collective farms. Because of this Tyurin was dishonorably discharged from the army and eventually arrested. Before his arrest, he took his younger brother to a street gang and asked them to show him how to survive. Even outside prison, the common Soviet citizen is forced to live like a criminal.

Tyurin tells the men to begin work and the most exhilarating part of the day takes place. Ivan lays bricks and is proud of the results. The men are late to return and have to be subjected to several counts, since the guards themselves could be imprisoned if they lost a man. The missing man is finally discovered, a Moldavian who fell asleep at his worksite. Although he is remorseful, he is sent to solitary confinement.

"The moon was really shining bright."

The rest of Ivan's day consists of earning more food by holding a place in the package line for Caesar, fighting his way past the orderly Clubfoot to get to his dinner, and buying tobacco with money he has made from odd jobs. He even gets Caesar's extra bread ration. Before roll call, Ivan feels pity for Fetyukov, who was beaten up for scrounging. He knows Fetyukov won't survive. He also feels sorry for Caesar, who might have most of the food from his package stolen, so he shows him how to hide it. The men are counted again before lights out. Caesar gives Ivan some of his goodies as thanks and Ivan shares with Aloysha. In bed Ivan hears Aloysha thank God and Ivan reviews his day, concluding that it was an unusually good one.

Characters

Alyoshka

Ivan's bunk mate, he is known by his religion. He represents the spiritual element that survives despite the atheism that is a cornerstone of Communism, in which the State is the only religion. He reads his Bible and is protected by Ivan, who respects his faith. In fact, Ivan wonders how Alyoshka can survive without extra rations and shares his cookie from Caesar with him.

The Baptist

See Alyoshka

Big Ivan

A tall, thin guard, he is the most easygoing of the lot.

Buynovsky

One of Ivan's bunk mates.

Captain Buynovsky

In the Russian navy, he was once a liaison officer on a British ship, since the British and Russians were allies during World War II. But after receiving a thank-you gift from a British officer for his good service, he was sentenced to twenty-five years of hard labor. Throughout the novel he changes from a die-hard military man to a clever inmate. When Buynovsky is sentenced to face ten days in solitary confinement for insubordination, Ivan wonders whether he will survive.

Clubfoot

As his name implies, he is handicapped, but uses his disability to secure a good job. He's as hardboiled as anyone can be and even earns enough money to pay an assistant.

Der

The foreman at the construction site, he treats his fellow prisoners badly, but Ivan's gang sticks together against him to keep him in check.

Estonians

These two seem like brothers although they first met in camp; both are tall, fair, and thin and sleep in the same bunk. One of the two, called Eino, fills Ivan's request for tobacco after first consulting with his best friend.

Fetyukov

A scavenger whom Ivan dislikes. He used to be a big shot in an office, but in prison he is beaten up for scrounging. In the end Ivan feels sorry for him.

Tom Courtenay as Ivan Denisovich brings bowls of gruel to his fellow prisoners in the motion picture One Day in the Life of Ivan Denisovich.

Gopchik

Only sixteen years old, he is enthusiastic and alert. Ivan thinks he will go far in the camps. Ivan lost his own son and seems to have fatherly feelings for Gopchik.

Stepan Grigoryevich

Although new, he is already known as a loudmouth, know-it-all doctor who believes work is the best cure for illness.

Ivan Kilgas

A Latvian and former bricklayer, he receives two packages a month, speaks Russian like a native, and jokes most of the time. He works well with Ivan, who realizes he has more in common with the Latvian than with his own family.

Senka Klevshin

A little deaf, the former Buchenwald inmate says if you fussed there, you were finished. Ivan works with him and respects him as a fellow survivor.

Kuzyomin

An old gang boss of Ivan's, he tells his men that the law of the jungle prevails in prison: the only way to survive is to not lick your bowl clean, not count on the infirmary, and not betray or "squeal on" other prisoners. Ivan took his advice to heart and never forgot it.

Caesar Markovich

Caesar was a cinematographer before his imprisonment. A rich intellectual, he receives packages that keep him well fed, yet he shares his food. Art is his god.

Moldavian

He falls asleep in a warm corner during the work day and fails to turn up for the count. When finally discovered, he is extremely remorseful but is nevertheless taken to solitary confinement, where rations are eight ounces of bread a day and a hot meal every third day. Shukhov says that after ten days in solitary, a man would be so weakened that he would have a difficult time getting back on his feet again.

Panteleyev

The man missing from the gang: no one knows if he is sick or a squealer.

Pavlo

The assistant gang boss from West Ukrainia, which was under Poland until after World War II and where the people are still polite, unlike the typical Soviet.

Shkuropatenko

Of beanpole physique, he is a prisoner paid to guard prefabricated panels against the prisoners pilfering them.

Ivan Denisovich Shukhov

The main character, Ivan is a peasant who was drafted during World War II. He managed to escape a German prison camp and return to Russia. For this he was imprisoned, since Soviet law considered any escapee a spy for the Germans. Although Ivan was innocent he thought it wiser to plead guilty, knowing that if he pleaded innocent, he'd be shot, but if he pleaded guilty, he'd go to prison. Ivan is forty years old, balding, and missing half his teeth. Although he'll do everything he can to survive, he maintains a strict personal code. For example, he will never take or give a bribe, betray others, or lick his bowl clean. He represents the common man in the Soviet Union, an inspiring Russian survivor.

Thin Tartar

Called by his nationality, he is one of the guards, thin and hairless, who threatens to send Ivan to solitary confinement but then relents and sends him to mop the warders' office. The cold doesn't seem to bother him.

Tyurin

On his second sentence, this gang boss does everything he can to take care of the gang. Ivan knew him at another camp but wasn't in his gang. Of all the men in the camp, Tyurin is the one man Ivan would never cheat; the gang boss is crucial to survival.

Nikolay Semyonovich Vdovushkin

Technically a medic, he spends the day writing poetry, thanks to Dr. Grigoryevich, his patron. The Russian love for poetry is evident here.

Lieutenant Volkovoy

A much-feared disciplinary officer with a reputation for using a whip. His name is derived from "wolf."

Media Adaptations

- *One Word of Truth* in videocassette form is a documentary narrated by Tom Courtney and produced by Anglo-Nordic Productions that recreates Solzhenitsyn's Nobel Prize speech.

- Caspar Wrede filmed *One Day in the Life of Ivan Denisovich,* starring Tom Courtney.

- Alexander Ford adapted *The First Circle,* considered by many the most autobiographical of Solzhenitsyn's novels, for film in 1973.

Y-81

An old prisoner who has survived with his dignity intact, he is Ivan's hero.

Themes

Man versus Society

Ivan represents the common man; the immediate society he lives in is prison. Every day he struggles to survive physically and psychologically. The prison supplies him with the bare necessities: food, shelter, and a job. His choices are few, but the one great choice is his: to live or to die. His choice to survive impacts the greater society: man can go on despite whatever cruelties society imposes.

The Truth versus the Lie

Ivan was imprisoned in the forced labor camp for the crime of high treason. During World War II, the Germans captured a great many Soviet soldiers. Ivan was one. However, he escaped and returned to his own lines. The Soviets believed he lied about escaping and was really spying for the Germans. Ivan realized if he told the truth, he'd be shot, but if he lied and said he was a spy, he'd be sent to prison. When one lie is stacked upon another, the light of truth is obscured. This is what happened under the tyranny of Josef Stalin, the So-

Topics for Further Study

- During the 1940s and '50s, a practice called "blacklisting" took effect in the film industry in Hollywood. Any writer, director, or actor who had previously belonged to the Communist party could not find work. Investigate this reactionary stage of American history and examine it from all sides: the government prosecutors, the accused, the informants, and the sympathizers.

- The word "Siberia" conjures up a vision of an endless snowcovered plain and cold blue sky. Make a map of the camp Solzhenitsyn describes and plan an escape. Then, using a real map, choose a place in Siberia where the camp might have been located and plan an escape route out of the former USSR to freedom.

- Compare and contrast capitalism and communism. Remember that capitalism needs a free-market society in order to operate. How does each philosophy regard man, how does it effect the resulting culture, and what are the economic pluses and minuses of each?

- Find copies of *One Day in the Life of Ivan Denisovich* by different translators and compare a section of text that could suggest subtle but slightly different interpretations. Discuss and demonstrate the problems of studying literature in translation.

---

viet leader—the vast majority of the Soviet people became accomplices to lies.

Life versus Death

Ivan chose living with lies over dying for truth. In his case, was the truth worth dying for or was surviving the better choice? What is the value of life and the value of the life Ivan is living? When is death of more value?

Good versus Evil

Every choice Ivan makes in his day is a moral one and is motivated by survival. He commits himself to his own survival by choosing to conserve his energy on a job that he doesn't want to do (mopping the floor for the inhuman warders) or to expand his energy on a job that gives him pleasure (bricklaying with the gang). He chooses who among the others should survive by selecting those who will receive his extra cookie or cigarette butt. His decision is always for the needy (for example, Alyoshka) instead of the greedy (Fetyukov).

The Individual versus the Unjust Law

In ancient Greece, Sophocles asked in his play *Antigone,* how does an individual deal with an unjust law? Should it be obeyed or flouted? To flout it one must be dedicated to a higher moral truth and one must be courageous. But in Ivan's world, this question is broader: how does an individual deal with an unjust system? Ivan gives his answer: survive it.

Style

On Translations

Most critics feel the best of the original translations of *One Day in the Life of Ivan Denisovich* is the Bantam book version. According to the translators, Max Haywood and Ronald Hingley, Solzhenitsyn's novella is written in the slang from the concentration camp and in the vocabulary of the Russian peasant. To express this in English, they have used American slang, such as "can" and "cooler" for solitary confinement, and unpolished diction in expressions like "Let em through" and "Get outa the way." Russian obscenities, never before printed in the Soviet Union, were for the most part translated into their English equivalents.

The Novella

A novella is longer than a short story but shorter than a traditional novel. In *One Day,* Solzhenitsyn presents his tale like a long short story. There are no chapters, only a flowing narrative. The visual breaks are the spacings signaling a change of place or a change of time. This form also suggests that the reader can finish the work in one sitting to get its full impact.

Socialist Realism

Literature under the Communists had to meet the standards of Socialist Realism; this meant not criticizing the Communist party. Therefore, content was more important than style, and since the party believed that religion was the "opiate of the peo-

Holding pictures of her parents, who were killed in Stalin's camps, a Russian woman joins demonstrators in observation of the Day of Political Prisoners (October 30) in Moscow.

ple," that capitalism was evil, and that socialism was superior to all other political systems, content was severely limited. Writings resulted in contradictions, hypocracies, and lies: "victory without defeat, radical social change without injustice, and complete centralization of power without autocracy," according to James Curtis in *Solzhenitsyn's Traditional Imagination.*

Point of View

Solzhenitsyn uses the third person, limited omniscient narrator. This means the story is told by a narrator who refers to all the characters as he, she, or they and describes the thoughts and feelings of the main character, in this case, Ivan. Therefore, the narrator is omniscient or all-knowing with regard to Ivan. However, he is limited with regard to the other characters who are only described externally, not internally. The third person allows the narrator to make general comments outside of the main character's mind. For example: "But now all at once something happened in the column, like a wave going through it…. The fellows in the back—that's where Shukhov was—had to run now … "

Chekhovian Technique

Christopher Moody in *Solzhenitsyn* points out that Solzhenitsyn uses Chekhov's technique of

"evoking a whole impression by means of a few … emotionally neutral" words. For example, from the very beginning of the book, the cold is mentioned as is the value of footwear, so by the time Ivan leaves with his gang for the outside and "the snow creaked under their boots," the complete setting of the pre-dawn, freezing cold in a stark, snowflattened landscape comes alive. The creaking is the warning sound that less than an inch of boot separates flesh from ice, and therefore life from death..

Russian Terms

There are a few terms used in the novella that are strictly Russian. *Zek* refers to a man serving in a forced-labor camp or one who has already served. The "free workers" are former zeks who have nowhere to go, so they work for the camp. *Kolkhozniks* are collective farmers and a *kolkhoz* is a collective farm. *Kulaks* are displaced farmers who rejected the collective farms.

Historical Context

Censorship in Russian Literature

The history of Russian literature has been one of censorship, first under the czars and then under

Compare & Contrast

- **1914:** Russia enters World War I against Germany and Austria-Hungary, enduring several crushing defeats.

- **1917:** The Russian Revolution refers to two revolutions. In March, starving rioters joined by the army overthrow the Romanov czars who ruled Russia for over three hundred years. In October, a second revolution led by Lenin put the Bolsheviks in power.

- **1918-20:** Russia pulls out of World War I.

- **1932-34:** Famine results from agricultural collectivization (communal farming); the government conceals this from the outside world so that no international aid can come to alleviate the situation. Cannibalism is rampant in the countryside and starving villagers attack nearby villages for food. Roughly 10 to 15 million people perish in the famine and the epidemics that follow.

- **1929-38:** Stalin purges the party of his enemies and supposed enemies; by 1937, he begins to purge the Red Army, resulting in millions of citizens being arrested and sentenced to the camps. (Anyone arrested has their family, friends and associates arrested; this accounts for every Soviet citizen having some personal involvement with the camps); by 1938 the Red Army, having lost its trained officers, is considerably weakened.

- **1941:** Stalin is considered responsible for the demoralization and decimation of the Red Army. Officers are shot if they refuse to lead impossible missions and soldiers who were captured by the German enemy and escaped are punished. Their families feel the consequences also. The Red Army is guessed to have lost 7 to 10 million men in the course of World War II according to J.N. Westwood in *Russia: 1917-1964.*

- **1942:** In the Battle of Stalingrad the Russians valiantly defeat the Germans, resulting in a turning point of World War II.

- **1945:** World War II ends and the Soviets begin accumulating 6 satellite countries of Eastern Europe.

- **1953:** Stalin dies.

- **1922-91:** The Union of Soviet Socialist Republics is created and becomes the most powerful Communist nation on earth. The USSR finally collapses, the satellite countries Russia dominated claim their independence, and Russia, too, becomes an independent nation again.

---

the Soviets. In the 19th century, the poet Pushkin, the novelists Turgenev, Tolstoy and Dostoyevski, and the dramatists Gogol and Chekhov, to name a few, elevated Russian literature to world renown, but these writers labored under the threat of exile, imprisonment, or death if their works were deemed politically unacceptable. Pushkin was exiled for a time. Dostoyevski had a crueler experience: he was condemned to the firing squad before the czar's messenger brought the order to commute the execution at the very last minute. In the 20th century, under the Soviets, censorship seemed even more severe and difficult to contain under the explosive advances of mass communication. But the Soviets felt that if communism wasn't the practical solution to all social ills, they would not allow that failing to come to the attention of the outside world. Soviet writers were forbidden to criticize the system; if they dared, they were silenced. A great writer like Bulgakov had his works banned, while the Nobel prize-winning Pasternak had his works smuggled out of the country to be published in the West.

The Penal Camps

One hundred years after Dostoyevski wrote *Notes from the House of the Dead* about his experiences in a penal camp, Solzhenitsyn wrote *One*

Day in the Life of Ivan Denisovich. According to critic Christopher Moody in *Solzhenitsyn,* after one hundred years the penal camps had become even more inhumane. In Dostoyevski's time, prisoners received sufficient food, enough time to devote to private activities, the opportunity to socialize with the nearby population, and the "certain knowledge of freedom at the end of their term." Solzhenitsyn's prisoners had no such guarantee. In fact, once free, they were exiled from their home towns.

Josef Stalin

The question arises: what happened in those hundred years to worsen things to such an inhumane degree? In a word, Stalin. Josef Stalin also spent time in these camps, but he was a man dedicated to political ideology. He clawed his way to the position of dictator over the bodies of his competitors, ruthlessly formed the Soviet Union into a world power, and earned the reputation of being perhaps the greatest mass murderer in Western civilization. Although Solzhenitsyn refers only once to Stalin in his novella, the ruler's demonic spirit permeates the camp. The paranoid laws that condemned so many of the men to camp were the same laws that condemned any real freedom outside of it.

Nikita Khrushchev

In 1950, Nikita Khrushchev, then premier of the USSR, wanted to de-Stalinize the Communist Party. He attributed the fact that Josef Stalin had destroyed more Soviet people than those who died in all Russian wars combined and yet retained his incredible hold over the Soviet people to "the cult of personality." Khrushchev wanted to put an end to Stalin's influence beyond the grave in order to strengthen his own power, and Solzhenitsyn's story seemed the perfect eulogy. Thanks to Solzhenitsyn's courage and continuing novels, the truth about Stalin was destined to live.

Critical Overview

Although Solzhenitsyn's work deals with politics from *One Day in the Life of Ivan Denisovich* to *The Gulag Archipelago,* perhaps what has been most detrimental to his reputation is his political statements. After being expelled from the Soviet Union and seeking refuge in Europe and the United States, he constantly criticized the West. Invited to give the commencement speech at Harvard Uni-

versity, Solzhenitsyn attracted one of the largest crowds in Harvard's history and was televised nationally. In his address, entitled "The World Split Apart," he called for unification, but his remarks seemed to create new splits and his speech was highly criticized.

Solzhenitsyn is a mathematician and physicist by training and a writer by profession. When asked to speak, however, he inevitably poses questions on politics and philosophy and freely gives his own answers. Although many of his criticisms are valid, he has a xenophobic vision of Russia, seeing it as morally superior to the West because Russia skipped the stage of competitive capitalism on her way to cooperative socialism. Many critics also believe that he misunderstands the inherent duality of western freedom, that it results in bad choices as well as good ones. Michael Scammell in *Solzhenitsyn: A Biography* quotes Solzhenitsyn as saying, "I cannot be regarded in political terms. A writer's view differs in kind from that of the politician or the philosopher." Yet, as Scammell concludes, Solzhenitsyn chooses not to take the stance of the writer, but instead embraces that of the political philosopher.

Solzhenitsyn's moral integrity remains unquestioned, his literary skills are laudable even in poor translations, and he is often forgiven much politicizing because he comes from the literary tradition of socialist realism. While his intellectual sweep is not generally considered all-encompassing, most critics do not expect it to be.

Criticism

Chloe Bolan

Bolan is an adjunct faculty member of Columbia College of Missouri extensions, a published writer of essays, short stories, and poems, and a playwright. In the following essay, she examines Ivan as the protagonist in One Day in the Life of Ivan Denisovich *and how this character affects setting, symbol, and theme in a literary, political, and personal way.*

When Aleksandr Solzhenitsyn wrote his testament to truth, *One Day in the Life of Ivan Denisovich,* he based it on his own experience, but he chose for a protagonist a Russian peasant. This choice of the common man, whose code of prison ethics is a blueprint for survival, affects the setting,

What Do I Read Next?

- Fyodor Dostoyevsky's *Notes from the House of the Dead,* written one hundred years prior to Solzhenitsyn's novella, provides a brilliant insight into the penal camps of the 19th century.

- *Man's Search for Meaning* by Viktor E. Frankl is a profoundly moving work on the Nazi concentration camps, shedding light on the psychological impact of camp life.

- *Alexander Solzhenitsyn: Stories and Prose Poems,* translated by Michael Glenny, contains the famous "Matryona's House" and "An Incident at Krechetovka Station" plus lesser-known pieces.

- In *Cancer Ward,* Solzhenitsyn used him own experience with cancer to write a polyphonic novel, that is, a novel with several main characters instead of just one.

- Solzhenitsyn's *The First Circle* is considered the most autobiographical of his novels and takes place in a "sharashka," a prison for scientists to do research while serving their sentences. The title is based on Dante's first circle of hell in *The Inferno.*

- *Stalin: The History of a Dictator* by H. Montgomery Hyde is a clearly written, suspenseful and Western view of that dictator's political and moral strengths and weaknesses.

- For a visceral understanding of Russia's pain and triumph in the Second World War, *Russia at War: 1941-45* by Vladimir Karpov has large, black and white photographs of battles and their aftermath.

- An unusual book because of its subject matter, *A Dance with Death: Soviet Airwomen in World War II* by Anne Noggle provides biographical essays and photographs of the first women in the world to fly combat missions.

- *A History of Soviet Russia* by Adam B. Ulam begins with the Bolsheviks and their selfless determination to free the masses and ends with *detente,* the peaceful coexistence of the USSR and the US in the 1970s.

---

symbol, and theme in a literary, political, and personal way.

In a literary and even political way, Ivan Denisovich Shukhov as the protagonist represents Russia more than any other type; his peasant wisdom goes unquestioned and his motive to survive needs no explanation. Hasn't the shrewd peasant existed for hundreds of years and endured innumerable, unbearable hardships? If Aloysha the Baptist were the protagonist, his every motive would have to be double-checked against religious restrictions; if Caesar were the protagonist, an artist's eye would color the perspective; if any of the non-Russians were protagonists, a cultural bias would be seen; a man of status like the Captain would be testing his military code against survival, and the gang leader or his assistant would constantly be looking out for the good of the gang. If Solzhenitsyn had based the protagonist on himself,

an intellectual who wrote poetry in the camps, Shukhov would be escaping to his mind instead of wrestling with his hostile environment.

Shukhov is a shrewd and daring peasant; whenever he breaks the rules—bringing in the steel wedge, hiding a tool—he knows not to get caught. So why wouldn't a man like this try to escape? Escape is never mentioned, but enough description makes escape from Siberia, the Devil's Island of the north, seem ludicrous. Surrounding the prison complex is a treeless plain of snow and ice, of darkness without warmth and a noonday sun that makes a zek sweat and then leaves him wet and cold. Siberia is a place to escape *from.* Although Shukhov finds his greatest joy bricklaying in the subzero weather, nightfall necessarily ends it as does his need for food. In fact, the endless tundra makes prison, where hunger and cold vie with each other for the bodies and souls of the zeks, a place

Joseph Stalin himself was exiled to Siberia several times between 1904 to 1917 for political activity as a Bolshevik. This photo, taken in 1920, shows a firing squad executing Bolsheviks.

Shukhov calls home. At least he's free from the biting wind and can grab a few minutes of free time.

The other setting, prison, reveals a variety of Soviet personalities, both Russian and satellite ethnicities, and, most importantly, the code Shukhov needs to survive. Because he's a hero without an attitude, the sadistic guards or warders swirling around him and the prisoners scrambling to survive physically and psychologically, from scrounger to gang leader to goner, are seen unblinkingly. So, too, is Shukhov. His only task is to survive and he's picked up all the tricks, from not losing his dignity by licking his bowl but using his crust to clean it, to earning an extra bowl of mush by holding another prisoner's place in the pick-up line for packages. Plotting for scraps of food and clothing or a few drags off someone else's cigarette fill up his day. Emotionally he can survive, too. He tells his family not to send him food, knowing they have none to spare, and he doesn't delude himself with sweet dreams of life after prison. First, he has no guarantee his prison sentence won't be extended; second, he's forbidden to go back to his home as all prisoners are automatically exiled from their hometown; third, his wife wrote him about the latest craze of painting carpets to support their meager earnings from the collective farm, but this

doesn't inspire him. In fact, the most likely outcome for Shukhov is becoming a "free worker," if he lives to get out.

Shukhov the peasant is symbolic of Russia; he resonates through her literature. In the 19th century, Turgenev humanized the serf, Tolstoy glorified him, and Chekhov laughed with him. In the 20th century, Solzhenitsyn politicizes him, suggesting he resonates through Russian history. Under the czars, his ancestors were slaves to the land; under the communists, he's a prisoner to the system. Shukhov symbolizes a man without hope— for a better day, a better life, an afterlife. Yet, he dares to go on. This is survival down to the marrow.

As in any work of art, many themes abound, but the one unfinished theme is reinforced by Shukhov as the protagonist. For there is no escape from the primary question *One Day in the Life of Ivan Denisovich* raises: how could the camps, filled with so many of the unjustly accused, exist? The answer falls into the political realm of *Stalinism*. Aleksandr Solzhenitsyn mentions Stalin only once, on an editorial recommendation; originally he was never mentioned—the reader was to supply his name. Still, the result is the same: the name Stalin is as much a part of the novel as the name Shukhov.

Now the question becomes clearer: how could the Soviet people allow Josef Stalin, possibly the greatest mass murderer in western civilization, to govern them?

The answer is found in Russian history with its clashes of political ideologies and its own evolution of Marxism. Before the fanatical Communists were the insular czars, the Romanoffs, unaccountable to their people for over 300 years. Although many peasant rebellions were put down by the czar's army, the system of serfdom kept four-fifths of the people enslaved, the exclusive property of their masters. Finally in 1861, the serfs were freed, but in the largest country on earth, they were not allowed to own land individually. From this the commune slowly evolved and decisions were made communally, drowning out individual voices and preparing the way for socialism.

Still, the starving peasants, this time joined by the army, finally had a successful revolution, the revolution of March, 1917. The October revolution in that same year, the one led by the Bolsheviks, is the famous one, but the March revolution was truly the voice of the most abused groups in Russia—her serfs and her soldiers. The Bolsheviks saw their opportunity to use the peasants, soon to be called workers, in the future for Communism just as the czars had used them in the past for the monarchy. The czars had claimed to be under God; the atheistic Bolsheviks had no such restrictions.

Marxism, the Bolshevik philosophy, proposes equality for all and an end of institutions including the withering away of the state; it is utopian in that it seeks an ideal solution to economic and political problems. However, revolutionaries like Lenin and Stalin were cold-blooded men who believed the ruthless attainment of putting their ideas in motion was justified by any evil means. A vicious civil war followed the revolution and Russia had to leave the First World War to the rest of Europe until she stabilized herself politically. The Bolsheviks renamed themselves Communists and Soviet history began.

When Lenin died, Stalin eventually replaced him and sought to radicalize the Soviet state by collectivization of agriculture, which was the basis of the economy, and industry, which was barely represented. His first five-year plan, which was based on expropriating food from the farm workers, failed, and the resulting famine was so invasive that cannibalism was common. Stalin passed a law that anyone stealing five ears of corn could be imprisoned for ten years or shot to death. From the re-

formist ideals of Marxism came a tyrant's reign of terror.

Unchecked because of his control of government, the army, and the secret police, Stalin exiled, jailed, or murdered anyone he perceived as a potential threat to his power. But he didn't stop at the offending person; he punished their family, friends, and acquaintances. To understand the rationale of a dictator, Lord Acton phrased it best: "Power corrupts and absolute power corrupts absolutely." To understand the reactions of the people, Solzhenitsyn shows it best: they're too busy trying to survive and too terrified to do much else.

Not until de-Stalinization in the 1960s was the bubble of truth, words in a magazine, *One Day in the Life of Ivan Denisovich,* allowed to rise into the forbidden air of Soviet lies. Behind the peasant descendant of serfs, the protagonist Ivan Denisovich, emerges the real giant-slayer. For Shukhov is the fiction of Solzhenitsyn, and it is Solzhenitsyn, former zek, who exposes Stalin in the most political, yet personal, theme of the novel.

Source: Chloe Bolan, in an essay for *Novels for Students,* Gale, 1999.

Alfred Cismaru

In the essay below, Cismaru reflects on the important role food plays in not only the physical but also the psychological survival of prisoners in the gulag.

The year 1983 marks the twentieth anniversary of Alexander Solzhenitsyn's *One Day in the Life of Ivan Denisovich.* Although this important work has benefited from numerous critical comments abroad, in this country there have been only cursory exegeses. With the hindsight of two decades it may be profitable to look at it again. Because the theme of physical survival is at the core of *One Day in the Life of Ivan Denisovich,* and because, so far, its importance has been eclipsed by critics in favor of that of spiritual victory, this essay will emphasize Solzhenitsyn's concern with food collection, ingestion, digestion, and with body preservation in general.

Those who know Solzhenitsyn are aware of the fact that he is a hearty eater, a gourmet and perhaps even a gourmand. But this is not the main reason for his preoccupation with food as a requirement for survival. Men who have experienced the gulag, or indeed any imposed confinement know that more than the rigors of climate, more than the forced marches and forced labor and the beatings and the spiritual deprivations, the incarcerated notes first and foremost the quasi-absence of food and the poor quality of that which is available. One need not go so far as Freud and proclaim that the mouth is the sexual organ *par excellence,* that eating is essentially a sexual act, in order to acquiesce in the centrality of food ingestion in man's daily routine. Moreover, no sort of spiritual well-being or preservation is possible for long on a starvation diet. It is this truism, more than Solzhenitsyn's own culinary concerns, that made him devote many a passage in *One Day in the Life of Ivan Denisovich* to the art of eating in prison.

Kuzyomin, the brigade foreman in the camp, a person with a twelve-year experience in the *modus vivendi* required by the gulag, has a formula for survival, one which he shares liberally with the others: "Here, fellows, *taiga* is the law." A Russian word meaning "virgin Siberian forest," *taiga* implies the law of the beasts of the jungle, the law that recognizes that only the fittest survive, and that fitness is the result of adequate food intake. No wonder, then, that the problems of hunger and diet are introduced as soon as the novel begins, in the description of the so-called breakfast shoved in front of the prisoners.

Ivan Denisovich Shukhov, with the accumulated tact of eight years of incarceration, looks upon eating as an artful endeavor whose gestures are meticulously performed, as befits the discipline of the artist:

> The only good thing about camp gruel was it was usually hot, but what Shukhov had was now quite cold. Even so, he ate it slow and careful like he always did. Mustn't hurry now, even if the roof caught fire....
>
> The fish was mostly bones. The flesh was boiled off except for bits on the tails and the heads. Not leaving a single scale or speck of flesh on the skeleton, Shukhov crunched and sucked the bones and spit them out on the table. He didn't leave anything—not even the gills or the tail. He ate the eyes too when they were still in place.

Though Shukhov must be a beast, Solzhenitsyn adds, "But when they 'the eyes' come off and were floating around in the bowl on their own he didn't eat them." This line asserts not so much a minimal awareness of the fact that even in the jungle there are traces of morality and ethics, as it points to the necessity that ingestion must maintain certain standards which would not conflict with proper digestion. Should nausea and vomiting result from certain unappetizing foods, or from their unappetizing presentation, the calories taken in

would be lost, at least partially. In his careful survival scheme Shukhov realizes that he cannot afford this risk.

Eating, then, is no longer an elemental activity, deriving from instinct and being pursued casually. It is a strategy replete with well-formulated tactics designed to afford the undernourished the best chances of retaining a viable body. More importantly, it becomes, without the hero's knowledge, a religious ritual which is approached with respect and quasi-reverence. Thus, during lunch, the process of chewing every mouthful is described minutely. Shukhov's hands, lips, tongue, taste buds and facial muscles participate in unison, slowly and deliberately, for the ultimate enjoyment of swallowing and digesting. Every single trace of food is scraped from the bowl with a piece of bread saved until last for this purpose. When Shukhov has finished, the bowl looks as if it has been washed and dried by the most thorough of hands.

Prior to lunch on the same day, Shukhov has been able, through astute maneuvering and well-planned tactics, to secure from the kitchen staff a few extra bowls of food for his brigade. He thus becomes entitled to a second helping. Therefore he eats his first portion even more slowly, trying not to feel as partially full as he does normally. Having conditioned his stomach to the proper introduction of the second ration, he proceeds to eat his mush with the acute pleasure of one who becomes sexually aroused again soon after experiencing climax. All his senses are now at play and extreme concentration is required in order for him to reach yet another gourmet's orgasm....

Post-meal euphoria is, however, ... short-lived. Soon reality sneaks back, and at times, in order to avoid it, the hero's thoughts revert to the past, before his incarceration. But even recollections of family and friends pale before those having to do with food:

> In the camp he often remembered how he used to eat in the village—potatoes by the panful and pots of kasha, and in the early days before that, great hunks of meat. And they swilled enough milk to make their bellies burst. But he understood in the camps this was all wrong. You had to eat with all your thoughts on the food, like he was nibbling off these little bits now, and turn them over on your tongue, and roll them over in your mouth—and then it tasted so good, this soggy black bread.

When it is come by easily, affluence provides less pleasure than scarcity which is well managed and calculatingly appropriated. Of course, Shukhov does not see the sour-grapes attitude involved in such reasoning. His need to think that he is making a go of camp life is so great that he has succeeded in conditioning himself psychologically to feelings and thoughts that make survival possible. Yet, at the same time, it may be concluded that this is all the more to his credit because the gulag affords no other means of overcoming starvation and death.

In fact, starvation in the gulag is not merely punishment for sins committed against the State; it is above all a way of having the prisoners compensate the State, a way of controlling and rendering more efficient their labor which enhances the economic well-being of the State. That is why the slave-labor force of the camp is divided into brigades and why the collective work of the brigade is considered rather than that of an individual prisoner. Each has to do his share of work, or else all members of the brigade have their rations cut or diminished:

> In the camp they had these 'brigades' to make the prisoners keep each other on their toes.... It was like this—either you all get something extra or you all starved. ("You're not pulling your weight, you swine, and I've got to go hungry because of you. So work, you bastard!").

Each *beast* in the camp must contribute, then, to the maintenance of survival based on food allotments, which in turn are based on the amount of daily work.

Not meeting a work quota even for one day involves a cut in rations. If the *beast* is not properly fed one day, the work quota cannot be met the next, which means that a vicious circle is created, leading to slow death by starvation. Hence *beast* pushes *beast* to do his best, the collective survival of all depending on the efforts of each. The gulag strips the person of even his most individualistic traits, and at the end of the tunnel, if ever one gets there, is a spoonful of mush.

The camp's currency is, of course, food. The State gets the work it wants done for the food it gives the prisoners; the authorities are bribed with food in parcels sent by relatives to the gulag; when a theft is committed food is always involved directly or indirectly. The emperor of the camp is the chief cook. He disposes of the food as he sees fit and puts on the airs of a French chef at a fancy resort. He controls innumerable assistants, acts pompously and authoritatively, yet all he actually does is boil water and groats, preparing a meal that any Boy Scout could fix over a campfire.

The importance of nourishment is presented with most vigor however in the oft-repeated or alluded to question of whether those who clear off the tables should lick the other prisoners' bowls thereby providing themselves with extra food. Kuzyomin's code forbids this, for it makes one dependent on scraps, and the humiliation of the act of licking is bound to strip one of any vestige of human dignity. Self-respect, though required for spiritual preservation, may be at odds with the caloric intake necessitated by the body. Shukhov is unable to choose easily: "And the worst thing was that if there was something left in the bowls you started to lick them. You couldn't help it." His concern for moral and esthetic standards conflicts with his appetite which is spurred by the continuous hunger within. But there is no transcendental reality in the gulag; there is no hereafter with its notions of reward and punishment. There is only the stark presence of starvation, the pain in the stomach emanating in the limbs and in the throat, the need to fill the void with something solid, with anything that will ease the hurt and make for life, or the semblance of life. There is nothing beyond the natural limits of the physical world here and now, and, within the confines of the camp, life is its own reward.

In addition, Kuzyomin's code may be wrong with reference to licking the bowls, reasons Shukhov, because it is wrong when it forbids a prisoner to spy on another prisoner. The code maintains that a stool pigeon cannot survive, but Shukhov's observation proves otherwise. He remarks: "About the secret spying he [Kuzyomin], of course, exaggerated. Exactly those [the stool pigeons] do survive." In the jungle there is no room for the niceties of principle, and those who live by the laws of the outside die inside. If Shukhov ultimately resists the temptation to lick the bowls, it is for the same practical reason that he would not eat the eyes of a fish floating in a soup: fear that physical repulsion would induce nausea and vomiting. The law of the *taiga* cannot be mellowed or modified, and Shukhov can only accept that part of it which helps physical survival. Kuzyomin cannot have it both ways; Shukhov will not even try, for the risk is personal annihilation.

In fact, the more one is confined in the gulag, the more animalistic his reaction to food becomes. For example, sniffing turns out to be the most efficient sensory mode for detecting the presence and the sort of food. When one of the prisoners, Caesar Markovich, receives a parcel from home, he need not unpack the contents in order for Shukhov to know exactly what they are:

> Like all the others he had the eyes of a hawk, and in a flash they ran over the things Caesar had laid out on the bed and on the locker. But though he still hadn't taken the paper off them or opened the bags, Shukhov couldn't help telling by ... a sniff of the nose that Caesar had gotten sausage, canned milk, a large smoked fish, fatback, crackers with one kind of smell and cookies with another, and about four pounds of lump sugar. And then there was butter, cigarettes, and pipe tobacco.

Shukhov's sense of smell is so precise that he can distinguish "crackers with one kind of smell" from cookies with another. In the gulag, the human being-become-beast develops the instincts of the latter, and, in time, uses them with the same degree of accuracy.

Finally, the sacramental quality that food has for the incarcerated is shown poignantly in a discussion the hero has with the prisoner Alyoskha. The latter, a devout believer in the Baptist Church and a practitioner of its codes, talks to Shukhov in an attempt to convert him to Christianity. His speech, replete with vocabulary that might be effective outside, is powerless in the confines of the camp. Where physical survival is paramount, it is useless to invoke the might of the spirit, the immortality of the soul, and the purity of Paradise. Evangelical metaphors, likewise, are ill-placed in the atmosphere of the gulag, and the miracle of moving mountains means little to someone whose every moment of continued existence is in itself a miracle. And so Alyoskha fails; but, significantly, when he refers to the daily bread in the Lord's Prayer, Shukhov properly asks: "You mean that ration [the daily one hundred gram bread allotment per man] we get?" Obviously, if that is all a person can hope for, or is permitted to ask of God, then, Shukhov reasons, there is not much point in prayer.

Shukhov's spirit, then, reduced by imprisonment to instinct, acts in order to attain measurable and immediate results: the maximum caloric intake to maintain physical viability, which allows him to work and avoid the ire of the other prisoners and the camp authorities. One can stay alive this way, and one can count the days that pass and those that remain in one's sentence. We meet Shukhov for only one day. We do not know if he will survive until he is released, or indeed if he will be released—the Soviet courts can renew a sentence if they so deem advisable. Still, we may conclude that his chances of self-preservation are good. After all,

the law of the *taiga* may have its shortcomings (Shukhov recognizes these himself), but it is a natural law, one that ought to work. Man's responsibility to his body may be secondary under normal conditions; within the narrow limitations of the gulag it becomes primordial.

Source: Alfred Cismaru, "The Importance of Food in *One Day in the Life of Ivan Denisovich*," in *San Jose Studies*, Vol. IX, No. 1, Winter, 1983, pp. 99–105.

Sources

David Burg, and George Feifer, *Solzhenitsyn*, Stein and Day Publishers, pp. 155-156.

James M. Curtis, *Solzhenitsyn's Traditional Imagination*, The University of Georgia Press, 1984, p. 185.

Max Hayward and Ronald Hingley, translators, *One Day in the Life of Ivan Denisovich*, Bantam Books, 1963, p. xviii.

Christopher Moody, *Solzhenitsyn*, Barnes and Noble, 1976, pp. 37-38.

Michael Scammell, *Solzhenitsyn: A Biography*, Norton, p. 981.

J. N. Westwood, *Russia 1917-1964*, Harper & Row, 1966, p. 122.

For Further Study

Steven Allaback, *Alexander Solzhenitsyn*, Taplinger Publishing Company, 1978.
> An informative look at the craftsmanship and genius of *One Day in the Life of Ivan Denisovich, The First Circle, The Cancer Ward,* and *August 1914.*

Francis Barker, *Solzhenitsyn: Politics and Form*, Barnes & Noble, 1977.
> The author traces Solzhenitsyn's rejection of Marxism and a willingness to explore democracy in his first novels to a reactionary political vision in his later ones.

Ronald Berman, editor, *Solzhenitsyn at Harvard*, Ethics and Public Policy Center, 1980.
> Solzhenitsyn's famous commencement address at Harvard is reprinted, followed by media comments and essays for a deeper analysis of that event.

Hans Bjorkegren, *Aleksandr Solzhenitsyn: A Biography*, The Third Press, 1972.
> Translated from the Swedish, this biography has the insight expected from an ever-vigilant neighbor.

Olga Carlisle, *Solzhenitsyn and the Secret Circle*, Holt, Rinehart and Winston, 1978.
> Born in Russia, American by marriage, and an enemy of Solzhenitsyn's, Olga Carlisle presents her assertion that she and her husband, a translator, were used by Solzhenitsyn.

Alex De Jonge, *Stalin and the Shaping of the Soviet Union*, William Morrow and Company, Inc., 1986.

De Jonge used archival material and living witnesses to trace Stalin's humble beginnings and his rise to despotism, his purges and liquidations, his role in World War II, and the subsequent expanding of the USSR map.

Helene Carrere D'Encausse, *Stalin: Order through Terror,* Longman, 1981.

In her second volume on the history of the Soviet Union, this Parisian professor examines the rise of Stalinism until Stalin's death.

John B. Dunlop, Richard Haugh, and Alexis Klimoff, editors, *Aleksandr Solzhenitsyn: Critical Essays and Documentary Materials,* Nordland Publishing, 1973.

This volume includes not only literary criticism of Solzhenitsyn in English but also four translated documents written by Solzhenitsyn about his philosophy and his craft.

John B. Dunlop, Richard S. Haugh, and Michael Nicholson, editors, *Solzhenitsyn in Exile,* Hoover Institution Press, 1985.

A collection of essays and documentary material of particular use to researchers. The critical essays examine Solzhenitsyn and his work; the documentary material consists of memoirs, interviews, and bibliographies.

John and Carol Gerrard, *Inside the Soviet Writers' Union,* Collier Macmillan, 1990.

The authors look inside one of the Soviet Union's most powerful tools for propaganda, the Writers' Union. Dedicated to the idea of Socialist Realism, this organization did its best to kill Russian creativity.

Paul Gray, "Russia's Prophet in Exile," *Time,* Vol. 134, No. 4, July 24, 1989, pp. 56-60.

An insightful interview with Solzhenitsyn on politics, literature, and religion.

Oakley Hall, *The Art & Craft of Novel Writing,* Writer's Digest Books, 1989.

Not only is this a well-thought analysis of how to write a novel, but it explains the techniques that lead the reader to the desired response.

K. P., "The Sage of Vermont," *Forbes,* Vol. 153, No. 10, May 9, 1994, p. 122.

A brief, unbiased overview of Solzhenitsyn's relationship to the United States.

Nikita S. Khrushchev, *Khrushchev Remembers: The Last Testament,* Little, Brown and Company, 1974.

The last volume of an oral history dictated by the former premier has a fascinating section on Stalin and his treatment of writers.

Vladislav Krasnov, *Solzhenitsyn and Dostoevsky,* University of Georgia Press, 1980.

Using the three earliest Solzhenitsyn novels, the author states that Solzhenitsyn is closer to Dostoevsky than Tolstoy, especially in the concept of the polyphonic novel where there is no main character, but rather several.

Georg Lukacs, *Solzhenitsyn,* The MIT Press, 1969.

A literary criticism that judges Solzhenitsyn in the tradition of Socialist Realism and the literary problems of the Stalinist era.

Judith Newman, "From Vermont, with Love," *People,* Vol. 41, No. 18, May 16, 1994, pp. 99-102.

The people of Vermont give a fond good-bye to the Solzhenitsyn family.

"Profile of Aleksandr Solzhenitsyn," *1988 Current Biography Yearbook,* H. W. Wilson Company, 1988.

A comprehensive sketch of the author which highlights milestones in his life and is accompanied by his photographs.

Edvard Radzinsky, *Stalin: The First In-Depth Biography Based On Explosive New Documents from Russia's Secret Archives,* Doubleday, 1996.

This very readable translation by H. T. Willetts of the life of Stalin is organized into three sections: one for each of Stalin's names (his childhood name, the teenage name he gives himself, and the name of Stalin, meaning "steel"). Each chapter is divided into subtitled sections.

Abraham Rothberg, *Aleksandr Solzhenitsyn: The Major Novels,* Cornell University Press, 1971.

An analysis of Solzhenitsyn's first three novels, this critique reaffirms the importance of the works from a moral, political, and artistic standpoint.

Marshall D Shulman, *Stalin's Foreign Policy Reappraised,* Harvard University Press, 1963.

A scholar of international politics, Shulman argues, contrary to popular opinion, that Russia's foreign policy began to become more flexible even before the death of Stalin.

Aleksandr Solzhenitsyn, *August 1914,* Farrar, Straus and Giroux, 1971.

This polyphonic novel examines the Battle of Tannenberg in World War I, a Russian defeat that showed the corruptions of the czarist system.

Aleksandr Solzhenitsyn, *Candle in the Wind,* University of Minnesota Press, 1960.

A play that examines scientific ethics: a scientist is confronted by a woman whose personality has been changed by biofeedback techniques.

Aleksandr Solzhenitsyn, *From under the Rubble,* Little, Brown and Company, 1974.

This collection of essays, edited by Solzhenitsyn and including two of his own essays, seeks to find a new, moral society. Soviet Russia is severely criticized and the West is seen as decadent.

Aleksandr Solzhenitsyn, *The Gulag Archipelago,* Harper & Row, 1973.

The "Gulag" is the acronym of secret police organizations including the camps. The author indicts this insidious segment of Soviet life using hundreds of characters and their stories.

Aleksandr Solzhenitsyn, *Lenin in Zurich,* Farrar, Straus and Giroux, 1975.

Chapters on Lenin in *August 1914,* Knot I, and in Knots II and III have now been enlarged and presented as a separate book, thanks to valuable research material Solzhenitsyn found in Zurich.

Aleksandr Solzhenitsyn, *Letter to the Soviet Leaders,* Harper & Row, 1974.
In "Nothing Changes for the Good," Solzhenitsyn predicts the destruction of Russia and the West. "War with China" is also a fascinating chapter and a cautionary tale for any country.

Aleksandr Solzhenitsyn, *The Oak and The Calf,* Harper & Row, 1979.
Solzhenitsyn's memoir of his writing career in Russia and how he had to confront even the KGB, the secret police. This English-language version, published four years after the Russian one, has added material.

Aleksandr Solzhenitsyn, *Solzhenitsyn: A Pictorial Autobiography,* Farrar, Straus and Giroux, 1974.
Solzhenitsyn has put together a book of snapshots, most of which are of him. The writing is a short and powerful recapping of his life under Soviet tyranny.

Aleksandr Solzhenitsyn, *Warning to the West,* Farrar, Straus and Giroux, 1976.
Solzhenitsyn begs the West to intervene in Soviet affairs for the future of the world.

B. H. Sumner, *A Short History of Russia,* Harcourt, Brace & World, Inc., 1949.
As the title implies, this is a brief overview of Russia divided into the following components: the frontier, the state, the land, the church, the Slavs, the sea, and the West.

Ragtime

E. L. Doctorow

1975

It often seems that there is a competition between popular literature and artistic literature, with each one claiming the right to call itself the greater benefit to society. *Ragtime* is one of the few novels that transcends this competition completely, having proven itself with undeniable success in both areas. Some critics have picked out miscellaneous faults, but the novel was received with widespread praise when it was published in 1975. Most reviewers agreed that Doctorow took the combination of historical and imaginary characters, a technique used often in historical novels but with only weak results, and manipulated it into a rich blend that is entertaining, challenging, and true to the spirit of the times. The reading public agreed: unlike many experimental works of art whose freshness makes them too difficult for widespread audiences, *Ragtime* became a best-seller in its initial hardcover edition. For a period of time in the mid-seventies, it seemed there was a copy in every home. E. L. Doctorow became a household name, and each new book he releases to this day is still considered a significant literary event, although it would be unreal to think that an event like *Ragtime* could occur more than once in one writer's lifetime. The novel's influence on popular culture continues today; it was adapted into a major Broadway musical in the late 1990s.

Author Biography

Edgar Lawrence Doctorow was born in the Bronx, in New York City, in 1931. Both of his parents were children of Russian Jewish immigrants, and the Jewish faith has been a powerful influence on his life and writing. He attended Brand High School of Science and then went on to Kenyon College in Ohio, which had a reputation as a good school for writers: while there, he studied under the poet John Crowe Ransom and met other writers who either were or would be famous. After receiving an A.B. in philosophy in 1952, he attended Columbia University in New York for a year, but then was drafted, and he spent the next two years in the army. Returning to civilian life, he married and worked a series of odd jobs, including reading novels for CBS Television and Columbia Pictures: "I was reading a book a day, seven days a week, and writing synopses of them," he told an interviewer years later. "I suppose each synopsis was no less than 1,200 words. I was getting an average of ten or twelve dollars a book, so I was making pretty good money—anywhere between seventy and one hundred dollars a week." In 1959 he started at New American Library, where in the next five years, he worked his way up to senior editor; his first novel, *Welcome to Hard Times,* was published in 1960. He left New American in 1964 to become editor-in-chief at Dial Press, and when he left Dial in 1969, he was a vice president. After that followed a series of teaching jobs intertwined with a series of awards for fiction. He won a Guggenheim Fellowship in 1972; the National Book Critics' Circle Award for *Ragtime* in 1976, and again for *Billy Bathgate* in 1990; the National Book Award for *World's Fair* in 1986; and the PEN/Faulkner Award for Fiction for *Billy Bathgate.* Like *Ragtime,* most of his books are based on historical facts: *The Book of Daniel,* for instance, is based on the true story of Julius and Ethel Rosenberg, who were executed as spies; and *Billy Bathgate* is a character associated with Prohibition-era gangster Dutch Schultz. Doctorow considers his 1966 science-fiction novel, *Big as Life,* to be a failure, and it is the only one of his books that is not in print today. Doctorow lives in New Rochelle, New York, in the house that was the model for the one described in the first pages of *Ragtime.*

Plot Summary

Section I

Ragtime is a novel about three families living in the early years of the twentieth century and how their members' separate lives intertwine within a wide, colorful quilt of personalities, some real and

E. L. Doctorow

some fictional. The book contains many different plotlines that begin and end in a jumble. It starts at the home of one family in New Rochelle, a New York suburb. The father of the house owns a company that manufactures fireworks and parade decorations, things used mostly on patriotic occasions. Father, as he is called, lives in the house with Mother and the Little Boy; also living there are Mother's Younger Brother and Grandfather. Introduced in the first chapter is the true historical story of Evelyn Nesbit, whose husband, millionaire Harry K. Thaw, shot her former lover, famed architect Stanford White, in a crowded restaurant one night in 1906. Younger Brother has pictures of Nesbit taped to his walls. One afternoon a car crashes into a telephone pole in front of the family's house. Driving the car is Harry Houdini, the famous escape artist; the car is all right, and Houdini is invited into the house until the radiator cools. As he leaves, the Little Boy tells him, for no obvious reason, "Warn the Duke." The next day, Father leaves to go on an expedition with Admiral Robert Peary to the North Pole. The narration shifts briefly to introduce an immigrant family, Mameh, Tateh, and the Little Girl, who are living in a tenement. In order to get more money, Mameh has sex with her employer, then disappears from the story when Tateh takes the Little Girl and leaves her. The main narrative follows Evelyn Nesbit, who testifies on her husband's behalf at his trial. One day she sees Tateh on a street corner, selling scissor-cut silhouettes, with the Little Girl tied to a rope to keep her from being stolen. She identifies with the girl, and forces herself on the family against Tateh's wishes, bringing them food. Tateh, a Socialist, takes Nesbit to a political meeting, where she meets Emma Goldman, another historical figure. Back at her apartment, Goldman explains her ideas about health and massages Evelyn, and Mother's Younger Brother, who has followed them, bursts in on them in a fury of sexual excitement. Evelyn Nesbit and Younger Brother become lovers. In the garden at the house in New Rochelle, Mother finds a newborn baby buried in the dirt. A police investigation quickly turns up the baby's mother, Sarah, a young black woman. To avoid breaking up the family, Mother takes Sarah and the baby to live with her family. Tateh and the Little Girl leave New York City, travelling on a series of streetcars from one city to another, until they end up in Massachusetts. At the end of this section, Houdini is introduced to Franz Ferdinand, Archduke of Austria-Hungary, whose assassination triggered World War I.

Section II

This section is mainly devoted to the story of Coalhouse Walker Jr., the father of Sarah's baby. Father returns from his Arctic exploration, and Younger Brother returns home after his affair with Evelyn Nesbit ends. Tateh works at a textile mill in Lawrence, Massachusetts, where he becomes involved in a strike and is battered by the police; escaping, he and the Little Girl end up in Philadelphia, where he sells a book of his artwork to the Franklin Novelty Company. Coalhouse Walker Jr. shows up at the house in New Rochelle, explaining that he heard that Sarah lived there. He is well-dressed and well-mannered and arrives in a clean new Model T. Sarah refuses to see him, and he returns again and again, once playing the piano for the family—he is a professional ragtime player in a nightclub. In the mean time, Younger Brother talks to Emma Goldman, and she teaches him the importance of revolutionary politics, and J. P. Morgan meets with Henry Ford to discuss his ideas, based in Egyptian religion, that certain individuals are meant to be leaders. Eventually, Sarah begins meeting with Coalhouse Walker, and she finally agrees to marry him.

The central event of the novel occurs one Sunday afternoon when Walker, driving home from visiting Sarah, is stopped in front of a volunteer fire department. He refuses to pay a "road toll" to the firemen who stand around threateningly and make racial slurs, and instead goes for a policeman. They return to find Walker's car vandalized, and when he argues, Walker is arrested. Over the next few weeks he tries to sue for damages, but he is treated badly by the courts because he is a black man. Sarah goes to see James Sherman, the vice-presidential candidate, because she thinks he is the President and can help the situation, but his bodyguards think she has a gun and they beat her. She later dies from her wounds. Walker then decides to take the law into his own hands: he and a band of men burn down the fire station and kill its inhabitants, but Willie Conklin, the fire chief who stopped him, is not there. They burn a few more fire stations, demanding that Walker's car be restored and Conklin be turned over to them. Because of the notoriety of the case, the family, with Sarah's baby, leaves town and stays at a hotel in Atlantic City. There they make the acquaintance of Baron Ashkenazy, a wealthy film maker, and his daughter, who turn out to be the characters previously known as Tateh and the Little Girl. When Walker and his gang, including Younger Brother, take control of the J. P. Morgan library, the police ask Father to come to New York to negotiate with him, fearful that he will destroy the library's priceless collection. After meeting with Booker T. Washington, Walker drops his demand for Conklin's life, and instead the fire chief and the damaged car are brought to the street in front of the library, where the chief has to work in the glare of public humiliation on restoring the car. Walker's men escape in the restored car.

Section III

Coalhouse Walker steps from the library and is shot down by the police. Younger Brother escapes to the southwest and eventually joins the band of revolutionary Mexican-rights leader Emiliano Zapata. J. P. Morgan dies of a cold caught from spending the night in a pyramid. Archduke Franz Ferdinand is assassinated, and Houdini, remembering the boy who years earlier had told him to "warn the Duke," realizes that in a life of make-believe magic tricks the boy's prediction had been his one true mystical experience. Father helps make munitions for the war, even though the U.S. is not involved in it yet, using plans for bombs that were developed by Younger Brother. After Father is killed in the sinking of the *S.S. Lusitania,* Mother marries Baron Ashkenazy, and they, their two children, and the child of Coalhouse and Sarah move to California together, the three families united.

Characters

Baron Ashkenazy

See Tateh

Willie Conklin

The fire chief of the Emerald Isle Company, and the instigator of the actions against Coalhouse Walker. When Coalhouse threatens to kill him, he goes into hiding in the Irish slums of New York, and Irish political leaders are called upon to bring him out and make him stand up to the humiliation of restoring Coalhouse's car in the street in front of the Morgan Library.

Father

Father owns a company that makes fireworks, flags, and other patriotic decorations. His own father had been irresponsible, cheerfully losing a fortune to bad investments, and as a result Father is presented as being cautious and conservative. He does, however, have a wild side that is attracted to danger. He is an explorer with a good reputation, invited to go along with Admiral Perry on an Arctic exploration. He returns from his adventure with a guilty conscience because he slept with an Eskimo woman. Father allows an unknown African-American girl, Sarah, to move into his house and to allow her boyfriend to come to the house to court her, but he is not good-hearted enough to have thought of these ideas himself. When Coalhouse Walker is assaulted at the fire station, Father hesitantly tries to get a lawyer he knows to help, and he offers to pay for the lawyer's services (the offer is refused). When Coalhouse and his confederates take over the Morgan Library, Father is called by the authorities to negotiate with the rebels. Father later finds a drawer full of blueprints for bombs and weapons in Younger Brother's desk at the fireworks plant. He becomes a consultant to the government, helping develop these weapons for use by American troops during World War I. He dies when a German submarine torpedoes the *S. S. Lusitania,* two years before America's entry into the war.

Sigmund Freud

A real-life character recognized as the Father of Psychoanalysis, he visits the United States early in the book, experiences popular culture, and declares, "America is a mistake, a gigantic mistake."

Harry Houdini

A real-life character who became famous as an escape artist, Houdini was a show-business phenomenon in his day, escaping from increasingly more difficult situations and tighter chains. The real-life Houdini, just like the character in the book, actually did buy one of the first airplanes available, and devoted the latter part of his life to unmasking fraudulent psychics, as described in the novel. Houdini plays a key role in the structure of the book: in the first chapter he arrives at the family's house, and the Little Boy tells him, ominously, "Warn the Duke." By the books' end, World War I has broken out over the assassination of Archduke Franz Ferdinand of Austria, whom Houdini meets at the end of Section 1. In the final pages of the novel Houdini remembers his encounter with the Little Boy as "the one genuine mystical experience of his life."

The Little Boy

Although the book's narrative travels all over, giving readers the thoughts and experiences of characters that most boys would never have met, the Little Boy turns out, when all is added together, to be the center of this story. It is his consciousness that grows throughout this story: when the first paragraph says "There were no Negroes. There were no immigrants," it is clearly not an objective fact but the impression of someone young and naive, an impression that will change throughout the story. It is the boy's life that is affected by all of the events in the story, since the Coalhouse Walker plot line and the Tateh plot line cross his life at different points and end up permanently affecting his future. The Little Boy is given some of the most mystical, intimate moments in the novel. Chapter 15 tells about his personal, peculiar outlook on the world, explaining that he "was alert not only to discarded materials but to unexpected events and coincidences," which indicates that his way of looking at the world is identical to the novel's unique structure. Throughout the book, the Little Boy is not a participant in the events around him, but an observer. The novel's most lyrical writing involves the boy's delight in befriending the Little Girl at the beach in Atlantic City over the course of the summer: "What bound them to each other was a fulfilled recognition which they lived and thought within so that their apprehension of each other could not be so distinct and separated as to include admiration for the other's fairness."

J. Pierpont Morgan

An actual historical figure who made millions of dollars in steel and finance, Morgan is presented

Howard Rollins in the movie Ragtime.

in this novel as a mystic who believes in the occult. In his urgency to share his enthusiasm for Egyptology with a peer, Morgan arranges a meeting with Henry Ford, the automobile magnate, but Ford is a practical, simple man who does not understand Morgan's complex theory. When reached at sea about Coalhouse Walker's demands while barricaded in the Morgan library, Morgan tells the police to "Give him his car, then hang him." Morgan spends a night alone in the great pyramid of Giza, hoping to absorb its mystical energy, and later dies of a cold contracted there.

Mother

Mother's sensibilities grow throughout this novel. At first, she is a dutiful suburban housewife, submitting to sex with her husband but avoiding it when she can, remembering the carefree days of her childhood. Mother's life changes when one day, walking through her garden, she finds a newborn baby buried in the dirt. She washes it off and takes it into her home and cares for it, and when the police locate Sarah, the baby's mother, Mother takes her into the household too. When Father returns home from his Polar expedition, expecting to find Mother angry and aloof, he is surprised: "He found instead a woman curious and alerted to his new being." A deep chasm opens between Mother and Father in the wake of Coalhouse Walker's first bomb-

ing attack, when she sympathizes with Coalhouse and Father curses him with angry racial epithets. When the family moves to Atlantic City to avoid the publicity associated with Coalhouse, Mother finds herself attracted to a fellow hotel patron, Baron Ashkenazy. After Father's death she marries Ashkenazy, and they and the three children move to California.

Mother's Younger Brother

He is a passionate and talented young man who cannot seem to find direction in life. At first, he works for his brother-in-law at the fireworks plant and dreams of Evelyn Nesbit, whose picture is in the newspapers frequently. When a meeting of the Socialist labor union, the Industrial Workers of the World, is disrupted by the police, he follows Nesbit and Emma Goldman, spying from a closet as Goldman massages the girl of his dreams until, overcome with excitement, he bursts into the room ejaculating. For a short time he and Nesbit date. When Coalhouse Walker begins his violent attacks, Younger Brother joins his band as a munitions expert and token white person. After that he travels to Mexico, fighting with legendary revolutionary Emiliano Zapata in the Mexican Revolution. The narrator explains throughout the book that many of the facts related here are known because they were recorded in Younger Brother's diary.

Evelyn Nesbit

Based on a historical person who was actually involved in the murder case described in the book, she was the wife of millionaire Harry K. Thaw, who walked into the restaurant atop Madison Square Garden one night in 1906 and shot her lover, famed architect Stanford White. The trial has remained one of the most famous of the century. In the novel, Nesbit becomes fascinated with the Little Girl, daughter of Tateh, who is suspicious of her attentions. She becomes romantically involved with Emma Goldman, who later, in a Socialist newspaper, describes her as a tool of the Capitalist system. She has a brief affair with Mother's Younger Brother. At her husband's murder trial she dutifully testifies to help him avoid execution with an insanity plea, but his lawyers refuse to give her the million-dollar divorce settlement they had promised.

Sarah

The young black woman who buried her newborn child, presumably to hide the fact that she gave birth to him out of wedlock. She agrees to live with the family that finds the child, living in their attic and hardly talking. When the baby's father, Coalhouse Walker, comes to court her, Sarah rejects him, presumably because he abandoned her when she was pregnant. It takes several months for her to become trusting enough to accept his marriage proposal. She tries to talk to the visiting vice-presidential candidate, but his bodyguards think she is an assassin when they see her approaching, and they beat her. She dies a few days later from the injuries received during the beating.

Tateh

The word "Tateh" is Yiddish for "father." When this character first appears in the novel, he is a "thirty-two-year-old geriatric artist" who sells silhouette portraits on the street corner. Evelyn Nesbit takes a liking to his daughter, although she just thinks of Tateh as a crazy old man; she visits their apartment frequently with food and gifts. Tateh is also a Socialist, and he takes Nesbit to a meeting where she becomes acquainted with Emma Goldman. He later packs all of his and his daughter's belongings and, taking one streetcar after another, travels to a succession of cities across the Northeast until they end up in Lawrence, Massachusetts, where Tateh takes a job at the wool mill that is the site of the famous Textile Mill Strike of 1912. He barely escapes the violence of the police during the strike and ends up destitute in Philadelphia, where he sells a book of pictures that he has

Media Adaptations

- An audio cassette version of *Ragtime* read by William Levine was released by Blackstone Audio.

- The 1981 film version of *Ragtime,* directed by Milos Foreman and with a screenplay by Michael Weller, was released on videocassette in 1991 by Paramount Home Video.

made to the Franklin Novelty Company for twenty-five dollars. When he next appears in the novel, he is a rich movie maker going by the name of Baron Ashkenazy. Romantic feelings bloom between himself and Mother one rainy afternoon in Atlantic City, and at the end of the book, after Father's death, he marries her.

Coalhouse Walker

A black musician from St. Louis, Coalhouse is a piano player with the Jim Europe Clef Club Orchestra, which plays regularly at the Manhattan Casino. He enters the story after Sarah and her baby are living with the family. The baby is his, and Coalhouse persists in coming to the house to court Sarah, eventually winning over her initial reluctance. He is a sharp dresser and drives a well-kept Model T convertible with a custom-made roof. Soon after Sarah agrees to marry him, Coalhouse is stopped on the road in front of the Emerald Isle volunteer fire station, where the firemen, led by their chief Willie Conklin, harass him by demanding he pay a toll. Coalhouse goes for a policeman and comes back to find his car vandalized, and the policeman arrests him for starting trouble. Lawyers will not help him sue for damages and the courts "lose" paperwork that he files himself. Sarah dies trying to talk to the vice-presidential candidate about the case, and Coalhouse Walker leads a band of rebels in action against the government, demanding that his car be restored and Willie Conklin be given over to him for punishment. His demands are signed with his name and the words "President, Provisional American Government."

His band bombs a few firehouses in the New Rochelle area, and then tries to take millionaire J. P. Morgan hostage, but ends up taking over the Morgan Library, which is adjacent to the Morgan house. Coalhouse negotiates the release of his supporters in exchange for dropping his demand for Conklin's life, and they drive away in his restored car. When Coalhouse surrenders, he is shot down in a hail of bullets.

Booker T. Washington

Washington, the founder of the first U.S. college for blacks, the Tuskegee Institute, spent his life supporting cooperation between the races, encouraging blacks to behave in ways that were socially proper in order to gain acceptance. In the novel, he enters the Morgan Library to talk to Coalhouse Walker and ask him, on behalf of his people, to surrender. "What will your recklessness cost me!" he asks Coalhouse in anger. "What will it cost my students laboring to learn a trade by which they can earn their livelihood and still white criticism! A thousand honest industrious black men cannot undo the harm of one like you." Out of respect for Washington, Coalhouse drops his demand for the fire chief's life, but he is not moved enough to give up in any other way.

Themes

Victims and Victimization

One of the central events in a novel that is packed with background incidents concerns the abuse and humiliation that Coalhouse Walker Jr. receives from the members of the Emerald Isle firehouse. Their actions against him are clearly based on classic bully mentality: he is different than them; they are jealous because he has a nicer car than most of them could afford; and they outnumber him. The novel is quite clear about the fact that early-1900s society allows the continued victimization of Coalhouse because he is black. Not only do the police refuse to help him when he wants justice for the damage to his car, but they actually arrest him, and the legal system is effective in tying up his civil litigation. At each step in the process, well-intentioned people advise him to drop his complaint and be thankful that the damage against him was not worse, even when his fiancée is killed for trying to talk to a white man on his behalf. Coalhouse is given the choice to accept victimization or to go to dangerous extremes to fight it, and in this context his violent rampage seems reasonable, if tragic.

Other characters in the book are presented as victims of society. Tateh's involvement in the textile mill strike at Lawrence is presented as a textbook example of how working people were abused by the people they worked for. The living conditions are deplorable: "Tateh stood in front of a loom for fifty-six hours a week. The family lived in a wooden tenement on a hill. They had no heat. They occupied one room overlooking an alley in which residents certainly dumped their garbage." When he tries to change his circumstance, though, the mill owners command the police to stage a violent attack against the strikers.

Even Evelyn Nesbit, who lives a life of financial luxury, is presented as a victim, a tool of powerful interests. Powerful men use her tragic story to sell newspapers and tickets to the motion pictures. Socialists and anarchists use her in their speeches as an example of how women are exploited by powerful men. None of these groups does anything to help her situation, leaving her in the position of having to aid her dangerously unstable husband, on trial for killing her lover, if she is to survive.

Culture Clash

Ragtime examines a time in American history when the old, established culture found itself especially vulnerable to new ideas. The move toward change came mostly from outside of the old culture's borders, but it also rose up from within, from those previously locked out of the mainstream. The attitude of mainstream culture is expressed on the book's first page: "There were no Negroes. There were no immigrants." That same paragraph goes on to mention some of the mysterious occurrences that did not make sense within this way of thought, and then to suggest that incomplete information was the reason. "Stories were hushed up and reporters were paid off by rich families," the novel explains. It then goes on to give a brief summary of the Evelyn Nesbit-Stanford White-Harry K. Thaw affair as an example of something that was clearly more complex than the dominant culture was willing to admit. "Apparently there *were* Negroes. There *were* immigrants," the paragraph concludes. No specific Negroes or immigrants had been mentioned, just suspicion of the mainstream culture's position.

The strongest symbol of the mainstream culture in the book is the Morgan library, packed with expensive historical artifacts, the cultural residue of Western civilization, tracing backwards through Europe to ancient Egypt. The greatest threat to these artifacts is, of course, the dynamite of the Coalhouse gang, ready to destroy centuries worth of culture in order to secure justice for a black man who has been excluded from the cultural system. Because he is intelligent, Coalhouse Walker is able to force the system to agree to his demands; because he is a cultural outsider, he is shot down in the street at the first chance. A worse fate befalls the immigrant workers of the wool mill in Lawrence, who go on strike to gain justice and are violently attacked by the police: after this episode the character known by the immigrant name of Tateh reappears later, having conquered American society by latching on to the newly-developing entertainment industry. Both Harry Houdini and the members of the Emerald Isle fire company are on the border between the old culture and the new. Houdini, like Tateh/Baron Ashkenazy, becomes wealthy in entertainment, and his wealth earns him acceptance into the mainstream culture, but he does not seem satisfied with social acceptance, pushing his performances to new levels of danger with "suspicions that his life was unimportant and his achievements laughable." The firemen are a part of the social order, but their relative newness to American culture is shown in the way that their firehouse name links them to Ireland. The fact that they pick on a black man, who is lower in social status than they are, indicates that they are not comfortable with their own social position.

Sex

In this novel there is no clear or easily-understood symbolic value for the function of sex. In the case of Mother, sex is an indicator of expanding thought, as she goes from prudishness to participation. Early in the second chapter, when the visit from Houdini interrupts sex between Mother and Father (referred to by the clinical term "coitus"), the novel explains that, "There was no sign from Mother that it was now to be resumed. She fled to her garden." Later, though, after finding a baby buried in that same garden revives her interest in life, Father returns from his Polar expedition to find her "in some way not as vigorously modest." Just when, ashamed of the sex he had with an Eskimo woman, he feels that she would have the right to reject him, she starts sleeping in his room and reaching out to him in bed. Evelyn Nesbit is presented as sexually promiscuous, sleeping with Stanford White, her husband Harry Thaw, Mother's Younger Brother, and a professional ragtime dancer, but the book considers her someone who is seeking fulfillment, an unhappy woman who is never as happy pleasing men as she seems to hope she will be. "She loved (Younger Brother) but she wanted someone who would treat her badly and

Topics for Further Study

- Study the music of Scott Joplin, Jelly Roll Morton, Eubie Blake, or another famous ragtime musician. Describe the characteristics of the music, and explain how it applies to the story the book tells.

- At the end of the book the family goes to live in California, which was just starting its long reign as the movie capital of the world. Research the early movie studios, before 1920, and report on who was making movies and what kind of movies they were making.

- Assemble as many pictures as you can from the years 1900-1915 and make a collage. Try to focus on one particular theme—clothes, sports, entertainment, or politics, for example.

- Explore the debate represented by the "isolationist" theories of W. E. B. Du Bois and the "assimilationist" theories of Booker T. Washington. Explain which of these men would be supported by famous black leaders in today's world, and why you think so.

whom she could treat badly," the book explains. Emma Goldman ascribes very little importance to her sexual liaisons, past and present: "In the room tonight," she tells Younger Brother, "you saw my present lover but also my former lovers. We are all good friends. Friendship is what endures." Despite what any of the characters tries to make of sex, it is mocked as nonsense in the book's most odd and memorable scene, when Goldman's long, slow, erotic massage of Nesbit is interrupted by Younger Brother, who cannot control his sexual urges, bursting out of the closet.

Style

Point of View

The point of view of this novel is uncertain. The prevailing consciousness is certainly that of the Little Boy—his personality is explained in detail, and much of the information that is given could have reached him, either from direct experience or through secondary sources, such as his uncle's diaries or newspaper clippings. When the narrative places itself in time as speaking "nearly fifty years after Houdini's death," it leaves open the possibility that the grown-up boy is telling the story (Houdini died in 1926, nearly fifty years before the book was published). On the other hand, there are many details here that the Little Boy really could not know, such as the intimate thoughts of prominent figures like J. Pierpont Morgan and Archduke Franz Ferdinand. Throughout the book the narrator speaks as an unidentified "we," presumably representing America. The narrator is given a distinct persona in the last chapter, when it speaks in the first person: "Poor Father, I see his final exploration." Contradictions abound, but most of the evidence indicates that, if the narrator is a particular person (as opposed to the omniscient narrator, who tells the story but is not part of it), it is probably the Little Boy.

Zeitgeist ("Spirit of the Time")

More important to the success of this novel than any particular characters or plotlines is the way that it creates a convincing sense of what life was like in America in the first years of the twentieth century. Although no novel or historical work could ever give readers the experience of exactly what it was like then, *Ragtime* struggles to make clear what the issues of social concern were and who the celebrities were, in order to give the flavor of the time. The structure of the book, with quick scenes and short chapters covering a wide variety of people and situations, helps readers to feel the new century's spirit of motion and confusion. One of the most irrelevant, yet symbolic events in the book involves novelist Theodore Dreiser, who appears in one paragraph at the end of Chapter 4 and then never again: "One day he decides his chair was facing the wrong direction. He gets up to move it, then moves it again, then again. Throughout the night Dreiser turned his chair in circles seeking the proper alignment." The uneven motion of the book and its characters has been compared to this exasperated circling. Each of the real-life people chosen to represent this time period—Harry Houdini, Harry K. Thaw, Sigmund Freud, Booker T. Washington, Emma Goldman, J. P. Morgan, and the rest—adds a slightly different, unique color to the overall picture, with no single story being more important than the overall effect.

Irony

This novel has a strong flair for irony, setting readers up to expect one thing but then leading to developments that, while logical, are quite different than expected. Usually, these reversals seem to deflate pomposity. Houdini, with the best intentions toward all humanity, offers money to subway workers who escaped a catastrophe, introducing himself as an "escapologist," and he is lifted off his feet and thrown out of the hospital. Morgan assembles America's wealthiest men to trade wisdom, and he finds them concerned with digestion, dozing off and muttering inanities: "Without exception the dozen most powerful men in America looked like horse's asses," he concludes. Archduke Franz Ferdinand, whose death triggered the global catastrophe of World War I, is so befuddled by his formal, ceremonious meeting with Houdini that he thinks the airplane Houdini brings with him is his own invention. After a lifetime of actions against the government, the event that leads to Emma Goldman's deportation is her commenting about the Coalhouse Walker affair. J. P. Morgan, seeking eternal knowledge in the pyramid, instead finds bedbugs and catches the cold that kills him. Any good novel will have a number of surprises, in order to avoid being predictable, but *Ragtime* consistently uses reversal of expectation to point out the weakness of the old ruling order, although the book's ironic tone continually pretends to be upholding the old notions.

Historical Context

Progressivism

The early part of the twentieth century, as *Ragtime* explains, saw a shift in public sentiment away from the values of the wealthy, the established fraternity of men who had run business and government with increasing disregard since the end of the Civil War. At the end of the nineteenth century, the wealth of the country was absorbed by a small number of financiers who owned interests in key industries and bought out or forced out competitors in order to establish monopolies. Among the most prominent of these men were John D. Rockefeller, who built a petroleum empire; Andrew Carnegie, who dominated the market in steel; Andrew Mellon, who controlled banking; and the most powerful of them all, John Pierpont Morgan, who appears as a character in the book. In 1882, Rockefeller established the first trust, and many other industries followed soon after. A "trust" is a legal agreement

Compare & Contrast

- **1909:** An interpreter for a French film company, attending the inauguration of President William Howard Taft, conceived the idea of presenting news events on film, which led to the practice of newsreels being shown in theaters across the world.

  1975: The integrity of the news divisions was a source of competition for the three major television networks.

  Today: There are specialized cable television channels for all sorts of special interests, including sports, weather, and local and national news.

- **1907:** At the height of one of the strongest waves of immigration in American history, 1.2 million people came into the country, mostly from Europe. The years between 1900 and 1914 saw an average of a million people per year. The percent of the U.S. population that was foreign-born hit an all-time high of fifteen percent.

  1975: Immigration, declining steadily since World War I, bottomed out at around five percent of the U.S. population.

  Today: The rise of multinational corporations and communication has created a smaller world and awareness of what is available: U.S. immigration is up, led by immigrants from Asian and Latin-American countries.

- **1908:** The Summer Olympics in 1908 had athletes from twenty-two nations competing.

  Today: Athletes from over 175 nations compete in the Olympics.

- **1901:** Booker T. Washington's autobiography, *Up from Slavery,* described conditions in the South after the Civil War. The existence of laws meant to keep blacks and whites separated, known as Jim Crow laws, created circumstances of intolerance and abuse toward blacks. Although the laws of the North were not as clearly against blacks, abuses were often tolerated.

  1975: After the Civil Rights movement of the 1950s and the confrontational race riots of the 1960s, the country began to slowly create a new, inclusive social order in the 1970s.

  Today: Although civil rights laws are generally enforced and bigotry is socially unacceptable, blacks and whites still have sharply contrasting views of the world, as indicated by the vast differences of opinion over the 1995 acquittal of accused murderer O.J. Simpson.

- **1910s:** The North American Woman's Suffrage Association struggled for a Constitutional amendment to grant women the right to vote. The amendment passed in 1919.

  1975: The Women's Liberation movement, then at the height of its influence, struggled to raise the consciousness of men and women alike regarding guarantees of political, economic, and social equality. Congress ratified the Equal Rights Amendment in 1972, but it failed to gain passage in enough states in the next ten years to make it a law.

  Today: Women enjoy many of the civil liberties that the Women's Movement has fought for, whether they identify themselves as feminists or not.

---

that allows one owner or corporation to control the stock of several companies within the same industry, thereby giving it control over the prices charged to consumers and the wages paid employees.

The mood of the country changed early in the twentieth century, favoring workers and those without political or social power. Across the world, Socialism had been gaining support since the 1870s, which led to the formation of groups such as the Industrial Workers of the World (the socialist trade union mentioned in the book in the Textile Mill Strike episode). The I.W.W. reached its peak in America between 1912 and 1917, when it had 60,000 to 100,000 members. A less radical, more

Workers on Ford Motor Company's production line assemble the Model T.

mainstream form of support for workers was known as Progressivism. Progressivism was the movement to establish fair living wages for workers, and to loosen the control that the trusts had on the economy. The figure most associated with Progressivism is Theodore Roosevelt, who was president from 1901 to 1909. He was known as a "trust-buster" for using the provisions of the Sherman Anti-Trust Act, which Congress had passed in 1890 but never enforced, to break up the business monopolies. In 1912, having been out of office for a term, Roosevelt ran for office again with a new political party that he called the Progressive Party. Progressivism was such a popular idea that the three U.S. presidents who held office between 1901 and 1921—Roosevelt, Taft and Wilson—identified themselves as Progressives.

While Progressivism opposed big business, it did so in order to promote the rights of the poor. Progressivism supported suffrage (the right to vote) for women, minimum wage laws, and child welfare regulations. Unlike Socialists like Tateh in the novel, who wanted sweeping changes in the structure of the government, and anarchists like Emma Goldman, who supported violence as a justifiable way to destroy the existing system, Progressives generally came from the middle class, like the nameless family from New Rochelle.

After Vietnam and Watergate

In 1975, the year *Ragtime* was published, the Unites States was dealing with losses suffered by two of its most powerful establishments, the military and the presidency. The year 1975 marked the fall of Saigon, the capitol of South Vietnam, which American forces had fought to defend against the Communist government in North Vietnam from 1961 to 1973. The Vietnam War was one of the central issues that had U.S. citizens protesting against the government during the tumultuous 1960s. Opposition to the war started on college campuses, where students who had grown up following the civil rights protests of the 1950s and early '60s applied the same methods to organize protests against the war. The protestors felt that the government's goal to "stop the spread of Communism in the world" was not a good enough reason for fighting. As the years wore on, with American soldiers dying by the thousands and no clear objective to be gained, more and more Americans agreed that the fighting should end. Military officials, many of whom began their careers as young men participating in the great American victories in World War II in the 1940s, could not accept the idea that America could lose in combat against a tiny country like North Vietnam. They did not want to leave without winning, and they expanded the war, spending more money and more lives and spreading the violence into the neighboring countries of Cambodia and Laos, which served to intensify the protests at home. President Richard Nixon, hoping to please both sides, promised that a settlement would be negotiated, but that America would not accept "peace without honor." In 1973 the U.S. troops were withdrawn. In 1975 the U.S. government stopped sending money and weapons to South Vietnam, and almost immediately the capitol city of Saigon was taken over by the Communists of the North. On television, U.S. citizens watched American diplomats in Saigon fleeing in terror, as army helicopters tried to carry them away—a strong visual image that the war had not been settled, giving the impression of America running away.

At the same time President Nixon was arranging the withdrawal of troops, he was concerned with the collapse of his own presidency. It started on June 17, 1972, when five men were arrested for breaking into the headquarters of the Democratic National Party in the Watergate Hotel in Washington, DC. Investigators soon found connections between the burglars and Nixon's re-election committee. As the 1972 presidential elections approached, stories associating the burglars with the Nixon White House trickled out, but citizens paid little attention, and in November Nixon defeated the Democratic candidate, George McGovern. Throughout 1973 and 1974, however, investigations continued to turn up incriminating evidence that connected the men who planned the break-in to higher government officials, including Cabinet officials and Nixon's Chief of Staff. These investigations also uncovered other crimes associated with Nixon, including tax problems and using government agencies to harass his political enemies. On August 9, 1974, Nixon resigned. The man who followed him as president, Gerald Ford, granted Nixon an unconditional pardon for any crimes he may have committed while in office. Disappointed that he had let Nixon go without making him stand trial for his crimes, the country voted Ford out of office in the 1976 elections. In 1975, while *Ragtime* was a huge success on the bestseller lists, the country was recovering from watching its social institutions unravel.

Critical Overview

It would be very difficult to find a piece of criticism that does not take *Ragtime* as a serious work of art. In his book-length survey of Doctorow's career, John G. Parks briefly mentions a few negative reviews of the book, including one by Roger Dale, who, in *The New York Times Book Review,* called it "all surface," and a piece by respected reviewer Hilton Kramer, who objected in *Commentary* to the novel's leftist political sensibilities. Parks identifies these critics as "second wave," who, having seen the glowing newspaper reviews and high sales figures after the novel was published, set out to go against popular opinion. Parks himself pays close attention to the themes of the book and finds it to be worthy of study and respect, in addition to being a "carnivalesque novel" that explores serious literary issues, such as the instability of history and the transitory nature of personality. Many other literary critics identified and applauded the book's ability to provoke thought without being too dense for general audiences, while still others looked at the same virtues from another direction, lauding it for being a popular book that is not afraid to touch on thought-provoking subjects. For example, Bernard F. Rogers, Jr., reviewing the book for *Chicago Review,* expressed his admiration for both the form and the content of *Ragtime:* he felt that the form appealed to critics and literati by experimenting with narrative, and to general audiences by striking a chord of familiarity; and that the content also played well to both audiences, struggling with serious themes while keeping readers entertained. Doctorow's novels are "simultaneously artistically venturesome and socially conscious," Arthur Seltzman wrote in a review called "The Stylistic Energy of E. L. Doctorow." "Like the Postmodernists," Seltzman asserted, "Doctorow extends the strategic possibilities of language; like the Naturalists, he employs language in the study of social ills."

Since most critics agree that *Ragtime* is an artistic as well as commercial success, most reviews throughout the years have tended to steer away from the question of whether the book succeeds and toward the study of how that success is brought about. David Emblidge, in a 1977 review, noted that Doctorow's very style made myths out of the incidents presented, even in cases where it seemed that myth-making was not his goal. Emblidge goes on to say that this is not necessarily bad for the author's works. David S. Gross thought that this mythological tone was actually a low-key satire of the kind of history lessons that are learned from schoolbooks, "wanting to destroy their easy and mystifying generalizations which prevent any accurate historical understanding." Paul Levine, in his book about Doctorow's career, takes note of the fact that much of what is done in *Ragtime* was done in a different form in John Dos Passos's *U.S.A. Trilogy*. Other critics, including Barbara Foley and John Seelye, examine the same connection, concluding that *Ragtime* surpasses the three-novel sequence by using contrasts to make its cynical point more quickly and efficiently. One of the sharpest critics of Doctorow's treatment of history is Greil Marcus, who wrote a review in the *Village Voice* pointing out the similarities between *Ragtime* and *Nashville,* a popular movie released at the same time that also used a large cast of characters to show the American dream faltering. The problem, as Marcus put it, was that both of these works were spun from their creators' theories of life, rather than from the writers' experiences. Most critics would agree, although most would say that this is not a bad thing if it is used well, as it is by Doctorow.

Criticism

David J. Kelly

David J. Kelly is a literature and creative writing instructor at several colleges in Illinois. In the following essay, he examines the relatively minor role that death plays in Ragtime *and finds it to be a function of Doctorow's ability to create characters.*

Steeped as it is in the past, slowed by the lazy, dreamy tone of things half-remembered, or half-forgotten, or only once implied, *Ragtime* doesn't impress one as a book about lives hanging in the balance. Oh, *life* is in it, and one comes away from reading the last pages with the feeling of having wandered through not just a few lives. But maybe as a result of the dreamy tone or maybe as the cause of it, life does not seem to be counterbalanced with its opposite. It isn't that characters in the book live forever, or that they can only be gotten rid of by going away and not coming back. At least six prominent characters die throughout the course of the story, starting with the early killing of Stanford White, gunned down in the stately restaurant he designed, and extending through to the news that Father sank with the *Lusitania*. But death does not carry much weight in this novel: it means little, surrounded as it is by the grandeur of life. In the end, the whole big complex world is just explained as being a neighborhood, and all the people, "white black, fat thin, rich poor, all kinds" are presented as "a society of ragamuffins, like all of us, getting into trouble and getting out again." Death is put forth here as just one more large patch of trouble to be gotten through.

There is nothing at all disturbing about the death of Stanford White. When it is first mentioned, on the second page of the book, it is quickly skipped across in a flow of esoterica about that long-ago time, sandwiched between Winslow Homer's seascapes and Charles Dana Gibson's newspaper drawing of Evelyn Nesbit resplendent in her fame and beauty. At his shooting, the narration never really settles on the murdered man, but swings past him: he's in the middle of the action, but not really central to it. We are told quite clearly that Harry Thaw wore a straw hat and a heavy black coat, and that Evelyn's underwear was white (presumably a visual to imply just how sudden and spastic her faint had been, that it could knock an ankle-length dress up that high). We are not told anything about how the victim looked.

If there is any possible sense of sorrow at this loss of life, it is over almost immediately. The story shifts to Evelyn, mentioning her underclothes and then the fact that she had been a famous beauty by age fifteen, and then it juxtaposes that youth and beauty and innocent-colored underwear with the revelation that the murdering millionaire "habitually whipped her." If White's life were not dismissed cleanly enough with that, he is brought back into the book later, to contrast the soft, indulgent lifestyle he led with the human misery that he was oblivious to right up to the day of his death. Newsman Jacob Riis goes to interview White about the possibility of designing buildings that would not breed disease, and finds the architect supervising a ship's unloading, anxious about the pricey cargo of art objects while shouting at immigrant workers and whacking them with his umbrella. While he dines at the roof garden at Madison Square and catches the opening of *Mamzelle Champagne*, the poor are suffering through a heat wave without any water in their buildings: "The sink at the bottom of the stairs was dry. Fathers raced through the streets looking for ice." His ignorance of their misery makes his murder seem a perfectly just reward.

The other famous characters from the pages of history who die in *Ragtime* are Archduke Franz Ferdinand and J. P. Morgan. The Archduke is an obscure and comical figure. He is weighed down with the silly outdated uniform of the future leader of the outdated Austro-Hungarian empire, which was to fall apart after his assassination in 1914.

What Do I Read Next?

- The character of Coalhouse Walker Jr. is based upon the character Michael Kohlhaas from an 1808 novella written by German author Heinrich von Kleist. "Michael Kohlhaas" is included in *Tales,* which is a collection of von Kleist's novellas, and also in *Twelve German Novellas,* edited and translated by Harry Steinhauer, published by the University of California Press in 1977.

- All of Doctorow's novels use *Ragtime*'s technique of intertwining history with fiction, to varying degrees. Especially noteworthy among them are *The Book of Daniel,* published in 1971, which resembles *Ragtime* in that it gives a rare look at dissident politics in America (it is loosely based on the 1951 execution of accused spies Julius and Ethel Rosenberg), and *The Waterworks,* published in 1994, which gives an eerily convincing sense of Now York society in the 1870s.

- The novels that John Dos Passos wrote in the 1920s and 1930s were similar to *Ragtime* in that they presented real-life characters and news events along with fiction. Dos Passos's most ambitious and experimental work was his trilogy of novels, *The Forty-second Parallel, 1919,* and *The Big Money,* published together as *The U.S.A. Trilogy.*

- The labor movement that Doctorow includes in the book is central to Upton Sinclair's 1906 masterpiece *The Jungle.* This book is a novel, but Sinclair researched the details the way a news reporter would, and it gives a good view of life in 1906. Most readers remember this book for its graphic scenes of disgusting conditions in Chicago's meatpacking facilities, but its real focus is on the struggle for workers' rights and the system used at that time to keep workers powerless.

- Doctorow's thoughts are expressed more directly in his essays than in his fiction, and readers interested in *Ragtime* might find it hard to put down his highly-regarded collection *Jack London, Ernest Hemingway and the Constitution: Selected Essays, 1977-1992.* Subjects covered, in addition to those referred to in the title, include writing in general, Henry David Thoreau, and Ronald Reagan.

Modern readers are amused by his plumed helmet and flat-top crewcut and big waxy moustache. Having been brought out to an airfield to watch Houdini fly an airplane, and never having seen a plane before, and having not, presumably, been a follower of the vaudeville circuit, he reasonably assumed that Houdini invented the contraption he was flying. In the real world, the Archduke's death triggered the horrors of modern warfare and was directly responsible for shifts in power that brought the world the Third Reich, Vietnam and Sarajevo, but within the context of the book the loss of this poor befuddled man, whose first reaction to his own assassination was "The day is ruined," is just another interesting detail. J. P. Morgan comes off as being a little more worth our sympathy, if only because the story spends quite a bit of space tracking his thoughts. He dies old and content—"he was far from unhappy, having concluded that his physical deterioration was exactly the sign for which he had been waiting." Morgan, a staunch believer in reincarnation, could not wait to die, so that he could be back on Earth again that much sooner.

One of the reasons that death is so undisturbing in this book is the recurring imagery of either life after death or an afterlife. It is not much of a book for symbolism, but there is mythology in the air, and among mankind's strongest myths are those that involve people who went to the other side and then came back. Here Doctorow presents his readers with the Myth of the Baby Who Grew in the Garden. It would be too simplistic to call this Christ-imagery, because we are not told what the baby grew up to be like, but we do know that he came out of his grave, and that he was in the garden, where good things like vegetables and flowers come up out of the dirt.

Father is not resurrected, but he does go on forever, "arriving eternally on the shore of his Self." He is discontent throughout the story, a fact symbolized by his going off on Polar explorations, literally searching the remotest corners of the globe to fulfill some need. The author could squeeze him out of the family with divorce, but he is sent to his reward in the end. As in the case of Morgan, death is presented as a type of fulfillment for those who have outlived their worldly purpose and deserve to go someplace better.

The deaths of Sarah and Coalhouse are not comical or gentle. In some sense, Coalhouse Walker's death could possibly be considered self-willed: not because he created the circumstances surrounding it, which he was only partly responsible for, but because he knows full well that he will be shot. His will is written, and "probably he knew that all he must do in order to end his life was to turn his head abruptly or lower his hands or smile." True to the novel's style, Walker's death is not presented directly, but is relayed from the point of view of non-witnesses: first, apparently, from news accounts, since we are told he "was said by police to have made a dash for freedom," and then from Father, who does not look outside until the shooting is all over. There is a fog of mystery around the specifics of Walker's death, just as there is around the death of Younger Brother. Both of them rise above any horror they go through to become mythical figures.

Sarah's is the only death presented as being truly tragic, painful, and unnecessary. She is not prepared, and is mystified about what happens to her: her death is a result of a misunderstanding touched off by bigotry. The murder of Sarah should have a more chilling impact on the reader, but it doesn't, because Sarah is the most poorly-realized character in the book. In theory, the details about her make for a good and reasonable story: the unwed mother who gives birth in secret and then tries to kill the baby, the jilted woman who resists her returning suitor's courtship, the naive girl who turns to the President to solve her problems. Too many factors have to be ignored, though, to believe what we are told about Sarah. Readers have to not wonder where she comes from. They have to accept the fact that she could live in the house and raise her child without speaking, or that the narrative, which can get into a private meeting between

Morgan and Henry Ford, would not know what she says. In the end, her death seems too fantastic, too convenient for the novelist's requirements, yet three shades more brutal than anything else in the world of the book, including the strike-breaking police. "Perhaps in the dark windy evening of the impending storm it seemed to Sherman's guards that Sarah's black hand was a weapon"—even though its first word tries to cloud reality, the statement rings false except on a symbolic level. The horror of her beating and death is weakened by the faint reminder that this is all fiction.

The fact that the deaths in *Ragtime* are presented in ways that do not shock is, in this case, a good thing: these characters are, for the most part, fulfilled by their deaths. In other cases this could be taken to indicate a world view on the part of the author that is serene, finding everything, even death, to have its place in the grand scheme of things. Doctorow uses a sarcastic tone, though, that implies anything but serenity. The reason the deaths in this book are not shocking is that they seem appropriate, which is a tribute to how well-drawn these characters are. Things here happen when it is their time—even the death of Coalhouse Walker, and even the death of Sarah. Doctorow brings these characters full circle, explaining their lives in ways that make their deaths the logical results. While another book might shy away from death or give death a dark, menacing presence, *Ragtime* presents it, but in this presentation it does not seem so bad.

Source: David J. Kelly, in an essay for *Novels for Students,* Gale, 1999.

Derek Wright

In the excerpt below, Wright investigates Doctorow's use of "pseudo-history" to create his story about marginalized men and women in American society.

Perhaps the crucial difference between E.L. Doctorow's *Ragtime* (1975) and other, more thoroughgoing fictional reinventions of history such as Barth's *Giles Goat-Boy* (1966) or Rushdie's *Shame* (1983) is that the latter use history to say something about fiction—they display the endlessly fertile capacity of the novelistic imagination to compensate for the stubborn limitations, or paucity, of facts—while Doctorow uses fiction to say something about history. Specifically, Doctorow calls into question the whole business of historicity and the origination of historical "fact" from possibly doubtful sources. Doctorow's metaphor for history in the novel is a "player piano" that plays its own tune, regardless of the style—classical, romantic, ragtime—which the pianist chooses to interpret it in. History, as the music of what happened, the events that actually took place, is not the same as history as it is received in the present from what historians have written down. Events are not scientifically mappable by "history" any more than, in Doctorow's novel, the North Pole is precisely locatable by the explorers of the Peary expedition or the correct alignment of the chair with the room by Theodore Dreiser. We put our flag or chair down anywhere: we make our own centers. As Doctorow, following Roland Barthes, has said in interview statements, there is no fiction or non-fiction, only narrative: the telling of a story.

Indeed, history, insofar as it is always narrowly partial and selective, is one of the least trustworthy and potentially one of the most fictional of narrative forms. As the opening pages of *Ragtime* demonstrate, whole racial groups have been written out of American history simply by not being mentioned, and the task of the novelist, as conceived by Doctorow, is to write them back in. The novelist's own pseudo-history parodies and then rewrites the falsely sentimental, nostalgic picture of the American past, as composed from the patriotic viewpoint of the dominant white middle-class culture which prevailed at the turn of the century. Not only are Doctorow's characters historically syncopated, fractionally offbeat on the historical chronometer like the base key which is marginally behind the melody in Scott Joplin's music (his Emma Goldman and Walker gang belong, in fact, to the 1960s), but his entire quasi-history is itself systematically unsynchronized or "in ragged time" with the school textbook, its facts always slightly askew from the received version. Against the known facts, Doctorow syncopates what he regards as "truthful fictions," which are poetically if not historically true: Freud and Jung mischievously shut up together in the Tunnel of Love on Coney Island and, on a more serious note, the Poverty Balls where guests dress in rags and the Stockyard Ball that is set in a mock-slaughterhouse. Concerning the latter two instances, which were certainly in the spirit of the times whether true or not, Doctorow's point is that in the early 1900s American reality was already becoming so incredible that it was most accurately located at the point where history fades into fiction, the factual into the fantastic.

History, Doctorow subsequently implies, is so patently fictional that there is no longer any felt need to preserve in separate categories fictional and historical plots and characters as, for example, Dos Passos had done in his trilogy *U.S.A.* (1937). Thus, all the canons of historical decorum are violated: personages from the newsreels and history books enter audaciously into the fictional life of the book either by performing fictional acts or meeting fictional characters.

And yet there are still a number of differences between the novel's fictional and historical material which assert themselves in its narrative form and serve to keep the two kinds of material in separate and clearly differentiated categories. Firstly, the historical vignettes of J. P. Morgan, Henry Ford, and Harry Houdini have a tendency to immobilize the narrative by the sheer mass of detailed information, to clutter it with blocks of fact, most notably in long accounts of the objects and properties the characters own. This draws attention obtrusively to the amount of undiluted factuality that has not been fictionalized, i.e., artistically shaped into dramatically interesting narrative material.

Secondly and more importantly, the abrupt shifts in locale in the historical material give the impression of history as a sprawling chaotic mass of unconnected facts. Doctorow's point, of course, is that history is plotless, playing its own heedless, incomprehensible music and plotted quite arbitrarily by the historian. But in practice this means that the novel acquires a sense of direction and causality, and indeed any coherence at all, only from the momentum of the fictional plots (of Tateh and Coalhouse Walker). Only then do we sense the presence of a causally related train of events and of mounting crisis, leading to a climax. The novel's underlying postulate, argues Barbara Foley [in her essay "From *U.S.A.* to *Ragtime*," in *E. L. Doctorow: Essays and Conversations,* edited by Richard Trenner, 1983], is that "whatever coherence emerges from the represented historical world is attributable to the writer's power as teller of his story, with the result that the process of historical reconstruction itself, rather than what is being represented, comes to the fore." What is implied by Doctorow's choice of form is a rather egotistical and paranoid view of history: that the only coherence history has is to be traced to the writer's superior talents as a storyteller.

Thirdly, there is the matter of characterization. We read of Tateh: "He began to create more and more intricate silhouettes, full-figured with backgrounds... With his scissors he suggested not merely outlines but textures, moods, character, despair." Tateh's brief silhouette-sketches illumine character in the light of background; they reveal personality in terms of the determining, victimizing forces acting upon it, and in this they act as a metaphor for the novelist's own flat, silhouettish, two-dimensional creations—in this case, the types of the Poor Jew and of the entrepreneurial Self-Made Man Tateh turns himself into once he has forsaken his victim-status. Doctorow's figures are essentially passive units impinged upon by social and economic forces, conductors of "the flow of American energy" which Tateh, like other American artists, learns to "point his life along," and the novelist seems to be as much interested in this current of historical energy as in the characters it pulses through. The outcome is that the semifictional cast of *Ragtime* are at times presented as the puppet-victims of history, jerked around in both comic and tragic ways by overwhelming forces, whether of repressed sexuality or institutionalized racism—Younger Brother by the rampant penis that "whips him about the floor" at the lesbian encounter of Evelyn Nesbitt and Emma Goldman, Coalhouse Walker by the firing squad that jerks his body about the street "in a sequence of attitudes as if it were trying to mop up its own blood."

The aesthetic price paid by Doctorow's historical fiction is that the characters, real or invented, are like historical characters: they are thinly textured creations, seen from the outside, not as intricate, complex individuals. Thus we never know if Younger Brother, in joining the Walker gang, is motivated by a burning passion for justice or simply by thrills and excitement ("I can make bombs"), because we are not admitted to his psychological dilemmas and crises. If we are surprised at the end to find that Walker is really not a revolutionary but just wants his car back, it is because we too have seen him, externally, through the public responses of the media, cinema newsreels, and newspapers features.

It would therefore be fitting that Walker should end his life as a historical character. In fact he does not. His fate is not that of the historical nineteenth-century visionary Hans Kohlhaas, who saw himself as a millenial revolutionary and an avenging agent of the Archangel Michael come to form a new world government. It is, instead, that of the eponymous hero of Kleist's novella *Michael Kohlhaas* (1810) about the sixteenth-century horse dealer Michael Kohlhaas (who here becomes "Coalhouse") and his pursuit of justice against the corrupt Junker Wenzel Von Tronka (here, Willie Conklin) over the wrecking of his horses (here, a car). Kleist's Kohlhaas simply wants his horses back but

he has to murder, rob, and loot in order to get the injustice redressed and the price, as in Coalhouse Walker's case, is his own execution: the shining new horses are paraded past him as he climbs the scaffold. Society finally pays its debt to him, and he to it, for his crimes. Coalhouse Walker, though he appears to be perceived in historical terms, is really a derived fiction, and he ends as one, paralleling the fiction in which he has his origin. He ends as a character in somebody else's book.

Source: Derek Wright, "*Ragtime* Revisited: History and Fiction in Doctorow's Novel," in *International Fiction Review*, Vol. 20, No. 1, 1993, pp. 14–16.

Marshall Bruce Gentry

In the next essay, Gentry interprets Doctorow's symbolic use of the automobile as a way to express individuality, yet still stay within the bounds of societal conventions.

The Model T automobile at the center of E. L. Doctorow's popular novel *Ragtime* may seem essentially sinister, the product of Henry Ford's assembly-line mentality and of an oppressive myth of American success. *Ragtime* might then seem the perfect example of a novelistic attack on automobile culture in America. One of Carol Yeh's drawings for the illustrated Bantam edition of *Ragtime* could be seen as expressing this view: Harry Houdini is bound and chained inside automobile tires, from which he will presumably make one of his not-quite-satisfying escapes. The novel's statement that Houdini never damages or unlocks the enchaining materials from which he releases himself could be taken as confirmation that the societal forces embodied in an automobile are unchanged by our temporary escapes. That the society of the ragtime era appeared to value automobiles more highly than people may even make the auto a grotesque symbol of a culture's collective neurosis, especially since the automobiles have names like Pope-Toledo Runabout or Pierce Arrow Opera Coach while human beings are named simply: Mameh and Tateh, Mother and Father, Mother's Younger Brother, the Little Girl and Little Boy.

David Emblidge argues for what is perhaps the most pessimistic reading of *Ragtime* possible, saying that "Life in the present in *Ragtime* is a continuous recapitulation of the past." Emblidge sees the novel as presenting us with a fascinating set of illusory indications of change that fails to effect any genuine change in mankind's hopeless condition. In this reading, the automobile and Ford's system of mass production are part of a "double apotheosis" (along with J. P. Morgan's theories about order) of the duplicable event. Another critical view of the automobile in *Ragtime* could be expressed in the terms of one of Father's observations during the final negotiations with Coalhouse Walker Jr.: "The car has no real value." For some readers the multiple significances of the automobile effectively empty it of meaning; in other words, the automobile is merely part of a whirlpool of chaotic, noisy, violent images in which human meaning is lost. For Geoffrey Galt Harpham, Coalhouse Walker's "Model T on whose uniqueness he paradoxically insists is actually a case of duplication so utter that there cannot even be said to be an original"; it seems to follow that *Ragtime* is "a book with no meaning." In this view the novelist Theodore Dreiser might seem like a human being pushed down to the status of a defective automobile, turning hopelessly "in circles seeking the proper alignment."

In contrast to these views, I would like to suggest that the automobile in *Ragtime* is crucial to Doctorow's vision of how human individuality and artistic value are created. Even as Doctorow's characters desperately use their autos as "getaway cars" or drive toward the chaos symbolized by water, we discover various ways in which the automobile is more than a toy that capitalism uses to distract and manipulate the masses. In Coalhouse Walker's receipt of a restored Model T, and in the Little Boy's visions of the car as a reflection of himself and of his society, we have definitions of how the self can do more than dissolve into a mass of humanity that makes America seem, as it does to J. P. Morgan at one point, merely part of "an empty universe" full of "horse's asses." Ultimately I think *Ragtime* says that we, like the Little Boy or Coalhouse, are like automobiles, that we are at least potentially individuals while paradoxically being all alike, and that this novel is itself an automobile. Like *Ragtime* as novel, we should be at once part of the mass (it was and is a popular novel) and in some sense unduplicable (although many novels mix historical "fact" and fiction fancifully, they also aspire to be original achievements). And when we become aware of how like an automobile we are and how like an automobile a novel is, we can discover more of the individuality of ourselves and of *Ragtime*.

Another way of stating my point is to say that *Ragtime* emphasizes the social origin of human individuality and of art. Just as the Model T is a product of a mass of working-class laborers, all the characters in *Ragtime*, all the readers of the novel, and the novel itself, are presented as products of a mass

of contributing forces. But this societal basis to reality does not destroy characters or readers or the novel; it simply shifts the rules by which we discover individualized significance. Even as we learn that Evelyn Nesbit's celebrity is an industrial construction, even as we realize that we readers have been trained to ignore many versions of American history, and even as we struggle with the multiple narrative points of view in the novel, we are given a new, more complex, more valid understanding of human personality, of the reader's role in the production of meaning, of authorship, and perhaps even of the American automobile. Martin Green has accused Doctorow of encouraging "nostalgia" for the early automobile, but I think Doctorow's treatment of the automobile demonstrates a fascinatingly complex understanding of the automobile's meaning.

Some historical background might make it easier to recognize the positive aspects of the automobile in *Ragtime*. In many ways, American culture has associated the automobile with freedom, and the Model T would be an especially good symbol of human freedom since it was, as Reynold M. Wik points out, "especially designed to travel over difficult terrain." Warren Belasco has even described the period from 1900 to 1920 (roughly the time period covered by *Ragtime*) as the era of anarchic "gypsying," of the use of automobiles to travel freely around the country without planning and to camp each night without expenses. Belasco concludes that "the automobile industry became the backbone of modern industrial capitalism, yet it was born in a spirit of rebellion against that system." If we recall that only 8,000 automobiles were registered in America in 1900 and that 8,000,000 were registered in 1920 [according to Mark S. Foster in his article "The Automobile and the City," in *The Automobile and American Culture,* edited by David L. Lewis and Laurence Goldstein, 1983], we might conclude reasonably that the automobile symbolizes an explosion of rebelliousness on the part of Americans....

The automobile in *Ragtime* often seems to be symbolically opposed to the sea, with the auto suggesting humanity's technological control and the sea suggesting chaos, irrationality, emotion. But in at least two significant instances, the symbols come together in ways that suggest positive qualities for the automobile—when Coalhouse Walker's car enters the Firehouse Pond, and when Mother drives herself, the Little Boy, and Coalhouse Walker III to Prout's Neck, Maine, home of Winslow Homer, who had once painted light associated with chaos:

Homer painted the light. It gave the sea a heavy dull menace and shone coldly on the rocks and shoals of the New England coast. There were unexplained shipwrecks and brave towline rescues. Odd things went on in lighthouses and in shacks nestled in the wild beach plum. Across America sex and death were barely distinguishable.

The early reference to Homer is significant because, during the Atlantic City storm that seems to bring Mother and Tateh together once and for all, she resembles "in her wet form the ample woman in the Winslow Homer painting who is being rescued from the sea by towline." I would suggest that the movement of the car towards water in both the Coalhouse Walker story and the story of the New Rochelle family symbolizes a complex interaction of forces in which the automobile, *like* the ocean to which it may *seem* to be opposed, is associated with some of the positive aspects of chaos.

As we turn to the issue of how the automobile provides a model for the achievement of human individuality, it may seem difficult to decide how seriously we are to take Coalhouse Walker Jr. as a heroic figure in what is sometimes considered the one traditional plot line in *Ragtime.* According to Martin Green, Doctorow's attitude toward Coalhouse Walker and toward Sarah is "uncritically romantic" and therefore flawed. While it may be true that Coalhouse Walker "defends his personal dignity fanatically, refusing to bend at all in the face of money-power and racial prejudice" [according to David S. Gross in his article "Tales of Obscene Power," in *E. L. Doctorow: Essays and Conversations,* edited by Richard Trenner, 1983], it is also true that he has accepted the dominant culture's belief that possessions like a Model T can add to his status and dignity, and when his car is desecrated and pushed into a pond by Willie Conklin and other volunteer firemen, who significantly have not yet made the switch from horses to motors, we may wonder how much Doctorow expects us to want Walker to regain the car. For Leonard and Barbara Quart, it is "a bit absurd" for Coalhouse Walker to be willing "to sacrifice and destroy lives with no larger political end than redeeming his car and gaining personal respect." Barbara L. Estrin makes this issue of Coalhouse Walker's heroism a major part of the novel's point. The story of Coalhouse Walker's occupation of the Morgan Museum "is undermined by the pervading feeling that its outcome was so predictable, its conclusion so forecast by the forces of a society bent on the preservation of the industrial system, that the action comes to nothing." Because of the "system of interchange-

able parts" that allows the easy replacement of Coalhouse Walker's car, Walker's death is unnecessary, "his death, like his revolution, a meaningless sacrifice. Nothing was changed by it." All the characters of *Ragtime* are, according to Estrin, "cogs on the wheels of time," and thus the novel seems to say "that we are all expendable."

I would like to suggest that Coalhouse Walker grows into his individuality, that it is precisely when Mother's Younger Brother is astonished to see Walker equating a mere car with justice that Walker has achieved heroism. It is crucial to the novel that Coalhouse Walker Jr. receives a car that is indeed a duplicate of his original Model T with the Pantasote top and at the same time a different car. Surely the car is more significant in its replacement form because the whole of New York's political establishment is watching it. The remade car is also different from the original in the sense that it is *not* produced by assembly line: "Fire Chief Conklin … piece by piece dismantled the Ford and made a new Ford from the chassis up." One might wonder whether Doctorow is claiming that this car produced by an individual is in some sense morally superior, or whether Doctorow is arguing for a return to the individual craftsman, and my answer would be yes but also no—it is impossible (following a logic that the novel suggests) to have individual craftsmanship, because Willie Conklin becomes the mass of society, "so ordinary as to be like all men," and, at least while he is building the car, he "become[s] Pierpont Morgan, the most important individual of his time." Even as Coalhouse Walker's demand is met, another Model T comes out of mass production. At the same time, it is worth noting that if a Ford cannot be produced by only one individual, not even Henry Ford can make a Ford by himself. The view that presents the Model T as a product of the entire society frees the automobile from Ford's tyranny to some extent. And there is something of a victory for Coalhouse even as the police equate him with the replaced car, complete with what might be considered the symbolically crucial customizing Pantasote top. He exchanges his life for the car *and* for the lives of his band of revolutionaries, all in a sense duplicates of Walker who call themselves Coalhouse.

The issues of the establishment of selfhood in a world of mass production are spelled out even more complexly in the story of the narrator, the Little Boy. *Ragtime* claims, through the Little Boy as narrator, that it is essential that one perceive (and maintain) the differences within apparent duplicates, as well as the similarities in things that seem chaotically dissimilar. Chapter 15 is crucial to an understanding of the Little Boy's fondness both for change, as taught by his grandfather, and for pattern. Not enough has been said critically about the significance for the boy of minor changes within pattern, of the rare occasion when the hairbrush or window does not remain still, of the slight changes that prove "even statues did not remain the same." The Little Boy seems to understand that the slight difference within sameness is the metaphor for his own individuality. Much has been made of the Little Boy's fondness for baseball because, he says, "The same thing happens over and over." According to Barbara L. Estrin, among others, baseball is a prime example of the sameness that rather depressingly underlies the appearance of change. But even here we see some delight in novelty, for as soon as the Little Boy praises the pattern, he is excited by the unusual occurrence of a foul ball that ends up in his hands. The point surely is that the Little Boy can always see both sides, and therein lies his power. Much has been said about the boy's vision of a "macrocephalic image of himself" in Houdini's headlight as a sign that the Little Boy is overly subjective, and some readers have been troubled by such a possibility. Barbara Foley criticizes *Ragtime* for implying that historical meaning as produced by this narrator is "chimerical and at best highly subjective," based on the notion "that whatever coherence emerges from the represented historical world is attributable to the writer's power as teller of his story." The Little Boy's amazing and initially obscure advice for Houdini, that he warn the Archduke Ferdinand of his coming assassination and of WWI, may even seem significant primarily for its pointlessness. In Estrin's interesting reading, the Little Boy's warning in the first chapter is a sort of failed authorial intrusion demonstrating the power of the machine over us all:

> With the insight he gains from subsequent experience, the little boy, pre-figuring the storyteller he later becomes, informs the magician. We live our lives in the illusion that we can change things, in the hope that we amount to more than insignificant parts of a vast machine moving inexorably toward doom. The child anticipates, simultaneously as the narrator reconstructs, history…. "Warn the Duke," he says, sounding a command that might alter the course of the novel we are about to read.

Although I do not agree with Barbara Cooper's description of the narrative persona of *Ragtime* as "anonymous," I agree with her idea that the narrator "transcends the limitations of a single human perspective." I would like to emphasize the idea

that the narrator's ability to combine points of view is more nearly the ground of his selfhood than a dilution of it. The narrator is at once a product of his time and an individual exercising some effect upon his time. His visions are not all of the sort that ends the first chapter and that Houdini somewhat pathetically reproduces near the novel's end. More should be made of the fact that the Little Boy's eyes are compared to a "school globe" and of the line in the description of Sarah's funeral that insists emphatically that the boy sees not just himself but the rest of this society: Sarah's hearse "was so highly polished the boy could see in its rear doors a reflection of the entire street." This line suggests that the Little Boy's visions are at once internal and external. Even in the episode in which the Little Boy stares at Houdini's headlight and sees himself, we can find more than an indication that the boy is at once able to predict world events and to be obsessed with his own head. Before he realizes that Houdini's car is approaching, the Little Boy equates the car visually with a fly. He fixes "his gaze on a bluebottle fly traversing the screen in a way that made it appear to be coming up the hill from North Avenue. The fly flew off. An automobile was coming up the hill from North Avenue." Perhaps the fascination with the fly is the result of the fly's possession of multiple eyes, in which case the boy's fascination with the car seems to be related to the automobile's multiplicities. The automobile in this passage suggests the value of multiple perspectives, not just the Little Boy's perspective. The narrator's possession of mystical powers seems far-fetched to some readers, but it does function to combine the options of reading *Ragtime* as mass-produced and of reading it as the production of an individual author. Although Geoffrey Galt Harpham says that the novel has "no consistent or even possible narrative persona," surely the key to understanding the narrative voice is in noticing, as Harpham himself points out, that the narrator "materializes miraculously at the very end as an older narrator." The point, I believe, is not so much that the Little Boy "will grow up to write the narrative" [as Paul Levine writes in his book *E. L. Doctorow,* 1985], as that he writes the narrative in *order* to grow up, that the construction of the novel is the construction of its creator as well, that the Little Boy achieves genuine individuality in duplicating—with a difference—the data produced by the assembly-line of ragtime America. Harpham claims that Mother and Tateh "most conspicuously" enjoy the "fate" of a "happy ending" as they "achieve individuation by mastering the processes of replication." While I accept the direction of Harpham's argument here, it also seems true that achievement and *mastery* are terms better applied to the Little Boy or Coalhouse than to Mother and Tateh, and Harpham does label the Little Boy the novel's "most successful character."

Angela Hague has argued that the duplicated event is "a way of overcoming—and, paradoxically, exemplifying—the fluidity of reality" and that the Little Boy's "attempt" at "self-duplication … accomplishes the negation of his own distinct personality." When he gazes into a mirror, the Little Boy feels that

> there were two selves facing one another, neither of which could claim to be the real one. The sensation was of being disembodied. He was no longer anything exact as a person. He had the dizzying feeling of separating from himself endlessly.

We need not consider this vision of multiplicity any more valid than the opposing sense of selfhood, however. It may be true that for a youngster, a sense of a fluid self is closer to the truth than the understanding such a child might have about wholeness, but it still ought to be possible to believe that the Little Boy as an adult will be able to balance the fluid and static impressions of the self. I think that Hague is absolutely correct in pointing out that motion pictures "both contradict and reinforce" the Little Boy's beliefs about change, but I am inclined to consider Doctorow to be more pleased than displeased about such a state of affairs.

The socialization of authorship involved in seeing a novel as an auto operated by a narrative persona at once himself and everybody is not all that different from what Doctorow [in his essay "False Documents," in *E. L. Doctorow: Essays and Conversations,* 1983] describes as the traditional novelistic device of "gaining authority for the narrative" through the dissociation of the individual author from it. Just as we may have more faith in a car produced by collective effort, we may trust the novel that presents the views of everyone in society, at least by implication. Even Barbara L. Estrin admits that *Ragtime* presents mass production as nothing new, that "it emerges simply as a different form of what existed long ago." It would seem to follow that the automobile cannot represent a decline in civilization, even in Estrin's reading; that it represents the duplication with a modern wrinkle of the ways in which human beings have always achieved meaning. *Ragtime* uses the automobile to suggest how we can satisfy our desire for individuality in spite of the societal forces demanding uniformity.

Source: Marshall Bruce Gentry, *"Ragtime* as Auto Biography," in *Kansas Quarterly,* Vol. 21, No. 4, Fall, 1989, pp. 105–112.

Sources

David Emblidge, "Progress as Illusion in Doctorow's Novels," *Southwest Review,* Vol. LXI, Autumn, 1977, pp. 397-409.

Barbara Foley, "From *U.S.A.* to *Ragtime:* Notes on the Forms of Historical Consciousness in Modern Fiction," *American Literature,* no. 50, 1978, pp. 85-105.

David S. Gross, "Tales of Obscene Power, Money and Culture, Modernism and History, in the Fiction of E. L. Doctorow," *Genre,* no. 13, 1980, pp. 71-92.

Paul Levine, *E. L. Doctorow,* Methuen, 1985.

John G. Parks, "Compositions of Dissatisfaction: *Ragtime,"* Continuum, 1991.

Bernard F. Rodgers Jr., "A Novelist's Revenge," *Chicago Review,* Vol. 27, 1976, p. 139.

John Seelye, "Doctorow's Dissertation," *The New Republic,* Vol. CLXXLI, April 10, 1976, p. 22.

Arthur Seltzman, "The Stylistic Energy of E. L. Doctorow," in *E. L. Doctorow: Essays and Conversations,* edited by Richard Trenner, Ontario Review Press, 1983.

For Further Study

Linda Donn, *Freud and Jung: Years of Friendship, Years of Loss,* Charles Scribner's Sons, 1988.
    This comprehensive and readable biography gives a good look at two of *Ragtime*'s minor characters, and how the world changed as the years passed.

Paul Levine, *E. L. Doctorow,* Methuen, 1985.
    This book, which covers Doctorow's works up to *Lives of the Poets,* is arranged thematically, with chapters such as "Politics and Imagination," "Fiction and Formulas," "Fiction and Radicalism," and "Fiction and History."

John G. Parks, *E. L. Doctorow,* Continuum, 1991.
    Parks's chapter about *Ragtime* is good but standard literary criticism. His chapter at the end of the book, "A Multiplicity of Witnesses," offers some real insight into Doctorow's overall style.

Richard Trenner, editor, *Essays and Conversations,* Ontario Review Press, 1983.
    The interviews in this collection represent a variety of interests and purposes, while the essays about Doctorow's works that comprise the last half of the book offer insights and in-depth analysis.

Siddhartha

Hermann Hesse

1922

Hermann Hesse referred to his novels as "biographies of the soul." In *Siddhartha* (1922), the title character is an exceptionally intelligent Brahman, a member of the highest caste in the Hindu religion, who seemingly has a well-ordered existence yet feels spiritually hollow. Siddhartha embarks on a journey of self-discovery that takes him through a period of asceticism and self-denial followed by one of sensual indulgence. An encounter with Buddha is intellectually meaningful but not spiritually affecting, and Siddhartha continues his own search, ultimately finding peace by a river. Siddhartha's search for truth and identity, the "inward journey" as Hesse referred to this recurring theme in his work, is reflective of the autobiographical and introspective nature of Hesse's writing. Hesse's works are distinctive, challenging, and unlike most of the works of Western writers. He has enjoyed periods of great popularity as well as periods of either neglect and even scorn. Although his receipt of the 1946 Nobel Prize for Literature spurred a flurry of translations, which included the 1951 English translation of *Siddhartha,* his works did not gain much recognition in the English-speaking world until the 1960s. Hesse excelled in the depiction of personal crisis and private agony; such literature seems to be particularly popular during periods of cultural crisis, which accounts by and large for Hesse's idolization in Germany immediately after two devastating wars. He was similarly venerated in the United States during the politically and socially chaotic 1960s and 1970s.

Author Biography

Born in Calw, Germany, in 1877, Hermann Hesse was influenced by his family's mix of background and beliefs. His father, a Pietist-Lutheran, believed that man is basically evil and requires austere discipline. His parents and grandparents had been missionaries in India and the Far East, and their homes yielded the flavors of Indian, Buddhist, and Mohammedan cultures. Hesse said, "From the time I was a child I breathed in and absorbed the spiritual side of India just as deeply as Christianity."

Hypersensitive, imaginative, and headstrong, Hermann behaved rebelliously while yearning to be a poet and magician. School authorities doubted his sanity, and he even fared poorly at schools for mentally challenged and emotionally disturbed children. Instead, he stayed at home, gardening, assisting in his father's publishing house, and reading books on Eastern philosophy and religion in his grandfather's library.

In 1899, Hesse, who had become something of a misfit, moved to Basel, Switzerland, determined to learn the art of living with other people. In 1904, he married and moved to remote Gaienhofen. Seven years later, he left for a trip to the East, expecting to find wisdom in India, which he considered to be a centerplace innocence; he also hoped to discover answers to his personal problems. Finding only poverty and commercialized Buddhism, he returned, suffering from heat exhaustion, dysentery, and disillusionment.

World War I left an already unsettled Hesse badly shaken. Nationalistic enough to hope for a German victory, he also abhorred war and argued for internationalism. That he volunteered his services to the German embassy in Bern and coedited two weeklies for German prisoners of war did little to dissuade his detractors among both the militarists and the pacifists. His father's death in 1916 further compounded his growing despair. At this time Hesse underwent Jungian psychoanalysis, a process that put him in touch with the irrational forces that lurk beneath both individuals and society at large as well as with the idea of a self-quest through synthesis of these forces.

In 1919, he settled alone in Montagnola, where *Siddhartha* was written. Persuaded that a postwar Germany was susceptible to change, Hesse helped to found and edit a periodical devoted to social reform, pacifism, and internationalism. Resurgent nationalism and spreading communism caused him to

Hermann Hesse

terminate his association with the monthly in 1921. Indignities and waning faith in Germany's political future persuaded Hesse to become a citizen of Switzerland in 1924. During this period, Hesse divorced his first wife, and, after a brief second marriage, married Ninon Dolbin, with whom he lived until his death.

During World War II, Hesse was again vilified by the German right-wing press. The bitterness and shock caused by the extermination of his wife's family by the Nazis stayed with Hesse for the rest of his life. Until his death from leukemia in 1962, he remained in Montagnola, rarely leaving it and never going outside of Switzerland, not even when he was awarded the Goethe Prize of Frankfurt am Main and the Nobel Prize for Literature in 1946.

Plot Summary

Hermann Hesse's novel *Siddhartha* tells the story of a young Brahman who explores the deepest meanings of life and the self. Siddhartha's quest for knowledge passes through several phases. During the first phase, he seeks wisdom in various religious philosophies such as Hinduism, asceticism, and Buddhism. He eventually abandons these paths, however, when he realizes that they all disrupt the unity of life by denying the physical body. After coming to this realization, Siddhartha pursues a life of physical pleasures and worldly success. He becomes a great lover and a successful businessman, but he eventually abandons these pleasures after they prove to be too superficial to satisfy his deeper spiritual side. In the third phase of his quest, he tries to reconcile the spiritual and physical sides of himself by becoming a simple ferryman. While performing his daily task of ferrying people across the river, he listens closely to the natural beauty of the river, and the river gradually teaches him how to recognize the essential unity of all life.

Part I—Siddhartha's Religious Quest for Knowledge

The first section of the novel describes Siddhartha's attempts to follow various religions. At first, he follows his father's example by performing the daily rituals of the Hindu religion. Everyone loves the handsome, happy, young Siddhartha, and they are convinced that he will soon become a successful Brahman like his father. Beneath Siddhartha's external devotion and contentment, however, he harbors an insatiable longing to explore the deeper meanings of life, which cannot be learned through codified religious rituals. When a group of wandering ascetics called Samanas pass through his village, he decides to leave his father's home and Brahman religion to follow after the Samanas' ascetic way of life. In addition, he persuades his closest friend, Govinda, to come with him and embrace this new path to knowledge. At first, Siddhartha's father is extremely angry and forbids Siddhartha to join the Samanas, but Siddhartha eventually wins his father's reluctant approval by demonstrating his firm determination to follow the Samanas' ascetic way of life.

Having already learned discipline and determination as a Brahman, Siddhartha immediately adapts to the Samanas' way of life, and he quickly masters the ascetic arts of fasting, suffering, meditation, and self-denial. He renounces all worldly pleasures and conquers the self's desires. Ultimately, however, he questions the Samanas' ascetic philosophies when he realizes that the path of self-denial can only bring temporary relief from suffering. When Siddhartha hears about another holy man, Gotama the illustrious Buddha, he convinces Govinda to go with him to learn about his new religious philosophy.

Together, Siddhartha and Govinda learn about the Fourfold Way, the Eightfold Path, and other Buddhist beliefs. Govinda is convinced by Gotama's teachings and decides to convert to the Buddhist religion, but Siddhartha remains unconvinced. In particular, he is troubled by a fundamental contradiction in the Buddha's philosophy. On one hand, the Buddha embraces the unity of all things, but on the other hand he denies this unity by seeking to overcome the physical world. Disillusioned with religions, Siddhartha forsakes all religious paths to knowledge. He sadly departs from Govinda and sets out on his own to find the meaning of life.

Part II—Siddhartha's Material Quest for Physical Pleasure

In the second section of the novel, Siddhartha turns away from religion and begins trying to learn from the physical pleasures of the material world. He wanders through the forest until he comes to a river, which he is ferried across by a kind old ferryman. He then wanders into the town where he eventually meets a beautiful young courtesan named Kamala. Kamala quickly convinces him to abandon the simple clothing of the ascetics and take up the fashionable dress of the wealthy. In addition, Kamala also helps Siddhartha get a job with Kamaswami, a rich merchant who lives in the town.

Siddhartha quickly learns the arts of business and becomes a successful trader, and as his success grows he also becomes Kamala's favorite lover. He learns the passionate arts of love from Kamala and the worldly pleasures that money can buy, but he always remains somewhat detached from this new life of pleasure. Unlike the ordinary people who take their business as a serious matter, Siddhartha always sees it as somewhat of a game that he enjoys playing but never takes seriously. Siddhartha does not care whether he wins or loses because he does not see this life as connected to the deepest core of his self. Consequently, even though he obtains all the worldly pleasures of love and money, Siddhartha begins to grow weary of this lifestyle as well, and he seeks to drown this weariness in gambling, drinking, and sexual pleasure. At the height of his disillusionment, he dreams that he finds Kamala's songbird dead in its cage. Interpreting this dream as a symbol of the death of his own self, Siddhartha leaves the town and forsakes his lifestyle of physical pleasure and worldly success.

Part III—Siddhartha's Vision of the Unity of All Life

In the third section of the novel, Siddhartha leaves Kamala's house and wanders through the forest until he returns to the ferryman's river, where he falls asleep under a tree. By pure coincidence, Govinda happens to pass by while he is sleeping, and Govinda stops to watch over him without knowing it is Siddhartha. When Siddhartha wakes up, he recognizes Govinda, and they are happy to meet again. After Govinda departs, Siddhartha reflects back upon the various paths that he has followed and recognizes that they are all transitory. Consequently, Siddhartha lets these previous experiences die as he contemplates the mystical word "Om" and the essential unity of all life. Having recognized that the river represents this oneness of life, Siddhartha decides to stay at the river with the ferryman, Vasudeva.

While Siddhartha is working for the ferryman, another group of pilgrims pass by on their way to Gotama's funeral, and Kamala is one of them. However, she dies after being bitten by a snake, leaving her eleven-year-old son, who turns out also to be Siddhartha's child; Kamala had become pregnant during her last night with Siddhartha and has named the boy after his father. Young Siddhartha, however, has been spoiled by a life of wealth, so he gets frustrated with Siddhartha's simple life and eventually runs away. At first, Siddhartha tries to control his son and get him to return, but eventually Vasudeva instructs Siddhartha to seek wisdom from the river. While contemplating the river, Siddhartha experiences a vision of the essential unity of all life. Just as the river flows into the sea only to return as rain, all of the various forms and aspects of life flow into each other to form a single whole. In a conversation with Govinda, Siddhartha describes the understanding that he gained from this visionary experience.

> "Listen, my friend! I am a sinner and you are a sinner, but someday the sinner will be Brahma again, will someday attain Nirvana, will someday become a Buddha. Now this 'someday' is illusion; it is only a comparison. The sinner is not on the way to a Buddha-like state; he is not evolving, although our thinking cannot conceive things otherwise. No, the potential Buddha already exists in the sinner; his future is already there. The potential hidden Buddha must be recognized in him, in you, in everybody. The world, Govinda, is not imperfect or slowly evolving along a long path to perfection. No, it is perfect at every moment; every sin already carries grace within it, all small children are potential old men, all sucklings have death within them, all dying people—eternal life. It is not possible for one person to see how far another is on the way; the Buddha exists in the robber and dice player, the robber exists in the Brahman. During deep meditation it is possible to dispel time, to see simultaneously all the past, present and future, and then everything is good, everything is perfect, everything is Brahman."

In this passage, Siddhartha explains how the endless cycles of birth and death are all part of a single grand unity in Brahman. Once time is overcome and the essential unity of all beings is recognized, everything can be seen in its true light as a manifestation of Brahman. Consequently, both life and death, both joy and sorrow, must be recognized as good. Nothing can be dismissed as inconsequential or unnecessary to the perfection of the whole.

The novel ends with Govinda returning to the river to seek wisdom from Siddhartha, who has now become a wise old sage. Siddhartha explains to Govinda, however, that wisdom cannot be taught and that verbal explanations are traps that keep people from true wisdom. Consequently, instead of discussing philosophies, Siddhartha instructs Govinda to kiss him on the forehead, and this kiss reveals to Govinda the unity of all things. Looking into Siddhartha's face, Govinda also receives a vision of all things becoming one. Thus, the two old friends achieve the wisdom that they had begun seeking together many years before as young men.

Characters

Buddha Gotama Buddha

Gotama Buddha is said to have brought to a standstill the cycle of rebirth. Before his enlightenment, he first had been an ascetic and then had turned to high living and the pleasures of the world. Siddhartha recognizes his radiance, but, despite his attraction to Gotama, Siddhartha is disinterested in his teaching and will not become a disciple. Siddhartha reminds the Buddha of his own quest for enlightenment, stating, "You have done so by your own seeking, in your own way, through thought, through meditation, through knowledge, through enlightenment. You have learned nothing through teachings, and so I think, O Illustrious One, that nobody finds salvation through teaching. To nobody, O Illustrious One, can you communicate in words and teachings what happened to you in the hour of your enlightenment." This is the central idea of the novel, that one can find the secret of self-realization only by going one's own way.

Gotama Buddha is a fictionalized version of the historical Gotama Buddha (approximately 563 B.C.–483 B.C.), born Prince Siddhartha Gotama.

Scene from the 1972 film version of Hermann Hesse's Siddhartha.

Gotama is the clan name, and Buddha, which means "to know," is the title which his followers gave to him.

Govinda

Govinda is Siddhartha's childhood friend and confidant. He loves everything about Siddhartha—his eyes, his voice, the way he walked, his grace. Govinda becomes Siddhartha's shadow. Like Siddhartha, Govinda must also go his own way. Siddhartha supports his friend's decision when Govinda leaves him to follow Gotama Buddha, stating, "Often I have thought: will Govinda ever take a step without me, from his own conviction? Now, you are a man and have chosen your own path." The friends meet at strategic points in their lives. After Siddhartha has attained eternal bliss, Govinda kisses his forehead, compelled by love and presentiment. It is through this kiss and not through Siddhartha's teaching that Govinda finally attains union with the universal, eternal essence.

Illustrious One

See Buddha Gotama Buddha

Kamala

Kamala, a well known courtesan, is beseeched by Siddhartha to teach him her art. She understands him more than even Govinda has; they are mirror images of each other. As Siddhartha tells her, "You are like me; you are different from other people. You are Kamala and no one else, and within you there is a stillness and sanctuary to which you can retreat any time and be yourself, just as I can. Few people have that capacity and yet everyone could have it." When she accuses Siddhartha of remaining a Samana in that he really loves no one, he acquiesces with the observation that "I am like you. You cannot love either, otherwise how could you practice love as an art? Perhaps people like us cannot love." But a time comes when she cannot hear enough about Gotama. Prophetically, she sighs, "One day, perhaps soon, I will also become a follower of this Buddha. I will give him my pleasure garden and take refuge in his teachings." When Siddhartha leaves, she is not surprised. She frees her caged bird and retires from her previous way of life. Having given birth to Siddhartha's son, she takes refuge in the teachings of Gotama. Years later, on hearing of the Buddha's impending death, she travels to see him. To appease her complaining son, she rests along the way near a river, the river where Siddhartha has become a ferryman. Kamala is bitten fatally by a snake; reunited with Siddhartha, she finds peace as she dies by looking into Siddhartha's eyes.

Media Adaptations

- *Siddhartha* was adapted as a film by Conrad Rooks, starring India's leading actor, Shashi Kapoor, Lotus Films, Columbia-Warner, 1972; cassette, Newman Communications, 1986.

Kamaswami

Kamaswami's name, which means "master of the material world," is an appropriate one for the rich merchant who employs Siddhartha. He is beginning to grow old, and Kamala implies, Siddhartha could become his successor. For twenty years, Siddhartha masters this life only to despair. Thinking of his father, Govinda, and Gotama, he wonders if he had left all of them in order to become a "kamaswami." Unlike Kamala, Kamaswami cannot understand that Siddhartha leaves his life of luxury willfully.

Perfect One

See Buddha Gotama Buddha

Sakyamuni

See Buddha Gotama Buddha

Samanas

The Samanas are wandering ascetics who practice self-denial and meditation. Fasting for days and sleeping naked in forests, they shun beauty, sensuality, and happiness as illusions and lies. They have only one goal, to become empty of thirst, desire, dreams, pleasure, and sorrow, and, thus, to let the Self die. Only this, they feel, will provide the experience of peace and pure thought, an awakening of the innermost Being that is no longer Self. Siddhartha is attracted to their ways, and, along with Govinda, travels with the Samanas for three years.

Siddhartha

Siddhartha is the precocious son of a Brahman, a member of the highest caste in Hinduism. Beloved by all but unable to find inner peace, he begins his personal search. Abandoning his devout father, he joins the Samanas. Although he learns some skills of spiritual survival from the Samanas, including thinking, waiting, and fasting, he concludes that asceticism is merely an escape from experience.

Siddhartha meets with Gotama the Buddha, who has reached that perfect state of being in which the transmigratory life cycle and agony of time are transcended. However, Siddhartha realizes that no spiritual teaching or doctrine can impart what he wants. He believes teachers and scripture have yielded only second-hand learning, not the first-hand experience from which real knowledge emanates. Thus, Siddhartha embarks on a life of pleasure with Kamala, who shows him the ways of carnal pleasures, and Kamaswami, who introduces him to the ways of material pursuits.

Decades later, Siddhartha feels worthless and alone. Realizing that he has traded his pursuit of Nirvana for its polar opposite, "Sansara," or the world of illusion, spiritual death, and ultimate despair, Siddhartha understands that the cause of his soul sickness is his inability to love.

Sidhartha turns to Vasudeva, the quiet ferryman, and learns from the river. Years of bliss are interrupted by a final encounter with Kamala and the son whom she bore Siddhartha, unbeknownst to him. Siddhartha loves his son, clings to him, and is desolate when he runs away. Again, Siddhartha listens to the river and hears the unity of voices and the word "Om," or perfection. From then on, Siddhartha is in harmony with the stream of life, full of sympathy and compassion, belonging to the unity of all things.

Hesse gives his protagonist the Buddha's personal Sanskrit name, Siddhartha, meaning "he who is on the right road" or "he who has achieved his goal." Hesse does not intend to portray the life of the Buddha but instead attempts to prefigure the pattern of his own hero's transformations. Both Siddharthas, Hesse's character and the religious figure, were unusual children. Buddha left his wife and son to become an ascetic, as Siddhartha leaves his beloved Kamala and his unborn son to take up the contemplative life. Both spent time among mendicant ascetics studying yoga. Buddha spent several years meditating by a river, and Siddhartha's last years are spent in ferryman's service on a river. Buddha's revelations came to him under a fig tree, whereas Siddhartha arrives at his final decision under a mango tree. Buddha had a visionary experience of all his previous existences and the interconnection of all things, and Siddhartha's final vision also embraces simultaneity and oneness.

Siddhartha's Father

Siddhartha's father, a handsome, teaching Brahman who practices meditation and ablutions in the river, is filled with pride because of his son, who is intelligent and thirsting for knowledge. The author's father, a clergyman, performed ritual ablutions similar to those practiced by Hesse's fictional creation of Sidhartha's father. Siddhartha's father sees his son growing up to be a great learned man—a priest, a prince among Brahmans. As a Brahman, he does not try to control his son through forceful and angry words, but when Siddhartha requests permission to follow the ways of the Samana, he is displeased.

Vasudeva

Vasudeva is another name for Krishna, who is the teacher of Arjuna, the principal hero of the *Bhagavad Gita* and a human incarnation of Vishnu, a Hindu deity. Vasudeva's name means "he in who all thinks abide and who abides in all." Siddhartha's first encounter with Vasudeva, the ferryman, occurs just after he departs from Gotama and Govinda. When Siddhartha remarks on the river's beauty, Vasudeva responds, "I love it above everything. I have often listened to it, gazed at it, and I have always learned something from it. One can learn much from a river." He predicts Siddhartha's return.

More than twenty years pass before Siddhartha does return to the river and contemplates suicide. When the river revives his spirit, Siddhartha determines to remain near it. Remembering the ferryman who so loved the river, he asks to become Vasudeva's apprentice. Vasudeva tells him, "You will learn, but not from me. The river has taught me to listen; you will learn it too." As time goes on, Siddhartha's smile begins to resemble Vasudeva's—radiant, childlike, filled with happiness. Travellers mistake them for brothers; sometimes, when they sit listening together to the river, they have the same thought.

When Siddhartha becomes distressed by his son's rebellion, Vasudeva encourages him to listen to the river and reminds him that he, too, left his own father to begin his path through life. After the young boy runs away, Vasudeva brings Siddhartha to the river so that he can hear that the "great song of a thousand voices consisted of one word: Om—perfection." When Vasudeva sees the look of serenity and knowledge shining in Siddhartha's eyes, he knows that it is time for him to go. "I have waited for this hour, my friend. Now that it has arrived, let me go. I have been Vasudeva, the ferryman, for a long time. Now it is over. Farewell hut, farewell river, farewell Siddhartha." Vasudeva then departs for the woods and the unity of all things.

Young Siddhartha

Raised without a father as a rich and spoiled mama's boy, young Siddhartha meets his father for the first time just before the death of his mother, Kamala. Disdaining his father's piety and simple lifestyle, the boy is arrogant and disrespectful. Finding his father's unconditional love and patience impossible to accept, he runs away. When Vasudeva reminds Siddhartha that his son must follow his own path, Siddhartha makes peace with his spirit.

Themes

The Search for the Meaning of Life

Hesse's works are largely confessional and autobiographical and deal with questions of "Weltanschauung," of a philosophy of life. Typically, as in *Siddhartha,* the individual's search for truth and identity through what Hesse called the "inward journey" is draped around the plot. Siddhartha, the obedient son of a rich Brahman, awakens one day to the realization that his life is empty and that his soul is not satisfied by his devotion to duty and strict observances of religious ordinances. He leaves home with his friend Govinda to begin his journey. First, he becomes an ascetic mendicant, but fasting and physical deprivation do not bring him closer to peace. Subsequently, he speaks with Gotama Buddha, who has attained the blissful state of Nirvana. Siddhartha realizes that he cannot accept the Buddhist doctrine of salvation from suffering or learn through the Buddha's teaching. He must proceed on his own path. Turning from asceticism, he lives a life of desire and sensual excitement but years later again finds himself disgusted and empty. Suicidal, Siddhartha finds his way back to a river he had once crossed. He stays there, learning from the ferryman to listen to the river. It is here that he finally achieves peace.

In Siddhartha's final conversation with Govinda, he tries to enumerate the insights he has gained. These include the idea that for each truth the opposite is equally true; that excessive searching—as practised by Govinda—is self-defeating; and that to "find" is, paradoxically, "to be free, to be open, to have no goal." One must simply love

Topics for Further Study

- Research the Indo-European family of languages, of which English, German, and Sanskrit are members. How does Pali, the language of Buddhism, fit in? What are other member languages? What migrations may have affected the history of this language group?

- Investigate C.G. Jung's concepts of the shadow, the *anima,* and the *animus.* Consider how the various characters in *Siddhartha* illustrate these concepts.

- Compare the Eastern ideas of simultaneity and totality as represented by the river with the philosophy of time and space that evolves out of Einstein's theory of relativity.

- Consider the father/son theme in *Siddhartha* in relation to Hesse's idea of synthesis.

---

and enjoy the world in all its aspects. Although Siddhartha may have reached the highest state of wisdom, he is unable to communicate its essence to Govinda. For another of his realizations is that although knowledge may be communicable, wisdom cannot be. He tells Govinda, "These are things and one can love things. But one cannot love words.... Perhaps that is what prevents you from finding peace, perhaps there are too many words, for even salvation and virtue, Samsara and Nirvana are only words, Govinda." It is only in an act of love, when Govinda kisses Siddhartha, that he too sees the "continuous stream of faces—hundreds, thousands, which all came and disappeared and yet all seemed to be there at the same time, which all continually changed and renewed themselves and which were yet all Siddhartha."

Although *Siddhartha* is set in India and engages with Buddhist thought, it would be naive to read the book as an embodiment or explanation of Indian philosophy. Written after World War I, *Siddhartha* is Hesse's attempt to restore his faith in mankind, to regain his lost peace of mind, and to

find again a harmonious relationship with his world. Siddhartha's way is his own, not Govinda's nor Buddha's nor even Hesse's, whose next major work, *Steppenwolf,* offers a complete contrast, replacing serenity with stridency, placing the individual problem in a social context, and stressing the contrast between the "inner" and "outer" worlds for grotesque and humorous effect.

Polarities and Synthesis

Hesse is fascinated by the dualistic nature of existence, particularly the world of the mind, which he calls "Geist," and the world of the body and physical action, which he calls "Natur." Siddhartha experiments with and exhausts both possibilities. In his father's house, he exercises his mind. With the Samanas, he seeks truth again through thinking and the extreme denial of the body. When these efforts fail to bring him peace, he tries another extreme. He immerses himself in material and carnal pursuits, but this life of the body brings him no closer to his goal. When he takes up his life by the river, he learns to transcend both the mind and the body by finding a third way, that of the soul. This synthesis, in fact, is what distinguishes Hesse's Siddhartha from Buddha. For Hesse, the river has part in both realms; it is not an obstacle to be crossed, as in Buddhist symbolism. Rather, Siddhartha is a ferryman who joins both sides of the river, which is the natural synthesis of extremes.

Love and Passion

The importance of love also distinguishes Hesse's Siddhartha from Buddhism. In 1931, Hesse commented, "The fact that my *Siddhartha* stresses not cognition but love, that it rejects dogma and makes experience of oneness the central point, may be felt as a tendency to return to Christianity, even to a truly Protestant faith." In many ways, the novel is about Siddhartha's learning to love the world in its particulars so that he can transcend them. The reader sees him in town with Kamala as they indulge their pleasures. "I am like you," he laments to her. "You cannot love either, otherwise how could you practice love as an art. Perhaps people like us cannot love." But in the end, Kamala gives up her life and follows the ways of the Buddha. On her pilgrimage, she is reunited with Siddhartha and, looking into his eyes before she dies, finds peace. Siddhartha feels keenly the loss of Kamala, but it is not sadness that is in his heart; he knows now that all life is indestructible and that, in a wider sense, Kamala has entered a new life that is in every blossom and in every breeze about him. Kamala also leaves Siddhartha with their son to love. "He felt indeed that this love, this blind love for his son, was a very human passion, that it was Samsara, a troubled spring of deep water. At the same time he felt that it was not worthless, that it was necessary, that it came from his own nature. This emotion, this pain, these follies also had to be experienced." Through Kamala and his son, Siddhartha learns to love the world. He tells Govinda, "I learned through my body and soul that it was necessary for me to sin, that I needed lust, that I had to strive for property and experience nausea and the depths of despair in order to learn not to resist them, in order to learn to love the world, and no longer compare it with some kind of desired imaginary world, some imaginary vision of perfection, but to leave it as it is, to love it and be glad to belong to it."

Om—Oneness, Totality, Unity

When Siddhartha despairs of ever finding peace, he contemplates suicide at the river. When the word "Om" comes to mind, he realizes the folly of his attempt to end his sufferings by extinguishing his physical being. Life is indestructible. Creation is an indivisible whole. He sees his great mistake in trying always to do something instead of just to be. Siddhartha comes to believe that all possible transformations or potentialities of the human soul are possible not only consecutively, but simultaneously. He explains this idea to Govinda by using the example of the stone: "This stone is stone; it is also animal, God, Buddha. I do not respect and love it because it was one thing and will become something else, but because it has already long been everything and always is everything. I love it just because it is a stone, because today and now it appears to me a stone." Siddhartha's Nirvana is the recognition that all being exists simultaneously in unity and totality.

Style

Setting

Hesse locates his tale in remote India of a time long past, but any realism in the narrative is the symbolic projection of an inner vision, an inner world, an "inward journey," and not an attempt to capture external reality. Hesse, in fact, criticized the tendency to attribute excessive importance to "so-called reality" in the shape of physical events. He intended to take his readers into an elevated, poetic, legendary or "magical" world. Using the landscape of India, the book achieves a unity of style, structure, and meaning that Hesse never again attained with such perfection. He called *Siddhartha* "an Indic poem"; some might call it an extreme of symbolic lyricism. The Indian milieu provides timeless, mythic validity—the legendary times allow the reader to lose the sense of differentiation and to come nearer to the oneness of the human race. The parallels to the Buddha's life are contributing factors to this legendary quality.

Style

Hesse uses an exotically formalized style, more noticeable in the original German but still apparent even in translation. The novel is borne along on a strong rhythmic current (like a river), on what seems an undertone of chant. All harsh sounds are avoided, while there is much alliteration and assonance. There is frequent use of parallelism in clause structure and repetition of words and phrases. The threefold repetitions, corresponding to the tripartite structure of the work, creates a liturgical aspect which is reminiscent of the Bible, but the language is not really biblical but rather reminiscent of Pali, the language used in the canonical books of the Buddhists. At points this language can achieve something of an incantatory effect, but for the most part it reflects the serene, balanced attitude of meditation. This antiquated, liturgical mode of expression enhances the gospel quality of this tale.

Structure

The short novel is divided into two parts with four and eight chapters. But it is quite obvious that the book falls into three thematic sections: Siddhartha's life at home, among the Samanas and with Buddha (four chapters); his life with Kamala and among the "child people" of the city (four chapters); and his life with Vasudeva on the river (four chapters). The river, which is the all-encompassing symbol of the novel, not only bears the burden of communication of truth but also provides the organizing structure. Temporally and spatially, the three parts of Siddhartha's search for meaning are delimited by his encounters with the river. These divisions are in keeping with Siddhartha's balanced progression from the realm of the mind, through that of the body, to that of the soul. The triadic structure is extended to the very mechanics of expression: to sentences, clauses, phrases, words, and paragraphs. And in keeping with this three-beat pulsation, Hesse even extends his customary projection of the actual self and one alternative to the actual self and three possibilities.

Siddhartha is Hesse's fictionalized self and Govinda, Buddha, and Vasudeva are the possibilities: Govinda is the self-effacing, institution-oriented person Siddhartha should not become; Buddha represents a laudable but undesirable life-denying model; and Vasudeva is an exemplary life-affirming ideal. When Siddhartha becomes this ideal, Vasudeva leaves the scene.

The novel's structure is also determined in part by its legendary form. Siddhartha is clearly regarded as a "saintly" figure. His reunification with the All at the end of the book corresponds to the miraculous union with God in Christian legends. As in Christian canonization trials, his saintliness is attested by witnesses—Vasudeva, Kamala, and Govinda—all of whom recognize in his face the aspect of godliness and repose.

Symbols

Often in literature, from Heraclitus to Thomas Wolfe, rivers are used as a symbol for timelessness. In Hesse's case this symbol of simultaneity is expanded to include the realm in which all polarity ceases: totality. It is a realm of pure existence in which all things coexist in harmony. Siddhartha expresses this idea of fluidity: "of every truth it can be said that the opposite is just as true." Siddhartha, as ferryman, helps people to cross the water which separates the city, the outer world of extroversion, superficial excitement, and wild pleasures, from the introverted, lonely, and ascetic world of forests and mountains. Siddhartha has himself crossed that river twice in the course of his search, and he has managed to reconcile those two worlds. The river with the city on one side and the forest on the other is a projection of Siddhartha's inner development onto the realm of space. In this way, the geography of the book becomes the landscape of the soul. In the final vision of the book, Hesse renders Siddhartha's fulfillment visually by reversing this process. As Govinda looks into Siddhartha's face at the end, what he perceives is no longer the landscape of the soul but rather the soul as landscape. Siddhartha has learned the lesson of the river so well that his entire being now reflects the totality and simultaneity that the river symbolizes. Govinda "no longer saw the face of his friend Siddhartha. Instead he saw other faces, many faces, a long series, a continuous stream of faces—hundreds, thousands, which all came and disappeared and yet all seemed to be there at the same time, which all continually changed and renewed themselves and which were yet all Siddhartha."

Historical Context

Ancient India

In the fifth century B.C., India consisted of sixteen major states in the north. The region's southern parts remained largely undeveloped. Kings or chiefs ruled individual states and acquired income through taxation and trade. The Brahmans, or religious leaders, held a very high position in each state and often had the authority to approve of the ruling class. On some occasions they were rulers themselves. In addition to the major states, there were dozens of smaller regions comprised of various tribes organized as oligarchies, each under a single ruling family. One of these oligarchies, in what is now Nepal, was ruled by the Shakya tribe, of which Siddhartha Gotama was a prince. Control of the Ganges Valley became a major issue between the northern Indian states during the sixth and fifth centuries B.C., and wars were continually fought over the rights to the lucrative trade routes. The state of Magadha established dominance in the region by the mid-fifth century B.C., but infighting continued into the next century. The nation of India was not unified until the establishment of the Mauryan Empire in 325 B.C.

The Story of Buddha

Siddhartha Gotama, who became known as Buddha, meaning the "Illustrious One" or "Enlightened One," founded Buddhism in approximately 500 B.C. Raised as a Brahman prince, he was married at sixteen to a neighboring princess, Yasodhara, who bore him at least one child. Despite his comfortable, even luxurious circumstances, a discontent grew in him. At the age of twenty-nine, he left home against his parents' will and began a spiritual quest.

At that time, wandering ascetics, who were also searching for a deeper meaning to life, travelled across northern India. They sought inner peace and freedom from attachment to the ordinary things of this world through the then-developing discipline of yoga. They came to be deeply respected by ordinary Indians. It is against this background that Siddhartha began his Great Renunciation. He meditated and practiced the extreme bodily asceticism which the Jains and others were advocating. He learned to "think, wait, and fast," but after six years he did not achieve enlightenment and, at the age of thirty-five, he abandoned the ascetic life and went to a place now called Bodh-Gaya, near the town of Uruvilva. He sat down to meditate at the foot of a fig tree, later to be referred to as the *bodhi* (enlightenment tree). The enlightenment he received was a profound awareness that all things are mutable, impermanent, insubstantial, and sorrowful, but that human beings tend to become attached to things as though they were substantial, abiding realities. Then, as the objects of these attachment disintegrate, humans are thrown into a state of panic and anguish. The Buddha was convinced that this insight would release him from craving and, by following the Middle Way between extremes of indulgence and denial, he could end the negative cycle of rebirths and free himself from the wheel of life.

Siddhartha promoted concepts of peace, love, and passive behavior as well as respect for all life. His teachings, known as the *dharma,* emerged in opposition to the violence, suffering, and inequality he witnessed in Indian society. He specifically denounced the Brahmans, who were supposed to be the spiritual and moral guides of society, for their participation in the killing of animals and for sanctioning war. He also felt that the caste system resulted in suffering and devalued life. The system, some of which remains in place to this day, is directly opposed to Buddhist beliefs in social equality and freedom of choice. Siddhartha, though of the highest Brahman caste himself, taught that all people are born equal and that everyone must fulfill his or her own destiny, which cannot be dictated by another.

During the forty-five years between the Buddha's enlightenment and death, he traveled and preached in central India and won many converts to the religion. After the Buddha's death, the Mallas of Kusinagara took his body, honored it with flowers, scents, and music, and then cremated it. The remains were divided among eight of the peoples of central India, who took their shares and constructed *stupas* (reliquary monuments) for them. These monuments were the forerunners of others that were later erected throughout India and that served as the centers for Buddhist devotees.

Turn-of-the-Century Germany

As the twentieth century began, Germany was marked by rapid industrialization. From 1895 to 1907, the number of industrial employees doubled and exports of finished goods rose from thirty-three to sixty-three percent. National wealth and urban populations soared, as did national pride. But working conditions were poor and industrial workers lacked full political rights. In Germany's social hierarchy, industrial workers and minorities were re-

Worshippers bowing before Buddha in Singapore, 1989.

garded as subservient members of society. When the economy slowed or cities became overpopulated, anti-Semitism surfaced and Jews were seen as outsiders.

By 1912 the German government had become increasingly militaristic and aggressive. The country's navy was second in might only to Great Britain's, and because of their newfound economic and military power, Germany began taking on the role of aggressor throughout Europe and North Africa. France, Great Britain, and Russia formed the Triple Entente alliance to ward off the potential threat of a German invasion. World War I erupted, though, after the heir to the Austrian throne, Archduke Francis Ferdinand, was assassinated by Serbian terrorists in 1914. The members of the Triple Entente found themselves in a fierce battle against a powerful German nation.

In 1918 World War I ended with German defeat. But it was not long before nationalism and aggression resurfaced in Germany. Capitalizing on the nation's desire to regain power after its loss, Adolf Hitler and fellow Nazis instilled strong feelings of anti-Semitism and fierce national pride in the German population. By 1921, Germany's government was denouncing writers such as Hesse, calling him and others "Jew-lovers" because of their anti-war and anti-prejudice view.

Critical Overview

After the 1904 publication of *Peter Camenzind,* Hermann Hesse's following grew with each subsequent book and began a popularity that rose and fell dramatically, as it still seems to continue to do. German readers felt comfortable with his traditional stories and poetry, and by 1914, when World War I broke out, he had become a pleasant reading habit. The tide changed with his wartime essays, which disparaged militarism and nationalism and censured Germany. Hesse was quickly reduced to an undesirable draft dodger and traitor. In the sociopolitically chaotic postwar years, the tide turned back. The apotheosizing of the individual and the apolitical gospel of self-knowledge and self-realization presented in *Demian* (published in 1919) struck a respondent chord in German youth, for whom Hesse became their idol and *Demian* their bible. But youth's exaltation was short-lived; spreading communism on one hand and budding National Socialism on the other proved to be too enticing. During the Weimar Republic, from 1919 to 1933, Hesse's popularity declined. By the mid 1930s, he was on the blacklist of virtually every newspaper and periodical in Germany. The scholarly interest in him also grew progressively less favorable and politically—tainted negative criticism began to be heard. Hesse now became a rank "Jew-lover" and an example of the insidious poisoning of the German soul by Freud's psychoanalysis. This trend culminated in the strident political and literary rejection of Hesse in Hitler's Germany between 1933 and 1945.

With the collapse of National Socialism in 1945 and Hesse's Nobel Prize in 1946, German critics and scholars, like Germany's reading public, rediscovered the author. For the next decade, he enjoyed both political and literary approval as never before. An undesirable German of questionable literary merits had become a man of insight, foresight, and humanity, an heir to the noblest heritage of the German people, a guide and inspiration for his fellow authors. Yet again, the fickle German literary community switched gears. By the late 1950s, there was a sudden and sharp decrease in scholarly and public interest and by the 1960s, Hesse was virtually dead as a writer of importance in Germany. But still another wave of interest in Hesse began to spread in Germany in the early 1970s. The occasion of this last revival, in which many of the most discerning studies of his work were done, was in large part the discovery of Hesse in America in the 1960s.

When Hesse was awarded the Nobel Prize in 1946, the English-speaking world barely knew who he was. His few translated works had not been well received. *Demian* (translated into English in 1923) was brushed aside as a "nightmare of abnormality, a crazed dream of a paranoiac." *Steppenwolf* (translated in 1929) was disposed of as "a peculiarly unappetizing conglomeration of fantasy, philosophy, and moist eroticism." In the 1950s, after Hesse won the Nobel Prize, publishers began scrambling for translations of his work, including *Siddhartha,* which was translated in 1951. Hesse himself was doubtful that the American public would ever be taken by his inward-directed individualism and, for a time, he seemed correct. In the 1960s, however, the American public became intrigued by Hesse. Those in middle age were disenchanted and the youth were rebellious. Skepticism and cynicism were widespread. For many, and for its youth in particular, America had become a stifling, excessively materialistic, morally and culturally bankrupt society. Hesse's individualism—his disparagement of modern society but firm faith in the meaningfulness of life—were a welcome antidote to the twentieth century's bleaker view of things. Hesse became a rallying point for protest and change, a kindred soul, an inspiration for an enthusiastic following of dissidents, seekers, and estranged loners who were drawn from both the establishment and the counterculture. By the time all of Hesse's novels, short stories, essays, poetry, and letters were available in English in the 1970s, the tide that had swept across America in the mid–1960s had peaked, but not before almost fifteen million copies of Hesse's works had been sold within a decade—a literary phenomenon without precedent in America.

American Hesse scholarship followed in the wake of the general public's attraction to him. Scholarly activity accelerated in the mid–1960s and crested in 1973–74, a few years after the reading community had already begun to lose its interest. Scholarly activity tapered off to a slow but steady flow. Still, American Hesse scholarship is now second in quantity only to its German counterpart and has outstripped it in quality.

Criticism

Robert Bennett

In the following essay, Bennett, a doctoral student at the University of California, Santa Barbara, and adjunct instructor in English, explains that while Siddhartha *draws heavily from Eastern religions in its themes, Hesse's philosophy diverges in some ways, and the author concludes that one's philosophy is a personal journey for each individual to discover.*

Clearly, the most obvious and significant aspect of Hermann Hesse's *Siddhartha* is its use of images, themes, and ideas drawn from Eastern religions. Having both traveled to India and studied extensively about Indian religions, Hesse was able to integrate a substantial understanding of Eastern religious traditions into his novel. In fact, *Siddhartha* does such a good job of developing Eastern religious themes that it has been published in India, and Indian critics have generally praised its sensitive understanding of their religious traditions.

From beginning to end, virtually every aspect of *Siddhartha* develops out of Hesse's knowledge of Eastern religions. For example, many of the characters are named after either Hindu or Buddhist gods:

Siddhartha is the personal name of the Buddha, Vasudeva is one of the names of Krishna, and Kamala's name is derived from Kama, the Hindu god of erotic love. In addition, Hesse bases most of the novel's themes on various Hindu or Buddhist principles. For example, Siddhartha seeks to gain an understanding of both Atman, the individual soul, and Brahma, the universal soul that unifies all beings. In order to achieve this understanding, however, he must experience a vision that reveals to him the true meaning of *Om,* the sacred word that Hindus chant when meditating upon the cosmic unity of all life. The vast majority of Sid-

dhartha's philosophical and religious questions develops out of his attempt to understand these religious principles or other themes drawn from Eastern religions such as meditation, fasting, renunciation, timelessness, transcending suffering, etc. While it would take an entire book to explain all of the religious ideas that Hesse develops in his novel, he generally presents at least a basic description of these ideas within the book itself. Consequently, readers can at least get a rudimentary understanding of these ideas even if they do not understand all of the subtle complexities of Eastern religious thought.

Not only does Hesse borrow names, themes, and ideas from Eastern religions, but he also bases and structures his narrative on the life of the historical Buddha. Much like Siddhartha in Hesse's novel, the historical Buddha was born into a wealthy family, but he renounced his wealth to live as an ascetic. After several years of self-denial, however, he came to realize the errors of asceticism. After leaving behind his austere life, he meditated under a Bodhi tree until he received Nirvana (or complete Enlightenment), and then he spent the rest of his life trying to help others reach Nirvana. This is very similar to the path that Siddhartha follows in the novel as he passes through similar stages of wealth, renunciation, meditation, enlightenment, and striving to teach others.

In addition to structuring the novel according to the Buddha's life, Hesse also structures the novel according to various principles found in the Buddha's teachings. In fact, several of the chapters are named after specific religious principles. For example, the chapter titled "Awakening" describes how Siddhartha comes to recognize the Buddhist belief that the path to enlightenment must be rooted in the here and now instead of focusing on other distant or transcendent worlds. In addition, the chapter titled "Samsara" describes how Siddhartha is caught in a continuous cycle of death and rebirth because he has not yet achieved a state of total enlightenment or Nirvana, and the chapter titled "Om" describes how Siddhartha eventually escapes from Samsara to achieve a vision of the essential unity of all things. These chapter titles accurately describe the spiritual development that Siddhartha undergoes in each chapter, and these stages of spiritual development provide the structure that organizes both the novel's development as a narrative and Siddhartha's development as a character. Even the chapters that are not titled after a specific religious principle usually represent Siddhartha's progress toward understanding some religious prin-

What
Do I Read
Next?

- The oldest speculative literature of the Hindus is the *Upanishads,* composed between 600 B.C. to 300 B.C. It is a collection of works on the nature of man and the universe.

- The *Bhagavad Gita* is part of the great Hindu epic the *Mahabharata* and has been called the New Testament of Hinduism. This discussion on the nature and meaning of life between the god Krishna, who appears as a charioteer, and Arjuna, a warrior about to go into battle, has had substantial impact on Western thought.

- The writer of *Ecclesiastes,* a book of the Old Testament, portrays his search for the meaning of life, his sense that all is vanity, and his own conclusions in his old age.

- Goethe's *Faust,* an 1808 play based on the legend of a German necromancer, Georg Faust, focuses on an old scholar who yearns to have not so much all knowledge but all experience. In order to do so, he must promise his immortal soul to the destructive tempting spirit, Mephistopheles.

- A different look at India is provided in E.M. Forster's 1924 novel, *A Passage to India.* The novel is notable for its strong mystical flavor and its treatment of Indian religions, including Islam and Hinduism.

- With the publication in 1904 of *Peter Camenzind* (translated 1961), Hesse established himself as an important German writer by winning the Bauernfeld Prize of Vienna. It is a poetic/realistic narrative of the gauche and inhibited misfit Camenzind and, in many ways, is Hesse's own veiled literary self-disclosure of his life in Basel.

- *Demian* was written by Hesse in 1919 and translated into English in 1923. The novel is a *bildungsroman* featuring Emil Sinclair, a young man who is troubled by life's conflicting forces. A mysterious boy, Max Demian, tells him of the devil-god Abraxas, who is the embodiment of good and evil.

- Hesse's 1927 novel *Steppenwolf* was translated into English two years later. It is a treatment of the artist as an outsider, a common theme in Hesse's fiction. Torn between his own frustrated artistic realism and the inhuman nature of modern reality, Harry Haller thinks of himself as a wolf of the Steppes.

- Many of Hesse's works focus on the interaction between characters with opposing temperaments. In his 1930 novel, *Narcissus and Goldmund* (translated 1932), the title characters represent, respectively, spirit and life. Set in a medieval monastery, half of this novel follows the friendship of the introverted, ascetic Narcissus and the extroverted sculptor Goldmund; the other half chronicles the latter's hedonistic adventures outside the cloister.

- Another Hesse *bildungsroman, Magister Ludi: (The Glass-Bead Game)* was written in 1943 and was translated in 1949. Josef Knecht lives in a utopian society of the twenty-third century that is dominated by a glass-bead game practiced in its highest form by an intellectual elite. Knecht eventually dies after departing to the outer world, the tragic result of a life dedicated entirely to the world of the spirit.

---

ciple, and many of these principles are taken directly from the Buddha's teachings about the Four Noble Truths or the Eightfold Path.

Nevertheless, even though Hesse develops both his themes and his narrative structure based on Eastern religious principles, there are several ways in which *Siddhartha* alters these concepts so that it is not simply an accurate description of Hin-

duism or Buddhism. For example, when the Buddha teaches Siddhartha about his religious beliefs, Siddhartha admires them, but he does not choose to follow them. Similarly, the historical Buddha finds enlightenment under the Bodhi tree, but Siddhartha's dream under the tree only helps him better understand the questions that he is seeking to understand. It provides him with new issues to consider, but it does not give him any final answers. In these respects, Hesse seems to suggest that he considers Eastern religions very useful guides to philosophical and spiritual understanding but ultimately considers knowledge a personal experience that cannot be codified into any religious rituals and dogmas. The conclusion to the novel makes this clear, when Siddhartha explains his fundamental distrust of all words and beliefs. He still embraces the goal of enlightenment and universal oneness, but he follows his own personal path instead of just following the Buddha's or anyone else's doctrines. In this sense, Hesse's novel develops an individualistic perspective that is perhaps more Western than Eastern. Because of these kinds of western elements, critics such as Mark Boulby, Robert Conrad, and Theodore Ziolkowski argue that *Siddhartha* advances more Western ideas than it does Eastern ones.

Although *Siddhartha* explores a wide variety of philosophical and religious themes, it focuses most specifically on three principal themes: the nature of the self, the nature of knowledge, and the essential unity of all things. From the very beginning of the novel, Siddhartha has a fierce longing to probe beneath the surface of life and discover the deeper layers of the self. Consequently, he refuses to simply follow the paths established by various religions—not because these religions are bad but because they focus on external rather that internal beliefs. Siddhartha is more interested in understanding his own self than he is in simply following the ideas created by others. As the novel progresses, Siddhartha explores deeper and deeper into the mysteries of the self as he rejects his home, his friend Govinda, all religious dogmas, and everything else that might cause him to compromise his intense personal vision. As Siddhartha abandons these hindrances to self-knowledge, he comes to understand the essential mysteries of the self.

In addition, Siddhartha is deeply concerned with the question of knowledge. Throughout the novel, he asks deep questions about the nature of knowledge: what is knowledge, how is it obtained, and how can it be taught to others? In fact, much of Hesse's interest in the self is intimately connected to his interest in the nature of knowledge since Hesse develops a view of knowledge that makes the self the primary means of discovering knowledge. Because Hesse locates the origin of knowledge in the self rather than in some set of beliefs, he is distrustful of any attempt to communicate or teach knowledge to others. As Siddhartha

explains to the Buddha after listening to his teachings, even if a person has experienced some vision of the essential nature of life, they cannot give that knowledge to someone else because they cannot give someone else the experiences through which they obtained their knowledge. They can talk about the ideas they have learned and the principles they believe, but they cannot communicate their personal experiences, aspects which Hesse believes are the most important part of knowledge.

By the end of the novel, Siddhartha has progressed to a point where the first two questions of the self and knowledge have become less important because he increasingly focuses on understanding the essential unity of all things. As Siddhartha explains to Govinda at the end of the novel, the self is a transitory being whose ultimate meaning can only be found by understanding its connection to all other beings instead of by exploring its own isolated, transitory, individual existence. Siddhartha experiences a vision of this oneness of life while he is meditating on the river. During this visionary experience, he comes to realize that endless flowing of the river symbolizes how all of the various forms and aspects of life flow into each other to form a single whole. The river, like Brahman and Buddha-nature, encompasses the entirety of existence in all of its diverse manifestations, and the meaning of this essential unity is best expressed through the sacred Hindu word, "Om." This word expresses a unity that transcends all barriers of time, difference, oppositions, and illusions to recognize the interconnectedness of all beings. While some critics see this final epiphany as expressing the essence of Eastern religions such as Buddhism or Hinduism, others see it as representing western philosophies such as Christianity or existentialism. Some even see it as Hesse's own personal religion, made up from an eclectic mixture of all of these traditions. Certainly, a good case can be made for each interpretation, so every reader must ultimately come to his or her own conclusion regarding how to interpret Siddhartha's final epiphany. In the end, however, it is perhaps less important to decide how to categorize Siddhartha's vision than to listen to it, think about it, and try to learn from it. Whatever its source, it offers profound insights into the human condition. Consequently, regardless of how it is interpreted, Siddhartha's vision presents a remarkable exploration of the deepest philosophical and spiritual dimensions of human existence.

Source: Robert Bennett, in an essay for *Novels for Students,* Gale, 1999.

Theodore Ziolkowski

In this excerpt, Ziolkowski explores the epiphanies that Siddhartha experiences.

Siddhartha's smile ... is the best example of the new dimension that we find in this novel. Here, in brief, we have the same story that we encountered in *Demian:* a man's search for himself through the stages of guilt, alienation, despair, to the experience of unity. The new element here is the insistence upon love as the synthesizing agent. Hesse regards this element as "natural growth and development" from his earlier beliefs, and certainly has no reversal or change of opinion. In the essay "My Faith" (1931) he admitted "that my *Siddhartha* puts not cognition, but love in first place: that it disdains dogma and makes the experience of unity the central point...." Cognition of unity as in *Demian* is not the ultimate goal, but rather the loving affirmation of the essential unity behind the apparent polarity of being. This is the meaning of Siddhartha's transfiguration at the end of the book. The passage goes on at length, developing all the images of horizontal breadth in space and vertical depth in time that we have indicated. But the whole vision is encompassed and united by "this smile of unity over the streaming shapes, this smile of simultaneity over the thousands of births and deaths."

The beatific smile is the symbol of fulfillment: the visual manifestation of the inner achievement. As a symbol, it too is developed and anticipated before the final scene in which Govinda sees it in Siddhartha's face. It is the outstanding characteristic of the two other figures in the book who have attained peace: Buddha and Vasudeva. When Siddhartha first sees Gautama he notices immediately that his face reveals neither happiness nor sadness, but seems rather "to smile gently inward." Everything about him, "his face and his step, his quietly lowered gaze, his quietly hanging hand, and even every finger on this quiet hand spoke of peace, spoke of perfection." When Siddhartha departs from the Buddha he thinks to himself:

> I have never seen a man gaze and smile, sit and walk like that.... truly, I wish that I too might be able to gaze and smile, sit and walk like him.... Only a man who has penetrated into his innermost Self gazes and walks in that way. Very well—I too shall seek to penetrate into my innermost Self.

Siddhartha acknowledges in the Buddha a conscious ideal, but it is Buddha's goal and not his path to which the younger man aspires. The symbol of this goal is the beatific smile behind which, almost like the smile of the Cheshire Cat, the individual disappears. The same smile appears again when Vasudeva is portrayed, and we see it grow on Siddhartha's own face.

> And gradually his smile became more and more like that of the ferryman; it became almost as radiant, almost as illumined with happiness, similarly glowing from a thousand little wrinkles, just as childlike, just as aged. Many travelers, when they saw the two ferrymen, took them to be brothers.

At the moment of Vasudeva's death the unity of this smile is clearly expressed: "His smile shone radiantly as he looked at his friend, and radiantly shone on Siddhartha's face, too, the same smile." The words here are not used in a figurative sense, for it literally is the same smile. The smile is the symbol of inner perfection, but inner perfection for Hesse means the awareness of the unity, totality, and simultaneity of all being. It is thus appropriate that the three men who share this perception should also share the same beatific smile, even though each reached his goal by following a completely different path....

Siddhartha's development to the point of loving affirmation is marked by a technique of modern fiction that James Joyce defined as the epiphany, but which occurs regularly in much prose, German and French as well as English, of the early twentieth century. In the epiphany the protagonist perceives the essence of things that lies hidden behind their empirical reality, and as such the epiphany is another symptom of the modern turn away from realism toward a new mysticism. The epiphany reveals the essential integral unity of a given object in a burst of radiance (what Joyce, in the words of Aquinas, calls the *integritas, consonantia,* and *claritas* of the object), and the observer is able to enter into a direct relationship of love with the object thus newly perceived. It is this element of loving perception, missing in the cooler cognition of *Demian,* that we find here in passage after passage. The most striking example occurs in the "awakening" scene of Chapter 4 after Siddhartha has made up his mind not to follow Buddha, but to seek his own way in the world of the senses:

> He looked around as though he were seeing the world for the first time. Lovely was the world, colorful was the world, strange and mysterious was the world! Here was blue, here was yellow, here was green. The sky flowed and the river, the forest towered up and the mountains, everything lovely, everything mysterious, and magical, and in the midst of it all—he, Siddhartha, the Awakening One, on the way to himself. All this, all this yellow and blue, river and forest, entered Siddhartha for the first time through his eyes,

was no longer the magic of Mara, no longer the veil of Maja, no longer the senseless and accidental multiplicity of the world of appearances, contemptible for the deep-thinking Brahman who disparages multiplicity and seeks unity. Blue was blue, the river was river, and even if the One and the Divine lay hidden in the blue and river within Siddhartha, it was still simply the manner of the Divine to be yellow here, blue here, sky there, forest there, and Siddhartha here. Sense and Essence were not somewhere behind the things. They were in them—in everything.

The points to be noticed in this and other epiphanies (including, of course, those written by the young Joyce) are, first, the impression of radiance aroused by the entire description, which here is created largely by words such as "blue," "yellow," and "sky." Then: these are all objects encountered constantly in daily life, but here *perceived* for the first time. And finally: what Siddhartha realizes is that the meaning of these things is inherent within them and not some abstract ideal that lies behind their reality. They are radiant and meaningful as manifestations of the One and the Divine, hence as symbols of unity and totality.

A further characteristic of the epiphany—one that is inherent in its very nature but not usually present in the actual epiphany scene—is the subject's feeling that words, phrases, and concepts detract from our ultimate perception of the object, that they lie as a veil between the viewer and true reality. (This is a syndrome that we discussed earlier as the language crisis.) In *Siddhartha,* as well as Hesse's works in general, we find this attitude, which provides the background for the experience of the epiphany. Siddhartha's final interview with Govinda makes it clear that he has been able to attain his affirmation and union with the All only because he eschews the easy way of convenient words and phrases as explanations of reality. "Words are not good for the secret meaning. Everything is always slightly distorted when one utters it in words—a little falsified, a little silly." He goes on to confide that he does not make distinctions between thoughts and words. "To be perfectly frank, I don't have a very high opinion of thoughts. I like *things* better." And he concludes by asserting that any ostensible difference between his views and those of Buddha is only illusory, the product of word-confusions. In essence, despite all superficial differences, they agree. The final vision, in which Govinda sees totality and simultaneity revealed in his friend's face, is also an epiphany: a direct revelation to Govinda of the essential unity of being

that Siddhartha was unable to convey through the medium of words.

It is through epiphanies that Siddhartha breaks out of the rigid schematism of Buddhism and Brahminism (their "highly bred reformation" quality of which Hesse speaks in the diary of 1920) and begins to enter into an immediate contact with the world, though it first leads him to the false extreme of sensualism. Since love is the new dimension of Siddhartha's world, he must, as his final trial, learn to affirm even the rejection of his love by his own son. Only after he has suffered the torment of rejection can he perceive the final truth, which had hitherto been purely intellectual: no two men have the same way to the final goal: not even the father can spare his son the agonies of self-discovery. When Siddhartha accepts this truth, he perceives with visionary clarity that in the realm of simultaneity and totality even he and his own father are one. Just as he had once deserted his father, so had his son left him.

> Siddhartha gazed into the water, and in the flowing water pictures appeared to him: his father appeared, lonely, grieving about his son; he himself appeared, lonely, he too bound by the bonds of longing to his distant son; his son appeared, he too lonely, the boy, storming covetously along the burning course of his young desires; each directed toward his goal, each possessed by his goal, each suffering.... The image of the father, his own image, that of the son flowed together; also Kamala's image appeared and merged with the stream, and the image of Govinda, and other images, and flowed one into the other, becoming one with the river....

Not until he has recognized and then affirmed the loss of his son is Siddhartha ready to enter the state of fulfillment. Only at this point does he affirm with love the insight which had been purely intellectual cognition when he departed from Buddha. For even in the case of his own son he is forced to concede that each man must find his own way in life, that no man's path can be prescribed. Thus the highest lesson of the novel is a direct contradiction of Buddha's theory of the Eightfold Path, to which ... Hesse objected in his diary of 1920; it is the whole meaning of the book that Siddhartha can attain Buddha's goal without following his path. If rejection of that doctrine is the essence of the novel, then it is futile to look to Buddhism for clues to the structural organization of the book. Rather, the structural principle is to be found precisely where the meaning of the book lies. Just as Siddhartha learns of the totality, and simultaneity of all being—man and nature alike—so too the development of the soul is expressed in geographical terms and, in turn, the landscape is reflected in the human face. The book achieves a unity of style, structure and meaning that Hesse never again attained with such perfection after *Siddhartha.*

It would be futile to deny, on the other hand, that this unity has been achieved at the expense of the narrative realism we customarily expect from fiction. Just as the characters and landscape have been stylized into abstractions by Hesse's poetic vision, likewise the dialogue and action have been reduced—or escalated—to symbolic essentials. As in *Demian* the action is almost wholly internalized: the excitement of this externally serene work is entirely within Siddhartha's mind. It is ultimately beside the point to judge this work by the criteria of the traditional realistic novel. Like Hermann Broch, who insisted that his *The Death of Vergil* was a "lyrical work" and that it be read and criticized as such, Hesse had good reasons for calling *Siddhartha* "an Indic poem." In both works there is a stratum of realistic narrative, but each as a whole represents the symbolic projection of an inner vision and not an attempt to capture external reality mimetically. Like his heroes, who vacillate between nature and spirit, Hesse as a narrator feels conflicting impulses toward realism and lyricism. In *Siddhartha* he reached an extreme of symbolic lyricism.

Source: Theodore Ziolkowski, "*Siddhartha:* The Landscape of the Soul—The Beatific Smile and The Epiphany," in his *The Novels of Hermann Hesse: A Study in Theme in Structure,* Princeton University Press, 1965, pp. 170-77.

Johannes Malthaner

In this excerpt, Malthaner points out the autobiographical nature of Siddhartha *and argues that the novel reflects Hesse's emphasis on faith as the only way for man to "penetrate to the source of light" and "find God."*

[Hesse's] novels do not have a strong plot around which the action revolves and therefore lack suspense or excitement. They are largely autobiographical and deal with questions of "Weltanschauung", of a philosophy of life. The plot is used by Hesse to drape his thoughts around it, to have an opportunity to present his innermost thoughts and the struggle for an understanding of the great problems of life. Hesse is, and always has been, a god-seeker; he has a message for his fellow-men, but one must "study" him, read and re-read his works carefully if one wants to get the full benefit of their message. His works are not so much for entertainment but rather want to give food for

thought; they have therefore a very strong appeal for the serious minded reader but not for the masses that crave excitement and entertainment instead of beauty and depth.

Herman Hesse's novel *Siddhartha* is just such a work of literature, and it is of special interest to the student of literature, and of Hesse in particular, because it marks an important step in the development of Hesse and is unique in German literature in its presentation of Eastern philosophy.

The novel is largely auto-biographical and has a long and interesting history. It is no doubt true of all great works of art that they do not just happen, that they are not products of chance. Great works of literature have their roots way back in the life of their writers, they have grown out of life and are part of the life of their creators; great works of literature are not factory products but grow and ripen slowly to full bloom. This is especially true of *Siddhartha.*

Siddhartha was published in 1922 but has its roots in the earliest childhood of Hesse. His parents had been missionaries to India, his mother having been born in India of missionary parents; but on account of the poor health of Hesse's father the family had to return to Europe and came to Calw, a small Black Forest town, to help the maternal grandfather of Hesse, Dr. Gundert, the director of their mission and a famous Indian scholar and linguist. Indian songs and books, frequent discussions about India with visiting missionaries and scholars, a large library of Indian and Chinese writings, also many objects of Eastern art created great interest and left a deep impression on Hesse ever since his childhood.

The first part of *Siddhartha,* up to the meeting with the courtesan Kamala, was written before 1919 and was first published in the literary magazine *Neue Rundschau.* Siddhartha is the son of a rich Brahman of India. He is a good obedient son and the joy of his parents, but one day be awakens to the realization that his life is empty, that his soul has been left unsatisfied by his devotion to duty and the strict observance of all religious ordinances. He wants to find God who so far has been to him only a vague idea, distant and unreal, although he tried to serve him with sincerity of heart to the best of his understanding. Young Siddhartha realizes that he is at a dead end and that he must break away. So he leaves home leaving behind him all that he so far had loved and treasured, all the comforts, giving up his high social position, and becomes a Samana, an itinerant monk, with no earthly possessions anymore, accompanied by his boyhood friend Govinda who has decided to follow Siddhartha's lead. By fasting and exposing his body to the rigors of the weather, Siddhartha wants to empty himself completely of all physical desires so that by any chance he may hear the voice of God speaking to his soul, that he may find peace.

Hesse's books are confessions, and the story of Siddhartha is his own story describing his own doubts and struggle. He, too, had rebelled: against the pietistic orthodoxy of his parents and the strict school system in Germany that destroyed any attempt of independence in its pupils. So he ran away to shape his own life. Self-education is the main theatre of most of the novels of Hesse, especially of the books of his youth. Self-education has been for centuries a very favorite theme in German literature and men like Luther, Goethe, Kant, and many other leading German writers and philosophers were the inspirers of German youth in their longing for independence.

It is significant that Hesse gave to a collection of four stories published in 1931, in which he included *Siddhartha,* the title of *Weg nach Innen,* Road to Within. Indeed, Siddhartha turns away from the outside observance of religious rituals and ordinances to a life of contemplation. So also does Hesse himself after the outbreak of World War I. Up to the war, Hesse had lived a rather quiet and self-satisfied life. After years of hard struggle to win recognition as a poet, he had found first success which brought him not only social recognition and financial security but also many friends and a home. But the war brought him a rather rude awakening out of his idylic life on the shore of Lake Constance where he had lived a rather happy and retired life. His apparently so secure and well ordered world came crashing down over his head. The vicious attacks by the German press and by many of his former friends for his stand against the war psychosis—Hesse was living at that time in Switzerland although he was still a German citizen—forced him to re-examine the fundamental truths on which he had built his life. He had become distrustful of religion as he saw it practised, and of education which had not prevented the western world of being plunged into a murderous war. Where was the truth? On what foundation could a man build his life? All had been found wanting.

Siddhartha is Hesse's attempt to restore his faith in mankind, to regain his lost peace of mind, and to find again a harmonious relationship with his world. A new more spiritual orientation takes place. He does no longer believe in the natural goodness of man, he is thrown back unto himself and comes to a new concept of God: No longer does he seek God in nature but, in the words of the Bible, he believed that "the Kingdom of God's is within you".

Hesse confesses that he had been pious only up to his thirteenth year but then had become a skeptic. Now he becomes a believer again, to be sure it is not a return to the orthodox belief of his parents, he wants to include in his new concept of religion not only the teachings of Jesus but also those of Buddha and of the Holy Scriptures of India as well....

Returning to our story, we find that Siddhartha also as a Samana has not come nearer his goal of happiness and peace. It seems to him that his religious fervor had been nothing but self-deception, that all the time he had been in flight from himself. The hardships which he had endured as a Samana had not brought him nearer to God.

At this period of his life, Siddhartha hears of Gotama Buddha of whom it was said that he had attained that blissful state of godliness where the chain of reincarnations had been broken, that he had entered Nirvana. Siddhartha goes to find him, hears him teach the multitude, and then has a private conversation with the Holy One; but it becomes clear to him that the way of salvation can not be taught, that words and creeds are empty sounds, that each man must find the way by himself, the secret of the experience can not be passed on. So he leaves also Gotama Buddha and all teachers and teachings. Govinda, his friend, stays with Gotama and so Siddhartha cuts the last link with his past. He is now all alone. And he comes to the sudden realization that all through the years so far he has lived a separate life, that he actually never had sought a real understanding of his fellow men, that he knew very little of the world and of life all about him. For the first time in many years he really looks about him and perceives the beauty of the world. The world about him, from which he had fled, he now finds attractive and good. He must not seek to escape life but face it, live it.

This is the startling new discovery Siddhartha makes and so he decides to leave the wilderness. He comes to the big city where he sees at the gate the beautiful Kamala, the courtesan. He finds her favor and she teaches him the ways of the world. He discards his beggar's clothes and becomes in short time a very successful merchant. But his heart is neither in his love nor in his business; all the pleasures of the world can not still the hunger of his soul. He finds the world wanting, too, and, moreover, he must realize after a few years that the worldly things, the acquiring of money, have gradually taken possession of his life, that he is being enslaved and harassed by the necessity of making money in order to satisfy his extravagant tastes, that he has become a busy and unfree man whose thoughts dwell less and less on the eternal things.

So he cuts himself loose from all that he had acquired, leaves once again everything behind him, and goes back to the river which he had crossed when he gave up his life as a Samana.

At this point there is a long interruption in the writing of *Siddhartha*. Hesse realized that his knowledge of Eastern philosophy was not sufficient; he devoted himself therefore to a very thorough study of Indian philosophy and religion. After a year and a half he takes up the writing of the story again. It is quite evident, however, that the emphasis has shifted. Description from now on is practically absent, and the tone is lighter, the language, too, is not so heavy, not so mystic but transparent and more elevated. The whole concentration is on the spiritual element. Instead of long discussions of philosophies and systems, we find the emphasis now on Faith. He perceives that only through faith, not by doing or by teaching, can man penetrate to the source of light, can he find God.

At the bank of the river Siddhartha sits for a long time and lets his whole life pass in review before him. He finds that even the evil things which he had done lately had been necessary as an experience in order to bring him to an understanding of what life really was. But he also becomes discouraged because all his endeavors so far had not given him the desired insight and peace of soul. There was nothing left in life that might entice him, challenge him, comfort him; he finds himself subject to an unescapable chain of cause and effect, to repeated incarnations, each of which means a new beginning of suffering. Will he ever be able to break this chain? Will he ever be able to enter Nirvana? He doubts it and is at the point of drowning himself when the mysterious word "OM" comes to his mind. "OM" means "having completed", in German "Vollendung". He realizes the folly of his attempt to try to find peace and an end to his sufferings by extinguishing his physical being. Life is indestructible. Siddhartha realizes, too, that all life is one, that all creation is an indivisible one, that trees and birds are indeed his brothers; he sees his

great mistake in trying always to do something instead of just to be.

He joins Vasudeva, the ferry man, who shows him the great secret of the river, namely that for the river the concept of time does not exist: The river just is, for the river there is no past, no future, no beginning, no end; for the river is only the presence. And for man, too, Vasudeva tells him, happiness is real only when causality—that is time—has ceased to exist for him. The problem is not, as Siddhartha had always understood it, to find perfection, but to find completion, "Vollendung".

One more lesson Siddhartha had to learn. When he left Kamala she had known that she would bear him a child, but she did not tell Siddhartha because she realized that she could not and must not hold him back, that Siddhartha had to go his own way. Later, too, she felt the emptiness of her life; so one day she decides to seek Gotama Buddha of whom she had heard. Her way leads her to the river where, unknown to her, Siddartha lived and stopping at the bank of the river to rest, she is bitten by a poisonous snake. Siddhartha finds her dying and recognizes her. After he had buried her, he takes his son, a boy of some twelve or fourteen years of age, to him. Siddhartha feels keenly the loss of Kamala, but it is not sadness that is in his heart for he knows now that all life is indestructible, that Kamala has only entered a new life, life in a wider sense, that in every blossom, in every breeze about him there is Kamala. He is not separated from her, never will be, in fact she is nearer to him now than ever before.

Siddhartha devotes himself to the education of his son but must make the painful experience that his love is not appreciated and his endeavors are repulsed. His son does not want the life Siddhartha thinks best for him, he wants to live his own life, and thus breaks away from his father as Siddhartha in his own youth had broken away from his own father. With the loss of his son, there is nothing left that binds Siddhartha to this world. He realizes that this had to come, so that he would no longer fight what he considered fate but give himself unreservedly to his destiny; thus Siddhartha has overcome suffering at last and with it has attained the last step of his completion, he has entered into Nirvana; now peace has come to Siddhartha at last.

Source: Johannes Malthaner, "Hermann Hesse: *Siddhartha*," in *The German Quarterly,* Vol. XXV, No. 2, March, 1952, pp. 103-09.

For Further Study

Mark Boulby, in *Hermann Hesse: His Mind and Art,* Cornell University Press, 1967.

A book-length study of Hesse's fiction with a chapter on *Siddhartha* that shows how Hesse's use of Indian themes promotes a Western, Christian world view.

Madison Brown, "Toward a Perspective for the Indian Element in Hermann Hesse's *Siddhartha,*" in *German Quarterly,* Vol. 49, No. 2, March, 1976, pp. 191-202.

An analysis of how *Siddhartha* draws on themes from Indian religious and cultural traditions but revises them to promote Hesse's own world view.

Harish Chander, "Hermann Hesse's *Siddhartha* and the Doctrine of Anatman," in *South Asian Review,* Vol. 2, No. 8, July, 1979, pp. 60-66.

An analysis of how *Siddhartha* develops Buddhist religious themes regarding the universal soul.

Robert C. Conrad, "Hermann Hesse's *Siddhartha, Eine indische Dichtung,* as a Western Archetype," *German Quarterly,* Vol. 48, No. 4, Fall, 1975, pp. 358-69.

An analysis of how Hesse uses Indian themes to develop Western archetypal patterns.

George Wallis Field, in *Hermann Hesse,* Twayne Publishers, Inc., 1970.

This book is a comprehensive and detailed study of Hesse's novels complemented by biographical and factual information.

Husain Kassim, "Toward a Mahayana Buddhist Interpretation of Hermann Hesse's *Siddhartha,*" in *Literature East and West,* Vol. 18, No. 2, March, 1974, pp. 233-43.

An analysis of how *Siddhartha* develops a Buddhist philosophy rather than a Christian one.

Celian LuZanne, *Heritage of Buddha: The Story of Siddhartha Gautama,* Philosophical Library, 1953.

This book provides historical information on the life of the Buddha, the model for Gotama Buddha in Hesse's novel.

Johannes Malthaner, "Hermann Hesse: 'Siddhartha'," in *German Quarterly,* Vol. 25, No. 2, March, 1952, pp. 103-09.

This article describes Siddhartha's spiritual journey and suggests that his quests reflect Hesse's attempt to regain his harmonious relationship with the world.

Joseph Mileck, "Hermann Hesse," in *Dictionary of Literary Biography, Vol. 66; German Fiction Writers, 1885-1913,* edited by James Hardin, Gale Research Company, 1988, pp 180-224.

This essay provides a comprehensive overview of Hesse's life and work by one of the great Hesse academic scholars.

Bhabagrahi Misra, "An Analysis of Indic Tradition in Hermann Hesse's *Siddhartha,*" in *Indian Literature,* Vol. 11, 1968, pp. 111-123.

An analysis of how *Siddhartha* draws on both Hindu religious beliefs and Western existentialism.

Ernst Rose, *Faith from the Abyss: Hermann Hesse's Way from Romanticism to Modernity,* New York University Press, 1965.

This volume provides poignant and significant biographical information and correlates Hesse's major works to corresponding periods in his life and state of mind.

Leroy Shaw, "Time and Structure of Hermann Hesse's *Siddhartha,*" in *Hermann Hesse: A Collection of Criticism,* edited by Judith Liebmann, McGraw-Hill, 1977, pp. 66-84.

An analysis of how the narrative structure of *Siddhartha* is patterned after Buddhist religious principles and an Eastern sense of timelessness.

Huston Smith, *The Religions of Man,* Harper & Row, 1958.

This classic study provides a comprehensive study of eight great world religions, including Buddhism and Hinduism.

Kamal D. Verma, "The Nature and Perception of Reality in Hermann Hesse's *Siddhartha,*" in *South Asian Review,* Vol. 11, No. 8, July, 1988, pp. 1-10.

An analysis of philosophical and metaphysical themes in *Siddhartha.*

Bernhard Zeller, *Portrait of Hesse,* Herder and Herder, 1971.

This biography is augmented by numerous photographs.

Theodore Ziolkowski, *The Novels of Hermann Hesse: A Study in Theme and Structure,* Princeton University Press, 1965.

This book explores the central themes that are woven through much of Hesse's work as well as the structure of individual novels, including *Siddhartha.*

The Stranger

Albert Camus

1942

Camus gave the world a new kind of hero when *The Stranger* and the accompanying essay collection *The Myth of Sisyphus* burst upon the literary scene in 1942. They were published in the dark days of World War II: France had surrendered to Hitler, the British were under siege, the Americans were still recovering from Pearl Harbor, and the Russians were on the defensive. With such a background, the work and philosophy of Albert Camus were appropriate responses to the tension of resisting the Germans. The individual's resistance was the very definition of freedom. Camus believed, and many agreed with him, that the world was meaningless, absurd, and indifferent. However, he also wrote that in the face of this indifference the individual must rebel against the absurdity felt by the mind and uphold traditional human values.

The Stranger was an immediate success and established Camus, incorrectly, as a major representative of the existentialist movement. The novel tells the story of Meursault, who kills an Arab in a reaction to the environment—the heat and glare of the sun. In the ensuing investigation, the law prosecutes Meursault for his failure to show proper feelings for his deceased mother, rather than for the crime of murder. Aghast at his apparent lack of love, they execute him. The novel, as well as the collection of essays, developed the concept of the absurd and the belief that a person can be happy in the face of the "absurd."

Author Biography

Albert Camus lived in a period of remarkable turmoil in the world—two world wars were fought, and colonized countries, notably India and Algeria, began independence struggles. Camus was born in the latter, a French colony in North Africa, in Mondovi, on November 7, 1913. When he was almost one, his father, Lucien Auguste Camus, was killed in the outbreak of World War I. Left fatherless, Albert lived with his mother Catherine Stintes Camus, his older brother Lucien, his Uncle Etienne Stintes, and his grandmother. They lived in a three-room apartment in the working-class Belcourt district of Algiers.

Camus's mother was a silent woman who rarely showed her sons affection and who expected Camus to work when he was old enough. Fortunately, there were two forces that helped Camus despite his mother's silence—school and sports. Albert excelled in school with the assistance the state provided him as a child of a fallen French soldier: he received free health care and money for his education. In fifth grade, his teacher, Louis Germain, became Albert's patron. Germain helped Camus to overcome the family's opposition to the pursuit of an education. He also assisted Camus with scholarship applications. The other formative force in the making of Albert Camus was soccer. Through team sports he developed social skills which his family life did not encourage.

His athletic career ended when he was diagnosed with tuberculosis in 1930. The doctor suggested that Camus move in with his Uncle Acault, who was a butcher. It was hoped that the access to red meat would help his condition. Uncle Acault also had more money to lend Albert for books. He withdrew his support, however, when Albert began seeing the scandalous Simone Hie.

Camus pursued a variety of activities throughout the 1930s. These included his studies, the beginnings of a literary career, active involvement with the Communist party, and writing for a theatrical troupe. Although Camus preferred drama to prose throughout his life, his plays are not as well known as his fiction. In 1933, he entered the University of Algiers, and submitted his thesis in 1936. From 1938 to 1940, he worked as a journalist with the *Alger-Republicain*. This occupation, as well as the popularity of American authors (like Hemingway), is reflected in the style of *The Stranger*, which Camus began at this time.

Albert Camus

In 1940, Camus divorced his wife—they had been separated for some time—and married Francine Faure. When France fell to Hitler, Camus joined the resistance in Paris. He became editor of the daily newspaper *Combat* and became the "conscience of France" through his popular editorials. Two years later, he published *The Stranger* and *The Myth of Sisyphus.* When France was liberated, Camus returned to Algeria.

After the war, he published an enlarged edition of *The Myth of Sisyphus,* as well as his most significant play, *Caligula.* In 1947, another literary classic, *The Plague,* was published. During the rest of his life, Camus struggled with his health, critics, issues of the Algerian war, and the strain on his marriage caused by his affair with the actress Maria Casarès. His best novel, technically speaking, was *The Fall,* published in 1956. That novel was followed by a collection of short stories, *Exile and Kingdom.* In 1957, he was awarded the Nobel Prize for Literature. Three years later, on January 4, 1960, he was killed in an auto accident.

Plot Summary

Part One

The Stranger opens with the narrator, Meursault, receiving a telegram telling him his mother has died. Departing on the afternoon bus from Algiers, he travels fifty miles to Marengo for the funeral. Upon arriving, he meets the director of the retirement home who leads him to the mortuary where his mother lies in a coffin. There Meursault begins a vigil that will last until the next morning. He dozes, awakening to the sound of his mother's companions at the home. They sit across from him, joining in the vigil. The night is punctuated by fits of crying and coughing by the residents. Meursault remains unemotional. The burial the next day becomes a blur of images for Meursault: the funeral procession in the hot desert sun, the village, the cemetery, the tears and fainting spell of Thomas Pérez—a male companion of his mother—and finally the bus ride back to Algiers. At one point in the day, a funeral helper asks him if his mother had been very old; Meursault gives a vague response because he does not know her exact age. Such seemingly superfluous details resurface with great significance later in the story.

The next morning at the beach, Meursault meets Marie, a former typist at his office. They make a date to see a comedic Fernandel film, after which Marie spends the night at Meursault's apartment. Alone on his balcony the next evening, Meursault concludes that the death of his mother has not changed his life at all. In the stairwell of his apartment building the next afternoon, Meursault encounters two of his neighbors: the aged Salamano, who is cursing his dog, and Raymond Sintès, a pimp. Raymond invites Meursault over for a meal. After dinner, Raymond asks Meursault to write a letter for him to his ex-mistress, a Moorish woman. Raymond wants to lure her back to punish her for having taken advantage of him. Earlier that day, Raymond had been in a fist fight with her brother. Meursault agrees to write the letter.

The next weekend Meursault and Marie hear screams coming from Raymond's apartment. With the hallway full of residents, a policeman arrives and talks to Raymond. His ex-mistress cries out that Raymond beat her. Raymond is given a summons and must go to the police station. Later that afternoon, Raymond asks Meursault if he will serve as a witness for him. Meursault assents and Raymond is eventually let off with a warning. That evening, Salamano tells Meursault that his dog is missing.

The following Sunday, Meursault, Marie, and Raymond take the bus out of Algiers to the coast. This excursion becomes a turning point in the plot. Earlier in the week, Raymond had invited them to a friend's beach house. A group of Arabs, among them the brother of Raymond's ex-mistress, watches them depart. At the beach Raymond and Meursault greet Raymond's friend Masson and his wife. After an early lunch, the three men take a walk on the beach. They encounter the brother and another Arab. A fight ensues. Raymond is cut by a knife and Masson must bring him to a doctor. Later in the afternoon, Raymond and Meursault again walk down the beach. They meet up with the two Arabs near a fresh-water spring. Raymond pulls out a revolver but Meursault convinces him to relinquish it. The two Arabs suddenly withdraw and Raymond and Meursault return to the beach house.

Preferring neither to walk up the stairs to the beach house nor to remain in the now scorching sun, Meursault decides to walk back along the beach. Struggling against the heat, he approaches the cool spring. Alone in the shade sits the brother. Feeling the breadth of the hot beach behind him, Meursault advances. The Arab pulls out his knife, the glint of which strikes Meursault. Oppressed by the heat, blinded by the flash of light and the sweat falling into his eyes, Meursault fires the revolver and kills the Arab. He pauses without reflection, then fires four more times into the inert body.

Part Two

Meursault is arrested and interviewed. A court lawyer is appointed to him and inquiries are made into his private life. Accusations of insensibility at his mother's funeral surface. Meursault explains to his lawyer that his nature is such that his physical needs often overpower his feelings. He had been tired the day of the funeral. Meursault observes that his mother's death has nothing to do with his crime. The lawyer responds that Meursault obviously has little experience with the law.

Meursault begins the first of many interviews with a magistrate. The magistrate first asks about Meursault's mother, then inquires as to why he paused between his first and second revolver shot. To this latter question Meursault has no answer. Pulling out a crucifix, the magistrate speaks of repentance; he discovers that Meursault does not believe in God. Responding to the magistrate's accusation that he has a hardened soul, Meursault remarks that rather than feeling regret at having killed the Arab, he experiences only a certain ennui, or sadness. Eleven months pass before the trial. Marie is allowed to visit him only once because they are not married. Meursault soon becomes accustomed to the prison routine and looks forward to the now cordial meetings with the magistrate.

With the summer sun and heat comes the trial. The first day, Meursault remarks upon the conviviality of the court scene. The lawyers and journalists mingle and greet one another like members of a club. Meursault watches in silence as witnesses are called forth to testify. The prosecution recalls details from the funeral: Meursault's calmness and lack of emotion, his quick departure after the burial, and the information, followed by a hush from the courtroom audience, that he did not know the age of his mother. The prosecutor characterizes Meursault as Raymond's conspirator: he both served as Raymond's witness at the police station and wrote the letter that set into motion the events that ended in the Arab's death. The prosecutor concludes that the murder was premeditated and that Meursault killed the Arab to help his friend Raymond. According to the prosecutor, Meursault's "irregular" relationship with Marie, begun the day after his mother's funeral, reveals his fundamental lack of respect for social values and reinforces his criminal nature. When Meursault's lawyer objects and questions whether his client is accused of having buried his mother or of having killed a man, the prosecutor retorts that he accuses Meursault of having "buried his mother with the heart of a criminal." Meursault is finally asked by one of the judges why he killed the Arab. Meursault responds that it was "because of the sun." The prosecutor demands the death penalty. The jury returns a verdict of premeditated murder and the judge sentences Meursault to be guillotined in a public square.

Lying in his cell, having refused three times to speak to the chaplain, Meursault contemplates the social mechanism determining his fate and posits the benefit he would derive from knowing that at least one person had managed to escape the inevitable course of events. Waiting for his appeal, Meursault allows the chaplain to enter his cell. After answering many questions concerning his lack of faith, Meursault suddenly cries out and grabs the chaplain by the collar. In a fit of rage he yells out his certitude about life and death, declaring that all are condemned to die, and that this common end renders life absurd and our choices meaningless. Following the outburst, Meursault is overcome with peace. His speech to the priest has purged him of bitterness and hope and he feels liberated. For his existence to be complete, Meursault only wishes for many spectators to be present the day of his execution and that they greet him with cries of hate:

"In the evening, Marie came to pick me up and asked me if I wanted to marry her. I said that it made no difference to me and that we could if she wanted to.

She wanted to know if I loved her. I answered as I already had before, that all that meant nothing but that undoubtedly I didn't love her. 'Then why marry me?' she said. I explained to her that marriage was of no importance and that if she wanted, we could get married. Besides, she was the one asking and I was just agreeing to say yes. She then remarked that marriage was a serious thing. 'No' I said. She was quiet for a moment and looked at me in silence. Then she spoke. She simply wanted to know if I would have accepted the same proposal coming from another woman for whom I would have held a similar affection. 'Of course' I said. She then wondered if she loved me. For my part, I could know nothing about it."

Characters

Marie Cardona

Formerly a typist in the same office as Meursault, Marie Cardona happens to be swimming at the same place as Meursault the day after his mother's funeral. She likes Meursault and their meeting sparks a relationship. She asks if he loves her but he tells her honestly that he doesn't think so. Still, he agrees to marry her, but then he is arrested.

Marie represents the happy life Meursault desires to live. In fact, she is the only reason he even considers regretting his crime. Meursault sees Marie's face in the prison wall—but the image fades after a time. Marie, for Meursault, was a comfort representing a life of "normality" that he might have lived. However, it did not happen. Instead he becomes certain only of life and death and is executed.

Caretaker

The caretaker takes a keen interest in Meursault. He stays by him throughout the vigil and provides him with explanations and introductions. He also tries to justify his life to Meursault. He explains that he has been to Paris and only became a caretaker when fate made him destitute.

It is the caretaker who provides the most damaging testimony at the trial. The caretaker testifies that Meursault "hadn't wanted to see Maman, that [he] had smoked and slept some, and that [he] had had some coffee." The prosecutor dwells on the caretaker's testimony and asks him to repeat the part about having a coffee and a cigarette with Meursault. It is during this testimony that Meursault "for the first time … realized that [he] was guilty."

Albert Camus directing actors Catherine Sellers and Marc Cassot in his stage adaptation of William Faulkner's novel Requiem for a Nun.

Céleste

Céleste owns the cafe at which Meursault customarily dines. He is called as a witness at Meursault's trial. His theory on Meursault's crime is that it was bad luck. He seems to be a fatalist, believing that one is more the victim of chance than a free agent.

Defense Counsel

The lawyer represents Meursault to the best of his ability. He seems to be the only person who understands the silliness of the trial and the difficul-

ties for someone like Meursault. After the examination of Pérez on the witness stand, he says, "Here we have a perfect reflection of this entire trial: everything is true, and nothing is true!" Unconsciously, the lawyer has just sided with Meursault—the truth of the court is arbitrary and meaningless.

Director of the Home

The director of the nursing home where Meursault's mother lived is a very matter-of-fact man. Death in his community means taking care of ceremony and keeping, as much as possible, the other patients from being too much on edge. Consequently, everything is done "as usual" so that while a funeral is a stress to the community, it is also a habitual ritual. The director accompanies the funeral procession to the gravesite and offers Meursault information about his mother's life at the home, but Meursault is not very interested.

Examining Magistrate

The magistrate, as an investigator, is interested in what other people think. This makes him the exact opposite of Meursault in psychological makeup. He examines Meursault's testimony for the insights they might provide about Meursault's mind, rather than making an effort to establish the facts of the murder. He tells Meursault that with God's help, he will try to "do something" for him. The magistrate asks Meursault if he loved his mother before asking about the five shots. Thus, the connection between Meursault's behavior at his mother's funeral and his act of murder is made concrete.

The magistrate then presents Meursault with a Bible and crucifix, hoping to save Meursault's soul. The ruse backfires because Meursault refuses to see the relevance of religion to the state's case against him. Having failed to "do something for him," the magistrate never brings up the matter again.

The magistrate is an important character in the story as the representative of society's law. He fails in his attempt to make Meursault acknowledge either the authority of law or that of religion. The magistrate is entirely unable to understand Meursault, and after a few sessions speaks only to his lawyer.

Lawyer

See Defense Counsel

Masson

Masson is the owner of the beach house to which Raymond takes Meursault and Marie for the day. Masson is an obese, carefree fellow who wants them all to live there in the vacation month of August and share expenses. He believes that lunchtime is when one is hungry and that it is good to do things when one wants and not according to schedule. Thus he is simply a man who likes to live well and to be happy.

Arthur Meursault

Meursault is a French Algerian clerk who learns that his mother has died. He attends the funeral and, on the following day, goes to the beach.

Media Adaptations

- There has been only one adaptation of Camus's novel to the screen. Directed by Luchino Visconti, *L'Etranger* was produced in 1967 by Paramount pictures. The film failed to capture the Camus's style, but fortunately, the role of Arthur Meursault is executed brilliantly by Marcello Mastroianni and Anna Karina delivers a fine performance as Marie Cardona.

There, he meets Marie, with whom he begins a relationship. A neighbor invites him to the beach where they encounter some Arabs. Meursault shoots one of the Arabs for no apparent reason. He is arrested, tried, and executed. Until the moment when the judge pronounces him guilty, Meursault is annoyingly indifferent to the activities of the real world. The judgement jars him into an examination of life, at the end of which he concludes that life is absurd. He finds peace and happiness in this acknowledgment. This conclusion of his analysis, Meursault discovers, is liberating.

The Stranger is the manifestation or incarnation of Camus's theory of the "absurd" man. Meursault reveals Camus's theory through his actions. That is, the protagonist Meursault possesses a curious psychology whose activity is of more interest than the fact of his crime. Meursault is an "outsider"—a person who lives in his own private world and maintains no interest in anyone else, least of all in how they view him. However, he is not unaware of others. Several crucial moments demonstrate this: at the opening, Meursault is aware that his boss shows him no sympathy upon hearing of his mother's death. Next, he is aware that one is expected to mourn the dead, which he refuses to do. He knows he could say he loved Marie and that she would accept his love, but he does not. Lastly, he is aware, throughout his own trial, that he ought to say certain things, but he does not.

Finally, as Camus himself said, Meursault is a Christ figure who dies for everyone who misunderstands him. Meursault becomes aware of the meaninglessness with which society pursues its notions of propriety, and, in the case of the prison chaplain, its dogmas. Meursault is convicted as much for his psychological indifference, his selfish and asocial behavior, and his lack of mourning for his mother, as for his crime. His position is not without logic. For example, when the magistrate tries to persuade him to believe in God so that he might be forgiven, Meursault asks what difference that makes when it is the state that will find him guilty and then execute him—not God.

It is before the priest, however, that he finally explodes: "none of [the priest's] certainties was worth one strand of a woman's hair. Living as he did, like a corpse, he couldn't even be sure of being alive. It might look as if my hands were empty. Actually, I was sure of myself, sure about everything, far surer than he; sure of my present life and of the death that was coming. That, no doubt, was all I had." Meursault dies because he knows this truth—he is killed because the others cling to their illusions.

Monsieur Thomas Pérez

Pérez is an old man who was a friend of Meursault's mother at the nursing home. He insists on attending the burial. Because of a limp and his age, Pérez falls behind the procession but still manages to attend. He is called as a witness at the trial and is unable to say whether or not he had seen Meursault cry.

Raymond

Raymond is a neighbor who asks Meursault to write a letter for him. Meursault agrees to do so because it is easier than saying no. Consequently, they become friends and Meursault even testifies to the police that Raymond's girlfriend was cheating on him. In response, the police let Raymond off (for beating her) with a warning. However, the girlfriend's brother is not so benevolent, and, along with a group of Arabs, starts following Raymond. A showdown takes place when Raymond and Meursault visit Masson's beach house. A fight ensues, and Raymond is cut. Shortly after this, Meursault shoots one of the Arabs.

Raymond represents the small-minded man who views things in terms of possession—he beats a woman for not being solely his; he insists that Meursault is his friend because he agreed to write the letter. Relationships, for Raymond, are his certainties and life fills in around them. It is Raymond, contrary to the evidence, who unquestioningly believes that Salamano's dog will return.

Salamano

Salamano is a disgusting older man who beats his dog. His routine walk with his mutt and his muttering give Meursault daily amusement. This routine is part of the general rhythm of tedium that is Meursault's universe. Sadly, the dog goes missing, and Salamano comes to Meursault for help. Meursault offers him none and Salamano acknowledges that his whole life has changed. The disruption of routine caused by the loss of the dog is one of many signs that Meursault's tedious universe has collapsed.

Themes

Absurdity

Absurdity is a philosophical view at which one arrives when one is forced out of a very repetitive existence. As Camus says in "An Absurd Reasoning" from his essay collection *The Myth of Sisyphus:*

> It happens that the stage sets collapse. Rising, streetcar, four hours in the office or the factory, meal, streetcar, four hours of work, meal, sleep, and Monday Tuesday Wednesday Thursday Friday and Saturday according to the same rhythm—this path is easily followed most of the time. But one day the "why" arises and everything begins in that weariness tinged with amazement.

This description characterizes Meursault perfectly. The essay collection explained the philosophy of the absurd, and the novel demonstrated the theory.

Meursault's repetitive life runs smoothly. Then, little by little, Meursault's happy stasis is pulled apart by the rest of the world's movement and collapse begins. His mother dies, and with her, a sense of stability he has had his whole life. He becomes involved with Marie, who asks him whether he cares for her and in asking nearly breaches his safe isolation. Raymond insists upon being his friend. Salamano's dog just disappears, thus disrupting a parallel repetitive rhythm. He shoots a man, and the law demands that he die. Each subtle disruption of Meursault's desire to be indifferently static brings him to a mental crisis. This crisis is resolved when he comes to understand the utter meaninglessness of his individual life within the mystery of the collective society. The events of his story only make sense that way. Any other explanation leads him to theology—represented by the priest—or fate.

In an expression of Camus's humanist logic, neither theology nor fate can offer men of intelligence (men like Meursault, willing to use only bare

Topics
For Further
Study

- Consider the element of time in the novel. Suggest some reasons why Camus chose not to establish the date or era. Keep in mind the historical context of the novel and the universal pretension of the theme.

- Consult psychological literature and create a profile of the "outsider." What sort of mental condition creates a person of moral indifference? Begin with the book *The Outsider* by Colin Wilson.

- Do some research on the condition of freedom of the press in France under Nazi occupation and the role of journals such as *Combat* in the resistance to this occupation. Does the refusal of Meursault to abide by the societal code of the world in which he lives have anything to do with the conditions under which Camus struggled?

- Read the *The Myth of Sisyphus*. What is the absurd man? Was Camus successful in creating a character in terms of his theory of the absurd? Does Meursault have a place in reality?

- Read the first American existential novel by Richard Wright, entitled *The Outsider* (1953), and compare to Camus's *The Stranger*.

- Often encyclopedic entries on existentialism will list Camus as a representative author. Select an existential novel (by such authors as de Beauvoir or Sartre) and compare its themes to Camus's theory of the absurd. Agree or disagree with such a categorization.

- Much has been made of the evident moral clash between Meursault and the magistrate or the priest. Do you think that Camus's project was the outlining of a moral code or the presentation of the absurd man?

---

logic to consider the question of life) an explanation for the absolutely senseless things that humans do—war, murder, and other heinous acts. The alternative, therefore, is absurdity. Meursault recognizes the "truth" that life is meaningless. That means life is just what one makes of it while being conscious of two certainties—life and death. In doing so, Camus argues, one would uphold traditional human values because they safeguard one's life. In other words, human values (what we understand today as "human rights") lead to the greatest happiness of the greatest number. When one is truly willing to face this Truth, one can be happy. Unfortunately, Meursault is executed before he can live in this fashion.

Colonialism

There are no hints which suggest that the novel takes place in a colonized country. There are, however, hints that racial tensions exist between French-Algerians and "Arabs." From the first page the reader knows that the novel is set in Algeria and that the date of publication is 1942. Therefore, it can be guessed that the novel occurs in a colonized setting. In addition, the narrator hints at the racial tension by telling the story as if it took place solely among some French people who happened to live in Algeria. Meursault only associates with French-Algerians, and the only people he names are French-Algerians. Then, for no apparent reason, he shoots an Arab.

While it could be argued, and usually is, that the issue of race and colonialism is not an important theme to the novel (because the novel is about the larger concern of absurd individuality), it is still important to note its existence. First, none of the Arabs in the book, including the murder victim, receive a name. In fact, the nurse at the nursing home is given no other attribute aside from having an abscess that requires her to wear bandaging on her face. The reader sees her as marked by this condition, and she is described as an "Arab." The reader gains little information about her. Another Arab woman is Raymond's girlfriend. She accuses him of being a pimp, and he beats her. She has no name. In fact, Meursault comments on her name, saying,

"[W]hen he told me the woman's name I realized she was Moorish." It does not bother him that his "friend" is having relations with an "Arab," nor does it bother him that Raymond wants to mark her for cheating on him. He wants to cut her nose off in the traditional manner of marking a prostitute. Finally, her brothers and his friends begin to follow Raymond. It is this nameless group of Arabs who Meursault, Masson, and Raymond encounter at the beach. One member of the group is found by Meursault alone and is shot.

The issue of race is the most troubling and unresolved issue of the novel. If one reads the novel solely in terms of the theme of absurdity, the action of the story makes sense—in a meaningless sort of way. However, read in terms of a lesson on human morality and the ethics of the Western tradition wherein a white man goes through a struggle—or *agon*—in the land of the "Other," then the story is very contradictory and highly problematic. Meursault certainly does arrive at a "truth," but that arrival was at the cost of a man's life as well as a ruined love.

Free Will

Though the possession of a free will is taken for granted by most people, the presentation of its "freeness" in *The Stranger* is rather unsettling. Meursault consistently expresses his awareness of his own will as free. In some instances, this might be interpreted as indifference, but Meursault is decidedly, perhaps starkly, free. He does not feel the temptation to encumber his reasoning with considerations or dogmas. For example, he is never worried and is repeatedly doing a systems check on his body—he declares states of hunger, whether he feels well, and that the temperature is good or the sun is too hot. These are important considerations to Meursault, and they pass the time. Conversely, the magistrate is frustrated, tired, and clings to his belief in God. Meursault discerns that the magistrate finds life's meaning only through this belief. But when the magistrate asks if Meursault is suggesting he should be without belief, Meursault replies that it has nothing to do with him one way or the other. This is because the only things that should concern Mersault, he decides, are elemental factors, such as keeping his body comfortably cool.

Style

Narrative

Psychological self-examinations are common in French first-person narratives, but Camus's *The*

Stranger gave the technique of psychological depth a new twist at the time it was published. Instead of allowing the protagonist to detail a static psychology for the reader, the action and behavior were given to the reader to decipher. Camus did this because he felt that "psychology is action, not thinking about oneself." The protagonist, along with a failure to explain everything to the reader, refuses to justify himself to other characters. He tells only what he is thinking and perceiving, he does not interrupt with commentary. By narrating the story this way, through the most indifferent person, the reader is also drawn into Meursault's perspective. The audience feels the absurdity of the events. However, other characters, who do not even have the benefit of hearing the whole of Meursault's story as the book's readers do, prefer their ideas of him. They are only too ready to make their judgments at the trial. Moreover, they readily condemn him to death as a heartless killer without regret

Structure and Language

Camus's narration was immediately recognized as extremely innovative. His language, while recognized as similar to the American "Hemingway style," was seen as so appropriate to the task as to be hardly borrowed. The style that Camus uses is one of direct speech that does not allow much description. He chose that style because it backed up his narrative technique. The reader is focused on the characters' reactions and behavior as they are related through Meursault.

Camus also divided the story at the murder. Part one opens with the death of Maman and ends with the murder of the Arab. In part two of the novel, Meursault is in prison and at the end is awaiting his execution. The division reinforces the importance of Meursault in the universe of the story. Normality is jarred throughout the first part until it dissolves into chaos because of the murder. The second half shows the force of law entering to reestablish meaning and therefore bring back order through the death of Meursault. The structure and the language, then, are technically at one with the greater theme of absurdity.

Setting

Environment is a very important element to Meursault. He reports the heat of rooms, the way that the sun affects him, and all the other conditions of the habitat he lives in. The story itself is set around the city of Algiers and the beach. It is always daytime and the sun is always out. Curiously, in the universe of *The Stranger* there is no

The Algerian Sahara Desert is the setting for Camus's novel The Stranger.

night, no darkness outside of mental obscurity. Things happen overnight, but no plot action occurs in the dark. The only moment when darkness does threaten is at the start of the vigil, but the caretaker dispels the darkness with the electric light. Other things that happen overnight include private encounters with Marie (we assume) and the verdict, which is read at eight o'clock at night. However, the novel's events occur during the day, long days that are hardly differentiated from each other. Such facts of time emphasize the absurdity of Meursault; everything is meaningless except for the current state of the body in the environment.

Foreshadowing

This technique is used to indicate a happening before it occurs, and this foretelling can be foreboding. A disturbing moment for Meursault, as well as the unsuspecting reader, occurs while Meursault is sitting near his Maman's coffin. "It was then that I realized they were all sitting across from me, nodding their heads, grouped around the caretaker. For a second I had the ridiculous feeling that they were there to judge me." Later, in part two, it is precisely his behavior at this funeral with which the state prosecution is concerned. The way in which Meursault honors his mother has everything to do with his guilt. In other words, the sense of

judgement he felt from those sitting across from him at the funeral vigil foreshadowed the solitary condemnation at the trial.

Historical Context

Algeria

Resuming a policy of imperialist expansion after the Napoleonic era, France invaded Algeria in 1830. The French soon controlled the city of Algiers and some coastal areas, but not until 1857 did they subdue the whole region. France sent settlers to colonize the conquered region, but even as late as 1940 the French in Algeria were outnumbered 9 to 1. During World War II the Algerians fought on the side of Germany, which occupied France. However, they were not too keen on resisting the Americans, and when General Eisenhower landed in November of 1942, he met little resistance. That invasion prevented Camus from leaving France and joining his wife in Algeria until the liberation of France in 1944. Throughout the rest of the war, the Algerian independence movement grew due to contact with other Westerners—British and American soldiers.

The independence movement continued to grow after the war but was violently put down by

Compare
&
Contrast

- **1942:** Algeria is a French colony under Nazi occupation.

  Today: The political party which established Algeria as an independent nation has lost power to more fundamentalist groups.

- **1942:** Mahatma Gandhi is imprisoned as a part of the British government crack-down on India's demand for independence.

  Today: Independent India has a population of just under billion people and, according to Bill

Gates, is soon to catch up with the United States in terms of technological sophistication. India's middle class is currently the largest of any nation on Earth.

- **1942:** Roosevelt's $59 billion-dollar budget called for $52 billion to be spent on the war effort.

  Today: In peace time, the U.S. spends 6 times that amount on military expenditure.

French troops. The struggle escalated when the National Liberation Front (FLN) wrote a new constitution in 1947. Unable to deliver on the promise of the new constitution, the FLN began a war of independence with France in 1954. By 1962, Charles de Gaulle agreed to grant the country independence.

World War II

World War II was in full swing in 1942, since America had declared war on Japan and Germany in response to the Pearl Harbor attack. However, the Allied cause did not look good. France had fallen to the Germans, and British troops were pushed from their holdings in the Pacific to India by the Japanese. On the Russian front, the Germans seemed to be on the verge of capturing Stalingrad when they attacked in February. This attack took the form of a gruesome siege. There was still hope, however, because both the British and the Russians refused to give in. Geography aided the Russians and the superiority of the Royal Air Force made the siege of Britain hazardous.

Summer began and the Allies started to gain against the Axis Powers. American troops were more successful than not in flooding the Allies with needed supplies through their base in Iceland. June brought real progress when the American Navy met the Japanese in the Battle of Midway. This decisive victory ended Japanese expansion in the Pacific and irreparably crippled their naval strength. In November, Eisenhower led a joint British-U.S.

force in a landing in Algeria. In Russia, the Germans were still unable to claim victory since the Russian army was refusing to give way. In the end Russia lost 750,000 soldiers throughout the year. The Germans gained against the Russians only to lose all but eighty thousand men, who survived by cannibalism, and surrendered by February of 1943. Slowly the tide was turning against the Germans.

Critical Overview

The success of *The Stranger* has been matched by an unceasing flow of criticism. Most of that criticism has been a positive affirmation of Camus's place as a master of French literature. One reviewer even described Camus as the writer America had been waiting for since Hemingway. The criticism has also had the effect, good or bad, of rendering the novel a moral treatise. This occurred early on when Jean-Paul Sartre reviewed the work in 1943 and said, among other things, that with this work "Albert Camus takes his place in the great tradition of those French moralists." Philip Thody, in a more recent article, says this is a misleading approach to *The Stranger* since in moral terms the novel is full of contradictions, whereas if read for its absurd theory, no breakdown exists.

Taking the cue from Sartre, other reviewers of the 1940s matched the novel with Camus's writings in *The Myth of Sisyphus* and criticized Camus's ability to handle Heidegger and Kierkegaard.

Richard Plant, however, did not seem to need the heavy guns of philosophy to enjoy the novel, according to his 1946 article "Benign Indifference." Instead, he claims, the novel presents the protagonist's philosophy as "nothing but a rationalization of his sublime indifference." Unfortunately, Plant seems to grow confused and therefore moves very quickly to compare Camus with the American style of writing. Plant says that the way Camus handles the shooting of the Arab should serve as a model to Americans of the "tough school." Finally, Plant says, "Camus emerges as a master craftsman who never wastes a word."

During the 1950s most critics were more concerned with Camus's political stance in response to the Algerian independence movement as well as his disagreement with French intellectuals—namely Sartre. The strife of the decade, accompanied by ailing health, gave Camus a horrendous writing block and left him silent but for a few rare occasions. Critics generally enjoyed *The Plague* of 1947 and *The Fall* of 1956. His Nobel prize was seen as well deserved.

Two exceptions to the above were Norman Podhoretz and Colin Wilson. The latter wrote a book in 1956 detailing the trend in modernity, and its fiction, toward a hero who stood for truth. Wilson entitled this work in honor of Camus's novel— in its British translation—as *The Outsider.* This character is defined as follows:

> The Outsider's case against society is very clear. All men and women have these dangerous, unnamable impulses, yet they keep up a pretense, to themselves, to others; their respectability, their philosophy, their religion, are all attempts to gloss over, to make look civilized and rational something that is savage, unorganized, irrational. He is an Outsider because he stands for [this] Truth.

Sartre wrote similarly about the phenomenon Camus's *Stranger* represented. However, Sartre believed such a being had a place in society whereas Wilson was simply recording a literary trend.

Podhoretz was also interested in this new hero. In 1958, he credited Camus with the correct identification of this new hero. "It was, of course, Camus who first spotted the significance of [the] new state of nihilism and identified it, in *The Stranger,* with the pathological apathy of the narrator Meursault—the French were far in advance of the Americans in seeing that the 'rebel' was giving way in our day to the 'Stranger.' "

Camus's death in 1960 shifted the discussion surrounding his work to an automatic respect, followed by criticism. Exemplifying the criticism that

arose in the face of his death, Henri Peyre wrote in a 1960 article, "Camus the Pagan," "the works of Camus, as they stand interrupted by fate, utter a pagan message which is to be set beside that of the great pagans of antiquity and that of some of the modern pagans to who Christianity owes an immense debt of gratitude." If Camus could be said to have had a religion, it would have been atheistic humanism. Writing in a 1962 introduction to "Camus: A Collection of Critical Essays," Germaine Bree commented: "Camus's rapid rise to celebrity between 1942 and 1945 is unparalleled in the history of French literature: *The Stranger, The Myth of Sisyphus,* and the two plays *Caligula* and *The Misunderstanding,* together with Camus's role in the Resistance and the widespread interest in his *Combat* editorials, started his career in meteoric fashion."

By the 1970s, criticism had returned to traveled, but still fruitful, paths of inquiry. In 1973, Donald Lazere wrote, "*The Stranger,* like the *Myth,* asserts the primacy of individual, flesh-and-blood reality against any abstract notion that claims to supersede it." But then with the rise of Post-Colonial criticism, there was a turn to aspects of *The Stranger* that were not often discussed. Philip Thody, in "Camus's *L'Etranger* Revisited" (1979), wrote that despite the fact that Camus championed the cause of Algerian independence in his journalism, he did not escape or confront colonialism in his fiction. For support Thody points to the obvious and striking absence of names for Algerians. Neither the nurse (who has an abscess), Raymond's girlfriend, nor the Arabs (who follow Raymond) have names. They are simply part of the scenery affecting Meursault when he pulls the trigger.

Criticism

Patrick J. Moser

Moser is an assistant professor at the University of California–Davis. In the following excerpt, Moser describes The Stranger *in terms of its Existential elements, Camus's philosophy of the absurd, and other viewpoints.*

The Stranger is probably Albert Camus's best known and most widely read work. Originally published in French in 1942 under the title *L'Etranger,* it precedes other celebrated writings such as the essays *The Myth of Sisyphus* (1943) and *The Rebel* (1951), the plays *Caligula* (1945) and *The Just Assassins* (1949), and the novels *The Plague* (1947)

What Do I Read Next?

- The obvious next step from *The Stranger* would be to read Camus's other 1942 work, *The Myth of Sisyphus.* There, through a collection of essays, he explains his position on the absurd at the time of writing *The Stranger.*

- Camus was regarded as the conscience of occupied France for his writings in *Combat.* For that paper he wrote such editorials as *Neither Victims Nor Executioners* (printed in the fall of 1946 and reprinted in 1968 by Dwight Macdonald). This piece argued the logical basis of an anti-war stance consistent with his own theories. He argued that murder is never legitimate, silence between those in disagreement is intolerable, and fear must be understood. In short, he defined a modest position "free of messianism and disencumbered of nostalgia for an earthly paradise."

- Camus's 1947 novel, *The Plague,* is seen by many to be a parable about World War II that demonstrates his moral philosophy. In this novel, a town is struck by plague but survives not by beliefs and prayer but through the rational investigation and practice of medical science.

- There are other works which deal with the theme of absurdity. One very famous work was a play written by an Irishman who also took part in the French Resistance. The play is *Waiting for Godot* (1952) by Samuel Beckett.

- A more properly existentialist work is the 1947 work, *The Age of Reason,* by Jean-Paul Sartre. Camus worked in the Resistance with Sartre but they had a falling out after the war. Sartre, more than Camus, exemplifies the philosophy of existentialism.

- Another existentialist was Simone de Beauvoir. She is best know for *The Second Sex.* In 1943, she wrote an existential novel entitled *She Comes to Stay.* It is an interesting contrast to Camus's novel of the year before.

---

and *The Fall* (1956). Set in pre-World War II Algeria, *The Stranger* nevertheless confronts issues that have preoccupied intellectuals and writers of post-World War II Europe: the apparent randomness of violence and death; the emptiness of social morality in the face of an irrational world; a focus on existential and absurd aspects of the human condition. Through the singular viewpoint of the narrator Meursault, Camus presents a philosophy devoid of religious belief and middle-class morality, where sentience and personal honesty become the bases of a happy and responsible life.

What perhaps strikes the reader first about *The Stranger* is the unemotional tone of the narrator, Meursault. The novel begins: "Today, mama died. Or maybe yesterday, I don't know. I received a telegram from the retirement home: 'Mother deceased. Funeral tomorrow. Deepest sympathy.' That tells me nothing. It could have been yesterday..." Meursault's flat response to the death of his mother conveys a sense of resignation, one supported by his lack of ambition at work and his indifference in personal relationships. Save for his tirade against the chaplain at the end of the novel, Meursault remains rather monotone throughout; his only pleasures are immediate and physical: the taste of a café au lait; the warmth of sun and water; the touch of his fiancée, Marie. Thus, from the opening words, Camus projects his remarkable philosophy through an unremarkable protagonist: since death is both arbitrary and inevitable, and since there is nothing beyond death, life only has importance in the here and now, in the day to day activities that make up our existence. Camus's simplistic narrative style, influenced by the journalistic tradition of Hemingway and his own experience as a reporter, helps to convey the sense of immediacy that lies at the foundation of his philosophy.

From a literary standpoint, *The Stranger* offers aspects that complement both modern and traditional sensibilities. With regards to the former, the story is presented as the subjective experience of a first-person narrator. We do not know his first name, what he looks like, or precisely when the action of the story takes place. He does not divulge much information about his past, nor does he attempt to present a cohesive view of, or opinion about, the society in which he lives and works. Such qualities are in stark contrast to the Realist novel tradition represented by such nineteenth century writers as Honoré de Balzac (1799-1850), whose works attempt to reproduce a complete account of French society through the eyes of a moralizing, omniscient third-person narrator.

In a more classical vein, *The Stranger* offers order and balance. The novel is organized into two parts of equal length, and the central episode of the book—the shooting of the Arab—is both preceded and followed by five chapters. Themes are maintained with strict focus: the story opens with the death of Meursault's mother, the murder lies at the exact center of the book, and the novel concludes with the death-sentence of Meursault. Within the story Camus creates scenes of explicit parallel and contrast. The tears and fainting of Thomas Pérez at the funeral, for example, offer a foil to Meursault's lack of emotion. The noise of Salamano cursing his dog directly precedes the screams of the Moorish woman as Raymond beats her; both relationships share qualities of physical love and abuse. One might argue that Camus's sense of literary balance is an attempt to put into practice an existential philosophy: the only order in a disordered world is the one we create for ourselves.

The Stranger and its author have often been linked to Existentialism, a post-World War II philosophy that has become synonymous with the name of Jean-Paul Sartre (1905-80). Although Camus was a one-time friend and supporter of Sartre, he denied being an existentialist. Nevertheless, there are clear existential themes in the *The Stranger,* a product of the intellectual climate of the times. Camus's preoccupation with the nature of being, for example, and his rejection of reason and order in the universe, are both existential concerns. When Camus presents the Arab's murder as the result of a random series of events, and Meursault refuses to lie in court to help win his case, we enter into existential realms of human action and responsibility. There is no outside force governing our lives, according to the existentialists; individuals must take responsibility for their own actions. Meursault's ultimate vindication is in having remained true to himself and to his feelings in a society that cultivates deception and hypocrisy.

Since its publication, critics have interpreted Meursault's plight in many ways. From a mythic or structuralist viewpoint, Meursault reenacts a timeless struggle of an individual caught up in the forces of fate, driven toward the murder by divine powers acting through the sun and the sea. In psychological readings, the protagonist acts out issues held by the author: an oedipal love for his mother and the desire to kill his father. Poststructuralist accounts concentrate on the novel's language and Meursault's inability to explain his actions adequately in court. This inability should be read as the failure of language, these latter critics argue, since it lies outside of reality, and not that of society's justice system or of its moral code. If there is a reading Camus himself preferred it was one that took into account his philosophy of the absurd. Many readers, following Sartre's first review of the novel in 1943, look to Camus's *The Myth of Sisyphus* for the most revealing commentary on the work. Published the year after *The Stranger,* the essay defines the absurd as arising from the meeting of two elements: the absence of meaning in the natural world, and mankind's inherent desire to seek out meaning. Meursault's ultimate dignity resides in the knowledge that his quest for meaning will always go unfulfilled; happiness is achieved only in a life without illusions. Notions of the absurd become an important part of post-World War II literary production in France, the principal writers, Samuel Beckett, Jean Genêt and Eugène Ionesco, forming what has become known as the "Theater of the Absurd."

Meursault's experiences with the natural world draw out elements of Camus's philosophy of the absurd. Meursault's name itself has been associated with the environment that affects him so strongly throughout the novel. In French, *mer* means "sea"; *sol* means "sun." Standing under the penetrating rays of the midday sun at the beach, "the same sun" that burned the day he buried his mother, Meursault faces off with the Arab. Suddenly scorched by a hot blast of wind from the sea, blinded by the sweat in his eyes, Meursault fires the revolver and shatters the silence of the day. Later, in court, he will tell the judge that he killed the Arab "because of the sun." He shows no remorse for the crime he has committed, realizing that it occurred only because of chance circumstances. This meeting between man and nature, like all such meetings, ends in a meaningless act. All that remains is for him to acknowledge what he has done.

Not surprisingly, much commentary has focused on the colonialist aspects of the novel, above all because the victim of the murder is an Arab. Camus's philosophy of the absurd may point to the murder as meaningless, but during a time of straining relations between Arabs and French (war broke out in 1954 between France and Algeria and concluded in 1962 with Algerian independence), the killing of an Arab by a French-Algerian could have been interpreted, and was, as a meaningful act indeed. A critic of colonialist oppression and a proponent of social justice for Muslims, Camus—a *pied-noir* or Frenchman born in Algeria—is nevertheless silent in his novel on the volatile political issues of the time. Although not depicted as social inferiors, Muslims in the novel are relegated to the periphery: a deformed nurse, an abused mistress, prisoners, and shiftless hangers-on. Camus considered himself an "Algerian" writer, yet his two-dimensional treatment of Arabs in the novel has, for some, aligned him more on the side of the French.

Early on in his career, Camus planned out the stages that his work would follow. *The Stranger* belongs to the first stage of his writing career, a period that also includes such titles as *The Myth of Sisigula* and *Caligula. The Stranger* projects a "zero point," according to the author, an "absurd" state of existence reduced to immediate sensations. Camus's later works, informed by his years working in the French Resistance and his experience with totalitarian governments, move beyond the leveling effect created by *The Stranger* and build upon positive social values. *The Just Assassins* and *The Plague,* belonging to the later period, recount tales of community, justice, and solidarity.

Source: Patrick J. Moser, in an essay for *Novels for Students,* Gale, 1999.

Susan Tarrow

In the following excerpt, Tarrow discusses the development of the novel's principal character, Meursault, "from an acquiescent figure who admits no limits to a combatant who claims the right to be different."

The Stranger, which grew out of the experiment of *A Happy Death* and was nourished by Camus's political experiences, constitutes an attack on the accepted norms of bourgeois society. It calls into question many aspects of an oppressive colonial regime: the use of the judiciary, religion, and above all, language to maintain dominance. It is an ironic condemnation of colonialist and racist attitudes. The novel also develops a theme with variations on indifference and difference, a theme rooted in the Algerian experience, as Camus's articles in *Alger-Républicain* have shown. If the hero Meursault has a moral message—and the reference to him as a Christ figure would suggest that he has—it is one that plays a constant role in Camus's thought; there are no absolutes to which one can adhere, only limits, and the vital nuances are played out within those limits. Total indifference and apathy allow others to act without limits. Meursault develops from an acquiescent figure who admits no limits to a combatant who claims the right to be different.

The story has a simple plot. Meursault, a clerk in an Algiers shipping office, attends his mother's funeral at an old people's home in Marengo. The following day he goes swimming, meets an old friend, Marie, takes her to see a Fernandel movie, and initiates an affair with her the same evening. With another friend, Raymond, he spends a Sunday on the beach with Marie, where they encounter three Arabs, one of whom has a grudge against Raymond. In the ensuing confrontation, Meursault shoots one of the Arabs.

The second half of the novel relates Meursault's trial and conviction, and his growing self-awareness during the months in prison. After being sentenced to death, he affirms his own system of values and rejects that of established society.

When *The Stranger* was first published in 1942 the aspect that evoked the most interest among critics was the use of the *passé composé,* the compound past tense, since the traditional tense used in literary narrative is the *passé simple.* Sartre, in his review of the book, comments that the effect of the *passé composé* is to isolate each sentence, to avoid giving any impression of cause and effect. Meursault's experience is a succession of presents. During the transition from Mersault to Meursault, Camus changed the form of the narrative: an omniscient author using the *passé simple* and the third person was replaced by a first-person narrative in the *passé composé.* The author leaves his hero in a situation where he is dominated by the power of language rather than in control of it; language is equivalent to destiny.

Camus's concern with language is evident in *The Stranger.* [The] use of language beyond [Meursault's] mastery reveals an intellectual confusion that stems from the limits of his education. It is true that Meursault was once a student; but in rejecting ambition, he also rejected the value of an intellectual life. Rational thought is not worth the linguistic effort involved. Ironically enough, misinterpretation is not limited to Meursault. The French authorities misinterpret too.

"Literature" obscures the true nature of reality: Meursault is someone who has "given up language and replaced it with *actual revolt*. He has chosen to do what Christ scorned to do: to save the damned—by damning himself." Viewed in this light, Meursault's deliberate firing of four more shots into the dead body is an act of revolt, a defiance of the society in which he lives. Meursault, who places no reliance on language, throws down the gauntlet but fails to justify his action in the eyes of the world.

[It] is obvious that Meursault is in conflict, albeit unconsciously, with all the norms of the French system; in response to his narration of events, the reader's sympathies lie with the Arabs defending their honor rather than with the unsavory Raymond. Meursault refuses to play the game, to be part of the family. The authority figures are all predisposed to be kind to Meursault: the soldier on whose shoulder he falls asleep on the bus, the director of the old-age home, his employer, the examining magistrate, his lawyer, the priest. It is only when he says no that they begin to resent him; he declines to view his mother's body, he turns down a promotion that would take him to Paris, he refuses to recognize the Cross, or to misrepresent the details of his case. When he says yes, it is to the "wrong" things: to a cup of coffee, to a Fernandel film, and to Raymond's sordid plan.

During the trial, it becomes clear that Meursault is being tried not for his action, but for his attitudes. The ironic presentation of the prosecutor's arguments, in which the narrator's use of free indirect discourse shows up the emptiness of the rhetoric, makes the trial seem farcical. Indeed one could assert that Meursault is innocent with respect to the invalid reasons for guilt attributed by the prosecution: "I accuse this man of burying a mother with a criminal heart." The implications of "the void in the heart that we find in this man" are enlarged to the scale of "an abyss into which society could sink." Meursault is accused of two crimes which he has not committed: burying his mother with a criminal heart (although psychoanalytical studies of this text have concluded there is some basis for his feelings of guilt at her death), and killing a father, since the prosecutor affirms in a flourish of rhetoric that he is responsible for the crime that will be tried in court the following day.

Bearing in mind the trials in Algeria that Camus covered as a journalist, one could conclude that the parodic deformation is mild, for in many of those cases the charges were politically motivated, the witnesses bribed, and the verdict a foregone conclusion. It is true that Meursault makes no effort to defend himself; but it is because he does not understand the ideas behind the verbiage, nor the consequences of his own words and deeds. The words used do not express reality, but Meursault and his friends are unable to counteract the force of their intent. They are verbally ill-equipped. The prosecutor, however, rejects such a defense before it is voiced. "This man is intelligent.... He can answer. He knows the value of words." In a sense, this is true. Meursault refuses to use words that do not precisely translate his feelings, words like *love, guilt, shame.* Society is accustomed to euphemism and lip-service.

Meursault finds a voice and an adequate command of language in the final pages of his narrative. The reader is led to suppose that his execution is imminent and that his voice will be silenced: the guillotine effectively dislocates the very source of speech.

Only in his final outburst does Meursault consciously evaluate other people, although still in a negative way. Camus called him "a negative snapshot." In an absurd world, all men are equal. It is through a kind of askesis, a narrowing down of his field of vision, that Meursault reaches an initial state of awareness, just as Mersault did. But Mersault is committed to death, and Meursault is committed to life.

Camus is playing ironically with ambiguity here, but this does not detract from the *moral* intent, to demonstrate that judgment is unjust because it is based on ambiguous data. Misinterpretation can be accidental or intentional, but in either case the consequences can prove fatal.

Metaphysical absurdity is mirrored by the social situation depicted in *The Stranger;* as Camus remarked, "*The Plague* has a social meaning and a metaphysical meaning. It's exactly the same. This ambiguity is also present in *The Stranger*." The injustice of that social situation is in turn reflected and complicated by the particular attributes of a colonial society. Meursault learns in the course of writing his life that it is not meaningless, and his desire to relive it is the first positive affirmation he makes.

One aspect of Meursault's statement, which will be a constant in Camus's ideas on rebellion, is the emphasis on the concrete and the present. The prison chaplain embodies exactly what Meursault rejects: a nonphysical relationship with the world and with human beings, a passive submission to the injustices of God and society, and a dogmatic faith in a better life in the future. Meursault is solidly involved in the here and now, convinced that joy is one of the most precious of human emotions, not to be sacrificed for some abstract and hypothetical goal. He sums up, but only for his readers, his notion of happiness during the final day in court: "While my lawyer went on talking, I heard the echoing sound of an ice-cream vendor's horn. I was overwhelmed by the memories of a life that was no longer mine, but in which I had found the simplest and most persistent joys...: the smells of summer, the neighborhood I loved, a certain evening sky, Marie's laughter and her dresses." The core of Camus's arguments in *The Rebel* is here in embryo.

Source: Susan Tarrow, "The Stranger," in her *Exile from the Kingdom: A Political Rereading of Albert Camus,* University of Alabama Press, 1985, 215 pp.

Ignace Feuerlicht

In the following excerpt, Feuerlicht analyzes the transformation of the protagonist's psyche—from indifference to an understanding of the world. He concludes that Camus's novel conceals a variety of possible interpretations.

The ambiguity of the novel starts with the title. With regard to whom or to what is Meursault a stranger or an alien? The word *étranger* is only used twice in the *récit,* but not for Meursault. Alienation or estrangement is said to be the mood of Camus's *L'Etranger,* and this short novel allegedly demonstrates a person's complete lack of relatedness to other human beings. Meursault, however, is not like Baudelaire's "Etranger," who has no friends, like the "stranger" in Schnitzler's short story "Die Fremde," or like the outsiders in Thomas Mann's early writings, who create an atmosphere of cold estrangement whenever they meet other people. Meursault is not odd, certainly not odder than, for instance, Salamano. True, Marie once calls him "bizarre," but this does not apply to his way of life, or his character, only to his unconventional views of love and marriage. He is not a stranger to Masson or to his boss. He has friends, such as Celeste, Emmanuel, Raymond; and his friends stay by him when he is in trouble. People in the neighborhood know him and he knows them. He is one of them.

Thus, it is rather obvious that Meursault is not a stranger to others. However, it is more difficult to determine whether he is a stranger to himself, as it has often been said.

There can be hardly any doubt, however, that Meursault is a stranger to society. As Camus states in his "avant-propos," "il est étranger à la société où il vit, il erre, en marge, dans les faubourgs de la vie privée, solitaire, sensuelle." (One might perhaps question both "errer" and "solitaire"). He is, according to Camus, not playing society's game, because he does not lie, even where and when everybody lies in order to simplify life, and because he rejects time-honored formulas, such as expressing regret after a crime, even when this rejection means the death sentence. Whether this actually stems from a "deep, though silent passion for the absolute and for truth" is debatable; this passion being too silent to be noticeable. To be sure, he is not only sincere when he refuses to pretend before the investigating judge that he feels genuine remorse, but also when he refuses to pretend to Marie that he loves her, and his sincerity makes him even say dogmatically that one is never allowed to pretend. Yet when he congratulates his lawyer in court, he is aware of not being sincere, and his testimony in behalf of Raymond at the police station is not a proof of his absolute sincerity either.

Meursault may also be termed a stranger to society because of his unconventional ideas about love, marriage, and how to get ahead in a job. Love, a conventional concept according to *Le Mythe de Sisyphe,* does not mean anything to him, and marriage, a conventional basis of society, is not a serious matter. He also declines the opportunity of going to Paris. Not to have any professional ambition is an affront to modern society. Meursault antagonizes society also by his "friendship" with the pimp Raymond and, above all, by not displaying the usual signs of grief at and after the burial of his mother.

Meursault is also a stranger to society because he sometimes feels left out. In the courtroom he has the bizarre impression of being just an intruder. Though he is sometimes tempted to "intervene" in the proceedings, he is told by his lawyer to keep quiet. His own trial seems to be held without him and his fate is decided without anyone asking him about his opinion. He is "reduced to zero" precisely by somebody who "acts" in his interest and who, according to convention, identifies himself with him by using "I" many times when he speaks of him. Meursault's helplessness during the proceedings in court may be symbolic of man's precarious place in a mass society whose workings he does not control nor even understand and whose leaders may speak in his name to further their own interests.

Meursault not only disregards some of society's time-honored conventions, but also some of its most valued achievements. Unlike another "stranger," Jean Péloueyre in Mauriac's *Le Baiser au lépreux,* he makes no reference to his former studies. Literature, philosophy, science, art do not seem to exist for him. No great personality, living or dead, is ever named in the book. Although he went to a university, there are only a very few instances which would indicate that his education might be more than elementary. Raymond obviously assumes that Meursault can write better to his prostitute mistress than he himself could. Meursault remembers having learned in school something about the guillotine and about the events of 1789 (the only historical fact mentioned in *L'Etranger*). He apparently read some mystery novels, and also thinks he should have read books dealing with executions. These are rather few and strange examples of the education society has given him. His short, "disconnected" sentences and his almost exclusive use of the *passé composé* may also be taken to be—among other things—a rejection of school rules and conventional writing.

This negative attitude toward culture perhaps reaches its climax in that unbelievable description of Paris, the cultural center of his nation: "C'est sale. Il y a des pigeons et des cours noires. Les gens ont la peau blanche." (It's dirty. There are pigeons and dark alleys. The men have white skin.) This is not meant to be funny. Meursault does not crack jokes and Marie does not laugh when she hears it, although she usually laughs at almost anything. It seems that *L'Etranger* is directed not only—as it has often been noted—against the *Pharisiens* but also against the *Parisiens.* Camus, of course, has often been critical of Parisian life and society, comparing it with the happier and more natural life in sundrenched Algeria.

However, this stranger to society never attacks society as such. He is not an anarchist or a rebel, he does not accuse or deride the judicial system, even praises some of its features, and is, according to the warden, the only prisoner who understands and approves certain punitive aspects of prison life. He is a law-abiding citizen, holds a steady job, works hard and well, and wears a black tie and a black armband as a tribute to convention. He is re-

spectful to everybody, including the authorities ("Oui, monsieur le Directeur," "Oui, monsieur le Président") and does not deny conventional politeness: he thanks the director for arranging a religious funeral and later for attending the funeral. He compliments Masson on his cabin and thanks the newspaperman for his friendly words. He never uses offensive language.

Meursault, the stranger to society, never speaks of "society," although the public prosecutor and the papers do. It is "the others" who have condemned him, that faceless, anonymous, undistinguishable group of people that sit in the jury box as well as in the streetcar and judge any new arrival.

A word that is stressed by Camus in connection with estrangement, especially in his *Le Mythe de Sisyphe,* and has perhaps become the most popular word of his philosophical vocabulary, is "absurd." It has confusingly different meanings, and often is synonymous with "indifferent" or "stranger"-like. Meursault, therefore, has also been called an absurd man, his style "style absurde," and *L'Etranger* an absurd novel or a novel of the absurd. In the novel the word is used only once. In his outburst at the end Meursault calls his life, not life in general, "absurd." But "absurd" has no meaning without the assumption of a meaning, and it is not clear which meaning Meursault thinks or feels his life has been lacking. This somewhat corresponds to the "poor joys" of his life he speaks about, which imply great and real joys, of which, however, there is not the slightest intimation in the novel.

According to the terminology and the illustrations of *Le Mythe de Sisyphe,* Meursault's basic indifference is absurd, since the absurd teaches that all experiences are indifferent. In addition, some of his experiences can be called absurd, such as that of the "inhuman landscape" and that of the independent reflection in the mirror of his tin can. In *Le Mythe de Sisyphe* Camus also calls the uneasiness absurd which one feels on discovering how non-human men really are and how mechanical their gestures can be. In *L'Etranger* Meursault is fascinated by the little woman who one day sits down at his table in the restaurant. Twice he calls her "bizarre," and he even follows her to watch her. Her gestures have the precision of an automaton. This woman automaton, as he calls her, observes him in court as intently and seriously as the young newspaperman. Since the latter is to some extent Meursault (and Camus) himself, this encounter with her may indicate his discovery of his own mechanical way of life. The jerkiness (*saccadé*) of her gestures also corresponds to the frequent jerkiness of his style. But the "femme automate" is not a "reflection" nor a "more extreme version of him." He lacks her "incredible" precision, speed, and assurance. Also, Meursault apparently sees "la mécanique qui écrasait tout" not in his life but in his execution. By the woman automaton Camus may have intended to symbolize the mechanization of modern life in this story that uses the style of modern American fiction.

"Indifference," which plays a key role in Camus's world, is a concept related to estrangement and absurdity and often synonymous with either. His teacher, Jean Grenier, wrote an essay "De l'Indifférence," and the original title of Meursault's story was "L'Indifférent." In the preface to the 1957 edition of *L'Envers et l'endroit,* Camus diagnoses a deep indifference in himself which is like a natural weakness and has to be corrected. In *Le Mythe de Sisyphe,* however, he finds a *noblesse profonde* in indifference and sees that man at an advanced stage will nourish his greatness with the wine of absurdity and the bread of indifference. The world reveals to him a serene indifference to everything. The sky, in particular, is indifferent, has an inane, indifferent smile, pursues with the earth an indifferent dialogue, and is even indifferent to the "atrocious victories and just defeat of Nazi Germany." But it also has charm, beauty, sweetness, and tenderness. This "explains" the paradoxical "tendre indifférence du monde" in the last paragraph, when Meursault looks at the starry sky.

Meursault is never called "indifferent" in the novel, but a group of hostile Arabs watch Raymond's house with indifference and the court reporters seem indifferent. It is clear from these two occurrences that indifference is not identical with apathy, but rather with lack of emotionalism. Meursault displays indifference at the death of his mother, at Raymond's offer of friendship, at Marie's desire to marry him, and at his employer's proposal to transfer him to a Paris office. After his mother's death "nothing has changed." One cannot change one's life; at any rate, all lives are of equal value. Meursault's indifference is probably not congenital, like Camus's, but the result of a drastic experience of an undisclosed nature. The break came when he had to give up his studies and ambitions. Now he knows that "all that" has no real importance and in various situations he repeats the slogan of indifference: "It's all the same to me." The prospect of impending death shakes his indif-

ference considerably, although he tries to maintain it by looking at the sky, and in his violent anger at the chaplain he even loses it to some extent, but only to regain and reaffirm it on a higher, lyrical, or mystical level. Again he maintains that nothing has any importance, that all lives and men are equal (because of death); but now with the "stars on his face," he feels that the world's "tender indifference" is penetrating him. As he finds the world brotherly now, it is a kind of mystical union, not with mother nature, but with brother world. Whereas the end of the first part, which leads to a violent death, is dominated by tension, hostility, destruction, and misfortune (*malheur* is the last word of this part), the end of the second part leads Meursault, who expects a violent death, to vague feelings of truce, peace, tenderness, brotherhood, and happiness. The last word (*haine*) is harsh again, but it means in its context the conquest of solitude and the reconquest of indifference.

Although Camus once states that "those are very poor who need myths" and that Algerians live without any myths, he himself reinterpreted or recreated old myths and perhaps created some new ones. In particular, his *L'Etranger* has been thought of as embodying various old and new myths. The multiplicity of mythical interpretations points definitely to the suggestive intensity of Camus's novel, but perhaps also to the elusive vagueness or to the abuse of "myth" as a literary term.

While representing the myths of modern man, of Oedipus and Sisyphus, Meursault is also said to be a reincarnation of the myth of Christ. Indeed, it is almost generally believed that this little office clerk, who cannot feel sad at his mother's death, who does not believe in a life hereafter, who kills a fellow-man, who does not seem to have any set of moral values, and who, consequently and perhaps not quite jokingly, is called "Mr. Antichrist" by the investigating judge, is a Christ figure, a tragic hero who takes upon himself the burden of humanity, a "sacrificial victim," or the "scapegoat of a society of pharisees and Pilates." Camus himself calls him—"paradoxically," as he says—"the only Christ we deserve." True, Meursault is like Christ a "victim of a judicial error," is like Christ unprejudiced toward social outcasts, and is executed at approximately the same age Christ was. But, in spite of Camus, one cannot see how Meursault "accepts to die for truth." He does not "incarnate truth," he does not die *for* the sake of sincerity, but *because* of his sincerity (whatever the causes of his sincerity may be), because his attitude is not "conventionnelle, c'est-à-dire comédienne." He does not live or die for anybody or anything, nor does he think he does, and his death does not change anything or anybody.

It is also rather difficult to see how the sea and the sun are used as "mythic religious symbols" in *L'Etranger* and especially how they are "associated in Camus's mind" with the mother and the father. The homonymy of *mère* and *mer* does not mean much, since most of the time Meursault calls his mother "maman." It is impossible to see the connection between the colorless, boring old woman, as Meursault sees his mother, whom he hardly cares to visit at the old age home, and the fascinating and beautiful Mediterranean, which he likes to watch and where he enjoys swimming. And while the sun is in *L'Etranger* the most powerful force, the father is weakness personified. All that Meursault knows about his father is that he vomited after witnessing the execution of a stranger, whereas his "stranger"-son finally expects his own execution with a feeling of near elation....

Camus in the "avant-propos" calls Meursault "un homme pauvre et nu." Indeed many a reader may sympathize when seeing poor Meursault suffer from an excess of light and heat, or dine on *boudin,* or "lost" in the forensic maze, or subjected to monstrous accusations. To be sure, there also are extenuating circumstances for his crime: the preceding scuffle, the beginning of a sunstroke, the lack of premeditation, the excessive consumption of wine, the feeling of the hostility of the world, the reflex (or defensive) nature of the first shot. But Meursault is no innocent, as most critics assume, unless one adopts the "absurdist" point of view, which "makes murder at least indifferent." Meursault's deed is not altogether an accident or a stroke of bad luck, as his friends in the courtroom and the magazines have called it. It comes as a climax: first, Masson, Raymond, and Meursault walk on the beach, then Raymond and Meursault, and finally, Meursault alone; at first, Meursault tries to prevent Raymond from shooting, then he thinks that one could shoot or not shoot, which is not a very innocent thought, and finally he does shoot. As he stands by the body of the dead man, he does not even feel that he has committed a crime. He understands that he has destroyed the equilibrium of the day and the exceptional silence of a beach—which is a credit to his feeling for nature—but he does not feel that he has also and above all destroyed a human life. He has to be told that he committed a crime and actually remains to the very end a "stranger to his crime."

Paradoxically Meursault gets even more elusive when he reaches what is generally assumed to be "lucidity" at the end. The light which illuminates for him his past life and life in general is not bright sunshine, but seems to come from the stars which he sees. His rejection of a future life, his reaffirmation of indifference, his contention that death equalizes all men and makes everything look unimportant, seem clear, in spite of the passionate tone; his lyrical reflections at the very end, when he has regained his calm and reached the height of lucidity, are the least clear passages of the whole novel....

Those who see in Meursault a Christ figure recall "the last moments of Christ, whose crucifixion was preceded by cries of hatred from the crowds." But then one must also explain why Meursault suddenly and consciously identifies himself with Christ or parodies him. When one thinks that Meursault deserves the hatred of the people because he "has denied their myths," and they see in him the symbol of their fate, which is usually masked by myths, one overlooks the fact that Meursault does not speak of *expecting,* but of *wishing* those cries of hate; also he has never been aware of his denying collective myths or of his being a symbol of something. When one believes that Meursault "wants the crowds to be there because he wants society to give some sign that it realizes how much he defies it," one forgets that the death penalty is a clear enough sign of how society regards him.

Meursault's strange last wish is above all proof of the firmness of his indifference in contrast to his attitude in court where the mere sight of people who, as he thought, detested him, made him feel like crying. He actually does not express that strange wish, but he feels the desirability or necessity of it; that wish probably means the ultimate height of tender indifference, which he thinks he has not achieved yet, but may or will very soon achieve.

The number and the violent reaction of the spectators are, of course, also a sign that people care about him, but a possible connection with the Salamano episode seems to be more enlightening. The only other time "haine" is employed in *L'Etranger* is to denote Salamano's feelings toward his dog. The old man even constantly uses what might be called "cris de haine" toward his dog: "Salaud, charogne." Since after his presumably violent death the hated dog makes his former master cry with affection and unhappiness, Meursault's possible identification with the generally detested dog may be an indirect way of expressing his desire to be remembered well by the people who despised him before his death. Meursault's identification with a dog at the time of his execution recalls Josef K., who in Kafka's *Der Prozeβ;* is executed at the end "like a dog."

Meursault's final illumination does not quite illuminate him in the eyes of the reader, who is left in the dark about the narrator's outward appearance (except his complexion), about his first name, and, above all, about his childhood and youth. In addition, Meursault shows baffling inconsistencies in his attitudes and actions. At ten in the morning he barely manages to walk three quarters of an hour because of the sun, but he walks the same distance at four o'clock the day before after a bus ride without any complaints; he takes a sunbath the day after, races after a truck and jumps on it at twelve-thirty two days later, and enjoys lying in the sun for hours. He shuns the "effort" to climb a few wooden steps, but instead takes a long walk in the broiling sun. He first wants to "see his mother right away," but then repeatedly declines to see her. He does not care about Sundays, but does not want to waste a Sunday visiting his mother. And why does he keep Raymond's revolver? And why does he (as well as the prosecutor) mistake the day of his mother's burial for the day of her death (is this another "burial of the burial")?

These are some of the puzzles which the numerous critics of the book have failed to solve or even to notice. Prompted by their philosophical preoccupations, some have in ingenious "superstructures" discussed ill-defined alienations or discovered non-existent myths and "absurdities," while they often failed to see obvious facts and to explain disturbing difficulties. One ventures to hope that careful and searching attention will turn to the "properly esthetic" facets of the book, such as the varied style and the enigmatic point of view. *L'Etranger* itself will continue radiating its charm and challenge.

Source: Ignace Feuerlicht, "Camus's *L'Etranger* Reconsidered," in *PMLA,* Vol. 78, No. 5, December, 1963, pp. 606-21.

Sources

Donald Lazere, *The Unique Creation of Albert Camus,* Yale University Press, 1973.

Henri Peyre, "Camus the Pagan," in *Yale French Studies,* Vol. 25, 1960, pp. 65-70.

Richard Plant, "Benign Indifference," in *The Saturday Review of Literature,* Vol. 29, No. 20, May 18, 1946, p. 10.

Jean-Paul Sartre, "An Explication of *The Stranger,*" in *Camus: A Collection of Critical Essays,* edited by Germaine Bree, Prentice-Hall, 1962, pp. 108-21.

Philip Thody, "Camus's *L'Etranger* Revisited," in *Critical Quarterly,* Vol. 2, Summer, 1979, pp. 61-69.

Colin Wilson, *The Outsider,* Houghton Mifflin, 1956.

For Further Study

Robert J. Champigny, *A Pagan Hero: An Interpretation of Meursault in Camus's 'The Stranger',* translated by Rowe Portis, University of Pennsylvania Press, 1969.

Champigny analyzes Mersault through several readings which show the character as innocent but whose characteristics set the stage of his guilt. Champigny also argues that Meursault's reaction to his guilt make him a hero.

Raymond Gay-Crosier, "Albert Camus," in *Dictionary of Literary Biography,* Volume 72: *French Novelists, 1930-1960,* edited by Catherine Savage, Gale Research, 1988, pp. 110-35.

The article presents an overview of the life and works of Albert Camus.

Adele King, *Notes on L'Etranger: The Stranger or The Outsider,* Longman York Press, 1980.

King offers an introduction to the novel, detailed summaries of the chapters, and brief critical commentary that touches on the most important parts of the novel: theme, historical context, structure, style, etc. An invaluable aid.

Patrick McCarthy, *Camus: A Critical Study of his Life and Work,* Hamish Hamilton, 1982.

A book-length investigation of Camus's life and works, placed within the historical context of war and struggle.

Norman Podhoretz, "The New Nihilism and the Novel" in his *Doings and Undoings,* Farrar, Straus, 1964, pp. 159-78.

According to Podhoretz, Camus was the first writer to identify the transition of the hero in twentieth-century fiction from rebel to stranger. In so doing, Camus spotted the significance of the new nihilism and identified it.

Jan Rigaud, "Depictions of Arabs in *L'Etranger,*" in *Camus's L'Etranger: Fifty Years On,* edited by Adele King, Macmillan, 1992.

In a collection of essays that spans many approaches to the novel—literary influence, textual studies, comparative studies—Rigaud's article highlights an important and often overlooked aspect of *The Stranger.*

English Showalter Jr., *The Stranger: Humanity and the Absurd,* Twayne, 1989.

A readable introduction to the novel that offers historical context, the work's importance, and an introduction to critical reception of the novel. The second half of the study presents a close reading of the novel.

Uncle Tom's Cabin

Harriet Beecher Stowe

1852

When *Uncle Tom's Cabin; or, Life among the Lowly* was first published in 1852, no one—least of all its author, Harriet Beecher Stowe—expected the book to become a sensation, but this antislavery novel took the world by storm. It was to become the second best-selling book in the world during the nineteenth century, second only to the Bible, and it touched off a flurry of criticism and praise. Stowe had written the novel as an angry response to the 1850 passage of the Fugitive Slave Law, which punished those who aided runaway slaves and diminished the rights of fugitive as well as freed slaves. Hoping to move her fellow Americans to protest this law and slavery in general, Stowe attempted to portray "the institution of slavery just as it existed." Indeed, *Uncle Tom's Cabin* was nearly unique at the time in its presentation of the slaves' point of view.

Stowe's novel tells the stories of three slaves—Tom, Eliza, and George—who start out together in Kentucky, but whose lives take different turns. Eliza and George, who are married to each other but owned by different masters, manage to escape to free territory with their little boy, Harry. Tom is not so lucky. He is taken away from his wife and children. Tom is sold first to a kind master, Augustine St. Clare, and then to the fiendish Simon Legree, at whose hands he meets his death. Stowe relied upon images of domesticity, motherhood, and Christianity to capture her nineteenth century audience's hearts and imaginations. In spite of the critical controversy surrounding the book, the char-

acters of Uncle Tom, Little Eva, and Simon Legree have all achieved legendary status in American culture. Often called sentimental and melodramatic, *Uncle Tom's Cabin* nevertheless endures as a powerful example of moral outrage over man's inhumanity to man.

Author Biography

Stowe seemed destined to write a powerful protest novel like *Uncle Tom's Cabin:* Her father was Lyman Beecher, a prominent evangelical preacher, and her siblings were preachers and social reformers. Born in 1811 in Litchfield, Connecticut, Stowe moved with her family at the age of twenty-one to Cincinnati, where she lived for eighteen years. In Cincinnati, across the Ohio River from slaveholding Kentucky, Stowe was exposed to the institution of slavery. Although she made just one brief trip to Kentucky—her only personal contact with the South—she knew freed and fugitive slaves in Cincinnati. She also had friends who participated in the underground railroad, the secret system for aiding runaway slaves in their flight to freedom. Stowe learned about slave life by talking to these people and by reading various materials, including slave narratives and antislavery tracts. She also saw Northern racial prejudice. Stowe began writing while living in Cincinnati. In 1836, she married Calvin Ellis Stowe, a distinguished biblical scholar and theology professor, and they had seven children. After marrying, Stowe continued to write, supplementing her husband's limited earnings.

In 1850, the United States Congress voted to pass the Fugitive Slave Law, which prohibited Northerners from helping slaves escape and required them to return slaves to their masters in the South. Stowe, having moved to Brunswick, Maine with her family, had been planning to write a protest of slavery since her experiences in Cincinnati. The passage of the Fugitive Slave Law proved a powerful catalyst. She began work on *Uncle Tom's Cabin* and published it first in serial form in the abolitionist magazine *The National Era.* The first installment appeared on June 5, 1851, but before the serial could be completed, the novel came out in a two-volume set in March 1852. The book became an immediate and extraordinary success, selling over one million copies in America and England before the year was out. Thus, Stowe became the most famous American woman writer of her day.

Harriet Beecher Stowe

In the United States, the novel incited controversy from both Northerners and Southerners: Northerners felt that Stowe portrayed the slaveholding South too kindly, while Southerners believed Stowe condemned their way of life. In 1853, responding to criticism that her novel was not grounded in reality, Stowe published *A Key to Uncle Tom's Cabin,* in which she pointed to factual documents—newspaper articles, court records, state laws—to substantiate her portrayal of slavery in *Uncle Tom's Cabin.* Less than a decade after the publication of *Uncle Tom's Cabin,* the Civil War began, largely due to the conflict over slavery. President Abraham Lincoln, upon meeting Stowe in 1862, is said to have declared: "So this is the little lady who brought on this big war." Stowe died on July 1, 1896, in Hartford, Connecticut, and is buried in Andover, Massachusetts. In spite of having published many works before and after its momentous appearance, she is remembered mainly for *Uncle Tom's Cabin.*

Plot Summary

Following three slaves and their experiences in and out of slavery, Stowe's novel deals with the effects of slavery on both blacks and whites in the antebellum, or pre-Civil War, South. *Uncle Tom's Cabin* can be seen in four uneven parts: Part I consisting of chapters one through nine, about the slave Eliza and her escape to freedom; Part II consisting of chapters ten through twenty-nine, about Uncle Tom and his relationship with Little Eva on the St. Clare plantation; Part III consisting of chapters thirty through forty-two, about Simon Legree and the death of Uncle Tom; and Part IV consisting of chapters forty-three through forty-five, which offer a resolution of the action and Harriet Beecher Stowe's appeal for the end of slavery.

Part I

Uncle Tom's Cabin was published in 1852 and was understood to take place in "real time," so the initial setting can be described as a plantation in Kentucky in 1852. The plantation owner, Mr. Shelby, is negotiating with a coldhearted slave trader named Mr. Haley to sell some of his slaves in order to pay his debts. Though it is considered a bad practice to sell slaves and break up families, Mr. Shelby agrees to sell Uncle Tom, a devoted and hard-working slave, as well as Harry, the five-year-old child of the house servant Eliza. When Eliza overhears the plan, she decides to run away from the plantation with Harry and to take the "underground railroad" to freedom in Canada. She tries to warn Uncle Tom of his danger and to persuade him to join her, but he refuses to violate Mr. Shelby's trust.

When Haley discovers that Eliza has run away, he chases her to the river, which is covered with floating ice. Eliza must jump from one slab of ice to the other in order to escape. She and Harry arrive on the other side, injured and exhausted, and are rescued by kind people who take them to a Quaker family. She and Harry are then reunited with Eliza's husband, George, who had run away previously. Together the family is placed on a ship bound for Canada, escaping the slave hunters that Haley has sent after them.

Part II

In this longest section of the book, Uncle Tom's saintly character is revealed as he accepts the indignity of being sold "down the river" to New Orleans. On the steamboat Uncle Tom makes friends with a little girl named Eva St. Clare, who is as good-hearted as he is. When Uncle Tom saves Eva after she falls into the river, her father agrees to purchase him in gratitude. Uncle Tom is taken to the St. Clare plantation where he lives a rela-tively easy life as the head coachman. The mistress of the house, St. Clare's sister Miss Ophelia, who moved from New England to the South, is extremely critical of lazy southern ways. St. Clare buys her an eight-year-old slave, Topsy, to distract her from reorganizing the household. Topsy is contrasted with Eva, who is the same age, but whose saintliness is the opposite of Topsy's rascally, naughty nature, just as Eva's blonde hair and white skin contrast with Topsy's black hair and black skin. Eva tries to reform Topsy, to no avail. Only when it is clear that Eva is slowly wasting away does Topsy promise to be good.

Before she dies, Eva makes her father promise to free all of his slaves. Eva gives each of the slaves a lock of her golden hair as a keepsake and begs them all to become Christians. St. Clare tells Uncle Tom he is going to be freed, but the old slave prefers to stay with St. Clare in order to convert him to Christianity. When St. Clare dies unexpectedly before freeing the slaves, his wife sells the slaves at public auction. Uncle Tom is bought by the villainous Simon Legree.

Part III

Stowe describes the slave auction at which Uncle Tom is sold for the benefit of her Northern readers who are not familiar with slavery. She explains why negroes appear to be happy in slavery when in reality they are not:

> The dealers in the human article make scrupulous and systematic efforts to promote noisy mirth among them, as a means of drowning reflection, and rendering them insensible to their condition. The whole object of the training to which the negro is put, from the time he is sold in the northern market till he arrives south, is systematically directed towards making him callous, unthinking, and brutal. The slave-dealer collects his gang in Virginia or Kentucky, and drives them to some convenient, healthy place—often a watering place—to be fattened. Here they are fed full daily; and, because some incline to pine, a fiddle is kept commonly going among them, and they are made to dance daily; and he who refuses to be merry—in whose soul thoughts of wife, or child, or home, are too strong for him to be gay—is marked as sullen and dangerous, and subjected to all the evils which the ill will of an utterly irresponsible and hardened man can inflict upon him. Briskness, alertness, and cheerfulness of appearance, especially before observers, are constantly enforced upon them, both by the hope of thereby getting a good master, and the fear of all that the driver may bring upon them if they prove unsalable.

Simon Legree is a brutal master who takes pleasure in tormenting his slaves. When Uncle Tom tries to help another slave, Lucy, by filling her bag with cotton after she has been beaten and cannot work anymore, Legree commands Uncle Tom to beat Lucy. Uncle Tom refuses, and Legree beats Tom so badly that he almost dies. Another slave, Cassy, comes to bind Uncle Tom's wounds and declares that God has forgotten the negro race, but Uncle Tom never loses his faith. Cassy develops a plan of escape and invites Uncle Tom to come along. Once again, Uncle Tom refuses to run away, seeing it as his Christian duty to stay behind and comfort the slaves who cannot escape. After Cassy drugs Legree so that she and another slave, Emmeline, can leave, Legree suspects that Uncle Tom knows where they have gone. In a scene that is reminiscent of Christ being tormented and spat upon before his crucifixion, Uncle Tom is taunted and spat upon before Legree delivers the blow that ultimately kills him.

In the meantime, George Shelby, the son of Uncle Tom's original owner, has been searching for him ever since he was sold down the river. George finds Uncle Tom in time to bid him farewell before he dies. In a fury, George threatens to charge Legree with murder, but Legree points out that no white person will convict another for killing a slave. George realizes sadly that Legree will go unpunished. But George vows to do "*what one man can do* to drive out this curse of slavery from my land!" He returns to Kentucky and frees all of his slaves, calling on them to "be as honest and as faithful a Christian as Tom was."

Part IV

Stowe ties up all the loose ends of her story. George and Eliza have been free for five years, and little Harry is going to a good school. Cassy, who turns out to be Eliza's mother, joins the family in Canada, and they all emigrate to Liberia. Topsy lives a happy life with Miss Ophelia in Vermont. In the final chapter, Stowe claims that although *Uncle Tom's Cabin* is fiction, it is based upon actual facts that have been enacted in the history of slavery many times. She makes a direct appeal to Southerners to release their slaves and to Northerners to become active in denouncing slavery. She argues that all Christian people, North and South, must unite in ridding America of this great evil for the sake of their souls. She believes that freed slaves should be trained and educated in the North and then sent to Liberia to begin life anew. She argues that the negro race, persecuted though it is, has done much to educate itself. "If this persecuted race, with every discouragement and disadvantage, have done thus much, how much more might they

do if the Christian church would act towards them in the spirit of her Lord!" Stowe ends *Uncle Tom's Cabin* with a warning that unless the slaves are freed, both North and South will suffer the wrath of Almighty God.

Characters

Adolph

Augustine St. Clare's personal slave, Adolph is something of a dandy. He wears his master's castoff elegant clothing and looks down on slaves whom he thinks are less refined than himself.

Mr. Bird

See Senator John Bird

Senator John Bird

Senator Bird votes for the Fugitive Slave Law in Congress, for which his wife chastises him. When runaway slave Eliza Harris and her little child Harry come to their house seeking shelter, the senator is moved by her plight and changes his mind about the law, helping her to escape capture.

Mrs. Mary Bird

The usually timid wife of Senator Bird surprises her husband by condemning slavery, arguing that it is un-Christian and anti-family. When Eliza Harris stops at their home in her flight from slavery, the Birds shelter her and help her to escape safely with little Harry.

Black Sam

See Sam

Misse Cassy

Misse Cassy is a slave owned by Simon Legree who has been Legree's mistress since she came to his plantation as a young girl. Cassy befriends Tom after he comes to live on Legree's plantation. Strong and dignified in spite of her enslaved state, Cassy calls herself "a lost soul" and tells Tom she does not believe in God. She is angry and bitter about her enslavement. Her two children were taken from her and sold. She killed her third child in its infancy to keep it from growing up in slavery. Cassy and young Emmeline finally escape from the plantation together after Tom dies and make their way to Canada. Cassy is reunited with

The Civil War was fought from 1861–1865 by soldiers, such as the Union soldiers pictured here.

Eliza Harris, whom she discovers to be her long-lost daughter.

Aunt Chloe

Uncle Tom's wife and the mother of his three children, Chloe is a slave and the head cook on the Shelby's Kentucky plantation. After Tom is sold down South, the Shelbys allow Chloe to hire herself out as a baker and save the money to buy Tom's freedom. When she finally earns enough money to rescue him, it is too late: Tom has died.

Dolph

See Adolph

Emmeline

Emmeline is a fifteen-year-old religious and innocent slave girl bought by Simon Legree to be his newest "mistress." In that role she replaces Cassy.

Eva

See Evangeline St. Clare

Miss Feely

See Ophelia St. Clare

Phineas Fletcher

A former backwoodsman who married into the Quakers, Phineas Fletcher is rough and daring but kind. He helps George and Eliza Harris, their son Harry, and their friend Jim and his aging mother, to escape the slave hunters.

George Mas'r

See George Shelby

George Master

See George Shelby

Rachel Halliday

Rachel is a gentle and maternal Quaker woman who shelters Eliza, George, and Harry as they hide from slave hunters.

Simeon Halliday

Husband of Rachel Halliday, Quaker Simeon helps to plot George and Eliza's escape from slave hunters.

Eliza Harris

Famous for her desperate flight across the frozen Ohio River, made by jumping barefoot along sheets of ice, Eliza is the novel's central symbol of motherhood. A refined and religious young slave

Media Adaptations

- Directed by William Robert Daly, the 1914 silent film version of *Uncle Tom's Cabin* starred Mary Eline, Irving Cummings, and Sam Lucas. Lucas was one of the first African-American actors to appear in a leading movie role.

- Another film version of *Uncle Tom's Cabin* (*Onkel Tom's Hutte*) was made in Yugoslavia in 1969 by Hungarian director Geza von Radvanyi and stars John Kitzmiller, O.W. Fischer, Herbert Lom, and Gertraud Mittermayr.

- A made-for-television version of Stowe's novel, directed by Stan Lathan, appeared in 1987. This version stars Avery Brooks, Kate Burton, Bruce Dern, Paula Kelly, Phylicia Rashad, Kathryn Walker, Edward Woodward, Frank Converse, George Coe, and Albert Hall.

- Following its publication in 1852, *Uncle Tom's Cabin* inspired numerous stage adaptations all around the world. In 1994, Garland Publishing published a new edition of George L. Aiken and George C. Howard's six-act musical play, *Uncle Tom's Cabin,* which was originally published by Samuel French in the 1850s.

woman owned by the Shelbys, Eliza is married to George Harris, a light-skinned slave on a neighboring plantation. Their only child, Harry, is the center of Eliza's life. When she learns Harry has been sold to a slave trader, Eliza panics and risks everything to protect and to keep him.

George Harris

The husband of Eliza and father of Harry, George is a slave belonging to the Harris family, neighbors of the Shelbys. Handsome and intelligent, George can no longer bear being a slave. His master, an ignorant man, is cruel to him, and slavery seems utterly irrational to George who exclaims: "My master! And who made him my master? ... What right has he to me? I'm a man as much as he is. I'm a better man than he is." Apologizing to his religious wife for his feelings, George explains to her that he cannot believe in a God who would let slavery exist. Unable to suffer any longer, George decides to run away to Canada. He and Eliza eventually find each other on their respective flights north. Once free, George obtains an education and ultimately takes his family to the African country of Liberia to "find [him]self a people."

Harry Harris

Harry is the beautiful and bright little son of Eliza and George Harris. He is carried by his mother across the frozen Ohio River to save him from being sold to a slave trader.

Mas'r Henrique

See Henrique St. Clare

Simon Legree

Simon Legree is Tom's final master, the brutal owner of a desolate Louisiana plantation whose slaves are abused and hopeless. Legree's name, which calls up images of greed, has become synonymous with evil and cruelty. His plantation represents the worst conditions that slavery can create: he beats, underfeeds, overworks, and bullies his slaves. He does not give them proper housing or warm enough clothing and forbids those slaves who are religious to view God as a power above himself. Legree attempts to corrupt Tom by enticing him with power over the other slaves, but Tom's Christian faith enables him to resist. Tom's resistance infuriates Legree, and he threatens to kill Tom for not recognizing him—instead of God—as his master. Legree's need for power and control over his slaves has made him a depraved monster, and his corruption exemplifies the demoralizing effects of slavery on slaveowners.

Lizy

See Eliza Harris

Tom Loker

Tom Loker is one of the slave hunters who chases after George and Eliza Harris, their son Harry, and two of the Harrises' friends.

Marks

Marks is the slave-hunting partner of Tom Loker.

Mas'r

See Mr. Arthur Shelby

Master

See Mr. Arthur Shelby

Missis

See Mrs. Emily Shelby

Miss Ophelia

See Ophelia St. Clare

Pussy

See Evangeline St. Clare

Quimbo

One of Simon Legree's slave henchmen, Quimbo participates in beating Tom to death, but then feels remorseful in the face of Tom's prayers and apologizes to Tom as he dies.

Sam

A slave of the Shelbys' who is known for comically overblown oratory, Sam is chosen along with another slave, Andy, to help Haley chase Eliza after she runs away. Sam keeps tricking Haley in order to slow down the chase and give Eliza time to escape.

Sambo

One of Simon Legree's slave flunkeys, Sambo assists in the beating death of Tom and, as Tom dies, repents and becomes converted to Christianity.

Mr. Arthur Shelby

Tom was given to Mr. Shelby as an infant; Mr. Shelby is Tom's first master. As the novel opens, Shelby is reluctantly making arrangements to sell Tom to Haley, the slave trader. Shelby is what is known in the world of slavery as "a kind master," and his reluctance to sell Tom reveals him to be "a man of humanity." He cares about Tom, but decides he needs the money that the sale will bring.

Mrs. Emily Shelby

Mrs. Shelby, a woman of "high moral and religious sensibility and principle," tries to convince her husband not to sell Tom and little Harry. She has raised Eliza from girlhood and has treated her as a particular favorite. Representative of the novel's strong domestic and moral emphasis, Mrs. Shelby feels it is important to allow slave families to stay together.

George Shelby

Young George Shelby, the only son of Mr. and Mrs. Shelby, loves the slaves with whom he has grown up—particularly Tom—and treats them almost like family. After Tom is sold to Haley, George vows to bring him back to his family one day and declares that he will never buy or sell slaves when he grows up. A few years after Tom leaves the Shelbys, George becomes the master of the Shelby plantation when his father dies suddenly. George nearly fulfills his promise to Tom, arriving at Legree's plantation just as Tom is dying. Upon his return home after burying Tom, George frccs the slaves on the Shelby place.

St. Clare

See Augustine St. Clare

Alfred St. Clare

Augustine St. Clare's twin brother and his physical and spiritual opposite, Alfred is a slaveholder and believes that the Anglo-Saxon race is "the dominant race of the world."

Augustine St. Clare

St. Clare is Tom's second master, for which Tom feels fortunate. Sensitive, kind and contemplative, St. Clare adores his daughter, Eva; tolerates his demanding wife, Marie; enjoys debating political issues with his cousin Ophelia; and indulges his slaves. Reflecting his name, St. Clare is "gay, airy, [and] handsome," but he is something of a fallen idealist. As a very young man, St. Clare's nature had been one of "romantic passion," but the defining event of St. Clare's life was the loss of his one true love. To his cousin's consternation, St. Clare refuses to read the Bible or to call himself a Christian. In spite of the fact that he is a "heathen" slaveholder, St. Clare has surprisingly humanitarian views that come to light when he discusses slavery and race relations with Ophelia, Marie, or his brother Alfred. St. Clare tells Tom that he plans to emancipate him, but he is unexpectedly killed before he can do so.

Evangeline St. Clare

Little Eva's full name, Evangeline, is a pointed reference to her evangelism, an activity which she shares with Tom. Eva is the delicately beautiful and angelic daughter of Augustine and Marie St. Clare, who befriends Tom and inspires love in all who know her. Often discussed as "Christlike," Eva does not seem meant for this world. She is described as being "spirit-like," with "large, mystic eyes." She is capable of converting even the seemingly amoral Topsy to Christianity, and she is persistent in her talks about going to heaven. Eva feels deeply for her fellow creatures, particularly those less fortunate than herself, such as her family's slaves. She often speaks to her father, mother, and cousins Henrique and Ophelia about her abomination of slavery. Just before she is to die, Eva calls all the members of the household to her bedside to tell them she is dying, to implore them to become Christians, and to give each of them a lock of her hair as a keepsake. Her deathbed scene, one of the most famous in literature, is the height of Victorian domestic melodrama, with Little Eva struggling for breath as her loved ones surround the bed, tears streaming down their faces.

Henrique St. Clare

While visiting his cousin Eva, spoiled Henrique is cruel to his young slave, Dodo, and sees nothing wrong with his behavior even when Eva reproves him for it.

Marie St. Clare

The selfish wife of Augustine St. Clare and mother of little Eva, Marie is a faded beauty who commands attention by complaining constantly about feeling ill. She becomes jealous of the attention Eva receives when she is dying. Cold-hearted, Marie views slaves as less than human and believes that her sensitive, kind husband never does enough for her.

Ophelia St. Clare

Miss Ophelia is Augustine St. Clare's middle-aged, unmarried cousin from Vermont whom he brings back to New Orleans to help look after Eva. Ophelia, a Christian, is a product of her orderly, quiet, precise New England home, and in her eyes the greatest sin is "shiftlessness." She loves her cousin Augustine in spite of his lackadaisical ways and the fact that he is not a Christian, and she often debates the issues of slavery and race relations with him. Although she deplores the practice of slaveholding, she holds prejudices against black people and would prefer to have little to do with them.

Ruth Stedman

Ruth is the young, sweet Quaker mother who helps to minister to Eliza and Harry after they escape from Haley.

Father Tom

See Uncle Tom

Uncle Tom

Tom is a slave who lives first with the Shelbys of Kentucky, then with the St. Clares of New Orleans, and finally on the plantation of Simon Legree in Louisiana. At the Shelbys', where Tom holds the affectionate name of Uncle Tom, he is married to Chloe, and they have three children. Stowe tried to show in this novel how slaves were capable of creating loving, Christian families, just like free whites. Uncle Tom's cabin is all hearth and family, with Chloe cooking at the stove, the children tumbling about on the floor, and Tom bouncing the baby on his knee. Tom is a converted Christian, and he is looked up to by the other slaves as a religious figure. He succeeds in converting others to his beloved Christianity. At the St. Clares', Tom and little Eva share a powerful belief in God and heaven.

Tom's faith is put to the ultimate test when he comes under Legree's power: The fiendish Legree vows to corrupt Tom, asking him "An't I yer master? ... An't yer mine, now, body and soul?", to which Tom replies, "My soul an't yours, Mas'r! ... It's been bought and paid for by one that is able to keep it ..." Legree is unable to disturb Tom's religious convictions.

When Tom dies at the hands of Legree and his henchmen, his death is Christlike. He forgives his tormentors and converts them even as his blood drips from their hands. Uncle Tom's name has become synonymous in American culture with fawning and flattering behavior, particularly on the part of a black person towards a white person. Tom is indeed the gentle, devoted, trustworthy slave to his kind masters, Mr. Shelby and Mr. St. Clare, but these qualities stem more from his Christian beliefs than from a lack of dignity. Viewed in the context of the book's nineteenth-century reading audience, Tom serves as a symbol of the support and sustenance that Christianity provides even in the most dire of circumstances.

Topsy

Topsy is a young slave girl who has been so abused and neglected by previous owners that she thinks cruel treatment is her birthright. Purchased for Ophelia by her cousin Augustine as a kind of educational experiment, Topsy is seen by Augustine as a blank slate: undisciplined, uneducated, and ready to be trained. Although reluctant to have anything to do with Topsy at first, Ophelia finally takes her on as a sort of project. Believing herself wicked and irreformable, Topsy proves a challenge to Ophelia's orderly ways, but she is finally "converted" to goodness by the Christ-like kindness and concern of little Eva.

Cousin Vermont

See Ophelia St. Clare

Mr. Wilson

Mr. Wilson is the factory owner who had employed George Harris while George was a slave. George meets Mr. Wilson again while he is en route to the North, attempting to escape slavery.

Themes

Human Rights

Slavery took many rights away from the enslaved. The loss of the basic right to have an intact family was perhaps its cruelest effect. Stowe targeted her white female audience in addressing this denial of human rights, knowing she would find empathy in this group that was devoted to family and home. In *Uncle Tom's Cabin,* she emphasizes the slaves' right to family by focusing on the destructive effect slavery has on several slave families. Speaking for Stowe, Mrs. Shelby asks her husband not to sell Harry and Uncle Tom because she believes slave families should be allowed to stay together. On her deathbed, little Eva tells her father that the slaves love their children as much as he loves her. Through Eliza's courageous escape with Harry across the frozen Ohio River, the tearful separation of Uncle Tom from his wife and children, and Cassy's devastating story about her children being sold away from her, Stowe powerfully demonstrates that slaves are human beings who need, desire, and deserve family attachments. By pairing white mothers like Mrs. Bird, Rachel Halliday, and Ruth Stedman with Eliza, Stowe contrasts the white mother's right to love and enjoy her children with the black mother's powerlessness to do the same.

God and Religion

Religion and faith play a central role in *Uncle Tom's Cabin.* A character's relation to Christianity—believer, lapsed believer, nonbeliever—is part of how that character is defined. Eliza, Tom, Mrs. Shelby, Eva, and Ophelia are all described as dedicated Christians, and they are mostly good.

Topics for Further Study

- Research mid-nineteenth-century American views of motherhood and domesticity and compare those views to Stowe's portrayal of mothers and motherhood.

- Look at actual nineteenth-century slave narratives written by both women and men, and consider the ways in which slavery was different for each sex.

- In what ways had slavery been built into an economic necessity in the agrarian antebellum South? Why might slaveholders sympathetic to the slaves' plight not have freed their slaves?

George, Augustine St. Clare, and Cassy are basically good in spite of their inability to believe in Christianity (they are presented as having justifiable excuses not to believe). Simon Legree's complete lack of religious faith is connected to his depravity. Christianity is linked in the novel to morality, humaneness, and generosity. The Christian faith of slaves gives them courage and the strength to go on. Tom's and Eva's religious convictions transform them into Christ-like figures, and their deaths, like Christ's, are meant to be redemptive. Although she dies of tuberculosis, Eva appears almost to give her life for the antislavery cause, as slavery pains her so profoundly. Tom converts Sambo and Quimbo to Christianity as he dies at their hands. In using religion to define her characters and her cause, Stowe speaks directly to her nineteenth-century audience. Slaves portrayed as pious and even saintly, are viewed more positively than their irreverent owners.

Love

Uncle Tom's Cabin explores the power of love, specifically love of God and love of family. A mother's love for her children is built up in the novel as the most powerful kind of love. This portrayal of love helps Stowe convey the inhumanity of slavery by depicting the anguish of slave mothers who are torn from their children.

A mother's love can be transformative: witness Eliza summoning the courage and strength to cross the river on the floating ice cakes. Her love for her child makes her almost superhuman. Love of God is also portrayed as being transformative. Although they are but a lowly slave and an innocent child, Tom's and Eva's powerful love of God raises them to the stature of Christ in their capacity for love, forgiveness, and moral valor. They die like saints, with Eva giving out locks of her hair like religious icons to her loved ones and Tom being tortured and killed by those who are galled by his faith. Love and prayer are the two most potent forces in the world of the novel.

Morals and Morality

Discussions of moral principles in *Uncle Tom's Cabin* converge in the central issue of slavery. Basically, the novel asks, is human slavery right or wrong? It is not difficult to see that the novel portrays the practice of slavery as immoral. Slavery breaks apart loving families, degrades slaves and their owners, and robs human beings of their freedom. While the novel presents not only an obviously evil, immoral master in Simon Legree, it also gives readers so-called "kind" masters like Mr. Shelby and St. Clare. However, it points out that, kind or not, a master is still a master, and one human being should not be allowed to own another.

More subtle than the blatant antislavery theme in the novel is the treatment of attitudes toward slavery. Here, Stowe presents some gray moral areas. What about the people who believe slavery is wrong and do not practice it but who despise blacks? And what about slaveholders who are uncomfortable with owning slaves but do not know what to do about it? In conversations about slavery between St. Clare and Ophelia, St. Clare asserts there is something immoral about the way Northern Christians condemn slavery but do not want anything to do personally with the blacks themselves. In St. Clare himself, Stowe expresses the difference between belief and action. He is troubled about the enslavement of blacks and believes that blacks are treated inhumanely, yet he does not free his own slaves. George Shelby and Little Eva are in a sense yardsticks for morality in the novel. Both characters truly love the black slaves in their families, vehemently oppose slavery, and attempt to persuade the adults around them to condemn slavery and free their slaves. As children, George and Eva are powerless to effect real change— George will finally free the Shelbys' slaves when

he grows up—but they are moral in that they believe in what is right (according to the moral code of the novel), and they live by their beliefs.

Race and Racism

In the world of Stowe's novel, characters are defined in large part by the color of their skin. In this kind of stereotyping, Stowe herself is guilty of a certain kind of racism. While white characters are not necessarily all good, as illustrated by the likes of slave trader Haley, Simon Legree, slave hunters Loker and Marks, and Alfred St. Clare and his son Henrique; black characters' virtue is related to the lightness or darkness of their skin. For example, slave mother Eliza Harris, set up as a model of piety and moral integrity, is a quadroon (one-quarter black), so light-skinned as to be almost white. Her husband, George, an admirable example of honor and decency, is also light-skinned, as is their son, Harry. Stowe presumes that her white nineteenth-century reader will be better able to identify with the Harris family because they look so much like her own. Stowe depends upon that identification of reader with character for the success of her novel. Darker-skinned figures, like Topsy, Aunt Chloe, and Black Sam, seem more like stock characters. They are simple, speak in dialect rather than standard English, and are more comic than heroic. Tom, although dark-skinned, is noble in his Christian humility and patience, but he is also characterized as simple, innocent, and uneducated. Stowe uses her white characters not so much as vessels of racism but more as mouthpieces of racist attitudes. In particular, Augustine St. Clare's conversations with others on the subject of slavery bring up many facets of the problem of racism. When he debates the issue of slavery with his Northern cousin Ophelia, readers see how hypocritical she is. While she opposes the institution of slavery, she also personally dislikes blacks. When St. Clare discusses their slaves with his wife, Marie, readers see Marie's belief that blacks are suited only for slavery. St. Clare's conversations about race with his brother Alfred reveal Alfred's position that the white race is meant to be dominant. While St. Clare's various discussions on racism often read like the texts of political debates, readers can see that Stowe is using these dialogues to shore up her antislavery message.

Style

Point of View

The third person ("they," "he," "she") omniscient or all-seeing narrative point of view is necessary to Stowe's novel, as the novel follows simultaneously the activity of several characters in different places. The point of view occasionally shifts to second person ("you") for the purpose of drawing the reader into the story at moments of high emotion. For instance, during the description of Eliza's flight with Harry from the Shelbys, the narrator suddenly confronts us: "If it were *your* Harry, mother, or your Willie, that were going to be torn away from you by a brutal trader, tomorrow morning ... how fast could *you* walk?" Since the success of *Uncle Tom's Cabin* depends upon the reader's ability to empathize with the characters—and particularly the black slaves—these shifts into second person point of view are crucial to Stowe's purpose. The omniscience of the narrator also enables the reader to empathize with the characters by showing the reader the emotions and motivations of the characters. When readers learn about how Tom feels upon hearing that St. Clare plans to free him, they can feel compassion for him: "He felt the muscles of his brawny arms with a sort of joy, as he thought they would soon belong to himself...."

Setting

Uncle Tom's Cabin is an antislavery novel, and the time and place of the novel provide an historically accurate context for considering the issue of slavery. The antebellum period in American history was characterized by slave-holding in Southern states. Stowe wrote her novel during this period in angry response to the practice of slavery. The novel is set primarily in Kentucky and Louisiana, which were slave states. Kentucky is across the Ohio River from the free states, so setting part of her novel in Kentucky allowed Stowe to show slaves escaping to free territory. Once in free territory, escaped slaves encounter the injustice of the Fugitive Slave Law—Stowe's incentive for writing the novel—as Eliza is chased by hired slave hunters. Tom is sold "down the river" to New Orleans, where he resides in relative peace with the St. Clares. After Tom is sold to Simon Legree, he experiences slavery at its worst. "Down the river" had a special, dreadful significance for slaves farther north, as it represented the distant unknown and the hard hot work of the large plantations.

Historical Context

The Fugitive Slave Law

In its early years as a nation, the United States gradually became divided into two main regions,

the North and South. These regions were growing increasingly more different in terms of their economic systems and ways of life. By the 1830s, the North was becoming more urban and industrial, employing free labor. The South was evolving into a more agrarian, or agricultural, culture that depended upon slave labor. The two regions shared less and less, and they began to disagree over the issue of slavery.

Following the Mexican War (1846-48), America grew by one-fifth through westward expansion. Congress was forced to confront the issue of slavery as it determined whether the newly acquired areas would be free states or slave states. Out of Congress's deliberations came the Compromise of 1850, which included five provisions concerning slavery, one of which was a more severe Fugitive Slave Law. This law radically diminished the rights of free blacks and required anyone who knew about a fugitive slave to return the slave to his or her owner. The Fugitive Slave Law appeased Southern slaveholding states but infuriated Northern abolitionists, who believed they should be free to help their fellow men and women escape from the bonds of slavery. Enraged by the passage of what she saw as an unjust law, Harriet Beecher Stowe was moved to write *Uncle Tom's Cabin*.

Although the entire novel is about slavery, it directly addresses the Fugitive Slave Law in chapter nine, "In Which It Appears That a Senator Is But a Man." Here Senator Bird is at home, fresh from the Congressional vote on the Compromise of 1850. Readers discover through his conversations with his kind-hearted wife that he voted in favor of this piece of legislation. His wife chides him for what she sees as his immoral vote: "'You ought to be ashamed, John! ... It's a shameful, wicked, abominable law, and I'll break it, for one, the first time I get a chance; and I hope I *shall* have a chance, I do!'" The senator defends himself by claiming that "'it's not a matter of private feeling—there are great public interests involved, there is such a state of public agitation rising, that we must put aside our private feelings.'" Ultimately, the senator's beliefs are put to the test when runaway slave Eliza and her little Harry appear in his kitchen, desperately seeking shelter and aid. Senator Bird, who is in truth a humane man, is touched by Eliza's plight and decides to help Eliza and Harry to escape. The journey toward freedom of Eliza, Harry, and eventually Eliza's husband, George, enables Stowe to show the injustice of the Fugitive Slave Law, as the runaways are constantly being chased by hired slave hunters, even after

Compare & Contrast

- **1850:** The U.S. Congress voted to pass the Fugitive Slave Law, which required Northerners to return runaway slaves to their Southern masters and tightened restrictions on free blacks as well as fugitive slaves.

  1950s: Jim Crow laws were still in effect in the southern states, limiting the rights of African Americans. Slowly, many of those laws began to be reversed in the 1950s, such as the 1954 Supreme Court decision that declared school segregation unconstitutional in *Brown v. Board of Education.*

  Today: Many African Americans now serve in Congress, sit on the Supreme Court, and have been considered credible candidates for president by both major political parties.

- **1850s:** American culture valued domesticity and the role of housewives in society. White middle-class women were expected to settle happily into marriage and motherhood and to tend to their families' spiritual and moral lives.

  1950s: While more career opportunities were beginning to open for women, middle-class women were still for the most part expected to marry young, quit working outside the home after marriage, and stay home to care for their children.

  Today: Society's expectations for women have changed with regard to marriage, working outside the home, and staying home with children. An increasing number of American women now choose to pursue a career along with raising children.

- **1850s:** The Second Great Awakening, a religious movement calling people to find redemption through Christ, motivated inspired followers to try to improve society through reforms, which often included antislavery efforts.

  1960s: The Reverend Dr. Martin Luther King Jr. wrote his stirring *Letter from Birmingham Jail,* in which he bemoaned the "laxity of the church" in the civil rights movement and called upon Christians to turn to "the inner spiritual church" and take up the civil rights cause.

  Today: Motivated by the problems affecting African-American communities, many religious leaders have become more involved in social reform. For instance, on October 16, 1995, Nation of Islam leader Louis Farrakhan arranged the Million Man March in Washington, D.C.—an event impelling black men of all ages and backgrounds to take responsibility for themselves and their families through spiritual means. The ceremonial "atonement" also encouraged the men to take advantage of educational opportunities, invest within their communities, and promote peace in their neighborhoods.

---

reaching free American territory. Escaped slaves are not truly free until they reach Canada.

Nineteenth-Century Views of Women

In the mid-nineteenth century, the home was the heart of American society. Women's work as housewives and mothers was considered valuable. The domestic novel, a genre that focused on housewives and their sphere, became extremely popular as well. Regarded as the spiritual and moral caretakers of their families, women also extended this moral guardianship outside the home to help the less fortunate. Many theologians of this period believed that the home was the most appropriate place for children's religious education and that mothers were responsible for training the future citizens of America. Thus housewives and mothers carried a certain amount of weight within American culture, as they were thought to possess a moral authority.

Life in Slavery

Slavery is often thought to have been universal in the antebellum period, but in 1860, slaves were held by only about one third of all white Southern families. Contrary to popular belief, only a small number of slaveholders owned over fifty slaves to work on their large plantation. Most slave-owning families did not own large plantations and held twenty slaves or fewer.

Life in slavery meant a life of restrictions, with no civil rights. Slaves had no control over their own lives and were considered property, just like cattle or other livestock. They were often sold at slave auctions, where they could be inspected from head to toe by potential buyers. Slave families were not recognized as valid. Though slaves might marry each other, slave marriages were not considered legal, and husbands and wives could be sold away from each other. Slave mothers and their young children could also be separated from each other, although a law supposedly prohibited this practice. Many slaves did not have adequate food, housing, or clothing, and many slaves were subject to physical abuses such as beatings or rapes in spite of laws limiting such mistreatment. Slave women were powerless to oppose their owners' sexual exploitation and often bore children fathered by their white owners.

In order to survive the oppression of slavery, slaves created a whole culture for themselves apart from mainstream American culture. For instance, slave songs, also called spirituals, sustained the slaves with images of the Promised Land, freedom, and God's protection and love. Folktales and other oral lore often reflected tales brought by earlier slaves from Africa. Some tales centered on such mischievous characters as Br'er Rabbit who were smart enough to trick their oppressors. Slaves living together on a farm or plantation often formed close–knit communities, as depicted in Stowe's novel with Uncle Tom, Aunt Chloe, and their fellow slaves at the Shelbys'. These human connections helped to sustain them as long as they were together.

Christianity in the 1850s

The first half of the nineteenth century saw a period of religious fervor known as the Second Great Awakening. The original Great Awakening of the eighteenth century had resulted in greater emphasis on the role of the individual in religion. Evangelical leaders of the Second Great Awakening exhorted followers to find personal redemption through Christ. Those who had been redeemed were inspired to look beyond themselves and to try to improve society. Reform movements emerged, calling for the end of such social problems as prostitution, alcoholism, and slavery.

This ca. 1850 engraving entitled "Southern Industry" seems almost an advertisement for Southern "goods" which, before the Civil War, included human beings. In 1852, when Uncle Tom's Cabin *was published, it was very unusual to outspokenly oppose slavery.*

Critical Overview

In 1853, Stowe published *A Key to Uncle Tom's Cabin,* with which she intended to quiet her critics' assertions that *Uncle Tom's Cabin* had been poorly researched. This second book cited actual documents, such as laws, court cases, and newspaper articles, that substantiated Stowe's portrayal of slavery in her novel. Accurate or not, *Uncle Tom's Cabin* hit a nerve in the United States and around the world. It maintained its popularity through the antebellum and Civil War years, inspiring translations into many languages as well as adaptations for the stage.

Although the notoriety of *Uncle Tom's Cabin* died down after the Civil War and emancipation of the slaves, it has endured as a mainstay of American literature. Stowe went on to write many other books, but her first book remained her most famous. Critics throughout the twentieth century have continued to examine *Uncle Tom's Cabin.* In his 1949 essay, "Everybody's Protest Novel," first published in *The Partisan Review,* James Baldwin criticized Stowe's novel, saying "it is a very bad novel" because of its "self-righteous, virtuous sentimentality ... [which] is the mark of dishonesty." Baldwin contends that the novel is driven by "theological terror, the terror of damnation" or "a fear of the dark." He claims that the novel equates darkness, or blackness, with evil, and therefore those characters with black skin—like Tom—are "born without the light [so that] only through humility, the incessant mortification of the flesh ... can [he] enter into communion with God or man." This treatment of black characters, Baldwin feels, denies them their humanity.

Langston Hughes, in his introduction to a 1952 illustrated edition of *Uncle Tom's Cabin*, praises the novel as containing "a good story, exciting in incident, sharp in characterization, and threaded with humor." Hughes narrates some of the background circumstances of the novel in order to illustrate the book's initial impact on readers and maintains that "the love and warmth and humanity that went into its writing keep it alive a century later from Bombay to Boston." Kenneth Lynn's 1961 introduction to another edition of *Uncle Tom's Cabin* proposes that Stowe's novel is "a tearjerker with a difference." By this, Lynn goes on to say, he means that "the novel's sentimentalism continually calls attention to the monstrous actuality [slavery] which existed under the very noses of its readers." Lynn claims that Stowe's novel departs from sentimental tradition in that it "aroused emotions not for emotion's sake alone ... but in order to facilitate the moral regeneration of an entire nation."

More recently, Madeleine Stern has written in her biographical 1982 essay "Harriet Beecher Stowe," that *Uncle Tom's Cabin* "is still the subject of intense critical examination" and that Stowe "has not lost her audience." Richard Yarborough's 1986 essay, "Strategies of Black Characterization in *Uncle Tom's Cabin* and the Early Afro-American Novel," is just one example of Stern's assertion that Stowe continues to interest scholars. Yarborough discusses the novel's treatment of black characters, saying that "Although Stowe unquestionably sympathized with the slaves, her commitment to challenging the claim of black inferiority was frequently undermined by her own endorsement of racial stereotypes." Yarborough agrees with Thomas Graham that this was true because, for Stowe, blacks were something of "'an enigma.'" Considering the novel's impact in terms of how it portrayed black characters, Yarborough also points to Leslie Fiedler's assertion that Stowe

"'invented American Blacks for the imagination of the whole world.'" Yarborough feels that these invented portraits are something "with which subsequent writers—black and white—have had to reckon."

Criticism

Sharon Cumberland

In the following essay, Cumberland, an assistant professor at Seattle University, explains that Stowe's novel cannot be understood outside of its historical context and the author's motives for writing it.

When *Uncle Tom's Cabin* was published in 1852, it created an immediate controversy in a United States that was divided—both geographically and politically—by the issue of slavery. It is impossible to understand the content or the importance of *Uncle Tom's Cabin* outside of the historical forces that prompted Harriet Beecher Stowe to write it.

The early settlers of the Thirteen Colonies were well aware of the problem that was developing for the young nation as more and more slaves were kidnapped in Africa and brought to America to supply agricultural labor for the underpopulated colonies. Due to a complex combination of economic need, political indecision, scientific ignorance, and prior custom, no action was taken to rid the country of slaves while there were still few enough of them to return to their homes in Africa. Thomas Jefferson said that America "had a tiger by the ears," meaning that the slaves were dangerous because, like a tiger in captivity, they would turn on the people who captured them if they were ever released. Jefferson concluded, as did most Americans in the eighteenth century, that the only way to control the "tiger" was to keep holding it tightly by the ears, as terrible as that dilemma was for both the slaves and the slave owners. Thus when Jefferson wrote in the Declaration of Independence in 1776 that "all men are created equal," he did not include the African slaves.

Jefferson did, however, lay the problem of slavery at the feet of George III, saying in his first draft of the Declaration that King George "has waged cruel war against human nature itself, violating its most sacred rights of life and liberty in the persons of a distant people who never offended him, captivating and carrying them into slavery in another hemisphere, or to incur miserable death in their transportation thither." Jefferson was forced to delete this passage from the final version of the Declaration, however, because of the fierce disagreement it caused between delegates from slave holding colonies in the South and delegates from colonies that had already outlawed slavery in the North. The argument between the northern and southern colonies threatened to precipitate secession and civil war just at the time when the thirteen colonies needed to be united in order to fight for independence against England. In effect, the Founding Fathers decided to leave the problem of slavery and civil war to their descendants. They believed that they were justified in doing this because freedom from the tyranny of England outweighed internal issues. They believed that when America was a nation in its own right it would have the peace and freedom to solve all of its domestic problems. What the Founding Fathers did not anticipate, however, was that the slave trade would become the source of economic security for an entire region, making it very difficult to abolish without bankrupting that region and seriously compromising the stability of the nation.

The "triangular trade" was extremely lucrative. It was called "triangular" because the path of a trading ship, if traced on a map, describes a triangle over the Atlantic ocean. The ships would take manufactured goods from England and Europe to trade in Africa for slaves. The slaves would then be transported to the Indies or the Americas (the notorious "middle passage") and traded for staples like cotton, sugar, rum, molasses, and indigo which would then be carried to England and Europe and traded for manufactured goods. This procedure, repeated again and again from the time of the first slaves' arrival in America in 1619 to the abolition of the slave trade in 1807, made traders at each stop on the triangle very wealthy. The Founding Fathers agreed, with a clause in the Constitution, to end the slave trade, but this did nothing to end the slave system. Slave owners simply continued to supply the slave markets through "natural increase." The loss of an external source of supply only made slaves more valuable.

Nevertheless, by the nineteenth century most of the world had come to believe that slavery was wrong. Enlightenment ideals concerning the brotherhood of mankind had changed social perceptions, and slavery had been abolished almost everywhere in Europe and its colonies. It was very difficult for Americans to imagine ending slavery, however, be-

What Do I Read Next?

- *Narrative of the Life of Frederick Douglass, an American Slave, Written by Himself,* Douglass's autobiography, was first published in 1845. Douglass tells of his life as a slave in the American South, the cruelty of Christian slaveholders, and how, after learning to read, he finally was able to escape to freedom.

- *Incidents in the Life of a Slave Girl,* written in 1861 by Harriet Jacobs, is the first slave narrative written by an African-American woman. Jacobs tells of the particular problems experienced by women in slavery—sexual exploitation, the separation of mother and children—and makes emotional appeals to her white female reading audience.

- *Our Nig; or, Sketches from the Life of a Free Black, in a Two-Story White House, North,* written in 1859 by Harriet Wilson, is the first published novel by an African-American woman. Wilson's novel focuses on the character of Alfredo, a young mixed-race woman living in the antebellum North who strives to maintain her Christian faith and to become independent from her unkind mistress.

- Published in 1853, *Clotel; or, The President's Daughter* by William Wells Brown is the first novel by an African American published. It tells the fictional story of the beautiful, genteel mixed-race daughter of Thomas Jefferson and her experiences in and out of slavery.

cause no one in the country had ever lived without it. In the seventy-five years since the foundation of the country, the North had gotten used to the idea that slaves were necessary to the South. Most of them believed that slave owners were kind to the slaves. They also believed that slaves were childlike and ineducable, and that if they were not kept as slaves they would not be able to take care of themselves. There was also the problem of what to do with the slaves if they were freed. No one, North or South, wanted to live with negroes. Thus, for a long time, it was easier to live with slavery rather than to try to change it.

As the United States expanded westward, however, slavery became a more pressing issue. Each new state entering the union shifted the balance of political power in Congress between slave states and free states. This, together with the rise of the Abolition Movement in the 1830s and the religious revival called the "Great Awakening," which saw slavery as evidence of national sin, created an atmosphere of tension between North and South that had been postponed since the founding of the nation. Into this atmosphere came Stowe's novel, which depicted the cruelties of slavery in a way that had never registered on the national consciousness before.

Harriet Beecher (1811-1896), born in Litchfield, Connecticut, belonged to a family of famous clergymen. Her father, Lyman Beecher, was a strict Congregationalist, and her brother, Henry Ward Beecher, became a famous preacher during a era when preachers were admired as much as film or television celebrities are admired today. Harriet Beecher was a retiring woman, however, married to Calvin Stowe, a professor at Lane Theological Seminary in Cincinnati, Ohio. For eighteen years, as she raised seven children, Stowe observed the effects of slavery in the slave state of Kentucky, just across the Ohio River from her home in the free state of Ohio. Stowe supplemented her family income with freelance writing. She developed the idea of writing a novel about the horrors of slavery after the Fugitive Slave Act was passed in 1850. Many Northerners were outraged by this law, which allowed slave owners to pursue their runaway slaves into free states in order to recover their "property." Stowe combined her religious background with her political beliefs by writing a book about a saintly slave who forgave his tormentors, just as Jesus Christ forgave His.

When *Uncle Tom's Cabin* was published it became an instant success, selling so many copies that it is considered today to be the first "best seller" in American publishing history. It was banned in the South, however, and prompted dozens of answering novels, essays, and poems by pro-slavery writers. Southern writers believed that Stowe exaggerated the condition of slaves in the South, representing the exceptional cruel master (Simon Legree) as the norm, and representing the kind master (Mr. Shelby) as too weak not to sell slaves in times of economic necessity. For nine years, between the time *Uncle Tom's Cabin* was published in 1852 and the start of the Civil War in 1861, a public relations war between Northern anti-slavery writers and Southern pro-slavery writers was waged. Though many anti-slavery works had been written before *Uncle Tom's Cabin,* most notably the fugitive slave narratives of Frederick Douglass, William Wells Brown and others, it was the combination of sentimentality and religious feeling in Stowe's novel that triggered the controversy that ended in Civil War. Abraham Lincoln's famous comment when he met Mrs. Stowe ("So you are the little lady who made this big war") implies that *Uncle Tom's Cabin* caused the war, but Stowe only articulated in a new way the deep-seated problem that had been present in America since the foundation of the colonies in the seventeenth century.

Uncle Tom's Cabin is not a work which can stand alone as a self-contained entertainment. It requires an understanding on the part of the reader of the conditions which made the author write it and which made the nation respond to it so passionately. It is difficult, today, to imagine a work of literature so powerful that it can truly be said to have hastened the onset of a war and the resolution of a problem so intractable that neither the Founding Fathers nor nearly a hundred years of Congresses could find a solution. The fact that Abraham Lincoln decided to emancipate the slaves in 1863 without addressing the related problems of where the freed slaves would live or whether the South would be bankrupt, is a testament to the fact that intense public feeling, rather than logic and negotiation, had made it possible for Lincoln to act unilaterally. *Uncle Tom's Cabin* contributed greatly—even primarily—to that change of feeling in the nation. The first approach to *Uncle Tom's Cabin,* therefore, must be the historical and biographical.

In the century and a half since *Uncle Tom's Cabin* was published, many scholars have reflected on the various ways one can read and understand this complex text, and how *Uncle Tom's Cabin* has been interpreted differently over the years, both before and after the Civil War. Cultural studies, such as Thomas F. Gossett's *"Uncle Tom's Cabin" and American Culture* and Moira Davison Reynolds' *"Uncle Tom's Cabin" and Mid-Nineteenth Century United States* provide the historical frame of reference needed to understand the religious, political, and racial issues addressed in the novel. Though early biographies of Stowe focus on the dramatic irony of a shy housewife making a massive impact on American history, more recent biographies, such as Joan D. Hedrick's *Harriet Beecher Stowe: A Life* place the facts of her career in the framework of the century and give the reader a history of an era in addition to a history of a life.

Once the historical frame is understood, however, the most central avenue of approach to *Uncle Tom's Cabin* is that which addresses its primary theme of sin and redemption. When the reader considers that Harriet Beecher Stowe came from a family of preachers, it becomes clear that she is as much a preacher in her novel as a minister in his pulpit. The character of Uncle Tom is unmistakably modeled on Jesus Christ, and everything that happens to him is designed to demonstrate how evil can be transformed into good by love. Little Eva is another model of saintly behavior, designed to prompt all who know her to change, like Topsy, from being bad to being good. Stowe intended the reader, including the southern slave owner, to read *Uncle Tom's Cabin* and "turn from sin and be saved."

The theme of sin and redemption can be expressed in more general terms as the struggle between good and evil, with slavery as the metaphor for all that is evil in the world. This is the approach taken by Josephine Donovan in *"Uncle Tom's Cabin": Evil, Affliction, and Redemptive Love.* The full range of evil, from the heartless cruelty of Simon Legree, the subtle weakness of Mr. Shelby, and the humorous rascality of Topsy are all transformed by the power of Uncle Tom's acceptance of his fate. It is for the reader to go out into the actual world and transform it.

Source: Sharon Cumberland, in an essay for *Novels for Students,* Gale, 1999.

Thomas P. Joswick

In the following excerpt, Joswick addresses Stowe's message about the problem of being moral and just within a corrupt social system of slavery.

The moral conclusion of *Uncle Tom's Cabin* is as uncontestable as it is everywhere obvious in the novel: the evils of slavery demand that it be abolished. We need to heed, however, the manner in which the argument is presented. At first glance it seems as if Stowe wishes to keep the injustice of slavery separate from the moral characters of those participating in it, for repeated in the novel is an assertion, rendered explicit in the Introduction to the 1881 edition, "that the evils of slavery were the inherent evils of a bad *system* and not always the fault of those who had become involved in it and were its actual administrators." As St. Clare says at one point, "The *thing itself* is the essence of all

abuse!" But laws and moral character are never far apart in Stowe's reasoning. Slave laws are wrong, she says in the last chapter, primarily because "there is, actually, nothing to protect the slave's life, but the *character* of the master," for the law will sanction the actions even of that owner "whose passions outweigh his interest." The slave's only "right" under the law is his or her economic value, and the "justice" of the law promotes only the owner's self-interest. Rather than emphasizing other notions of rights and obligations, however, Stowe repeatedly charges that the system would crumble of its own accord were it not for the moral sanction given it by benevolent masters. "For pity's sake, for shame's sake, because we are men born of women … many of us do not, and dare not … use the full power which our savage laws put into our hands," St. Clare concludes; but "it is you considerate, humane men," says another character, "that are responsible for all the brutality and outrage wrought by these wretches like (Simon Legree); because, if it were not for your sanction and influence, the whole system could not keep foot-hold for an hour.… It is your respectability and humanity that licenses and protects Legree's brutality."

What these remarks underscore is a conviction not only that human character is at the root of any social system but that moral character, by its pervasive influence, is the real authority in a society. The laws that define rights and obligations here and elsewhere in the novel are usually reduced to matters of self-interest and are often imaged as unstable structures that would collapse without the support of a higher moral authority. The truth of slavery, Stowe is saying, is to be found in the moral influence of those who lend it tacit support and in the moral degradation of those who use the power of law to vent their brutal passions. Thus, if slavery is to be abolished, the appeal will not be so much to a declaration of rights as to a conversion of character. As [critic Jane P.] Tompkins puts it [in a 1981 *Glyph* article], in Stowe's view reality "can only be changed by conversion in the spirit because it is the spirit alone that is finally real." Owners (and readers), then, ought not merely to forgo the use of power in the law; they must undergo a change of heart directed toward an authority higher than the law.

The final authority toward which the conversion is directed is, of course, an eternal and transcendent God, but this divine authority is given both a communal context and a morally persuasive power in the novel. And as most readers could readily say, divine authority has its worthy representatives in the mothers who appear in the novel, for motherly love, not law, is the novel's highest authority for directing all ethical choices and all communal responsibilities....

Motherly love is all-powerful precisely because it relinquishes the rights of power. Spurn a mother's love, and its comforts are transformed into fears of judgment, not because love will assert a rightful indignation, but because love will always be self-sacrificing and forgiving. The "bad soul" is thereby compelled to see "herself," that is, to see its own truth against the measure of its own *feminine,* unwavering ideal. Equally important, the inner truth is known by seemingly palpable forms, as if the soul "herself" were an apparition of a mother visiting her child. Thus, a conscience originates out of *self-evident* measures of good and evil, for the separation from motherly love divides the soul from itself, a division which is itself "direst despair" and which is made palpable in the psychological phenomenon of visions.

The conversion of heart that the novel demands, then, consists in turning to the authority of motherly care as the principle for ethical action. How forms of moral reasoning likewise change in this conversion can be seen in tracing the transformation of Eliza from slave to free woman. Early in the novel Eliza holds those notions of justice and religious obligation that govern and sanction the slave laws: "I always thought that I must obey my master and mistress, or I couldn't be a Christian," she says with mournful resignation at one point. Her obedience and religious piety are directed by a concept of authority restricted to a distinct and fixed social position, and the ordering principle of this authority likewise fixes distinct social classes to which people resort for a sense of personal identity and for guidance on how to act. Eliza finds this authority persuasive and valuable not so much because she fears punishment (although that too) but because she feels obliged to reciprocate the kindness of the master and mistress with obedience to their authority. Lawrence Kohlberg calls this form of moral sense "instrumental hedonism" or "reciprocal fairness," for most of the reasoning about obligations centers on the actual benefits (or punishments) that ground moral exchanges. Thus Eliza's husband George says he can see "some sense" in Eliza's reasoning because, as he tells her, "they have brought you up like a child, fed you, clothed you, indulged you, and taught you, so that you have a good education; that is some reason why they should claim you."

This notion of justice is employed also to defend the Fugitive Slave Law. Senator Bird, for example, reasons that it is "no more than Christian and kind" to treat "our brethren in Kentucky" with reciprocal fairness by trying "to quiet the excitement" stirred up by the excessive acts of "reckless Abolitionists." But this form of reasoning need not result in only one conclusion about either slavery or the Fugitive Slave Law. When Eliza has crossed the Ohio, for instance, she is aided by a man who turns out to be a neighbor to the Shelbys. He admires her courage and declares that by her daring she has "arnt" (earned) her liberty and that he will not return her to Shelby. He adds, "Shelby, now, mebbe won't think this yer the most neighborly thing in the world; but what's a feller to do? If he catches one of my gals in the same fix, he's welcome to pay back." Again, fair reciprocity justifies a moral choice, but this choice is one Stowe obviously approves; because of his lack of instruction in legal niceties, the "heathenish Kentuckian ... was betrayed into acting in a sort of Christianized manner, which, if he had been better situated and more enlightened, he would not have been left to do." Although conclusions are different, the same form of moral reasoning is operating, especially in the recognition that notions of law derive from an authority fixed in a particular socioeconomic class.

Source:: Thomas P. Joswick, "'The Crown without the Conflict': Religious Values and Moral Reasoning in *Uncle Tom's Cabin,*" in *Nineteenth-Century Fiction,* Vol. 39, No. 3, December, 1984, pp. 257–74.

Elizabeth Ammons

In the following excerpt, Ammons discusses the important role of Stowe's female characters as opponents of slavery.

The opening episode of *Uncle Tom's Cabin* introduces Stowe's argument by portraying mothers, black and white, as active opponents of slavery. The system itself, this first scene makes clear, is basically masculine: white men buy and sell black people while the white woman stands by powerless to intervene. This may not be the pattern in every case but, in Stowe's opinion, it is the model, as her prime and detailed treatment of it suggests. When the slave-holder, Mr. Shelby, gets himself into debt and decides that he must sell some property, he settles on Eliza's son, Harry, and Uncle Tom. Shelby, it is true, does not *want* to sell the pretty child or the kind man who raised him from a boy; but sell he does, and to a trader he knows to be so callous, so "'alive to nothing but trade and profit ... [that] he'd sell his own mother at a good per centage.'" Figuratively Shelby would do the same, as his selling of Tom demonstrates, and Stowe emphasizes how fine the line is that separates the "benevolent" planter Shelby and the coarse trader Haley, whose favorite topic of conversation (to Shelby's discomfort) always has to do with slave mother's aggravating attachment to their children, whom Haley is in the business of selling away from them. Shelby is in the same business, one step removed, but would rather not admit it. His wife confronts him. Although helpless to overrule him legally, she cries out against his refined brutality, calling slavery "'a bitter, bitter, most accursed thing!—a curse to the master and a curse to the slave! I was a fool to think I could make anything good out of such a deadly evil.... I never thought that slavery was right—never felt willing to own slaves.'" When her mate suggests they sneak off on a trip to avoid witnessing the black families' grief at separation, her resistance crystallizes. "'No, no,' said Mrs. Shelby; 'I'll be in no sense accomplice or help in this cruel business.'" Likewise Tom's wife, Aunt Chloe, reacts rebelliously, supporting Eliza in her decision to run away with her child and urging Tom to go with her. These two maternal antagonists of slavery secure Eliza's flight. Because Mrs. Shelby surreptitiously encourages the slaves to sabotage the search for Eliza, and because Aunt Chloe stalls the pursuit by producing culinary disasters which keep the search party at dinner for hours, Eliza is able to make her break for freedom across the frozen Ohio, baby in arms.

Due to the conspiracy of the two mothers, one white and one black, followed by the equally crucial assistance of stalwart Mrs. Bird, wife of a wrong-headed Ohio Senator and herself a recently bereaved mother, Eliza and child arrive safely at a Quaker station on the route to Canada. The community serves as a hint of the ideal in *Uncle Tom's Cabin*. It is family-centered, nonviolent, egalitarian; and especially impressive among its members are two hearty matrons, significantly named Ruth and Rachel. Stowe remarks: "So much has been said and sung of beautiful young girls, why don't somebody wake up to the beauty of old women?" For Stowe Rachel Halliday's beauty issues from her perfection as a mother and from the way she uses her power in what is in practice a matriarchal (because completely home-centered) community. Stowe plays with the idea of Rachel as a mother-goddess, calling her a figure much more worthy of a "cestus" than the overrated Venus whom "bards" like to sing about, and then immediately follows that remark with a glimpse of Rachel's husband

happily "engaged in the anti-patriarchal operation of shaving." Of course, Stowe is being whimsical here, but only in the sense that she is too confident a Christian to need to appeal seriously to pagan concepts to express the principle incarnate in Rachel, whose earthy maternal love Stowe will bring to transfigured life in the two unlikely but motherly Christ-figures, Eva and Tom. As a matter of fact the Quaker community is "anti-patriarchal" in its pacifism and its matrifocal social structure, and that is its beauty for Stowe. "Rachel never looked so truly and benignly happy as at the head of her table. There was so much motherliness and full-heartedness even in the way she passed a plate of cakes or poured a cup of coffee, that it seemed to put a spirit into the food and drink she offered." Rachel Halliday, sitting at the head of her family's table in a scene that brings to mind Christ's ministry at the Last Supper, illustrates how humane and spiritually nourishing mother-rule might be.

Eliza and her family escape their white masters. Most slaves did not, and Harriet Beecher Stowe places particular emphasis on the horrors suffered by the system's maternal victims. The first slave auction in the book focuses on an aged mother and teen-aged son who are sold apart over the old woman's pleas and sobs. A young black woman whose baby is stolen and sold drowns herself in the Mississippi, her only obituary an entry in a slave trader's ledger under "losses." A middle-aged slave, her twelve children auctioned away, drinks to silence memory of her thirteenth baby who was starved to death; drunk once too often, the woman is locked in a cellar until the smell of her corpse satisfies her owners' wrath. The degradation of Cassy, Simon Legree's chattel concubine, began with a white lover's clandestine sale of her two small children. Cassy spared her next baby; in her own words, "'I took the little fellow in my arms, when he was two weeks old, and kissed him, and cried over him; and then I gave him laudanum, and held him close to my bosom, while he slept to death.... I am not sorry, to this day; he, at least, is out of pain.'" These cruelly severed ties between mothers and children recur throughout Stowe's exposé of slavery for several reasons: to stir Abolitionist passion within parents in Stowe's audience, to assert the humanity of the black race in the face of racist myths that blacks do not share the emotions of whites, to show that women suffer horrible tortures in the midst of a society boastful about its chivalry toward the "gentle sex," and—most important—to dramatize the root evil of slavery: the displacement of life-giving maternal values by a profit-hungry masculine ethic that regards human beings as marketable commodities. Planters, traders, drivers, bounty hunters, judges, voters—all are white, all are men, all are responsible; and the mothers and motherless children in *Uncle Tom's Cabin* show the human cost of the system.

No character illustrates Stowe's charge more starkly than Topsy. Motherless all her young life and systematically kept ignorant by whites, what can the child believe except that she "just growed"? It is a miracle that she has managed that. For years her owners have routinely beaten her with chains and fireplace pokers, starved her, and locked her in closets until she can respond to nothing but pain and violent abuse. The child has been crippled psychologically by an entire social structure purposely designed to strip her (and her black brothers) of all sense of human selfhood. Stowe defends Topsy as a credible character in [her] *A Key to Uncle Tom's Cabin* (1853): "Does any one wish to know what is inscribed on the seal which keeps the great stone over the sepulchre of African mind? It is this,— which was so truly said by poor Topsy—'NOTH-ING BUT A NIGGER!' It is this, burnt into the soul by the branding-iron of cruel and unchristian scorn, that is a sorer and deeper wound than all the physical evils of slavery together. There never was a slave who did not feel it."

It is significant that only Evangeline St. Clare can dress Topsy's "wound" and awaken in the motherless black girl feelings of tenderness, trust, and self-respect. To understand the ethereal blonde child's life-renewing influence, one must take seriously the unearthly qualities Stowe attaches to Eva. She is not a realistic character any more than Hawthorne's preternatural Pearl in *The Scarlet Letter* (1850) or Melville's Pip in *Moby Dick* (1851). Stowe, too, relies on Romantic convention in *Uncle Tom's Cabin*, first published serially in 1851–52. She consistently describes Eva as dreamy, buoyant, inspired, cloud-like, spotless; and flatly states that this child has an "aerial grace, such as one might dream of for some mythic and allegorical being." Stowe is clear that her mythic and allegorical character resembles Jesus. Tom, who "almost worshipped her as something heavenly and divine," often gazes on Eva "as the Italian sailor gazes on his image of the child Jesus,—with a mixture of reverence and tenderness." Eva's Mammy considers her a "blessed lamb" not destined to live long. Stowe calls her a "dove" and associates her with the morning star. Ophelia describes her as "Christ-like" and hopes that she has learned "something of the love of Christ from her." Tom, before

her death, visualizes Eva's face among the angels; and after she is gone he has a dream-vision of the saintly child reading Christ's words to him, words of comfort which end with "'I am the Lord thy God, the Holy One of Israel, thy Saviour.'" Even while alive Eva's selflessness seems supranatural. Sights and stories of slavery's atrocity make "her large, mystic eyes dilate with horror...." and move her to lay her hands on her breast and sigh profoundly. She explains, "'these things *sink into my heart.*'" The child identifies with the slaves' misery, telling Tom finally: "'I can understand why Jesus *wanted* to die for us.... I *would die* for them, Tom, if I could.'" On the figurative level—the only level on which Eva makes sense—she gets her wish. Stowe contrives her death to demonstrate that there is no life for a pure, Christlike spirit in the corrupt plantation economy the book attacks.

None of this means that Eva "is" Christ. But I think it does mean that she reflects by way of her name a type of Christ, and Stowe's unusual typology vivifies the moral center of *Uncle Tom's Cabin*.

Source: Elizabeth Ammons, "Heroines in *Uncle Tom's Cabin,* in *American Literature,* Vol. 49, No. 2, May, 1977, pp. 165–79.

Sources

Langston Hughes, introduction to *Uncle Tom's Cabin* in *Critical Essays on Harriet Beecher Stowe,* edited by Elizabeth Ammons, G.K. Hall, 1980, pp. 102-4.

Kenneth S. Lynn, introduction to Harriet Beecher Stowe's *Uncle Tom's Cabin; or, Life among the Lowly,* The Belknap Press of Harvard University Press, 1962, pp. vii-xxiv.

Madeleine B. Stern, "Harriet Beecher Stowe," in *Dictionary of Literary Biography, Volume 12: American Realists and Naturalists,* edited by Donald Pizer and Earl N. Harbert, Gale Research, 1982, pp. 425-33.

Richard Yarborough, "Strategies of Black Characterization in 'Uncle Tom's Cabin' and the Early Afro-American Novel," in *New Essays on Uncle Tom's Cabin,* edited by Eric J. Sundquist, Cambridge University Press, 1986, pp. 45-84.

For Further Study

Nina Baym, et al., eds., *The Norton Anthology of American Literature,* 4th ed., Vol. 1, Norton, 1994.
    An anthology containing Jefferson's first draft of the Declaration of Independence, showing his initial condemnation of slavery.

Josephine Donovan, *Uncle Tom's Cabin: Evil, Affliction and Redemptive Love,* Twayne, 1991.

This is a good general introduction to the themes and historical context of *Uncle Tom's Cabin,* with a reading of the text in terms of the problem of evil.

Ann Douglas, *The Feminization of American Culture,* Avon, 1978.

A classic study of American culture during Stowe's era, which relates the religiosity of the times both to the abolitionist movement and the marginalization of women.

Thomas F. Gossett, *Uncle Tom's Cabin and American Culture,* Southern Methodist University Press, 1985.

A cultural study of *Uncle Tom's Cabin* beginning with the political environment surrounding Stowe from her birth in 1811 to the reception of the novel from 1852 to the present.

John D. Hedrick, *Harriet Beecher Stowe: A Life,* Oxford University Press, 1994.

The most recent scholarly biography with an extensive bibliography and sixteen pages of photographs.

Theodore R. Hovet, *The Master Narrative: Harriet Beecher Stowe's Subversive Story of Master and Slave in Uncle Tom's Cabin and Dred,* University Press of America, 1988.

A book which relates American slavery to patriarchal themes and concepts of the "fallen world." Allows *Uncle Tom's Cabin* to be seen in the context of the western patriarchal tradition dating back to Plotinus in the third century.

Mason I. Lowance, Jr., Ellen E. Westbrook, and R. C. DeProspo, eds., *The Stowe Debate: Rhetorical Strategies in Uncle Tom's Cabin,* University of Massachusetts Press, 1994.

Discusses the three main debates generated by *Uncle Tom's Cabin* over the years: slavery, critical reception, and theory. Contains many useful articles on such topics as race and slavery, domesticity and sentimentality as rhetorical strategies, and various theoretical approaches to *Uncle Tom's Cabin.*

Moira Davison Reynolds, *Uncle Tom's Cabin and Mid-Nineteenth Century United States,* McFarland, 1985.

A description of the political environment that surrounded the publication of *Uncle Tom's Cabin.*

Harriet Beecher Stowe, *The Key to Uncle Tom's Cabin,* Arno Press & New York Times, 1968.

Originally published in 1854, *The Key to Uncle Tom's Cabin* presents Stowe's own source book of facts for *Uncle Tom's Cabin* that she complied to corroborate her claims and to demonstrate to skeptical readers that all of the characters and events in the novel were based upon actual people and phenomena of slavery.

Forrest Wilson, *Crusader in Crinoline: The Life of Harriet Beecher Stowe,* J. B. Lippincott, 1941.

A dated popularization of Stowe's life, which should be used only with more current biographies, but which contains many interesting photographs and contemporary drawings.

The Woman Warrior

Maxine Hong Kingston

1976

The Woman Warrior experienced immediate success upon its publication in 1976. It became an instant bestseller and secured a place in the top ten nonfiction books of the decade. Because Maxine Hong Kingston deals with stories of growth in individuals and among generations in two different cultures, teachers from various disciplines utilize the book to supplement their instruction. Some use it to discuss women's topics, while others find it serves well to encourage and support dialogue regarding sociological, historical, literary, and ethnic issues. Critics praise Kingston's ability to deal with the concerns of identity formation in Chinese women who have long been oppressed by Chinese male tradition. In addition, her skill at story telling continues the Chinese art of "talk story" but advances the oral custom to a written treasure to be passed down through generations.

The Woman Warrior has also received negative reviews because critics find its content difficult to categorize. While Knopf published the book as nonfiction, many reviewers claim that Kingston includes too many nonspecific memories for the book to be considered anything but fiction. Kingston admits that the main sources of information for her books are her mother's tales and her father's reticence, along with her own memories and imagination. Kingston defends her technique, however. She says that the book is not specifically an autobiography but combines truth and fiction in an autobiographical form.

Whether readers love the book for its inspiring message about female empowerment or despise it for its sometimes cruel themes, most will agree with Pin-chia Feng, who wrote in the *Dictionary of Literary Biography,* "Kingston's writing ... embodies the collective spirit of the Chinese American community."

Author Biography

Maxine "Ting Ting" Hong Kingston grew up in a working-class neighborhood in Stockton, California. Born in 1940 to Tom Hong and Brave Orchid, Kingston is the oldest of her parents' six American-born children. Kingston's parents serve as the primary sources for the imaginative stories she writes.

Kingston's father came to America as a scholar and teacher but made his early living in this country washing windows, and later, as part owner in a New York laundry. After losing his share of the business, Hong relocated in 1940 to Stockton, California, to manage an illegal gambling business. Brave Orchid, who had just joined her husband in America, accompanied him. Until World War II, Hong alternately ran gambling houses and suffered arrests for it. After the war, Hong opened his own laundry and provided a good life for his Chinese-American family. Hong told his daughter little about his life in China. The stories Kingston tells of her father have been pieced together from her mother's stories and her own memories.

Kingston's mother, on the other hand, was as vocal about life in China as her husband was quiet. Having managed to break free of the bonds that held her in the role of a traditional Chinese woman, Brave Orchid became a respected doctor, fighting the "ghosts" in her life and in others' lives. When she moved to America, she traded her doctor's role for one of laundry woman, cannery worker, maid, tomato picker, and mother. She would "talk stories" to her children at bedtime, offering tales of ghosts and family history as well as myths and legends. Her yarns provided her children with their connection to Chinese tradition and stimulated their imaginations. While her stories "warned" her children of the Chinese hatred for women, they also equipped them with knowledge of women who overcame the limits of traditionalism.

The "ghosts" in Kingston's stories represent the remains of these Chinese traditions present in

Maxine Hong Kingston

her life as a young child and teenager. Her ghosts are the images of the American life that her parents tried to deny and of the Chinese life that they tried to forget. As a very young child, Kingston struggled with her Chinese heritage and her American existence. She did not speak English until she started school. She failed kindergarten because she did not talk and covered her school paintings with black paint. In sixth grade, Kingston attacked another Chinese girl for her refusal to speak. After this incident, Kingston spent 18 months in bed. Late in her teen years, Kingston confronted her mother, finding a strength to defy the heritage she hated.

Since her teen years, Kingston has found a different voice for her memories. Through her writing, she translates the oral tradition of her community and gives substance to the "ghosts" in her life. In doing so, Pin-chia Feng says in a biography of Kingston's life, she "unsettles both Chinese American sexism and American racism."

Plot Summary

No Name Woman

Maxine Hong Kingston's autobiography begins with her mother telling her a story which she must never repeat about the aunt she never knew she had. In China the aunt had become pregnant long after her husband and brothers had celebrated their "hurry up" weddings and left for America. The weddings had been to ensure that all the men who went to America would come home and resume their places in Chinese society, but the aunt's adultery had disrupted that society. When the pregnancy became obvious, the enraged villagers had raided the family house, breaking and destroying their possessions as the aunt had broken and destroyed social order. That night, after the raid the aunt gave birth to her baby in a pigsty and then drowned herself and the child in the family well. The family never mentions her, pretending she was never born.

Unable to ask questions about the unmentionable aunt, Kingston speculates about her, trying to imagine what she might have been like and what might have motivated her actions. She wonders whether her aunt, a traditional Chinese woman accustomed to taking orders, was raped by one of the village men who then later joined in the raid on her home. She also wonders if her aunt, unable to seek adventure as her brothers had done by going to America, had crossed a different sort of boundary, looking for romance. She imagines the pain and isolation that her aunt must have endured giving birth to the child alone in the pigsty. Finally she realizes that her family has not mentioned her aunt not just to hide their shame but also to punish her aunt. Forgetting her aunt is the real punishment. Kingston realizes that she had unknowingly participated in this punishment, and she says that she feels her aunt haunting her now that she is the only one telling her story.

White Tigers

Kingston remembers the Chinese folktales her mother used to tell her about amazing warrior women who could battle whole armies and save their families. She particularly remembers the chant of Fa Mu Lan, and she slips into a fantasy in which she is Mu Lan. As Mu Lan she is a little girl who one day strays from her family's home while following a bird, and ends up in the mountains where she meets an old couple who takes her in and trains her to become a warrior. For fifteen years she stays with them and studies martial arts, meditation, and magic. Occasionally the old man shows her a magic drinking gourd in which she can see her family, and also the enemies that oppress them. In this gourd she sees her childhood lover marry her, even though she is not there for the ceremony. Finally

she returns to her family and tells her elderly father that she will take his place in the war he has been drafted into. Before she goes, her parents carve words on her back which tell of all the wrongs done to them. Then Mu Lan dresses like a man and leads an army into battle. They win many battles, and for a time her husband joins her and they have a baby. Then he takes the baby back to his family while she returns to battle. Finally her army beheads the emperor who has been oppressing them and appoints a peasant in his place.

Emerging from her fantasy, Kingston reflects on what a disappointment her American life has been. The good grades she earns in school do not seem as glorious as the deeds of the woman warrior, and they do nothing to stop the pain she feels when she hears her parents say that girls are worthless. She struggles with her mixed feelings about her Chinese culture and with her uncertainty about how to blend the two cultures of which she is a part. Ultimately she realizes that she, as a writer, has much in common with the woman warrior. What they have in common are the words at their backs. Telling her story is her way of avenging herself and her family.

Shaman

Shaman is largely about Kingston's mother. Kingston discusses how her mother, Brave Orchid, went to a medical college for women in China. Kingston's mother quickly became known among the other women as a brilliant student, but she made her greatest impression on the other students when she offered to spend a night in a haunted room. During the night she was visited by a "sitting ghost" which nearly smothered her, but she was too strong for the ghost, and in the morning she told the other students a fabulous tale about the event and then led them all in purging the room of the ghost. When Brave Orchid returned to her village, she became known as a great healer. In America, however, Brave Orchid cannot practice medicine and she sees all the Americans as ghosts. In the final section of this chapter, Kingston recalls her last visit to her parents. Brave Orchid, now an old woman, wants her children all at home and not wandering, but Kingston explains that she has found some places that are ghost-free and that she thinks she belongs there, where she is happier.

At the Western Palace

When she is sixty-eight years old, Brave Orchid finally manages to bring her sister, Moon Orchid, to America. Moon Orchid's husband has been in America for many years, but he has never sent for his wife or daughter. When Moon Orchid finally arrives, her daughter and Brave Orchid are there to meet her, but it soon becomes clear that Moon Orchid will not be able to make the transition to America easily. She is an old woman and unaccustomed to work, and she cannot do even the simplest of the tasks at the laundry. Finally Brave Orchid insists that Moon Orchid confront her husband. They drive down to Los Angeles, where he is a doctor with a new, younger wife who knows nothing about Moon Orchid. They trick him into coming out to their car, but when he sees them he is furious. He will continue to give his wife money, but he will not acknowledge her. Brave Orchid returns home, but soon she hears that Moon Orchid, who has stayed with her daughter, is becoming paranoid. Brave Orchid asks her sister to come back to her home and tries to cure her, but her sister is going insane, imagining that everyone she sees is planning to kill her. Finally Moon Orchid is committed to a mental asylum, where she seems happier, but where she finally dies.

A Song for a Barbarian Reed Pipe

Kingston tells how, when she was a baby, her mother cut her tongue so that she would not be tongue-tied, but Kingston thinks she cut too much because now she has a terrible time overcoming her shyness and talking. She realizes that silence has something to do with being a Chinese girl, as all the Chinese girls in school are quiet. Kingston grows to hate one particularly silent girl, seeing her as an embodiment of her own weakness and silence. One day she corners the girl in the bathroom and taunts her and tries, unsuccessfully, to force her to talk. Kingston comes to think that talking is what distinguishes crazy people from sane people. Crazy people are unable to explain themselves. There are a number of crazy girls in her neighborhood, and she thinks perhaps every family must have one. She doesn't want to be the crazy one, but she also doesn't want to conform to the traditional Chinese roles she thinks her parents want to force on her. She doesn't want to be married off or sold as a slave if they go back to China. She finally confronts her mother and complains that her mother's stories confuse her, that she can't tell what is true and what is just a story. She ends by announcing that she is going to college and that her mother can't stop her from talking. Her mother, also a champion talker, responds and they end up yelling at each other.

Kingston ends the book by telling a story that her mother told her, but which she ends in her own way. Brave Orchid tells her how the family always attended the theater in China, which Kingston's grandmother believed would keep them safe from all danger. Kingston likes to think that in some of those performances they heard the songs of Ts'ai Yen, a Chinese poetess who was captured by the Barbarians and kept by them for many years. During all those years she was unable to communicate with her captors, until she heard them playing on their reed pipes and joined them, adding her mournful voice to their songs. When she was returned to her people she brought the song for the Barbarian reed pipe back with her, and it translated well.

Characters

Aunt

See Moon Orchid

Brave Orchid Hong

Brave Orchid, Maxine's mother, tells stories like no other person can. Her "talk stories" lull her children to sleep with visions of mythical characters, historical fact, family tales, and legendary heroes and heroines. At the beginning of *The Woman Warrior*, Brave Orchid warns Maxine about the sins of adultery through her story of her husband's sister. Because this unmarried sister became pregnant—and ultimately, committed suicide—the family never speaks of her or even acknowledges her life. The sister brought disgrace to the family, and Brave Orchid cautions Maxine to keep silent about her knowledge, and more importantly, to avoid the same mistake.

Brave Orchid's own story begins in China, after her husband has left for America. She is a pretty young woman with naturally curly hair, thick eyebrows, and full lips. Her eyes have a direct and serious gaze. A strong person, Brave Orchid bears the pain of her first two children's deaths alone. After ten years of waiting for her husband's return, she decides to use the money she has saved to attend medical school in a distant city. She completes her studies in two years and returns to her village, a respected doctor. She stays in China and practices medicine and midwifery until 1939.

Leaving her medical practice behind her in China, Brave Orchid moves to America. Shortly after arriving in New York in 1940, she and her hus-

Morning traffic on a congested corner of the Shanghai business district in the 1930s.

band relocate to Stockton, California. There, she works with him in their laundry and picks tomatoes to supplement their income. She raises her six American-born children to know their Chinese roots, expecting them to adhere to Chinese customs. She frightens them with her talk of "ghosts" and warns them to avoid the "White Ghosts" in particular. When her children disobey her for any reason, Brave Orchid disciplines them with a firm hand and a sharp tongue. Maxine thinks her mother is hardest on her. Brave Orchid tells Maxine she is stupid, ugly, noisy, and humorless. She accuses Maxine of leading her sisters astray, and calls her "unusual." Even after Maxine reaches adulthood and moves away from home, a white-haired, heavy-set Brave Orchid continues with "talk stories" intended to show her children true Chinese ways.

Maxine Hong

Maxine's earliest memories are of the stories her mother told her. They include accounts of Maxine's father's sister, a nameless aunt who brought disgrace to the family, and of the brave Fa Mu Lan, a young Chinese girl who fought battles for her own father. The stories prompt Maxine to create tales of her own, myths woven around images of herself as a girl trained to be a woman warrior who becomes a legendary heroine. In reality, Maxine is a Chinese girl born in America, struggling to make sense of two sets of traditions and values.

Maxine suffers continual disappointment when she tries to please her mother with her Americanized accomplishments such as good grades in school. She does not understand why her mother berates her and calls her "bad girl." She is confused by the special treatment her younger brothers receive. Their births merit special celebrations; they learn to speak English. She wonders why her mother cut her tongue and not those of her brothers and sisters.

When Maxine starts kindergarten, she speaks no English and must endure taunting from the other children. Her teachers worry that she has psychological problems because she is so silent and covers her drawings in black paint. Maxine is in the sixth grade when her Chinese differences, reflected in another quiet Chinese girl, cause her to act aggressively. She pulls the girl's hair, pinches her cheeks, and tries to torment her into speaking. Maxine does not get the girl to speak, and Maxine, herself, ends up in bed for eighteen months. She never feels comfortable in American schools, where Chinese customs are neither understood nor valued.

Working in her father's laundry, Maxine experiences more confusion about her heritage. When she attempts to talk to her mother about her feelings, her mother tells her to quit talking. Maxine keeps her thoughts to herself, feeling guilty about the things she has done and the questions she has that she cannot discuss with anyone. Finally, when she can bear the guilt no longer, she spills her emotions to her mother, who tells her to leave.

The distance Maxine puts between herself and her family enables her to look at her heritage in a different light. She begins to unscramble her memories to try to resolve which experiences she has imagined and which ones are real, which experiences are representative of Chinese families and which are just family, and which experiences are typical of childhood and which ones are particular to her own childhood. Through reflection, she feels cleansed and hopeful. She discovers that she can think about going home again and even visiting China.

Fa Mu Lan

Fa Mu Lan is the mythical woman warrior about whom Brave Orchid tells her children. Fa Mu Lan disguises herself as a man and goes to battle in place of her aged father. She returns to her village victorious, a heroine for all Chinese women. Her story empowers women to seek more out of life than being the wives and slaves of men who would claim to own them. As a young girl, Maxine envisions herself as Fa Mu Lan, enabling her to escape from the disappointments of her American life.

Moon Orchid

Moon Orchid, Brave Orchid's sister, arrives in San Francisco after having waited for thirty years for her husband to send for her. Moon Orchid's daughter, Brave Orchid's children, and Brave Orchid watch for her arrival at the airport. Brave Orchid expects some change in her sister after thirty years but is surprised to see the little old woman who acknowledges their greeting. Moon Orchid seems to have gotten shorter, and she is very thin. She has tiny fluttering hands and wears her gray hair in a bun. Most unsettling of all, Brave Orchid sees that Moon Orchid is old, even though she, herself, is one year older.

Although Moon Orchid expected her husband to invite her to come to America, he never did. He has, however, always sent money, provided servants, and supported their daughter. Brave Orchid, in the meantime, has worked constantly to get her sister to America. Now that Moon Orchid has arrived, Brave Orchid thinks that Moon Orchid

Media Adaptations

- Kingston reads *The Woman Warrior* on an audio cassette entitled *Maxine Hong Kingston Reading The Woman Warrior [and] China Men (Excerptsaudio Cassette).* American Audio Prose Library produced the tape in June 1987.

---

should reclaim her husband from his new wife. Moon Orchid does not want to take the new wife's place. She even says that the new wife can stay with them as a servant. Brave Orchid thinks her sister is lovely but useless and not very intelligent. Brave Orchid devises a plot to get the two back together. Moon Orchid reluctantly allows her sister to convince her to go along with the scheme but tells her that she is not quite ready for it.

Meanwhile, Moon Orchid tries to adjust to life in America. Her sister's children confuse her. Because they accept her compliments, they appear rude. They have white hair and smell like cow's milk. In addition, she does not understand the work her sister's family does. She cannot help at the laundry because she has no skills.

After a few months, Moon Orchid's daughter decides to go back to Los Angeles to her family, which is also where Moon Orchid's husband lives. Even though Moon Orchid tells her sister that she is happy living with her, Brave Orchid insists that it is time for them to put their plan into action. Upon arrival in Los Angeles, Brave Orchid enters the husband's office, where he practices medicine. The beautiful, young nurse is his wife. Brave Orchid tricks the doctor into coming down to the car for a supposed emergency. There, he is shocked to see his Chinese wife. He tells her that he wants nothing to do with her and that there is no room for her in his new American life.

Moon Orchid goes to live with her daughter. Brave Orchid hears nothing from her for months. When she does, she learns that Moon Orchid has become afraid of everything. She brings Moon Orchid back to her own home, convinced that she can help her overcome her fear. Moon Orchid, however, slips into a world of her own. She becomes so ill that Brave Orchid commits her to a mental asylum, where she lives for the short remainder of her life.

Mother

See Brave Orchid Hong

No Name Aunt

No Name Aunt was Maxine's aunt who disgraced the family years before Maxine's birth. The aunt was Maxine's father's sister. No one speaks of this aunt. If family members spoke of her, then they would be admitting that she ever existed. According to Chinese tradition, a person who disgraces a family is a person whose existence is denied. According to the Hongs, this aunt never lived.

No Name Aunt's husband left for America in 1924 with Maxine's father. The aunt and her husband had just married. Years after the aunt's husband left, however, Maxine's mother noticed that the aunt looked pregnant. The family pretended not to see it and did not discuss it among themselves or with her. For the aunt to be pregnant so long after her husband had left was unthinkable—a disgrace to the family and to the village in which they lived.

Angry that the aunt should disgrace them, the village people raided the family's property on the night that the baby was to be born, killing their animals and destroying their home. They tore down doors, smeared blood on the walls, demolished food and furniture, and destroyed everything that belonged to the aunt. While no one knew the identity of the aunt's lover, the village people meant the destruction for him, too. The violence demonstrated to the aunt and her lover that the people did not tolerate the couple's breaking tradition. Families were supposed to stay whole. When families allowed outsiders to break their homes apart, everyone suffered the consequences.

The family angrily denounced the aunt after the villagers had left. They told her that she no longer existed for them, calling her "ghost" and wishing death upon her. She ran outside to the pigsty where she went into labor and delivered the baby. Knowing that she and the baby would have no home and would never be accepted, she chose to end its life and her own. She drowned her baby and herself in the family's well. In death, she became the "the drowned one," a weeping ghost whom Chinese fear because the ghost waits by the well to pull in a substitute.

Second Aunt

See Moon Orchid

Ting-Ting

See Maxine Hong

Ying Lan

See Brave Orchid Hong

Themes

Identity and Search for Self

People form their personal identities through life experiences and interactions with the people around them. *The Woman Warrior* collects five stories from Kingston's life that contribute to her growth as a person and the development of her identity.

From the time Maxine is a small child, she questions who she really is, and where she belongs in her family, Chinese culture, and American culture. As a kindergartner, Maxine does not speak. She does not talk to her classmates or to her teachers. She struggles to overcome her inability to talk, trying to discover herself and to connect to her Chinese and American communities. Her mother's "talk stories" and admonitions about "ghosts" keep Maxine suspended between Chinese and American cultures. For three years, her silence is total. Underscoring the strangeness of her silence, she covers her school paintings in black paint. Her teachers fear for her sanity.

Maxine questions her mother's love for her, too. She sees that her parents treat the girls in the family differently than they treat the boys. For example, the family holds special birthday celebrations for the boys and praises their accomplishments. On the other hand, the family members insult the girls and ignore them at every opportunity. Maxine's mother, especially, sends her messages that make her feel powerless. She berates Maxine, telling her that she is stupid and ugly. Yet, in a contradictory way, Maxine's mother tries to empower her, too, by allowing her glimpses of a different life. She tells Maxine stories of Fa Mu Lan, the famous girl warrior, who is strong, smart, and brave. Hearing these stories gives Maxine an idea that women might live lives entirely different from the one she lives or the one her mother lives. She dreams of herself as a woman warrior.

Maxine's mother, too, suffers an identity crisis. In China, Brave Orchid left her role as a traditional Chinese woman to attend medical school in a distant city. Upon graduation, she practiced medicine as a respected doctor and midwife. She comes to America, however, and finds herself the same mother, wife, and slave that she was before she became a doctor.

When Maxine reaches the sixth grade, her silent frustrations catch up with her and prompt her to attack another quiet Chinese girl, who reminds Maxine too much of herself. As a result, Maxine discovers and releases her angry voice, which she later uses to confront her mother. In voicing her frustrations, anger, and fears, Maxine reviews the indignities she has suffered. Her irate mother tells her to leave.

At a distance from her mother and her Chinese traditions, Maxine begins to reconcile her Chinese self and her American self. She comes to terms with her family and begins to understand her heritage. She even begins to "talk story" herself. She at last claims an identity of her own.

Flesh vs. Spirit

Maxine's mother cautions her constantly about the various "ghosts" among whom she must live in America, warning Maxine not to imitate them. As a result, Maxine fears all the White Ghosts from the Taxi Ghost to the Police Ghost. She most fears the Newsboy Ghost, however. He stands in the street without his parents; she marvels at this blatant disobedience and runs from him in fear. Her mother reminds her, too, that Chinese ghosts exist in their own family and that she should absolutely avoid their mistakes. The No-Name Aunt, for one, represents family disgrace brought on by an overt act of defiance of tradition.

Though the ghosts in Maxine's life are not the supernatural kind, they cause her to experience the same kind of breathlessness people feel when they think they have encountered the supernatural. She feels smothered by the sheer number of American ghosts who surround her every day.

Only after Maxine reaches adulthood does she realize that her mother's talk of ghosts was really only Brave Orchid's denial of her life in America and a refusal to let go of her Chinese self. Eventually, Maxine's mother releases the image of the old China, accepting that it is not the same China that she knew in her past. As a result, Maxine can free the "ghosts" that have haunted her all her life and no longer fears China. When she does this, she

Topics for Further Study

- Compare and contrast the Chinese tradition of "talking story" to traditions of oral storytelling in other cultures. Describe the relative importance of the tradition in various cultures and explain the purposes the tradition serves for different peoples.

- Research the history of Chinese immigration in the United States. When did it begin? For what reasons did the Chinese leave their own country? Where are the largest populations of Chinese in the United States? How have they adapted to this culture?

- Explore the history of Chinese laundries in the United States. Why did many Chinese immigrants find employment in this particular industry?

- Read about the role of women in China. Compare and contrast the role of women in China to the role of women in the United States.

- In the novel *The Woman Warrior,* Kingston recalls her early years in school, particularly her kindergarten year when teachers were disturbed by her black paintings and her silence. Assume the role of a child psychologist and offer an informed opinion of her reasons for these actions. Then, prescribe a course of action for the teachers and her parents.

- Take Kingston's position and defend your silence and black paintings. Defend your actions from the viewpoint of your life experiences and their contributions toward making you the successful adult you now are.

- Why do you think that Kingston spent eighteen months in bed after she confronted the silent Chinese girl? Defend your answer.

finds she is able to accept both her mother and her own Chinese heritage.

Sexism

Maxine receives mixed messages from her mother regarding a woman's role in society. Sharing talk-story myths about the famous woman warrior, Fa Mu Lan, Brave Orchid permits Maxine to imagine herself as the victorious heroine. She dashes Maxine's dreams, however, with repeated stories such as the No Name Aunt's. Brave Orchid reminds Maxine through these stories that traditions live on in China, and traditions cannot be broken without punishment. Chinese women spend their lives serving their husbands and, especially, their in-laws. As is symbolized by the Chinese tradition of foot-binding, Chinese women are bound to a lifetime of self-denial. A proper Chinese woman allows her husband to provide for her while she serves as his maid and mistress.

Even in America, Chinese families nurture misogyny, or hatred of women. The grandfather of Maxine's cousins, for example, calls the girls "maggots." The woman-warrior image taunts Maxine, who despises the special treatment her brothers receive. The families hold big celebrations for the boys' birthdays and buy them wonderful gifts, like bicycles. They ignore the girls on their birthdays. When girls do get gifts, they receive such things as typewriters, which prepare them for service. Maxine sees these discrepancies and reacts to them in a confrontation with her mother. Maxine would like to be the woman warrior, the Chinese woman who successfully breaks tradition.

Style

Style

Literary experts both praise and criticize Kingston's writing style. She combines fact with fiction—relying on her own memories, her mother's "talk stories," and her own vivid imagination—to create a view of what it is like to grow up a Chinese-American female. The critics who appreciate her ability to mold stories in this way especially like the way she reworks traditional myths and legends to modernize their messages. This technique irritates other critics, however, especially those who are Asian Americans. They argue that Kingston's retelling of Chinese myths and legends detracts from the original purposes they were meant to serve. In addition, these critics state that her dependence on so much inventiveness renders her writing difficult to classify as autobiography or fiction.

Structure

In addition to having a unique writing style, Kingston also uses an unusual structure in her organization of *The Woman Warrior*. The central theme focuses on a young Chinese girl's growing up in America and being pulled by the forces of both Chinese and American customs. Yet Kingston creates the drama of the girl's life through five separate stories of events through which the girl has matured. These five episodes help to show how the girl forms an identity for herself through the relationships she has with the women in her life.

Point of View

Kingston's use of the five separate stories allows her to change voices, or to tell the stories from different points of view. She tells four of the five stories from the first-person point of view. Through her own narrative, Kingston can take a stand and report events the way she sees them, speaking out against social and racial injustice. The one story that Kingston tells in the third-person narrative gives her silent aunt, Moon Orchid, a voice. Moon Orchid, never able to adjust to American life, suffers from mental illness. Telling Moon Orchid's story enables Kingston to appease Moon Orchid's "displaced spirit."

Setting

The narrator grows up in Stockton, California, where she was born in 1940. The events that actually occur in her life take place in California. Her imagined warrior life and her mother's "talk stories," however, take place in China. For example, the story of No-Name Aunt, the ghost aunt, occurs in China from about 1924 to 1934. In the chapter "White Tigers," Kingston's imagined self as a woman warrior lives in ancient China. "Shaman" is Brave Orchid's story about her life in China as a medical student and doctor, prior to her coming to America in 1939.

Symbolism

Symbolism provides substance for two of the five stories in *The Woman Warrior*. At the beginning of "Shaman," Brave Orchid is attending medical school after having spent the last decade or more of her adult life serving her husband and family as a traditional Chinese woman. When her fellow students challenge her to investigate a dormitory room that is supposedly haunted, she accepts the dare and spends the night in the room. The next day, she claims to have fought a fierce battle with "Sitting Ghost." She tells her friends that it still

Compare & Contrast

- **6th Century BC-1911 AD:** Confinement and oppression of Chinese women abounds.

- **1912-1928:** Last Chinese monarchy ends. Sun Yat-sen and his successor Yuan Shikai attempt to restore monarchy and are rivaled by warlords.

- **1917-1921:** Revolution in Chinese thought and culture known as the May Fourth Movement. Also, Marxism arrives in China and the Chinese Communist Party begins with Mao Zedong (Mao Tse-tung) in attendance.

- **1921-1927:** Chinese Nationalists (Kuomintang) and Russian Communists join forces.

- **1925:** Chiang Kai-shek takes over military command of Kuomintang.

- **1937:** Japanese invasion of China.

- **1937-1945:** Rapid growth of the Chinese Communist Party, with Mao a national leader. Many Chinese come to the United States under a new immigration law that permits 105 Chinese per year to enter.

- **1949:** People's Republic of China forms with Mao Zedong as chairman.

- **1965:** The Chinese immigration quota is abolished.

- **1966-1969:** The Chinese Cultural Revolution is led by Mao to destroy the liberal elements in China.

- **Today:** The 1990 Immigration Act raises the quota for Chinese immigrants and reorganizes the entrance preference system.

---

threatens them and convinces the girls to help her fight and conquer it. The group holds a ritual that rids the room of the dangerous spirit. This act symbolizes Brave Orchid's battle with the confining role of Chinese women.

In "At the Western Palace," Moon Orchid has arrived from China to live with her sister in California. Moon Orchid epitomizes the traditional Chinese woman. She allows her sister to manipulate a forced meeting between Moon Orchid and her Americanized husband. She does not assert herself in any way. The tiny, gray-haired, old woman keeps quiet about everything and eventually fades away in a mental asylum. Her name, Moon Orchid, symbolizes her nonentity.

Figurative Language

Brave Orchid uses the word "ghost" in a figurative way. That is, the ghosts to which she refers most often are not supernatural beings, but Americans. She warns her children about White Ghosts of all kinds: Teacher Ghosts, Coach Ghosts, Taxi Ghosts, Police Ghosts, the Newsboy Ghost, and so on. Black Ghosts exist, too, but the children could fear them less because they were more distinct;

Black Ghosts could not sneak around as easily as White Ghosts could. Other ghosts to whom Brave Orchid refers less frequently are those Chinese who have brought disgrace upon themselves or their families. No Name Aunt represents these Chinese ghosts.

While Brave Orchid warns her children about American ghosts, she does not mean to belittle Americans. She just refuses to accept her position in America and hates to release her image of herself as a respected Chinese woman.

Historical Context

Women in Chinese Society

Kingston takes revenge on centuries of Chinese female oppression in *The Woman Warrior*. Additionally, she comes to terms with her family and their place in American society. Through her "talk stories" about herself and her female relatives, Kingston paints a picture of Chinese tradition that portrays women as objects controlled by men and used as slaves. From the days of Confucius, and

Life was not easy for Chinese immigrants living in California during the 1930s. Here, unemployed Chinese workers march in Sacramento's Hunger Parade, presenting demands to the California State Legislature.

reaching into the early twentieth century, the Chinese placed family above social order, and men above women. When people married, new family ties formed, and new wives became particularly subservient to their grooms' parents. Women from the higher classes lived extremely secluded lives and suffered such treatments as foot-binding. The Chinese chose young girls who were especially pretty to undergo foot-binding to keep their feet as small as possible. The binder bent the large toe backward, forever deforming the foot. Men favored women with bound feet, a sign of beauty and gen-

tility, because it signified that they could support these women who were incapable of physical labor. While Kingston includes some stories of such subservient women, she also offers glimpses of mythical Chinese women who have broken the bonds of slavery to become warriors, heroines, and swordswomen. Kingston's own mother has offered her these visions. According to critic Diane Johnson in the *New York Review of Books,* Kingston "has been given hints of female power, and also explicit messages of female powerlessness from her mother, who in China had been a doctor and now toiled in the family laundry." Henry Allen, in the *Washington Post,* calls the resulting stories "a wild mix of myth, memory, history and lucidity which verges on the eerie." Mary Gordon gives Kingston credit for the technique, saying in the *New York Times Book Review,* "the blend ... [is as] ... relentless as a truth-seeking child's."

Chinese Political History

The Woman Warrior opens with Kingston's mother telling the story of her husband's sister who disgraced the family by having a child out of wedlock and then committing suicide. The year was 1924, when many men left China for America. China was experiencing political unrest at the time. After living under more than 3,000 years of imperialistic rule, Chinese revolutionaries forced the last Qing emperor to abdicate the throne. Sun Yat-sen became the temporary president of the Chinese Republic, supported by even the most conservative Chinese. Yuan Shikai succeeded Sun Yat-sen but died in 1916. From that time until 1928, warlords ruled China. Even though the government was unstable, the people of China began to think more liberally, adopting many Western ideas, denouncing imperialism, and attacking the social order established by Confucius. Historians refer to this nationalistic period as the May Fourth movement. At the same time, though, many Chinese embraced the newly-introduced Marxism, with Mao Zedong (Mao Tse-tung) leading the first Chinese Communist Party.

Even though China now boasted a Communist party, Russian Communists did not support it. They instead rallied behind the Nationalist Party because it had more members and more political clout. Their intent was to rid China of the warlord influence and make way for socialism. Sun Yat-sen led this Nationalist Party, or the Kuomintang (Guomindang), from 1912 until 1925. In 1923, the Russian Communists and Kuomintang demanded that Chinese individuals join their ranks, and the Kuomintang began to adhere more closely to Russian Communism. This alliance did not last long, however, because the Kuomintang troops attacked the Chinese Communist Party and the Shanghai labor movement in a bloody massacre. Chiang Kai-shek, who had been Sun Yat-sen's military advisor, led the massacre and took over the Kuomintang when Sun died in 1925. It was Chiang and his troops who, during the Northern Expedition, destroyed the power of Chinese warlords. Kingston refers to both the warlords and the Communist rule in the chapter entitled "White Tigers." In a blending of ancient Chinese myth and modern Chinese history, she envisions herself as the female warrior who avenges the wrongs her family and country have suffered at the hands of the revolutionaries and Communists.

Critical Overview

Kingston finished writing *The Woman Warrior* during her seventeen-year stay in Hawaii. At the same time that she was working on *The Woman Warrior,* she was also writing *China Men.* She told Timothy Pfaff of the *New York Times Book Review* that she thinks of the two books as "one big book. I was writing them more or less simultaneously." She hesitated to send *The Woman Warrior* to publishers, however, because she did not know what they would think of it. While publishers seldom print a writer's first attempt, Alfred A. Knopf, Inc., took a chance on Kingston and her book's unusual style and content. The company published *The Woman Warrior* in 1976 as nonfiction. Surprisingly, the public liked the book so much, it promptly made the bestseller list. It also earned the National Book Critics Circle Award for nonfiction that year and held the honor of being one of the top ten nonfiction books of the 1970s.

Critics applaud Kingston for her strong feminist voice and her ability to battle social and racial injustices through her use of words. In the *Dictionary of Literary Biography,* Pin-chia Feng calls Kingston "one of the most outspoken contemporary feminist writers" and a "word warrior." Critics also credit Kingston's expertise for translating stories told in oral form into written stories that maintain the unique characteristics of the Cantonese dialect that is spoken in her community. She does a thorough job of telling about a Chinese-American girl's growing up and being torn between Chinese traditions and American customs. Through a combination of myth and reality, she uncovers the Chinese tradition of male dominance and female oppression, and a Chinese-American girl's battle against it. In a *Washington Post Book World* review, William McPherson describes *The Woman Warrior* as "a strange, sometimes savagely terrifying and, in the literal sense, wonderful story of growing up caught between two highly sophisticated and utterly alien cultures, both vivid, often menacing and equally mysterious." Yet Kingston also builds the less-alien image of an important, though seldom-voiced, strength in ties between a Chinese-American girl and her mother. A good example of the result of a modern-thinking Chinese mother's influence on her Chinese-American daughters occurs at the end of Moon Orchid's story, *At the Western Palace,* in *The Woman Warrior.* Kingston writes, "Brave Orchid's daughters decided fiercely that they would never let men be unfaithful to them. All her children made up their minds to major in science or mathematics." Kingston's blend of legend and personal truths results in a work so unique that it is difficult to classify as fiction or nonfiction, biographical or autobiographical. Paul Gray says in *Time,* "Art has intervened here. The stories may or may not be transcripts of actual experience."

The very traits that earn the book favorable reviews, though, are also the ones that reap criticism. For example, many reviewers appreciate Kingston's attempts to tell about the Chinese-American woman's experience in America through the author's own life stories. Others, however, do not think that her stories present the truth for the community of all Chinese-American women. These critics think that Kingston combines too much fiction with the truth in her stories to be able to claim that she's reporting the Chinese-American woman's reality. Another aspect of Kingston's style that earns both approval and disapproval is her blending of traditional Chinese myths and legends with the events of her own life. Asian-American reviewers and scholars who study Chinese customs, history, language, and literature very much disapprove of this technique. They say that Kingston is twisting long-time Chinese history and legend, changing them to fit her needs. The best example of this in *The Woman Warrior* occurs in the chapter "White Tigers." The original legend tells of a woman who replaces her elderly father in a military draft. Kingston's version, however, makes the woman an aggressor who takes revenge on male dominance by killing the emperor. Critics view this misrepresentation as Kingston's most crucial mistake because it makes the book generic, unbelievable, and not true to Chinese heritage. Paul Gray, a critic for *Time,* agrees with the Asian-American critics and scholars, saying the book is "drenched in alienation" and "haunts a region somewhere between autobiography and fiction."

While critics cannot agree to appreciate the methods Kingston used to write *The Woman Warrior,* they can agree on its power. The book invokes a broad range of emotions—including rage, pride, enchantment, and inspiration. As a result, *The Woman Warrior* has won many awards, and educators use it extensively not only in literature classes, but also in women's studies, sociology, ethnic studies, and history classes.

Criticism

Donna Woodford

Donna Woodford is a doctoral candidate at Washington University and has written for a wide variety of academic journals and educational publishers. In the following essay she discusses how the theme of the power of language unites the stories that make up Kingston's autobiography.

Maxine Hong Kingston's autobiography, *The Woman Warrior: Memoirs of a Girlhood among Ghosts,* differs from most autobiographies in that it is not a first-person narration of the author's life. Rather, it is a form of nonfiction that, as Paul Mandelbaum says, "allows for—even thrives on—the vagaries of memory, translation, and point of view." Kingston tells her own life story by telling the stories of other women whose lives have impacted hers. This work of nonfiction is made up of memories, fantasies, and speculations about these women. In telling the stories of her mother, her aunts, the folk figure Fa Mu Lan, and the historical figure Ts'ai Yen, Kingston is seeking to find "ancestral help" which will allow her to understand her own life. If she can see their lives "branching into" her own, then she can better understand her own place in the world. In telling these stories she is also struggling to reconcile her identity as a member of two cultures, Chinese and American, who does not feel entirely at home in either culture. As a Chinese American woman she struggles to combat what Shirley Geok-Lin Lim has called "the cultural silencing of Chinese in American society and … the gendered silencing of women in Chinese society." She combats both of these forms of silence through the telling of stories about women who are either literally or mythically her ancestors, and because words are her weapons against silence, racism, and sexism, the power of language becomes a central and unifying theme in the book and the means through which Kingston can discover and relate her own identity.

The first chapter of Kingston's autobiography tells the story of the "no name woman," her aunt who disgraced the family by committing adultery, having a baby, and then drowning herself in the family well. Because this is a secret, shameful

What Do I Read Next?

- *China Men* follows Kingston's *The Woman Warrior.* While Kingston actually started this book prior to *The Woman Warrior,* Knopf did not publish it until 1980. *China Men* tells stories of Kingston's male ancestors. Kingston wrote this book to restore her Chinese family history and to take a new look at it in relation to American history.

- Kingston's *Tripmaster Monkey,* published by Knopf in 1989, continues her mix of Chinese mythology with fiction. The main character, Wittman Ah-Sing, is a fifth-generation Californian, Berkeley graduate, and playwright who "trips" his way from city to city trying to create his own theatre. In his drug-induced state, he imitates the Monkey King from Chinese mythology. Critics recognize this book for its diverse use of language.

- *The Joy Luck Club,* published by Putnam's Sons in 1989, is a story written by Chinese-American author Amy Tan. The book tells the stories of four Chinese-American daughters and their relationships with their Chinese mothers. These stories provide a good basis for comparison with Kingston's female characters in *The Woman Warrior.*

- Amy Tan's second novel, *The Kitchen God's Wife,* was published by Putnam in 1991. This book deals with female-female relationships and the effects Chinese male tradition and abuse can have on those relationships.

- The Chinese sister in Amy Tan's 1996 novel, *The Hundred Secret Senses,* convinces her American-born sister that she can communicate with the dead. The "ghosts" in this book evoke images of the "ghosts" in Kingston's *The Woman Warrior.*

---

story, the chapter and the book begin with Kingston's mother telling her, "You must not tell anyone what I am about to tell you." Thus even the opening line of the book suggests the immense power of language. Kingston, in thinking about this story, says, "I have thought that sex was unspeakable and words so strong and fathers so frail that 'aunt' would do my father mysterious harm." But she comes to realize that the silence is not only a way of protecting her father and the family from shame, but also a way of punishing her aunt. Denying her aunt their voices and refusing to tell her story or even to acknowledge that she was born is the harshest form of punishment the family can inflict, and Kingston, by including her aunt's story as part of her autobiography, is reversing that punishment, but she is also endangering herself. She may become the "substitute" for her aunt. Her mother has told her this "story to grow up on" as a warning that if she is rebellious like her aunt, she could also be denied a story that ties her to her family and her culture. The story of her aunt highlights the dangers of speaking out even as it emphasizes the power of language.

The second chapter also emphasizes the power of language and story telling, but in a more positive manner. Although Kingston is distressed at the many Chinese expressions which compare girls to maggots or slaves, she also acknowledges that the Chinese stories her parents tell her offer another image of women. Girls can grow up to be "heroines, swordswomen." Kingston realizes that when she is listening to her mother tell stories she is "in the presence of great power." The story of Fa Mu Lan, which begins as one of stories told to Kingston by her mother and continues as a fantasy in which Kingston becomes Fa Mu Lan, makes the power of language even clearer. Fa Mu Lan becomes a representative of the power of language not only because she is a figure "told of in fairy tales," remembered and revered, unlike Kingston's no-name aunt, but also because of the words which are carved on her back, "words in red and black files, like an army." The words themselves become soldiers in the war, and they also turn Fa Mu Lan's body into a weapon, a living testament of the wrongs done to her family. The words furthermore connect Kingston, the writer, to Fa Mu Lan, the woman warrior, since both use words as weapons: "what [they] have in common are the words at [their] backs." If the story of Kingston's no-name aunt illustrated that refusing to tell stories could be a form of punishment, Kingston's version of the Fa Mu Lan story shows that telling a story can be a form of vengeance: "The idioms for revenge are 'report a crime' and 'report to five families.' The reporting is the vengeance—not the beheading, not the gutting, but the words." Kingston, through her writing, discovers that she, like her mother and Fa Mu Lan, has the great power of story telling.

In the third chapter, "Shaman," Kingston gives a more detailed picture of her mother's powerful use of language. She tells the story of her mother as a young woman who, like Fa Mu Lan, leaves her family to be educated and then returns to serve her community. She tells of how her mother and the other women at the medical school are "new women, scientists who changed the rituals" and who learn to chant the "horizontal names of one generation" instead of the traditional chant of ancestor's names. Brave Orchid's courage in forging these new trails connects her, like her daughter, to the woman warrior. And, like her daughter and the Woman Warrior, Brave Orchid is able to use language in battle, as when she fights the sitting ghost. Her fight against the ghost is primarily one of language, insults which she hurls at the ghost even as it is crushing her. She defeats the ghost, as Sidonie Smith has noted, with "the boldness of her word and the power of the images she voices to taunt him into submission and cowardice." Her command of language not only allows her to defeat the ghost but also to describe the battle to her friends in such a way that she makes herself seem stronger and nobler. In Smith's words, she "author[s] herself as a powerful protagonist." It is this same powerful authoring that Kingston will inherit from her mother, and this is how her mother's story becomes Kingston's story and provides her with ancestral help. The chapter closes with Kingston realizing how much she and her mother have in common: "I am really a Dragon, as she is a Dragon, both of us born in dragon years. I am practically a first daughter of a first daughter." Their use of language and storytelling connects them and empowers both of them.

The fourth chapter tells the story of another aunt, Brave Orchid's sister, Moon Orchid, who lacks the story telling power of her sister and niece. Moon Orchid, unlike her sister, is not brave enough to venture alone into new territories. She waits for thirty years for her husband to send for her. Nor does she have the brave, commanding voice of her sister. When forced to confront her husband she cannot even manage to speak: "her voice was fading to a whisper." Her lack of language becomes the weapon her husband uses against her when he tells her that he has important guests who come into his house and "you can't talk to them. You can barely talk to me." Not only is she unable to leave the confines of her family and create a new path, as Brave Orchid did, but her lack of language also prevents her from maintaining her role within her family. She is speechless and therefore helpless. Without the security of her husband and her traditional place in Chinese society, Moon Orchid goes insane, which Brave Orchid recognizes by the change in her story telling: "The difference between mad people and sane people … is that sane people have variety when they talk story. Mad people have only one story that they talk over and over." But if Moon Orchid is not able to empower herself through story telling, her story does become a source of empowerment for her nieces. Kingston weaves the simple story of her aunt into a complicated knot which gives her ancestral help by showing her the importance of being strong and vocal like her mother and not weak and quiet like her aunt, and all the girls vow never to let a man be unfaithful to them. Their aunt has become another family story for them to grow on, a warning of the danger of weakness and silence just as the story of the no name aunt was a warning of the danger of breaking boundaries.

The final chapter is full of powerful stories about language. Kingston describes her difficulties in speaking up for herself, and she wonders if it is because her mother cut too much of her tongue in an attempt to ensure that she would never be tongue-tied. She also tells how she cornered the quiet girl in the bathroom at school, taking her fear of her own silence out on the only person quieter and weaker than she felt herself to be. Additionally Kingston confesses that she is ashamed of her mother's loud voice and the way she is always insisting that Kingston translate embarrassing things for her. She reveals how her difficulty with speaking is connected to her confusion over her place in two different cultures: "Normal Chinese women's voices are strong and bossy. We American-Chinese girls had to whisper to make ourselves American-feminine. Apparently we whispered even more than the Americans." But the story with which she ends this chapter, and the book, resolves these conflicts. The story of Ts'ai Yen, a poet alone in a foreign land, becomes the story of Kingston and her mother. Both of them are, like Ts'ai Yen, women using language to help them make a place for themselves in a foreign land. And like Ts'ai Yen, they are, through language, able to bring their two cultures together, to "translate well" between them.

Thus, though Kingston's book is not a traditional autobiography, it does relate her struggle to understand herself as a member of two cultures, and it details her search for a voice of her own. As Sidonie Smith has said, Kingston recognizes the "inextricable relationship between an individual's sense of 'self' and the community's stories of selfhood, [and] self-consciously reads herself into existence through the stories her culture tells about women." As a member of more than one culture, Kingston cannot "read herself into existence" with only one story. Since language is such a crucial part of her identity, the stories with which she chooses to define herself must also convey the power of language. By weaving together the stories of these women and the impact of language and story telling on their lives, Kingston is truly telling the story of her own life, and the story of her struggle to find a language in which to tell her story.

Source: Donna Woodford, in an essay for *Novels for Students*, Gale, 1999.

Malini Schueller

In this excerpt, Schueller examines the way in which The Woman Warrior *questions accepted cultural definitions of female and ethnic identity.*

Ever since its publication in 1976, Maxine Hong Kingston's *The Woman Warrior* has been praised as a feminist work. But while critics have written extensively about the articulation of female experience in *The Woman Warrior,* they have been unable to deal simultaneously with the questions of national and racial identity that the book so powerfully raises. However, if we approach women's writing as centrally concerned not strictly with gender but with oppression, we can fruitfully examine the conjuncture and relationship between female and ethnic identity, an important issue not only for this text but for feminist theory as well. I will briefly examine the politicization of female identity offered by some feminist critics and then examine *The Woman Warrior* as a dialogic text, one

which subverts singular definitions of racial and ethnic identity and which valorizes intersubjectivity and communication....

Feminist critics have long recognized that what constitutes female experience is not biological gender or a specific female psyche but the constraints and limitations felt by women as a result of the cultural constitution of gender and the phallocentric organization of society. To write socially and politically as a woman is therefore to question the truth status and ostensible ideological neutrality of cultural norms and institutions.... What is politically important for women and racial minorities is not to frame correct definitions of female and ethnic identity but to question all such definitions. Above all it means to reject the concept of a stable and autonomous self upon which such definitions depend....

Few contemporary American writers are as aware of the need to question and subvert accepted cultural definitions as Maxine Hong Kingston. *The Woman Warrior* is a sustained subversion of cultural, racial and gender definitions and an affirmation of a radical intersubjectivity as the basis of articulation.

The Woman Warrior is a collection of "memoirs" of Kingston's experiences of growing up in an immigrant family in Stockton, California. Kingston reveals the squalor and poverty of Chinatowns, the endemic racism, the traumas of acculturation in a hostile environment, and her own attempt to subvert gender hierarchies by imaginative identification with the woman warrior. But although Kingston writes polemically against the subjugation of women and the racial hostility experienced by Chinese Americans, she does not do so from a position of stability or unity. Articulation itself is a complex issue in the text. The very act of speaking involves breaking through the gender and race barriers that suppress voicing from the margins. But the voice Kingston speaks through is not isolated and autonomous. It refracts, echoes, and is creatively conjoined with the numerous voices with which it interacts. This undefined basis of narration dramatizes Kingston's determination not to create singular definitions of ethnic identity in order to combat the impoverishing stereotypes to which Chinese Americans are subject, not to postulate the foundations of a new hierarchy.

It is clear at the very outset that the act of articulation itself will be a major concern in the book. Kingston begins her memoirs with a secrecy oath imposed on her by her indomitable mother: "You must not tell anyone," and a moral drawn from the story of the adulterous aunt who has been banished from family memory. "Don't humiliate us. You wouldn't like to be forgotten as if you had never been born." Kingston is aware of the temerity involved in the very act of her writing. To articulate herself she must break through the numerous barriers that condemn her to voicelessness. The unnamed narrator thus begins her recollections with the act of listening rather than speaking. Sworn to silence, she hears the tale of the unnamed aunt who gives "silent birth" to "save her inseminator's name." This initial story establishes the denial of expression women are condemned to in patriarchy and the cultural stranglehold the narrator must fight in order to express herself....

But the anxiety of articulation is also peculiarly a racial one. Kingston is sensitive to the brutality and degradation experienced by Chinese immigrants. *China Men* records the heroism of Chinese railroad workers and sugarcane planters who survive hostility and violence. Living in a culture that had for long grouped Orientals with imbeciles and denied Chinese immigrants legal and naturalization rights, the present-day immigrants in *The Woman Warrior* still live in fear. Immigrants thus "guard their real names with silence" and even after years of living in America avoid signing innocuous permission slips for their children at school. The narrator realizes that "silence had to do with being a Chinese girl." In the American school she is overcome by dumbness, her voice reduced to a whisper. In the Chinese school she finds her voice but it is a strained one: "You could hear splinters in my voice, bones rubbing jagged against one another."...

Kingston's voicelessness is a symbolic expression of the culture's refusal to give her voice legitimacy. But the alternative to this disempowerment, Kingston knows, is not to create a "true" Chinese woman's voice or to define a singular Chinese identity to celebrate, but to question the very political structures that make positions of power and powerlessness possible. Kingston deconstructs oppositions between American and Chinese, male and female, and most importantly between Self and Other by articulating herself through a language in which opposed and diverse voices constantly coexist. By doing so, Kingston questions the values of the autonomous self and definitions of racial and sexual identity, and simultaneously presents dialogic intersubjectivity and community as the realm of hope and possibility....

Kingston deals with the necessity of maintaining and creating multiple ideological positions, of always letting the numerous voices echo in her own articulations. For Kingston this refraction of other voices is an affirmation of community and diversity. Thus it is appropriate that the final story of the book emphasizes differences and communicative interaction. "Here is a story my mother told me ... recently, when I told her I also talk story. The beginning is hers, the ending, mine." As opposed to the beginning of the book where the mother silences her, here the narrator emphasizes how their voices are inextricably and dialogically linked, even if they are different....

The narrating voice as it emerges in *The Woman Warrior* is thus highly provisional, always full of echoes of other voices, and never autonomous. Kingston does not merely wish to appropriate power and write an authoritative "marginal" text. She wishes to celebrate marginality as a position of writing and not to postulate a new source of authority or a new hierarchy.... Denying universality, absolute values, and an autonomous self are crucial to writings of all marginal groups.

Just as it is important for Kingston to treat gender as a site of difference, it is vital for her to treat race too as a play of differences. Indeed to view *The Woman Warrior* as a book about an essential, abstract, female self beyond culture and society is to miss the point entirely. The immigrant experience is an integral part of the book. Kingston is sensitive to the dehumanizing definitions Chinese Americans are subject to and is determined not to perpetuate the same by merely inverting the hierarchies. At the base of such definitions is the destructive binary logic which hierarchically divides male and female, self and other, white and non white. [In his book *Orientalism,* Random House, 1978] Edward Said has compellingly demonstrated how such hierarchies have operated in depictions of the "Oriental" as the passive and denatured Other. In *The Woman Warrior* Kingston questions and undoes oppositions that make such sterile racial definitions possible.

The narrator of *The Woman Warrior* is uniquely positioned to dialogically question racial oppositions. She is the daughter of Chinese immigrants for whom America is temporary exile, and China home, but who nevertheless will stay in America. Her only reality is America, but it is the America of the margins (Kingston makes no bones about Stockton being a racial and economic ghetto). She goes to Chinese school and to American school. Her own undefinable position is a metaphor for the way in which ethnicity will operate: "I learned to make my mind large, as the universe is large, so that there is room for paradoxes.... The dragon lives in the sky, ocean, marshes, and mountains; and the mountains are also its cranium.... It breathes fire and water; and sometimes the dragon is one, sometimes many." ...

On an obvious level Kingston obviously creates clear cultural oppositions, indeed as if she were speaking in the voice of the monocultural reader. American life is logical, concrete, free, and guarantees individual happiness; Chinese life is illogical, superstition-ridden, constricted by social roles, and weighted down by community pressures. The American school teaches that an eclipse is "just a shadow the earth makes when it comes between the moon and the sun"; the Chinese mother prepares the children to "slam pots and lids together to scare the frog from swallowing the moon" during the next eclipse. American culture promises the young girl opportunity for excellence if she gets straight 'A's. She can go to college. But she also has the freedom to be a lumberjack in Oregon. In China the girl fears she will be sold as a slave; or within the immigrant community she will be married off to a Fresh Off the Boat Chinese. Indeed the structure of hierarchical oppositions is so cleverly set up that the narrator's growth might be equated with being fully "American."

But Kingston sets up these hierarchies only to subvert and make undecidable these singular oppositions. "To make my waking life American-normal, I turn on the lights before anything untoward makes an appearance. I push the deformed into my dreams, which are in Chinese, the language of impossible dreams." But just as the conventional American reader might begin to feel at ease with the comfortable hierarchy (American-normal, Chinese-deformed), Kingston challenges it. "When the thermometer in our laundry reached one hundred and eleven degrees on summer afternoons, either my mother or my father would say that it was time to tell another ghost story so that we could get some good chills up our backs." American-normal reality gets so nightmarish that Chinese ghost stories are needed to chase it away into imaginary chills. Not only is the cultural hierarchy subverted but the traditional associations of logicality and dreams are suspended....

Kingston's questioning of oppositions and her resistance to definition are intensely political strategies. For the marginal writer who is often the sub-

ject of singular definition, such a dialogic stance is often a strategy of survival. Kingston thus problematizes and subverts racial definitions in order to reveal the dangers of maintaining them....

[Kingston] presents Chinese culture as a conglomeration of diverse, multiple, often contradictory values that she does not attempt to unify into an easy explanation. Such unities, for Kingston, are the hallmarks of tourist propaganda, not lived culture. Kingston does not believe in the possibility of representing Chinese culture because that assumes that there is a simple "Chinese" reality and culture easily available for representation. As Kingston said [in Marilyn Yalom, *Women Writers of the West Coast: Speaking of Their Lives and Careers,* Capra Press (Santa Barbara), 1983], "There are Chinese American writers who seek to represent the rest of us; they end up with tourist manuals or chamber of commerce public relations whitewash." In *The Woman Warrior* every aspect of Chinese culture and Chinese immigrant life is so diverse that it resists generalization. The striking contrast between the strength of the narrator's mother, Brave Orchid, who becomes a doctor in China and fights for her rights in America and Moon Orchid who accepts the role of abandoned wife, is only one of several. Immigrant Chinese range from the wealthy, Americanized husband of Moon Orchid, to the Stockton Chinese who maintain their native village affiliations, to refugees from the revolution. And the difference between the immigrant Chinese and the Chinese from the narrator's village is so vast that to the untutored eyes of Moon Orchid, the former appear like foreigners. "I'm glad to see the Americans talk like us" says Moon Orchid to her sister. "Brave Orchid was ... again startled at her sister's denseness. 'These aren't the Americans. These are the overseas Chinese'."...

The Woman Warrior thus subverts all forms that have the potential of providing cultural stability and unity.... Kingston writes polemically as a Chinese-American woman confronting and battling with the patriarchal, white American culture but she does so from a position that is radically unstable. She writes as a woman, but destabilizes the concept of gender; she speaks as a Chinese American, but questions racial definitions. Authorship therefore becomes a complicated question because Kingston refuses to give us a traditional position from which she articulates. This does not mean that the text is apolitical or socially meaningless. Gender and race are important to Kingston, but not as transcendent and true categories. Kingston does not dismiss or destroy these categories, but radically transvalues them by making them dialogically interactive. And because she subverts these categories only in relation to the singular definitions imposed by the dominant culture and does not attempt to lay the foundations of another (more pure or true) set of categories, she resists impoverishing the issues of gender and race.

Source: Malini Schueller, "Questioning Race and Gender Definitions: Dialogic Subversions in *The Woman Warrior,*" in *Criticism,* Vol XXXI, No. 4, Fall, 1989, pp. 421–437.

Amy Ling

In the following article, Ling contrasts the role of woman as victim and victor in Kingston's The Woman Warrior.

In *Autobiographical Occasions and Original Acts* [1982], Albert Stone identifies several situations which he calls "occasions" for the writing of autobiography. The first is "the situation of an old man looking back over a long career and significant stretch of history to recapture the personal past against the background of sweeping cultural change." As examples of this type, Stone discusses *The Education of Henry Adams* and the *Autobiography of W. E. B. Du Bois,* though the most famous example, of course, would be Benjamin Franklin's *Autobiography....* Stone's second autobiographical occasion is the account of one's spiritual growth or journey, as Henry David Thoreau's *Walden* (1854), *Black Elk Speaks* (1931), and more recently Annie Dillard's *Pilgrim at Tinker Creek* (1974). A third occasion is physical or psychic violence, as recorded in the lives of Helen Keller, Maya Angelou, Malcolm X, and Alexander Berkman's *Prison Memoirs of an Anarchist.* Stone's fourth occasion is the need to bridge a psychic split between private and public self, a "split in social experience (which) ... defines women's identities even more painfully—and creatively—than it does for other groups ... tensions between old conventions and new circumstances, between rigid social stereotypes and the urge to define oneself in wider terms." This is the situation which occasioned Maxine Hong Kingston's critically acclaimed book, *The Woman Warrior* (1976).

Constructing a plausible self-identity is, according to Stone, an original act, an act of creation or recreation, necessarily involving an examination of the cultural myths and national contexts which shaped this self. And since "myth and ideology, as Warren Susman has argued, are equally essential to history in general, their presence and weight must be traced in personal history as well." All of

this Kingston does. For some readers, her self-recreation is a confusing act because she does not remain within the traditional bounds of any genre. *The Woman Warrior* is not structured by chronology, the usual method, nor is its mode strictly factual; instead, the narrative is fractured, and fact and fiction are mingled. Kingston blends myth and history, not the confirmable myths of the Chinese people, but myths as filtered to her through her mother's consciousness and memory, actually what Kingston remembers of her mother's stories. As E. L. Doctorow inserted facts, historical figures, into his fiction *Ragtime,* Kingston incorporates fiction (the legend of Fa Mulan) into her facts.... On a fundamental level, *The Woman Warrior* is made coherent by thematic threads: woman as both victim and victor, and voice as power.

Woman as victim is dramatically established in the very first episode, which begins with an injunction and a simple disclosure:

> "You must not tell anyone," my mother said, "what I am about to tell you. In China your father had a sister who killed herself. She jumped into the family well. We say that your father has all brothers because it is as if she had never been born...." Kingston is told this story at puberty as a lesson and a warning; a woman must guard her chastity and honor or she will be cast off. Her own family's silence negates the rebellious aunt's existence and is greater punishment than the havoc wreaked on the family home by angered villagers.

However, instead of accepting the story as a moral lesson and keeping it to herself, as an obedient Chinese daughter should, Kingston, the American, not only disobeys her mother's injunction by telling the story but even elaborates on it. She speculates on the circumstances that would bring a woman to an affair, moving from the most conventional explanations to the most shocking. Perhaps it was coercion and "some man had commanded her to lie with him and be his secret evil" or perhaps, a dreamer like Kingston herself, she fell in love with an ephemeral aspect:

> She looked at a man because she liked the way the hair was tucked behind his ears, or she liked the question-mark line of a long torso curving at the shoulder and straight at the hip. For warm eyes or a soft voice or a slow walk—that's all—a few hairs, a line, a brightness, a sound, a pace, she gave up family. She offered us up for a charm that vanished with tiredness, a pigtail that didn't toss when the wind died. Why the wrong lighting could erase the dearest thing about him. Or she might have been "a wild woman" who "kept rollicking company," or perhaps it was incest. Kingston imagines how this aunt must have felt watching the enraged villagers defile, de-

stroy and loot her family's home and sympathetically and practically wonders if a general famine had anything to do with the punishment's taking the form of stealing the family provisions. She recreates with a heroic cast the aunt's experience of giving birth alone at night under the stars, suckling her baby and finally hardening herself and jumping with it into the family drinking well. The suicide was paradoxically an act of love and caring, for the fate of an unwanted female orphan in old China would invariably be a miserable one.

For twenty years, Kingston had remained silent, joining the rest of her family in punishing this aunt, but now, in telling her story, in calling this outcast "my forerunner," Kingston not only acknowledges her but identifies with this woman who dared to defy conventions, to break taboos, to be her own person. Though victor and vanquished, or victim for our purposes, are generally diametrically opposed, in this instance they may be found in the same person. The no-name aunt is undoubtedly a victim of the conventions of her society, her family, or her personal weakness, but at the same time, in a small measure, she is a victor through her own suicide, for by jumping into the family well, she polluted the family drinking water and gained her revenge. In a larger measure, however, Kingston's telling of her story gains her aunt a victory, for not only is the family silence broken and the aunt restored to her place, but through her speculations, Kingston has extended, to this earlier rebel, not only understanding and sympathy, but even tribute.

The second chapter, "White Tigers," clearly presents woman as victor. Kingston elaborates extensively on the original Chinese legend, which comprises only a dozen lines. Her embellishment includes a mystical Taoist training for the woman warrior's childhood, a life of sacrifice and discipline on a mountain top with an old couple who possess superhuman powers. For Mulan, Kingston borrows a striking event from a legend of a male general, Yueh Fei—the carving of the battle cause in characters on her bare back. In Kingston's version, though Mulan is playing the male role successfully, nonetheless, she does not deny herself female satisfactions, for her fiance joins her on her campaigns, marries her and in secret she bears a child whom she sends back home with her husband until she is able to join them.

These departures from the original ballad, however, are minor. What is significant is that Fa Mulan is clearly a victor in every possible way: on the spiritual as well as physical planes, in both the traditionally male and female spheres of action. She has developed mystical powers as well as military prowess and is both a successful warrior, as well as a wife and mother.

The no-name aunt and Fa Mulan, both introduced to Kingston by her mother, represent the polar extremes of social behavior available to a woman: the victim aunt was obviously the example to avoid; the victorious Mulan, a model to follow. But how, Maxine as a girl wondered, was one to be a woman warrior in the United States, especially when one was so shy among Caucasians that one never said a word and was told she had an I.Q. of zero? Where was one's village to defend? Who were the tyrants and villains? How was a Chinamerican girl to reconcile the stories of her mother's Cantonese past with the realities of her Stockton, California present and forge a harmonious identity out of these conflicting forces?

Kingston raises these questions but does not answer them directly. Instead, she continues with her stories, and in all of them the victor / victim theme is evident.

The author's mother, Brave Orchid, is clearly cut from the heroic, even a mythic stamp, a victor in many ways. She is described in terms of hardness and strength, with "eyes strong as boulders," unsmiling in her photographs, with no time for frivolities "My mother is not soft … does not have smiling eyes … has not learned to place decorations and phonograph needles." Finding that her husband in America does not send for her year after year, though he continues to send her money, she decides to use the money to put herself through a two-year medical school and she becomes one of thirty seven graduates out of an entering class of one hundred and twelve. At medical school, Brave Orchid earns a reputation for being naturally brilliant, by studying in secret, and for courage by successfully exorcising a ghost that terrified all the women in the dormitory. As a doctor, she is committed, hardworking, respected, fearless, delivering monsters without blinking an eye. Finally joining her husband in the United States, she incredibly bore six children after the age of forty-five and worked in the family laundry from 6:30 A.M. to midnight. After the laundry was torn down through urban renewal, even though she could have retired on social security, she worked in the fields, picking tomatoes and potatoes.… Brave Orchid was indeed well-named, and her victorious exploits and accomplishments are a modern equivalent of Fa Mulan's.

Her sister, Moon Orchid, was, by contrast, a victim. In the chapter called "At the Western

Palace," at Brave Orchid's insistence and with her savings, Moon Orchid comes from Hong Kong to the United States to reclaim her "rightful" position as the first wife of her long-estranged, now remarried husband. By old Chinese custom, the husband and all his wives could live under the same roof, with the first wife having preeminence and authority. In America, of course, this cannot be. Brave Orchid's interference in her sister's affairs results in Moon Orchid's humiliation, madness and finally her death. Moon Orchid is a woman in the old-fashioned Chinese mold, having lived a soft life, in a sense by reflected light, on the money sent her from America by this straying husband, she cannot adapt to the American ways of independence and self-assertion, of doing everything for herself, of abandoning the past. She cannot face the shock of harsh reality and her mind gives way.

With all the female models from the distant past and recent history established, Kingston moves on to her own story, showing the ignorance, the bafflement, the conflicts, the self denigration, the stifling she suffered growing up female and Chinamerican under the smothering wings of a strong, willful mother. In this section, the voice becomes the central symbol of identity and power. Those with voices and stories to tell, like her mother, are powerful; those without, herself as a child, are powerless. Throughout her childhood, Kingston believed that her mother had cut her frenum. When Kingston identified with her mother, she was proud: "Sometimes I felt very proud that my mother committed such a powerful act upon me." When considering her personal situation, however, Kingston feared that she had suffered the female equivalent of castration: "At other times I was terrified—the first thing my mother did when she saw me was to cut my tongue." Her mother said she did it to loosen her tongue, to allow it to move in all directions, in any language, but the effect was just the opposite: Maxine became tongue-tied. When she began school and had to speak English for the first time, she became silent. And even today, as an adult, though she admits she is getting better, she says, "A dumbness—a shame—still cracks my voice in two." Her silence was so complete that for three years she even covered all her drawings in a layer of black paint, like a discreet curtain over her privacy. When she found out she was supposed to talk, school became a misery. "The other Chinese girls did not talk either, so I knew the silence had to do with being a Chinese girl." In Chinese school, from 5 to 7:30 P.M. every day, she and the other girls had no difficulty talking, even screaming and

yelling. The problem was only with English, the language of the "foreign ghosts," and was most acute in the early years of school when her mother's influence was strongest.

In the last chapter, "A Song For a Barbarian Reed Pipe" Kingston tells the painful story of her bullying another twelve-year-old Chinamerican classmate whom she hated for being so quiet, so clean, so soft … so much like the model set up for herself. Kingston tries to force the girl to speak up but though she pinches her, pulls her hair, and screams at her, the girl does nothing but cry and will not say a word. The author's own exasperation and self-hatred are vented on this unfortunate classmate but to no avail except to leave Kingston guilty and bed-ridden for the next eighteen months. In this case, the victim was the victor.

In the final episode of the book, Kingston retells a story of a Chinese poetess Ts'ai Yen, born in 175 A.D. who at 20 was kidnapped by a raiding nomadic tribe. She lived twelve years with these barbarians and bore two children who did not speak Chinese but only imitated her sounds and laughed. The only music these people had were crude flutes they attached to their arrows, which sang in flight. One night she heard the flutes, "yearning toward a high note, which they found at last and held—an icicle in the desert" and she began to sing: "a song so high and clear, it matched the flutes. Ts'ai Yen sang about China and her family there. Her words seemed to be Chinese, but the barbarians understood their sadness and anger. Sometimes they thought they could catch barbarian phrases about forever wandering." In finding her voice and singing the stories of her own past, in creating art out of history, the victim Ts'ai Yen, exiled and alone amidst strangers, became a victor. Her children no longer laughed at her but learned her words and sang with her.

In writing *The Woman Warrior,* of course, Maxine Hong Kingston finds and exercises her voice and makes, out of the ghosts of her past—the stories her mother filled and confused her with in childhood—a work of art, a song that becomes "an icicle in the desert," an ephemeral, unlikely, unexpected event. Though "barbarians" may not understand the language, they can understand the emotions behind this song. The ethnicity that was once a handicap, that set her apart from the others, that made her feel inferior and strange is at the same time her heritage, her treasure, and her strength. The same mother that humiliated her by sending her out to demand candy to "rectify" the drugstore's "crime" of making a wrong delivery of medicine (thus bringing illness to the house, according to her mother's way of thinking) is also the source of all these beautiful Chinese legends of feminine valor and courage, resourcefulness and pride. The same mother that tells her that girls were sold as slaves in China and that "it is more profitable to feed geese than daughters" is also the woman who put herself through medical school, who studied while the other students slept, who fearlessly delivered monsters. The mother who filled her life with ghosts from the past and made ghosts of her present ("mailman ghost," "garbage collector ghosts," etc.) was also the one who dared to spend a night in the haunted room and who, with considerable effort, exorcised a ghost that had terrified the entire dormitory.

Throughout the book, Maxine Hong Kingston contrasts her strong, dominant, and domineering mother's talk-story, and her own inability to talk. The belief that her mother had actually cut her frenum, is the powerlessness she suffered in relation to this powerful mother. The book's impetus is the daughter's need to separate herself from her mother, to stand apart, to be her own person, to find her own voice, to reveal her own power. Giving voice to the prodigal aunt's experience in the opening chapter is to assert not only the aunt's existence but Kingston's own. That Kingston's voice is finally so much entangled with her mother's talk-story is inevitable, for most of the stories are the ones her mother told her, embellished by her own imagination. Modestly, Kingston in a 1977 interview [with Nan Robertson, "Ghosts of Girlhood Lift Obscure Book to Peak of Acclaim," *New York Times,* February 12, 1977] said, "My mother is the creative one—the one with the visions and the stories to tell. I'm the technician. She's the great inspiration. I never realized it until I finished the book." However, the final story of Ts'ai Yen is an act of collaboration, which Kingston acknowledges thus, "Here is a story my mother told me, not when I was young, but recently, when I told her I also talk-story. The beginning is hers, the ending, mine."

The Woman Warrior itself is the reconciliation between daughter as victim and mother as victor, but it is simultaneously an acceptance of a difficult past when mother may also be seen as a victim of sorts, crippled in the New World by outdated customs and out-of-place reactions from the Old World. The book is an assertion of the daughter's victory through the printed word despite the tongue whose frenum was cut, as though the voice that was dammed up for so many childhood years had suddenly broken through. Recounting so many of her mother's stories, the author is recognizing her indebtedness, and making of her book an offering of love and peace not only to her mother but to the world. Between the poles of woman as victim and as victor, as humiliated and as heroic, as voiceless and as singer, Maxine Hong Kingston makes her place. *The Woman Warrior* is the record of her struggle to come to terms with all the elements of her Chinese background and their uneasy, often conflicting, relationship to her American self. The resolution is finally the realization that the very elements which made her a "victim" in this society are also the elements that, by her giving them voice and shape and beauty, now make her a "victor." ...

Source: Amy Ling, "Thematic Threads in Maxine Hong Kingston's *The Woman Warrior,*" in *Tamkang Review,* Vol. XIV, Nos. 1–4, Autumn, 1983-Summer, 1984, pp. 155–164.

Sources

Henry Allen, review in *Washington Post,* June 26, 1980.

Mary Gordon, review in *New York Times Book Review,* April 23, 1989.

Paul Gray, review in *Time,* December 6, 1976.

Diane Johnson, review in the *New York Review of Books,* February 3, 1977.

Maxine Hong Kingston, "At the Western Palace," *The Woman Warrior,* Vintage International, 1989, p. 160.

William McPherson, review in *Washington Post Book World,* October 10, 1976.

Timothy Pfaff, review in *New York Times Book Review,* November 7, 1976.

Pin-chia Feng, "Maxine Hong Kingston," in *Dictionary of Literary Biography, Vol. 173: American Novelists Since World War II, Fifth Series,* Gale Research, 1996, pp. 84-97.

For Further Study

Frank Chin, "Come All Ye Asian American Writers of the Real and the Fake," in *The Big Aiiieeeee!: An Anthology of Chinese American and Japanese American Literature,* edited by Jeffery Paul Chan, Frank Chin, Lawson Fusao Inada, and Shawn Wong, Meridian, 1991, pp. 1-92.

> Chin criticizes Kingston for demeaning Chinese culture by altering traditional Chinese myths and by writing an autobiography, which he does not consider an "authentically Chinese" genre.

Elisabeth Croll, *Changing Identities of Chinese Women: Rhetoric, Experience, and Self-Perception in Twentieth-Century China,* Zed Books, 1995.

> This book addresses the raising of Chinese daughters through and across generations before, during, and

after the Revolution. Combining case-study accounts with historical data, the author describes growing up across gender-related and cultural boundaries.

Patricia Buckley Ebrey, *The Cambridge Illustrated History of China,* Cambridge University Press, 1996.

The author traces Chinese traditions from prehistory through modern times, focusing on the arts, culture, economics, foreign policy, emigration, and politics. Of particular interest is the author's discussion of Chinese society's treatment of women.

Elizabeth Fox-Genovese, "Women in Society," in Grolier Multimedia Encyclopedia [CD-ROM], Grolier Interactive, Inc., 1998.

The author explains Chinese women's lowly position in society through the early twentieth century. She notes, in particular, women's relationships with their husbands and their husbands' families, and describes the effects of their low status.

Yan Gao, *The Art of Parody: Maxine Hong Kingston's Use of Chinese Sources (Many Voices: Ethnic Literatures of the Americas, Vol. 2),* Peter Lang Publishing, 1996.

This author provides an analysis of Kingston's use of Chinese sources in her novels, focusing on the advantage Kingston's bicultural upbringing brings to her unique observations of Chinese and American traditions.

Donn V. Hart, "Foot Binding," in Grolier Multimedia Encyclopedia [CD-ROM], Grolier Interactive, Inc., 1998.

Hart gives a vivid description of the Chinese tradition of foot binding, explaining its purposes as well as the process.

Shirley Geok-Lin Lim, "'Growing with Stories': Chinese American Identities, Textual Identities," in *Teaching American Ethnic Literatures: Nineteen Essays,* edited by John R. Maitino and David R. Peck, University of New Mexico Press, 1996, pp. 273-91.

Lim offers a useful analysis of the themes and structure of Kingston's autobiography before discussing approaches to teaching the book.

Paul Mandelbaum, "Rising from the Ashes: A Profile of Maxine Hong Kingston," in *Poets and Writers,* Vol. 26, no. 3, May/June, 1998, pp. 46-53.

An article detailing Kingston's life and work, including the 156-page manuscript she lost when her Oakland home burned to the ground. Mandelbaum praises Kingston's ability to travel "deep into the borderland that encompasses both fact and fantasy."

Paul Outka, "Publish or Perish: Food, Hunger, and Self-Construction in Maxine Hong Kingston's *The Woman Warrior,*" in *Contemporary Literature,* Vol. 38, no. 3, Fall, 1997, pp. 447-82.

Outka traces Kingston's search for selfhood and its connection to the theme of hunger in the book.

Tracy Robinson, "The Intersections of Gender, Class, Race, and Culture: On Seeing Clients Whole," in *Journal of Multicultural Counseling and Development,* Vol. 21, no. 1, January, 1993, pp. 50-58.

This article relates identity formation to the effects of a person's race, culture, and class.

Malini Schueller, "Questioning Race and Gender Definitions: Dialogic Subversions in *The Woman Warrior,*" in *Criticism,* Vol. 31, 1989, pp. 421-37.

Schueller commends Kingston for her unique form of autobiography and for questioning simple definitions of female and ethnic identities.

Sidonie Smith, "Maxine Hong Kingston's *Woman Warrior:* Filiality and Woman's Autobiographical Storytelling," in *Feminisms: An Anthology of Literary Theory and Criticism,* edited by Robyn R. Warhol and Diane Price Herndl, Rutgers University Press, 1997, pp. 1117-37.

Smith praises Kingston's work for capturing the connection between gender and genre in autobiography and calling *The Woman Warrior* "an autobiography about women's autobiographical story telling."

Howard J. Wechsler, "History of China," in Grolier Multimedia Encyclopedia [CD-ROM], Grolier Interactive, Inc., 1998.

The author provides a detailed description of China's history from its earliest days through modern times. Of particular importance to this novel are the author's discussions of the Nationalist Movement, the Chinese Communists, and the Kuomintang.

Gayle Wurst, "Cultural Stereotypes and the Language of Identity: Margaret Atwood's *Lady Oracle,* Maxine Hong Kingston's *The Woman Warrior,* and Alice Walker's *The Color Purple,*" in *Cross-Cultural Studies: American, Canadian, and European Literatures: 1945-1985,* edited by Mirko Jurak, Filozofska Fakulteta (Yugoslavia), 1988, pp. 53-64.

Wurst compares Kingston's *The Woman Warrior* with Atwood's *Lady Oracle* and Walker's *The Color Purple,* noting that in all three works the narrator strives to break down cultural stereotypes.

Glossary of Literary Terms

A

Abstract: As an adjective applied to writing or literary works, abstract refers to words or phrases that name things not knowable through the five senses.

Aestheticism: A literary and artistic movement of the nineteenth century. Followers of the movement believed that art should not be mixed with social, political, or moral teaching. The statement "art for art's sake" is a good summary of aestheticism. The movement had its roots in France, but it gained widespread importance in England in the last half of the nineteenth century, where it helped change the Victorian practice of including moral lessons in literature.

Allegory: A narrative technique in which characters representing things or abstract ideas are used to convey a message or teach a lesson. Allegory is typically used to teach moral, ethical, or religious lessons but is sometimes used for satiric or political purposes.

Allusion: A reference to a familiar literary or historical person or event, used to make an idea more easily understood.

Analogy: A comparison of two things made to explain something unfamiliar through its similarities to something familiar, or to prove one point based on the acceptedness of another. Similes and metaphors are types of analogies.

Antagonist: The major character in a narrative or drama who works against the hero or protagonist.

Anthropomorphism: The presentation of animals or objects in human shape or with human characteristics. The term is derived from the Greek word for "human form."

Antihero: A central character in a work of literature who lacks traditional heroic qualities such as courage, physical prowess, and fortitude. Antiheroes typically distrust conventional values and are unable to commit themselves to any ideals. They generally feel helpless in a world over which they have no control. Antiheroes usually accept, and often celebrate, their positions as social outcasts.

Apprenticeship Novel: See *Bildungsroman*

Archetype: The word archetype is commonly used to describe an original pattern or model from which all other things of the same kind are made. This term was introduced to literary criticism from the psychology of Carl Jung. It expresses Jung's theory that behind every person's "unconscious," or repressed memories of the past, lies the "collective unconscious" of the human race: memories of the countless typical experiences of our ancestors. These memories are said to prompt illogical associations that trigger powerful emotions in the reader. Often, the emotional process is primitive, even primordial. Archetypes are the literary images that grow out of the "collective unconscious." They appear in literature as incidents and plots that repeat basic patterns of life. They may also appear as stereotyped characters.

Avant-garde: French term meaning "vanguard." It is used in literary criticism to describe new writing that rejects traditional approaches to literature in favor of innovations in style or content.

B

Beat Movement: A period featuring a group of American poets and novelists of the 1950s and 1960s—including Jack Kerouac, Allen Ginsberg, Gregory Corso, William S. Burroughs, and Lawrence Ferlinghetti—who rejected established social and literary values. Using such techniques as stream of consciousness writing and jazz-influenced free verse and focusing on unusual or abnormal states of mind—generated by religious ecstasy or the use of drugs—the Beat writers aimed to create works that were unconventional in both form and subject matter.

Bildungsroman: A German word meaning "novel of development." The *bildungsroman* is a study of the maturation of a youthful character, typically brought about through a series of social or sexual encounters that lead to self-awareness. *Bildungsroman* is used interchangeably with *erziehungsroman,* a novel of initiation and education. When a *bildungsroman* is concerned with the development of an artist (as in James Joyce's *A Portrait of the Artist as a Young Man*), it is often termed a *kunstlerroman.* Also known as Apprenticeship Novel, Coming of Age Novel, *Erziehungsroman,* or *Kunstlerroman.*

Black Aesthetic Movement: A period of artistic and literary development among African Americans in the 1960s and early 1970s. This was the first major African-American artistic movement since the Harlem Renaissance and was closely paralleled by the civil rights and black power movements. The black aesthetic writers attempted to produce works of art that would be meaningful to the black masses. Key figures in black aesthetics included one of its founders, poet and playwright Amiri Baraka, formerly known as LeRoi Jones; poet and essayist Haki R. Madhubuti, formerly Don L. Lee; poet and playwright Sonia Sanchez; and dramatist Ed Bullins. Also known as Black Arts Movement.

Black Humor: Writing that places grotesque elements side by side with humorous ones in an attempt to shock the reader, forcing him or her to laugh at the horrifying reality of a disordered world. Also known as Black Comedy.

Burlesque: Any literary work that uses exaggeration to make its subject appear ridiculous, either by treating a trivial subject with profound seriousness or by treating a dignified subject frivolously. The word "burlesque" may also be used as an adjective, as in "burlesque show," to mean "striptease act."

C

Character: Broadly speaking, a person in a literary work. The actions of characters are what constitute the plot of a story, novel, or poem. There are numerous types of characters, ranging from simple, stereotypical figures to intricate, multifaceted ones. In the techniques of anthropomorphism and personification, animals—and even places or things—can assume aspects of character. "Characterization" is the process by which an author creates vivid, believable characters in a work of art. This may be done in a variety of ways, including (1) direct description of the character by the narrator; (2) the direct presentation of the speech, thoughts, or actions of the character; and (3) the responses of other characters to the character. The term "character" also refers to a form originated by the ancient Greek writer Theophrastus that later became popular in the seventeenth and eighteenth centuries. It is a short essay or sketch of a person who prominently displays a specific attribute or quality, such as miserliness or ambition.

Climax: The turning point in a narrative, the moment when the conflict is at its most intense. Typically, the structure of stories, novels, and plays is one of rising action, in which tension builds to the climax, followed by falling action, in which tension lessens as the story moves to its conclusion.

Colloquialism: A word, phrase, or form of pronunciation that is acceptable in casual conversation but not in formal, written communication. It is considered more acceptable than slang.

Coming of Age Novel: See *Bildungsroman*

Concrete: Concrete is the opposite of abstract, and refers to a thing that actually exists or a description that allows the reader to experience an object or concept with the senses.

Connotation: The impression that a word gives beyond its defined meaning. Connotations may be universally understood or may be significant only to a certain group.

Convention: Any widely accepted literary device, style, or form.

D

Denotation: The definition of a word, apart from the impressions or feelings it creates (connotations) in the reader.

Denouement: A French word meaning "the unknotting." In literary criticism, it denotes the resolution of conflict in fiction or drama. The *denouement* follows the climax and provides an outcome to the primary plot situation as well as an explanation of secondary plot complications. The *denouement* often involves a character's recognition of his or her state of mind or moral condition. Also known as Falling Action.

Description: Descriptive writing is intended to allow a reader to picture the scene or setting in which the action of a story takes place. The form this description takes often evokes an intended emotional response—a dark, spooky graveyard will evoke fear, and a peaceful, sunny meadow will evoke calmness.

Dialogue: In its widest sense, dialogue is simply conversation between people in a literary work; in its most restricted sense, it refers specifically to the speech of characters in a drama. As a specific literary genre, a "dialogue" is a composition in which characters debate an issue or idea.

Diction: The selection and arrangement of words in a literary work. Either or both may vary depending on the desired effect. There are four general types of diction: "formal," used in scholarly or lofty writing; "informal," used in relaxed but educated conversation; "colloquial," used in everyday speech; and "slang," containing newly coined words and other terms not accepted in formal usage.

Didactic: A term used to describe works of literature that aim to teach some moral, religious, political, or practical lesson. Although didactic elements are often found in artistically pleasing works, the term "didactic" usually refers to literature in which the message is more important than the form. The term may also be used to criticize a work that the critic finds "overly didactic," that is, heavy-handed in its delivery of a lesson.

Doppelganger: A literary technique by which a character is duplicated (usually in the form of an alter ego, though sometimes as a ghostly counterpart) or divided into two distinct, usually opposite personalities. The use of this character device is widespread in nineteenth- and twentieth-century literature, and indicates a growing awareness among authors that the "self" is really a composite of many "selves." Also known as The Double.

Double Entendre: A corruption of a French phrase meaning "double meaning." The term is used to indicate a word or phrase that is deliberately ambiguous, especially when one of the meanings is risqué or improper.

Dramatic Irony: Occurs when the audience of a play or the reader of a work of literature knows something that a character in the work itself does not know. The irony is in the contrast between the intended meaning of the statements or actions of a character and the additional information understood by the audience.

Dystopia: An imaginary place in a work of fiction where the characters lead dehumanized, fearful lives.

E

Edwardian: Describes cultural conventions identified with the period of the reign of Edward VII of England (1901-1910). Writers of the Edwardian Age typically displayed a strong reaction against the propriety and conservatism of the Victorian Age. Their work often exhibits distrust of authority in religion, politics, and art and expresses strong doubts about the soundness of conventional values.

Empathy: A sense of shared experience, including emotional and physical feelings, with someone or something other than oneself. Empathy is often used to describe the response of a reader to a literary character.

Enlightenment, The: An eighteenth-century philosophical movement. It began in France but had a wide impact throughout Europe and America. Thinkers of the Enlightenment valued reason and believed that both the individual and society could achieve a state of perfection. Corresponding to this essentially humanist vision was a resistance to religious authority.

Epigram: A saying that makes the speaker's point quickly and concisely. Often used to preface a novel.

Epilogue: A concluding statement or section of a literary work. In dramas, particularly those of the seventeenth and eighteenth centuries, the epilogue is a closing speech, often in verse, delivered by an actor at the end of a play and spoken directly to the audience.

Epiphany: A sudden revelation of truth inspired by a seemingly trivial incident.

Episode: An incident that forms part of a story and is significantly related to it. Episodes may be either self-contained narratives or events that depend on a larger context for their sense and importance.

Epistolary Novel: A novel in the form of letters. The form was particularly popular in the eighteenth century.

Epithet: A word or phrase, often disparaging or abusive, that expresses a character trait of someone or something.

Existentialism: A predominantly twentieth-century philosophy concerned with the nature and perception of human existence. There are two major strains of existentialist thought: atheistic and Christian. Followers of atheistic existentialism believe that the individual is alone in a godless universe and that the basic human condition is one of suffering and loneliness. Nevertheless, because there are no fixed values, individuals can create their own characters—indeed, they can shape themselves—through the exercise of free will. The atheistic strain culminates in and is popularly associated with the works of Jean-Paul Sartre. The Christian existentialists, on the other hand, believe that only in God may people find freedom from life's anguish. The two strains hold certain beliefs in common: that existence cannot be fully understood or described through empirical effort; that anguish is a universal element of life; that individuals must bear responsibility for their actions; and that there is no common standard of behavior or perception for religious and ethical matters.

Expatriates: See *Expatriatism*

Expatriatism: The practice of leaving one's country to live for an extended period in another country.

Exposition: Writing intended to explain the nature of an idea, thing, or theme. Expository writing is often combined with description, narration, or argument. In dramatic writing, the exposition is the introductory material which presents the characters, setting, and tone of the play.

Expressionism: An indistinct literary term, originally used to describe an early twentieth-century school of German painting. The term applies to almost any mode of unconventional, highly subjective writing that distorts reality in some way.

F

Fable: A prose or verse narrative intended to convey a moral. Animals or inanimate objects with human characteristics often serve as characters in fables.

Falling Action: See *Denouement*

Fantasy: A literary form related to mythology and folklore. Fantasy literature is typically set in non-existent realms and features supernatural beings.

Farce: A type of comedy characterized by broad humor, outlandish incidents, and often vulgar subject matter.

Femme fatale: A French phrase with the literal translation "fatal woman." A *femme fatale* is a sensuous, alluring woman who often leads men into danger or trouble.

Fiction: Any story that is the product of imagination rather than a documentation of fact. Characters and events in such narratives may be based in real life but their ultimate form and configuration is a creation of the author.

Figurative Language: A technique in writing in which the author temporarily interrupts the order, construction, or meaning of the writing for a particular effect. This interruption takes the form of one or more figures of speech such as hyperbole, irony, or simile. Figurative language is the opposite of literal language, in which every word is truthful, accurate, and free of exaggeration or embellishment.

Figures of Speech: Writing that differs from customary conventions for construction, meaning, order, or significance for the purpose of a special meaning or effect. There are two major types of figures of speech: rhetorical figures, which do not make changes in the meaning of the words, and tropes, which do.

Fin de siecle: A French term meaning "end of the century." The term is used to denote the last decade of the nineteenth century, a transition period when writers and other artists abandoned old conventions and looked for new techniques and objectives.

First Person: See *Point of View*

Flashback: A device used in literature to present action that occurred before the beginning of the story. Flashbacks are often introduced as the dreams or recollections of one or more characters.

Foil: A character in a work of literature whose physical or psychological qualities contrast strongly with, and therefore highlight, the corresponding qualities of another character.

Folklore: Traditions and myths preserved in a culture or group of people. Typically, these are passed on by word of mouth in various forms—such as legends, songs, and proverbs—or preserved in customs and ceremonies. This term was first used by W. J. Thoms in 1846.

Folktale: A story originating in oral tradition. Folktales fall into a variety of categories, including legends, ghost stories, fairy tales, fables, and anecdotes based on historical figures and events.

Foreshadowing: A device used in literature to create expectation or to set up an explanation of later developments.

Form: The pattern or construction of a work which identifies its genre and distinguishes it from other genres.

G

Genre: A category of literary work. In critical theory, genre may refer to both the content of a given work—tragedy, comedy, pastoral—and to its form, such as poetry, novel, or drama.

Gilded Age: A period in American history during the 1870s characterized by political corruption and materialism. A number of important novels of social and political criticism were written during this time.

Gothicism: In literary criticism, works characterized by a taste for the medieval or morbidly attractive. A gothic novel prominently features elements of horror, the supernatural, gloom, and violence: clanking chains, terror, charnel houses, ghosts, medieval castles, and mysteriously slamming doors. The term "gothic novel" is also applied to novels that lack elements of the traditional Gothic setting but that create a similar atmosphere of terror or dread.

Grotesque: In literary criticism, the subject matter of a work or a style of expression characterized by exaggeration, deformity, freakishness, and disorder. The grotesque often includes an element of comic absurdity.

H

Harlem Renaissance: The Harlem Renaissance of the 1920s is generally considered the first significant movement of black writers and artists in the United States. During this period, new and established black writers published more fiction and poetry than ever before, the first influential black literary journals were established, and black authors and artists received their first widespread recognition and serious critical appraisal. Among the major writers associated with this period are Claude McKay, Jean Toomer, Countee Cullen, Langston Hughes, Arna Bontemps, Nella Larsen, and Zora Neale Hurston. Also known as Negro Renaissance and New Negro Movement.

Hero/Heroine: The principal sympathetic character (male or female) in a literary work. Heroes and heroines typically exhibit admirable traits: idealism, courage, and integrity, for example.

Holocaust Literature: Literature influenced by or written about the Holocaust of World War II. Such literature includes true stories of survival in concentration camps, escape, and life after the war, as well as fictional works and poetry.

Humanism: A philosophy that places faith in the dignity of humankind and rejects the medieval perception of the individual as a weak, fallen creature. "Humanists" typically believe in the perfectibility of human nature and view reason and education as the means to that end.

Hyperbole: In literary criticism, deliberate exaggeration used to achieve an effect.

I

Idiom: A word construction or verbal expression closely associated with a given language.

Image: A concrete representation of an object or sensory experience. Typically, such a representation helps evoke the feelings associated with the object or experience itself. Images are either "literal" or "figurative." Literal images are especially concrete and involve little or no extension of the obvious meaning of the words used to express them. Figurative images do not follow the literal meaning of the words exactly. Images in literature are usually visual, but the term "image" can also refer to the representation of any sensory experience.

Imagery: The array of images in a literary work. Also, figurative language.

In medias res: A Latin term meaning "in the middle of things." It refers to the technique of beginning a story at its midpoint and then using various flashback devices to reveal previous action.

Interior Monologue: A narrative technique in which characters' thoughts are revealed in a way that appears to be uncontrolled by the author. The interior monologue typically aims to reveal the inner self of a character. It portrays emotional experiences as they occur at both a conscious and unconscious level. Images are often used to represent sensations or emotions.

Irony: In literary criticism, the effect of language in which the intended meaning is the opposite of what is stated.

J

Jargon: Language that is used or understood only by a select group of people. Jargon may refer to terminology used in a certain profession, such as computer jargon, or it may refer to any non-sensical language that is not understood by most people.

L

Leitmotiv: See *Motif*

Literal Language: An author uses literal language when he or she writes without exaggerating or embellishing the subject matter and without any tools of figurative language.

Lost Generation: A term first used by Gertrude Stein to describe the post-World War I generation of American writers: men and women haunted by a sense of betrayal and emptiness brought about by the destructiveness of the war.

M

Mannerism: Exaggerated, artificial adherence to a literary manner or style. Also, a popular style of the visual arts of late sixteenth-century Europe that was marked by elongation of the human form and by intentional spatial distortion. Literary works that are self-consciously high-toned and artistic are often said to be "mannered."

Metaphor: A figure of speech that expresses an idea through the image of another object. Metaphors suggest the essence of the first object by identifying it with certain qualities of the second object.

Modernism: Modern literary practices. Also, the principles of a literary school that lasted from roughly the beginning of the twentieth century until the end of World War II. Modernism is defined by its rejection of the literary conventions of the nineteenth century and by its opposition to conventional morality, taste, traditions, and economic values.

Mood: The prevailing emotions of a work or of the author in his or her creation of the work. The mood of a work is not always what might be expected based on its subject matter.

Motif: A theme, character type, image, metaphor, or other verbal element that recurs throughout a single work of literature or occurs in a number of different works over a period of time. Also known as *Motiv* or *Leitmotiv.*

Myth: An anonymous tale emerging from the traditional beliefs of a culture or social unit. Myths use supernatural explanations for natural phenomena. They may also explain cosmic issues like creation and death. Collections of myths, known as mythologies, are common to all cultures and nations, but the best-known myths belong to the Norse, Roman, and Greek mythologies.

N

Narration: The telling of a series of events, real or invented. A narration may be either a simple narrative, in which the events are recounted chronologically, or a narrative with a plot, in which the account is given in a style reflecting the author's artistic concept of the story. Narration is sometimes used as a synonym for "storyline."

Narrative: A verse or prose accounting of an event or sequence of events, real or invented. The term is also used as an adjective in the sense "method of narration." For example, in literary criticism, the expression "narrative technique" usually refers to the way the author structures and presents his or her story.

Narrator: The teller of a story. The narrator may be the author or a character in the story through whom the author speaks.

Naturalism: A literary movement of the late nineteenth and early twentieth centuries. The movement's major theorist, French novelist Emile Zola, envisioned a type of fiction that would examine human life with the objectivity of scientific inquiry. The Naturalists typically viewed human beings as either the products of "biological determinism," ruled by hereditary instincts and engaged in an endless struggle for survival, or as the products of "socioeconomic determinism," ruled by social and economic forces beyond their control. In their works, the Naturalists generally ignored the highest levels of society and focused on degradation: poverty, alcoholism, prostitution, insanity, and disease.

Noble Savage: The idea that primitive man is noble and good but becomes evil and corrupted as he becomes civilized. The concept of the noble savage originated in the Renaissance period but is more closely identified with such later writers as

Jean-Jacques Rousseau and Aphra Behn. See also Primitivism.

Novel of Ideas: A novel in which the examination of intellectual issues and concepts takes precedence over characterization or a traditional storyline.

Novel of Manners: A novel that examines the customs and mores of a cultural group.

Novel: A long fictional narrative written in prose, which developed from the novella and other early forms of narrative. A novel is usually organized under a plot or theme with a focus on character development and action.

Novella: An Italian term meaning "story." This term has been especially used to describe fourteenth-century Italian tales, but it also refers to modern short novels.

O

Objective Correlative: An outward set of objects, a situation, or a chain of events corresponding to an inward experience and evoking this experience in the reader. The term frequently appears in modern criticism in discussions of authors' intended effects on the emotional responses of readers.

Objectivity: A quality in writing characterized by the absence of the author's opinion or feeling about the subject matter. Objectivity is an important factor in criticism.

Oedipus Complex: A son's amorous obsession with his mother. The phrase is derived from the story of the ancient Theban hero Oedipus, who unknowingly killed his father and married his mother.

Omniscience: See *Point of View*

Onomatopoeia: The use of words whose sounds express or suggest their meaning. In its simplest sense, onomatopoeia may be represented by words that mimic the sounds they denote such as "hiss" or "meow." At a more subtle level, the pattern and rhythm of sounds and rhymes of a line or poem may be onomatopoeic.

Oxymoron: A phrase combining two contradictory terms. Oxymorons may be intentional or unintentional.

P

Parable: A story intended to teach a moral lesson or answer an ethical question.

Paradox: A statement that appears illogical or contradictory at first, but may actually point to an underlying truth.

Parallelism: A method of comparison of two ideas in which each is developed in the same grammatical structure.

Parody: In literary criticism, this term refers to an imitation of a serious literary work or the signature style of a particular author in a ridiculous manner. A typical parody adopts the style of the original and applies it to an inappropriate subject for humorous effect. Parody is a form of satire and could be considered the literary equivalent of a caricature or cartoon.

Pastoral: A term derived from the Latin word "pastor," meaning shepherd. A pastoral is a literary composition on a rural theme. The conventions of the pastoral were originated by the third-century Greek poet Theocritus, who wrote about the experiences, love affairs, and pastimes of Sicilian shepherds. In a pastoral, characters and language of a courtly nature are often placed in a simple setting. The term pastoral is also used to classify dramas, elegies, and lyrics that exhibit the use of country settings and shepherd characters.

Pen Name: See *Pseudonym*

Persona: A Latin term meaning "mask." *Personae* are the characters in a fictional work of literature. The *persona* generally functions as a mask through which the author tells a story in a voice other than his or her own. A *persona* is usually either a character in a story who acts as a narrator or an "implied author," a voice created by the author to act as the narrator for himself or herself.

Personification: A figure of speech that gives human qualities to abstract ideas, animals, and inanimate objects. Also known as *Prosopopoeia.*

Picaresque Novel: Episodic fiction depicting the adventures of a roguish central character ("picaro" is Spanish for "rogue"). The picaresque hero is commonly a low-born but clever individual who wanders into and out of various affairs of love, danger, and farcical intrigue. These involvements may take place at all social levels and typically present a humorous and wide-ranging satire of a given society.

Plagiarism: Claiming another person's written material as one's own. Plagiarism can take the form of direct, word-for-word copying or the theft of the substance or idea of the work.

Plot: In literary criticism, this term refers to the pattern of events in a narrative or drama. In its simplest sense, the plot guides the author in composing the work and helps the reader follow the work. Typically, plots exhibit causality and unity and have a beginning, a middle, and an end. Sometimes, however, a plot may consist of a series of disconnected events, in which case it is known as an "episodic plot."

Poetic Justice: An outcome in a literary work, not necessarily a poem, in which the good are rewarded and the evil are punished, especially in ways that particularly fit their virtues or crimes.

Poetic License: Distortions of fact and literary convention made by a writer—not always a poet—for the sake of the effect gained. Poetic license is closely related to the concept of "artistic freedom."

Poetics: This term has two closely related meanings. It denotes (1) an aesthetic theory in literary criticism about the essence of poetry or (2) rules prescribing the proper methods, content, style, or diction of poetry. The term poetics may also refer to theories about literature in general, not just poetry.

Point of View: The narrative perspective from which a literary work is presented to the reader. There are four traditional points of view. The "third person omniscient" gives the reader a "godlike" perspective, unrestricted by time or place, from which to see actions and look into the minds of characters. This allows the author to comment openly on characters and events in the work. The "third person" point of view presents the events of the story from outside of any single character's perception, much like the omniscient point of view, but the reader must understand the action as it takes place and without any special insight into characters' minds or motivations. The "first person" or "personal" point of view relates events as they are perceived by a single character. The main character "tells" the story and may offer opinions about the action and characters which differ from those of the author. Much less common than omniscient, third person, and first person is the "second person" point of view, wherein the author tells the story as if it is happening to the reader.

Polemic: A work in which the author takes a stand on a controversial subject, such as abortion or religion. Such works are often extremely argumentative or provocative.

Pornography: Writing intended to provoke feelings of lust in the reader. Such works are often condemned by critics and teachers, but those which can be shown to have literary value are viewed less harshly.

Post-Aesthetic Movement: An artistic response made by African Americans to the black aesthetic movement of the 1960s and early '70s. Writers since that time have adopted a somewhat different tone in their work, with less emphasis placed on the disparity between black and white in the United States. In the words of post-aesthetic authors such as Toni Morrison, John Edgar Wideman, and Kristin Hunter, African Americans are portrayed as looking inward for answers to their own questions, rather than always looking to the outside world.

Postmodernism: Writing from the 1960s forward characterized by experimentation and continuing to apply some of the fundamentals of modernism, which included existentialism and alienation. Postmodernists have gone a step further in the rejection of tradition begun with the modernists by also rejecting traditional forms, preferring the anti-novel over the novel and the antihero over the hero.

Primitivism: The belief that primitive peoples were nobler and less flawed than civilized peoples because they had not been subjected to the tainting influence of society. See also Noble Savage.

Prologue: An introductory section of a literary work. It often contains information establishing the situation of the characters or presents information about the setting, time period, or action. In drama, the prologue is spoken by a chorus or by one of the principal characters.

Prose: A literary medium that attempts to mirror the language of everyday speech. It is distinguished from poetry by its use of unmetered, unrhymed language consisting of logically related sentences. Prose is usually grouped into paragraphs that form a cohesive whole such as an essay or a novel.

***Prosopopoeia*:** See *Personification*

Protagonist: The central character of a story who serves as a focus for its themes and incidents and as the principal rationale for its development. The protagonist is sometimes referred to in discussions of modern literature as the hero or antihero.

Protest Fiction: Protest fiction has as its primary purpose the protesting of some social injustice, such as racism or discrimination.

Proverb: A brief, sage saying that expresses a truth about life in a striking manner.

Pseudonym: A name assumed by a writer, most often intended to prevent his or her identification as the author of a work. Two or more authors may work together under one pseudonym, or an author may use a different name for each genre he or she publishes in. Some publishing companies maintain "house pseudonyms," under which any number of authors may write installations in a series. Some authors also choose a pseudonym over their real names the way an actor may use a stage name.

Pun: A play on words that have similar sounds but different meanings.

R

Realism: A nineteenth-century European literary movement that sought to portray familiar characters, situations, and settings in a realistic manner. This was done primarily by using an objective narrative point of view and through the buildup of accurate detail. The standard for success of any realistic work depends on how faithfully it transfers common experience into fictional forms. The realistic method may be altered or extended, as in stream of consciousness writing, to record highly subjective experience.

Repartee: Conversation featuring snappy retorts and witticisms.

Resolution: The portion of a story following the climax, in which the conflict is resolved. See also *Denouement.*

Rhetoric: In literary criticism, this term denotes the art of ethical persuasion. In its strictest sense, rhetoric adheres to various principles developed since classical times for arranging facts and ideas in a clear, persuasive, appealing manner. The term is also used to refer to effective prose in general and theories of or methods for composing effective prose.

Rhetorical Question: A question intended to provoke thought, but not an expressed answer, in the reader. It is most commonly used in oratory and other persuasive genres.

Rising Action: The part of a drama where the plot becomes increasingly complicated. Rising action leads up to the climax, or turning point, of a drama.

Roman a clef: A French phrase meaning "novel with a key." It refers to a narrative in which real persons are portrayed under fictitious names.

Romance: A broad term, usually denoting a narrative with exotic, exaggerated, often idealized characters, scenes, and themes.

Romanticism: This term has two widely accepted meanings. In historical criticism, it refers to a European intellectual and artistic movement of the late eighteenth and early nineteenth centuries that sought greater freedom of personal expression than that allowed by the strict rules of literary form and logic of the eighteenth-century neoclassicists. The Romantics preferred emotional and imaginative expression to rational analysis. They considered the individual to be at the center of all experience and so placed him or her at the center of their art. The Romantics believed that the creative imagination reveals nobler truths—unique feelings and attitudes—than those that could be discovered by logic or by scientific examination. Both the natural world and the state of childhood were important sources for revelations of "eternal truths." "Romanticism" is also used as a general term to refer to a type of sensibility found in all periods of literary history and usually considered to be in opposition to the principles of classicism. In this sense, Romanticism signifies any work or philosophy in which the exotic or dreamlike figure strongly, or that is devoted to individualistic expression, self-analysis, or a pursuit of a higher realm of knowledge than can be discovered by human reason.

Romantics: See *Romanticism*

S

Satire: A work that uses ridicule, humor, and wit to criticize and provoke change in human nature and institutions. There are two major types of satire: "formal" or "direct" satire speaks directly to the reader or to a character in the work; "indirect" satire relies upon the ridiculous behavior of its characters to make its point. Formal satire is further divided into two manners: the "Horatian," which ridicules gently, and the "Juvenalian," which derides its subjects harshly and bitterly.

Science Fiction: A type of narrative about or based upon real or imagined scientific theories and technology. Science fiction is often peopled with alien creatures and set on other planets or in different dimensions.

Second Person: See *Point of View*

Setting: The time, place, and culture in which the action of a narrative takes place. The elements of setting may include geographic location, characters' physical and mental environments, prevailing cultural attitudes, or the historical time in which the action takes place.

Simile: A comparison, usually using "like" or "as", of two essentially dissimilar things, as in "coffee as cold as ice" or "He sounded like a broken record."

Slang: A type of informal verbal communication that is generally unacceptable for formal writing. Slang words and phrases are often colorful exaggerations used to emphasize the speaker's point; they may also be shortened versions of an often-used word or phrase.

Slave Narrative: Autobiographical accounts of American slave life as told by escaped slaves. These works first appeared during the abolition movement of the 1830s through the 1850s.

Socialist Realism: The Socialist Realism school of literary theory was proposed by Maxim Gorky and established as a dogma by the first Soviet Congress of Writers. It demanded adherence to a communist worldview in works of literature. Its doctrines required an objective viewpoint comprehensible to the working classes and themes of social struggle featuring strong proletarian heroes. Also known as Social Realism.

Stereotype: A stereotype was originally the name for a duplication made during the printing process; this led to its modern definition as a person or thing that is (or is assumed to be) the same as all others of its type.

Stream of Consciousness: A narrative technique for rendering the inward experience of a character. This technique is designed to give the impression of an ever-changing series of thoughts, emotions, images, and memories in the spontaneous and seemingly illogical order that they occur in life.

Structure: The form taken by a piece of literature. The structure may be made obvious for ease of understanding, as in nonfiction works, or may be obscured for artistic purposes, as in some poetry or seemingly "unstructured" prose.

***Sturm und Drang*:** A German term meaning "storm and stress." It refers to a German literary movement of the 1770s and 1780s that reacted against the order and rationalism of the enlightenment, focusing instead on the intense experience of extraordinary individuals.

Style: A writer's distinctive manner of arranging words to suit his or her ideas and purpose in writing. The unique imprint of the author's personality upon his or her writing, style is the product of an author's way of arranging ideas and his or her use of diction, different sentence structures, rhythm, figures of speech, rhetorical principles, and other elements of composition.

Subjectivity: Writing that expresses the author's personal feelings about his subject, and which may or may not include factual information about the subject.

Subplot: A secondary story in a narrative. A subplot may serve as a motivating or complicating force for the main plot of the work, or it may provide emphasis for, or relief from, the main plot.

Surrealism: A term introduced to criticism by Guillaume Apollinaire and later adopted by Andre Breton. It refers to a French literary and artistic movement founded in the 1920s. The Surrealists sought to express unconscious thoughts and feelings in their works. The best-known technique used for achieving this aim was automatic writing—transcriptions of spontaneous outpourings from the unconscious. The Surrealists proposed to unify the contrary levels of conscious and unconscious, dream and reality, objectivity and subjectivity into a new level of "super-realism."

Suspense: A literary device in which the author maintains the audience's attention through the buildup of events, the outcome of which will soon be revealed.

Symbol: Something that suggests or stands for something else without losing its original identity. In literature, symbols combine their literal meaning with the suggestion of an abstract concept. Literary symbols are of two types: those that carry complex associations of meaning no matter what their contexts, and those that derive their suggestive meaning from their functions in specific literary works.

Symbolism: This term has two widely accepted meanings. In historical criticism, it denotes an early modernist literary movement initiated in France during the nineteenth century that reacted against the prevailing standards of realism. Writers in this movement aimed to evoke, indirectly and symbolically, an order of being beyond the material world of the five senses. Poetic expression of personal emotion figured strongly in the movement, typically by means of a private set of symbols uniquely identifiable with the individual poet. The principal aim of the Symbolists was to express in words the highly complex feelings that grew out of everyday contact with the world. In a broader sense, the term "symbolism" refers to the use of one object to represent another.

T

Tall Tale: A humorous tale told in a straightforward, credible tone but relating absolutely impossible events or feats of the characters. Such tales were commonly told of frontier adventures during the settlement of the west in the United States.

Theme: The main point of a work of literature. The term is used interchangeably with thesis.

Thesis: A thesis is both an essay and the point argued in the essay. Thesis novels and thesis plays share the quality of containing a thesis which is supported through the action of the story.

Third Person: See *Point of View*

Tone: The author's attitude toward his or her audience may be deduced from the tone of the work. A formal tone may create distance or convey politeness, while an informal tone may encourage a friendly, intimate, or intrusive feeling in the reader. The author's attitude toward his or her subject matter may also be deduced from the tone of the words he or she uses in discussing it.

Transcendentalism: An American philosophical and religious movement, based in New England from around 1835 until the Civil War. Transcendentalism was a form of American romanticism that had its roots abroad in the works of Thomas Carlyle, Samuel Coleridge, and Johann Wolfgang von Goethe. The Transcendentalists stressed the importance of intuition and subjective experience in communication with God. They rejected religious dogma and texts in favor of mysticism and scientific naturalism. They pursued truths that lie beyond the "colorless" realms perceived by reason and the senses and were active social reformers in public education, women's rights, and the abolition of slavery.

U

Urban Realism: A branch of realist writing that attempts to accurately reflect the often harsh facts of modern urban existence.

Utopia: A fictional perfect place, such as "paradise" or "heaven."

V

Verisimilitude: Literally, the appearance of truth. In literary criticism, the term refers to aspects of a work of literature that seem true to the reader.

Victorian: Refers broadly to the reign of Queen Victoria of England (1837-1901) and to anything with qualities typical of that era. For example, the qualities of smug narrowmindedness, bourgeois materialism, faith in social progress, and priggish morality are often considered Victorian. This stereotype is contradicted by such dramatic intellectual developments as the theories of Charles Darwin, Karl Marx, and Sigmund Freud (which stirred strong debates in England) and the critical attitudes of serious Victorian writers like Charles Dickens and George Eliot. In literature, the Victorian Period was the great age of the English novel, and the latter part of the era saw the rise of movements such as decadence and symbolism. Also known as Victorian Age and Victorian Period.

W

Weltanschauung: A German term referring to a person's worldview or philosophy.

Weltschmerz: A German term meaning "world pain." It describes a sense of anguish about the nature of existence, usually associated with a melancholy, pessimistic attitude.

Z

Zeitgeist: A German term meaning "spirit of the time." It refers to the moral and intellectual trends of a given era.

Cumulative
Author/Title Index

Cumulative Author/Title Index

Cumulative
Nationality/Ethnicity Index

Le Guin, Ursula K.
The Left Hand of Darkness: V6
Lee, Harper
To Kill a Mockingbird: V2
Lowry, Lois
The Giver: V3
Mason, Bobbie Ann
In Country: V4
McCullers, Carson
The Heart Is a Lonely Hunter: V6
Morrison, Toni
Beloved: V6
The Bluest Eye: V1
O'Connor, Flannery
Wise Blood: V3
Plath, Sylvia
The Bell Jar: V1
Potok, Chaim
The Chosen: V4
Rölvaag, O. E.
Giants in the Earth: V5
Salinger, J. D.
The Catcher in the Rye: V1
Sinclair, Upton
The Jungle: V6
Steinbeck, John
Of Mice and Men: V1
The Pearl: V5
Stowe, Harriet Beecher
Uncle Tom's Cabin: V6
Tan, Amy
The Joy Luck Club: V1
Twain, Mark
*The Adventures of Huckleberry
Finn*: V1
The Adventures of Tom Sawyer: V6
Tyler, Anne
*Dinner at the Homesick
Restaurant*: V2
Vonnegut, Kurt, Jr.
Slaughterhouse-Five: V3
Walker, Alice
The Color Purple: V5
Wharton, Edith
Ethan Frome: V5
Wright, Richard
Black Boy: V1

Asian American
Kingston, Maxine Hong
The Woman Warrior: V6
Tan, Amy
The Joy Luck Club: V1

Asian Canadian
Kogawa, Joy
Obasan: V3

British
Austen, Jane
Pride and Prejudice: V1

Blair, Eric Arthur
Animal Farm: V3
Brontë, Charlotte
Jane Eyre: V4
Brontë, Emily
Wuthering Heights: V2
Conrad, Joseph
Heart of Darkness: V2
Dickens, Charles
Great Expectations: V4
A Tale of Two Cities: V5
Forster, E. M.
A Passage to India: V3
Golding, William
Lord of the Flies: V2
Hardy, Thomas
Tess of the d'Urbervilles: V3
Huxley, Aldous
Brave New World: V6
Marmon Silko, Leslie
Ceremony: V4
Orwell, George
Animal Farm: V3
Shelley, Mary
Frankenstein: V1
Swift, Jonathan
Gulliver's Travels: V6

Canadian
Atwood, Margaret
The Handmaid's Tale: V4
Kogawa, Joy
Obasan: V3

Chilean
Allende, Isabel
The House of the Spirits: V6

Colombian
García Márquez, Gabriel
Love in the Time of Cholera: V1
One Hundred Years of Solitude:
V5

Dominican
Alvarez, Julia
*How the García Girls Lost Their
Accents*: V5

European
American
Hemingway, Ernest
The Old Man and the Sea: V6
Stowe, Harriet Beecher
Uncle Tom's Cabin: V6

French
Camus, Albert
The Stranger: V6
Hugo, Victor
Les Misérables: V5

German
Hesse, Hermann
Siddhartha: V6
Remarque, Erich Maria
All Quiet on the Western Front: V4

Hispanic American
Cisneros, Sandra
The House on Mango Street: V2

Jewish
Bellow, Saul
Seize the Day: V4
Malamud, Bernard
The Natural: V4
Wiesel, Eliezer
Night: V4

Mexican
Esquivel, Laura
Like Water for Chocolate: V5

Native American
Dorris, Michael
A Yellow Raft in Blue Water: V3
Erdrich, Louise
Love Medicine: V5
Marmon Silko, Leslie
Ceremony: V4

Nigerian
Achebe, Chinua
Things Fall Apart: V3

Norwegian
Rölvaag, O. E.
Giants in the Earth: V5

Romanian
Wiesel, Eliezer
Night: V4

Russian
Dostoyevsky, Fyodor
Crime and Punishment: V3

Solzhenitsyn, Aleksandr
  *One Day in the Life of Ivan
    Denisovich:* V6

South African

Gordimer, Nadine
  July's People: V4

Paton, Alan
  Cry, the Beloved Country: V3

West Indian

Kincaid, Jamaica
  Annie John: V3

Subject/Theme Index

For Reference

Not to be taken from this room